RESEARCH IN
COMPOSITION
AND RHETORIC

RESEARCH IN COMPOSITION AND RHETORIC

A Bibliographic Sourcebook

Edited by
Michael G. Moran
and
Ronald F. Lunsford

GREENWOOD PRESS
Westport, Connecticut • London, England

Library of Congress Cataloging in Publication Data

Main entry under title:

Research in composition and rhetoric.

Bibliography: p.
Includes indexes.
1. English language—Rhetoric—Study and teaching—
Bibliography. 2. English language—Composition and
exercises—Study and teaching—Bibliography.
3. English language—Rhetoric—Study and teaching—
Research. 4. English language—Composition and exer-
cises—Study and teaching—Research. I. Moran,
Michael G. II. Lunsford, Ronald F.
Z2015.R5R47   1984   016.808′042′07   83-22568
[PE1404]
ISBN 0-313-23308-X (lib. bdg.)

Library of Congress Catalog Card Number: 83-22568
ISBN: 0-313-23308-X

First published in 1984

Greenwood Press
A division of Congressional Information Service, Inc.
88 Post Road West
Westport, Connecticut 06881

Printed in the United States of America

10 9 8 7 6 5 4 3 2 1

Contents

Preface

The purpose of *Research in Composition and Rhetoric* is to make the research tradition in composition more explicit. This tradition, though now vigorous, languished for many years in part because the field lacked a strong sense of its historical development. The research is now being conducted, but it often appears in journals and books in diverse fields, such as psychology, philosophy, sociology, literacy theory, literature, education, and rhetoric. This volume pulls together this research material, in many cases for the first time, with the ultimate goal of defining the field of composition more precisely for both the composition teacher and researcher.

The volume follows in the tradition of Gary Tate's *Teaching Composition: Ten Bibliographical Essays* (Fort Worth: Texas Christian University Press, 1976). We have not repeated the subjects surveyed in that volume, with the exception of the chapter on basic writing. Instead we have chosen many areas of composition that have received little serious attention from writing specialists on the college level: punctuation, vocabulary development, spelling, and usage, for instance. With so much emphasis on concerns such as the writing process and invention, these other areas, often associated with the return-to-basics movement, have not received the attention they deserve.

In addition to selecting such neglected areas of composition, we have also asked scholars to place composition within larger intellectual traditions and to consider the relationship between composition and philosophy, psychology, literature, and reading theory. Thus we hope these chapters will guide composition scholars currently extending their research into these other disciplines.

In the first chapter, "The Writing Process," John Warnock reviews the current research on the composing process, one of the most significant developments in writing pedagogy during the past two decades. By defining a new term, *writing*,* Warnock focuses his chapter not on good, great, or bad writing but on any act that we can truthfully call "writing." We have access, he argues, to the results of writing but not to the cognitive processes that produce the written product. The problem researchers face, therefore, is that they cannot have access to the most important parts of the process that they claim to study. Warnock discusses and analyzes new movements such as "naturalistic" and ethnographic research, as well as other recent developments that determine whether these methods can provide us with non-trivial, context-independent information about the writing process.

In "Cross-Sections in an Emerging Psychology of Composition," Louise Wetherbee Phelps surveys the mammoth field of psychology to establish an emerging sub-field of the psychology of composition. She covers areas such as discourse theory and text production within larger psychological and sociological contexts; the roles of memory, hemisphericity, abstraction, and egocentrism in writing; and current work in psycho-linguistics. Although Phelps does not construct a psychology of composition, she points the way towards such a synthesis. In conclusion, she suggests that composition study must move beyond considerations of the discourse modes and the composing process to establish a theoretical framework that will characterize "the relationships between the growth and learning of written language and other aspects of cognitive, affective, moral, and linguistic development."

In "Research on Writing Blocks, Writing Anxiety, and Writing Apprehension," Lynn Z. Bloom explores the narrower but important concern of writing anxiety, the psychological blocking that prevents writers from functioning. She discusses the methods available for measuring writing anxiety, the causes of the phenomenon, the studies conducted on it in composition and psychology, and ways for teachers to help students overcome the problem. As Bloom argues, more work needs to be done on anxious as well as non-anxious writers to determine the role that anxiety plays in successful writing and the ways that teachers can help the blocked writer.

John C. Briggs turns in "Philosophy and Rhetoric" to another broad field that has influenced research in rhetoric and composition, often only indirectly. Taking a broadly historical view, Briggs traces the important philosophical issues affecting composition and rhetoric from ancient times to the present. As he demonstrates, composition cannot be seen apart from the philosophical issues that have informed it throughout history, and unless researchers recognize these issues, composition can easily degenerate into a series of techniques divorced from broad humanistic and intellectual concerns.

William L. Stull in "Literature, Literary Theory, and the Teaching of Composition" deals with the related issue of the relationship between composition and literature. As the profession of English gradually splits into two competing, often hostile segments, we all should recognize that both areas have much to offer each other. As Stull shows, for instance, recent literary critics interested in the nature of reading and the interpretation of texts provide the composition researcher and teacher with new theoretical frameworks for viewing the subject.

This is the general question that Jasper Neel's "Reading and Writing" takes up. To help composition scholars examine new critical and reading theories, Neel provides an introduction to issues such as decoding theory; modern textual theory and its philosophical, psychoanalytic, and linguistic roots; and their influence on contemporary views of the reading process.

Although the first six chapters place composition in relation to other disciplines, the next three chapters concern themselves with major issues in the field itself. Christopher Burnham's "Research Methods in Composition" uses a historical perspective to trace the development of research methodologies in the field. Burnham examines and evaluates the important research studies, such as Richard Braddock and his colleagues' *Research in Written Composition* (1963), W. Ross Winterowd's *Contemporary Rhetoric* (1975), Gary Tate's *Teaching Composition* (1976), and the most recent research methodologies such as ethnographic research, to show a steady progress towards establishing a distinctive research tradition.

Robert W. Reising and Benjamin J. Stewart in "Grading and Evaluation" do a similar survey of evaluation methods, both those available to classroom teachers and those available to the administrators of large composition programs. Reising and Stewart delineate the numerous direct assessment methods of measuring actual essays, including analytic scoring, holistic scoring, various essay scales, Primary Trait Scoring, T-unit analysis, and other important approaches. They conclude with an outline of the promising directions that evaluation research should take in the future.

Lynn Beene in "Assignment Making" reviews the research on constructing effective assignments that help students produce strong essays. She first discusses the guidelines and criteria that assignments should follow and then evaluates specific kinds of writing assignments for narration and description, analysis, argumentation, persuasion, and library papers. She also examines research on designing writing sequences that require students to write a series of related essays. As Beene notes in the opening of her chapter, researchers have not devoted as much attention to this important area of composition theory as they should.

The next seven chapters deal with what has often been pejoratively termed the "Basics." Matters such as teaching punctuation, vocabulary, sentence structure, spelling, and paragraphing were once considered the only important elements of composition and therefore received an undue emphasis in the classroom. To the general public, control over these elements still is the primary mark of good writing. As composition specialists reacted against this attitude, turned to larger rhetorical concerns, and began to view writing as process, as a method of discovery, and as a mode of thought, less attention was given to these fundamentals. However, we still must teach them in our classrooms, and each area has its own intellectual and research tradition that deserves our attention.

Because these fundamentals are most often associated with Basic Writing (BW), this group of chapters opens with Glynda A. Hull and David Bartholomae's "Basic Writing." This chapter extends Mina Shaughnessy's work in

Tate's *Teaching Composition* by examining the more recent material published on the subject. The authors cover concerns such as the nature of basic writers and their prose, the relation between the development of writing abilities and cognitive growth, and the research on teaching and preparing to teach BW. They also argue that the teaching of BW has important connections with the teaching of other kinds of writing and that the work of basic writers is in many ways similar to that of better prepared students.

Although the other chapters in this section are often associated with BW, they cover the fundamentals any writing teacher should be cognizant of when entering even the most advanced composition classroom. Frank J. D'Angelo in "The Sentence" examines the various views of English sentence structure from the nineteenth century to the present. He covers the tradition of dividing sentences into types (simple, compound, complex, compound/complex), Christensen generative grammar based on structural linguistics, sentence combining with its generative-transformational roots, rhetorical approaches to the sentence, the sentence in relation to the modes of discourse, and other pedagogies of the sentence. At the beginning of his chapter, D'Angelo asserts that the sentence has largely been neglected by researchers, and this area deserves further study.

James Beggs in "The Role of Spelling in Composition for Older Students" surveys the research on spelling, another area that has largely been neglected by college-level composition researchers. He surveys the traditional methods of teaching spelling using word lists and drill, as well as newer methods based on research in phonics and modern linguistics. Although the new methods have promise, Beggs finds that the research studies validate the older ones. He also covers some of the research on teaching the learning disabled, foreign students, and those with dialect interference.

In "Vocabulary Development," Mary Hurley Moran surveys the research in another largely neglected area of composition, the teaching of vocabulary. Although few composition courses seriously teach vocabulary, studies show that this aspect of writing and speaking is closely correlated with professional success and development. Moran defines two major, interacting traditions in vocabulary instruction. The direct method relies on word lists and drills, and the more recent indirect method ties instruction to reading, discussion, and other such methods patterned after the ways people naturally learn new words.

Greta Little surveys still another largely unexamined area of research in "Punctuation." Although many teachers consider it a mere mechanical concern, Little, using a broad historical perspective, demonstrates that punctuation has three distinct traditions that form the unarticulated basis of our current pedagogies. The first is the rhetorical tradition that used punctuation to control how texts were to be read aloud. The second, the grammatical tradition, ties punctuation to grammatical patterns and sentence structure. Finally, the typological tradition grows from the conventions of printers and typesetters, who have greatly influenced our current views on punctuation.

In "Usage," Marvin Ching reviews research in this thorny area, emphasizing the kinds of materials with which the composition teacher should be familiar. He cites works in the history of the English language, semantics, lexicography, language variation, and contemporary linguistic studies of usage to suggest that teachers should take a flexible, informed approach to this subject. Since many composition teachers have not read widely in these areas, Ching argues that they must develop a comprehensive approach based on current research, not on unexamined assumptions.

The final chapter, Michael G. Moran's "English Paragraph," examines the research on this subject from the nineteenth century to the present. The nineteenth-century theorists such as Bain, Lewis, Genung, Scott and Denney, and Wendell established the basic concepts of traditional paragraphing that were not seriously challenged until the work of Francis Christensen, A. L. Becker, and Paul C. Rodgers, Jr., of the 1960s. Moran also selectively reviews the research of fields such as reading theory, educational psychology, and linguistics, which is beginning to influence contemporary views of the paragraph. In general, the profession is beginning to recognize that the paragraph is controlled by a set of flexible conventions rather than by a set of inflexible rules.

The volume concludes with two appendices designed to help composition teachers select textbooks and handbooks. The first, Donald C. Stewart's "Textbooks Revisited," continues his research published in "Composition Textbooks and the Assault on Tradition," *College Composition and Communication*, 29 (1978), 171–76. In Appendix A Stewart reviews 32 textbooks falling under the categories of best-sellers, university-press composition texts, and innovative texts. He concludes that not much has changed since 1978, because many textbooks still do not reflect the current findings of composition research. Appendix B, Marvin Ching's "Evaluating Usage Manuals," reviews the most influential or popular textbooks and trade books on this subject. He discusses books designed for the specialist and the teacher, as well as for the student.

A listing of the abbreviations of journals and books, and organizations used in the book follows the preface. The volume also provides both an Author Index and a Subject Index and an annotated listing about the contributors.

We hope that this collection proves useful to those who teach and conduct research in composition and rhetoric. We would like to thank the many people who contributed to the book. They worked long and hard to provide overviews of their assigned areas, and many of them had to do this with little or no previous work to guide them. Other people also deserve our thanks: M. Thomas Inge, the head of Clemson's English department; Marilyn Brownstein, acquisitions editor at Greenwood Press, who encouraged the project from the outset; Gary Tate, who offered advice and early support; and Joyce Keenum, who worked hard to standardize the reference lists.

Michael G. Moran

Abbreviations

A Psychol	American Psychologist
Acad Ther	Academic Therapy
ADE Bul	ADE Bulletin
AEB	Arizona English Bulletin
AEDS J	Association for Educational Data Systems Journal
AI	American Imago
AJOT	American Journal of Occupational Therapy
AJPs	American Journal of Psychology
ALLC Bul	Association for Literary and Linguistic Computing Bulletin
AM	Atlantic Monthly
Am Educ Res J	American Educational Research Journal
Am J Philol	American Journal of Philology
Am Sch	American Scholar
Am Sp	American Speech
Appl Psycholiguist	Applied Psycholinguistics
Ach Gesch Phil	Archiv Für Geschichte Der Philosophie
Augustin Stud	Augustinian Studies
Bal Sheet	The Balance Sheet
Behav Brain Sci	The Behavioral and Brain Sciences
Brit J Educ Psychol	British Journal of Educational Psychology
BRT	Behavior Research and Therapy
Bul Mod Hum Res Assoc	Bulletin of the Modern Humanities Research Association
Bul Sch Ed. Indiana Univ	Bulletin of the School of Education, Indiana University
Bus Educ Forum	Business Education Forum

Bus Educ World	*Business Education World*
C&T	*Composition and Teaching*
Calif J Ed Res	*California Journal of Educational Research*
Can J of Psychol	*Canadian Journal of Psychology*
CCC	*College Composition and Communication*
CCR	*Community College Review*
CE	*College English*
CEA	*CEA Critic*
CEAF	*College English Association Forum*
Chem Eng News	*Chemical Engineering News*
Chron Higher Educ	*Chronical of Higher Education*
Class J	*Classical Journal*
Class Philol	*Classical Philology*
Clear H	*Clearing House*
Cog Psychol	*Cognitive Psychology*
Cog Sci	*Cognitive Science*
Cog Therapy Res	*Cognitive Therapy and Research*
Comm Mon	*Communication Monographs*
Comp Stud Hist & Soc	*Comparative Studies in History and Society*
Comput Hum	*Computer and Humanities*
Conn E J	*Connecticut English Journal*
Couns Psychol	*Counseling Psychologist*
Crit I	*Critical Inquiry*
CSS J	*Central States Speech Journal*
DAI	*Dissertation Abstracts International*
Develop Psychol	*Developmental Psychology*
E Rec	*English Record*
Ed Res (Brit)	*Educational Research (British)*
Educ Horizons	*Educational Horizons*
Educ Lead	*Educational Leadership*
Educ Tech	*Educational Technology*
EER	*Elementary English Review*
EEJ	*English Journal*
El Sch J	*Elementary School Journal*
Elem Eng	*Elementary English*
Engl Lang Teach J	*English Language Teaching Journal*
Engl Stud	*English Studies*
ER	*Educational Review*
ERIC	*Educational Resources Informational Center*
ERQ	*Educational Research Quarterly*
Ex E	*Exercise Exchange*
EEN	*Freshman English News*
Focus: Teach Eng Lang Arts	*Focus: Teaching English Language Arts*

Ga R	Georgia Review
Gifted Child Q	Gifted Child Quarterly
Grade Teach	Grade Teacher
Greek Rom & Byz Studies	Greek, Roman, and Byzantine Studies
H Points	High Points
Harv Stud Class Phil	Harvard Studies in Classical Philology
Harvard Educ Rev	Harvard Educational Review
Human Dev	Human Development
ILL E B	Illinois English Bulletin
Improv Coll & Univ Teaching	Improving College and University Teaching
Ind Read Q	Indiana Reading Quarterly
Instr	Instructor
Int Encycl Social Sc	International Encyclopedia of Social Science
Int J Psychol	International Journal of Psychology
Int Rev Educ	International Review of Education
Interact	Interaction
J Bus Ed	Journal of Business Education
J Comm	Journal of Communication
J Creat Behav	Journal of Creative Behavior
J Dev Rem Ed	Journal of Developmental and Remediial Education
J Educ	Journal of Education
J Educ Method	Journal of Educational Method
J Educ Psychol	Journal of Educational Psychology
J Educ Res	Journal of Educational Research
J Exp Educ	Journal of Experimental Education
J Exp Psychol	Journal of Experimental Psychology
J Exp Psychol Hum Learn Mem	Journal of Experimental Psychology: Human Learning and Memory
J Exp Psychol Hum Perc Perf	Journal of Experimental Psychology: Human Perception and Performance
J Exp Soc Psychol	Journal of Experimental Social Psychology
J Gen Ed	Journal of General Education
J Learn Dis	Journal of Learning Disabilities
J Linguist	Journal of Linguistics
J Lit Seman	Journal of Literary Semantics
J PERS	Journal of Personality
J Pers Soc Psychol	Journal of Personality and Social Psychology
J Psychol	Journal of Psychology
J Read	Journal of Reading
J Read Behav	Journal of Reading Behavior
J Res Dev Ed	Journal of Research and Development in Education

J Soc Psychology	*Journal of Social Psychology*
J Speech Hear Res	*Journal of Speech and Hearing Research*
J Tech Writ Comm	*Journal of Technical Writing and Communication*
J Verb Learn Verb Behav	*Journal of Verbal Learning and Verbal Behavior*
J Youth Ado	*Journal of Youth and Adolescence*
JAAC	*Journal of Aesthetics and Art Criticism*
JAC	*Journal of Advanced Composition*
JBTEP	*Journal of Behavioral Therapy and Experimental Psychology*
JBW	*Journal of Basic Writing*
JCCP	*Journal of Consulting and Clinical Psychology*
JEGP	*Journal of English and Germanic Philology*
JETT	*Journal of English Teaching Techniques*
JHE	*Journal of Higher Education*
JHI	*Journal of the History of Ideas*
JOP	*Journal of Occupational Psychology*
JQ	*Journalism Quarterly*
Lang	*Language*
Lang Arts	*Language Arts*
Lang L	*Language Learning*
Lang S	*Language and Style*
Learn Dis Q	*Learning Disability Quarterly*
LF	*Langue Française*
Li Li	*Zeitschrift für Literaturwissenschaft und Linguistik*
Linguistic Phil	*Linguistics and Philosophy*
Minn Engl J	*Minnesota English Journal*
MLN	*Modern Lanbguage Notes*
Mod Lang J	*Modern Language Journal*
MP	*Modern Philology*
N&Q	*Notes and Queries*
Nat Soc Study Ed Yrbk	*National Society for the Study of Educational Yearbook*
Nation's Sch & Coll	*Nation's Schools and Colleges*
Natl El Prin	*National Elementary Principal*
NCF	*Nineteenth Century Fiction*
NCTE	National Council of Teachers of English
NDEJ	*Notre Dame English Journal*
New Scholas	*New Scholasticism*
NLH	*New Literary History*
NOTE	*Notes on Teaching English*

NY R B	New York Review of Books
Ohio Eng Lang Arts Bul	Ohio English Language Arts Bulletin
PBSA	Papers of the Bibliographic Society of America
PCTE	Pennsylvania College Teachers of English Bulletin
Perc Motor Skills	Perceptual and Motor Skills
Phi Del Kap	Phi Delta Kappan
Phi Phenomenol Res	Philosophy and Phenomenological Research
Phil Rev	Philosophical Review
Phil Rhet	Philosophy and Rhetoric
Phil Today	Philosophy Today
PJE	Peabody Journal of Education
PMLA	Publications of the Modern Language Association
Po T	Poetics Today
Prt Ink	Printer's Ink
PSA	Pennsylvania Speech Annual
Psy Q	Psychiatric Quarterly
Psy R	Psychoanalytic Review
Psychol Rep	Psychological Reports
Psychol Rev	Psychological Review
Q J Wxp Psychol	Quarterly Journal of Experimental Psychology
QJS	Quarterly Journal of Speech
QJSE	Quarterly Journal of Speech Education
Read Horizons	Reading Horizons
Read Res Q	Reading Research Quarterly
Read Teach	Reading Teacher
Read World	Reading World
Reading Improv	Reading Improvement
RES	Review of English Studies
Res Lang Arts	Research in Language Arts
Rev Educ Res	Review of Educational Research
Rev Metaphysics	Review of Metaphysics
RR	Rhetoric Review
RSQ	Rhetorical Society Quarterly
RTE	Research in Teaching English
Sat Rev	Saturday Review
SB	Studies in Bibliography
Sch	School
Sch & Com	School and Community
Sch P	Scholarly Publishing
Sch Rev	School Review
Sch & Soc	School and Society

SECOL B	*SECOL Bullletin*
SP	*Studies in Philology*
Speech Mon	*Speech Monographs*
SQ	*Shakespeare Quarterly*
SSpCJ	*Southern Speech Communication Journal*
Stud Lang & Lang Behav	*Studies in Language and Language Behavior*
TAJ	*Transactional Analysis Journal*
TCR	*Teachers College Record*
Teach Col J	*Teachers College Journal*
Teach & Writ Mag	*Teachers and Writers Magazine*
TESOL Quarterly	*Teachers of English to Speakers of Other Languages Quarterly*
TETYC	*Teaching English Association in the Two-Year College*
Times Educ Sup	*Times Educational Supplement*
TLS	*Times Literary Supplement*
Univ of Edinburgh J	*University of Edinburgh Journal*
Use Engl	*Use of English*
UTQ	*University of Toronto Quarterly*
Visibl Lang	*Visible Language*
Western J Speech Comm	*Western Journal of Speech and Communication*
Westminster Rev	*Westminster Review*
WPA	*Writing Program Administrator*
Writ Instr	*Writing Instructor*
Yale Rev	*Yale Review*

Part I

Current Research

The Writing Process

JOHN WARNOCK

Writing is a complex process, but for the writer of an essay which purports to review work on the writing process, that is only part of the problem. Though "writing" is often used with an apparent confidence that we all know what we mean by the term, that confidence is as unwarranted as our sometime confidence about the term "literacy." We shall have to try to find a definition of writing we can settle on for this essay.

Assuming we do not define "writing" trivially, we shall have another problem: the problem of how we can know that we are indeed observing an instance of writing, and how we can study it once we have found it. This is a problem in any study of "process," as it is with any study of "competence."

About Writing* and "Process"

Definitions of *writing* vary by culture; by social, economic and political context; and by time—historical time, developmental time, and composing time. Among the studies from social science that support this observation are Sylvia Scribner and Michael Cole's *Psychology of Literacy* (1981); Michael Stubbs's "Written Language and Society," in *What Writers Know* (1982); and the essays in Part I, "The Socio-Cultural Functions of Writing," in *Writing*, volume 1 (1981). Donald H. Graves (1982a) gave an account of how children define *writing* differently over time. Protocols, as in the reports of Linda Flower and John R. Hayes (1980) and S. Perl (1979), show writers defining *writing* differently as they move through the process. More polemical analyses of the problem of defining *writing* and *literacy* are found in Richard Ohmann, *English in America*

I want to thank Thomas Newkirk and Linda Flower for comments on an earlier draft of this chapter and Tilly Warnock for help all along the way.

(1976) and Robert Pattison *On Literacy* (1982). The Pattison book provides, among other things, a provocative adumbration of the nature of the problem of defining *literacy* and a graceful and scholarly account of how literacy has been found in Western history; an excellent selected annotated bibliography is also provided.

For the purposes of this exploration, the term writing* means the least a machine or a person would have to be able to do to enable us to say truthfully of that machine or person that it was actually writing in the way we know all human beings are able to do in enabling situations. Writing,* then, is not to be confused with the products of writing,* not with Great Writing, not even with good or effective writing, the sort of thing that gets one high ratings from the socialized readers in Princeton. The 1's may be as much a product of writing* as the 9's are.

As to whether a particular act amounts to "actually writing," we might differ more than we would differ about whether a particular utterance was "well formed" in Noam Chomsky's sense (1957). This variation we could take as further evidence that our ideas of writing* are tied to social and cultural factors. I think we would agree, however, that the proverbial apes at the typing machines are not writing,* nor, so far, are the computers that write poetry, no matter how plausible their products.

In defining *writing* in this way, I have taken sides, for the purposes of this chapter, in one active controversy about writing*—whether it is natural or artificial. If by "natural" we mean that anybody can do it—when circumstances don't prevent it—without being taught to do it (we now assume that the ability to speak a language is natural, in this sense), I take writing to be natural. It is hard to know what sort of study would prove writing to be natural or artificial. The position one takes in the discussion has important pedagogical consequences: The best adumbration of the pedagogical assumptions that follow from taking writing to be natural is Janet Emig's "Non-Magical Thinking" in *Writing*, volume 1 (1981). Emig's essay also sets out some criteria for "enabling situations." Other criteria are set out in John Warnock's "New Rhetoric and the Grammar of Pedagogy" (1976a).

The notion of a writing* machine is introduced here not to take a position in the debate about whether human beings are "only machines" but to highlight the wonderful complexity of our subject and to remind us how far writing* lies beyond our present technological competence. I hope it might also suggest the sense I have that the meanest act of writing* calls for a moment of thanksgiving, whatever else it may call for.

How do we know that we are observing an instance of writing*? A cartoon on a graduate student's door pictures a newspaper editor-bird in the first panel standing near his wastebasket of a desk, a question mark in his mind-balloon; in the next panel he stares with lidded eyes at his typewriter; in the third panel he is sailing a paper airplane; in the fourth panel he is leaning back in his chair apparently asleep; in the fifth panel he is hunched in his chair in obvious deep depression; in the sixth panel a secretary-bird approaches to ask him something, but she is stopped by the "perfesser"-bird who explains: "Better not bother him now, Muffy. He's writing" (Jeff MacNelly, *Shoe*, date unknown).

We can point to a page in a book and say with some confidence that that page is the product of writing,* but only with some confidence, since the page could be the product of a glitch in the word processor or the proverbial ape at the typing machine. We can point to students pushing pens across pages, and we can say with some confidence that they are writing,* but only with some confidence, since they might be moving their pens just to hear the scratching noises. For a discussion of several analytical treatments of this question, see Margaret A. Boden's *Purposive Explanation in Psychology* (1972), especially pages 263–81.

We go by appearances; we infer writing* from them. In principle, however, we are not incorrect in any of our suppositions that we see writing* going on outside ourselves. Not even if we had a writing* machine would we be incorrigible, since a machine that could write* could presumably, like people, not write* as well. Empirical research into writing* proceeds by defining particular observable and describable acts as constituting writing,* or some sub-process of writing* like planning. This analytical point seems important when we are attempting to derive teaching methods from what we know about the writing process.

Another important point about studying process may be seen in K. S. Lashley's comment in "The Behavioristic Interpretation of Consciousness" (1923) that "no activity of the mind is ever conscious." This statement is interpreted by Daniel Dennett in *Brainstorms* (1978), page 165, to mean that "we have access— conscious access—to the *results* of mental processes, but not to the processes themselves." The relationship of "that of which we are conscious" to the actual processes of which such conscious contents are only a part is not taken up much in the literature on writing.* In fairness, little could be said with certainty about such relationships. Still, we might acknowledge more than we do the need for such an account before we pretend to have the kind of knowledge that would enable us to produce a writing* machine.

The shift from product to process cannot mean a shift entirely away from the products of writing. We know writing only through its products. There is no other way. The shift means, among other things, that we have broadened our notion of what are the interesting products of writing to include much besides the results of a writer's last acts before publication. It means also that we have complicated our notion of what are the producers of writing* to include more than hypostases such as "thoughts" and "assignments."

The shift began, for people in composition, with Janet Emig's study *The Composing Processes of Twelfth Graders* (1971). As Emig noted in her review of the literature, the final products of writing—the books we read, the papers students hand in—are remarkably opaque when we try to use them as a way of seeing into writing.* Writing* covers its tracks, for one thing. J. Derrida in *Of Grammatology* (1976) has made much of this property of texts.

One move, then, would be to look at the drafts of writers, but they too are opaque. Although they show us what people actually uttered before achieving their final products, they do not tell us much about the timing or the order of the changes in a given draft, nor do they tell us what writers had in mind when they wrote what they did. Drafts have been and are being studied by literary scholars, but the purpose of their study is to argue artistic intention—meaning—and not to understand writing.* See for instance M. Groden's *Ulysses in Progress* (1977).

Two moves might help answer the deficiencies of drafts. One would be to observe writers during a particular act of writing, taking pictures and timing the acts of the writer, if time and technology permitted. The research of A. Matsuhashi is our best example of an attempt to use the data produced in this way. See "Explorations in the Real-Time Production of Written Discourse" in *What Writers Know* (1982). As Matsuhashi pointed out, if one only observes writers writing, one is far short of being able to interpret securely the observed behaviors. When one attempts to solve this problem by, for example, asking writers what was in their minds as they wrote, a number of other problems arise.

Humans have proven to be quite unreliable in after-the-fact explanations of behavior. For a while this unreliability gave introspection in general a bad name among psychological researchers, as Richard E. Nisbett and Timothy DeCamp Wilson argued in "Telling More Than We Can Know" (1977). Introspection has made a partial come-back; it has become respectable to ask subjects to report, not to explain, what is, not was, in their minds. The theoretical and empirical justification for this move is argued in Eliot R. Smith and Frederick D. Miller's "Limits on Perception of Cognitive Processes" (1978) and in K. Anders Ericcson and Herbert Simon's "Retrospective Verbal Reports as Data" (1978) and "Thinking-Aloud Protocols as Data" (1979).

This particular kind of introspective report is the thinking-aloud protocol associated with the research of Flower and Hayes ajnd others. Although we have good reason to accept these reports as reflecting what was in fact in peoples' minds at the time they were reporting, we do not now have any good account of the relationship of these conscious products of writing to what is happening in the brain. A fascinating speculation on this subject—both playful and scientifically profound—is found in Douglas Hofstadter's *Godel, Escher, Bach* (1979). Among the research that has employed thinking-aloud protocols is that of Emig (1971), Perl (1979), S. Pianko (1979), Flower and Hayes (1980, 1981a, 1981b), and A. Matsuhashi (1981).

Having to report the contents of consciousness in words might distort the contents of consciousness and might also fail to capture aspects of awareness relevant to writing* that are nevertheless non-, sub-, or pre-verbal. Furthermore, not all shifts of attention would be marked by shifts in observable behavior, for example, pauses. This has prompted a search for ways of marking shifts in attention that do not require verbal reports or pauses. John Warnock and Tilly

Warnock (unpublished research) have attempted this with a device they call "changing pencils."

These methodologies allow us to look with some delicacy at single episodes of writing.* As Donald Graves remarked (1975, page 227), researchers had paid very little attention to such episodes themselves until Emig (1971). Much more common was work that looked at the textual outcomes of many such episodes, attempting not so much to understand what went into them as to draw conclusions about the efficacy of a particular method of instruction. Such studies did not succeed in the purpose they did not have, the purpose of understanding writing,* but they did not succeed either as a rule in the purpose they did have, that of evaluating methods of instruction, as Richard Braddock, Richard Lloyd-Jones, and Lowell Schorer suggested in *Research in Written Composition* (1963).

Researchers interested in writing* might also want to widen the study to include the products of a number of writers or lengthen it to include a number of episodes by a single writer or by several writers. This last is the move of those who undertake "horizontal" study. Walter Loban's *Language Development: Kindergarten through Grade Twelve* (1976) is a good example of a study that looks out wide and long. So are the studies of the National Assessment of Educational Progress. Both of these studies are text-centered; they do not deal in, for example, protocols. It is a long step from conclusions about writing to conclusions about writing.*

Yet another move is entailed in the case-study method. In case study, researchers take the horizontal view, but usually they also broaden their sense of what data are relevant to the particular episodes of writing* studied. A case study may be text-centered, or it may include what a writer says about things, or the results of tests of attitude or apprehension, or socio-economic data—in fact anything hypothesized to cause variation in the products of writing.* Opening up in this way the possibilities for what counts as data creates challenging problems for researchers. Any number of factors might be related causally to variation in the products of writing*; one problem is how to limit the scope of one's investigation without trivializing it. When one is studying "situation," "context," "community," "culture," one has the problem also of deciding what are the appropriate categories for the situation being observed. These categories must not only be appropriate for the situation being observed—internally valid—but they will be hoped somehow to be significant to observers in other situations, contexts, and so on—externally valid. For context-dependent research, the problem of external validity is the more intractable. If such research aspires to be naturalistic, it has also the problem of defining and maintaining the natural quality of the performances being observed. Perhaps since it is difficult to argue the naturalness of *any* research situation, researchers have begun to refer to the "ecology" of such situations; the researcher is often recognized to be not just an observer but a "participant-observer," which calls for an account of how the researcher affects the data.

These are the problems of the emerging field of ethnographic research. A good discussion of the problems and promise of such research, together with citations to much of the work of this sort that has been done so far, is found in Kenneth J. Kantor, Dan R. Kirby, and Judith P. Goetz's "Research in Context" (1981). A thought-provoking statement of the difference in the interpretive stance of such researchers is found in Clifford Geertz's *Interpretation of Cultures* (1973). Research of this sort is currently underway at, among other places, the Writing Process Laboratory at the University of New Hampshire (Donald Graves, Lucy Calkins, Susan Sowers), at the American Research Institute in Washington, D.C. (Dixie Goswami, Lee Odell), at the University of Georgia (Kenneth Kantor, Dan Kirby, Judith Goetz), and at the City University of New York (S. Perl).

Both science and development proceed through feats of abstraction. But in abstraction, we trade reality for power, as James Moffett (1968) among others pointed out. Some of the recent methodological developments in composition may be seen as efforts to regain a reality that has been lost through a too thorough commitment to one kind of experimental research. "Quasi-experimental" research has the objective of finding ways of justifying conclusions without the Procrustean bed of laboratory conditions. "Action" research envisages research in circumstances where the researcher does not simply observe the phenomenon to understand it but attempts to understand the phenomenon to be able to act upon it. Research done in the context of UNESCO's mission of achieving "world literacy" is claimed to be "action" research. Sometimes (in UNESCO's case, not often enough) such research recognizes and embraces a complex relationship between the observer of phenomena and the participant in events; teachers of writing might also recognize and embrace such complexity.

The shift from product to process, then, has meant that we have accepted much more as potentially useful data in our attempts to make perspicuous inferences about writing.* Qualitatively, the shift is one from ends to means, a strategem characteristic of creative work, as D. N. Perkins argued in *The Mind's Best Work* (1981). Concurrently, we have developed or accepted new methodologies that accommodate our new sense of what counts as data in a study of writing.*

But we may need to remind ourselves of two points about this shift from product to process: no matter how deep or how far we go, we shall be inferring writing* from its products, never simply describing it; and since process in motion for its own sake is either divine or pathological, we have undertaken this shift *for* something. We could name this end in a number of ways. R. M. Pirsig, in *Zen and the Art of Motorcycle Maintenance* (1974), called it "Quality."

Research Results

A useful survey of research into the composing process appeared in Ann Humes's "Research on the Composing Process," in *Writing* (1982). Readers may find there a more detailed account of some of the methods and findings of individual researchers than will appear here. Here we spend more time considering certain assumptions sometimes made in conducting this research.

We can and do speak of the results of research into pre-writing and re-writing, but we ought to pause a moment to ask about the ontological status of these stages of writing.* They have a kind of beginning-middle-end quality, which makes them serviceable for scheduling a class hour, or semester, but what is their relation to writing* and the learning of writing*? Flower and Hayes (1981a) criticized these categories for representing the product of writing not the process; it may be more to the point to say that these categories represent the product of teaching rather than the process of writing. Would we expect our writing* machine to pre-write, write, and re-write? That would depend on what task it had set for itself and where it was at the time. If it was in school, we might indeed expect it to write that way, depending on, among other things, what teachers it had had and what their power was.

Writing* begins. And writing* ends. Where those two points lie we may have great trouble saying, unless we stipulate them, as we may have to do in school, in business, in publishing. We may have just as much difficulty specifying in objective terms where the parts of writing that we call ''pre-writing'' and ''re-writing'' begin and end and what precisely distinguishes one from the other.

Re-writing, we might think, can be clearly enough ascertained. You can re-write only what has been once written. You can't alter the spelling of a thought. You can, however, alter the thought of a thought, if you can keep it in mind long enough. Most would agree that the most significant re-writing is that which involves re-thinking. So even though we recognize that having a written text may be especially convenient for thinking, we need to ask in what significant respect does significant re-writing differ from re-thinking? Coming at the matter from the other end, isn't most pre-writing a matter of re-thinking? We might even wonder if there is any thinking that isn't re-thinking. On a number of grounds, it is not unreasonable to assume that, in principle, there is no difference in kind between pre-writing and re-writing, except in those matters that have to do with coding proprieties. When professional writers talk about their processes, some such conclusion seems not far off, as in Donald M. Murray, ''Internal Revision,'' in *Learning by Teaching* (1982); and William Stafford, *Writing the Australian Crawl* (1978).

A most interesting and difficult question, however, is: taking thought to be the content of pre-writing, if not also of re-writing, what is the relation to thought of what I have above called ''coding proprieties''? Here we encounter some of the thorniest and actively controversial issues going, although you wouldn't know it to read many textbook discussions of writing.* Some of the issues are epistemological and some empirical. Among them: What is the relation of language, whatever that is, to thought, of speech to thought, of thought and language to social life? Some philosophers who have inquired into this matter are Ludwig Wittgenstein, *Philosophical Investigations* (1953); and W.V.O. Quine, *Word and Object* (1960). Empirical work relevant to this inquiry is L. S. Vygotsky's *Thought and Language*

(1962) and *Mind in Society*, edited by Michael Cole and others (1978). Another important discussion is G. H. Mead's *Mind, Self, and Society* (1934).

Other hard questions are: how exactly do capacities for thought develop? The proposals of Jean Piaget have gained a wide following (see, for example, *The Psychology of Intelligence* [1953] but see also an important critique in Margaret Donaldson's *Children's Minds* [1978]. See also Jerome Bruner's *On Knowing* [1962]).

Is it possible to learn to think? Is it possible to teach people to think? If it is possible to learn to think, are there technologies for thinking—techniques of invention—that are independent of the particular problem encountered? If such technologies do exist, are the best ones systematic or unsystematic, open or closed? On this topic, see the excellent bibliographical survey of Richard Young, "Invention," in Gary Tate's *Teaching Composition* (1976). Another excellent discussion is W. Ross Winterowd's "Topics and Levels in the Composing Process" (1967).

Finally, what *is* thinking? One discussion is M. Heidegger's *What Is Called Thinking?* (1968).

Some of the questions now most important to researchers concerning revision are: how old do you have to be to do it? R. J. Bracewell and colleagues argued in "The Development of Audience Awareness in Writing" (1978) that you had to be 14 to revise for an audience, but Donald Graves (1979b) shows this to be possible much earlier.

Are there two kinds of revision: one for the writer, one for the reader; or one for the thought, one for the "conventions"? Murray, in "Internal Revision" (1982) suggested that there are two kinds; Elsa Jaffe Bartlett made a similar proposal in "Learning to Revise," in *What Writer's Know* (1982). We now accept the fact that there is more than one kind of revision. But perhaps we should ask whether these are "kinds" of revision or rather something more like different frames of mind, and whether there are two of these frames or as many frames as there are frames of mind.

Can you teach revision through requiring specific tasks? G. Hillocks (1982) said yes. Murray said no. This would seem to be one avatar of the question that bedevils composition teachers in all areas of writing:* What should be the nature of the tasks we specify, or should *we* specify any tasks for students learning to write?

These questions about revision are also central to investigations of pre-writing. The identity suggests that we ought to think less of investigating the properties of these two stages and think more of what common set of actions they might both be a part of.

When we survey the findings of research into the composing process, we may be left, as Humes said in "Research on the Composing Process" (1982), wondering if it was "all for naught." Most findings seem to have exceptions: The finding that good writers plan about two-thirds of their writing time (Carol Berkenkotter, "Decisions and Revisions" [1982]) can be matched with the finding that both the good and the bad letter writers planned about two-thirds of the time (John D. Gould, *Cognitive Processes in Writing* [1980]). The finding that good writers review and revise a lot (Perl [1979]; Nancy Sommers [1980]) can be matched with the finding that revisions of poor writers often do not make things better (Mina Shaughnessy, [1977]; S. Perl, [1980]). As our understanding of the components of the process increases, we seem to be faced with the real possibility that no process, as such, will make for better writing.*

An important distinction is thus suggested. We need an adequate notion not only of how writing* is done but of how it is learned. In this account the distinction between *learning* and *acquisition* would seem to be crucial, a point that is argued by John Warnock in "New Rhetoric and the Grammar of Pedagogy" (1976a). So also, by implication, would an account of the role of conscious knowledge versus what might be called practical knowledge be crucial. A theoretical statement that reveals the complexity and importance of this issue is found in Michael Polanyi, *Personal Knowledge* (1958).

Not all writing programs or writing teachers face squarely the need for an account of how writing* is learned. Many teachers seem to assume that learning happens by virtue of the way we are accustomed to teach. Little effort is devoted to making explicit our assumptions about how our subject is learned. One program that offers an explicit account is the Huntington Beach Writing Project, directed by W. Ross Winterowd. His workshop/lab model is based upon an assumed distinction between *acquisition* and *learning*, as outlined by S. D. Krashen in "Formal and Informal Linguistic Environments" (1976), and a delineation of the domains of writing* activity where each could be expected to operate. The New Jersey Writing Project, directed by Linda Waitkus, also emphasizes the centrality of developmental learning while urging a role for learning theory and research. The Wyoming Writing Project proposes that teachers of writing articulate their theories of writing as part of the developmental process of changing teaching, on the argument that only articulated theories are subject to certain kinds of criticism and revision, or confirmation.

Furthermore, an account of how writing is learned would have to include, if D. N. Perkins (1981) is right, an explanation of what makes someone want to write well. A premise here is offered by William E. Coles, who argued in "The Circle of Unbelief" (1969) that we cannot hope for good writing unless we teach from what writing means to us. This argument demands more of us than skill in the application of an adequate technology. It implies that we cannot hope finally to save ourselves or our students from bad writing by "approaches" or "strategies" or, to use the language of the Ontario Institute for Studies in Education (OISE) group, by "procedural facilitation."

Nevertheless, in spite of what we may or may not hope for from accounts of the writing process, much research is now being done in an attempt to develop a model of the process and to distinguish what good or expert writers do from what the not-so-good writers do. This research is both interesting and skilled.

In some discussions, but not often in the field of composition, *model* has a precise meaning. In composition, the word might include what others have meant by "schema," or "scheme" (Piaget [1953]), or "hypothesis" (Frank Smith [1971]), or "construct" (G. A. Kelly [1955]), or "theory." *Theory* in composition has meant everything from "model" (see Nancy Sommer's "The Need for Theory in Composition Research" [1979]) to "taxonomy" (see James L. Kinneavy's *A Theory of Discourse* [1971]) to something like "motive" (see Warnock's "Who's Afraid of Theory" [1976b]).

In the philosophy of science, a *model* is distinguished from a *theory* by its hypothetical nature. A *scientific theory* according to Ronald N. Giere in *Understanding Scientific Reasoning* (1979) is "a definition of a kind of natural system" (page 68). A *theoretical hypothesis* asserts that "Such-and-such real system is a system of the type defined by the theory" (page 70). This assertion is then tested in any way the researcher can think to test it.

Models, then, in this context, are not descriptions of real systems, nor are they definitions of a kind of natural system. Rather they are working definitions, proposed to see what they might suggest about ways of exploring a question and to see whether the assertions that can be deduced from the model are validated by observation. Thus a model can't count as a model in this context unless it is stated so that it can be tested by observation.

I am not proposing that we in composition restrict our use of model to that employed in empirical science. It is crucial, however, to distinguish between models for research and models for teaching and not to make easy assumptions about connections between the two. Sometimes, for example, easy assumptions are made about the relation of a model or theory to conduct. If we have not known enough from experience to be skeptical, we have learned about the difference between the words and deeds of teachers in *Functions of Language in the Classroom*, by Courtney Cazden and others (1972). The research that led psychologists to be skeptical of the validity of introspection might also support some skepticism toward whether one's articulated theories of writing and teaching are those one in fact writes and teaches by.

In recent years, several research models of writing* have been proposed. These models are scientific in the sense outlined above: They aim to suggest empirically testable propositions about writing.* They appear to aspire to be simulation models: That is, their proponents have attempted to state them in such a way that a machine might be programmed to operate according to the model so that it can be observed whether the traces produced by the machine resemble those produced by writers.* A variation on the theme of simulation is found in M. Scardamalia and C. Bereiter's "Development of Dialectical Processes in Composition" (1981) in which a "model is 'run' on human subjects who are not already 'programmed' to run that way, [to see if the results are] compatible with those of an expert writer whose performance is taken as criterial" (p. 30).

In the community of researchers seeking to develop models of this kind, it is now commonplace that any satisfactory scientific model of the writing process must be multi-level, iterative, and recursive. A *multi-level model* would allow for operations at more than one level, apparently simultaneously (for example,

at the sensori-motor, morphemic, syntactic, and pragmatic levels; we do not know how many levels there are or even if "levels" is the best metaphor for us here), with some operations being automatic and some conscious and controlled, and with the "executive capacity" of the writer being allocated differently at different times. An *iterative model* would allow for operations to repeat themselves (for example, allowing planning or revising to take place repeatedly at different times during a course of writing). A *recursive model* would allow certain operations to be repeated at different levels during composing. (It is common in writing on composition to confuse "recursiveness" with "iteration"; *recursiveness* entails repetition at different levels.)

From the point of view of scientific research into writing,* the linear fixed-stage models of the writing process have been so thoroughly discredited as to have the status of straw men, as Gould noted in *Cognitive Processes in Writing* (1980). The challenge to such models began, as did so much in the field, with Moffett (1968) and Emig (1971). The bad press that fixed-stage models have received in the research community has not prevented such models from remaining dominant in many classrooms. The fact that fixed-stage models do not serve the needs of researchers does not necessarily mean that such models might not serve the needs of teachers or (we must not too easily identify these two communities of interest) of students learning to write. Even a lecture on writing might serve the needs of some students some time. What is disheartening is the overwhelming reliance by teachers, in the past and at present, on lecture and conventional writing assignments as the means of teaching everything, as documented in Kenneth Sirotnik's "What You See Is What You Get" (1983). Also disheartening is many teachers' unbelief in the validity of their methods, as adumbrated by William E. Coles in "The Circle of Unbelief" (1969).

The research models I specify here are those of Linda Flower and John Hayes (1981a, 1981b) and Scardamalia and Bereiter (1981). Gould (1980) and Ellen Nold (1980) have proposed models similar in general outline to that of Flower and Hayes.

For this chapter, it seems much less useful to compare these models in detail or to evaluate their completeness and validity with respect to one another than to point out general similarities and to discuss an important aspect of writing that none of them deals with.

Flower and Hayes's model is presented in "A Cognitive Process Theory of Writing" (1981a) and developed in more detail in "Plans that Guide the Composing Process" (1981b) and "The Cognition of Discovery" (1980). In this model, writing is characterized as a kind of "problem solving." The writing process is seen as consisting of the basic sub-processes of planning, translating, and reviewing. All of these components are placed in the context of the "task environment" and "the writer's long-term memory."

Planning is the part of the writing process that has received the most attention in Flower and Hayes's work so far. They used a notion of plan (an "internal representation") that is widely employed among researchers into cognition. The initial specification of this sense of the nature of plans is found in George Miller, Eugene Galanter, and Kenneth Pribram's *Plans and the Structure of Behavior* (1960). This notion of plans has of course been important to people in artificial intelligence. See, for instance, R. C. Schank and R. P. Abelson's *Scripts, Plans, Goals, and Understanding* (1977). A good brief discussion of the use of the notion of plans among psychologists is Boden's *Purposive Explanation in Psychology* (1972), pages 194–98.

In Flower and Hayes's model of writing,* plans are further analyzed into plans for generating, plans for organizing, and (plans for?) goal-setting. In another essay, "Plans that Guide the Composing Process," in *Writing*, volume 2 (1980), Flower and Hayes proposed to understand writers as having plans for generating ideas and plans for producing texts, and they found evidence that the two kinds of plans can be in conflict. In *Writing Without Teachers* (1973), Peter Elbow testified to such a conflict in his own experience, and there have been other testimonials, such as Stafford's in *Writing the Australian Crawl* (1978).

The model of Scardamalia and Bereiter characterizes the whole of the composing process as a matter of planning. They analyzed this planning into a Compare-Diagnose-Operate process, highly reminiscent of the Test-Operate-Test-Exit process proposed in Miller, Galanter, and Pribram's *Plans and the Structure of Behavior* (1960). It is indeed not easy to see how Flower and Hayes's sub-processes of translating and reviewing would not themselves involve "internal representations," and thus it is not always easy to see how planning could be taken to be only one component of the writing process. Yet the three components of Flower and Hayes's model do seem to characterize three kinds of conscious attention in a way that the model of Scardamalia and Bereiter does not.

In the third sub-division of planning in the model of Flower and Hayes—goal-setting—we encounter a particularly problematical aspect of putting the matter in the way these researchers do. Does it not stretch the metaphor to speak of "plans" for goal-setting? This stretching happens precisely at the most important point of the model, in terms of affecting outcomes of writing.* If we accept the conclusions of Perkins in *The Mind's Best Work* (1981), "The essence of invention isn't process, but purpose. . . . Purpose shapes process. . . . Discovery depends not on special processes but on special purposes" (p. 100). The intractability of the problem of understanding how purpose arises for writing* has led one researcher, E. D. Hirsch, to propose in *The Philosophy of Composition* (1977) that as writing teachers we have no business with a writer's intention, only with the "relative readability" of the writing. Hirsch faced the problem more squarely than some, although his solution to it has not struck many as satisfactory.

It is common in cognitive research to characterize writing* as "goal-directed." But none of the researchers we are considering here offered an account of where goals come from or how they are set. Only Flower and Hayes, as far as I know, have published in their account of writing* any indication that this is a serious deficiency. There is reason to believe that until we have a way of approaching

this question, we are unable to "teach" writing,* no matter how sophisticated our knowledge of its processes may be.

The research models of writing* have produced a good deal of excitement among writing teachers and researchers but also a good deal of skepticism. There can be no doubt that the work of these researchers has advanced our understanding of writing.* Whether it has also advanced our writing or our teaching of writing is a subject that must be treated elsewhere.

Also creating excitement and controversy today is the naturalistic research of Donald Graves and his colleagues Lucy McCormick Calkins and Susan Sowers, at the Writing Process Laboratory at the University of New Hampshire. See the articles of Graves, Calkins, and Sowers in this chapter's References, and Graves's *Writing* (1982b). This research does not aim to produce simulation models of cognitive processes. Rather, it aims to let us see, in rich detail, what writers do in context when left largely to their own devices. This research produces models by dint of extensive observation over time, with the observational categories being developed as much from the experience of observation as from any preliminary hypotheses. But despite their empirical basis, the models produced here, it may be argued, do not count as scientific. They contain a great deal of information, and many teachers have learned much from this work about what children do naturally, with different kinds of help, without being assigned particular "learning" tasks. Indeed, as Thomas Newkirk (personal letter) pointed out, this work has undercut many of the claims of developmental incapacity made by the experimental researchers.

But this naturalistic-observational work does not offer us any prospect of a deductive system; we might say instead that it presents us with a dramatistic scene. It offers us not so much the prospect of control as the prospect of a more thorough participation in the actuality of language learning with children.

Nor will the ethnographic research now going on in a number of places produce research models. Teachers, however, seem to find the images of such research more useful than the research models. To report this observation is by no means to sneer at research models; it is to suggest that the kind of knowledge that is most useful to performers may differ from the kind of knowledge that is useful to inquirers.

If this research has emerged out of an investigation of the cognitive processes of writers,* another line of research has emerged out of the study of language. For a while, some students of writing* thought that linguistics held great promise for researchers and teachers of writing,* in spite of Chomsky's disclaimers of any connection between his grammar and what is going on in the mind. It is increasingly recognized that Chomsky is "systematically ambiguous" on this point. Robert de Beaugrande, in "Psychology and Composition," in *What Writers Know* (1982), argued that an account of "performance" will not suffice as an account of writing* and that linguistics, in its Chomskyan form, won't do either. Greater promise is found in "text linguistics." See de Beaugrande, *Text, Discourse, and Process* (1980). It is proving necessary, however, to define *text* in terms of context: de Beaugrande's own definition (1980, page 2) places *text* within the world of "discourse" (the "set of mutually relevant texts") and *discourse* within the "universe of discourse" (the "total constellation of discourse in a group or society"). Although it is not clear how serviceable such definitions are, it is clear that much that is interesting might be gained from this shift of focus from "language" as it is defined by Chomsky to "text." Yet if the goal is to understand writing,* it seems unlikely that in the last analysis scientists will be able to do with anything less than an account of mind in society; de Beaugrande's definitions of *text* extend the usual understandings of the word in that direction. He believes that the emerging field of cognitive science will make the most significant contributions to a "science of composition." This may be so. His proposals, however, like the others mentioned in this section, lack an account of what makes writers want to write well. Any science of composition that gives us no help in this respect will not give us a world of writers* that is to be preferred to the one we already have.

The research model—formal, operationally stated, empirically testable—can seem to be the ideal that teachers, as well as scientists, should be aspiring to in all contexts. But this aspiration leads teachers seriously astray. When one's goal is a scientific understanding of writing,* the usefulness of holding oneself to the standards of the research models seems clear. But to understand writing* in this way is not to be able to do it or to teach it. To propose that we might do our job as teachers of writing by giving to our students copies of the diagrams of Flower and Hayes would be worse than silly.

In "Bluspels and Flalansperes," in his *Selected Literary Essays* (1969), C. S. Lewis argued that two kinds of metaphors are employed in teaching and learning. *Magistral metaphors* are those teachers use, presumably with full knowledge of their inadequacy to a final account of what-is-to-be-learned; *pupillary metaphors* are used by learners to give them something-to-hold-onto during learning. The difference between the two is that teachers recognize the metaphorical nature of the device and presumably could, if they wanted, employ other metaphors as a way of trying to get at what-is-to-be-learned, but learners may not recognize the metaphorical nature of the device or have any other way of grasping the matter. When a teacher (or a researcher) "forgets" the metaphorical source of his or her model, no harm is done, provided the teacher (or researcher) has other metaphors with which to approach what-is-to-be-learned. But if the teacher or researcher—or writer—comes to take the metaphor for *the* truth, the working situation becomes a nightmare as we struggle to act while in the grip of the dead hand of the dead metaphor.

I would add to Lewis's account another description, one that, like his, carries with it a warning. Whatever metaphor, or model, we choose, we do not choose it without consequence to whom we are. Whatever we may learn to do with language, we are also done to by it. Viewing language as no more than an instrument of communication obscures this fact. The point has been argued for many years in many ways by Kenneth Burke. Burke is a literary or, perhaps

one should say, a rhetorical man; but the point has also been argued recently by a computer scientist, Douglas Hofstadter, in *Godel, Escher, Bach* (1979). The writing teacher whose own writing shows the most profound awareness of the personal commitments entailed in various ways of talking about writing* is William E. Coles, Jr. For me the most telling of his many statements on this subject is his enactment in three voices, "An Alternative to Losing," given at the Wyoming Conference on Freshman and Sophomore English, Laramie, Wyoming, June 1982.

Research models will be faulted when they are found to be untrue, when predictions they suggest do not test out. Teaching models, if we take them to be metaphors of the kind specified by Lewis, ought not to be criticized for being untrue, since that is taken for granted. Instead they might be chided for being trivial or unchallenging, or for holding up the show, or, perhaps most importantly, for pretending to *be* true.

In the literature on composition, teaching models abound. Most, like that of Dorothy Augustine in "Geometries and Words" (1981), would not count as research models, since they are not stated operationally, and they do not permit empirical testing. But they seem to aspire to research-model status, and thus they fail the tests of the teaching models too. It is important for workers in composition to be aware of the radical difference in the two kinds of models.

A number of teachers might exemplify how we can encounter the research models and yet remain free of them. Donald M. Murray is not shy of working from a "model" of the composing process in workshops for teachers, a model that he characterizes as his own, although not only his. But in his technique of teaching by conference, Murray may go even farther than Moffett, for example, in attempting to give "author-ity" to students. See Murray's "Teaching the Other Self" (1982) and his textbook *Write to Learn* (1983). Another textbook that enacts Lewis's freedom from dead metaphor without denying the relevance of the research models is W. Ross Winterowd's *The Contemporary Writer* (1975). Other such textbooks exist, but their market appeal may be limited by the nature of the play they require with writing.* Such books do not permit the teaching of writing as if it were no more than a skill.

Writing* and Development

Development is a term that plays an important part in many discussions of writing.* It is important to discuss the concept here, since it is becoming clear that the writing process is in important respects a process of development. However, like so many of the terms we have been dealing with here, *development* can mean a number of things, and we cannot always be sure which is meant in a particular instance.

"Development" implies change over time. Also present in most instances is an implication that the change is meliorative. The strongest sense of the word is the one associated with Jean Piaget, outlined in, for example, *Psychology and*

Intelligence (1953). This sense of development specifies progressive change taking place in a necessary order, within approximate time frames, in "stages." Developmental stages are characterized by specific disabilities (for example, the inability to conserve) that cannot be eliminated by learning in the strict sense (that is, gaining knowledge) but only by learning in the larger sense (that is, changes in the way of knowing).

The work of Piaget has acquired a special authority in the schools. Unfortunately, this has happened just at the moment that a number of the specific conclusions reached by Piaget about the capabilities of children are being seriously challenged. An especially important critique of Piaget (of his findings, not his epistemology) is Margaret Donaldson's *Children's Minds* (1978). Donaldson has found that children can indeed do much of what Piaget found they could not, when they are invited to act in a situation that makes sense.

Walter Loban's *Language Development* (1976) is a study that uses "development" in something less than its strong sense. Loban has collected information on linguistic developments (for example, number of words used, number of adjectival and adverbial modifiers per communication unit, and much more) in the speech and writing of his subjects. Loban's interesting results might help us predict group performance, in linguistic terms; they do not support any conclusions about linguistic development, in the strong sense, nor does Loban make an attempt to provide a cognitive theory that might account for the linguistic phenomena observed.

Studies of language acquisition in children, although they provide firm and fascinating findings about the facts of language development, may offer little to students of writing,* since, among other things, they do not offer a theory the cognitive development of which the language growth is a part. One of the classic studies of language acquisition in children is Roger Brown's *A First Language* (1973).

Some recent studies of writing* such as B. M. Kroll's "Cognitive Egocentrism and the Problem of Audience Awareness in Written Discourse" (1978) have employed concepts associated with the strong sense of development. There is reason to be concerned that in using "egocentrism" to "explain" the actions of writers we may be begging the question or, if not that, explaining the unknown by the more unknown. One wonders about the ontological status of this egocentrism that supposedly bedevils our students, and one wonders also what one does to fix it. Donaldson's critique of Piaget suggests that we should spend more time looking at the meaningfulness of the situations as students than we might, if we diagnose "their" problem as "egocentrism."

One significant study concerned with development is that of the British Schools Council Writing Research Project, reported in, among other places, James Britton and his colleagues' *Development of Writing Abilities, 11–18* (1975). Relying on Moffett, Vygotsky, Emig, and others, these researchers develop a highly elaborated scheme for classifying texts that is both multi-dimensional and developmental. It is multi-dimensional in that texts are classified according to function and audience, with other axes of classification suggested, and developmental in that an order of development in kinds of writing is suggested. In the schools studied, the writing of the children was indeed found to change in both audience and function. It was also found to be seriously impoverished in terms of the options taken up by student writers. As with Loban's study, however, the findings of this group do not support conclusions about the development, in the strong sense, of writing.* A discussion of the limits of the findings of this research group is found in John Warnock's "Brittonism" (1979).

The Schools Council group relied importantly on the earlier work of L. S. Vygotsky and James Moffett. Vygotsky was concerned not with the development of writing abilities as such but with the development of conceptual thought and its relationship to language. It is Vygotsky's concern with language that distinguishes him importantly from Piaget, who thought that the importance of language in education was greatly overrated. Vygotsky proposed in *Thought and Language* (1962) and *Mind in Society* (1978) that a crucial facet of development was the transformation of "inner speech" (which is characterized by the predominance of sense over meaning, of sentence over word, and of context over sentence) into speech that bears an authentic relationship to true concepts, a relationship that is acquired by the use of language in society. In "The Prehistory of Writing" in *Mind and Society*, Vygotsky proposed that we understand writing not as a development from reading, as is commonly done, but as a development from gesture, with writing first appearing in the form of first-order *signs* and later going to second-order *symbols*. Vygotsky's writings were unavailable for 30 years after he published them because of censorship in his country and, for many of us, because of the language barrier. In the last 20 years, his work has had a powerful influence on students of writing.*

Moffett's scheme of development, offered in *Teaching the Universe of Discourse* (1968), focuses upon development in discourse, not just in writing. Relying upon Vygotsky as well as Piaget and other students of child development, Moffett proposed that discoursers learn to differentiate the universe of discourse by means of apprehending progressively more abstract relations to audience (the I-You relation) and subject (the I-It relation). Moffett's scheme has proved to be of much more interest to researchers than to teachers, perhaps because the conclusions Moffett reached about the pedagogy of discourse challenge so radically conventional skills teaching. His proposals are powerful; they do not, however, fit neatly into the worlds of the hard scientists or the purely practical pedagogues.

Two current centers of interest in development are the one in Toronto at the Ontario Institute for Studies in Education (OISE) and York University and the one at the University of New Hampshire, headed by Donald Graves. The two groups take cognizance of each other's work, but they seem to have important differences in both method and motive.

The broadest proposal about development I've seen from the Toronto group is Carl Bereiter's "Development in Writing" (1979). In this scheme, we progress from the "associative" to the "epistemic" by means of the integration of lower skills into higher. In integration, the lower skills become automatic; this releases the attention of the writer for the demands of the higher skill. Bereiter was tentative in this proposal, and Bereiter and Scardamalia were always careful to limit their sense of the word *development* to something less than the Piagetian one. A more specific proposal is found in "From Conversation to Composition" (in press). Here it is proposed that development in writing* consists of becoming able to supply one's own interlocutor, a proposal made also in historical and developmental terms by OISE's David Olson in "From Utterance to Text" (1977). One aspect of this kind of development is documented in Scardamalia and Bereiter's "Development of Dialectical Processes in Composition" (1981).

The Toronto group takes the position that there is, in fact, no naturalistic study of the composing process. Carl Bereiter and Marlene Scardamalia in "From Conversation to Composition" (in press) urged sensitivity to the "ecology" of the research and the instructional setting. Although they were interested, then, in both the ecology and development of writing,* they seemed to be committed to developing instructional procedures that can succeed in spite of the teacher or situation, procedures that are suitable, moreover, for students on what they called "the low road." See the conclusion to Carl Bereiter and Marlene Scardamalia's "Does Learning to Write Have to Be So Difficult?" (1980). The New Hampshire group shares OISE's concern with the ecology of teaching, but their work has different pedagogical aspirations.

The New Hampshire group, working in the Writing Process Laboratory at the University of New Hampshire, under the direction of Donald Graves, has been particularly forceful in its advocacy of naturalistic research-in-context. An accessible argument in justification of the naturalistic approach may be found in Grave's "Research Update" (1979a). A more detailed description and justification will appear in Lucy Calkin's *Lessons from a Child* (1983).

An indirect argument in support of research of this kind is found in the graceful, rich, and jargon-free "Research Updates" of the work of Graves, Calkins, and Sowers, which have appeared in the pages of *Language Arts* in recent years. See the References under these authors' names. Other work in the same tradition is Glenda Bissex, *Gnys at Wrk* (1980), and Marie M. Clay, *What Did I Write* (1975). These descriptions and others have provided a rich documentation of children developing as writers, demonstrating their capacities and incapacities, showing children to be capable of what they have been commonly thought to be incapable, like planning and revising (see Graves, 1978 and 1979b). Their accounts demonstrate also the labile quality of the processes of development they are studying, as well as the remarkable individuality of these new writers.

The result of their work is not a particular scheme of development so much as an array of possibilities: possible views children have of what writing is; possible ways they have of getting started, of revising, of making writing "hard," and much more. Graves (1975) concluded with an argument like that of Moffett: that the development of writing* in children is so various as to render otiose the requirement of any particular tasks or procedures for writing.* Upon reading the results of this work, one does not so much conceive the possibility of building a writing* machine as stand in awe of what would be necessary should one ever be built.

Another context in which the development of writing is discussed is the mission for worldwide adult "functional" literacy sponsored by UNESCO. In these discussions, the cognitive, the economic, and sometimes even the spiritual tend to get mixed up. Assumptions are routinely made that acquiring literacy means acquiring everything from special cognitive capacities to a higher standard of living to a fuller life. Some of the most responsible claims for the special powers of literacy may be found advanced in Olson's "From Utterance to Text" (1977); in the works of Walter Ong, S.J. (1967, 1977); and in Jack Goody's *The Domestication of the Savage Mind* (1977). Critiques of these positions are advanced in Scribner and Cole's *The Psychology of Literacy* (1981) and in an important new book, *On Literacy*, by Robert Pattison (1982). Neither of these critics wanted to deny that learning to write makes some things possible or easy that before were impossible or hard. But they denied that learning to write *necessarily* results in some of the benefits that have been claimed by the proponents named above, and they further argued that *not* learning to write does not necessarily result in the mental and functional disabilities some people think it does.

With tact and grace, and with skillful scholarship, Pattison argued that each culture defines its own literacy, a crucial aspect of which is the relation the culture posits between language and the world. Thus Pattison subjected developmental thinking to an existential critique, suggesting once again that whatever our knowledge of writing,* we probably cannot hope to teach it without choosing what we want to make writing* be for.

Conclusion

Rhetoric was practiced, we may be sure, before it became a subject, something that could be discussed as in this chapter. To become a subject, rhetoric had to be abstracted from particular instances of itself. Writing* could become a subject only in the same way—by being abstracted from particular instances, from writers and texts. This abstraction is a feat of mind that is performed not without sacrifice, the nature of which is sometimes hinted at by colleagues in literature who argue that the study of writing as distinct from the study of particular worthy texts is, if not impossible, certainly undesirable and non-humanistic. So it is not—not humanistic, that is—if we students of writing* forget that in abstracting from texts, although we may gain power, we may lose reality. Presumably, we would like to conduct our research into writing* in a way that would enable us not to lose the hope of either of these gifts.

References

Augustine, Dorothy. "Geometrics and Words: Linguistics and Philosophy: A Model of the Composing Process." *CE*, 43 (1981), 221–31.

Bereiter, Carl. "Development in Writing." In *Testing, Teaching, and Learning*. R. W. Tyler and S. H. White (chairs). Washington, D.C.: National Institute of Education, 1979.

―――, and M. Scarmadalia. "Does Learning to Write Have to Be So Difficult." In (Title to be announced). Ed. I. Pringle, J. Yalden, and A. Freedman. New York: Longman, 1980.

―――. "From Conversation to Composition: The Role of Instruction in a Developmental Process." In *Advances in Instructional Psychology*. Vol. 2. Ed. R. Glaser. Hillsdale, N.J.: Erlbaum (in press).

Berkenkotter, Carol. "Decisions and Revisions: The Planning Strategies of a Publishing Writer." Paper presented at the Conference on College Composition and Communication, San Francisco, Calif., March 1982.

Bissex, Glenda. *Gnys at Wrk: A Child Learns to Write and Read*. Cambridge, Mass.: Harvard University Press, 1980.

Boden, Margaret A. *Purposive Explanation in Psychology*. Cambridge, Mass.: Harvard University Press, 1972.

Bracewell, R. J., M. Scardamalia, and C. Bereiter. "The Development of Audience Awareness in Writing." *Resources in Education*. 1978. ERIC ED 154 433.

Braddock, Richard, Richard Lloyd-Jones, and Lowell Schorer. *Research in Written Composition*. Urbana, Ill.: NCTE, 1963.

Britton, James, T. Burgess, N. Martin, A. McLeod, and H. Rosen. *The Development of Writing Abilities, 11–18*. London: Macmillan, 1975.

Brown, Roger. *A First Language: The Early Stages*. Cambridge, Mass.: Harvard University Press, 1973.

Bruner, J. *On Knowing: Essays for the Left Hand*. Cambridge, Mass.: Belknap, 1962.

Burke, Kenneth. *Language as Symbolic Action*. Berkeley: University of California Press, 1966.

―――. *Dramatism and Development*. Barre, Mass.: Clark University Press, 1972.

Calkins, Lucy McCormick. "Andrea Learns to Make Writing Hard." *Lang Arts*, 56 (1979), 569–76.

―――. *Lessons from a Child: On the Teaching and Learning of Writing*. Exeter, N.H.: Heinemann Educational, 1983.

Cazden, C. B., V. P. John, and Dell Hymes. *Functions of Language in the Classroom*. New York: Teachers College Press, 1972.

Chomsky, Noam. *Syntactic Structures*. The Hague: Mouton, 1957.

Clay, Marie M. *What Did I Write*. Aukland: Heinemann, 1975.

Cognitive Processes in Writing: An Interdisciplinary Approach. Ed. Lee Gregg and Erwin Steinberg. Hillsdale, N.J.: Erlbaum, 1980.

Cole, Michael, and Sylvia Scribner. *Culture and Thought: A Psychological Introduction*. New York: Wiley, 1974.

Coles, William E., Jr. "The Circle of Unbelief." *CE*, 31 (1969), 134–42.

―――. *Composing: Writing as a Self-Creating Process*. Rochelle Park, N.J.: Hayden, 1974.

―――. *The Plural I: The Teaching of Writing*. New York: Holt, Rinehart, Winston, 1979.

―――. "An Alternative to Losing: Literacy for the Eighties." Paper presented at the Wyoming Conference on Freshman and Sophomore English. Laramie, Wyo. 7 July 1981a.

Coles, William E., Jr. *Composing II: Writing as a Self-Creating Process*. Rochelle Park, N.J.: Hayden, 1981b.

―――. "Psychology and Composition." In *What Writers Know*. Ed. Martin Nystrand. New York: Academic Press, 1982.

de Beaugrande, Robert. *Text, Discourse, and Process*. Norwood, N.J.: Ablex, 1980.

Dennett, Daniel. *Brainstorms: Philosophical Essays on Mind and Psychology*. Montgomery, Vt.: Bradford, 1978.

Derrida, J. *Of Grammatology*. Trans. G. C. Spivak. Baltimore: Johns Hopkins University Press, 1976.

Donaldson, Margaret. *Children's Minds*. New York: Norton, 1978.

Elbow, Peter. *Writing Without Teachers*. New York: Oxford University Press, 1973.

Emig, Janet. *The Composing Processes of Twelfth Graders*. NCTE Research Report No. 13. Urbana, Ill.: National Council of Teachers of English, 1971.

―――. "Non-Magical Thinking: Presenting Writing Developmentally in the Schools." In *Variation in Writing: Functional and Linguistic-Cultural Differences*. Ed. Marcia Farr Whiteman. Vol. 1 in *Writing: The Nature, Development, and Teaching of Written Communication*. Hillsdale, N.J.: Erlbaum, 1981.

Ericcson, K. Anders, and Herbert A. Simon. "Retrospective Verbal Reports as Data." C.I.P. Working Paper No. 388. Carnegie-Mellon University. 4 Aug. 1978.

―――. "Thinking-Aloud Protocols as Data." C.I.P. Working Paper No. 397. Carnegie-Mellon University. 12 Jan. 1979.

Flower, Linda, and John R. Hayes. "The Cognition of Discovery: Defining a Rhetorical Problem." *CCC*, 30 (1980), 21–32.

―――. "A Cognitive Process of Writing." *CCC*, 32 (1981a), 365–87.

―――. "Plans that Guide the Composing Process." In *Writing: Process, Development, and Communication*. Ed. Carl H. Frederiksen and Joseph F. Dominic. Vol. 2 in *Writing: The Nature, Development, and Teaching of Written Communication*. Hillsdale, N.J.: Erlbaum, 1981b, 39–58.

―――. "The Pregnant Pause: An Inquiry into the Nature of Planning." *RTE*, 15 (1981c), 229–243.

Geertz, Clifford, *The Interpretation of Cultures: Selected Essays*. New York: Basic, 1973.

Giere, Ronald N. *Understanding Scientific Reasoning*. New York: Holt, Rinehart, Winston, 1979.

Goody, Jack. *The Domestication of the Savage Mind*. Cambridge: Cambridge University Press, 1977.

Gould, John D. "Experiments in Composing Letters." In *Cognitive Processes in Writing*. Ed. Lee W. Gregg and Erwin Steinberg. Hillsdale, N.J.: Erlbaum, 1980.

Graves, Donald H. "An Examination of the Writing Process of Seven-Year-Old Children." *RTE*, 9 (1975), 227–41.

―――. *Balance the Basics: Let Them Write*. New York: Ford Foundation, 1978.

―――. "Research Update: Research Doesn't Have to Be Boring." *Lang Arts*, 56 (1979a), 76–80.

―――. "Research Update: What Children Show Us about Revision." *Lang Arts*, 56 (1979b), 312–19.

―――. "Research Update: How Do Writers Develop?" *Lang Arts*, 59 (1982a), 173–79.

―――. *Writing: Teachers and Children at Work*. Exeter, N.H.: Heinemann, 1982b.

Groden, M. *Ulysses in Progress*. Princeton, N.J.: Princeton University Press, 1977.

Heideigger, M. *What Is Called Thinking?* Trans. J. G. Gray. New York: Harper, Row, 1968.

Hillocks, G. "The Interaction of Instruction, Teacher Comment, and Revision in Teaching the Composing Process." *RTE*, 16 (1982), 261–78.

Hirsch, E. D. *The Philosophy of Composition*. Chicago: University of Chicago Press, 1977.

Hofstadter, Douglas. *Godel, Escher, Bach: An Eternal Golden Braid*. New York: Basic, 1979.

Humes, Ann. "Research on the Composing Process." In *Writing: Policies, Problems, and Possibilities*. Ed. Bruce Cronnell and Joan Michael. Los Alamitos, Calif.: Southwest Regional Laboratory of Educational Research and Development, 1982.

Kantor, Kenneth J., Dan R. Kirby, and Judith P. Goetz. "Research in Context: Ethnographic Studies in Education." *RTE*, 15 (1981), 293–309.

Kelly, G. A. *The Psychology of Personal Constructs*. 2 vols. New York: Norton, 1955.

Kinneavy, James. *A Theory of Discourse*. Englewood Cliffs, N.J.: Prentice-Hall, 1971.

Krashen, S. D. "Formal and Informal Linguistic Environments in Language Acquisition and Language Learning." *TESOL Quarterly*, 10 (1976), 157–68.

Kroll, B. M. "Cognitive Egocentrism and the Problem of Audience Awareness in Written Discourse." *RTE*, 12 (1978), 269–81.

Lashley, K. S. "The Behavioristic Interpretation of Consciousness." *Psychol. Rev.*, 30 (1923), 237–72, 329–53.

———. "The Problem of Serial Order in Behavior." In *Cerebral Mechanisms in Behavior: The Hixon Symposium*. Ed. L. A. Jeffress. New York: Wiley, 1951, pp. 112–35.

Lewis, C. S. "Bluspels and Flalansferes: A Semantic Nightmare." In *Selected Literary Essays*. Ed. Walter Hooper. Cambridge: Cambridge University Press, 1969, pp. 251–65.

Loban, Walter. *Language Development: Kindergarten through Grade Twelve*. NCTE Research Report No. 18. Urbana, Ill.: National Council of Teachers of English, 1976.

Matsuhashi, A. "Pausing and Planning: The Tempo of Written Discourse Production." *RTE*, 15 (1981), 113–34.

Mead, G. H. *Mind, Self, and Society*. Chicago: University of Chicago Press, 1934.

Miller, George, Eugene Galanter, and Kenneth Pribram. *Plans and the Structure of Behavior*. New York: Holt, Rinehart, Winston, 1960.

Moffett, James. *Teaching the Universe of Discourse*. Boston: Houghton Mifflin, 1968.

Murray, Donald M. *Learning by Teaching: Selected Articles on Writing and Teaching*. Montclair, N.J.: Boynton/Cook, 1982.

———. "Teaching the Other Self." In *Learning by Teaching*. Montclair, N.J.: Boynton/Cook, 1982, pp. 164–72.

———. *Write to Learn*. New York: Holt, Rinehart, Winston, 1983.

Nagel, Ernest. *The Structure of Science: Problems in the Logic of Scientific Explanation*. Indianapolis: Hackett, 1979.

Nisbett, Richard E., and Timothy DeCamp Wilson. "Telling More Than We Can Know: Verbal Reports on Mental Processes." *Psychol. Rev.*, 84 (May 1977), 231–59.

Nold, Ellen. In *Cognitive Processes in Writing*. Ed. Lee Gregg and Erwin Steinberg. Hillsdale, N.J.: Erlbaum, 1980.

Odell, Lee, and Dixie Goswami. "Writing in a Non-academic Setting." *RTE*, 16 (1982), 201–24.

Ohmann, Richard. *English in America: A Radical View of the Profession*. New York: Oxford University Press, 1976.

Olson, David. "From Utterance to Text: The Bias of Language in Speech and Writing." *Harvard Educ. Rev.*, 47 (1977), 257–81.

Ong, Walter, S. J. *The Presence of the Word*. New Haven, Conn.: Yale University Press, 1967.

———. *Rhetoric, Romance, Technology*. Ithaca, N.Y.: Cornell University Press, 1971.

———. *Interfaces of the Word*. Ithaca, N.Y.: Cornell University Press, 1977.

Pattison, Robert. *On Literacy: The Politics of the Word from Homer to the Age of Rock*. New York: Oxford University Press, 1982.

Perkins, D. N. *The Mind's Best Work*. Cambridge, Mass.: Harvard University Press, 1981.

Perl, S. "The Composing Process of Unskilled College Writers." *RTE*, 13 (1979), 317–36.

———. "Understanding Composing." *CCC*, 31 (1980), 363–69.

Piaget, Jean. *Psychology of Intelligence*. Trans. M. Piercy and D. E. Berlyne. London: Routledge, Kegan Paul, 1953.

Pianko, S. "A Description of the Composing Process of College Freshman Writers." *RTE*, 13 (1979), 5–22.

Pirsig, R. M. *Zen and the Art of Motorcycle Maintenance: An Inquiry into Values*. New York: Morrow, 1974.

Polanyi, Michael. *Personal Knowledge: Towards a Postcritical Philosophy*. Chicago: University of Chicago Press, 1958; rev. ed. New York: Harper Torchbooks, 1964.

———. *The Tacit Dimension*. Garden City, N.Y.: Doubleday, 1966.

Quine, W.V.O. *Word and Object*. Cambridge, Mass.: Technology Press of MIT, 1960.

Scardamalia, M., and C. Bereiter. "Development of Dialectical Processes in Composition." Paper presented at Conference on the Nature and Consequences of Literacy, Ontario Institute for Studies in Education. Toronto, Ontario. Oct. 1981.

———. "The Development of Evaluative, Diagnostic, and Remedial Capabilities in Children's Composing." In *The Psychology of Written Language: A Developmental Approach*. Ed. M. Martlew. London: Wiley, (in press).

Schank, R. C., and R. P. Abelson, *Scripts, Plans, Goals, and Understanding: An Inquiry into Human Knowledge Structures*. Hillsdale, N.J.: Erlbaum, 1977.

Scribner, Sylvia, and Michael Cole. *The Psychology of Literacy*. Cambridge, Mass.: Harvard University Press, 1981.

Shaughnessy, Mina. *Errors and Expectations: A Guide for Teachers of Basic Writing*. New York: Oxford University Press, 1977.

Sirotnik, Kenneth A. "What You See Is What You Get: Consistency, Persistency, and Mediocrity in Classrooms." *Harvard Educ. Rev.*, 53 (1983), 16–31.

Smith, Eliot R., and Frederick D. Miller. "Limits on Perception of Cognitive Processes: A Reply to Nisbett and Wilson." *Psychol. Rev.*, 85 (1978), 355–62.

Smith, Frank. *Understanding Reading: A Psycholinguistic Analysis of Reading and Learning to Read*. New York: Holt, Rinehart, Winston, 1971.

Sommers, Nancy. "The Need for Theory in Composition Research." *CCC*, 30 (1979), 46–49.

————. "Revision Strategies of Student Writers and Experienced Adult Writers." *CCC*, 31 (1980), 378–88.

Sowers, Susan. "Reflect, Expand, Select: Three Responses in the Writing Conference." In *Understanding Writing: Ways of Observing, Learning, and Teaching, K–8*. Ed. Thomas Newkirk and Nancie Atwell. Chelmsford, Mass.: Northeast Regional Exchange, 1982.

Stafford, William. *Writing the Australian Crawl: Views on the Writer's Vocation*. Ann Arbor: University of Michigan Press, 1978.

Teaching Writing: Ten Bibliographical Essays. Ed. Gary Tate. Fort Worth: Texas Christian University Press, 1976.

Understanding Writing: Ways of Observing, Learning, and Teaching, K–8. Ed. Thomas Newkirk and Nancie Atwell. Chelmsford, Mass.: Northeast Regional Exchange, 1982.

Vygotsky, L. S. *Thought and Language*. Ed. and trans. Eugenia Hanfmann and Gertrude Vakar. Cambridge, Mass.: MIT Press, 1962.

————. *Mind in Society: The Development of Higher Psychological Processes*. Ed. Michael Cole et al. Cambridge, Mass.: Harvard University Press, 1978.

Warnock, John. "New Rhetoric and the Grammar of Pedagogy." *FEN*, 5 (1976a), 1–22.

————. "Who's Afraid of Theory." *CCC*, 27 (1976b), 16–20.

————. "Brittonism." *RSQ*, 9, No. 1. (1979), 7–15.

What Writers Know: The Language, Process and Structure of Written Discourse. Ed. Martin Nystrand. New York: Academic Press, 1982.

Winterowd, W. Ross. "Topics and Levels in the Composing Process." In *Ideas for English 101*. Ed. R. Ohmann and W. B. Coley. Urbana, Ill.: NCTE, 1967, pp. 132–40.

————. *The Contemporary Writer: A Practical Rhetoric*. New York: Harcourt, 1975.

Wittgenstein, Ludwig. *Philosophical Investigations*. Trans. G.E.M. Anscombe. Oxford: Blackwell, 1953.

Writing: The Nature, Development, and Teaching of Written Communication, vol. 1, *Variation in Writing: Functional and Linguistic-Cultural Differences*. Ed. Marcia Farr Whiteman; and vol. 2, *Writing: Process, Development, and Communication*. Ed. Carl H. Frederiksen and Joseph F. Dominic. Hillsdale, N.J.: Erlbaum, 1981.

Writing: Policies, Problems and Possibilities. Ed. Bruce Cronnell and Joan Michael. Los Alamitos, Calif.: Southwest Regional Laboratory of Educational Research and Development, 1982.

Cross-Sections in an Emerging Psychology of Composition

LOUISE WETHERBEE PHELPS

There is at present no commonly recognized body of work that falls within the domain of a "psychology of composition." The problem is not categorical but conceptual: we must discover what we are looking for. The grammar of the term invites us to think about our relationships to other disciplines in a new way, on an integrative rather than an additive principle. Instead of simply borrowing knowledge from psychology, we would assimilate information from multidisciplinary sources to an intrinsically rhetorical perspective on psychological issues. This chapter seeks to define a psychology of composition as a disciplinary structure with its own integrity and to suggest how we might give that concept substantive content.

We can start by locating a psychology of composition as the point of intersection between two dimensions. On one dimension, composition picks out written language from the spectrum of symbolic activity in which human beings engage. In the second dimension, psychology selects a particular plane of analysis for studying human activity. Such planes of analysis constitute complementary perspectives that allow us to build up adequately complex understandings of interactive phenomena. On this axis a psychology of composition contrasts to other coherent perspectives on written language—to a biology, sociology, rhetoric, or pedagogy of composition.

This definition implies a conception of composition as a discipline that needs to be made explicit. Composition, also called "rhetoric" or "literacy," has only recently emerged from its matrix in a teaching tradition and despite the talk of a new paradigm has yet to settle on its distinctive subject matter and its responsibilities. I take it here to be broadly concerned with studying and facilitating the development of written language as a personal and interpersonal function of human life. A psychological perspective looks at that function as a power of the mind that individuals develop and use. Although historically composition research and teaching have emphasized writing over reading, the two are not functionally separable, so we will assume that a psychology of composition must deal with both and with their relationships.

Before elaborating this definition we should consider the alternative of constituting a psychology of written discourse within a cross-discipline of cognition and communication. (The term "cross-discipline" is introduced by Teun van Dijk and János Petöfi, "Editorial Introduction" [1981].) Robert de Beaugrande spoke for this position in "Psychology and Composition" (1982a). He called for an interdisciplinary effort to create a hierarchy of sciences concerned with language, cognition, and action, through a principle of antecedence. At the top of the hierarchy would be a unified science of cognition and communication, subsuming in turn a science of language or discourse and sciences of writing and reading.

Research on the psychology of discourse has in fact moved decisively to locate itself within a cross-discipline of cognitive science, with the intersection of linguistics, psychology, and artificial intelligence as its stable core and a shifting group of other fields on its fringe. The institutionalization of this discipline is marked by the founding of the Cognitive Science Society in 1979: papers from its first conference are collected in *Perspectives on Cognitive Science*, edited by Donald Norman (1981b). Besides the journal of this society, *Cognitive Science* (1977), two other journals founded to integrate various disciplinary perspectives on cognition and language are *Discourse Processes* (1978) and *Text* (1981). De Beaugrande attempted a comprehensive synthesis of multidisciplinary work on "texts" (referring to communicative acts, not inscription) in his book *Text, Discourse, and Process* (1980), which makes linguistics the pivotal discipline. His more recent *Text Production* (1982b) promises a similar integration for a science of composition.

Whereas researchers outside the field are working explicitly toward an integration of psychology and language, there are few precedents for thinking of a psychology of composition as an active schema by which the discipline can mediate knowledge from other fields. However, such mediation is the paradigmatic problem of the composition scholar-teacher.

As an academic specialty, composition differs from other language-related disciplines in the unusual link between what it studies and what it teaches. Linguists and psychologists seek knowledge for its own sake, and their teaching transmits the same knowledge they inherit and create. Compositionists teach not a body of knowledge but a skilled performance. The motive that prompted the revival of rhetoric and the establishment of composition as a modern field of scholarship was to base teaching on a fundamental understanding of writing (and, more recently, reading) as performance or process. But in the course of searching for knowledge at this level, it has discovered a deeper sense of its mission. Compositionists now view literacy as both more and less than a craft or even an art—although it is both at its higher levels, where we speak of rhetoric and the interpretation of literature. Literacy is most profoundly a function of human mental and social life, and the mission of composition as a discipline is not so much to teach performance as to help individuals realize and extend natural capacities for literacy. (See John Warnock's discussion on the naturalness of writing in his chapter in Part I of this volume.)

Viewed functionally, written language is even in its simplest instance an incredibly complex interaction of the individual and the social, cognition and culture, organism and environment, system and process. The mission of composition requires that it develop specifically interactional knowledge to account for complex actualities. This means focusing on relational rather than componential understanding, accommodating any kind of knowledge that might become relevant rather than defining logical boundaries for the discipline, and addressing discourse at many levels of analysis—as cognitive process, social event, biological structure, cultural code, developmental process, and so on. Such knowledge does not arise exclusively in one discipline, even a cross-discipline.

Furthermore, although a cross-discipline does develop genuinely interactional knowledge, insofar as it is a science, that knowledge will be general. The mission of composition, however, guarantees that the compositionist is interested in being able to understand richly and to affect unique and particular instances of those interactive realities, indeed becoming a part of them. There is therefore no real research focus (with respect to general or scientific knowledge), including writing process, that belongs distinctively to composition as a discipline; insofar as it is basic and general, composition research will contribute to other disciplines or to a cross-discipline like cognitive science, semiotics, or rhetoric. What is unique to composition research is its synthesizing thrust and its pragmatic, ad hoc interpretation of scientific and humanistic knowledge with respect to the issues and problems of its mission. In this respect it is more like medicine than the arts and sciences.

To construct a psychology of composition intrinsic to the discipline, then, would be to create a perspectival structure, an integrated understanding, organically related to the mission of composition. It is the inescapable condition of such an effort that it attempts to make incomplete knowledge the basis of principled action (that is, it is a fundamentally rhetorical task). This is true whether we speak of an individual constructing a personal synthesis from small samples of the available information or the concerted effort of the field to develop a consensus view of the information that filters into its collective consciousness—information that is itself fragmented, conflicting, partial, tentative, constantly changing.

At the lowest level of interpretation, composition scholars largely summarize and organize information from other fields that might bear on a psychology of composition. This serves a useful purpose in marking out relevant bodies of research for other researchers but does not reflect any schema intrinsic to the discipline. Such a schema, which is by definition comprehensive—not in amount of information but in its integrative scope—organizes psychological issues in relation to broader disciplinary conceptions and commitments as understood by a particular theorist and thus serves to reformulate, reinterpret, modify, elaborate, and evaluate information from other sources. We have so far only a few efforts to construct explicitly such schemas relating psychology and composition. Two that may be contrasted are those of E. D. Hirsch, *The Philosophy of Composition* (1977), and George Dillon, *Constructing Texts* (1981).

Hirsch introduced many in composition to psycho-linguistic literature on the cognitive processing of prose. His concept of "relative readability" refers to the efficiency by which language can be processed by readers at the sentence level; good writing is better because it requires less effort for readers to understand the same meaning. Although provocative and challenging in its use of research in the psychology of language, Hirsch's work has been widely criticized for reducing composition to the teaching of style. It is in effect an effort to construct a psychology of composition that is limited both by its significant omissions (for example, epistemic functions of writing) and by what has turned out to be an incomplete account of how readers read. The processing of text, as discourse researchers (and Hirsch himself) have discovered, cannot be explained in terms of cognitive universals, without reference to readers' situational and cultural knowledge, personal skills, purposes, and other contextual factors.

Dillon wrote in part to refute psycho-linguistic assumptions he attributed to Hirsch, while drawing extensively on more recent cognitive research that pictures readers as actively constructing texts in response to linguistic cues. He built a psychology of composition ("constructing texts") around the notion of "convention" in the sense of cultural, learned expectations about discourse and writing that discoursers share. The primary conventions for Dillon are those that govern writing, or "Text," as opposed to speech or "Utterance": here he followed both Hirsch and David Olson (see "From Utterance to Text" [1977]). Among the more specific genres which conventions define, Dillon took the expository essay as most fully exemplifying "Text." Dillon differs from Hirsch in emphasizing esthetic values and the shaping of readers' experiences over the efficient processing of information and in more fully acknowledging the role of global discourse structures as contexts for sentence construction. Nevertheless, he, too, is largely concerned with perceptual strategies at the micro-level of text, that is, with a psychology of style rather than (as he acknowledged) a theory of text production, much less a more comprehensive psychology of composition.

Frank D'Angelo in "Rhetoric and Cognition" (1982) attempted an ambitious synthesis, although only in outline, of a theory of rhetorical competence in relation to cognitive processes, building on his earlier studies of paradigms. His theory projects the categories of a variety of rhetorical schemes—the *topoi*, modes, and the tropes (related to Freud's unconscious dream mechanisms)— onto a diachronic scheme representing genetic development (reflecting the paradigms of several major psychologists). He saw the patterns of development as prefiguring adult cognitive processes and forms of discourse.

Despite these pioneer efforts, compositionists have as yet no broadly shared schema for making sense of the flood of current work on psychological aspects of written language. However, the cross-disciplinary thrust I have pointed out in much of that research suggests it is beginning to have an internal coherence in its effort to account for more and more of the natural complexities and interactions of different aspects of language use and learning. The rest of this chapter will attempt to bring out that coherence and articulate it in the context of our disciplinary needs.

To explore even suggestively the increasingly rhetorical emphasis in discourse studies by the cognitive and social sciences, I am ironically forced to neglect the important convergences between that work and theories of written language and reading developing in the humanities, especially literary theory in its relationship to semiotics, linguistics, and the rhetorical tradition. Readers will have to pursue these connections themselves; Jasper Neel's discussion of literary theories of text in his chapter in Part I of this volume is a good place to start.

"The Interpretive Turn"

For much of the twentieth century the human sciences have taken the natural sciences as their model and have each dreamed of reaching the "paradigm" state of a mature science based on positivist principles. Their failure to make any progress in this direction is brilliantly analyzed by Susanne Langer in "Idols of the Laboratory," a chapter in the first volume of her monumental work *Mind* (1967). She identified the five "idols of the laboratory" as Physicalism, Methodology, Jargon, Objectivity, and Mathematization; and she argued that worship of these idols has prevented the mental and social sciences from developing philosophically sound conceptual foundations, which might lead them in a direction different from that of the hard sciences.

To teacher-scholars of composition looking to the human sciences for knowledge to ground practical action, this has meant trying to fit their own experiential grasp of complex realities in human discourse and learning to a Procrustean bed of theories, mainly psychological and linguistic. However elegant and initially attractive they are, these theories often turn out to have only trivial application to composition because they use a reductionist language-game. See Paul Ricoeur's review, "A Critique of B. F. Skinner's *Beyond Freedom and Dignity*" (1973); compare de Beaugrande (1982a).

The characteristic method of a positivist mental or social science is componential or modular, aiming to treat each part in isolation from its whole and postpone consideration of their interaction until an understanding has been built up of each fragment. By the same token it decontextualizes, or isolates a whole structure from its surrounding field. It often entails adopting a stative rather than a dynamic view of the object of study. (This method characterizes both generative grammar and much work in psychology and artificial intelligence on semantic networks. See Dwight Bolinger, "The Atomization of Meaning" [1965]; Jeffrey Franks, "Toward Understanding Understanding" [1974]; and Hubert Dreyfus, *What Computers Can't Do* [1972] for critiques from different viewpoints.) The componential approach operates at all levels of analysis. In linguistics, for example, it meant separating syntax from semantics, removing the sentence from its linguistic context, and studying language in isolation from other cognitive processes (memory, perception, problem-solving), actual discourse events, and the social milieu.

A significant move away from this model and toward building up a more integrative knowledge of discourse occurred when groups of scholars began to define new branches of traditional disciplines relating cognition to language or language to social context: for example, psycho-linguistics, socio-linguistics, and ethnomethodology. As some of this work began to focus on language comprehension, reading, and—very recently—writing, it became necessary to invoke the knowledge and viewpoints of more and more disciplines to explain the complex events being studied. This pattern shows up with particular clarity in interdisciplinary collections from which I have drawn throughout this chapter, many of them published by Erlbaum, Ablex, and Academic. These volumes are often landmarks in the convergence of research on discourse and are enlightening for the clash and play of disciplinary perspectives. Here are some important examples.

Language Comprehension and the Acquisition of Knowledge, edited by Roy Freedle and John Carroll (1972), is an early example of reports from a conference bringing together linguists, psychologists, and education specialists at a time when attention was just beginning to shift from the sentence to the discourse level. Freedle has since edited four volumes in an important series called *Advances in Discourse Processes: Discourse Production and Comprehension*, edited by Freedle (1977); *New Directions in Discourse Processing*, edited by Freedle (1979); *The Pear Stories*, edited by Wallace Chafe (1980a); and *Text, Discourse, and Process*, edited by Robert de Beaugrande (1980).

Volume 1 of *Cognition and the Symbolic Processes*, edited by Walter Weimer and David Palermo (1974), includes both formal papers and extensive discussion from a conference that reflects the emergence of a constructivist view in psychology and a revealing encounter between linguists and psychologists. The second volume of this series appeared in 1982. Another important collection on language comprehension is *Cognitive Processes in Comprehension*, edited by Marcel Adam Just and Patricia Carpenter (1977), which is based on a multidisciplinary conference at Carnegie-Mellon University.

Work focused specifically on reading is more likely to include educational specialists in conferences and edited collections. One example is the three-volume set of papers *Theory and Practice of Early Reading*, edited by Lauren Resnick and Phyllis Weaver (1979), in which psychologists, linguists, instructional designers, and reading and special-education experts debate sharply conflicting views of reading models and their application to education. *Theoretical Issues in Reading Comprehension*, edited by Rand Spiro, Bertram Bruce, and William Brewer (1980), is a strongly focused collection in which the editors try to reveal a synthesis of viewpoints (from cognitive psychology, linguistics, artificial intelligence, and education) about higher levels of reading.

Finally, three volumes show the recent increase in attention to writing or text production. *Cognitive Processes in Writing*, edited by Lee Gregg and Erwin Steinberg (1980), reports on a symposium at Carnegie-Mellon University bringing together researchers from psychology, linguistics, education, and English to define the current state of research in writing so as to plan for future interdisciplinary inquiry. Two recently published companion volumes entitled *Writing* present research from an extremely broad base of disciplines, including anthropology, linguistics (particularly psycho-linguistics and socio-linguistics), psychology (cognitive, developmental, and educational), education, literature, and rhetoric. Volume 1, *Variation in Writing*, edited by Marcia Whiteman (1981) has a socio-cultural focus, and volume 2, *Writing*, edited by Carl Frederiksen and Joseph Dominic (1981), has a focus on the individual.

These increasingly interdisciplinary efforts to study written discourse as a complex of processes and influences, which culminate in the formation or revitalization of cross-disciplines, coincide with a broad shift across the human sciences that has been called the "interpretive turn." Paul Rabinow and William Sullivan, a philosopher and an anthropologist, respectively, set forth this concept powerfully in "The Interpretive Turn" (1979), which introduces *Interpretive Social Science*, edited by Rabinow and Sullivan (1979), a book of seminal readings. The authors argued that the human sciences must develop knowledge of a kind different from that of the natural sciences, knowledge that concerns most deeply the world of intersubjective meanings. ("Human sciences" translates the German word "Geisteswissenschaften," which evokes a whole philosophic tradition: see H. P. Rickman's entry in the *Encyclopedia of Philosophy* [1967].) The meanings of this cultural world exist only as part of a field or whole and can be understood only through interpretation founded on participation by the interpreter. Such interpretation does not aim at discovering rules or universal laws but at revealing the richness of meaning and variation in context-bound activity, particularly symbolic action. At this level, the interpretive view is epistemological, with strong methodological implications.

At another level, the interpretive view produces a different kind of knowledge, or "understanding" (*verstehen*), of human life and discourse. It presents an image of human beings as situated in a world wherein literacy and language use develop as functional, purposeful activities that exhibit persons as constructive or interpretive organisms. As mental processes, language activities are strategic and value-laden rather than (like machines) governed solely by the logical relations of symbolic systems, and they are highly interactive with perception and other higher mental functions. Intersubjectively, an individual's acts of symbolization participate in a larger web of signification or cultural meanings. Biological, cognitive, linguistic, and social dynamics interact with the physical world to produce human experience.

This image strikingly harmonizes a number of themes that emerge strongly, if unevenly, from contemporary studies of discourse. The themes of that work may be summarized in a set of key ideas or terms. Briefly, modern discourse studies see written language as *ecological* or *contextualized*; *constructive*; *functional* and *strategic*; *holistic*, with a strong *tacit* component; *dynamic*; and *interactive*.

Two authors who use the term constructivist broadly to refer to an interpretive framework are Jesse Delia and A. Jon Magoon. In "Constructivism and the Study of Human Communication" (1977), Delia presented the principles of this approach as they relate to the philosophy of science and in their application to communications research. In the communication researchers' version of the interpretive view, a concept of the organism as an actively developing structural whole is important (a structural-developmental position influenced by psychologists such as Jean Piaget, Heinz Werner, and George Kelly). Magoon's article "Constructivist Approaches in Educational Research" (1977) reviews the same theme in the history and philosophy of the social and behavioral sciences and discusses its application to educational research.

A brief synthetic statement of many of these themes is found in Spiro, Bruce, and Brewer (1980), in the introduction to their volume on reading comprehension. They described reading as a multi-level interactive process, constructive, strategic, and partly tacit. In introducing a later section, they pointed out the commitment of contributors to an "intentionalist" position, which treats linguistic structures as devices for communicating intentions rather than as abstract formal objects. (See Jerry Morgan and Manfred Sellner, "Discourse and Linguistic Theory" [1980].) Frederiksen and Dominic's introduction to *Writing* (1981) stresses similar ideas about writing, presenting their collection as viewing writing from four perspectives: as cognitive process; as a particular form of language; as a communicative process; and as a context-bound, purposeful activity.

Attempts to articulate cognitive science as a cross-discipline have stimulated serious reflection on epistemological problems and on framing assumptions about the relationships among organism, environment, and observer. In the volume *Perspectives on Cognitive Science*, edited by Norman (1981b), many contributors echoed the interpretive themes and probed the inadequacies of too mechanistic a view of human language and cognition: see, for example, Donald Norman's effort to broaden the scope of cognitive science to include emotion, learning, consciousness, and other unorthodox topics, in "Twelve Issues for Cognitive Science" (1981a); and Terry Winograd's narrative of his growth toward a more interpretive view of language and a new focus on the domain of human action and interaction in "What Does It Mean to Understand Language?" (1981).

Among the fullest and most important statements of the interpretive themes in the composition literature are those of Roger Shuy and Janet Emig. In Shuy's article, "A Holistic View of Language" (1981), he argued that language is primarily functional and only secondarily formal. He described this view as "holistic" rather than componential, "constructivist" rather than reductionist: always examining language and language skills in relation to their context. Shuy tied this view to research in natural learning of oral and written language and drew strong conclusions about the failure of writing instruction to address language skills in the context of meaning.

Emig's article, "The Tacit Tradition" (1980), traces the interdisciplinary roots that she believes make up the tacit tradition of a modern composition theory and finds in them the same themes we have been considering. She called that tradition "constructivist" and "transactionalist," meaning that the writer as learner actively makes meaning through transactions with experience.

Under the editorship of Julie Jensen, the journal *Language Arts* has for some years been steadily emphasizing a functional, contextualized, and constructivist view of writing and reading in the classroom. Its "Research Updates" reflect the emergence of the interpretive view in research that focuses on children learning to write and read naturally: for example, Donald Graves, "A New Look at Writing Research" (1980) and "Writing Research for the Eighties" (1981); Martha King and Victor Rental, "Conveying Meaning in Written Texts" (1981); and Marie Clay, "Learning and Teaching Writing" (1982).

The interpretive emphasis on social context at first sight raises some troublesome problems for a psychology of composition in its relationship to the image of the individual mind as actively constructing its own reality. Are not these ideas incompatible? First, to say that these themes recur and converge in the literature is not to say that all researchers accept their coherence. Some regard the emphasis on the constructive power of the mind as competing with rich views of the environment or the text. Second, the notion of context has many interpretations, one of which is cognitive. Third, for those who believe discourse to be both constructive and context-bound, the concepts of strategy (purpose, function) and interaction resolve the conflict.

The term *context* expresses in its most general sense the notion of a field that gives meaning to objects or elements in it: a whole that is greater than the sum of its parts and within which its parts take their definition. It is also the ground against which a figure stands out. (See Dreyfus [1972] on the significance of context or world to human intelligence; he argued that without a living body and a world, a computer can never achieve true intelligence.)

Obviously, context can be defined at different levels of detail and generality. For example, Donald Graves (1981) distinguished three contextual categories: the Writing Episode, the Life of the Child Who Writes, and the Social-ethnographic Context of the Episode. One can also distinguish a spatiotemporal and socio-cultural context. The latter includes those aspects of the culture that are actually significant to a given instance of discourse for its participants: see Ivana Markova, introduction to *The Social Context of Language* (1978), a collection of essays thematizing context in communication. Louise Wetherbee Phelps, in "Acts, Texts, and the Teaching Context" (1980), combined these discriminations, drawing on definitions from several disciplines to analyze *scene* as setting, situation, and world. This analysis points out the complications of defining *context* in written language: see discussions by Olson (1977), Hirsch (1977),

Dillon (1981), and Paul Ricoeur, *Interpretation Theory* (1976). Probably the most subtle and richly elaborated discussion of context and discourse is that of Kenneth Burke in his treatment of scene as an element in the Pentad: see *A Grammar of Motives* (1969).

Two other notions of context are linguistic and cognitive. Linguistic context for a sentence is simply the language preceding or following it or the whole unit of discourse in which it appears. The cognitive sense of context views all of these other kinds of context as they are represented in the long-term memory or knowledge base of the individual and brought to bear in understanding or producing a particular instance of discourse. Cognitive scientists are not always careful to distinguish the cognitive from the environmental sense of context; if context is viewed as nothing but the cognitive map of an individual, one can miss important facts about the interactions of language and social life. See Elinor Ochs, "Social Foundations of Language" (1979) on the cognitive bias of language research; and Peter Berger and Thomas Luckmann, *The Social Construction of Reality* (1967) on the intersubjectivity of the individual's world as given largely through language.

As long as this distinction is maintained, the cognitive representation of context forms one bridge between assertions of the primacy of context on the one hand and the constructive power of the human mind on the other. Another bridge between them is the concept of function in language: the idea that language is strategic in operation (even in processing details) because it serves both conceptual and pragmatic purposes in a social world. Composition has been strongly influenced by a functionalist tradition in British linguistics through its effect on British education. See, for example, M.A.K. Halliday, "Language Structure and Language Function" (1970); James Britton, "The Composing Process and the Functions of Writing" (1978), *Language and Learning* (1970), and *Prospect and Retrospect* (1982); and James Britton and others, *The Development of Writing Abilities, 11–18* (1975).

The concepts of holism and interaction need brief clarification. In one interpretation, *holism* refers to the internal integrity of structures, as in structuralist conceptions of language as a closed system. Rabinow and Sullivan pointed out that this step is crucial but not sufficient to account for the relation of a structure to the larger field. In Shuy's usage *holism* means understanding parts or elements through their relation both to an immediate meaningful whole and to the real social context. This relation implies a dynamic capacity for wholes to grow and change through their participation in the larger field: see Jean Piaget on assimilation, accommodation, and equilibration as interpreted by Hans Furth, *Piaget and Knowledge* (1981). A number of processes connected with written language are explained in terms of a development from global wholes to differentiated and then hierarchically integrated structures. (See Barry Kroll, "Developmental Relations between Speaking and Writing" [1981], and D'Angelo [1982], who traced this idea to Heinz Werner.)

The componential approach to studying discourse is losing ground in many disciplines, because it rests on an inadequate model of human systems and processes. Many researchers now advocate taking the interactivity of the system itself as the primary object of inquiry, its elements being not static components but aspects of the way the system functions in a given situation. See, for example, Lars-Göran Nilsson's argument for the interactive nature of cognition in "Functions of Memory" (1979). William Brewer gives experimental evidence against the separability of thought, perception, and language in "The Problem of Meaning and the Interrelations of the Higher Mental Processes" (1974). Similar arguments undermine the sharp separation of syntax, semantics, and pragmatics in linguistic theories.

Compositionists, who have long professed an interactionist view of discourse, are only now beginning to articulate all of its ramifications and their radical implications. In "Dialectics of Coherence" (forthcoming), Louise Wetherbee Phelps proposed that to deal with interactive realities, composition must build up theories from inherently integrative concepts: for example, coherence as a relation between text, reader, and writer. See Phelps (1980) and Barbara O'-Keefe, "Writing, Speaking, and the Production of Discourse" (1981); see also the transactional views of writing in this chapter. Barry Kroll, in "Developmental Perspectives and the Teaching of Composition" (1980), applied an interactionist perspective to teaching, based on synthesizing nurture-and-nature explanations of human development. See also Nan Elsasser and Vera John-Steiner, "An Interactionist Approach to Advancing Literacy" (1977, 1980).

In its epistemological aspect, an interpretive view often constitutes an attack on positivist science as a paradigm for human studies. Although some researchers maintain the positivist orientation while taking constructive, holistic, functional, or interactive views of discourse, the logic of the interpretive position is reflexive. Most philosophical or abstract presentations of an interpretive view draw strong conclusions for a different methodology in the human sciences: besides Rabinow and Sullivan (1979) and Delia (1977), see Charles Taylor, "Interpretation and the Sciences of Man" (1971, 1979), and Elliot Mishler, "Meaning in Context" (1979). These works variously critique "variable analysis"; suggest goals for social science other than prediction; emphasize conceptual analysis, participants' perspectives, and particularity; and propose alternate notions of empirical validation.

Two important exchanges on the interpretive view and methodology reveal conflicts in composition about the kinds of truth our discipline can develop or look for in other research on discourse. Janet Emig's essay "Inquiry Paradigms and Writing" (1982) apparently sets out simply to compare three types of "governing gaze": positivist, phenomenological, and transactional-constructionist. (The latter two are compatible with respect to the themes discussed in this chapter.) But her essay goes on to develop a critique of conventional empirical science and a case for phenomenological methods of studying discourse, specifically case study and ethnography, which study discourse in its ecological context.

In "Composition Studies and Science" (1983), Robert Connors took issue with Emig in an article that sends mixed signals. On the one hand he argued that composition studies are not and cannot be scientific, limiting the term to its positivist sense. But he seemed to wish that they were, reaching what he spoke of as "glum conclusions" about the possibility for cumulating certain knowledge about written discourse. Acknowledging at the end of his essay the dangers of trying inappropriately to imitate the natural sciences, he nevertheless did not seem to view the interpretive stance as a positive alternative producing a different order of knowledge. In contrast, Taylor (1971) and Clifford Geertz, "Thick Description" (1973) saw the social sciences as developing a kind of knowledge that is different from that of experimental science but equally valid: knowledge not as prediction according to causal laws but as explication of cultural meanings.

The same controversy is played out more pointedly in *Rhetoric Society Quarterly* between authors representing naturalistic inquiry and an extreme positivism. James Kinney in "Composition Research and the Rhetorical Tradition" (1980) took a pluralistic position on research methods but in comparing experimental science to naturalistic inquiry saw the latter as appropriate for composition, because it is essentially rhetorical. N. Scott Arnold replied in "Research Methods and the Evaluation of Hypotheses" (1980) that there is only one standard for science, and that is truth, which he identified with the objective verification of hypotheses by observation and experiment. See Roger Straus, "The Theoretical Frame of Symbolic Interactionism" (1981), and Anthony Giddens, "Hermeneutics, Ethnomethodology, and Problems of Interpretive Analysis" (1976), for views of the positivist and interpretive approaches as complementary models for natural and social science.

Kenneth Kantor, Dan Kirby, and Judith Goetz provided an excellent introduction to these issues as they affect composition in "Research in Context" (1981), a comprehensive review of recent ethnographic research on written language. The authors rejected any dichotomy between quantitative and qualitative research and examined the ways in which qualitative research methods can be rigorous.

Cross-Sections

The recurrent themes I have described are revealed by looking at psychological issues that cut across the usual topical boundaries in studies of written language. This method allows us to sample a broad range of research while focusing on the relationships that integrate different aspects of textual events, in particular the commonalities and reciprocities of writing and reading. The four cross-sections involve these issues:

1. Constructive processes
2. The role of memory

3. The tacit-focal relation

4. Hemisphericity, abstraction, and egocentrism

We saw earlier that for some scholars the term constructivist refers broadly to an interpretive framework for the human sciences in general and communication in particular. It has a compatible but narrower meaning for some cognitive psychologists, who apply the term constructive to the relationship between the human organism and the environment without necessarily subscribing to the epistemological and methodological conclusions drawn by interpretive theorists. Constructive accounts of writing and reading, largely as developed by cognitive scientists, are having considerable impact on composition studies.

An excellent and readable overview of the constructive conception of human understanding is given by John Bransford and Nancy McCarrell in "A Sketch of a Cognitive Approach to Comprehension" (1974). Like most psychologists' discussions of a constructivist view, theirs focuses on receptive processes, perception, and language comprehension rather than action and language production, perhaps because this is the logical point of attack on a behaviorist tradition that pictured the organism as passively acted upon (also because receptive processes are thought simpler; research on reading far outweighs that on writing). Bransford and McCarrell presented a picture of the organism as seeking the "click" of meaning. In their view, meaningfulness has to do with relational information, information about how entities relate to other objects and events. In perception, comprehenders use relational knowledge about abstract entities together with contextual information to produce significances. Linguistic understanding is similarly interactive. Language serves to cue and constrain a person's effort to create meanings, that is, to create a situation that realizes the abstract relations specified by sentences. Meaning is a construction that the comprehender builds from world knowledge (of relations among entities) and contextual information guided by linguistic cues. Bransford and McCarrell cited a number of experiments that demonstrate the enormous cognitive contribution that comprehenders make to textual meaning, including the important role of inference in adding meaning to what is "directly" expressed.

Subsequent work explores these inferential processes: see, for example, Herbert Clark, "Inferences in Comprehension" (1977); Herbert Clark and Susan Haviland, "Comprehension and the Given-New Contract" (1977); and Allan Collins, John Seely Brown, and Kathy Larkin, "Inference in Text Understanding" (1980). More recent work, including the last article, questions highly text-based conceptions of inference (for example, Clark and Haviland's notion of "bridging" between sentences), and proposes that readers construct situational models to connect ideas in texts. Compare the critique of text-based inference by A. J. Sanford and S. C. Garrod in *Understanding Written Language* (1981).

Sanford and Garrod's book is one of the most comprehensive treatments of issues in the comprehension of prose and is useful both for its summaries and critiques of other research and for its own contributions on the issue of reference.

(See Herbert Clark and Eve Clark, *Psychology and Language* [1977], an invaluable summary of experimental research in psycho-linguistics.) Rand Spiro's article "Constructive Processes in Prose Comprehension" (1980) gives a useful historical review of the development of the constructive position on comprehending prose. He described construction as a process of "knowledge-based, contextually influenced, and purposeful enrichment" for which the text acts as a blueprint (p. 245). According to Spiro, the "meaning-in-the-text" position was undermined in psychology by the work on inference already cited and by the demonstration of the importance of theme or gist to readers' understanding.

There remain some dissenters to the constructivist position among cognitive psychologists and reading specialists. Researchers influenced by J. J. Gibson's theory of perception have argued forcefully against extreme constructivism, sometimes identified as an "information-processing view" (although that term is slippery). See for example, Eleanor Gibson, "How Perception Really Develops" (1977), and discussions of Gibsonian ideas by William Mace, M. T. Turvey, and others at the Weimer and Palermo conference (*Cognition and the Symbolic Processes*, Vol. 1 [1974]). Their highly sophisticated theories, which emphasize the directness of perception and the richness of the perceptual array offered by the environment, have impressed constructivists enough to modify their own views: see, for example, Ulric Neisser, *Cognition and Reality* (1976).

Although Gibsonians grant that language understanding must be constructive, the same disagreement about the relative importance of the organism and the environment appears in the "top-down" and "bottom-up" controversies in reading theory. Models that assume that fluent reading is "data-driven," that is, a passive receptive process determined by the stimulus and occurring in linear stages (from textual features to meaning), seem to have been outmoded by the discovery that individuals' world knowledge in the form of global schemas organizes reading at higher levels from which decoding of sentences follows. Researchers have moved toward a model of reading as an interaction between text-based and knowledge-based processes. But the controversy continues with respect to teaching reading, since instructional strategies respond to children's learning processes rather than following from the characteristics of skilled performance. In early reading research, most researchers still emphasize attention to the linguistic code: see the three volumes of *Theory and Practice of Early Reading*, edited by Resnick and Weaver (1979).

The realization that reading is a constructive process has led researchers in composition as well as other fields to emphasize the similarities between writing and reading as meaning-making activities. The conception of writing as the discovery or invention of meanings is well known in composition and currently dominates research if not teaching (see Maxine Hairston, "The Winds of Change" [1982], and James Berlin, "Contemporary Composition" [1982], for two views). The force of this new view of reading is to treat the two processes as comparable acts of composition or understanding, because, as Anthony Petrosky put it, "understanding is composing," a view he developed eloquently in his article

"From Story to Essay" (1982). The impact of this concept has yet to be fully realized: it is potentially a powerful heuristic for understanding both processes and for unifying composition as a discipline of literacy.

Comparisons of work on writing and reading processes suggest many ways in which they are similar, meaning-making activities. Both are linguistic ways for the organism to deal with the novel in terms of what is known. More specifically, each involves a relationship between what I will call "forethought" and adaptivity to environmental feedback in terms of evolving purposes. Deborah Tannen, "What's in a Frame?" (1979), surveyed work on "frames" (theories of knowledge and comprehension) in terms of the concept of "expectations" that guide human activity. Neisser (1976) gave an elegant account of how this works for perception in what he called the "perceptual cycle": a schema (structure of expectations) directs exploration in which the organism samples available information, which then modifies the schema. See also the concept of a TOTE (test-operate-test-exit) unit or feedback loop in George Miller, Eugene Galanter, and Karl Pribram, *Plans and the Structure of Behavior* (1960), which has influenced models of the writing process.

This notion of expectations is carried out in theories of both reading and writing. In reading, Frank Smith in *Understanding Reading* (1982) described fluent reading in terms of hypotheses, prediction, and anticipation. This theme is repeated in accounts of reading based on schema theory. In research on the writing process, cognitively based models build on the concepts of planning and goals, which involve structured expectations and willed efforts to realize them. See, for example, the work of John Hayes and Linda Flower (discussed by Warnock in his chapter in Part I of this volume) and Bertram Bruce's discussion, in "Plans and Social Actions" (1980), of how readers comprehend writers' and characters' plans. Along with Miller, Galanter, and Pribram, Roger Schank and Robert Abelson's *Scripts, Plans, Goals and Understanding* (1977) is a seminal work. In less formal accounts, Sondra Perl in "Understanding Composing" (1980) developed the concepts of "projective" structuring (forethought) and "retrospective" structuring (recomposing in response to feedback) in the composing process, and the more organic treatments of revision describe it in terms of relating intentions to effectiveness as perceived through the feedback of reading one's own writing: for example, see Nancy Sommers, "Revision Strategies of Student Writers and Experienced Adult Writers" (1980), and Donald Murray, *Learning by Teaching* (1982).

In their logical extension, concepts of forethought, prediction, planning, and expectation lead some researchers to view both writing and reading as problem-solving activities. Although this notion is problematic because of differences in how people define *problem-solving* (and *plans*, for that matter), it reflects a new agreement that what is happening in reading and writing has a lot more to do with other cognitive and social activities than had been thought. Rather than requiring special explanation as unique activities, writing and reading can be seen in large part as applications of general abilities to perceive, think, and interact socially. These ideas emerge, for example, in the transactional views of written language discussed next and in many models of writing process or invention.

The constructive framework also leads to another view of writing and reading as mutually related processes that are shaped to one another and interact to produce joint meanings. Martin Nystrand developed such an interactive view of communication in his conception of a "textual space" of shared consciousness between writer and reader: see *What Writers Know* (1982). Often this conception rests on a broader notion of interactive relationships between organisms and their worlds: see, for example, Louise Wetherbee Phelps, "The Dance of Discourse" (1982), which relates such a notion of discourse to the world view of modern physics.

Many writers have emphasized the transactional, contractual character of written language as the basis for writer-reader interactions. Gary Olson, Robert Mack, and Susan Duffy gave an exceptionally clear statement of this idea in "Cognitive Aspects of Genre" (1981). Beginning with the "Guidance Principle," which expresses the mutual understandings of writers and readers about how textual communication works, they derived a list of conventions of composition for simple texts. Terry Winograd presented a similar view in "A Framework for Understanding Discourse" (1977), which describes language as fundamentally reflexive, designed by the writer for the reader to analyze as intentional. An excellent summary of these ideas for teachers is given by Robert Tierney and Jill LaZansky in "The Rights and Responsibilities of Readers and Writers" (1980).

The formulation of this basically rhetorical position by cognitive scientists seems to be largely independent of the rhetorical and literary traditions or current scholarship in the humanities, although they draw on some of the same sources, including speech act theory (J. L. Austin, John Searle, and various linguists) and H. P. Grice's theory of implicatures and the Cooperative Principle. Many compositionists, notably W. Ross Winterowd, have been influenced by these theories: the most up-to-date synthesis, drawing particularly on the work of linguists K. Bach and R. M. Harnish, is that of Martin Steinmann, "Speech-Act Theory and Writing" (1982).

Despite a convergence by many researchers on a view of writing and reading as mutually shaping and complementary activities, their accounts differ considerably in ways that reflect ancient and perhaps undecidable controversies about the relationships among individuals and their environment or among biology, culture, and the self. For example, arguments often focus on the appropriate metaphor for discourse processes and the experience of meaning. Michael Reddy in "The Conduit Metaphor" (1979) described the English language as riddled with metaphorical expressions of the idea that communication is the transmission of information and language is the conduit. This idea is related to the notion of humans as symbolic processors comparable to digital computers. Humanists have always questioned this metaphor: now we find cognitive scientists like Terry

Winograd (1981), Donald Norman (1981), and Walter Weimer, "Overview of a Cognitive Conspiracy" (1974), doing so. They and others ask questions like these: How should models of discourse processes balance the individual's constructive effort against the power of social institutions and conventions, especially linguistic ones, and the power of the text itself to determine meaning? To what degree should we refer to biologically determined needs and limitations, that is, processing limitations, to explain discourse processes and choices? What is the relative importance of propositional knowledge and other aspects of discourse such as esthetic purposes and effects? How rule-governed are discourse processes, and how free are they? (See Robert de Beaugrande's criteria for reading theories in "Design Criteria for Process Models of Reading" [1981].)

As some investigators have remarked, language permeates and enacts human life to the degree that a theory of language may be indistinguishable from a theory of mind in relation to culture. To build even the current primitive models of writing and reading processes, it has been necessary to implicate the whole range of mental phenomena and functions—perception, imagination, consciousness, logical inference, for example—and to consider their relationship to experience and action. I use *memory* as a probe for these interactions, partly because of its salience in psychological research into discourse processes but also because the ferment in memory studies reveals clearly the thematic tendencies I have set forth.

The topic of memory cuts across models of writing and reading, although by far the greatest attention has gone to comprehension. Its centrality to current discourse studies suggests that we might restore memory to its status as a department of rhetoric, along with invention, arrangement, and style—but only if we reorient these categories to apply to reading as well as writing and texts. Curiously, this possibility is raised not by a rhetorician but by an educational psychologist, M. C. Wittrock. His article "The Generative Processes of Memory" (1977) summarizes the history of arts of memory (drawing on the work of Frances Yates) as support for his own theory that learning in schools involves active construction of meanings depending on both verbal and imaginal processing.

My discussion sorts the work on memory into three baskets, admittedly oversimplifying the controversies and perhaps giving them more of a direction than they actually have. I consider memory as a performance factor in writing and (mainly) reading, a knowledge base for both, and a function of cognition, in a special sense.

As a performance factor, memory is treated as a constraint on writing and reading processes. This view depends on two assumptions: the metaphor of memory as space, or storage, and a stage view of cognitive processing as moving information from one space to another. The two together mean that any aspect of writing or reading involves competition for cognitive resources, both space and time (reflected in experiments that draw conclusions from how long it takes discoursers to carry out some tasks reflecting understanding, summarized in Clark and Clark [1977]).

The intertwining of these two concepts, memory spaces and processing sequence, were most accessibly summarized by Smith (1982), although he went on to modify them. He described three aspects of memory, revealingly called "bottlenecks": sensory store, short-term memory (STM), and long-term memory (LTM).

Sensory store is a construct postulated to account for the persistence of incoming perceptual information while it is worked on and identified. (For a different and plausible view of this kind of memory as simply perception, thought of as inherently temporal, see Gunnar Johansson, "Memory Functions in Visual Event Perception" [1979].)

Short-term memory is a buffer for storing whatever the individual is currently attending to. Items in STM will remain there only as long as they are rehearsed or worked on: hence the term *working memory*. Since George Miller's famous article "The Magical Number Seven, Plus or Minus Two" (1956), psychologists have accepted a limit of about five to seven items on the capacity of STM although it has been suggested recently that perhaps this capacity is flexible and somewhat context-dependent (see discussion in de Beaugrande, [1981]). This limit is stretched in any case by the possibility of "chunking" items into larger units.

Finally, *long-term memory* is a relatively stable base of knowledge and beliefs about the world, often divided into *semantic memory* (categorical and abstract knowledge) and *episodic memory* (memory for events). There is disagreement about whether everything that happens is stored in an individual's LTM, but if so there is still the problem of retrieving it. Smith spoke of the long time it takes to code items into LTM (about five seconds) as another bottleneck, but if others are right about LTM accepting all of the organism's experiences, this difficulty must be one of organization—relating new information to old information so that it will be accessible later—rather than input.

In information-processing models of reading, these concepts of memory appear literal rather than metaphorical. Smith, however, rejected notions of different kinds of memory, parts of the brain, or stages in processing and conceptualized working memory as a part of long-term memory—essentially, attention to a current situation, with two-way interactions between STM and LTM. The advent of schema theory meant that top-down schematic models largely displaced the bottom-up, stage views of reading associated with a literal conception of different storage spaces in memory. The schema models rapidly modulated into interactive theories, postulating that the organism's knowledge and the textual cues operate simultaneously, redundantly, and in concert, affecting one another continuously at all levels (Spiro, Bruce, and Brewer [1980]). But the concept of STM as a limited workspace persists. The reason is that the constraints originally defined in terms of memory boxes and sequential transfer from one space to another can be translated into more continuous frameworks where working memory merges with concepts of attention, consciousness, backgrounding and foregrounding, salience, and tacit knowledge. However, the notion of a limited workspace as a performance constraint is subject to modification by the concept of parallel processing and the possibility of automatic (unconscious or unattended) processes in discourse: see the tacit-focal issue below.

In a series of articles, Wallace Chafe developed a more complex view of memory and attention in reading and listening (discussed below). Two neglected and highly original articles are "Language and Memory" (1973) and "Language and Consciousness" (1974), which treat memory during comprehension in terms of backgrounding and foregrounding in consciousness. Chafe made finer discriminations regarding experiential time and its relation to language than do most psychologists, and he had the imagination to relate his discussion of memory to a parallel organization of expectations.

Early attempts to develop models of composing began with the same kinds of assumptions about stages in a linear process and, to a lesser extent, resource limitations, although with less formal modeling in flow charts than the reading theorists (but see John Hayes and Linda Flower, "Identifying the Organization of Writing Processes" [1980]). Vigorous criticism has modified the stage theories toward recursivity, but writing models are only beginning to deal with the interactivities between text and writer, not to mention simultaneities and mutual influences among cognitive functions and levels of processing. One of the most interesting of recent efforts to describe writing at this level is that of Marlene Scardamalia, Carl Bereiter, and Hillel Goelman, "The Role of Production Factors in Writing Ability" (1982), which specifically addresses the question of production factors in writing, including possible memory loss and interference from mechanisms competing for resources. Their conclusions present a complex picture of the relations among production factors, mental representations of text, and memory, arguing that people do not store a single representation of text during writing but construct and reconstruct different ones as needed. Another important non-sequential or integrative model for the production process is that of Ann Matsuhashi, "Explorations in the Real-Time Production of Written Discourse" (1982). Linda Flower and John Hayes also discussed resource limitations as constraints within a non-stage model in "The Dynamics of Composing" (1980).

Research on memory has affected studies of writing mainly in an indirect way by specifying at a cognitive level the ancient insight that skilled writing adapts language to the way readers read, both to make meanings understandable and to shape readers' experiences. A body of work of continuing importance considers how language, both as system and as style in an individual text, adapts itself to the memory characteristics, attentional limits, and other processing needs of human minds. Hirsch (1977) introduced such notions to compositionists, giving the support of modern psychology to many maxims of traditional rhetoric. (See also Joseph Williams, *Style* [1981], for detailed applications of these insights to stylistic decisions.) As pointed out earlier, Dillon (1981) criticized an overemphasis on textual choices as responding to readers' cognitive limitations.

The thrust of much work on language from this perspective is to identify mechanisms that help readers to attach incoming information from text to existing cognitive structures. The work of Walter Kintsch and Teun van Dijk offers specific models for this process, in which readers use "microstructures" (information at the sentence level) to build up a "macrostructure," a representation of the gist or propositional content of the text. Among the works that present their theory in successive stages of its development are two books by van Dijk, *Text and Context* (1977) and *Macrostructures* (1980a), and a joint article, "Toward a Model of Text Comprehension and Production" (1978).

Other work focuses on specific linguistic phenomena that appear to adapt language to processing needs. Many of these fall under the category of cohesive devices as described by M.A.K. Halliday and Ruqaiya Hasan in *Cohesion in English* (1976). The phenomenon of reference is one example of how language guides readers to relate new information to what is "old" or "given" (information they are presumed to know from context, either earlier text or relevant situational and generic knowledge). Sanford and Garrod (1981) treated reference as a memory problem, as did S. R. Rochester and J. R. Martin in "The Art of Referring" (1977). Definite and indefinite description is another linguistic feature that is understood to adapt to readers' memory limitations: see, for example, Keith Stenning, "Articles, Quantifiers, and Their Encoding in Textual Comprehension" (1977). Work on inferencing, discussed earlier, treats the activity of integration by which readers attach new information to old; see also Patricia Carpenter and Marcel Adam Just, "Integrative Processes in Comprehension" (1977), and Carol Walker and Bonnie Meyer, "Integrating Information from Text" (1980).

Let us turn now to the view of memory as a knowledge base from which to comprehend or produce writing—essentially a turn from short-term memory to long-term memory, which tends to shift attention from the bottleneck represented by the first to the great resources that the second gives to the writer or reader in producing and comprehending text.

According to Perry Thorndyke and Frank Yekovich, "A Critique of Schema-Based Theories of Human Story Memory" (1980), frame or schema-based (top-down) theories of discourse processes derive from two lines of research: efforts to simulate human intelligence, specifically language comprehension, on computers and memory for prose studies, which merge into studies of prose comprehension. (So far this work refers largely to reading, but see Wallace Chafe, "Creativity in Verbalization and Its Implications for the Nature of Stored Knowledge" [1977], on language production.) The first body of work, in artificial intelligence, focuses mainly on characterizing the knowledge base itself. Psychological studies are more diverse: some attempting to establish the constructive nature of comprehension by showing how much readers add to "literal meanings"; others modeling the way that memory schemas function in comprehension, storage of information, and recall. Both approaches have already been discussed here: for example, the work of Bransford and his colleagues on inferences and memory (reviewed in Clark and Clark [1977]) and the models of Kintsch and van Dijk. To the latter we can add the work of Bonnie Meyer on memory for prose structure, for example, "What Is Remembered from Prose" (1977) and *The Organization of Prose and Its Effects on Memory* (1975); and studies of story comprehension, for example, by David Rumelhart, "Notes on a Schema for Stories" (1975) and "Understanding and Summarizing Brief Stories" (1977); see a special interdisciplinary issue of *Poetics* (1980) with an introduction, "Story Comprehension" (1980b) by Teun van Dijk and a useful "Story Processing Bibliography" (1980) by Perry Thorndyke.

Thorndyke and Yekovich's critique (1980) is only one of a number of excellent reviews that summarize and compare the work by Marvin Minsky, Winograd, Schank and Abelson, and Rumelhart (among others) on schema theories, all traced to the seminal ideas of F. Bartlett, *Remembering* (1932). Others are Marilyn Jager Adams and Allan Collins, "A Schema-Theoretic View of Reading" (1979), and David Rumelhart, "Schemata" (1980), both introductions; Sanford and Garrod (1981); Spiro, (1980) and "Remembering Information from Text" (1977); and two that relate these theories to education, Dolores Durkin, "What Is the Value of the New Interest in Reading Comprehension" (1981), and Richard Anderson, "The Notion of Schemata and the Educational Enterprise" (1977). Three important primary works are Schank and Abelson (1977); Marvin Minsky, "A Framework for Representing Knowledge" (1975); and David Rumelhart and Andrew Ortony, "The Representation of Knowledge in Memory" (1977), a synthesizing effort. From these works we may draw the following common elements of schema theories.

A *schema* is a hierarchical package or cluster of knowledge, a data structure, that represents complex concepts in memory. These concepts are generic, that is, they represent a set of concepts and associations that characterize a typical or normal situation, event, or object. Rumelhart compared the schema to a play script that can be enacted or instantiated by specific actors. Variables correspond to characters in the play. Since the variables and knowledge about them specifies a great deal about a situation or object, they allow people to fill in information when a given instance of the concept does not supply it; as soon as they can recognize, for example, a restaurant scene, they can make inferences about waiters, menus, food, and so on. Schemas are active structures that accommodate to as well as assimilate new information and change over time. They occur at all levels of abstraction, referring to objects, events, actions, scenes, and so on, embedding other schemas and combining with one another in complex ways.

The major contribution of schema theories to an understanding of writing and reading is to make clear how important people's prior knowledge is in these processes. It is now widely accepted that schemas make comprehension, learning, and composing possible and that they are the currency in which previous experience and present experience and action are mediated, although there is little detailed idea how. (Spiro [1980] listed unanswered questions for research, largely about how schemas actually work, where and how they don't work, how they are formed and modified, and how they are related to attitude.) Simulations or models of how schemas operate in actual language use (mainly reading) still seem remote from human experience, even though they capture more of it than the bottom-up models seemed to. One reason is that schema theory remains often very text-based and rule-governed, for example, in assuming that all default variables or slots in a schema must automatically be filled.

A promising variant of schema theories suggests that humans use schemas to construct mental models of symbolic situations (described or referred to in texts) that can evolve and expand in very rich ways, not confined to slots in a discourse schema or propositions in a text base. Such a concept of language use is inherently less propositional and potentially better able to deal with factors such as value, emotion, and purpose. This idea attracts researchers of very different orientations: see, for example, Collins, Brown, and Larkin (1980); Sanford and Garrod (1981); Donald Norman, "Perception, Memory, and Mental Processes" (1979); and Richard Bjornson, "Cognitive Mapping and the Understanding of Literature" (1981). An interesting addition is P. N. Johnson-Laird's article, "Thinking as a Skill" (1982), which bases informal logic on mental modeling.

To deal with all of the questions raised by schema theory, the concept of memory must become more dynamic. In artificial intelligence work there has often been a collapsing of process and structure, such that knowledge structures are simultaneously programs for remembering or thinking or acting (see Donald Norman, David Rumelhart, and the LNR Research Group, *Explorations in Cognition* [1975]). A number of researchers are now supporting a "reconstructive" conception of memory, which says that memory structures are not static but change continuously, meaning that active construction occurs not only during perception and comprehension but during retention and recall. This position was argued by Spiro (1980) and, very accessibly, by Mary diSibio, "Memory for Connected Discourse" (1982), who presented it in an educational context. This view of memory intersects with other work on learning from prose, which questions many of the assumptions about learning that follow from traditional traceviews of memory; see, for example, John Bransford, Kathleen Nitsch, and Jeffrey Franks, "Schooling and the Facilitation of Knowing" (1977). They and others in the same volume (*Schooling and the Acquisition of Knowledge*, edited by Richard Anderson, Rand Spiro, and William Montague [1977]) believe that theories of memory have failed to deal with the way knowledge is acquired and drawn from memory in subsequent thought and action, particularly skilled or expert activity.

Some recent work on memory collected in *Perspectives on Memory Research*, edited by Lars-Göran Nilsson (1979b), suggests reconceptualizations of memory that may respond to such demands. Nilsson's article "Functions of Memory" (1979a) gives a useful review of paradigms in memory research and ends by rejecting the computer analogy that led researchers to see memory in spatial terms. He said that concepts of STM and LTM as spaces have been abandoned and indeed that memory can no longer be conceived as either storage place, process, or thing. Rather, memory is a function of cognition in a given situation, not separate from but interactive with other functions such as perception, language, and thinking. These functions are not separate entities but aspects of a single system, corresponding to the specific functions it performs in a given case. He further asserted that memory is an ecological concept in that memory function is an effect of the interaction of the cognitive system and the environment (consider, for example, the concept of "memorability"). This view is elaborated to philosophical depths by M. T. Turvey and Robert Shaw, "The Primacy of Perceiving" (1979) in the same volume. Note also Ulric Neisser's collection of articles on remembering in natural contexts, *Memory Observed* (1982), which calls for a turn toward more realistic studies of memory.

Fergus Craik and Larry Jacoby, "Elaboration and Distinctiveness in Episodic Memory" (1979), also in the Nilsson volume, discussed a concept of memory as stage setting which they attributed to J. D. Bransford and his colleagues ("Toward Unexplaining Memory" [1977]). Memory is the cognitive system in its function of "setting the stage" or acting as a tacit background for interpreting present events, both novel and familiar. Turvey and Shaw suggested that this need not replace the notion of memory as a set of records; rather, the cognitive system can work in a range of modes to focus on comprehension (with learning as the background to new events) or on remembering (with new events as background to recalling earlier events or ideas). The idea of memory as an "attuned organism" is one of many ways in which current research on discourse makes use of the concept of tacit knowledge in relation to focus or attention.

In its cognitive sense, context refers to knowledge a writer or reader invokes to understand or compose meanings. In the section on memory we saw researchers trying to characterize that knowledge and—very abstractly—its role in discourse processing. They quickly got themselves into very deep waters. The question of how prior knowledge functions in writing or reading raises some of the most difficult issues of cognition, including attention, consciousness, and the relations between concepts—or generic knowledge—and particulars of experience. It becomes clear in discussions of memory and schema theory that most of the interaction between prior knowledge and currently experienced events takes place outside the narrowly circumscribed "space" of consciousness, or focal attention. In addition, a great deal of our knowledge is inaccessible to conscious awareness. Many rhetoricians, linguists, psychologists, and others, adopting terminology from Michael Polanyi, make a distinction between "tacit" knowledge and "focal" attention to discuss the role of inexplicit or subconscious structures and processes in linguistic events. (See Noam Chomsky's concept of competence as tacit knowledge of a grammar, *Aspects of the Theory of Syntax* [1965].)

Polanyi presented conceptions of tacit knowledge and a tacit-focal relation in his book *The Tacit Dimension* (1966, 1967); they are related to his central preoccupation with the personal and communal bases of all knowing, explored in *Personal Knowledge* (1962) and many other works. The concept of tacit knowledge is relational rather than absolute, that is, it pertains to attention within an act of knowing rather than to a quality in knowledge itself. In this configuration of attention, something focal in consciousness is understood through or in terms of knowledge that remains inexplicit or tacit. In Polanyi's words, we attend *from* one thing *to* another. This structure has a number of different aspects or manifestations in different contexts—for example, we attend from particulars (notes in a melody) to their joint meaning, from a tool (a hammer) to its functioning (hitting), or from a theory to an understanding of objects or to a practice.

The theory of tacit knowing is extended through notions of "indwelling" and "personal knowledge." *Indwelling* is the activity of interiorization by which we make knowledge tacit or instrumental, thereby ensuring that we are not (in the act of knowing) aware of it as such. To become conscious of tacit knowledge (if that is possible) is to momentarily disable our capacity for grasping something else for which it forms the particulars, background, or context. Polanyi argued that all scientific discovery, all claims to truth, depend on tacit integrations of one's own body and skills, tools, ideas, communal frameworks and values, so that all knowing becomes a personal act of faith and responsibility.

In her article "The Tacit Tradition" (1980), whose title plays on Polanyi's concept, Janet Emig identified him as one of those who inspire the current development of composition as a scholarly field. Polanyi's influence on rhetoric is explored in a special issue of the journal *Pre/Text* edited by Sam Watson (1981). (See also Watson's "Polanyi and the Contexts of Composing" [1980].) Among those who most fully draw on Polanyi's ideas as they relate to composition theory are James Britton (1978; with others, 1975) and Louise Wetherbee Phelps (1980).

Polanyi's influence combines with a phenomenological perspective to energize Hubert Dreyfus's critique of artificial intelligence (1972), which opposes the computational metaphor for cognition. Dreyfus, psychologists, linguists, and the artificial intelligence community would agree that there are knowledge structures that must operate tacitly in given language acts and indeed are not available to conscious awareness at all; they would further agree (although more recently) that many automatic and subconscious processes must go on in parallel during cognition. The difference is in their conception of this knowledge (as formal rules and relations or as holistic, perhaps perceptual structures) and of what is going on below the surface of consciousness. Dreyfus described a number of activities (for example, pattern recognition and chess) where human intelligence draws on global, unformalizable knowledge, not (he said) through rapid subconscious calculations comparable to those of a digital computer but through a kind of "short-cut processing made possible by fringe-consciousness [tacit knowing], insight, and ambiguity tolerance" (p. 213).

Some of these arguments—highly controversial among cognitive scientists—receive at least partial support from some recently proposed views of the brain, which see it as functioning holistically rather than digitally. See, for example, James Anderson, "Neural Models with Cognitive Implications" (1977), which suggests a different electronic metaphor, the transistor radio, and Kenneth Pelletier, *Toward a Science of Consciousness* (1978), which discusses holistic perspectives representing a convergence of brain research, modern physics, and Eastern world views. A. R. Luria, in *The Working Brain* (1973), denied the mechanistic analogy and argued that higher mental processes are not localized, but distributed, with different parts of the brain making contributions to complex functional systems.

Although the mainstream of cognitive science favors more digital views, Polanyi's terms (if not always the conceptual framework underlying them) have surprising currency among cognitive scientists. Walter Weimer (1974) identified tacit knowledge as the theme of the first Weimer and Palermo conference, and in his overview of the conference he said that "the entire problem of tacit knowledge is nothing more, nothing less, than the problem of meaning" (p. 428). Jeffrey Franks' rich article in the same volume (1974) argues for the notion that "All overt responses and phenomenal experiences presuppose underlying [holistic] tacit meaning structures" (p. 234). In this view, experiences such as motor response, symbolization, and images are all products or surface manifestations of tacitly known relations. These specific tacit "meanings" (corresponding to Chomskyan "deep structures") in turn are activations of a tacit system of generative relations, which represents our relatively static situational knowledge of the world (corresponding to a generative grammar). Despite drawing this analogy, Franks denied that tacit meanings or knowledge (that is, semantics) resemble symbol-manipulation systems like language. He described them as generative, recursive, Gestalt patterns, basically perceptual. But we can only be aware of, or talk about, our tacit knowledge in terms of symbols, that is, elements and relations—their surface manifestations in consciousness. See M. T. Turvey, "Constructive Theory, Perceptual Systems, and Tacit Knowledge" (1974).

Even researchers who describe human cognition in terms of a computational metaphor now recognize the significance of both tacit knowledge and tacit processes, those that go on below the level of awareness and may not be available to introspection. For example, D. Alan Allport in "Conscious and Unconscious Cognition" (1979) described cognition in terms of a "control structure" that combines parallel organization and a completely global data base acting as a central processor through which interactions are channelled, for example, in the simultaneous top-down and bottom-up processing of reading. Allport suggested that episodic awareness of information in current consciousness results from "pre-attentive" processes that are not governed by constraints on attentional capacity. William Woods, in "Multiple Theory Formation in Speech and Reading" (1980), also made a case for automatic pre-attentive processes, which he characterized as involving the formation and evaluation (through comparison and mutual influence) of many alternative partial hypotheses. Such processes must be either very rapid, highly parallel, or both. Interestingly, he suggested that our introspective knowledge about such tacit processes develops just like any other knowledge, in that we have direct knowledge of certain mental events and must make inferences from those about others.

The interest in tacit knowledge has perhaps stimulated consideration of a complementary concept, *metacognition*. In one of its senses, the term refers to deliberate and conscious control of one's cognitive acts (see Ann Brown, "Metacognitive Development and Reading" [1980]), and it is often associated with an "executive" on control structure in computer modeling of language and cognition. This notion of control is not identical with that of explicit knowledge about one's cognitive acts: the metacognitive ability to think about, plan, and modify mental activities may itself be seen as drawing on tacit metacognitive knowledge. In some cases, such knowledge can be made explicit (perhaps in the same sense Franks spoke of, in terms of its products or surface, conscious manifestations). Brown gave a useful review of work on metacognition, which has focused on how children develop metacognitive skills, or abilities to monitor mental processes: for example, predicting, checking, planning, problem recognition, and strategies to deal with performance constraints. Another review is by Steven Yussen, Samuel Mathews, II, and Elfrieda Hiebert, "Metacognitive Aspects of Reading" (1982).

The concept of a tacit-focal relation underlies an important body of work at the micro-level of written language that is concerned with the way linguistic cues accomplish certain kinds of pragmatic weighting of ideational content. (See the discussion of cues responding to memory constraints above.) The specific pragmatic function I want to connect to the tacit-focal relation is that of salience, or "attention-drawing." First I must deal with the radical confusion of terminology that marks the research on this function.

A relationship between focal or salient elements and backgrounded parts of text has been described in terms of many polarities, including "given" versus "new" information, "topic" versus "comment," "theme" versus "rheme," "foregrounding" versus "backgrounding," or under more comprehensive labels like "staging" and "packaging." Among the originators of these terms are M.A.K. Halliday, "Notes on Transitivity and Theme in English," Part 2 (1967); linguists of the Prague School (for example, see Frantisek Daneš, editor, *Papers on Functional Sentence Perspective* [1974]); and text linguists (see Joseph Grimes, *The Thread of Discourse* [1975] and de Beaugrande [1980] for syntheses). The linguist Wallace Chafe has also contributed to the conceptual discussions in a number of important papers, including "Givenness, Contrastiveness, Definiteness, Subjects, Topics, and Point of View" (1976) and "The Deployment of Consciousness in the Production of a Narrative" (1980a). William Vande Kopple reviewed some of this work from the point of view of a compositionist in "Functional Sentence Perspective, Composition, and Reading" (1982); and Dillon (1981) offered his own version of these distinctions and their significance for composition.

The proliferation of terminology about this subject is formidably confused and confusing. It is not clear whether we are dealing with different labels for a few functions or many different functions. The most lucid summaries and definitions I know are those given by researchers in developmental pragmatics, who are concerned with establishing a basic developmental relationship between communicative functions and surface grammatical forms. Elizabeth Bates and Brian MacWhinney's "A Functional Approach to the Acquisition of Grammar" (1979) is one of the best in an important volume, *Developmental Pragmatics*, edited by Elinor Ochs and Bambi Schieffelin (1979). After discussing the variety of semantic and pragmatic functions, or different types of meaning, that compete for the limited channel of the sentence, Bates and MacWhinney presented a detailed analysis of what they decided is a single pragmatic function, which they called the "topic-comment" relation. (A useful chart compares the usages of different researchers). This function places some information in a "point-making" relation to other information, such that the second (comment) represents a point made about the first (topic), and the topic represents a context or perspective from which the comment is understood. They argued that all other dimensions discussed by researchers are factors that influence the selection of topics and comments, which are communicated by an impressive variety of syntactic and morphological cues.

Another point of view is given by Martin Atkinson in the same collection, in "Prerequisites for Reference" (1979). He described a pragmatic function of "attention-drawing," which he (and others in the volume) believed is ontogenetically more basic than making statements of propositions. The idea is that the addresser uses linguistic cues to make sure that the addressee is attending to an intended entity, putting the two in a relationship of "reciprocal attention." This phenomenon is related in adult language to a complex (and largely unconscious) effort by the speaker, or for us the writer, to manage the experience the addressee has of the kinds of relationships already described. On the basis of all of this work, we might generalize tentatively that they concern, on the one hand, the way information flows into memory and consciousness, connects with tacit knowledge structures, and is maintained somehow on the fringes of consciousness as a context for new information; and on the other hand, the role such information plays as the inexplicit or played-down ground for new information.

All of these manifestations of the tacit-focal relation have important implications for education. For example, some see metacognition as a key to understanding difficulties that children have in reading and writing, especially when these activities are looked at in their highly skilled later development: see, for example, Scardamalia, Bereiter, and Goelman (1982) and Robert Bracewell, "Writing as a Cognitive Activity" (1980). Current interest among compositionists in functional sentence perspective and cohesion suggests, as Dillon (1981) explicitly proposed, giving pedagogical attention to how the packaging of propositional content affects readers' comprehension and response at the micro-level and in turn accounts for more global aspects of meaning construction.

More broadly, the problem of tacit knowledge raises an important issue for teaching, in that it is associated with learning by acquisition, as in the case of speech, rather than by conscious, effortful attention. A conflict persists in composition pedagogy between those who emphasize the natural acquisition and sub-

sequent highly tacit use of compositional skills and those who believe that
students can usefully learn rules, strategies, or forms and apply them to some
degree consciously in writing. One way to relate the two approaches is to treat
some components of the writing task as tacit and others as focal. For example,
under the influence of the monitor theory of Stephen Krashen, a view of second
language acquisition extended to writing ("On the Acquisition of Planned Discourse" [1978]), the Huntington Beach Project of W. Ross Winterowd has
adopted a model of teaching that distinguishes between the workshop, where
messy rhetorical interactions take place during composing processes (that is, the
generation of text), and the lab, where editing (of surface features of text) is
focally learned and practiced. (See Winterowd's "Developing a Composition
Program" [1980]). Phelps (1980) suggested developing a more highly differentiated model of consciousness in language use based on a functional definition
of the tacit-focal relation. This model would aim to describe the shifts in level
of indwelling that become possible or necessary in the effort to acquire and
practice expertise, comparable to the gradient of tacit-focal relations experienced
by performers such as musicians, actors, and athletes. See Bransford, Nitsch,
and Franks (1977).

Finally, H. S. Broudy, in "Types of Knowledge and Purposes of Education"
(1977), pointed out the profound implications of a theory of tacit personal knowledge for the goals of education, or learning. He distinguished three kinds of
knowledge: knowing how, knowing that, and (Polanyi's) knowing with. Regarding knowing with, education from the student's point of view can be described as the building up of contexts to indwell them in later thought and action.
Contextual knowing serves to "restore the unity that abstract learning necessarily
ruptures" (p. 16). He suggested that viewing learning, especially learning from
texts, in terms of these continuing and value-saturated interactions between
abstract knowledge structures and experiences would have radical implications
for schooling.

Three psychological topics have attracted special attention from compositionists: hemisphericity, abstraction, and egocentrism. This complex of topics, which
cannot be treated in the depth it deserves, serves to raise some important issues
about relationships between brain, cognition, and language, where composition
is peculiarly susceptible to the problems of misusing concepts from other fields.

In the 1970s tremendous advances in research on the brain attracted increasing
attention from psychologists and people in education, and a number of works
appeared that made this research accessible to compositionists. Among them are
The Human Brain (1977) and *The Brain and Psychology* (1980), both edited by
M. C. Wittrock, and *Education and the Brain* (1978), edited by Jeanne Chall
and Allan Mirsky. These collections include authoritative and clearly written
discussions of the implications of recent brain studies for educational topics such
as attention, motivation, brain dysfunctions, and dyslexia. Prominent composition researchers have drawn attention to the importance of brain studies for

composition: see, for example, Janet Emig's well-known essay "Hand, Eye, Brain" (1978).

Compositionists have been most excited by studies of hemisphericity, the lateralization of cognitive functions in the left and right hemispheres: see Sally P. Springer and Georg Deutsch, *Left Brain, Right Brain* (1981), for an up-to-date review of this research. Briefly, studies of patients with *split-brains* (where the corpus callosum connecting the two hemispheres had been cut), along with other techniques developed later for normal populations, have revealed that the two hemispheres appear to specialize in different kinds of cognition, embodying different approaches to the processing of experience and to action. The *left hemisphere* (in most right-handed people) seems superior at analytical, sequential, time-dependent tasks, taking major responsibility for language, and the *right hemisphere* is better at holistic, simultaneous tasks such as recognition of faces.

These characterizations are of course oversimplified and are constantly being refined by new studies. But composition has not been immune to the temptation to distort this research or speculate far beyond the current data. Its remarkable impact stems from the fact that these differences in hemispheric function appear to explain and support ancient human polarities, arising in many cultures, between two modes of consciousness and thought (for example, mystical and rational, Eastern and Western, metaphor and metonymy, and so forth). Two researchers who have been careful to distinguish speculation from knowledge are W. Ross Winterowd, in his seminal article, "Brain, Rhetoric, and Style" (1979), and Benjamin Glassner, in the recent review "Writing as an Integrator of Hemispheric Function" (1981). Their articles reveal that hemisphericity functions most powerfully as a metaphor that has helped us to revalue intuitive, holistic modes of consciousness (appositional thought) as a personal cognitive style, a type of discourse organization, a state of awareness, and a component or dimension of writing and reading acts complementary to the linear, hierarchical, discursive qualities that language contributes to thought. (See James Moffett, "Writing, Inner Speech, and Meditation" [1981].)

The concepts of abstraction and egocentrism were introduced together into composition by James Moffett, in a book that remains one of the most subtle and suggestive discussions of language and thought in the field: *Teaching the Universe of Discourse* (1968). Moffett defined abstraction as the processing of experience through symbols, beginning with perception and moving up a hierarchy or ladder of abstraction reflecting greater and greater processing by the human mind, culminating in abstractions about lower abstractions, or meta-language. He described the *abstractive processes* as operations of hierarchical organization, which rank material through criteria of class inclusion and concreteness, and of selective attention, which summarize, reorganize, and integrate perception and memories.

Discourse then represents symbolic action as a structure of two relations, the *I-it relation* (abstracting *from* experience) and the *I-you relation* (abstracting *for* an audience). Moffett's modes of discourse exhibit an order of abstraction, or hierarchy, structured by these two relations and representing a greater and greater decontextualization of both through increasing distance between writer and subject, writer and audience. Moffett argued that social experience (participating in a great range of oral and written discourse) as it acts upon and responds to cognitive growth is the way in which individuals learn to actualize these increasingly decontextualized relations.

Moffett invoked Piaget's concept of egocentrism to characterize a movement in maturation toward greater capacity to differentiate self from others and to take others' perspectives. (He was also interested in the connections drawn from L. S. Vygotsky in *Thought and Language* [1962] between an egocentric stage of social speech and its internalization as "inner speech.") Unlike some later compositionists who took up this term, Moffett did not use it as a blanket explanation for the inability of young or inexperienced writers to deal skillfully with audiences. Broadly, children are thought to "decenter" or become less egocentric as they mature (and gain social experience), although new situations and cognitive demands recapitulate the problem of egocentrism at higher levels on into adulthood. Moffett extended the notion of decentering along both axes of discourse, as an increasing ability to detach oneself from the immediate existential situation of face-to-face discourse in order to handle more abstract, critical, and public relations between self and world, self and audience. Moffett associated decreasing egocentrism with a growing consciousness of abstraction, which both signals and makes possible flexible and skillful control of this spectrum of discourse (see the discussion of metacognition above).

Moffett's theory is informal, built on his extensive experience in the classroom, although he cited some psychological research. But he was prescient within the profession in trying to connect literacy with cognition and specifically with what I call here "disembedded thinking" after Margaret Donaldson in *Children's Minds* (1978), because this effort has become an important and controversial theme in disciplines ranging from classics to psychology and anthropology (recently reviewed by C. Jan Swearingen for compositionists at the 1983 Conference on College Composition and Communication). Donaldson's book (in the context of a Piagetan critique) reinterprets Piaget's observations, and cites others, to support her contention that it is difficult for both adults and children to manage logical operations and rhetorical relations apart from their normal embedding in the context of human situations and purposes. Like Moffett, she believes such reasoning requires a meta-awareness of language and cognition that is stimulated and supported by schooling and by the technology of writing in particular.

The argument currently rages over what indeed are the precise relationships among literacy, literacy practices, schooling, other features of a culture, the capacity for formal operations, and the performance of decontextualized thinking in particular circumstances: for a review, see the introduction to Sylvia Scribner and Michael Cole, *The Psychology of Literacy* (1981), a monumental study of literacy practices among the Vai in West Africa, with complex conclusions. A further issue, raised particularly by the work of A. R. Luria, *Cognitive Development* (1976) and L. S. Vygotsky, *Mind in Society* (1978), is how closely the impact of literacy on a whole society, especially in the transition to a literate culture, parallels the relationships between literacy and cognitive growth in an individual living in a high-literate society. The latter issue is especially salient for compositionists working in American schools because of their need to facilitate literacy for groups who do not fully participate in the high literacy of the culture as a whole. (The problem presents itself differently, of course, in contexts such as the Third World; see the work of Paolo Freire, for example, *Education for Critical Consciousness* [1981] and *Pedagogy of the Oppressed* [1982].) The controversy over these relationships picks up, from a different perspective, themes we have been following throughout this chapter, namely, the primacy of context and the functional nature of language.

The Significance of a Developmental Perspective

It was my original intention in this chapter to treat each topic from two points of view: the first, a process perspective, where process refers to fairly discrete, time-limited acts of writing and reading: the second, a developmental perspective, which would consider how writing and reading abilities develop as a function of both cognitive growth and social experience. (The latter perspective implies a notion of "natural" acquisition without excluding schools as natural contexts; it also suggests a related interest in factors that block natural development of literacy powers in a literate culture.) As it turned out, this plan was never practical and not simply because it would have doubled the length of an already overstuffed chapter. It soon became apparent that, on the one hand, composition has only very recently begun to address seriously the subject of development, so there was little research to cite (but see Warnock's consideration of issues in the development of writing in the first chapter of this volume); on the other hand, I lack at present the breadth and depth of knowledge in other fields that should be brought to bear. These constraints give my chapter an undesired bias that my conclusion is intended to counter by calling attention to the significance of developmental research to a psychology of composition and giving some sense of its possible impact.

Despite references by some compositionists to theories of developmental psychology, at present most of us have not studied this work in sufficient depth to undertake synthetic and creative thinking about its meaning for composition. One significant exception to this superficiality is the work of Janet Emig, already cited. Other interesting efforts to relate developmental psychology to composition are Kroll (1980); Loren Barritt and Barry Kroll, "Some Implications of Cognitive-Developmental Psychology for Research in Composing" (1978); and Andrea Lunsford, "Cognitive Development and the Basic Writer" (1979, 1981), a controversial extension of developmental concepts from Piaget and Vygotsky to adults.

Recently, there has been a great upsurge of interest in studying the way children naturally acquire the ability to write and read, both in school and at home: two publications that report such studies are Donald Graves, *Writing* (1982), and Denny Taylor, *Family Literacy* (1983); and Warnock cited others in the first chapter of this volume. To support inquiries of this sort we need a theoretical framework that moves beyond discourse modes and even theories of composing process to characterize the relationships between the growth and learning of written language and other aspects of cognitive, affective, moral, and linguistic development. To this end we must go further than the borrowing of a few concepts here and there, to develop both an appreciative and a critical knowledge of the developmental research in general and the great psychologists in particular: I am thinking of Freud, Erikson, Piaget, Werner, Jerome Bruner, Luria, and Vygotsky, among others. We will need to correlate this work with the contributions of anthropologists, linguists, social psychologists, educators, and others if we are to grasp development of literacy as both a personal and a cultural phenomenon and contribute ourselves to its understanding.

Developmental studies promise to be a key to understanding the processes of writing and reading in general. This path of inquiry encourages the kind of contextualized, interactive models that scientists and teachers have been seeking to account for the relationships between cognitive processes and social life. It may eventually lead us to see writing and reading episodes less componentially and more organically in relation to the mental life of the individual: as moments abstracted from a continuity, the ongoing stream of oral, written, and inner speech.

L. S. Vygotsky offered one model of the relationships between developmental studies and process studies in his *Mind and Society* (1978). He believed that developmental studies were the primary theoretical and empirical means for revealing complex processes. In his experimental-genetic method, Vygotsky attempted to pose tasks and sometimes to intervene in them to provoke learning, telescoping development so that he could observe the dynamics of change in intellectual development.

Vygotsky saw parallels between children's play and their activity in schools, both situations that exploit "zones of proximal development," a kind of mental space between an actual and a potential developmental level. In these zones, development occurs through problem solving with adult guidance or peer collaboration, facilitated by discourse; this is what Vygotsky stimulated and observed through his innovative experimental methods. Thus developmental research presents a model for education as well as inquiry. The importance of developmental studies for composition lies in part in the fact that composition, as I suggested at the beginning of this chapter, is more than the study of literacy; it is a facilitating praxis, a pedagogy, based on ethical commitments. Thus a psychology of composition treats writing and reading as simultaneously windows on the mind (Chomsky's view of language in general) and functional powers that, for the sake of psychological and social health, composition teachers work to develop and enhance. Developmental studies not only make possible a richer and deeper understanding of the psychology of writing and reading, but they may enable the development of what Jerome Bruner, in "The Growth of Mind" (1973), called a "psychology of assisted growth."

References

Adams, Marilyn Jager, and Allan Collins. "A Schema-Theoretic View of Reading." In *New Directions in Discourse Processing*. Vol. 2 in *Advances in Discourse Processes*. Ed. Roy O. Freedle. Norwood, N.J.: Ablex, 1979, pp. 1–22.

Allport, D. Alan. "Conscious and Unconscious Cognition: A Computational Metaphor for the Mechanism of Attention and Integration." In *Perspectives on Memory Research: Essays in Honor of Uppsala University's 500th Anniversary*. Ed. Lars-Göran Nilsson, Hillsdale, N.J.: Erlbaum, 1979, pp. 61–89.

Anderson, James A. "Neural Models with Cognitive Implications." In *Basic Processes in Reading: Perception and Comprehension*. Ed. David Laberge and S. J. Samuels. Hillsdale, N.J.: Erlbaum, 1977, pp. 27–90.

Anderson, Richard C. "The Notion of Schemata and the Educational Enterprise: General Discussion of the Conference." In *Schooling and the Acquisition of Knowledge*. Ed. Richard C. Anderson, Rand J. Spiro, and William E. Montague. Hillsdale, N.J.: Erlbaum, 1977, pp. 415–31.

———, Rand J. Spiro, and William E. Montague, eds. *Schooling and the Acquisition of Knowledge*. Hillsdale, N.J.: Erlbaum, 1977.

Arnold, N. Scott. "Research Methods and the Evaluation of Hypotheses: A Reply to Kinney." *RSQ*, 10 (1980), 149–55.

Atkinson, Martin. "Prerequisites for Reference." In *Developmental Pragmatics*. Ed. Elinor Ochs and Bambi B. Schieffelin. New York: Academic, 1979, pp. 229–49.

Barritt, Loren S., and Barry M. Kroll. "Some Implications of Cognitive-Developmental Psychology for Research in Composing." In *Research on Composing: Points of Departure*. Ed. Charles R. Cooper and Lee Odell. Urbana, Ill.: NCTE, 1978, pp. 49–57.

Bartlett, F. C. *Remembering: A Study in Experimental and Social Psychology*. Cambridge: Cambridge University Press, 1932.

Bates, Elizabeth, and Brian MacWhinney. "A Functionalist Approach to the Acquisition of Grammar." In *Developmental Pragmatics*. Ed. Elinor Ochs and Bambi B. Schieffelin. New York: Academic, 1979, pp. 167–211.

Berger, Peter L., and Thomas Luckmann. *The Social Construction of Reality: A Treatise in the Sociology of Knowledge*. Garden City, N.Y.: Doubleday, Anchor, 1967.

Berlin, James A. "Contemporary Composition: The Major Pedagogical Theories." *CE*, 44 (1982), 765–77.

Bjornson, Richard. "Cognitive Mapping and the Understanding of Literature." *Sub-Stance*, 30 (1981), 31–62.

Bolinger, Dwight. "The Atomization of Meaning." *Lang*, 40 (1965), 555–73.

Bracewell, Robert J. "Writing as a Cognitive Activity." *Visibl Lang*, 14 (1980), 400–422.

Bransford, John D., Kathleen E. Nitsch, and Jeffrey J. Franks. "Schooling and the

Facilitation of Knowing.'' In *Schooling and the Acquisition of Knowledge*. Ed. Richard C. Anderson, Rand J. Spiro, and William E. Montague. Hillsdale, N.J.: Erlbaum, 1977, pp. 31–55.

————, and Nancy S. McCarrell. ''A Sketch of a Cognitive Approach to Comprehension: Some Thoughts About Understanding What It Means to Comprehend.'' In *Cognition and the Symbolic Process*, Vol. 1. Ed. Walter B. Weimer and David S. Palermo. Hillsdale, N.J.: Erlbaum, 1974, pp. 189–230.

————, et al. ''Toward Unexplaining Memory.'' In *Perceiving, Acting, and Knowing: Toward an Ecological Psychology*. Ed. Robert Shaw and John Bransford. Hillsdale, N.J.: Erlbaum, 1977, pp. 431–66.

Brewer, William F. ''The Problem of Meaning and the Interrelations of the Higher Mental Processes.'' In *Cognition and the Symbolic Process*, Vol. 1. Ed. Walter B. Weimer and David S. Palermo. Hillsdale, N.J.: Erlbaum, 1974, pp. 263–98.

Britton, James. *Language and Learning*. Baltimore: Penguin, 1970.

————. ''The Composing Process and the Functions of Writing.'' In *Research on Composing: Points of Departure*. Ed. Charles R. Cooper and Lee Odell. Urbana, Ill.: NCTE, 1978, pp. 13–28.

————. *Prospect and Retrospect: Selected Essays of James Britton*. Ed. Gordon M. Pradl. Montclair, N.J.: Boynton/Cook, 1982.

————, et al. *The Development of Writing Abilities, 11–18*. London: Macmillan, 1975.

Broudy, H. S. ''Types of Knowledge and Purposes of Education.'' In *Schooling and the Acquisition of Knowledge*. Ed. Richard C. Anderson, Rand J. Spiro, and William E. Montague. Hillsdale, N.J.: Erlbaum, 1977, pp. 1–17.

Brown, Ann. J. ''Metacognitive Development and Reading.'' In *Theoretical Issues in Reading Comprehension: Perspectives from Cognitive Psychology, Linguistics, Artificial Intelligence, and Education*. Ed. Rand J. Spiro, Bertram C. Bruce, and William F. Brewer. Hillsdale, N.J.: Erlbaum, 1980, pp. 453–81.

Bruce, Bertram C. ''Plans and Social Actions.'' In *Theoretical Issues in Reading Comprehension: Perspectives from Cognitive Psychology, Linguistics, Artificial Intelligence, and Education*. Ed. Rand J. Spiro, Bertram C. Bruce, and William F. Brewer. Hillsdale, N.J.: Erlbaum, 1980, pp. 367–84.

Bruner, Jerome S. ''The Growth of Mind.'' *A Psychol*, 20 (1965), 1007–17. Rpt. in Jerome S. Bruner, *Beyond the Information Given: Studies in the Psychology of Knowing*. Ed. Jeromy M. Anglin. New York: Norton, 1973, pp. 437–51.

Burke, Kenneth. *A Grammar of Motives*. 1945; rpt. Berkeley: University of California Press, 1969.

Carpenter, Patricia A., and Marcel A. Just. ''Integrative Processes in Comprehension.'' In *Basic Processes in Reading: Perception and Comprehension*. Ed. David Laberge and S. Jay Samuels. Hillsdale, N.J.: Erlbaum, 1977, pp. 217–63.

Chafe, Wallace L. ''Language and Memory.'' *Lang*, 49 (1973), 261–81.

————. ''Language and Consciousness.'' *Lang*, 50 (1974), 111–33.

————. ''Givenness, Contrastiveness, Definiteness, Subjects, Topics, and Point of View.'' In *Subject and Topic*. Ed. Charles N. Li. New York: Academic Press, 1976, pp. 25–55.

————. ''Creativity in Verbalization and Its Implications for the Nature of Stored Knowledge.'' In *Discourse Production and Comprehension*. Vol. 1 in *Discourse Processes: Advances in Research and Theory*. Ed. Roy O. Freedle. Norwood, N.J.: Ablex, 1977, pp. 41–55.

————. "The Deployment of Consciousness in the Production of a Narrative." In *The Pear Stories: Cognitive, Cultural, and Linguistic Aspects of Narrative Production.* Ed. Wallace L. Chafe. Vol. 3 in *Advances in Discourse Processes.* Ed. Roy O. Freedle. Norwood, N.J.: Ablex, 1980a, pp. 9–50.

————, ed. *The Pear Stories: Cognitive, Cultural, and Linguistic Aspects of Narrative Production.* Vol. 3 in *Advances in Discourse Processes.* Ed. Roy O. Freedle. Norwood, N.J.: Ablex, 1980b.

Chall, Jeanne S., and Allan F. Mirsky, eds. *Education and the Brain: The Seventy-Seventh Yearbook of the National Society for the Study of Education.* Part 2. Chicago: National Society for the Study of Education, 1978.

Chomsky, Noam. *Aspects of the Theory of Syntax.* Cambridge, Mass.: M.I.T. Press, 1965.

Clark, Herbert H. "Inference in Comprehension." In *Basic Processes in Reading: Perception and Comprehension.* Ed. David Laberge and S. Jay Samuels. Hillsdale, N.J.: Erlbaum, 1977, pp. 243–63.

————, and Eve V. Clark. *Psychology and Language: An Introduction to Psycholinguistics.* New York: Harcourt, 1977.

————, and Susan E. Haviland. "Comprehension and the Given-New Contract." In *Discourse Production and Comprehension.* Vol. 1 in *Discourse Processes: Advances in Research and Theory.* Ed. Roy O. Freedle. Norwood, N.J.: Ablex, 1977, pp. 1–40.

Clay, Marie J. "Research Update: Learning and Teaching Writing: A Developmental Perspective." *Lang Arts,* 59 (1982), 65–70.

Cognitive Science: A Multidisciplinary Journal of Artificial Intelligence, Psychology, and Language. Vol. 1. Norwood, N.J.: Ablex, 1977.

Collins, Allen, John Seely Brown, and Kathy M. Larkin. "Inference in Text Understanding." In *Theoretical Issues in Reading Comprehension: Perspectives from Cognitive Psychology, Linguistics, Artificial Intelligence, and Education.* Ed. Rand J. Spiro, Bertram C. Bruce, and William F. Brewer. Hillsdale, N.J.: Erlbaum, 1980, pp. 385–407.

Connors, Robert J. "Composition Studies and Science." *CE,* 45 (1983), 1–20.

Craik, Fergus I. M., and Larry L. Jacoby. "Elaboration and Distinctiveness in Episodic Memory." In *Perspectives on Memory Research: Essays in Honor of Uppsala University's 500th Anniversary.* Ed. Lars-Göran Nilsson. Hillsdale, N.J.: Erlbaum, 1979, pp. 145–66.

Daneš, F., ed. *Papers on Functional Sentence Perspective.* The Hague: Mouton, 1974.

D'Angelo, Frank J. "Rhetoric and Cognition: Toward a Metatheory of Discourse." *Pre/Text,* 3 (1982), 105–19.

de Beaugrande, Robert. *Text, Discourse, and Process: Toward a Multidisciplinary Science of Texts.* Vol. 4 in *Advances in Discourse Processes.* Ed. Roy O. Freedle. Norwood, N.J.: Ablex, 1980.

————. "Design Criteria for Process Models of Reading." *Read Res Q,* 2 (1981), 216–315.

————. "Psychology and Composition: Past, Present and Future." In *What Writers Know: The Language, Process, and Structure of Written Discourse.* Ed. Martin Nystrand. New York: Academic, 1982a, pp. 211–67.

————. *Text Production: Toward a Science of Composition.* Norwood, N.J.: Ablex, 1982b.

Delia, Jesse G. "Constructivism and the Study of Human Communication." *QJS*, 63 (1977), 66–83.

Dillon, George L. *Constructing Texts: Elements of a Theory of Composition and Style*. Bloomington: Indiana University Press, 1981.

Discourse Processes: A Multidisciplinary Journal. Vol. 1. Norwood, N.J.: Ablex, 1978.

diSibio, Mary. "Memory for Connected Discourse: A Constructivist View." *Rev Educ Res*, 53 (1982), 149–74.

Donaldson, Margaret. *Children's Minds*. New York: Norton, 1978.

Dreyfus, Hubert L. *What Computers Can't Do: A Critique of Artificial Reason*. New York: Harper, 1972.

Durkin, Dolores. "What Is the Value of the New Interest in Reading Comprehension?" *Lang Arts*, 58 (1981), 23–43.

Elsasser, Nan, and Vera John-Steiner. "An Interactionist Approach to Advancing Literacy." *Harvard Educ Rev*, 47 (1977), 353–69. Rpt. in *Thought and Language, Language and Reading*. Cambridge, Mass.: Harvard Educational Review, 1980, pp. 451–65.

Emig, Janet. "Hand, Eye, Brain: Some Basics in the Writing Process." In *Research on Composing: Points of Departure*. Ed. Charles R. Cooper and Lee Odell. Urbana, Ill.: NCTE, 1978, pp. 59–71.

———. "The Tacit Tradition: The Inevitability of a Multi-Disciplinary Approach to Writing Research." In *Reinventing the Rhetorical Tradition*. Ed. Aviva Freedman and Ian Pringle. Conway, Ark.: L and S, 1980, 9–17.

———. "Inquiry Paradigms and Writing." *CCC*, 33 (1982), 64–75.

Flower, Linda S., and John R. Hayes. "The Dynamics of Composing: Making Plans and Juggling Constraints." In *Cognitive Processes in Writing*. Ed. Lee W. Gregg and Erwin R. Steinberg. Hillsdale, N.J.: Erlbaum, 1980, pp. 31–50.

Franks, Jeffrey J. "Toward Understanding Understanding." In *Cognition and the Symbolic Processes*. Vol. 1. Ed. Walter B. Weimer and David S. Palermo, Hillsdale, N.J.: Erlbaum, 1974, pp. 231–61.

Frederiksen, Carl H., and Joseph F. Dominic. "Introduction: Perspectives on the Activity of Writing." In *Writing: Process, Development, and Communication*. Ed. Carl H. Frederiksen and Joseph F. Dominic. Vol. 2 in *Writing: The Nature, Development, and Teaching of Written Communication*. Hillsdale, N.J.: Erlbaum, 1981, pp. 1–20.

Freedle, Roy O., ed. *Discourse Production and Comprehension*. Vol. 1 in *Discourse Processes: Advances in Research and Theory*. Ed. Roy O. Freedle. Norwood, N.J.: Ablex, 1977.

———, ed. *New Directions in Discourse Processing*. Vol. 2 in *Advances in Discourse Processes*. Ed. Roy O. Freedle. Norwood, N.J.: Ablex, 1979.

———, and John B. Carroll, eds. *Language Comprehension and the Acquisition of Knowledge*. Washington, D.C.: Winston, 1972.

Freire, Paulo. *Education for Critical Consciousness*. New York: Continuum, 1981.

———. *Pedagogy of the Oppressed*. Trans. Myra Bergman. Ramos. New York: Continuum, 1982.

Furth, Hans G. *Piaget and Knowledge: Theoretical Foundations*, 2nd ed. Chicago: University of Chicago Press, 1981.

Geertz, Clifford. "Thick Description: Toward an Interpretive Theory of Culture." In *The Interpretation of Cultures*. New York: Basic, 1973, pp. 3–30.

Gibson, Eleanor J. "How Perception Really Develops: A View from Outside the Network." In *Basic Processes in Reading: Perception and Comprehension*. Ed. David Laberge and S. Jay Samuels. Hillsdale, N.J.: Erlbaum, 1977, pp. 155–73.

Giddens, Anthony. "Hermeneutics, Ethnomethodology, and Problems of Interpretative Analysis." In *Studies in Social and Political Theory*. New York: Basic, 1976, pp. 165–78.

Glassner, Benjamin M. "Writing as an Integrator of Hemispheric Function." In *Exploring Speaking-Writing Relationships: Connections and Contrasts*. Ed. Barry M. Kroll and Roberta J. Vann. Urbana, Ill.: NCTE, 1981, pp. 142–53.

Graves, Donald H. "Research Update: A New Look at Writing Research." *Lang Arts*, 57 (1980), pp. 913–19.

———. "Research Update: Writing Research for the Eighties: What Is Needed?" *Lang Arts*, 58 (1981), 197–206.

———. *Writing: Teachers and Children at Work*. Exeter, N.H.: Heinemann, 1982.

Gregg, Lee W., and Erwin R. Steinberg, eds. *Cognitive Processes in Writing*. Hillsdale, N.Y.: Erlbaum, 1980.

Grimes, Joseph, *The Thread of Discourse*. The Hague: Mouton, 1975.

Hairston, Maxine. "The Winds of Change: Thomas Kuhn and the Revolution in Teaching of Writing." *CCC*, 33 (1982), 76–88.

Halliday, M.A.K. "Notes on Transitivity and Theme in English." Part 2. *J Linguist*, 3 (1967), 199–245.

———. "Language Structure and Language Function." In *New Horizons in Linguistics*. Ed. John Lyons. Baltimore: Penguin, 1970, pp. 140-65.

———, and Ruqaiya Hasan. *Cohesion In English*. London: Longman, 1976.

Hayes, John R., and Linda S. Flower. "Identifying the Organization of Writing Processes." In *Cognitive Processes in Writing*. Ed. Lee W. Gregg and Erwin R. Steinberg. Hillsdale, N.J.: Erlbaum, 1980, pp. 3–30.

Hirsch, E. D. *The Philosophy of Composition*. Chicago: University of Chicago Press, 1977.

Johansson, Gunnar. "Memory Functions in Visual Event Perception." In *Perspectives on Memory Research*. Ed. Lars-Göran Nilsson. Hillsdale, N.J.: Erlbaum, 1979, pp. 93–103.

Johnson-Laird, P.N., "Thinking as a Skill." *Q J Exp Psychol*, 34A (1982), 1–29.

Just, Marcel Adam, and Patricia A. Carpenter, eds. *Cognitive Processes in Comprehension*. Hillsdale, N.J.: Erlbaum, 1977.

Kantor, Kenneth J., Dan R. Kirby, and Judith P. Goetz. "Research in Context; Ethnographic Studies in English Education." *RTE*, 15 (1981), 293–309.

King, Martha L., and Victor M. Rental. "Research Update: Converging Meaning in Written Texts." *Lang Arts*, 58 (1981), 721–28.

Kinney, James. "Composition Research and the Rhetorical Tradition." *RSQ*, 10 (1980), 143–48.

Kintsch, Walter, and Teun A. van Dijk. "Toward a Model of Text Comprehension and Production." *Psychol Rev*, 85 (1978), 363–94.

Krashen, Stephen D. "On the Acquisition of Planned Discourse: Written English as a Second Dialect." In *Claremont Reading Conference*, 42nd Yearbook. Ed. Malcolm P. Douglass. Claremont, Calif.: Claremont Reading Conference, 1978, pp. 173–85.

Kroll, Barry M. "Developmental Perspectives and the Teaching of Composition." *CE*, 41 (1980), 741–52.

———. "Developmental Relationships Between Speaking and Writing." In *Exploring Speaking-Writing Relationships: Connection and Contrasts*. Ed. Barry M. Kroll and Roberta J. Vann. Urbana, Ill.: NCTE, 1981, pp. 32–54.

Langer, Susanne K. *Mind: An Essay on Human Feeling*, Vols. 1–3. Baltimore: Johns Hopkins University Press, 1967, 1972, 1982.

Lunsford, Andrea A. "Cognitive Development and the Basic Writer." *CE*, 41 (1979), 39–46, Rpt. in *The Writing Teacher's Sourcebook*, Ed. Gary Tate and Edward P. J. Corbett. New York: Oxford University Press, 1981, pp. 257–67.

Luria, A. R. *Cognitive Development: Its Cultural and Social Foundations*. Trans. Martin Lopez-Morillas and Lynn Solotaroff. Ed. Michael Cole. Cambridge, Mass.: Harvard University Press, 1976.

———. *The Working Brain: An Introduction to Neuropsychology*. Trans. Basil Haigh. New York: Basic, 1973.

Mace, William. "Ecologically Stimulating Cognitive Psychology: Gibsonian Perspectives." In *Cognition and the Symbolic Processes*. Ed. Walter B. Weimer and David S. Palermo. Hillsdale, N.J.: Erlbaum, 1974, pp. 137–64.

Magoon, A. Jon. "Constructivist Approaches in Educational Research." *Rev Educ Res*, 47 (1977), 651–93.

Markova, Ivana. "Introduction." In *The Social Context of Language*. Chichester, England: Wiley, 1978, pp. 1–15.

———, ed. *The Social Context of Language*. Chichester: Wiley, 1978.

Matsuhashi, Ann. "Explorations in the Real-Time Production of Written Discourse." In *What Writers Know: The Language, Process, and Structure of Written Discourse*. Ed. Martin Nystrand. New York: Academic, 1982, pp. 269–90.

Meyer, Bonnie J. F. *The Organization of Prose and Its Effects on Memory*. Amsterdam: North Holland, 1975.

———. "What is Remembered from Prose: A Function of Passage Structure." In *Discourse Production and Comprehension*. Vol. 1 in *Discourse Processes: Advances in Research and Theory*. Ed. Roy O. Freedle. Norwood, N.J.: Ablex, 1977, pp. 307–36.

Miller, George A. "The Magical Number Seven, Plus or Minus Two: Some Limits on Our Capacity for Processing Information." *Psychol Rev*, 63 (1956), pp. 81–92.

———, Eugene Galanter, and Karl H. Pribram. *Plans and the Structure of Behavior*. New York: Holt, 1960.

Minsky, Marvin. "A Framework for Representing Knowledge." In *The Psychology of Computer Vision*. Ed. Patrick Henry Winston. New York: McGraw-Hill, 1975, pp. 211–77.

Mishler, Elliot F. "Meaning in Context: Is There Any Other Kind?" *Harvard Educ. Rev*, 49 (1979), 1–19.

Moffett, James, *Teaching the Universe of Discourse*. Boston: Houghton Mifflin, 1968.

———. "Writing, Inner Speech, and Meditation." In *Coming on Center: English Education in Evolution*. Montclair, N.J.: Boynton/Cook, 1981, pp. 133–81.

Morgan, Jerry L., and Manfred B. Sellner. "Discourse and Linguistic Theory." In *Theoretical Issues in Reading Comprehension: Perspectives from Cognitive Psychology, Linguistics, Artificial Intelligence, and Education*. Ed. Rand J. Spiro,

Bertram C. Bruce, and William F. Brewer. Hillsdale, N.J.: Erlbaum, 1980, pp. 165–200.

Murray, Donald M. *Learning by Teaching: Selected Articles on Writing and Teaching.* Montclair, N.J.: Boynton/Cook, 1982.

Neisser, Ulric. *Cognition and Reality.* San Francisco: Freeman, 1976.

———, ed. *Memory Observed: Remembering in Natural Contexts.* San Francisco: Freeman, 1982.

Nilsson, Lars-Göran. "Functions of Memory." In *Perspectives on Memory Research: Essays in Honor of Uppsala University's 500th Anniversary.* Ed. Lars-Göran Nilsson. Hillsdale, N.J.: Erlbaum, 1979a, pp. 3–15.

———, ed. *Perspectives on Memory Research: Essays in Honor of Uppsala University's 500th Anniversary.* Hillsdale, N.J.: Erlbaum, 1979b.

Norman, Donald A. "Perception, Memory, and Mental Processes." In *Perspectives on Memory Research: Essays in Honor of Uppsala University's 500th Anniversary.* Ed. Lars-Göran Nilsson. Hillsdale, N.J.: Erlbaum, 1979, pp. 121–44.

———. "Twelve Issues for Cognitive Science." In *Perspectives on Cognitive Science.* Ed. Donald A. Norman. Norwood, N.J.: Ablex, 1981a, pp. 265–95.

———, ed. *Perspectives on Cognitive Science,* Norwood, N.J.: Ablex, 1981b.

———, David E. Rumelhart, and the LNR Research Group. *Explorations in Cognition.* San Francisco: Freeman, 1975.

Nystrand, Martin. "The Structure of Textual Space." In *What Writers Know: The Language, Process, and Structure of Written Discourse.* Ed. Martin Nystrand. New York: Academic, 1982a, pp. 75–86.

———, ed. *What Writers Know: Language, Process, and Structure of Written Discourse.* New York: Academic, 1982b.

Ochs, Elinor. "Social Foundations of Language." In *New Directions in Discourse Processing.* Vol. 2 in *Advances in Discourse Processes.* Ed. Roy O. Freedle. Norwood, N.J.: Ablex, 1979, pp. 207–21.

———, and Bambi B. Schieffelin, eds. *Developmental Pragmatics.* New York: Academic, 1979.

O'Keefe, Barbara J. "Writing, Speaking, and the Production of Discourse." In *Exploring Speaking-Writing Relationships: Connections and Contrasts.* Ed. Barry K. Kroll and Roberta J. Vann. Urbana, Ill.: NCTE, 1981, pp. 134–41.

Olson, David R. "From Utterance to Text: The Bias of Language in Speech and Writing." *Harvard Educ Rev,* 47 (1977), 257–81.

Olson, Gary M., Robert L. Mack, and Susan Duffy. "Cognitive Aspects of Genre." *Poetics,* 10 (1981), 283–315.

Pelletier, Kenneth R. *Toward a Science of Consciousness.* New York: Delacorte, 1978.

Perl, Sondra. "Understanding Composing." *CCC* 31 (1980), 363–69.

Petrosky, Anthony. "From Story to Essay: Reading and Writing." *CCC,* 33 (1982), 19–36.

Phelps, Louise Wetherbee. "Acts, Texts, and the Teaching Context: Their Relations Within a Dramatistic Philosophy of Composition." Diss. Case Western Reserve University, 1980.

———. "The Dance of Discourse: A Dynamic, Relativistic View of Structure." *Pre/Text,* 3 (1982), 51–83.

———. "Dialectics of Coherence: Toward an Integrative Theory." *CE,* forthcoming.

Poetics, 9, No. 1–3 (1980). Special issue on story comprehension. Ed. Teun A. van Dijk.

Polanyi, Michael. *Personal Knowledge: Towards a Post-Critical Philosophy*. Chicago: University of Chicago Press, 1962.

———. *The Tacit Dimension*. 1966; rpt. Garden City, N.Y.: Doubleday, 1967.

Pre/Text: An Inter-Disciplinary Journal of Rhetoric, 2, No. 1-2 (1981). Special issue on Michael Polanyi. Ed. Sam Watson.

Rabinow, Paul, and William M. Sullivan. "The Interpretive Turn: Emergence of an Approach." Introduction to *Interpretive Social Science; A Reader*. Ed. Paul Rabinow and William M. Sullivan. Berkeley: University of California Press, 1979.

———, eds. *Interpretive Social Science: A Reader*. Berkeley: University of California Press, 1979.

Reddy, Michael J. "The Conduit Metaphor: A Case of Frame Conflict in Language About Language." In *Metaphor and Thought*. Ed. Anthony Ortony. Cambridge: Cambridge University Press, 1979, pp. 284–321.

Resnick, Lauren B., and Phyllis A. Weaver, eds. *Theory and Practice of Early Reading*, Vols. 1–3. Hillsdale, N.J.: Erlbaum, 1979.

Rickman, H. P. "Geisteswissenschaften." *Encyclopedia of Philosophy* 3-4 (1967).

Ricoeur, Paul. "A Critique of B. F. Skinner's *Beyond Freedom and Dignity*." *Phil Today*, 17 (1973), 166–75.

———. *Interpretation Theory: Discourse and the Surplus of Meaning*. Fort Worth: Texas Christian University Press, 1976.

Rochester, S. R., and J. R. Martin. "The Art of Referring: The Speaker's Use of Noun Phrases to Instruct the Listener." In *Discourse Production and Comprehension*. Vol. 1 in *Discourse Processes: Advances in Research and Theory*. Ed. Roy O. Freedle. Norwood, N.J.: Ablex, 1977, pp. 245–69.

Rumelhart, David E. "Notes on a Schema for Stories." In *Representation and Understanding: Studies in Cognitive Science*. Ed. Daniel B. Bobrow and Allan Collins. New York: Academic, 1975, pp. 211–36.

———. "Understanding and Summarizing Brief Stories." In *Basic Processes in Reading: Perception and Comprehension*. Ed. David Laberge and S. Jay Samuels. Hillsdale, N.J.: Erlbaum, 1977, pp. 265–303.

———. "Schemata: The Building Blocks of Cognition." In *Theoretical Issues in Reading Comprehension: Perspectives From Cognitive Psychology, Linguistics, Artificial Intelligence, and Education*. Ed. Rand J. Spiro, Bertram C. Bruce, and William F. Brewer. Hillsdale, N.J.: Erlbaum, 1980, pp. 33–58.

———, and Andrew Ortony. "The Representation of Knowledge in Memory." In *Schooling and the Acquisition of Knowledge*. Ed. Richard C. Anderson, Rand J. Spiro, and William E. Montague. Hillsdale, N.J.: Erlbaum, 1977, pp. 99–135.

Sanford, A. J., and S. C. Garrod. *Understanding Written Language: Explorations of Comprehension Beyond the Sentence*. Chichester, England: Wiley, 1981.

Scardamalia, Marlene, Carl Bereiter, and Hillel Goelman. "The Role of Production Factors in Writing Ability." In *What Writers Know: The Language, Process, and Structure of Written Discourse*. Ed. Martin Nystrand. New York: Academic, 1982, pp. 173–210.

Schank, Roger C., and Robert P. Abelson. *Scripts, Plans, Goals, and Understanding*. Hillsdale, N.J.: Erlbaum, 1977.

Scribner, Sylvia, and Michael Cole. *The Psychology of Literacy*. Cambridge, Mass.: Harvard University Press, 1981.

Shuy, Roger W. "A Holistic View of Language." *RTE*, 15 (1981), 101–11.

Smith, Frank. *Understanding Reading: A Psycholinguistic Analysis of Reading and Learning to Read*, 3rd ed. New York: Holt, 1982.

Sommers, Nancy. "Revision Strategies of Student Writers and Experienced Adult Writers." *CCC*, 31 (1980), 378–88.

Spiro, Rand J. "Remembering Information from Text: The State of Schema Approach." In *Schooling and the Acquisition of Knowledge*. Ed. Richard C. Anderson, Rand J. Spiro, and William E. Montague. Hillsdale, N.J.: Erlbaum, 1977, pp. 137–165.

———. "Constructive Processes in Prose Comprehension and Recall." In *Theoretical Issues in Reading Comprehension: Perspectives from Cognitive Psychology, Linguistics, Artificial Intelligence, and Education*. Ed. Rand J. Spiro, Bertram C. Bruce, and William F. Brewer. Hillsdale, N.J.: Erlbaum, 1980, pp. 245–278.

———, Bertram C. Bruce, and William F. Brewer. Introduction to *Theoretical Issues in Reading Comprehension: Perspectives from Cognitive Psychology, Linguistics, Artificial Intelligence, and Education*. Ed. Rand J. Spiro, Bertram C. Bruce, and William F. Brewer. Hillsdale, N.J.: Erlbaum, 1980, pp. 1–5.

———, Bertram C. Bruce, and William F. Brewer, eds. *Theoretical Issues in Reading Comprehension: Perspectives from Cognitive Psychology, Linguistics, Artificial Intelligence, and Education*. Hillsdale, N.J.: Erlbaum, 1980.

Springer, Sally P., and Georg Deutsch. *Left Brain, Right Brain*. San Francisco: Freeman, 1981.

Steinmann, Martin, Jr. "Speech-Act Theory and Writing." In *What Writers Know: The Language, Process, and Structure of Written Discourse*. Ed. Martin Nystrand. New York: Academic, 1982, pp. 291–323.

Stenning, Keith. "Articles, Quantifiers, and Their Encoding in Textual Comprehension." In *Discourse Production and Comprehension*. Vol. 1 in *Discourse Processes: Advances in Research and Theory*. Ed. Roy O. Freedle. Norwood, N.J.: Ablex, 1977, pp. 193–212.

Straus, Roger A. "The Theoretical Frame of Symbolic Interactionism: A Contextualist, Social Science." *Symbolic Interaction*, 4 (1981), 261–72.

Tannen, Deborah. "What's in a Frame? Surface Evidence for Underlying Expectations." In *New Directions in Discourse Processing*. Vol. 2 in *Advances in Discourse Processes*. Ed. Roy O. Freedle. Norwood, N.J.: Ablex, 1979, pp. 137–81.

Taylor, Charles. "Interpretation and the Sciences of Man." *Rev Metaphysics*, 25 (1971), 3–51. Rpt. in *Interpretive Social Science: A Reader*. Ed. Paul Rabinow and William M. Sullivan. Berkeley: University of California Press, 1979, pp. 25–71.

Taylor, Denny. *Family Literacy: Young Children Learning to Read and Write*. Exeter, N.H.: Heinemann, 1983.

Text: An Interdisciplinary Journal for the Study of Discourse. Vol. 1. The Hague: Mouton. 1981.

Thorndyke, Perry W. "Story Processing Bibliography." *Poetics*, 9 (1980), 329–32.

———, and Frank R. Yekovich. "A Critique of Schema-Based Theories of Human Story Memory." *Poetics*, 9 (1980), 23–49.

Tierney, Robert J., and Jill LaZansky. "The Rights and Responsibilities of Readers and Writers: A Contractual Agreement." *Lang Arts*, 57 (1980), 606–13.

Turvey, M. T. "Constructive Theory, Perceptual Systems, and Tacit Knowledge." In *Cognition and the Symbolic Processes*. Vol. 1. Ed. Walter B. Weimer and David S. Palermo. Hillsdale, N.J.: Erlbaum, 1974, pp. 165–80.

————. "The Primacy of Perceiving: An Ecological Reformulation of Perception for Understanding Memory." In *Perspectives on Memory Research: Essays in Honor of Uppsala University's 500th Anniversary*. Ed. Lars-Göran Nilsson. Hillsdale, N.J.: Erlbaum, 1979, pp. 167–222.

van Dijk, T. A. *Text and Context: Explorations in the Semantics and Pragmatics of Discourse*. London: Longman, 1977.

————. *Macrostructures: An Interdisciplinary Study of Global Structures in Discourse, Interaction, and Cognition*. Hillsdale, N.J.: Erlbaum, 1980a.

————. "Story Comprehension: An Introduction." *Poetics*, 9 (1980b), 1–21.

————, and János S. Petöfi. "Editorial Introduction." *Text*, 1 (1981), 1–3.

Vande Kopple, William J. "Functional Sentence Perspective, Composition, and Reading." *CCC*, 33 (1982), 50–63.

Vygotsky, L.S. *Thought and Language*. Ed. and trans. Eugenia Hanfmann and Gertrude Vakar. Cambridge, Mass.: M.I.T. Press, 1962.

————. *Mind in Society: The Development of Higher Psychological Processes*. Ed. Michael Cole et al. Cambridge, Mass.: Harvard University Press, 1978.

Walker, Carol H., and Bonnie J. F. Meyer. "Integrating Information from Text: An Evaluation of Current Theories." *Rev Educ Res*, 50 (1980), 421–37.

Watson, Sam, Jr. "Polanyi and the Contexts of Composing." In *Reinventing the Rhetorical Tradition*. Ed. Aviva Freedman and Ian Pringle. Conway, Ark.: L and S, 1980, pp. 18–25.

Weimer, Walter B. "Overview of a Cognitive Conspiracy: Reflections on the Volume." In *Cognition and the Symbolic Processes*. Vol. 1. Ed. Walter B. Weimer and David S. Palermo. Hillsdale, N.J.: Erlbaum, 1974.

————, and David A. Palermo, eds. *Cognition and the Symbolic Processes*. 2 vols. Hillsdale, N.J.: Erlbaum, 1974, 1982.

Whiteman, Marcia, ed. *Variations in Writing: Functional and Linguistic-Cultural Differences*. Vol. 1 in *Writing: The Nature, Development, and Teaching of Written Communication*. Hillsdale, N.J.: Erlbaum, 1981.

Williams, Joseph. *Style: Ten Lessons in Clarity and Grace*. Glenview, Ill.: Scott, Foresman, 1981.

Winograd, Terry. "A Framework for Understanding Discourse." In *Cognitive Processes in Comprehension*. Ed. Marcel Adam Just and Patricia A. Carpenter. Hillsdale, N.J.: Erlbaum, 1977, pp. 63–88.

————. "What Does It Mean to Understand Language?" In *Perspectives on Cognitive Science*. Ed. Donald A. Norman. Norwood, N.J.: Ablex, 1981.

Winterowd, W. Ross. "Brain, Rhetoric, and Style." In *Linguistics, Stylistics, and the Teachings of Composition*. Ed. Donald McQuade. Akron, Ohio: L and S, 1979, pp. 151–81.

————. "Developing a Composition Program." In *Reinventing the Rhetorical Tradition*. Ed. Aviva Freedman and Ian Pringle. Conway, Ark.: L and S, 1980, pp. 157–71.

Wittrock, M. C. "The Generative Processes of Memory." In *The Human Brain*, by M. C. Wittrock et al. Englewood Cliffs, N.J.: Prentice-Hall, 1977, pp. 153–84.

————, ed. *The Brain and Psychology*. New York: Academic, 1980.

————, et al. *The Human Brain*. Englewood Cliffs, N.J.: Prentice-Hall, 1977.

Woods, William A. ''Multiple Theory Formation in Speech and Reading.'' In *Theoretical Issues in Reading Comprehension: Perspectives from Cognitive Psychology, Linguistics, Artificial Intelligence, and Education*. Ed. Rand J. Spiro, Bertram C. Bruce, and William F. Brewer. Hillsdale, N.J.: Erlbaum, 1980, pp. 58–82.

Yussen, Steven R., Samuel R. Mathews II, and Elfrieda Hiebert. ''Metacognitive Aspects of Reading.'' In *Reading Expository Material*. Ed. Wayne Otto and Sandra White. New York: Academic, 1982, pp. 189–218.

Research on Writing Blocks, Writing Anxiety, and Writing Apprehension

LYNN Z. BLOOM

In *The Plague* (1971), Albert Camus epitomized one type of anxious writer in M. Joseph Grand, a talented man plagued by perfectionism. His lowly clerical status even in midlife is due, he believes, to his "inability to find the right words" and thereby to write the great novel that he expects to bring him esteem and fame. Year after frustrating year he attempts to perfect this unwritten work so that its quality will be evident from the first sentence. For months he labors over that single sentence, with "excruciating pains spending evenings, whole weeks . . . on one word . . . Sometimes on a mere conjunction!" But alas, although Grand's friends have admired various of his innumerable versions of that sentence, Grand himself believes that it doesn't "quite hit the mark as yet," and by the year's (and novel's) end, he has progressed no farther, although he continues to try (pp. 95–96).

Blocked writers are legion among literati; those who have commented specifically on their particular problems include diverse authors such as Herman Melville, E. M. Forster, Dorothy Parker, William Styron, and George Orwell. Although the case histories of some impeded writers have been known to psychoanalysts for decades, only within the past decade has the attention of writing researchers focused on blocked or anxious writers. This chapter provides a review of the research literature to consider the types of questions researchers ask about anxious writers, the problems they see as central, and the answers they provide. It emphasizes those studies or types of studies that writing teachers at various levels and across the disciplines should find useful in helping their students to write with greater ease, efficiency, and comfort.

In addition to this chapter, the only other comprehensive annotated bibliographic survey of relevant research is John Daly's "Writing Apprehension," in *Writing Process Problems* (1984). Daly's essay is more concerned with technical aspects of methodology and data analysis than is this chapter, which focuses somewhat more on specific problems and possible solutions. Both bibliographies emphasize the research literature, primarily of the 1970s and early 1980s, when most of the work was done, and both include dissertations and ERIC documents; this one excludes unpublished works.

Definitions

Three major terms emerge in the research literature—*writing apprehension, writing anxiety,* and *writer's block.* There is no consensus on what these terms mean. Indeed, since some writers on the subject use them interchangeably, readers of the literature often have to infer the particular parameters of meaning from the discussion at hand.

John Daly said that he and Michael Miller coined the term *writing apprehension* in "The Empirical Development of an Instrument to Measure Writing Apprehension" (1975a). People with high apprehension of writing, claimed Daly and Miller, avoid writing whenever they can. They seek occupations, college courses, and extra-curricular activities requiring little writing and avoid situations that demand writing. They "fear evaluation of their writing . . . feeling that they will be negatively rated on it. . . .They expect to fail in writing" and consistently cut writing classes and neglect to turn in their compositions (p. 246). They write more poorly than less apprehensive writers (John A. Daly, "Writing Apprehension and Writing Competency" [1978]). On the contrary, explained Daly and Deborah Wilson, "Low apprehensives represent the other end of the continuum. They don't mind writing, are confident in their abilities to do so, and often enjoy it" ("Writing Apprehension, Self-Esteem, and Personality" [1983], p. 327). This view of apprehensive writers shows them to be analogous to people suffering from math anxiety in their dislike, anxiety about, and avoidance of the subject, as analyzed by Sheila Tobias in *Overcoming Math Anxiety* (1978).

Research by Lynn Z. Bloom and others uses the term *writing anxiety* to describe people who exhibit a cluster of attitudes, behaviors, and lack of knowledge about writing that creates writing problems. Using case studies and the Daly and Miller 26-item writing-apprehension scale, Bloom's findings corroborate Daly's that anxious writers "do not enjoy thinking about writing, the writing itself, or discussing their writing with others," or having it evaluated ("Teaching Anxious Writers" [1980b], p. 50). They are procrastinators, who may in fact write very well (contrary to Daly's view), but who have difficulty in organizing their papers and in giving sufficiently high priority to their writing tasks and time. According to estimates by Bloom, Daly, and Mike Rose, anxious writers comprise about 10 percent of the general student population—struggling with undergraduate and graduate papers, dissertations, and theses. Bloom found such writers in professional contexts as well, despite the predictions of Daly and Wayne Shamo that because of their negative attitudes toward writing, apprehensive writers would choose academic majors and occupations that involved little or no writing ("Academic Decisions as a Function of Writing Apprehension [1978], and "Writing Apprehension and Occupational Choice" [1976]).

Mike Rose defined *writer's block* as "an inability to begin or continue writing for reasons other than a lack of skill or commitment," in *Writer's Block* (1983, p. 3), a volume based on this research. Blocking, Rose said, in *Writer's Block*,

is not simply measured by the passage of time (for writers often spend productive time toying with ideas without putting pen to paper), but by the passage of time with limited functional/productive involvement in the writing task. Certain behaviors (i.e. missing deadlines) are associated with blocking. Feelings of anxiety, frustration, anger, or confusion often characterize this unproductive work. Blocking can be manifested in a variety of ways: some blockers produce only a few sentences; others produce many more, but these sentences will be false starts, repetitions, blind alleys, or disconnected fragments of discourse; still others produce a certain amount of satisfactory prose only to stop in mid-essay. . . . Some blockers might eventually produce quality papers (p. 3).

Rose considered writer's block broader than writing apprehension, for not all blockers are poor writers or avoid writing, although writing apprehension may sometimes cause blocking or be a reaction to it. "Blocking and apprehensiveness," he said, "(and low-blocking and non-apprehensiveness) are not synonymous, not necessarily coexistent, and not necessarily causally linked" (*Writer's Block*, p. 4). In "Writing Apprehension" (1984), Daly also discriminated between blocking, which "occurs when the individual, willing to write," finds that "during the composing activity nothing comes," and other dimensions of apprehensiveness. In contrast to Rose, Daly considered writing apprehension a much broader concept than blocking.

This lack of agreement among researchers on definitions of terms reflects the newness of the field. As more research is conducted, perhaps usage will settle down and de facto consensus will be reached. Until that time, let readers beware.

Measures of Writing Apprehension and Writer's Block

Research in writing anxiety often begins by forming distinct and mutually exclusive groups, such as those who are very highly anxious and those who are low in anxiety. A researcher could use any single instrument (such as one of those described below) to identify the people who make scores on the extreme ends of the scale, thereby preventing overlap in the two groups. Once two such distinct groups are identified, the researcher can empirically discover other factors that characterize one but not the other. For example, a research design could be constructed to explore the question of whether high-anxious or low-anxious people would be more likely to take advanced writing courses. Because the two groups are empirically distinct, associated characteristics that are not part of the original definition can be measured.

Several researchers have developed empirically based, standardized questionnaires to help identify apprehensive or blocked writers. They consist of between 26 and 52 items that use a Likert-type response sequence and can be answered on a five-point continuum from either "strongly agree" to "strongly disagree" or "almost always" to "almost never."

The most widely used instrument is John Daly and Michael Miller's (1975a) writing-apprehension scale, an attitudinal measure based on models derived from speech communication and interpersonal communication. It focuses mostly on "anxiety about writing in general" ("I avoid writing." "I like to write down my ideas."); and anxiety over evaluation of writing by teachers, peers, or professional editors ("I am afraid of writing essays when I know they will be evaluated"; "I like to have my friends read what I have written.") Scores may range from a low of 26 (indicating a person with extremely low writing apprehension) to a high of 130. Daly uses this highly reliable scale in his research with various groups, and because he obtains new mean scores for each group, the lowest score identifying a highly apprehensive writer changes with each project, depending on the standard deviation from the mean, and ranges between 68 and 90.

Teachers often use the Daly-Miller scale as a quick way to pick out apprehensive writers in their classes to be able to treat them with extra understanding in hopes of reducing their apprehension. A note of caution is in order. This scale, like others, depends on relative norms; except for extremes at either end, absolute score numbers may not necessarily distinguish apprehensive writers. However, high scores on one or more of the following items usually identify anxiety-related problems to which the teacher can respond (numbers correspond to the Daly-Miller numbers):

1. I avoid writing.

2. I am afraid of being evaluated.

7. My mind goes blank when I start to write a composition.

13. I'm nervous about being evaluated.

16. I can't write my ideas clearly.

21. I have a terrible time organizing my ideas.

23. It's hard for me to write a good composition.

24. I don't think I write as well as others.

25. I don't like my compositions to be evaluated (p. 246).

A further note of caution is in order. In some research the investigator has determined the mean Daly-Miller score for his population and then arbitrarily labeled all of those with scores above the mean as "high apprehensives" and all of those with scores below the mean as "low apprehensives" (see Roy Fox [1980]). Labels assigned in this way, without employing standard deviations, make inappropriate, unreliable distinctions.

Three other measures of writing apprehension reported in the literature are similar to the Daly-Miller scale. Merle O. Thompson, in "The Development and Evaluation of a Language Study Approach to a College Course in Freshman Composition'' (1978), developed a 30-item scale that, she said, stresses ''the writer's feelings about the writing process and its consequences'' (p. 13). Barry Kroll created a 25-item self-report measure (its reliability not indicated), used primarily by the college freshmen on whom he reported in ''Assessing Students' Attitudes Toward Writing'' (1979). In ''Assessing English and Language Arts Teachers' Attitudes Toward Writers and Writing'' (1976), R. W. Blake reported the results from his 20-item, internally consistent measure that focused on skills of writing, varieties of writing, and kinds of writers. In ''Writing Apprehension'' (1984) Daly said these items correlate highly with his own scale.

Rose developed a 24-item scale to determine five salient ''cognitive/behavioral'' and ''cognitive/attitudinal'' features of writer's block, which he used to select subjects for the research on ''The Cognitive Dimensions of Writer's Block'' (1981a) and *Writer's Block* (1983). He identified the significant features of this measure as:

Blocking (this subscale provides a set of behavioral indicators of writer's block). ''There are times when I sit at my desk for hours, unable to write a thing.'' ''While writing a paper, I'll hit places that keep me stuck for an hour or more.'' *Lateness* (i.e., missing deadlines. A behavioral subscale, not as consistent an indicator of writer's block as Blocking). ''I have to hand in assignments late because I can't get the words down on paper.'' ''I run over deadlines because I get stuck while trying to write my papers.'' *Premature Editing* (i.e., editing too early in the composing process. A cognitive/behavioral subscale). ''I'll wait until I've found just the right phrase.'' ''Each sentence I write has to be just right before I'll go on to the next sentence.'' *Strategies for Complexity* (i.e., not possessing adequate strategies for interpreting and writing on complex material. A cognitive/behavioral subscale). ''There are times when I'm not sure how to organize all the information I've gathered for a paper.'' ''I have trouble figuring out how to write on issues that have many interpretations.'' *Attitudes* (i.e., feelings and beliefs about writing and evaluation. A cognitive/attitudinal subscale). ''I think my writing is good.'' ''My teachers are familiar with so much good writing that my writing must look bad by comparison'' (pp. 19–20).

The publication of this carefully designed scale should provide a diagnostic tool particularly useful in its designation of specific features of writing problems. Teachers who are aware that some students find ''It is hard for me to write on topics that could be written about from a number of angles,'' while other students claim that ''Each sentence I write has to be just right before I'll go on to the next sentence,'' can offer specific assistance to accommodate diverse aspects of individual writing processes. The Daly-Miller scale is less relevant to writing processes and consequently is less useful as a diagnostic tool for process-related problems.

Causes of Writing Anxiety

What causes writing anxiety or writer's block? What sustains or exacerbates it? Why do some people develop apprehensiveness about writing while others with similar abilities (or lack thereof) do not? To what extent do the contexts in which a person writes (at home, at school, at work) and the intended audience (self, teacher, boss, general public) affect the writer's anxiety? To date there has been surprisingly little research into these fundamental questions.

In one of the earliest explorations of the subject, "Psychological Barriers to Writing" (1956), B. H. Weil and J. C. Lane attributed "stagefright in writers" to several causes. Writers overestimate their deficiencies. When they don't clearly understand the purpose of their writing, they think it's a waste of time. Their writing is often rushed and subjected to editorial criticism they consider excessive and arbitrary. P. G. Aldrich's 1979 survey, "Adult Writers," reveals that people become appropriately anxious about their writing if they don't know how to do it or how to handle the writing demands of their jobs. C. R. Duke's "Writing Apprehension" (1980) corroborates these findings.

Zena C. Harvley-Felder attempted in "Some Factors Relating to Writing Apprehension" (1978) to identify the causes of writing apprehension in elementary and high school children. Through administration of the Daly-Miller scale and a questionnaire focusing on the causes, Harvley-Felder arrived at three principal categories. The first, *Positive Reinforcement/Punishment in School*, not surprisingly revealed that teachers' negative reactions to student writing exacerbated anxiety ("My papers have come back with a lot of red marks"). Counteracting influences came from the second category, *models* such as teachers, parents, and peers who provided positive reinforcement ("A friend of mine practices writing outside of school"). The third category, *Communication Seeking Behavior in the Classroom*, pertained to the students' freedom and ability to ask teachers about their writing, such as to explain paper assignments they didn't understand or to substitute interesting paper topics for dull ones. Less anxious students sought such communication far more often than the more anxious students—but it's hard to tell which are the effects and which are the causes of such behavior.

John Daly also offered, in "Writing Apprehension" (1984), a "comparison deficiency" explanation. He hypothesized (although without evidence) that writers become apprehensive when they "consistently believe that what they have written inadequately matches what they had in mind as they composed," or what they had spoken aloud, and so avoid writing. Lynn Bloom, in "Teaching Anxious Writers" (1980b), identified a number of myths that plague anxious writers. They include the beliefs that "Most other people write better than I do" (p. 51) and "Writing is hard for me and easy for everyone else. Therefore, something is wrong with me" (p. 52). Teachers and textbooks that oversimplify writing processes or make them seem more uniform and linear than they actually are contribute to these problems, said Bloom. In "Sophisticated, Ineffective Books" (1981b), Mike Rose expanded on this. He showed how most composition textbooks, however sophisticated, reduce "the process of composing to rules, stages, and operations that belie the richness" and fluidity of actual writing behavior (p. 69). This "dismantling of process" exacerbates blockers' characteristic problems. Teachers and textbooks that encourage flexible writing processes adapted both to differences among individuals and various academic disciplines can help to overcome these difficulties.

Correlation Studies

Correlation studies use statistical means to measure how closely two or more qualities, phenomena, or characteristics are related. Correlation studies of anxious or apprehensive writers use various measures, usually Daly and Miller's, to define their characteristics, diagnose their problems, predict their current and future behavior, and assess their performance. Correlation researchers take for granted the axiom "Correlation is not causation"—a caveat that others who would apply their findings in different contexts would do well to remember.

The correlational studies of John A. Daly, a professor of speech communication at the University of Texas, Austin, and various associates are the most diverse and the best known. This is not the place to discuss Daly's statistical techniques and methods of data analysis, except to say that his studies involve large numbers of people, usually 100 to 500 college students, randomly sampled from particular whole classes. Daly employed his scale, along with various other instruments, to generate the data that form the basis of many of his numerous studies. They are carefully designed, the data thoroughly and responsibly analyzed according to standard procedures (sometimes ingeniously applied to tease out meaning), and are therefore presumably readily replicable. Daly and his associates do not make sweeping claims that exceed the limits of their data, and they leave open the possibilities of alternative interpretations and additional research.

Daly and Miller do suggest, however, that their test may be a better predictor of "predisposition towards writing" and "expectations of success in writing" than the SAT. In "Further Studies on Writing Apprehension" (1975b), they demonstrated that there is little correlation between SAT scores, which measure aptitude, and writing apprehension scores, which measure attitude. Most of the SAT-Verbal "deals not with writing, but . . . with vocabulary, reading, and analysis," unlike the Daly-Miller scale, which focuses exclusively on writing and is therefore, they claim, a more suitable measure (p. 250).

One major focus of correlational research has been to discover differences between high- and low-apprehensive writers. Daly and Miller (1975b) also found that women were less apprehensive about writing than men; that less apprehensive students thought they wrote better than more apprehensive students and voluntarily took advanced writing courses that the high apprehensives avoided. In "Writing Apprehension and Writing Competency" (1978), Daly reported that "low apprehensive writers scored significantly better on a comprehensive test of grammar, mechanics and larger concerns in writing skills" than high apprehensives did (p. 10). Lester Faigley, John Daly, and Stephen P. Witte identified other differences in "The Role of Writing Apprehension in Writing Performance and Writing Competence'' (1981). They found that high apprehensives scored significantly lower than low apprehensives on tests for general verbal ability, reading comprehension, usage, and mastery of the conventions of writing. These findings were corroborated by inverse correlations between writing apprehension and composite ACT scores identified by B. Fowler and B. M. Kroll in "Relationship of Apprehension About Writing to Performance as Measured by Grades in a College Course on Composition" (1980).

Faigley, Daly, and Witte (1981) also found that highly anxious writers wrote personal narrative or descriptive essays significantly shorter and less syntactically mature than those of less anxious writers. The authors attributed the fact that there were no significant differences in the argumentative essays of either group to the greater syntactic complexity and less personal style demanded of all writers by argumentative writing. E. M. Richardson's "Quality of Essays Written for Distant and Intimate Audiences by High and Low Apprehensive Two-Year College Freshmen" (1980) corroborates these findings, likewise demonstrating no significant difference in the quality of argumentative essays written by high and low apprehensives.

Robert C. Garcia's "Investigation of Relationships: Writing Apprehension, Syntactic Performance, and Writing Quality" (1977) analyzed the syntactic features of the essays written by a small number (32) of high- and low-apprehensive students. Although these groups differed significantly on infinitives, gerunds, prepositional phrases, participles, and adjectival, adverbial, and nominal clauses, both groups wrote equal numbers of words, t-units, clauses per t-unit, words per t-unit, and words per clause. (For a related study, see also John Daly, "The Effects of Writing Apprehension on Message Encoding" [1977].)

Other correlational studies relate writing apprehension to academic and occupational decisions. In "Writing Apprehension and Occupational Choice" (1976), Daly and Shamo found that undergraduates with high writing apprehensiveness chose occupations "with low writing requirements," and low writing apprehensives thought they could cope with more writing on the job (p. 56). Likewise, in "Academic Decisions as a Function of Writing Apprehension" (1978), Daly and Shamo not surprisingly corroborated the above research with the finding that "High apprehensive writers indicated that their chosen majors were significantly lower in writing requirements than those selected by [low apprehensives]" (p. 124)—a socially useful form of natural selection that impels some students to study science and engineering (p. 125). Teachers, even in elementary school, said Daly in "Writing Apprehension in the Classroom" (1979), may reinforce student predispositions by evaluating highly apprehensive writers less positively than low apprehensives and by considering students who avoid or dislike writing as less successful academically and "less likely to succeed in the future" (p. 42).

The different teaching styles of apprehensive writing teachers versus their non-apprehensive counterparts may strongly influence both their students' levels of apprehensiveness and their ability to write well. Highly apprehensive secondary school teachers, for instance, make only one-third the number of writing assignments a year in comparison with non-apprehensive teachers, 7.0 versus 19.9, reported S. H. Claypool in "Teacher Writing Apprehension" (1980).

Apprehensive writing teachers differ from non-apprehensive writing teachers in what they consider relevant and important in student writing. Ann R. Gere, B. F. Schuessler, and R. D. Abbott reported their research in "Measuring Teacher Attitudes Toward Instruction in Writing" (1981). They measured teacher attitudes toward the importance of (1) standard English in writing instruction (sentences shouldn't begin with *and, or, few*, or *but*); (2) evaluating papers (grades are crucial; every error should be marked); (3) student self-expression; and (4) linguistic maturity, which emphasized a process approach and positive writing behaviors, such as constructive teacher-pupil conferences. Gere and her colleagues found that low-apprehensive teachers were more liberal than highly apprehensive teachers about style, self-expression, and non-traditional writing processes. The more highly apprehensive teachers, especially women, buttress their insecurity about the subject by holding rigidly onto unyielding beliefs about writing instruction and evaluation. They approach their subject dogmatically through focusing on form and usage rather than on process, style, and individual variations in each.

Not all writing anxiety is bad. Case studies (see below), reinforced by the observations of Daly and Joy Lynn Hailey ("Putting the Situation into Writing Research," in *New Directions in Composition Research* [1984]), agree that "Moderate amounts of anxiety enhance performance. Too much or too little detracts from the quality of the product" (p. 272). William G. Powers, John A. Cook, and Russell Meyer showed, in "The Effect of Compulsory Writing on Writing Apprehension" (1979), that compulsory basic or regular Freshman English will make less anxious students significantly more anxious, while maintaining the high anxiety levels of already anxious students. Yet despite these authors' views, if the "What, me worry?" kids become more concerned, a particular need of many basic writers (witness Mina Shaughnessy's efforts throughout *Errors and Expectations* [1977]), they may spend more time and effort on their writing and may actually improve (see Lynn Bloom, "The Composing Processes of Anxious and Non-Anxious Writers" [1980a]).

Psychological and Psychoanalytic Research

Because most writing researchers regard writing anxiety as a situation-specific problem that does not interfere with a person's ability to function effectively in other areas of life, they do not regard it as particularly pathological or neurotic—contrary to the premise of the psychological and psychoanalytic research discussed below (see Martin Bloom, "Anxious Writers" [1980]). It is nevertheless useful to be aware of the work that is being done from this clinical perspective, if only to realize how different professional fields treat the same phenomena.

The pathological aspects of neurotic anxieties of all kinds have received considerable discussion in psychological and psychoanalytic literature during recent decades. Since most writing teachers are not practicing psychotherapy with or without a license, it is sufficient to note that a number of recent studies are concerned with eliminating "exam fear" and "test anxiety," partly through enabling people fearful of taking tests to "realistically reevaluate imaginally presented test-taking situations" (Marvin R. Goldfried, Marsha M. Linehan, and Jean L. Smith, "Reduction of Test Anxiety Through Cognitive Restructuring" [1978], p. 32). Many other studies are devoted to treating writer's cramp severe enough to prevent the writer from writing legibly, if at all. These studies involve either long-term psychotherapy (see, for instance, A. H. Crisp and H. Moldofsky, "A Psychosomatic Study of Writer's Cramp" [1965]); aversion therapy (see L. A. Liversedge and J. D. Sylvester, "Conditioning Techniques in the Treatment of Writer's Cramp" [1955]); or a combination of "systematic desensitization and biofeedback training" to reduce "muscular tension in the act of writing" (see Kikuo Uchiyama, Martin Lutterjohann, and Mumtaz Daniel Shah, "Biofeedback-Assisted Desensitization Treatment of Writer's Cramp" [1971] p. 169; and E. Sanavio, "An Operant Approach to the Treatment of Writer's Cramp" [1982]).

Studies of particular writing problems and blocked writers are somewhat more relevant. Paul Federn's analysis of "The Neurotic Style" (1957) points out stylistic faults that suggest psychological disturbances rather than blocked style. Lawrence Kubie's *Neurotic Distortions of the Creative Process* (1973) discusses several cases of writers whose neuroses blocked their writing, but they appear idiosyncratic and are therefore hard to draw generalizations from. Marvin Rosenberg's psychoanalytic study "Releasing the Creative Imagination" (1976) reports that hypnosis enabled blocked playwrights to exercise their creative imagination blocked by cultural conditioning. Edmund Bergler's psychoanalytic studies of writer's block define *creative writing* as an unconscious defense against oral-masochistic conflicts; writer's block results from the breakdown of this defense. See Bergler's *The Basic Neurosis* (1949); "Does 'Writer's Block' Exist?" (1959); *The Writer and Psychoanalysis* (1954); and "Unconscious Mechanisms in 'Writer's Block' " (1955).

Other psychological case studies have some possible relevance for the teaching of writing. Richard H. Passman, in "A Procedure for Eliminating Writer's Block in a College Student" (1976), reported using positive reinforcement to enable a student to complete six English papers necessary for her graduation from college. After determining that she was a chronic procrastinator, the therapist suggested that she allot time each day to sit at her desk and write one paragraph of an assignment. As soon as she finished the paragraph, she could reward herself with an unspecified amount of time spent on her favorite pastimes. This method enabled her (with some setbacks) not only to finish the required papers but to complete the rest of her college work during a 30-week period without difficulty. Using a paradigm of transactional analysis, A. C. Jones reported a plan for eliminating procrastination through a contract between the writer and the therapist, specifying in detail the subject, amount of writing to be composed each day, and deadlines for first and final draft ("Grandiosity Blocks Writing Projects" [1975]). Teachers could easily employ a contractual schedule of writing and rewards to encourage all students, anxious or not, to get their writing done expeditiously and to enjoy it.

Mary B. Harris's "Accelerating Dissertation Writing" (1974) reveals an ingenious application of "productive avoidance technique," also known as "contingency management." This "involves having a person's productive behavior lead to postponement of an aversive outcome" (p. 984). The subject and the therapist drew up a contract, stating that every Wednesday for ten weeks the subject had to submit to the therapist five or more completed pages of her dissertation, which she had avoided finishing for two years. If she didn't, the therapist would mail $5 of the subject's money to a detested charity. If she turned in the pages, she got to keep the $5. Within eight weeks, the subject had completed her dissertation. But when she procrastinated for six weeks on the revisions the ante was raised. If they remained overdue, not only would the remaining contributions be sent, but they would be accompanied by a note requesting that a proselytizer call upon the subject. Within six days she had finished everything satisfactorily.

Robert Boice used a contingency management program over an extended time to enable six blocked academic writers to change their beliefs about writing and to write more ("Increasing the Writing Productivity of 'Blocked' Academicians" [1982]). Behavioral therapy involving relaxation, breathing exercises, and "flooding" (practice in the activity combined with the expectation of positive results) is discussed by F. Menks in "Behavioral Techniques in the Treatment of a Writing Phobia" (1979).

It would be ethically hazardous for English teachers to use productive avoidance techniques, systematic desensitization, and behavioral therapy to get students to finish their writing, especially in courses not taken for therapeutic reasons, however great the anticipated benefits of completion. Constructive scheduling, encouragement, and other positive rewards fit the academic paradigm better and are well within the control of most teachers.

Case Studies

What characterizes the writing processes of anxious writers? In what ways are they like those of non-anxious writers? In what ways are they different? What aspects of their writing processes are particularly problematic? What can teachers or the writers themselves do to resolve these difficulties?

Although correlational studies can show characteristics, trends, and tendencies among large numbers of people, individuals often get lost in these overviews of the forest. Case studies of writing processes, given prominence and respectability by Janet Emig's pioneering *The Writing Processes of Twelfth Graders* (1971), have provided a needed corrective, despite the difficulty of generalizing from single individuals or small numbers. The protocols analyzed in numerous studies by Linda Flower and John Hayes, such as in *A Process Model of Composition* (1979), give us some sense of what typical writing processes are like.

Most of the case studies cited below provide vivid portraits of their subjects trying to write, writing, or not writing in ways that readers, and teachers especially, can call vividly to mind. Through understanding the problems concerning impeded or inefficient writing processes of these writers, researchers and teachers alike are beginning to explore solutions, as the research cited in both this and the next section reveal. The case studies are considered according to the developmental sequence of the student subjects.

Donald Graves's "Blocking and the Young Writer" (1984) asks, How do the writing processes of elementary schoolchildren, ages six to nine, develop? Where does *blocking* (which Graves defined not as a permanent impediment but a temporary halt to allow the writer to learn something new or to resolve a difficulty) occur? His research involved a two-year ethnomethodological observation and case studies of the writing processes of 16 children. Children learning to write are dealing simultaneously with problems involving spelling, the appearance of of the writing on the page, convention (marking off meaning units with spaces and punctuation), topic/information, and revision. Very young children write in short, two- to three-minute installments, usually to illustrate their drawings, on which they spend more time than on the writing. At this stage they are self-confident and rarely block.

As children gain more experience with writing, perhaps by second grade, their writing becomes more complex, although they still write a given piece in a series of short sittings. Now they think about their composing when they are not writing; as they become aware of more choices for inserting and deleting information, they move from mechanical to intellectual concerns. With more options come more opportunities for blocking. The process of revising enables them to unblock and move on. At any point, however, the teacher can create "major blocks" by expecting more from the children than they know how to do.

Next, developmentally, they write "bed-to-bed" stories (narratives proceeding from when they wake up until they return to bed at night). They gradually learn to "add, heighten, select, delete," and thereby to focus and shape their materials for external readers but may block if they ignore this sequence. As children get older and "do harder things, the writing gets harder"; they grow by solving the problems, surmounting the blocks—"necessary by-products of any creative endeavor," and moving on.

Helen F. Heaton's "A Study of Writing Anxiety Among High School Students" (1980) was based on a study conducted to determine the causes of writing anxiety and its relationship to the quality of student writing in grades 9 to 12 of a rural school. Twice as many boys were anxious as girls. The causes of the presence or absence of anxiety, for both boys and girls, were teachers' writing assignments, students' lack of composition skills, and teachers' grades and comments. These findings corroborate Harvley-Felder's investigations (1978). But

Heaton's case studies contradict the findings of Daly and Miller (1975) that highly anxious students will have low standardized test scores and low school achievement and vice versa. Neither group necessarily seeks help from their writing teachers.

In "Diagnosing Writing Process Problems" (1984), Muriel Harris made a compelling case for analyzing protocols of students' oral composing as a way of aiding their writing process. She recommended teaching college students how to compose aloud, perhaps following the teacher's model, to enable an analysis of what they don't say about their writing as well as what they do say. She showed that protocol analysis can reveal problems such as lack of appropriate decision-making strategies, which may lead students to write copiously and delete most of what they've written; indecision about what the teacher wants, which can cause other students to spend "long, agonizing, unproductive hours trying to compose"; and lack of invention strategies that cause still other students to re-read "incessantly" and distractingly as they compose. Harris offered a number of considerations to guide teachers in examining the recorded protocols:

1. Are the students' composing strategies sufficiently varied, flexible, and complex?
2. Are the students' composing strategies productive?
3. Is there anything missing or inadequate in the students' composing processes? (For instance, have the writers asked themselves inadequate questions, set skimpy goals, settled for undeveloped ideas? Do they lack adequate means to record fleeting thoughts or lack techniques for reorganizing materials retrieved from long-term memory?)

Cynthia L. Selfe, in "An Apprehensive Writer Composes" (1984), attempted to answer some of these questions through an extended case study of Bev, a highly anxious college freshman. Selfe identified a "limited repertoire of composing skills and strategies" as characteristic of unskilled writers and postulated a link between these deficiencies and high writing apprehension. Bev feared "academic writing" and procrastinated until the last minute, until "her anxiety became strong enough to act as a 'special kind' of motivating device." She then wrote her required Freshman English essay in a "mad, frantic, get-everything-you-can-down-on-paper rush," concerned far more with speed than with substance, in hopes that a focus would emerge from her hasty freewriting. Typical of unskilled writers, Bev mistook "mechanical correctness for organizational and logical soundness." She spent nearly 25 percent of her composing time in editing the mechanical minutiae, which inappropriately distracted her attention from the content; she substituted editing for real revising.

Selfe's research provided not only the above study but her doctoral dissertation "The Composing Processes of Four High and Four Low Writing Apprehensives" (1981) and the related paper "The Composing Processes of High and Low Writing Apprehensives" (1981). In both of these works she reported that the two highly apprehensive students (Bev included) extracted less information from the writing assignment (concerning content and adaptation to audience) and did less planning and less written "prefiguring" than the two low-apprehensive students. They spent less time writing individual sentences and less time editing and revising.

Lynn Bloom's "The Composing Processes of Anxious and Non-Anxious Writers" (1980) corroborates some aspects of Selfe's research. Bloom's case studies of college students at various levels reveal that the non-anxious writers work more efficiently and productively, are less self-distracting, and "exploit various aspects of the composing process more fully" than anxious writers do, including developing ideas, organizing, revising, and rewriting extensively (p. 17). Some students are so anxious that they refuse to write at all and drop or avoid courses involving writing rather than deal with their difficulties.

Several other case studies by Bloom and by Mike Rose propose solutions to the problems discovered and are discussed in the next section.

Overcoming the Difficulties: Possible Solutions

Research into the composing processes of anxious writers offers some of the most illuminating analyses of their problems and some of the most theoretically sound and practical solutions. In a major research work, *Writer's Block* (1983), the only book-length study of the subject to date except for his compilation of essays in *Writing Process Problems* (1984), Mike Rose insightfully and engagingly presented the essence of his award-winning doctoral dissertation "The Cognitive Dimension of Writer's Block" (1981a). From ten case studies Rose obtained a great deal of information about the writing processes of college students with and without writing blocks. While each subject wrote for an hour on a university-level topic, two videotape cameras recorded, respectively, the student and the student's emerging text. After the writing session, Rose and the student viewed the two tapes simultaneously on a split screen; each could stop the tape to comment on and discuss the process. Their dialogue was audiotaped, corroborated by larger group data that included questionnaire self-reports, "measurements of prewriting, pausing, and planning time, tabulations of words produced and deleted, evaluations of student essays" (p. 30) and tabulations of a variety of cognitive and cognitive behavioral entities and events including rules, plans, assumptions, premature editing, conflict, and self-evaluation.

Rose found that some writers block for one or more of the following reasons: (1) The rules by which they guide their composing processes are rigid, inappropriately invoked, or incorrect. ("You're not supposed to have passive verbs." "Word choices should not be too simple.") (2) Their assumptions about composing are misleading. (A spontaneous essay is better than one planned in advance, because planning, a "diabolical" activity, sacrifices "truth and real feelings.") (3) They edit too early in the composing process in some cases, repeatedly and distractedly, while they're writing the first draft. (4) They lack appropriate planning and discourse strategies or rely on inflexible or inappropriate strategies (which range from little or no planning to planning so elaborate that it impinges drastically on the writing time and impedes the flow of words). (5) They invoke conflicting rules, assumptions, plans, and strategies; sometimes they understand formulas but can't use them to solve problems. (6) They evaluate their writing with inappropriate or inadequately understood criteria. ("If you can singsong your writing, it's not good stylistically.")

On the first five of these dimensions Rose found conspicuous differences between blockers and non-blockers. For instance, blockers expressed 4 times more non-functional, rigid rules ("Word choices should not be too simple") as non-blockers, and the non-blockers expressed 17 times as many functional (flexible, heuristic) rules ("Get something written before worrying about editing") as blockers. Yet on the sixth dimension, blockers and non-blockers expressed about the same number of positive and negative evaluations of their work, a finding that supports Rose's cognitive orientation and challenges an affective one.

Rose's research suggests a number of precepts to enable writing teachers to help students avoid blocking and write better essays. Teachers need to be aware of (1) "The rich functional differences in composing"—that is, varied composing strategies and processes—particularly among their own students. (2) "Certain general realities that seem to hold for most writing" (such as the fact that one's best writing is not necessarily spontaneous but "built on slowly acquired technical virtuosity, prethinking, and rehearsal"). (3) Counterproductive procedures (such as lack of planning or premature editing) (p. 89). Among the applications of these precepts are several corollaries: (a) Because writing is psychologically and sociologically complex, "few writing rules can be stated absolutely. Most rules should be taught flexibly and contextually," such as those concerning passive constructions. (b) Teachers should emphasize discourse instead of "correctness." (c) Teachers should give students "a realistic picture of the composing process" and flexible, multi-purposed planning strategies that will enable them to manipulate and modify fundamental frames of discourse, such as comparison and contrast essays (pp. 90–98).

Mike Rose's "Rigid Rules, Inflexible Plans, and the Stifling of Language" (1980), derived from the same research, analyzes the difficulties that blocked college student writers encounter in trying to compose with rules or planning strategies that impede rather than enhance the writing process. In contrast are non-blockers who use less rigid rules and more flexible plans. The blocked writers follow rules ("Grab your audience with a catchy opening") as though they are "algorithms, absolute dicta, rather than the loose heuristics" they are intended to be. Or they make questionable heuristics ("Always make three points in an essay") algorithmic. Some students habitually impose a linear organization on all of their essays, where this preconceived set is sometimes functional, sometimes not. Students sometimes inappropriately allow "inflexible and static cognitive blueprints" (p. 398) to govern their thinking rather than use fluid, multi-directional plans to enhance open, "adventurous exploration . . . with strategies that allow re-direction once 'dead ends' are encountered" (p. 399).

Blocked students are likely to become immobilized by conflicting rules rather than use such conflicts as an impetus to problem-solving, as non-blockers do. Rose's solutions are similar to those in his *Writer's Block* (1983).

Merle O. Thompson offered a language study curriculum as a solution to the difficulties of anxious writers in her dissertation "The Development and Evaluation of a Language Study Approach to a College Course in Freshman Composition" (1978) and in related conference papers: "Writing Anxiety and Discrimination in Freshman Composition" (1979); "Classroom Techniques for Reducing Writing Anxiety" (1980a); "A Study of Writing Anxiety" (1979); and "Writing Anxiety and Discrimination in Freshman Composition" (1980b). She contrasted five approaches to teaching composition: the Traditional Rhetorical approach, the Traditional Organic approach, the Interview/Tutor approach, and the Self-Instructional/Unit approach.

The Language Study approach focused on reading and writing about language, with writing instruction presented through lecture, discussion, and peer group. Letter grades were assigned; revision was optional. Thompson found that only this approach, including discussions of procrastination, concentration, and establishing a "personal writing rhythm" reduced writing anxiety significantly. In addition to "reducing the mystery surrounding the writing process," Thompson aimed to "reduce the mystery surrounding language" through means such as providing information about standard English and dialects, thereby relieving apprehensiveness about standards of language correctness.

The experience of simply taking a writing course and writing frequently in it decreases writing apprehension significantly. So indicate the investigations of D. D. Basile ("Do Attitudes About Writing Change as Composition Skills Improve?" [1982]); L. M. Schultz and G. D. Meyers ("Measuring Writing Apprehension in Required Freshman Composition and Upper-Level Writing Courses," [1981]); and Roy F. Fox ("Treatment of Writing Apprehension and Its Effects on Composition" [1980] and his doctoral dissertation of the same title [1978]). This is particularly true, said Fox, in a student-centered, sequential workshop setting as opposed to a traditional, teacher-centered classroom. G. Craven suggested, in "Motivating Reluctant Students to Write" (1980), that students will be less anxious if they read and write about what they're interested in and if they have an external audience for their writing through publication. David Bartholomae found that by teaching basic writers to read as well as to write responses to the readings, their anxiety was reduced significantly ("Teaching Basic Writing" [1979]). But for contrary findings, see Powers, Cook, and Meyer (1979).

In four related case studies of anxious graduate student and post-graduate writers, the only research on such persons to date, Lynn Bloom found still other causes of writing difficulties related to their age and status. (See "Doctoring and Mastering Graduate Writing" [1981a]; "Why Graduate Students Can't Write" [1981b]; and "Anxious Writers in Context" [1984].)

Bloom observed that for many graduate students the stakes of writing successfully are very high indeed, for on the quality and timing of their performance hinges their professional future. Many graduate students, bright and characteristically high achievers, are plagued by their very accomplishments and subject themselves to unrealistically perfectionistic standards. Sometimes they procrastinate or stop writing altogether, immobilized by fear of exposing their ignorance or of their school's presumably terrifyingly high standards for graduate work.

Students often lack knowledge about the form, style, organization, research methods, and bibliographic format of graduate or professional papers—an innocence of which their professors may be unaware. They don't know how to choose a topic manageable in the extended length of a thesis or dissertation, how to conduct research or write over the protracted and unstructured time that these works often require, or how to satisfy the varied methodological or intellectual demands of diverse advisors.

Graduate students are likely to have the conflicting and multiple demands of jobs, families, and community responsibilities in addition to their student roles. Their mixture of dependence and independence, freedom and responsibility, sometimes makes them unable to give appropriate priorities to their research and writing. The momentum to finish protracted writing often diminishes as both the project and the writer age, especially if the writer leaves the academic context.

Some solutions lie with graduate schools and their faculties. Graduate programs can incorporate thesis and dissertation methodology, research, even writing, into courses and can thereby provide for systematic, scheduled, supervised work. Advisors can teach students how to find key resources first and what criteria their work must meet in the way of breadth, depth, originality, and quality. Graduate schools can provide realistic but firm deadlines for completion of courses and degrees.

Graduate students, too, can assume much of the responsibility for their writing projects. They should feel free to ask their professors anything, however trivial or obvious, about the scope, emphasis, length, and research methodology of their writing. Students should ask for a realistic time schedule for submitting work and receiving commentary on it perhaps chapter by chapter, instead of waiting until everything is done. They should try to finish their work on time, and on campus, and under the aegis of professors who will settle for the best work in the time available, rather than demand an unattainable perfection.

Questions for Future Research

Among matters yet to be explored more fully are the following:

1. Are writing anxiety, writing apprehension, and writer's block necessarily the dysfuctional phenomena that most researchers assume? Might too relaxed a writer produce little or nothing?

2. Is there an optimum state, somewhere on a continuum between highly anxious and

thoroughly relaxed, that is best for any given writer? Or for a particular writer in particular circumstances? Or for writers in general?

3. To what extent does the experience of being a research subject make writers more anxious than they might otherwise be, and to what extent does this influence their writing processes and the research thereon?

4. Do anxious writers really write less well than non-anxious writers? What would writing process studies of anxious versus non-anxious professional writers reveal about this?

5. To what extent are anxieties about writing related to difficulties with reading? If they are related, should they be dealt with simultaneously, perhaps by team teachers in reading and writing?

6. What can adults learn from the writing processes (and learning sequences) of children?

7. What are the effects of different contexts (physical, social, psychological) on writing processes and writing blocks?

8. Should anxious writing students be taught with regular students, or would they be better off in special classes adapted to their particular difficulties?

9. What can teachers of non-anxious students learn from the research on anxious writers?

10. How does "adult" writing anxiety originate? Does it become exacerbated over time? How can it be prevented?

11. Is blocking likely to increase as writers become more skilled and take more risks?

References

Aldrich, P. G. "Adult Writers: Some Factors That Interfere with Effective Writing." 1979. ERIC ED 209 675.

Bartholomae, David. "Teaching Basic Writing: An Alternative to Basic Skills." *JBW*, 2 (1979), 85–109.

Basile, D. D. "Do Attitudes about Writing Change as Composition Skills Improve?" *CCR*, 9 (1982), 22–27.

Bergler, Edmund. *The Basic Neuroses*. New York: Grune, Stratton, 1949.

———. *The Writer and Psychoanalysis*. 2nd ed. New York: Brunner, 1954.

———. "Unconscious Mechanisms in 'Writer's Block.' " *Psy R*, 42 (1955), 160–67.

———. "Does 'Writer's Block' Exist?" *AI*, 7 (1959), 43–54.

Blake, R. W. "Assessing English and Language Arts Teachers' Attitudes Toward Writers and Writing." *E Rec*, 27 (1976), 87–97.

Bloom, Lynn Z. "The Composing Processes of Anxious and Non-Anxious Writers." 1980. ERIC ED 185559. 1980a.

———. "Teaching Anxious Writers: Implications and Applications of Research." *C&T*, 2 (1980b), 47–60.

———. "Doctoring and Mastering Graduate Writing." *JETT*, 12 (1981a), 74–81.

———. "Why Graduate Students Can't Write: Implications of Research on Writing Anxiety for Graduate Education." *JAC*, 1–2 (1981b), 103–17.

———. "Anxious Writers in Context: Graduate Students and Beyond." In *Writing Process Problems*. Ed. Mike Rose. New York: Guilford, 1984.

Bloom, Martin. "Anxious Writers: Distinguishing Anxiety from Pathology." 1980. ERIC ED 172 254.

Boice, Robert. "Increasing the Writing Productivity of 'Blocked' Academicians." *BRT*, 20 (1982), 197–207.

Camus, Albert. *The Plague*. Tr. Stewart Gilbert. New York: Knopf, 1971.

Claypool, S. H. "Teacher Writing Apprehension: Does It Affect Writing Assignments Across the Curriculum?" 1980. ERIC ED 216 387.

Craven, G. "Motivating Reluctant Students to Write." 1980. ERIC ED 198547.

Crisp, A. H., and H. Moldofsky. "A Psychosomatic Study of Writer's Cramp." *British Journal of Psychiatry*, 3 (1965), 841–858.

Daly, John A. "The Effects of Writing Apprehension on Message Encoding." *JQ*, 54 (1977), 566–72.

———. "Writing Apprehension and Writing Competency." *J Educ Res*, 72 (1978), 10–14.

———. "Writing Apprehension in the Classroom: Teacher Role Expectancies of the Apprehensive Writer." *RTE*, 13 (1979), 37–44.

———. "Writing Apprehension." In *Writing Process Problems*. Ed. Mike Rose, New York: Guilford, 1984.

———, and J. L. Hailey. "Putting the Situation into Writing Research: State and Disposition as Parameters of Writing Apprehension." In *New Directions in Composition Research*. Ed. R. Beach and L. Bidwell. New York: Guilford, 1983.

———, and Michael D. Miller. "The Empirical Development of an Instrument to Measure Writing Apprehension." *RTE*, 9 (1975a), 242–49.

———. "Further Studies in Writing Apprehension: SAT Scores, Success Expectations, Willingness to Take Advanced Courses, and Sex Differences." *RTE*, 9 (1975b), 250–56.

———, and Wayne Shamo. "Academic Decisions as a Function of Writing Apprehension." *RTE*, 12 (1978), 119–26.

———. "Writing Apprehension and Occupational Choice." *JOP*, 49 (1976), 55–56.

———, and D. Wilson. "Writing Apprehension, Self-Esteem, and Personality." *RTE*, 17 (1983), 327–341.

Duke, C. R. "Writing Apprehension: (II) Where Does Fear of Writing Come From?" *Ill E B*, (1980), 16–23.

Emig, Janet. *The Writing Processes of Twelfth Graders*. Urbana, Ill.: NCTE, 1971.

Faigley, Lester, John A. Daly, and Stephen P. Witte. "The Role of Writing Apprehension in Writing Performance and Writing Competence." *J Educ Res*, 75 (1981), 16–21.

Federn, P. "The Neurotic Style." 1930. Rpt. in *Psy Q*, 31 (1957), 681–89.

Flower, Linda, and John R. Hayes. *A Process Model of Composition*. Technical Report #3. Document Design Project. Pittsburgh: Carnegie-Mellon University, 1979.

Fowler, B., and Barry M. Kroll. "The Relationship of Apprehension about Writing to Performance as Measured by Grades in a College Course on Composition." *Psychol Rep*, 46 (1980), 583–86.

Fox, Roy F. "Treatment of Writing Apprehension and Its Effects on Composition." Diss. University of Missouri-Columbia, 1978.

———. "Treatment of Writing Apprehension and Its Effects on Composition." *RTE*, 14 (1980), 39–49.

Garcia, Robert J. "An Investigation of Relationships: Writing Apprehension, Syntactic Performance, and Writing Quality." Diss. Arizona State, 1977.

Gere, Ann R., B. F. Schuessler, and R. D. Abbott. "Measuring Teacher Attitudes Toward Instruction in Writing." 1981. ERIC ED 199 717.

Goldfried, Marvin R., Marsha M. Linehan, and Jean L. Smith. "Reduction of Test Anxiety Through Cognitive Restructuring." *JCCP*, 48 (1978), 32–39.

Graves, Donald. "Blocking and the Young Writer." In *Writing Process Problems*. Ed. Mike Rose. New York: Guilford, 1984.

Harris, Mary B. "Accelerating Dissertation Writing: Case Study." *Psychol Rep*, 34 (1974), 984–86.

Harris, Muriel. "Diagnosing Writing Process Problems: A Pedagogical Application of Speaking-Aloud Protocol Analysis." In *Writing Process Problems*. Ed. Mike Rose, New York: Guilford, 1984.

Harvley-Fedler, Zena C. "Some Factors Relating to Writing Apprehension: An Exploratory Study." Diss. University of North Carolina-Chapel Hill, 1978.

Heaton, Helen F. "A Study of Writing Anxiety Among High School Students Including Case Histories of Three High and Three Low Anxiety Students." Diss. University of Wisconsin-Madison, 1980.

Jones, A. C. "Grandiosity Blocks Writing Projects." *TAJ*, 5 (1975), 415.

Kroll, Barry M. "Assessing Students' Attitudes Toward Writing." *Eng R*, 30 (1979), 6–9.

Kubie, Lawrence. *Neurotic Distortions of the Creative Process*. New York: Noonday, 1973.

Liversedge, L. A., and J. D. Sylvester. "Conditioning Techniques in the Treatment of Writer's Cramp." *Lancet*, 7 (1955), 1147–49.

Menks, F. "Behavioral Techniques in the Treatment of a Writing Phobia." *AJOT*, 33 (1979), 192–7.

Passman, Richard. "A Procedure for Eliminating Writer's Block in a College Student." *JBTEP*, 7 (1976), 297–98.

Powers, William G., John A. Cook, and Russell Meyer. "The Effect of Compulsory Writing on Writing Apprehension." *RTE*, 13 (1979), 255–30.

Richardson, E. M. "The Quality of Essays Written for Distant and Intimate Audiences by High and Low Apprehensive Two-Year College Freshmen." Diss. University of Cincinnati, 1980.

Rose, Mike. "Rigid Rules, Inflexible Plans, and the Stifling of Language: A Cognitive Analysis of Writer's Block." *CCC*, 31 (1980), 389–401.

———. "The Cognitive Dimension of Writer's Block: An Examination of University Students." Diss. University of California-Los Angeles, 1981a.

———. "Sophisticated, Ineffective Books: The Dismantling of Process in Composition Texts." *CCC*, 32 (1981b), 65–74.

———. *Writer's Block: The Cognitive Dimension*. Urbana, Ill.: NCTE; and Carbondale, Ill.: Southern Illinois University Press, 1983.

———, ed. *Writing Process Problems: Writing Blocks, Writing Anxiety, Writing Apprehension*. New York: Guilford, 1984.

Rosenberg, Marvin. "Releasing the Creative Imagination." *J Creat Behav*, 10 (1976), 203–9.

Sanavio, E. "An Operant Approach to the Treatment of Writer's Cramp." *JBTEP,* 13 (1982), 69–72.

Schultz, L. M., and G. D. Meyers. "Measuring Writing Apprehension in Required Freshman Composition and Upper-Level Writing Courses." 1981. ERIC ED 203 326.

———. "An Apprehensive Writer Composes." In *Writing Process Problems*. Ed. Mike Rose. New York: Guilford, 1984.

Selfe, Cynthia L. "The Composing Processes of Four High and Four Low Writing Apprehensives: A Modified Case Study." Diss. University of Texas-Austin, 1981. Also 1981. ERIC ED 216 534.

Shaughnessy, Mina P. *Errors and Expectations*. New York: Oxford University Press, 1977.

Thompson, Merle O. "The Development and Evaluation of a Language Study Approach to a College Course in Freshman Composition." Diss. American University, 1978.

———. "A Study of Writing Anxiety: The Effects of Several Classroom Strategies." 1979. ERIC ED 206 339.

———. "Writing Anxiety and Discrimination in Freshman Composition." 1980b. ERIC ED 183 235.

———. "Classroom Techniques for Reducing Writing Anxiety: A Study of Several Cases." 1980a. ERIC ED 188 681.

Tobias, Sheila. *Overcoming Math Anxiety*. New York: Norton, 1978.

Uchiyama, Kiuko, Martin Lutterjohann, and Mumtaz D. Shah. "Biofeedback-Assisted Desensitization Treatment of Writer's Cramp." *JBTEP*, 8 (1971), 169–71.

Weil, B. H., and J. C. Lane. "Psychological Barriers to Writing." *Chem Eng News* (1956), 6244–48.

Philosophy and Rhetoric

JOHN C. BRIGGS

Entitling a chapter ''Philosophy and Rhetoric'' risks introducing notorious problems of definition by evoking a long history of active and latent controversy. The variable meaning of and the shifting relationship between each term press a world of significance into the little word *and*, whose portentous meaning in such a title cannot be unpacked in any straightforward way. Does *and* signify the conjunction of philosophy and rhetoric as harmonious, perhaps congruent theories and practices, or does it announce that they are really combatants? To interpret these terms and their relationship, despite the difficulties attending such an effort, is to seek the foundations of modern conceptions of rhetoric and their relevance for the theory and practice of composition.

Stereotypical views of the relation between philosophy and rhetoric can be reduced to three, if we are content for now to define *rhetoric* as the study and practice of the means of persuasion and *philosophy* as the theory and practice of the love of wisdom. Although such definitions soon prove insufficient, they are commonly ventured opinions. But their very commonness and persistence in a tradition of debate makes them significant places to begin our investigation.

The first view claims that rhetoric's enlightenment and persuasion of various audiences, especially those made up of non-specialists, are subordinate to philosophy's pursuit and discovery of knowledge itself. The second, contrary position insists that rhetoric is more fundamental than philosophy, perhaps because truth is essentially subjective or because knowledge supposedly must be communicated effectively to be coherent even to itself. The third position maintains that rhetoric and philosophy are so complementary and interdependent that neither is of predominant importance. Plato and post-Renaissance philosophers are usually identified with the first camp; the sophists, some Renaissance humanists, and a few moderns with the second; Isocrates, Cicero, Quintilian, other Renaissance humanists, and many modern rhetorical theorists with the third.

To draw such neat patterns of associations is to see how inadequate they are.

Closer investigation reveals that the meanings of philosophy and rhetoric vary among theorists and eras. Moderns tend to identify or contrast philosophy with empirical science or mathematical logic, whereas medieval logicians merge it with theology. Even though the resultant medieval conception of dialectic is largely inspired by Aristotle's definitions of demonstrative, "scientific" philosophy, it is in turn ridiculed by fifteenth– and sixteenth-century humanists who allege that it demonstrates no interest in truth but rather reduces all learning indifferently into dogmatic theology or contentious, rule-ridden dialectic, neither of which contributes to the genuine instruction of others. The humanists' new doctrines joining wisdom and eloquence have in turn proved controversial, since scholars now take opposing views on the meaning and relative importance of rhetoric and philosophy in humanist theory and practice.

From age to age, rhetoric undergoes its own set of metamorphoses complicated by the disappearance of a name for rhetoric or the deceptive persistence of a name despite changes in definition. Thus rhetoric, which seems distinct from the technical dialectic of disputation among the schoolmen, becomes so entwined in the Renaissance conceptions of dialectic and poetics that it is difficult to distinguish confusion from purposeful redefinition. Today *rhetoric* and *philosophy* sometimes seem to be used interchangeably in opposite theories. The changing circumstances and motivation behind the use of the words require that we be attuned to possible differences between apparent and actual definition, as well as the modification of the apparent substance of a theory in the way that theory is presented.

Rhetoric, like philosophy, has been identified with all three parts of the trivium—grammar, logic, and rhetoric—and a host of specialized studies derived from each one. Like philosophy, rhetoric has sometimes taken on the character of an arch-discipline ruling over the entire trivium and all specialized sciences. A study of the elusive history of both terms and the relation between them begins to disclose the interdependence of grammar, logic, and rhetoric in the traditional trivium, as well as the tendency for "trivial" conceptions of rhetoric, logic, and grammar to grow into specialized sciences that sometimes aspire to architechtonic mastery of all arts, methods, and subject matters.

If the phrase "philosophy and rhetoric" means anything today, it does so because the flux of words and terms, motives, and circumstances has not destroyed the desire to frame questions about the relationships between truth-seeking, persuasion, learning, and the grammatical medium of language—all of which have to do with the relationship of understanding and the presentation of understanding. Even some theorists' refusals to entertain a topic like "philosophy and rhetoric," insisting that it is a worn-out phrase provoking mere logomachy, often seem to generate new pairings of terms (for example, discovery/presentation) in which the old questions persist. Outlines of some of these issues can be found in P. Albert Duhamel's "The Function of Rhetoric as Effective Expression" (1949), Douglas Ehninger's "On Systems of Rhetoric" (1968), and the works of Richard McKeon.

Douglas B. Park's recent essay "Theories and Expectations" (1979) observes how an endemic desire among researchers to build theories of rhetoric and composition, apply them directly to pedagogy, and witness the revolutionary perfection of a discipline has led to debilitating swings between extremes of anxiety and euphoria. In what follows, I have assumed that a serious study of the relationship between philosophy and rhetoric, with applications to the theory and practice of composition, can help temper these fickle vacillations, especially if it returns our attention to major texts that have grown out of a tradition of inquiry and debate. Otis M. Walter provided an excellent starting point for such a project in "On Views of Rhetoric, Whether Conservative or Progressive" (1963), an essay insisting that the study of rhetorical theories makes no sense unless we seek to discover the questions and circumstances that generated them.

I have attempted to build upon the useful bibliography compiled by Richard Young in the first chapter of Gary Tate's collection, *Teaching Composition* (1976). Young focused on rhetorical invention, no doubt a major interest of most modern rhetorical theorists, largely because it is ostensibly the most philosophical of the traditional stages of rhetorical theory and practice. However, Young's list tends to defer general questions about rhetoric and philosophy and to favor the work of specialized sciences, especially cognitive psychology. My assumption has been that a selection of basic texts with broader affinities to the concerns of the trivium offers more provocative responses to the most basic questions we can ask about the foundations of rhetoric and the relation of rhetoric to philosophy.

I have concentrated on finding secondary material that might elude researchers limiting themselves to the familiar lists of classic articles and standard histories. However, I have reviewed those sources to include as many works as possible that are especially helpful. I have benefitted from the historical and critical surveys by George Kennedy (*The Art of Persuasion in Greece* [1963] and *The Art of Rhetoric in the Roman World* [1973]), Wilbur Samuel Howell (*Logic and Rhetoric in England, 1500–1700* [1956] and *Eighteenth-Century British Logic and Rhetoric* [1971]), James Murphy (*Rhetoric in the Middle Ages* [1974]), and C. S. Baldwin (*Ancient Rhetoric and Poetic* [1924], *Medieval Rhetoric and Poetic* [1928], and *Renaissance Literary Theory and Practice* [1939]). Important works giving relatively sustained attention to the relationship between philosophy and rhetoric and containing helpful bibliographies are *The New Rhetoric* by Chaim Perelman and Olbrechts-Tyteca (1969), Edward P. J. Corbett's *Classical Rhetoric for the Modern Student* (1971), James Kinneavy's *A Theory of Discourse* (1971), and Wayne Booth's *Modern Dogma and the Rhetoric of Assent* (1974), which develops a rich set of footnotes. The most complete bibliographies having to do with the interaction of modern rhetorical theories and philosophy are in *Philosophy, Rhetoric, and Argumentation*, edited by Henry Johnstone and Maurice Natanson (1965), and *Contemporary Theories of Rhetoric*, edited by Richard L. Johannesen (1971).

My organization is chronological, because the progression of major texts is in some sense a debate and a collective inquiry; but the bibliography will inevitably fix itself upon important principles and issues as they emerge and develop. The modern tide of interest in sophistic rhetoric—the first influential conception of rhetoric with profound philosophical implications—makes the sophistic movement an appropriate place to begin such a project.

Philosophy and/or Rhetoric: Sophists, Anti-Sophists, Protosophists

Although very few of the original sophists' texts survive, fragments of their work have been preserved, along with the portrait of the sophists that Plato gives us in dialogues such as the *Gorgias, Phaedrus, Sophist, Protagorus*, and Aristotle's apparent reference, in the early pages of the *Rhetoric*, to sophistic handbooks of rhetoric. Some scholars believe that the sophists have no single position regarding affinities or antagonisms between philosophy and rhetoric, that the accuracy of Plato's severe critique of their work is uncertain, because he probably invented the speeches by which they defend themselves.

Werner Jaeger presented in the *Paideia* (1954–1961) his famous overview and defense of the sophistic movement as an emphasis on rhetorical training that prepared the way for modern "humanistic" education (Vol. 2, Chapter 3). He attempted to overcome Plato's allegations of moral and philosophical weakness in the sophists by demonstrating that their achievements as founders outweigh their defects as practitioners. Yet Jaeger recognized the force of Plato's criticisms by avoiding analysis of the work of Gorgias, the most prominent and controversial of the sophists, and by noting the limits of his praise: "Sophists are the inventors of intellectual culture and the art of education which aims at producing it. At the same time it is clear that whenever their new culture went beyond formal or factual education, whenever their political training attacked the deeper problems of morality and the state, it was in danger of teaching half-truths" (p. 293).

A good way to move beyond Jaeger's observation is to study the actual fragments of Gorgias's work and the critique Isocrates offered of one of them. As Charles P. Segal pointed out in "Gorgias and the Psychology of the Logos" (1962), the orations are demonstrations of the principles and methods of Gorgias's sophistic rhetoric. Each touches on the problem of relating philosophy and rhetoric.

In reading the *Encomium to Helen* by Gorgias (available in the Loeb edition of Isocrates, Vol. 3, pp. 55–57), we are immediately faced with determining how seriously Gorgias addressed the question at hand. Is the oration an elaborate joke, purposely defending an impossible position (that Helen of Troy is unquestionably virtuous) so that Gorgias's brilliant persuasiveness can be better admired? Does it in fact make a serious claim for the superiority of rhetoric over philosophy or perhaps the reverse? His first lines seem to merge all of these possibilities when they playfully venture the idea that discourses are embellished by means of truth, just as souls are embellished by wisdom. He wanted "by rational calculation" to reveal the truth about Helen, but his brief and pointed presentation leads up to the argument that force—particularly persuasion's power to overwhelm susceptible natures—absolves the weaker nature from any blame. Persuasion, like poetry and religious incantation, is a powerful charm or drug. Those it dominates are naturally moved by leaders who rule just as the gods rule over men, surpassing them in power and everything else: "It is a law of nature that . . . the weaker is subjugated and dominated by the stronger; the stronger is the leader, which is the entreater" (p. 56). The argument is an oracular, disarming embodiment of the notion that might is right.

Jonathan Barnes (*The Presocratic Philosophers*, Vol. 2 [1979], pp. 221–28), commented on this and another Gorgian text, *Concerning Nature*, a summary of which is available in his Volume 1 (pp. 173–74), and in K. Freeman, *Ancilla to the Pre-Socratic Philosophers* (1956, pp. 128–29). The traditional charge that Gorgias was a nihilist, that he relied on an ethic of force, largely stems from his alleged statement, "first, that nothing exists; second, that even if anything exists, it is incomprehensible to mankind; third, that even if it is comprehensible, at all events it is incommunicable and inexpressible to a neighbor" (Barnes [1979], Vol. 1, p. 173). But G. B. Kereferd's brief, lucid book *The Sophistic Movement* (1981) speculates that Gorgias's defense of force is an attempt to discover the best means of persuasion in a world he has defined as though the *logos*—the very proofs, language, and substance of his discourse—were distinct from, in fact utterly deprived of, the existence of truth. Recent rhetorical theorists have seized upon this argument because of its apparent affinity to the modern rejection of Enlightenment faith in the objective powers of reason and its tendency to grant the highest status to human powers of fabrication, which seem blessed in the famous saying of another sophist, Protagoras, that "man is the measure of all things." However, the meaning of sophistic rhetoric is not easily recovered when sufficient study is not given to the ancient controversy among the sophists, Isocrates, Plato, and Aristotle.

One of the most significant interpretations of Gorgias and sophistic rhetoric in general is that of Isocrates, for in reading his *Helen* we can see how he both attacked and defended his teacher Gorgias, with the knowledge that the famous sophist may have corrupted as well as taught him. Isocrates's ambition to make a legitimate institution out of rhetorical education makes him, in Jaeger's terms, the archetypal sophist. In fact, the *Helen*, along with his other orations touching on the sophists (*Against the Sophists,* the *Panegyricus,* the *Antidosis*), should be of compelling interest if we are to understand the influential tradition, running from Isocrates through Cicero and Quintilian, which attempts to combine philosophy and rhetoric without falling into the Gorgian or stereotypically anti-Gorgian camps.

In the *Helen*, Isocrates vigorously objected to all argumentation traditionally associated with the sophists and endeavored to make rhetoric philosophically respectable for the education of Greek youth and the renovation of Greek politics. However, his oration takes advantage of the Gorgian notion that ascribes virtue and wisdom to superior force, as though power might justify itself. Thus Isocrates's defense of Helen almost entirely by the distant means of praising her first lover Theseus (the supremely heroic Greek ruler who did so much to enhance the power and reputation of Greece) oscillates between anti-Gorgian and Gorgian arguments: what makes Theseus virtuous is what he does, which includes loving Helen, and yet Helen is virtuous not because of what she does, but because her lover Theseus's heroic nature is so impressive. Isocrates tried to confirm his proof by evoking Greek respect for Theseus and the pan-Hellenic, public virtue stimulated in the war that Helen provoked when she went to Troy. To determine whether he succeeded, we must ask whether he genuinely transcended the problem of arguing for the virtue of Helen by praising the eminent virtue of Theseus.

Socrates's favorable yet tentative reference to Isocrates in Plato's *Phaedrus* is an important sign that Plato thought Isocrates to be standing precariously between the worlds of Gorgian and anti-Gorgian rhetoric. Plato's most explicitly anti-sophistic dialogues, read in the light of Isocrates's problematic stance and our knowledge of Isocrates's powerful influence on Cicero and Quintilian, take on additional importance as responses to the tradition of reconciliation between philosophy and rhetoric, a tradition that has gained a new life in modern conceptions of a "New Rhetoric."

In contrast to the lack of modern interest in Isocrates's orations as important documents about rhetorical theory, the recognition given by rhetorical theorists to Plato's work has been so regular as to become perfunctory. A good antidote to hackneyed opinions is Edwin Black's essay "Plato's View of Rhetoric" (1958), which points out Socrates's reluctance to condemn rhetoric in general. Plato directed his critique of sophistic rhetoric, in Black's view, toward the misleading application of rhetoric, not toward rhetoric itself. But although Black focused on the distinction between principle and application of principle, it was Richard Weaver, in the opening chapter of *The Ethics of Rhetoric* (1953), who confronted both the powerful sophistic attacks on philosophy and Platonic philosophy's serious challenges to any defense of rhetoric. Weaver elucidated the means by which rhetoric and Plato's philosophical dialectic interact in the *Phaedrus*, but for him that interaction was so strenuous and complex it bore no resemblance to the Isocratean compromise. A review of recent controversy over rhetoric and dialectic in the *Phaedrus* is Michael C. Leff's "Re-interpreting Plato's *Phaedrus*" (1971).

The Platonic dialogues particularly concerned with sophistic rhetoric, such as the *Gorgias, Phaedrus*, and *Protagoras*, are read most productively not by merely extracting propositions made by individual speakers but by taking into account the dialogues' essentially dramatic character. For example, the characterization of the sophist Protagoras through gesture as well as speech and the development of a particular setting for Protagoras's interaction with Socrates imply much more about Plato's view of sophistic rhetoric than we can glean from isolated speeches. The circumstances of the dialogue's beginning, the reasons for its abortive close, the presence of an enthusiastic crowd that Protagoras was eager to please even if he had to submit to Socrates's questions for a while—all help to disclose what only a lengthy commentary can begin to elucidate. An admirable attempt to write such a commentary is Ronna Burger's *Plato's "Phaedrus"* (1980). Stanley Rosen's commentary *Plato's Symposium* (1968) is also a revealing aid to the study of dramatic rhetoric and philosophy in the *Gorgias*, *Phaedrus*, and *Protagorus*. A recent book-length commentary on the *Gorgias* was written by Ilham Dilman: *Morality and the Inner Life* (1979).

The funny, relatively straightforward *Protagorus* is a good introduction to the more complex *Gorgias* and *Phaedrus*, both often alleged to be self-contradictory and at cross-purposes with each other. If the *Gorgias* is about rhetoric, why is so much of it devoted to ethics? If the *Phaedrus* is a definitive discussion of rhetoric, why are its speeches all about *eros*? If the *Gorgias* supposedly proclaims that all rhetoric is corrupt, why does the *Phaedrus* seem to propose the use of a philosophical rhetoric in harmony with Platonic dialectic? It is apparent, however, that the *Gorgias* is not strictly an anti-rhetorical work. Socrates was surprisingly deferential toward Gorgias himself, implying that Gorgias might be capable of saying something to dispel Socrates's doubts. Gorgias seems to have been ruled by a conventional morality; he wanted rhetoric to be respectable and tried at first to answer Socrates's questions to satisfy philosophical inquiry into what he did. His deeper, possibly nihilistic views are hidden and for the most part under control. But his ruthless student Polus and the tyranny-loving public official Callicles freely endorsed the notion that persuasion is really force. Gorgias's conventional morality had no hold on them. Believing that rhetoric and philosophy can accommodate to one another by means of good intentions, Gorgias apparently taught rhetoric with good intentions and disastrous results. The question the dialogue poses is whether even a high-minded rhetoric can be taught that does not poison its students or serve as an excuse for those interested merely in subjugation. Since Cicero and other commentators have remarked how Socrates himself relied increasingly on speechmaking as the dialogue progresses, an answer to this question would have to judge the rhetoric of Socrates himself.

The *Phaedrus* counters this dark interchange with what is in some sense a completion of it: Socrates's encounter with the enthusiastic but easily corrupted Phaedrus, leading up to the positive although elusive definition of *philosophical rhetoric* as the power to define "dialectically" and to present the knowledge gained by that power by means of a knowledge of souls in their various kinds and magnitudes. But the web of the drama makes the meaning and application of this principle complex, since Plato's reputation for uncompromising insistence on the predominance of philosophy is qualified by the enactment of the philosopher's being forced to discourse with audiences often far less philosophical than himself, both because of his constant desire to seek truth in dialogue and because audiences regularly requested or demanded that he engage their interests up to the moment of his death.

Aristotle's *Rhetoric* responds more directly to Plato's suggestion in the *Phaedrus* that such a rhetoric might be possible. It counters the negative portrait of *rhetoric* in the *Gorgias*, where it is defined as the mere "counterpart" of cookery, by calling rhetoric the "counterpart" of dialectic—for Aristotle the art of discussing *endoxa*, or probable truths. (See "References to Plato in Aristotle's *Rhetoric*" [1924] by W. Rhys Roberts.) In fact, Aristotle's willingness to call rhetoric a counterpart of dialectic most appropriate for large, usually non-philosophical, audiences opens the possibility of its involvement with scientific definition and demonstration, both of which in Aristotle's works are not rigidly distinguished from dialectic. "Rhetoric, Dialectic, and Syllogistic Argument" by Sally Raphael (1974) maintains that because Aristotle never adequately systematized the connections between his conceptions of science, dialectic, and rhetoric, he in fact confused them. But her discussion provides ample evidence for a different view taken up by Richard J. Burke ("Aristotle on the Limits of Argument" [1967]). Burke tried to show that despite Aristotle's occasionally strict separation of scientific demonstration from dialectic and rhetoric, he made science "social"— a "matter of argument" that has to do with "teaching and learning"—that resolves intellectual impasses. Hence Aristotelian science, in some sense the most philosophical of endeavors, is profoundly dialectical, even rhetorical. It is heavily dependent on common sense and "what everyone knows" for its starting points. Skeptical sophists should not require it to give a reason for everything; they do not understand the necessity of science's beginning in "things known to us" as it moves toward those things that are known without qualification. Burke conceded that there are grounds for the modern belief that Aristotelian intuitionism invites mere circularity, even error, but he was not inclined to answer those claims with additional discussion of the role of *nous* or insight into what Aristotle considered the starting points of science. Nor did he pursue the general question of how dialecticians and rhetoricians can rise from *endoxa* toward scientific truth. For a discussion of the controversial nature of ancient dialectic and its relation to Aristotle's concept of science and rhetoric, see "Dialectic" in M. Adler's *Syntopicon* (1971), the complex definition of *endoxa* in the *Topics* (I.i.), and the general discussion in *Aristotle on Dialectic* edited by G.E.L. Owen (1968), *Aristotle's* "The Academy and Dialectic" by Gilbert Ryle (1971), and *Aristotle's Concept of Dialectic* by J.D.G. Evans (1977). The relationship of noetic and dialectical truth in Plato and Aristotle is explored in Richard Weaver's *The Ethics of Rhetoric* (1953) and in Stanley Rosen's critique of a recent tendency to collapse intuition and "ordinary language," as well as philosophy and rhetoric, into each other (*Nihilism*, [1969]).

A provocative attempt to show the kinship of scientific demonstration and dialectic (and by implication the connection of both to rhetoric) is the tiny book by Ernst Kapp, *Greek Foundations of Traditional Logic* (1942). Indeed, Kapp's Chapter 5 identifies ancient logic with ancient academic conversation by contrasting them with modern logic exemplified in the work of John Stuart Mill. Ancient logic, including dialectic, "found its subject matter in the sphere of conversation, and . . . it concentrated almost exclusively on such logical operations as are capable of external performance or external experimentation between two people" in their use of words in dialogue (p. 84). Its foundations are thus "fairly solid . . . because of their palpability" (p. 84). In contrast to modern logic, they may seem "rather scanty and incoherent and scarcely fit or sufficient to support more than comparatively few separate parts of a modern logical system"; but their limitations contrast with "a certain one-sidedness of modern logic" that rejects any essential function for the communication of ideas (p. 87). Mill's "solitary rational being," denying its highest functions the exercise of logical discussion, is constantly in danger of becoming incoherent and confusing to itself.

These secondary sources make more accessible the primary texts by Aristotle that complement the *Rhetoric*: for example, the *Posterior Analytics,* which focuses on what Aristotle called the "scientific" or "demonstrative" philosophy closest to mathematics; the *Topics*, which is a guide for academic discussion of probable truths (dialectic); and the *Sophistical Refutations*, the companion to both works that outlines fallacious arguments and, just as importantly, introduces means of confronting and eluding, in the sometimes fluid circumstances of discussion, what may seem to be dialectical discussion but is really a display of contentiousness. To Aristotle, the *Refutations* was an aid to philosophical and rhetorical dimensions of discourse. It was not simply a means for "scientific" logic to purge discourse of "merely rhetorical" or dialectical fallacies. Aristotle assumed that sophistry, or pseudo-dialectic, shadows every discussion, even the most controlled philosophical dialogue, threatening to denature or corrupt even the anti-sophist's discourse. There is no tool of logic that can merely reveal it; it is a potential malignancy, actualized when the general vigor of rhetoric and dialectic is allowed to decline.

Aristotle's works on these subjects are notorious for their compressed presentation of difficult concepts, but there are sections that help the reader open up the ancient arguments that reveal Aristotle's equally proverbial common sense. Each work's opening chapter, the *Posterior Analytics'* discussion of definition, and Book 8 of the *Topics* on rhetorical aspects of dialectical discussions are good guides. The relation between these books and the *Rhetoric* can be clarified by testing a double hypothesis: (1) that Aristotle distinguished between scientific (demonstrative) philosophy, dialectic, and rhetoric and yet cultivated the possibility that rhetoric and dialectic might remain open to philosophy; (2) that he assumed scientific demonstration depends upon dialectical, even rhetorical, discourse to examine and to test the credibility of its own axioms. (See McKeon's "The Hellenistic and Roman Foundations of the Tradition of Aristotle in the West" [1979].)

The controversy over the scientific status of rhetoric and dialectic emerges in discussion of the *Rhetoric* when readers ask how Aristotle's anti-sophistic focus on proofs and invention in Book 1 can harmonize with his focus on psychology, arrangement, and style in Books 2 and 3. Since in Book 1 Aristotle chided the sophists for their dependence on superficial appeals to the emotions rather than proofs, critics have asked whether the rest of his treatise contradicts or genuinely extends his main argument.

Resolution of this issue depends largely on Aristotle's conception of the emotions, to which he gave increasing attention in Books 2 and 3. What is the relation of the feelings, if any, to the intellectual operation of proof emphasized in Book 1? William W. Fortenbaugh supplied helpful notes and bibliography for an answer in "Aristotle's *Rhetoric* on Emotion" (1970). A related issue has to do with the meaning of *pisteis*, variously translated as "belief" or "proof" or both. The matter is of obvious relevance to the broader question whether Aristotle's discussion of proof and emotion is unified. Joseph T. Lienhard performed the service of summing up the opposing views of two other articles on this subject, one asserting that the nature of all *pisteis* is essentially philosophical, the other claiming that Aristotle's use of the word in the later stages of the *Rhetoric* is purely pragmatic ("A Note on the Meaning of *Pisteis* in Aristotle's *Rhetoric*" [1966]). The major elaboration of the former view is William M. A. Grimaldi's commentary *Studies in the Philosophy of Aristotle's Rhetoric* (1972). The standard commentaries by Edward M. Cope and Lane Cooper tended to support the latter position insofar as they assumed that the *Rhetoric* is essentially a handbook for which the question of theoretical unity is irrelevant. (For a strident elaboration of this view, see F. Hill's "The Amorality of Aristotle's *Rhetoric*" [1981].) Grimaldi (1972) tried to demonstrate the *Rhetoric*'s philosophical seriousness by revealing its "intimate articulation of matter and form," reason and suasion, in its characteristically Greek conception of discourse as the logos (p. 1). The *Rhetoric*'s purpose is fully intellectual, not merely emotive or pragmatic. It aspires "not to persuade but to discern the possibly suasive in the subject" and thus "creates an attitude in another's mind, a sense of the reasonableness of the position proposed, whereby the auditor may make his own decision" (p. 27). Larry Arnhart's *Aristotle on Political Reasoning* (1981) is a new commentary, in partial sympathy with Grimaldi's assumptions, designed to define the high level of political and philosophical seriousness in the *Rhetoric*.

Since the *enthymeme* is for Aristotle the essential form of proof in rhetoric, its definition and its relation to dialectical and demonstrative forms of proof are technical issues that turn out to be points of focus for readers of the *Rhetoric* investigating the relation between scientific demonstration, dialectic, and rhetoric. Insofar as "enthymeme" derives from *thumos*—the complex term for the seat of anger, courage, the will or "heart," spiritedness, and in some sense the soul—its appeal as a form of proof is difficult to understand without confronting the problem of relating philosophy and rhetoric. (See Edward H. Madden's discussion in "The Enthymeme" [1952], and Stephen E. Lucas's "Notes on Aristotle's Concept of Logos" [1971].)

Arguments over the meaning of the topics, the "places" from which dialectic and rhetoric have traditionally drawn material for discourse, have divided scholars into what may be called "scientific" and "rhetorical" camps. In *Teaching Composition*, edited by Gary Tate (1976), Richard Young's bibliographical essay "Invention" analyzes this division between those who see the topics as "cognitive," inherent in the thinking process, and those who consider them to be forms of behavior inculcated by social conditioning. Both views are in one sense scientific, although in another they stem from or lead to rhetorical principles that are profoundly Gorgian: by making topical thought seem either totally innate or totally conditioned, both camps have made it seem eminently susceptible not only to instruction but also to manipulation.

In "The Tradition of the Logical Topics" (1962), Otto Bird explained the attempt by some medieval commentators to purify Aristotle's topics by strictly separating the universal, formal inferences from the "material" ones contingent on meanings and contexts. This uncompromising version of the Platonic distinction between philosophy and rhetoric is resisted by John of Salisbury, who saw the quest for universal, necessary principles of inference in the topics as a misguided embrace of necessity. (For Bird's treatment of Stephen Toulmin's *Uses of Argument* [1958] as an unconscious echo of John of Salisbury's arguments, see his "Rediscovery of the Topics" [1961].) Eleanore Stump's edition of Boethius's work on the topics, *Boethius's "De Topicis Differentiis"* (1978), is also a study of the problem of consistently distinguishing between "logical" and rhetorical topics. Jean M. Lechner's survey *Renaissance Concepts of the Commonplaces* (1962) is full of evidence, if not analysis, of this difficulty in the later age.

Cicero: Synthesis or False Compromise?

The post-classical tendency to separate "logical" from "rhetorical" elements in rhetoric and dialectic partially obscures the interrelation of Aristotelian science, dialectic, and rhetoric. But whereas Aristotle invited the drawing of connections between the *Rhetoric,* the *Topics,* the *Posterior Analytics,* and the *Sophistical Refutations,* he refrained from systematizing them in a single, explicit doctrine that joins rhetoric to philosophy. Cicero, on the other hand, took the resonance of these works to be a single note. In fact, Cicero's works on oratory and philosophy have been called attempts to fuse *ratio* and *oratio* in order to capture the philosophical dimension of Aristotle's *Rhetoric*, the philosophical principles of the *Phaedrus* (which the *De Oratore* supposedly imitates), and the predilection toward philosophy in the work of Isocrates. (See Friedrich Solmson's "The Aristotelian Tradition in Ancient Rhetoric" [1941].) However, Samuel Ijsseling's account of Ciceronian rhetoric (*Rhetoric and Philosophy in Conflict* [1976], Chapter 5) concentrates on evidence for Cicero's ultimate disdain for philosophy and his consequent inability to construct a theory of rhetoric in a spirit of genuine synthesis. A far more authoritative refutation of Solmson's perspective is Richard McKeon's essay "The Hellenistic and Roman Foundations of the Tradition of Aristotle in the West" (1979). McKeon saw in Cicero's *De Oratore* and *De Inventione* a refashioning of Aristotle that makes philosophy and rhetoric so absolutely congruent that they are in some sense profoundly confused. On the one hand, Cicero pressed into the service of the orator all that he thought essential in philosophy. On the other hand, he assumed that oratory is essentially philosophical. McKeon's detailed comparison of Aristotle's *Rhetoric* with corresponding sections of Cicero's work concludes that a consequence of Cicero's enlargement of the powers and duties of philosophical orators is the diminishment of later ages' understanding of the *Rhetoric*'s articulation of Aristotelian science, dialectic, and rhetoric.

McKeon argued that the result of the Ciceronian redefinition of *rhetoric, dialectic,* and *philosophy* is the conversion of specialized sciences, which Aristotle often distinguished from rhetoric, into rhetorical endeavors concentrating on the presentation of their subject matter in oratory. Paradoxically, Cicero also made philosophical investigation the foundation and structure of rhetoric. He explained rhetorical invention as though it consisted of immediate philosophical inquiry into the existence and truth of subject matters rather than the collection of Aristotelian dialectic and rhetoric. In the process, philosophy is made to seem eminently accessible to the study and practice of rhetoric at the same time that Cicero put it aside by narrowing the horizon of rhetoric, abandoning much of Aristotle that seems irrelevant to the immediate concerns of oratorical practice. In a parallel movement, Cicero made Aristotelian rhetoric seem essentially practical, while in fact raising it to the status of a master method of invention and judgment that absorbs and rules all arts, methods, and subject matters.

Augustine and the Medieval Dialecticians: Humbling and Spiritualizing Rhetoric

The Ciceronian fixation on the philosophical orator's practical mastery of discourse tends to discount non-discursive factors in Aristotle's and Plato's conceptions of philosophy and rhetoric, particularly Aristotle's conception of noetic insight—what he believed to be the source of scientific axioms that were in turn examined and propagated by dialectic and rhetoric—and Plato's notion of the erotic aspiration leading the philosopher momentarily into sight of the blinding sun and then somehow influencing his rhetoric when he returns to the cave. It is Augustine who restored and vastly expanded the non-discursive dimension of rhetoric when he rehabilitated Cicero for the sake of Christian theology and rhetoric. Indeed, Augustine's rhetoric develops in light of the tremendous problem of integrating Christian revelation, which is utterly beyond the reach of traditional proof and persuasion, into Christian preaching for the sake of that revelation. (For a lucid introduction to the circumstances and trains of thought that led philosophers and rhetoricians away from Cicero's philosophical-rhetorical synthesis, see the first chapter of Rosemary Radrod Ruether's *Gregory of Nazianzus* [1969].)

Joseph A. Mazzeo in "St. Augustine's Rhetoric of Silence" (1962) tried to explain Augustine's resolution of rhetorical and religious claims, in Book IV of *De Doctrine*, and other writings, as a subordination of means to ends, of rhetoric to religion. Although eloquent exposition of "natural" signs created by God and the "conventional" signs of language made by men are extremely important, the Christian revelation absolutely transcends them. Rhetoric ultimately begins and ends in silence, so there exists no real conflict between rhetoric and Christianity or between pagan and Christian rhetoric, because one absorbs the other.

In opposition to Mazzeo's analysis, the essay "St. Augustine's Rhetoric of Silence Revisited" (1978) by Marcia L. Colish cites precedents in the rhetorical tradition that she maintained drew Augustine toward a more traditional position. Looking beyond *De Doctrine*, toward Augustine's brief treatises on lying (*De Mendacio* and *Contra Mendacium*), she noted his strenuous efforts to reconcile an absolute prohibition on lying with the exigencies of projecting God's message. The seriousness with which Augustine took that problem of reconciliation is evident in the intense interest that he showed throughout his works in the interpretation of indirection, silence, and apparent falsehood.

Ernest L. Fortin developed a similar set of assumptions to argue that Augustine's radical insistence on truth-telling, despite his close imitation of Cicero's writings on rhetoric, is a profound rejection of a Ciceronian compromise between rhetoric and philosophy. (See Fortin's "Augustine and the Problem of Christian Rhetoric" [1974].) Cicero embraced that compromise, according to Fortin, because he knew and admitted (in *De Oratore* III, 137) that philosophical ideas and rhetorical practice will never genuinely coincide:

this can only mean that in addressing his fellow citizens the orator is compelled to adopt an ironic posture. Although his teaching does not correspond fully to what he himself knows to be true, it is essential that it be perceived as a true teaching by his hearers. He will be successful to the extent to which others remain ignorant of the fact that what he does is the one thing that he cannot claim to be doing [as a philosopher]. There is an element of high comedy in the highest form of oratory. Cicero's perfect orator is a liar, not because he wants to [be], but because he has no choice in the matter. (p. 91)

If Augustine both imitates and transforms Cicero, his work might be seen as the fruition of Cicero's efforts to preserve the *paideia*. The title of W. R. Johnson's article demonstrates his desire to show that possibility is a fact: "Isocrates Flowering" (1976). By calling Augustine the blossom of the *paideia* tradition, Johnson meant that Augustine pushed that tradition to its extremes, first by assuming that the rhetor's audience is truly universal and second by giving the rhetor the mission of somehow opening to view everything that pertains to the confrontation of that audience's soul with the Bible's message, from the structure of the Biblical language to the news of its most mystical teachings. Precisely how Augustine intended this perfection of Isocratean–Ciceronian rhetoric to move or touch its universal audience, given Augustine's contradictory commitment to the pre-eminence of faith, was taken up by James J. Murphy. "The Metarhetorics of Plato, Augustine, and McLuhan" (1971) suggests that Augustine relied on evocation rather than suasion to solve the dilemma. For a universal audience conceived as a collection of individuals who must by themselves come to the faith or strengthen their existing faith, Augustine created a theory and practice of rhetoric focused on a Christian understanding of *imitatio* rather than on instruction. Evocative rhetoric allows the universal audience to confront what Augustine called "natural" and "conventional" signs in order to understand the Christian message, the signs being at once significant of God's will and utterly separate from it. The new rhetoric is in this sense less conventionally directive, although it attempts to evoke an understanding in audiences of the radically strenuous imperative, foreign to traditional rhetoric, that they make use of signs in the exercise of their faith without falling into the sin of ever identifying a mere sign with the will of God.

The implications of this radical transformation of Cicero's philosophical rhetoric that focuses on things into a theological rhetoric that focuses on signs are analyzed in Richard McKeon's "Rhetoric in the Middle Ages" (1942). McKeon's article is also a pivotal explanation of the later decline of rhetoric after enthusiasm for specialized theological disputation helped draw attention and approval away from public oratory. But a paradoxical aspect of this subordination of rhetoric to medieval dialectic was the increasingly rhetorical nature of dialectical method the more it denied the rhetorical dimension of its dialectical disputation—a development that parallels Augustine's magnification of rhetoric's role in appearing to subordinate rhetoric to the soul's struggle with the Christian message. (S. Roberts touched on some of these developments in "Rhetoric and Dialectic" [1957].)

The Humanists: Philosophy as Pedagogy; Rhetoric as Philosophy; Both as Poetry

Many of the classical, Augustinian, and scholastic controversies emerge in Renaissance humanism, but their shapes conform to new cultural contexts and new motivations. In this sense, they are also evident in the work of later scholars trying to determine the meaning of the humanists' goal of eloquence. The modern re-enactment of the humanists' debate over the meaning of that goal can be traced in a series of articles on key humanist texts addressing the problem of relating philosophy and rhetoric, some of the most prominent being Petrarch's letter to Caloria (ca. 1335), Pico Della Mirandola's attack on rhetoric (1485), Ermalao Barbaro's reply (1485), Melanchthon's seconding of Barbaro (1558), Agricola's *Dialectica Libri Tres* (1521), and Petrus Ramus's numerous works (especially the *Scholae in Liberales Artes* [1569]). (Accessible translations of some of these texts are listed in this chapter's References.)

Emphasizing the predominance of the humanists' concern for eloquence, whatever their apparent views on the relation of philosophy and rhetoric, Hannah H. Gray documented their aim to resuscitate Ciceronianism in order to join wisdom and speech ("Renaissance Humanism" [1963]). However, the neo-Ciceronian definition of *eloquence*, typified by Erasmus's claim that true eloquence is "wisdom speaking copiously" (Gray [1963], p. 513) has frequently been considered controversial and problematic. Quirinus Breen, in "Giovanni Pico Della Mirandola on the Conflict of Philosophy and Rhetoric" (1952), pointed out what appears to be serious disagreement between Pico and Melanchthon about the relative status of philosophy and rhetoric. Her interpretation of Pico's letters on the subject follows Melanchthon's opinion that Pico clearly championed philosophy. Breen's conclusion angered J. R. McNally, who identified some of the complexities of Pico's motives and circumstances, as well as the depth of his irony, arguing that the texts have been misread. (See *"Rector et Dux Populi"* [1969].) His analysis of personae and multiple ironies in several humanist texts invites the conclusion that tactics of indirection were chosen by self-conscious authors aware of the temptation toward self-contradition inherent in eloquent defenses of philosophy and carefully argued expositions on the powers of rhetoric. Pico and Barbero in particular seemed to be trying to answer the question of how they could write about eloquence when ordinary debate on the subject tended immediately to label the writer a hypocrite or a dogmatist. The density of their artifice shades their argument into artifact. However, the addition of a poetic dimension to the debate by no means displaces controversy between philosophy and rhetoric with the creation of a work of literature. In fact, Pico and Barbero may have expanded the ramifications of the issue by employing a medium of discourse they assumed to be at one with philosophy and rhetoric. (See Elizabeth Tuve's *Elizabethan and Metaphysical Imagery* [1947] for an argument for the interrelationship of poetic, rhetoric, and philosophy in English Renaissance poetry.) A complementary joining of pedagogy and invention is assumed in Rodolphus Agricola's *De Inventione Dialectica Libri Tres*, which is analyzed in McNally's article, *"Dux Illa Directrixque Artium"* (1966). See Donald Weinstein's useful series of book reviews touching on many of these matters ("In Whose Image and Likeness" [1972]) and Jerrold E. Seigel's *Rhetoric and Philosophy in Renaissance Humanism* (1968).

A particularly thorny hedge of criticism has grown up around Ramus's *Dialecticae* (1555), in which he assumed that dialectic is equivalent to what Aristotle called "scientific demonstration," and that it therefore must be cleansed of the rhetorical confusions that Aristotle and others allegedly tolerated. Ramus's new dialectic seems to have contributed to the modern era's dismissal of rhetoric as the theory and practice of "mere" style and delivery and in the process appears to have collapsed what was left of the Aristotelian distinction between scientific ("apodeictic") discourse and dialectical discourse about probable truths. The operations of invention and arrangement, which some Renaissance theorists cultivate in both rhetoric and dialectic, Ramus restricted to dialectic. Style, memory, and delivery he relegated to rhetoric, while claiming that his new dialectic revealed apodeictic method and truth to anyone interested in studying it. Whether Ramus's perfected dialectic is a revolutionary or debasing combination of rhetoric and philosophy is a matter of significance for modern theories of exposition, many of which draw from a Ramistic heritage.

A basic source for studying Ramus's treatment of philosophy and rhetoric, Walter J. Ong's *Ramus, Method, and the Decay of Dialogue* (1958), argues that Ramus's success as an educator paradoxically contributed to the modern abandonment of logocentric education and in the process discouraged interest in the entire trivium: rhetoric, logic, and the conception of grammar that led to minute "grammatical" analyses of the meaning and structure of individual utterances.

However, in *Renaissance Concepts of Method* (1960), Neal W. Gilbert described the disputes over Ramus's ideas as though they were only artificial conflicts between philosophers and pedagogues. Ramus's famous reduction of philosophical, dialectical, and rhetorical method to a single law—that the first "in nature" should come first and the things less clear afterward—is in one sense simply a pedagogical rule of thumb for presenting philosophical and scientific discoveries to students. If opposing polemicists had recognized this fact, no conflict might have arisen. On the other hand, Gilbert admitted, Ramus's rule was a philosophical assertion about the ordering of all knowledge and so could not be tolerated as a "merely rhetorical" guideline. Gilbert concluded that had the traditionalists and the revolutionary Ramists possessed the methodology we now call "scientific," they could have clearly distinguished between arts of communication and arts of discovery and had access to ways of removing falsehoods from the era's "body of knowledge" (pp. 222–23). However, the depth to which Gilbert went to discover the cause of Ramus's influence indicates how deeply the controversy is involved in problems endemic to several basic intellectual issues, problems the empirical sciences do not necessarily resolve. (See especially Gilbert's Part II.) Lisa Jardine (*Francis Bacon* [1974]) observed that many of the roots of modern science existed hundreds of years before the seventeenth century's "discovery" of empirical, inductive inquiry, but that even Bacon's theories of rhetoric, dialectic, and science cannot divorce themselves from a powerful, traditional tendency to intermingle poetry, rhetoric, dialectic, and apodeictic.

The case of Bacon is pivotal for the study of these issues, since he absorbed so much of the Renaissance controversy over rhetoric and philosophy into his ingenious program for a "New Organon"—a complete renovation of Aristotle's *Organon* and of the *Rhetoric*. Bacon's *Advancement of Learning* (1605) proclaimed the importance of this undertaking, and the inner workings of his program are set out in works such as the *Novum Organum* (1620) and the later books of the *Advancement*. As Bacon worked to create excitement and hope in a new enterprise of useful, experimental science, he attempted to create a new theory and practice of communication to free learning of its traditional dependence on pre-existent knowledge and to establish a heuristic "machine" that forces the new scientist away from error. As he tried to persuade new learners to follow new methods, without sacrificing philosophy's devotion to truth, he took extraordinary measures to guard the new science from those whose inability to learn for themselves would damage its objectivity. To orchestrate such a host of cross-purposes, each one setting some aspect of philosophy and rhetoric at odds, Bacon attempted in each work to make and practice a theory of discourse that would escape self-contradiction.

James Stephens outlined a few of these problems in *Francis Bacon and the*

Style of Science (1975), a valuable introduction to Bacon's theories of inquiry and communication, especially his attempt to establish (1) a disjunctive, aphoristic discourse of observations to produce independent, scientific thinking; (2) a literature and rhetoric that conceal, reveal, and transform scientific discoveries; and (3) a general theory of rhetorical presentation at once Machiavellian and open-spirited. Broader studies of Bacon that devote space to these matters are by Brian Vickers (*Francis Bacon and Renaissance Prose* [1968]) and Karl R. Wallace (*Francis Bacon on Communication and Rhetoric* [1943]). Bacon's own *New Atlantis* (1626) fictionalizes the problem of revealing a new, greatly beneficial science without exposing that science to an unenlightened public's damaging scrutiny.

Other works about Bacon have explored these subjects mostly on the level of style: the most grammatical of the five traditional "stages" of rhetorical composition and in some sense the most poetical. (For the long-established precedents that associate grammar and poetic, see McKeon's "Rhetoric in the Middle Ages" [1942].) Again, concentration on the poetic dimension of Bacon's work is not necessarily an abandonment or even subordination of philosophical and rhetorical issues. Some of the most revealing literature on the tension between philosophy and rhetoric is available in studies of the late sixteenth- and seventeenth-century debate over the proper style for harmonizing language and thought, form and subject matter. See, for example, Stanley E. Fish's examination of Bacon's prose (*Self-Consuming Artifacts* [1972]) and *The Senecan Amble* by George Williamson (1951).

The Modern Era: The Emergence of New Rhetorics Amidst Science and Religion

The great irony of the Baconian legacy is that the founders of the Royal Society, which was to be the institution of the new science, are openly contemptuous of rhetoric. Despite some notable exceptions, their successors in science and philosophy are increasingly dominated by ideals of empirical, inductive investigation and rigorous skepticism toward uses of language that do not mirror that method of investigation. As Garard A. Hauser reminded us in "Empiricism, Description, and the New Rhetoric" (1972), however, the new emphasis on empirical (what Aristotle called "non-artistic") criteria for proof is accompanied in the eighteenth century by the resurgence of a characteristically rhetorical interest in understanding and appealing to the passions.

The complex results of that parallel development on major rhetorical theorists, George Campbell, for example, have been variously interpreted. Wilbur S. Howell concluded that Locke's arguments for the natural, compelling correspondence of ideas and "the reality of things" triumphs in several eighteenth-century works, including Campbell's *Philosophy of Rhetoric* (1776). (See Howell's "John Locke and the New Rhetoric" [1967].) Nevertheless, Joseph Priestley's discussion of method in Part 2 of the *Course of Lectures on Oratory and*

Criticism (1777) pointed out the potential for concealment or complex double purposes in inductive and deductive methods of scientific discourse. Moreover, Lloyd F. Bitzer's "A Re-evaluation of Campbell's Doctrine of Evidence" (1960) draws attention to Campbell's own resistance to Locke's "natural" objectivity, especially the consequences for rhetoric of a radical skepticism that is the unacknowledged consequence of Locke's effort to combat religious dogmatism in *An Essay Concerning Human Understanding* (1690). Part of the background for Bitzer's argument is Otis M. Walter's article noting a continuity in the progression from Descartes's program of radical doubt, through Locke's attack on preconceived ideas, and then to Hume's extension of the implications of radical skepticism, which undermines the grounds for Locke's residual faith in a natural correspondence between ideas, sensations, and the natural reality of things. (See Walter's "Descartes on Reasoning" [1951].) Walter argued that Descartes and Locke, despite their obvious differences, endorsed a way of using language that ultimately removes the ground for discussing convictions and beliefs that are neither scientific nor purely intuitional or subjective. Bitzer tried to show that George Campbell met this problem three ways: (1) by constructing a rhetoric heavily reliant on figures and tropes, rather than demonstrative proofs, for the sake of producing "lively and glowing ideas" that dominate the senses and their derivative ideas; (2) by extending Hume's notions of a shared human sympathy so that sympathy derives from common-sense morality rather than eloquence per se; and (3) by invoking the criterion of common sense, set out in Thomas Reid's *Enquiry into the Human Mind on the Principles of Common Sense* (1764), as a general basis for proof when the modern, scientific philosophy is incapable of judgment.

A Humean critique of Campbell, concluding that the *Philosophy of Rhetoric* fails to distinguish rhetoric from the modern paradigm of scientific reasoning, has been presented by Clarence W. Edney ("Campbell's Theory of Logical Truth" [1948]). The broader issue in assessing a theory like Campbell's— whether any modern theory of rhetoric distinct from science is possible—is the subject of Vico's famous analysis of the foundations of Cartesian science. *On the Study Methods of Our Time* (1709) answers Descartes with a defense of the essential importance of rhetorical copiousness. Whereas systematic doubt fragments the ground of discourse, only the rhetoric of copiousness unifies, orders and even creates cultural history by means of a knowledge of verisimilitudes. (See James D. Schaeffer, "Vico's Rhetorical Model of the Mind" [1981].)

One of the most penetrating studies of Locke's profoundly unsettling influence on the theory and practice of rhetoric is Perry Miller's examination of the implications of Locke's theory of sensations for any notion that ideas must have a basis in something other than sensation ("Edwards, Locke, and the Rhetoric of Sensation" [1950]). Miller first explained Berkeley's extension of Locke's implicit skepticism as Berkeley's effort to affirm a definite, theological perspective by altogether denying the reality of the material world. To create a rhetoric that avoided these extremes and yet was both Lockean and theological, Jonathan

Edwards worked out a mode of preaching to allow words to convey "sensible concepts" about the Christian message, a preaching that Miller asserted helped stimulate (and perhaps wreck) New England's Great Awakening.

The most revealing practical evidence of the interaction of modern rhetoric and science is Descartes's own exploitation of the rhetorical power inherent in the radical skepticism of the *Discourse on Method* (1637). The *Discourse* is a brilliant example of how a sustained, high-minded polemic—admitting to concealing key points of Descartes's method while claiming to confine itself to the clearest facts of his personal enlightenment—can create the conviction that Descartes has purified his treatise of all rhetoric.

In the early nineteenth century, the problem of relating philosophy and rhetoric on an explicit theoretical level emerges in the work of Kant, Whately, and Kierkegaard and takes forms that are often parodied in recent inquiries and debates. Samuel Ijsseling briefly reviewed the thoroughgoing rejection of rhetoric in Kant's *Critique of Judgment* (1790). (See *Rhetoric and Philosophy in Conflict* [1976], Chapter 12.) For Kant, the rules, preaching, and suasion of rhetoric stand totally opposed to both critical thought and the liberating art of poetry; rhetoric contradicts the meaning of the Enlightenment, which was supposed to have released human beings once and for all from "tutelage." But Kant's sundering of the understanding from any prospect of true certainty imposes the monumental task of constructing a rhetoric for making judgments convincing. Thus the *Critique of Judgment* imposes upon itself the necessity of becoming a rhetorical *tour de force*, the general Kantian project being to convince the understanding that it can be satisfied in knowing a priori truths wholly distinct from what had been conventionally understood to be more or less certain.

Kierkegaard also found conventional ideas about persuasion intolerable, because they deny audiences true freedom of choice (*Concluding Unscientific Post-Script to the Philosophical Fragments* [1846]); but unlike Kant he did not hesitate to advocate a form of Augustine's radically paradoxical theological rhetoric, using "indirect communication" and "edifying discourse" to obliterate rhetorical and poetic illusions with an apprehension of one's own relation to Christian truth and the necessity of an existential choice that renders all forms of persuasion irrelevant. (Raymond E. Anderson discussed some of these matters in "Kierkegaard's Theory of Communication" [1963].)

Richard Whately, who wrote the modern age's most elegant neo-Aristotelian rhetoric, reviewed many of the commonplaces in the old debate (*Elements of Rhetoric* [1828], revised seventh edition published in 1846). But the greater import of that work is its tendency to separate completely the logic of scientific inquiry from the procedures of rhetorical communication. (See D. Ehninger's introduction to the 1963 re-issue of *The Elements*.) Whately's abdication of rhetoric's earlier interest in science would not necessarily have diminished the philosophical seriousness of his work in the eyes of twentieth-century theorists, had he not failed to pursue the philosophical implications of rhetorical invention. His neo-Aristotelian *via media* between scientific-philosophical skepticism and religious intuitionism seems to be, according to a critic such as I. A. Richards, mere ornament for a handbook of prudential rules that must give way to a modern, comprehensive investigation of the sentence-level causes of verbal understanding and misunderstanding (*The Philosophy of Rhetoric* [1936]).

Like Whately, Kant and Kierkegaard have provoked strong reactions that variously extend and combine a disdain for rhetoric with a conscious or unconscious desire to construct a theory of discourse so profound it will be accepted as universal. The most prominent representative of both modes in combination is Nietzsche's *The Will to Power* (1895), which discloses the paradoxical extremes of a theory of rhetoric based both on absolute skepticism and an equally radical "will to truth." In *Rhetoric and Philosophy in Conflict* (1976), Samuel Ijsseling analyzed this strange rebirth and metamorphosis of sophistic, Gorgian rhetoric: "According to Nietzsche, there can be no philosophy other than rhetorical philosophy, since the philosopher 'decrees' the truth. The philosopher should recognize this, however, and the fact that he refuses to do so constitutes precisely the decadence of philosophy" (p. 108). The Nietzschean goal of exercising a muscular nihilism that somehow creates truth by fiat finds its converse in theories of language that assume thought and language are ultimately fused by social history, perhaps by the engine of Marxism. (See Vygotsky's *Thought and Language* [1962], Chapter 4.)

The leading modern argument for the power of language itself to tyrannize over its users by dictating reality, even over those who declare that they are conscious of and hence to some degree in control of language's power, resides in the post-*Tractatus* work of Ludwig Wittgenstein, especially *Philosophical Investigations* (1953). But some readers allege that Wittgenstein himself offered a tyrannical solution that is at once radically scientific and rhetorical: the replacement of the conceptual traps of rhetoric, grammar, and logic with silence, or an "ordinary language" we cannot truly talk about. (See Stanley Rosen's *Nihilism* [1969].)

Kenneth Burke, more than any other twentieth-century theorist of rhetoric, absorbed and confronted Nietzschean and Marxist methods and assumptions in his attempt to transcend what he conceived to be a logomachy between philosophy and rhetoric. Burke observed, lamented, and reveled in rhetoric's power "to prove opposites" for the sake of sheer advantage, social revolution, and comic entertainment. But the alchemy in Burke's proving of opposites is supposed to show philosophy and rhetoric transformed into each other and back again so that a philosophical and even religious dimension can be restored to rhetoric, saving it from trivialization at the hands of science, egocentricity, and Marxism, and revealing the inroads rhetoric makes into philosophy and religion. (See Burke's Introduction to *A Grammar of Motives* [1945] and the play of philosophy and rhetoric as opposites as well as congruent perspectives in "The Range of Rhetoric," a chapter in *A Rhetoric of Motives* [1950].) Whether Burke's system is ultimately sophistic, Nietzschean, or Marxist, despite the mildness of his stated goals; whether it is essentially an extension of Aristotelian rhetoric, as he sometimes claimed (see Laura Holland's *Counterpoint* [1959]); or whether his project resolves for good the logomachy between philosophy and rhetoric—all are questions pursued in William Rueckert's collection *Critical Responses to Kenneth Burke, 1924–1966* (1969). The fact that "dramatism" is Burke's optic on these matters implies a possible transvaluation of all such issues into the realm of the poetic and hence the subordination of rhetoric and philosophy—or their concealment—in a theory of man as a symbol-making animal. For one of Burke's difficult, enigmatic treatments of the possibility of a dominant poetic in his work, see "Rhetoric, Poetics, and Philosophy" (1978).

Burke's attempts to reconcile and yet celebrate the differences between philosophy and rhetoric, like Nietzsche's absolutist nihilism and radically ambiguous fusion of rhetoric and philosophy, is a reaction to the total separation of philosophy and rhetoric supposedly exemplified by Kant. Positivists like Bertrand Russell, on the other hand, responded to the Kantian heritage by assuming that his distinction does not go far enough, that his concept of philosophy is essentially subjective, and that he cannot give critical attention to the search for absolute, scientific certainty. However, Russell's adamant suppression of non-scientific philosophy is accompanied by a plethora of presuppositions his empiricism and skepticism do not seem capable of substantiating. The paradoxes arising from his attempts to establish credible arguments, given the degree of his skepticism and his remarkable eagerness to make evaluative pronouncements, are explored by Wayne Booth in *Modern Dogma and the Rhetoric of Assent* (1974). *The Limits of Analysis* (1980), Stanley Rosen's critique of modern logical positivism, is in part an examination of a philosophical rhetoric like Russell's that absolutely denies its own existence.

A leading phenomenologist, Maurice Merleau-Ponty, implicitly condemned Kant's attitude toward rhetoric for a somewhat different reason: Kant allegedly deprived philosophical language of any prospect of revealing truth and hence denied the philosopher any real desire for moving in or toward truth. The phenomenological solution to the Kantian dilemma is in some ways akin to those found in Kierkegaard and Nietzsche: a greatly heightened emphasis on the effects of performance on conviction. Truth is not remote or pre-existing but resident in the act of risking oneself. An utterance, for example, is to be "validated by being performed." "We take our fate in our hands" both by reflection on our history and by "a violent act . . . on which we stake our life" (Merleau-Ponty, "What is Phenomenology" [1969], p. 29). In this spirit, the very manifestation or performance of philosophy creates "being," even though or rather because "it remains faithful to its intention, never knowing where it is going" in revealing "the mystery of the world and of reason" (p. 30). Moderated versions of these ideas can be found in Michael Polanyi's *Personal Knowledge* (1958), a major influence on Wayne Booth's *Modern Dogma and the Rhetoric of Assent* (1974) and the focus of a spirited discussion of rhetorical theory in Samuel D. Watson's "Michael Polanyi and the Recovery of Rhetoric" (1973).

Recent, highly influential attempts to join philosophy and rhetoric by means of a more conventional framework—jurisprudence—do not necessarily elude the controlling influence of phenomenology or positivism. Two prominent examples of this trend are *The New Rhetoric* by Chaim Perelman and L. Olbrechts-Tyteca (first published 1958, first English translation 1969) and Stephen Toulmin's *Uses of Argument* (1958). (The Johannesen bibliography, *Contemporary Theories of Rhetoric* [1971], is particularly helpful regarding Perelman, Toulmin, Burke, Weaver, and Richards.) Wayne Brockriede and Douglas Ehninger have endorsed and explicated Toulmin's effort to simplify and correct many applications of mathematically oriented modern logic ("Toulmin on Argument" [1960]), whereas Peter T. Manicas criticized his system for being more rigidly analytical and arbitrary than the concept of argument it seeks to replace. (See Manicas's "On Toulmin's Contribution to Logic and Argumentation" [1971].)

Useful introductions to Perelman are "The Philosophical Basis of Chaim Perelman's Theory of Rhetoric" by Ray D. Dearin (1969), "Rhetoric and Its Rehabilitation in Contemporary Philosophy" by Vasile Florescue (1970), and "Argumentation and Philosophical Clarification" by Nathan Rotenstreich (1972). The most accessible introduction to Perelman's views is his own article, "The New Rhetoric" (1970), with extensive footnotes. There he separated himself not only from what he considered to be the Cartesian reduction of philosophy to the tyranny of mere mathematics but also from the "subjective" tendencies of modern existentialism, presumably including aspects of phenomenologies like Merleau-Ponty's. But Perelman's stress on continuous, open-ended argumentation, which fundamentally rejects "mechanical" Cartesian logic as well as subjectivism, also relies on the finality of willful acts and an ideally rational, "universal" audience that holds facts and truths unquestionably in common, hence making absolutely valid agreement seem possible. (See "Perelman's Universal Audience" [1978] by John W. Ray.) Perelman's analysis of argumentative "loci," or topics, is equally ambiguous to the extent that his project categorizes scientifically the prevailing topics of persuasion and argument and analyzes them as though they were fundamentally contingent. (See Perelman's "New Rhetoric," p. 286.) His essay "Rhetoric and Philosophy" (1968) draws attention to the affinity between this position and Kant's anchoring of practical reason in a deliberate, categorical imperative rather than conformity to rationality per se: "the truth of the rules of action" (p. 22). Thus on the one hand, Samuel Watson could allege that the New Rhetoric fails to shed Perelman's old positivist clothes, and on the other hand, a supporter of the New Rhetoric such as Henry Johnstone could chafe at Perelman's apparent satisfaction with consensus on what Johnstone called non-philosophical, even "trivial," issues not related to the pursuit of absolute certainty.

Many of Johnstone's own arguments for a New Rhetoric have been assembled in his *Validity and Rhetoric in Philosophical Argument* [1978]. The unstable bonding of positivistic and phenomenological-existentialist philosophy that tends to occur in modern attempts to fuse rhetoric and philosophy is evident in the collection's final essay, "The Philosophical Basis of Rhetoric." In a searching analysis of all of Johnstone's writings, Walter M. Carleton claimed that Johnstone joined philosophy and rhetoric by assuming that philosophy is a particular form of rhetoric (Carleton, "Colloquy/Theory Transformation in Communication" [1975]).

For examples of studies akin to phenomenological-rhetorical theories like those of Perelman but that reveal a deeper affinity for sophistic rhetoric than Perelman's ostensibly judicial perspective, see Robert L. Scott's "On Viewing Rhetoric as Epistemic" (1967), Harold Zyskind's "Some Philosophical Strands in Popular Rhetoric" (1970), Bruce E. Gronbeck's "Gorgias on Rhetoric and Poetic" (1972), Walter Carleton's "What Is Rhetorical Knowledge?" (1978), and Sharon Crowley's "Of Gorgias and Grammatology" (1979). Conversely, Ernesto Grassi's "Rhetoric and Philosophy" (1976) demonstates how easily a phenomenological orientation can convert into a quasi-religious conception of rhetoric's function, as though rhetoric were identical to prophesy, revelation, and the basis of all proofs.

In this context of high hopes for a synthesis of philosophy and rhetoric, followed by extremely unstable realizations of those hopes in theories of discourse, some rhetorical theorists have found a speech-act theory of language especially appealing. J. L. Austin's key text, *How to Do Things with Words* (1962), and John R. Searle's *Speech Acts* (1969) are to some degree projects for restoring a rhetoric to positivism and ordinary language analysis and at the same time forcing analytic rigor on existential or religious notions of "authentic" expression. Thus Austin began by assuming that all utterances are precise references, clear instrumentalities, or immediately self-fulfilling expressions like "I implore you," but he soon began to mix categories. (See John Stewart's "J. L. Austin's Speech Act Analysis" [1973].) However, such theories impose severe limitations on themselves by relying upon sentence-level analysis. More important, they do not account for a disharmony between their own strongly analytic biases and their emphasis on the effective meaning of discourse. (See Konstantin Kolenda's "Speech Acts and Truth" [1971].)

New aspirations to join rhetoric and philosophy systematically, often for the purpose of restoring rhetoric's stature, are evident in recent discussions of "metarhetoric," although the many meanings of *meta* (after, beyond, among, behind) introduce new problems of definition often not taken into account. For James J. Murphy ("The Metarhetorics of Plato, Augustine, and McLuhan" [1971]), metarhetoric relates to rhetoric much as Aristotle's metaphysics relates to physics or epistemology to "the science of method and grounds of knowledge" (p. 201). It is supposedly a study of first principles, but Murphy did not seem aware of how the pattern of discussion in Aristotelian dialectic, with affinities for both to philosophy and rhetoric, carries out a similar function. Conversely, Maurice Natanson ("Rhetoric and Philosophical Argumentation" [1962]) posited a radically phenomenological, metarhetorical foundation in the philosopher's self, especially his attempt "to uncover something about himself" (p. 152) by considering his "primordial choice of styles of philosophizing," which can be communicated only by means of a Kierkegaardian "indirect argumentation" emanating from a philosophical rhetoric of "involvement" with truth (p. 156). Martin Steinmann's influential essay "Rhetorical Research" (1967) insists that metarhetorical theory be a projection of the sciences of linguistics and behavioral psychology into the deepest source of linguistic meaning, where more ordinary grounds of rhetorical meaning are presumably inconceivable. For Otis M. Walter, however, the true metarhetoric rises out of the more accessible assumptions that come to light only in a careful study of key works in the history of rhetoric ("On Views of Rhetoric, Whether Conservative or Progressive" [1963]). Richard Ohmann adopted a similar position in regard to the history of the New Rhetoric ("In Lieu of a New Rhetoric" [1964]), as did Kenneth Burke in "Rhetoric—Old and New" (1967) and W. S. Howell in "Renaissance Rhetoric and Modern Rhetoric" (1958). The text-centered, metarhetorical criticism of Plato by Richard Weaver in *The Ethics of Rhetoric* (1953) is part of a larger body of work by Weaver receiving renewed attention in recent analyses by Donald P. Cushman and Gerard A. Hauser ("Weaver's Rhetorical Theory" [1973]) and John Bliese ("Richard Weaver's Axiology of Argument" [1979]).

By far the most comprehensive metarhetorical approach to the history and theory of rhetoric and its relation to philosophy has been developed by Richard McKeon, whose numerous essays on these issues are catalogued in Booth's *Modern Dogma and the Rhetoric of Assent* and in the *Philosopher's Index* (1978). (See "McKeon's Philosophy of Communication" [1973] by G.A. Hauser and D. P. Cushman.) McKeon offered relatively accessible overviews of some of his thinking in "The Uses of Rhetoric in a Technological Age" (1971) and "Creativity and the Commonplace" (1973). These writings attempt to reopen consideration of Aristotle's articulation of philosophical demonstration, dialectic, and rhetoric and to establish the history of Aristotle's metamorphosis in later ages. Hauser and Cushman (1973) claimed that McKeon revised Aristotle so that Aristotelian rhetoric would become the architectonic principle for all sciences (p. 221). Whatever the case, the gradual rediscovery of the fertile complexity of Aristotle's conception of dialectic as a mediating dimension of discourse, in some sense neither absolutely philosophical nor absolutely rhetorical, bodes well for the recovery of a sense of bearing in matters of rhetorical theory. (See Richard Burke's "Rhetoric, Dialectic, and Force" [1974] and some of the work of Gilbert Ryle, such as "Formal and Informal Logic" [1954].)

Running parallel to contemporary interest in metarhetoric is the desire among teachers and researchers in composition to substantiate their pedagogy with a powerful theory of discourse. However, the traditionally pedagogical orientation of laborers in the field of composition has tended to bend almost all theoretical endeavors toward immediate application in the classroom. The result is often a conflation of theory and practice that obscures the problematic relationship not only between inquiry and presentation but also between philosophy and rhetoric. Paradoxically, the aspiration of the dedicated pedagogue to move to a theory of composition beyond or behind the daily practice of teaching is often expressed by embracing the method and subject matter of a specialized science like linguistics or a quasi-religious conception of human creativity. In other cases, rhetoric becomes a meta-science like metaphysics and so presumes to dominate all methods and subject matters. A concern for pedagogy then either disappears or utterly dominates the result. Either outcome leads its champions to dismiss the long tradition of often fruitful controversy over the proper relation between philosophy and rhetoric.

Since that tradition helps to raise broader, newly insistent questions relevant to composition—concerning, for example, the relation of the entire trivium to the study and practice of the sciences—contemporary research in composition has unfortunately denied itself the nurture of its own past. Even a work as old and apparently remote as John of Salisbury's *Metalogican* (1159), for example, is of great potential value for contemporary theory and pedagogy of composition, because its learned, humorous polemic is an attack on two extreme positions that are common today: the impatient conviction that one must seize upon scientific or religious principles while neglecting the fundamental studies of grammar, logic, and rhetoric; and the notion that one should forever study and teach only a narrowly defined trivium, even though such a fixation dulls and limits the intelligence that has no other aspirations.

E. D. Hirsch's recent definition of grammatical readability (*The Philosophy of Composition* [1977]) takes a more moderate position by linking considerations of grammar with those of rhetoric and logic, thus returning to the study of the trivium to understand readability in different kinds of specialized and non-specialized discourse. Many specialists in composition have objected to Hirsch's theory because of its apparent lack of empirical verifiability or explicit enthusiasm for creative expression or direct application to pedagogy. But the very controversy that the book has generated has raised a host of questions concerning the importance of the trivium and the connections between rhetoric, science, and philosophy itself. These are issues we should seek to understand.

References

Agricola, Rodolphus. *De Inventione Dialectica Libri Tres*. See McNally.

Anderson, Raymond E. "Kierkegaard's Theory of Communication." *Speech Mon*, 30 (1963), 1–14.

Aristotle. *The "Rhetoric" of Aristotle*. Ed. and trans. Lane Cooper. New York: Appleton-Century-Crofts, 1932.

———. *The Works of Aristotle*. 12 vols. Ed. W. D. Ross. Oxford: Clarendon, 1959.

Arnhart, Larry. *Aristotle on Political Reasoning: A Commentary on the "Rhetoric."* Dekalb: Northern Illinois University Press, 1981.

Augustine. *The Works of Aurelius Augustine*. 15 vols. Ed. and trans. M. Dods. Edinburgh: T and T Clark, 1871–1883.

Austin, J. L. *How to Do Things with Words*. Cambridge, Mass.: Harvard University Press, 1962.

Bacon, Francis. *The Works of Francis Bacon*. 14 vols. Ed. James Spedding. New York: Garrett, 1968.

Baldwin, C. S. *Ancient Rhetoric and Poetic*. New York: Macmillan, 1924.

———. *Medieval Rhetoric and Poetic*. New York: Macmillan, 1928.

———. *Renaissance Literary Theory and Practice: Classicism in the Rhetoric and Poetic of Italy, France, and England, 1400–1600*. Ed. D. L. Clark. New York: Columbia University Press, 1939.

Barbaro, Ermolao. "E. Barbaro to Giovanni Pico della Mirandola." See Breen.

Barnes, Jonathan. *The Presocratic Philosophers*. 2 vols. London: Routledge, Kegan Paul, 1979.

Bird, Otto. "The Re-Discovery of the Topics." *Mind*, NS 70 (1961), 534–39.

———. "The Tradition of the Logical Topics: Aristotle to Ockham." *JHI*, 23 (1962), 307–23.

Bitzer, Lloyd F. "A Re-Evaluation of Campbell's Doctrine of Evidence." *QJS*, 46 (1960), 135–40.

Black, Edwin. "Plato's View of Rhetoric." *QJS*, 44 (1958), 361–74.

Bliese, John R. E. "Richard Weaver's Axiology of Argument." *SSpCJ*, 44 (1979), 275–88.

Booth, Wayne. *Modern Dogma and the Rhetoric of Assent*. Notre Dame, Ind.: University of Notre Dame Press, 1974.

Breen, Quirinus. "Giovanni Pico Della Mirandola on the Conflict of Philosophy and Rhetoric." *JHI*, 13 (1952), 384–426. (Includes translations of letters by Pico della Mirandola [1485], E. Barbaro [1485], and P. Melanthon [1558].)

Brockriede, Wayne, and Ehninger, Douglas. "Toulmin on Argument." *QJS*, 46 (1960), 44–53.

Burger, Ronna. *Plato's "Phaedrus": A Defense of a Philosophic Art of Writing*. University: University of Alabama Press, 1980.

Burke, Kenneth. *A Grammar of Motives*. New York: Prentice-Hall, 1945.

———. *A Rhetoric of Motives*. New York: Prentice-Hall, 1950.

———. "Rhetoric—Old and New." *J Gen Ed*, 5 (1951), 202–9. Also in *New Rhetorics*. Ed. Martin Steinmann. New York: Scribner, 1967, pp. 59–76.

———. "Rhetoric, Poetics, and Philosophy." In *Rhetoric, Philosophy and Literature: An Exploration*. Ed. Don M. Burks. West Lafayette, Ind.: Purdue University Press, 1978, pp. 15–33.

Burke, Richard J. "Aristotle on the Limits of Argument." *Phil Phenomenol Res*, 27 (1967), 386–400.

———. "Rhetoric, Dialectic, and Force." *Phil Rhet*, 7 (1974) 154–65.

Campbell, George. *The Philosophy of Rhetoric*. Ed. Lloyd F. Bitzer. Carbondale: Southern Illinois University Press, 1963.

Carleton, Walter M. "Colloquy/Theory Transformation in Communication: The Case of Henry Johnstone." *QJS*, 61 (1975), 76–88.

———. "What is Rhetorical Knowledge? A Response to Farrell—And More." *QJS*, 64 (1978), 313–28.

Cicero. *The Basic Works*. Ed. Moses Hadas. New York: Modern Library, 1951.

———. *Rhetorica ad Herennium*. Trans. Harry Caplan. Cambridge, Mass.: Harvard University Press (Loeb Classical Library), 1954.

———. *De Oratore*. 2 vols. Trans. E. W. Sutton and H. Rackham. Cambridge, Mass.: Harvard University Press (Loeb Classical Library), 1959.

Colish, Marcia L. "St. Augustine's Rhetoric of Silence Revisited." *Augustin Stud*, 9 (1978), 15–24.

Cope, Edward M. *The "Rhetoric" of Aristotle with Commentary*. 3 vols. Ed. John E. Sandys. Cambridge: Cambridge University Press, 1877.

Corbett, E.P.J. *Classical Rhetoric for the Modern Student*. New York: Oxford, 1971.

Crowley, Sharon. "Of Gorgias and Grammatology." *CCC*, 30 (1979), 275–84.

Cushman, Donald P., and G. A. Hauser. "Weaver's Rhetorical Theory: Axiology and Adjustment of Belief, Invention, and Judgment." *QJS*, 59 (1973), 319–29.

Dearin, Ray D. "The Philosophical Basis of Chaim Perelman's Theory of Rhetoric." *QJS*, 55 (1969), 213–24.

Descartes, René. *The Philosophical Works of Descartes*. 2 vols. Trans. E. S. Haldane and G.R.T. Ross. Cambridge: Cambridge University Press, 1931.

"Dialectic." *The Great Ideas: A Syntopicon of the Great Books of the Western World*. 2 vols. Eds. Mortimer J. Adler and William Gorman. Chicago: Encyclopaedia Britannica, 1971, Vol. 1, 345–57.

Dilman, Ilham. *Morality and the Inner Life: A Study of Plato's Gorgias*. London: Macmillan, 1979.

Duhamel, P. Albert. "The Function of Rhetoric as Effective Expression." *JHI*, 10 (1949), 344–56.

Edney, Clarence W. "Campbell's Theory of Logical Truth." *Speech Mon*, 15 (1948), 19–38.

Ehninger, Douglas. "On Systems of Rhetoric." *Phil Rhet*, 1 (1968), 131–43.

Evans, J.D.G. *Aristotle's Concept of Dialectic*. Cambridge: Cambridge University Press, 1977.

Fish, Stanley E. *Self-Consuming Artifacts: The Experience of Seventeenth-Century Literature*. Berkeley: University of California Press, 1972.

Florescue, Vasile. "Rhetoric and Its Rehabilitation in Contemporary Philosophy." Trans. Barbara Johnstone. *Phil Rhet*, 3 (1970), 193–224.

Fortenbaugh, William W. "Aristotle's *Rhetoric* on Emotions." *Arch Gesch Phil*, 52 (1970), 40–70.

Fortin, Ernest L. "Augustine and the Problem of Christian Rhetoric." *Augustin Stud*, 5 (1974), 85–100.

Freeman, K. *Ancilla to the Pre-Socratic Philosophers*. Oxford: Basil Blackwell, 1956.

Gilbert, Neal W. *Renaissance Concepts of Method*. New York: Columbia University Press, 1960.

Grassi, Ernesto. "Rhetoric and Philosophy." *Phil Rhet*, 9 (1976), 200–216.

Gray, Hannah H. "Renaissance Humanism: The Pursuit of Eloquence." *JHI*, 24 (1963), 497–514.

Grimaldi, William M. A. *Studies in the Philosophy of Aristotle's "Rhetoric."* Hermes-Einzelschriften No. 25. Wiesbaden: Franz Steiner Verlag, 1972.

Gronbeck, Bruce E. "Gorgias on Rhetoric and Poetic: A Rehabilitation." *SSpCJ*, 38 (1972), 27–38.

Hauser, G. A. "Empiricism, Description, and the New Rhetoric." *Phil Rhet*, 5 (1972), 24–44.

———, and D. P. Cushman. "McKeon's Philosophy of Communication." *Phil Rhet*, 6 (1973), 211–34.

Hill, F. "The Amorality of Aristotle's *Rhetoric*," *Greek, Rom & Byz Studies*, 22 (1981), 133–47.

Hirsch, E. D. *The Philosophy of Composition*. Chicago: University of Chicago Press, 1977.

Holland, Laura V. *Counterpoint: Kenneth Burke and Aristotle's Theories of Rhetoric*. New York: Philosophical Library, 1959.

Howell, Wilbur S. *Logic and Rhetoric in England, 1500–1700*. Princeton, N.J.: Princeton University Press, 1956.

―――. "Renaissance Rhetoric and Modern Rhetoric: A Study in Change." In *The Rhetorical Idiom*. Ed. D. C. Bryant. Ithaca, N.Y.: Cornell University Press, 1958, pp. 53–70.

―――. "John Locke and the New Rhetoric." *QJS*, 53 (1967), 319–33.

―――. *Eighteenth-Century British Logic and Rhetoric*. Princeton, N.J.: Princeton University Press, 1971.

Ijsseling, Samuel. *Rhetoric and Philosophy in Conflict*. The Hague: Martinus Nijhoff, 1976.

Isocrates. *Isocrates*. 3 vols. Trans. George Nolin. Cambridge, Mass.: Harvard University Press, 1954–1956.

Jaeger, Werner. *Paideia: The Ideals of Greek Culture*. 3 vols. Trans. Gilbert Highet. New York: Oxford University Press, 1954–1961.

Jardine, Lisa. *Francis Bacon: Discovery and the Art of Discourse*. Cambridge: Cambridge University Press, 1974.

Johannesen, R. L., ed. *Contemporary Theories of Rhetoric: Selected Readings*. New York: Harper, Row, 1971.

John of Salisbury. *Metalogicon*. Trans. Daniel D. McGarry. Berkeley: University of California Press, 1955. (MS completed in 1159).

Johnson, W. R. "Isocrates Flowering: The Rhetoric of Augustine." *Phil Rhet*, 9 (1976), 217–31.

Johnstone, Henry W. *Validity and Rhetoric in Philosophical Argument: An Outlook in Transition*. University Park, Pa.: Dialogue, 1978.

―――, and Maurice Natanson, eds. *Philosophy, Rhetoric, and Argumentation*. University Park: Pennsylvania State University Press, 1965.

Kant, Immanuel. *The Critique of Judgment*. Ed. and trans. James C. Meredith. Oxford: Clarendon, 1953.

Kapp, Ernst. *Greek Foundations of Traditional Logic*. New York: Columbia University Press, 1942.

Kennedy, George. *The Art of Persuasion in Greece*. London: Routledge, Kegan Paul, 1963.

―――. *The Art of Rhetoric in the Roman World, 300 B.C.–A.D. 300*. London: Oxford University Press, 1973.

Kereferd, George B. *The Sophistic Movement*. London: Cambridge University Press, 1981.

Kierkegaard, Soren. *Concluding Unscientific Post-Script to the Philosophical Fragments*. Trans. David F. Swenson and Walter Lowrie. Princeton, N.J.: Princeton University Press, 1944.

Kinneavy, James. *A Theory of Discourse: The Aims of Discourse*. New York: Norton, 1971.

Kolenda, Konstantin. "Speech Acts and Truth." *Phil Rhet*, 4 (1971), 230–41.

Lechner, Jean M., Sr. *Renaissance Concepts of the Commonplaces*. New York: Pageant, 1962.

Leff, Michael C. "Re-interpreting Plato's *Phaedrus.*" *QJS*, 57 (1971), 344–46.

Lienhard, Joseph T. "A Note on the Meaning of *Pisteis* in Aristotle's *Rhetoric.*" *Am J Philol*, 87 (1966), 446–54.

Locke, John. *An Essay Concerning Human Understanding.* Peter H. Nidditch, ed. Oxford: Clarendon, 1975.

Lucas, Stephen E. "Notes on Aristotle's Concept of Logos." *QJS*, 57 (1971), 456–58.

Madden, Edward H. "The Enthymeme: Crossroads of Logic, Rhetoric, and Metaphysics." *Phil Rev*, 61 (1952), 368–76.

Manicas, Peter T. "On Toulmin's Contribution to Logic and Argumentation." In *Contemporary Theories of Rhetoric.* Ed. Richard L. Johannesen. New York: Harper, Row, 1971, pp. 256–70.

Mazzeo, Joseph Anthony. "St. Augustine's Rhetoric of Silence." *JHI*, 23 (1962), 175–96.

McGuire, Michael. "The Ethics of Rhetoric: The Morality of Knowledge." *SSpCJ*, 45 (1980), 133–48.

McKeon, Richard. "Rhetoric in the Middle Ages." *Speculum*, 17 (1942), 1–32.

———. "The Uses of Rhetoric in a Technological Age." In *The Prospect of Rhetoric.* Eds. Lloyd F. Bitzer and Edwin Black. Englewood Cliffs, N.J.: Prentice-Hall, 1971, pp. 44–63.

———. "Creativity and the Commonplaces." *Phil Rhet*, 6 (1973), 199–210.

———. "The Hellenistic and Roman Foundations of the Tradition of Aristotle in the West." *Rev Metaphysics*, 32 (1979), 677–715.

McNally, J.R. "*Dux Illa Directrixque Artium:* Rudolph Agricola's Dialectical System." *QJS*, 52 (1966), 337–47.

———. "Rudolph Agricola's *De Inventione Dialectica Libri Tres:* A Translation of Selected Chapters." *Speech Mon*, 34 (1967), 393–422.

———. "*Rector et Dux Populi*: Italian Humanism and the Relationship between Rhetoric and Logic." *MP*, 67 (1969), 168–76.

Melancthon, Philip. "Reply of P. Melancthon in Behalf of Ermolao." See Breen.

Merleau-Ponty, Maurice. "What is Phenomenology?" In *Phenomenology of Religion.* Ed. Joseph D. Bettis. New York: Harper, Row, 1969, pp. 13–30.

Miller, Perry. "Edwards, Locke, and the Rhetoric of Sensation." In *Perspectives of Criticism.* Ed. Harry Levin. Cambridge, Mass.: Harvard University Press, 1950.

Murphy, James J. "The Metarhetorics of Plato, Augustine, and McLuhan: A Pointing Essay." *Phil Rhet*, 4 (1971), 201–14.

———. *Rhetoric in the Middle Ages: A History of Rhetoric Theory from Saint Augustine to the Renaissance.* Berkeley: University of California Press, 1974.

Natanson, Maurice. "Rhetoric and Philosophical Argumentation." *QJS*, 48 (1962), 23–30.

Nietzsche, Freidrich. *The Will to Power.* Trans. Walter Kaufmann and R. J. Hollingdale. New York: Random House, 1967.

Ohmann, Richard. "In Lieu of a New Rhetoric." *CE*, 26 (1964), 17–22.

Ong, Walter. *Ramus, Method and the Decay of Dialogue.* Cambridge, Mass.: Harvard University Press, 1958.

———. Introduction to *Scolae in Liberales Artes.* By Petrus Ramus. Hildesheim: Georg Olms Verlag, 1970.

Owen G.E.L., ed. *Aristotle on Dialectic: The Topics.* Oxford: Oxford University Press, 1968.

Park, Douglas B. "Theories and Expectations: On Conceiving Composition and Rhetoric as a Discipline." *CE*, 41 (1979), 47–86.

Perelman, Chaim. "The New Rhetoric: A Theory of Practical Reasoning." In *The Great Ideas Today*. Ed. Mortimer Adler and Robert M. Hutchins. New York: Arno, 1970.

———. "Rhetoric and Philosophy." *Phil Rhet*, 1 (1968), 15–24.

———, and L. Olbrechts-Tytecha. *The New Rhetoric: A Treatise on Argument*. Notre Dame, Ind.: University of Notre Dame Press, 1969. (Originally published as *La Nouvelle Rhetorique: Traite de la Argumentation*. Paris: Presses Universitares de France, 1958.)

Petrarca, Francesco. "To Tommaso of Messina, Against Old Dialectic Cavilers." In *The Renaissance Philosophy of Man*. Ed. E. Cassirer, P. Kristeller, and J. M. Randall. Chicago: University of Chicago Press, 1948, pp. 134–39.

Philosopher's Index: A Retrospective Index to U.S. Publications from 1940. 3 vols. Bowling Green, Ohio: Bowling Green State University, 1978.

Pico della Mirandolla. "G. Pico della Mirandola to his Friend E. Barbero." See Breen.

Plato. *The Dialogues. The Works of Plato*. Trans. B. Jowett. New York: Tudor, 1937.

Polanyi, Michael. *Personal Knowledge*. Chicago: University of Chicago Press, 1958.

Priestley, Joseph. *A Course of Lectures on Oratory and Criticism*. London: J. Johnson, 1777.

Quintilian. *The Instituto Oratoria of Quintilian*. 4 vols. Trans. H. E. Butler. Cambridge, Mass.: Harvard University Press, 1953.

Ramus, Petrus (Pierre de la Ramee). *Scholae in Liberales Artes*. Hildesheim: Georg Olms Verlag, 1970.

Raphael, Sally. "Rhetoric, Dialectic, and Syllogistic Argument: Aristotle's Position in *Rhetoric* I–II." *Phronesis*, 19 (1974), 153–67.

Ray, John W. "Perelman's Universal Audience." *QJS*, 64 (1978), 361–75.

Reid, Thomas. An *Inquiry into the Human Mind on the Principles of Common Sense*. Ed. Timothy Duggan. Chicago: University of Chicago Press, 1970.

Richards, I. A. *The Philosophy of Rhetoric*. New York: Oxford University Press, 1965. (Lectures delivered in 1936).

Roberts, S. "Rhetoric and Dialectic: According to the First Latin Commentary on the *Rhetoric* of Aristotle." *New Scholas*, 31 (1957), 484–98.

Roberts, W. Rhys. "References to Plato in Aristotle's *Rhetoric*." *Class Philol*, 29 (1924), 342–46.

Rosen, Stanley. *Plato's Symposium*. New Haven: Yale University Press, 1968.

———. *Nihilism: A Philosophical Essay*. New Haven: Yale University Press, 1969.

———. *The Limits of Analysis*. New York: Basic, 1980.

Rotenstreich, Nathan. "Argumentation and Philosophical Clarification." *Phil Rhet*, 5 (1972), 12–23.

Rueckert, W. H., ed. *Critical Responses to Kenneth Burke, 1924–1966*. Minneapolis: University of Minneapolis Press, 1969.

Ruether, Rosemary Radford. *Gregory of Nazianzus: Rhetor and Philosopher*. Oxford: Oxford University Press, 1969.

Ryle, Gilbert. "Formal and Informal Logic." In *Dilemmas*. Cambridge: Cambridge University Press, 1954, Chapter 8. Also in *Essays on Rhetoric*. Ed. Dudley Bailey. New York: Oxford University Press, 1965, pp. 250–67.

—————. "The Academy and Dialectic." In *Collected Papers*. Vol. 1. London: Hutchinson, 1971, pp. 89–125.

Schaeffer, James D. "Vico's Rhetorical Model of the Mind." *Phil Rhet*, 14 (Summer 1981), 152–67.

Scott, Robert L. "On Viewing Rhetoric as Epistemic." *CSS J*, 18 (1967), 9–17.

Searle, John R. *Speech Acts: An Essay in the Philosophy of Language*. Cambridge: Cambridge University Press, 1969.

Segal, Charles P. "Gorgias and the Psychology of the Logos." *Harv Stud Class Phil*, 66 (1962), 99–155.

Seigel, Jerrold E. *Rhetoric and Philosophy in Renaissance Humanism: The Union of Eloquence and Wisdom, Petrarch to Valla*. Princeton, N.J.: Princeton University Press, 1968.

Solmson, Friedrich. "The Aristotelian Tradition in Ancient Rhetoric." *Am J Philol*, 62 (1941), 35–50, 169–90.

Stephens, James. *Francis Bacon and the Style of Science*. Chicago: University of Chicago Press, 1975.

Steinmann, Martin, Jr. "Rhetorical Research." In *New Rhetorics*. Ed. Martin Steinmann. New York: Scribner, 1967, pp. 17–32.

Stewart, John. "J. L. Austin's Speech Act Analysis." In *Philosophers on Rhetoric: Traditional and Emerging Views*. Ed. Donald G. Douglas. Skokie, Ill.: International Textbook, 1973, pp. 192–205.

Stump, Eleanore. *Boethius's "De Topicis Differentiis."* Ithaca, N.Y.: Cornell University Press, 1978.

Tate, Gary, ed. *Teaching Composition: 10 Bibliographical Essays*. Fort Worth: Texas Christian University Press, 1976.

Toulmin, Stephen. *The Uses of Argument*. Cambridge: Cambridge University Press, 1958.

Tuve, Elizabeth. *Elizabethan and Metaphysical Imagery*. Chicago: University of Chicago Press, 1947.

Vickers, Brian. *Francis Bacon and Renaissance Prose*. Cambridge: Cambridge University Press, 1968.

Vico, Giambattista. *On the Study Methods of Our Time*. Trans. E. Gianturco. Indianapolis: Bobbs-Merrill (The Library of the Liberal Arts), 1965.

Vygotsky, Lev. *Thought and Language*. Cambridge, Mass.: M.I.T. Press, 1962.

Wallace, Karl R. *Francis Bacon on Communication and Rhetoric*. Chapel Hill: University of North Carolina Press, 1943.

Walter, Otis M. "Descartes on Reasoning." *Speech Mon*, 18 (1951), 47–53.

—————. "On Views of Rhetoric, Whether Conservative or Progressive." *QJS*, 49 (1963), 367–82.

Watson, Samuel D. "Michael Polanyi and the Recovery of Rhetoric." Diss. University of Iowa, 1973.

Weaver, Richard. *The Ethics of Rhetoric*. Chicago: Regnary, 1953.

Weinstein, Donald. "In Whose Image and Likeness? Interpretations of Renaissance Humanism." *JHI*, 33 (1972), 165–76.

Whately, Richard. *Elements of Rhetoric*. Ed. Douglas Ehninger. 1846; rpt. Carbondale: Southern Illinois University Press, 1963.

Williamson, George. *The Senecan Amble*. Chicago: University of Chicago Press, 1951.

Wittgenstein, Ludwig. *Philosophical Investigations*. Trans. G.E.M. Anscombe. New York: Macmillan, 1953.

Young, Richard. "Invention: A Topographical Survey." In *Teaching Composition: 10 Bibliographical Essays*. Ed. Gary Tate. Fort Worth: Texas Christian University Press, 1976, pp. 1–43.

Zyskind, Harold. "Some Philosophic Strands in Popular Rhetoric." In *Perspectives in Education, Religion, and the Arts*. Ed. Howard E. Kiefer and Milton K. Munitz. Albany: SUNY Press, 1970, pp. 373–95.

Literature, Literary Theory, and the Teaching of Composition

WILLIAM L. STULL

"Of all our current fake polarities," Wayne Booth wrote in "The Common Aims That Divide Us" (1981), "perhaps the one that would surprise our ancestors most is that between 'composition' and 'literature.' It would have surprised them because they could never have dreamed that one might try to teach scholars to write well without at the same time trying to teach them to read and enjoy what is well written" (p. 1). Nevertheless, as the profession of English passes its first centennial, a polarity, real or "fake," seems to be widening between teachers of composition and teachers of literature, both of whom once claimed to be teachers of the same thing: English.

The NCTE *Statement on the Preparation of Teachers of English and Language Arts* (1976) notes that in the 1960s *English* was defined "as a discipline comprising language, literature, and composition—the familiar 'tripod.' Today, that metaphor has all but disappeared" (p. 1). More recently, in "The Winds of Change" (1982), Maxine Hairston used Thomas Kuhn's term *paradigm shift* to describe the changeover. Few teachers of writing have failed to notice that W. Ross Winterowd observed in "Getting It Together in the English Department" (1977): "Until very recently, the English department rhetorician has lived in the ghetto" (p. 28). Likewise, most would agree that, as Sondra Perl wrote in "The State of the Art in Composition" (1980), composition "is an exciting field these days" (p. 44). For these reasons, not all may wish the "familiar tripod" restored.

But the emergence of composition as a discipline explains only one side of the literature-composition polarity. The titles of two books by literary theorist

In preparing this chapter, I received valuable suggestions from the following scholars: Ann E. Berthoff, University of Massachusetts; Donald A. Daiker, Miami University (Ohio); Charles Gullans, University of California–Los Angeles; Muriel Harris, Purdue University; Winifred Bryan Horner, University of Missouri; and Richard A. Lanham, University of California–Los Angeles; as well as Leo Rockas and Charles L. Ross, both of the University of Hartford. I thank each one for his or her contributions, but I assume full responsibility for the errors and omissions that remain.

Geoffrey H. Hartman indicate a second "paradigm shift" in recent English studies. The first, ushering in the 1970s, in *Beyond Formalism* (1970); the second, marking our current decade, is *Criticism in the Wilderness* (1980). Beyond the New Critical formalism that some of us who teach writing remember as the *only* criticism stretches the wilderness of reception aesthetics, structuralism, deconstruction, and beyond.

Given these rapid developments in both literature and composition, it is no wonder that further specialization and separation strike some as inevitable. If either the newly emerged composition specialist or the postmodern critic had the last word, the fractious profession of English, which once encompassed not only literature and composition but also speech, linguistics, and "communications," might well fracture again. But a number of English teachers, including scholars like Booth, E. D. Hirsch, Richard A. Lanham, and J. Hillis Miller, have begun decrying the current polarity as "fake." It is fake, they argue, because the paradigms in both fields have shifted in the same direction. During the 1970s, literary theorists and composition researchers alike shifted their attentions from the products of writing, texts once assumed to be "finished," to the dynamic processes of reading and writing. In "From Story to Essay" (1982), Anthony Petrosky summarized how the new paradigms in both literary theory and composition reconnect the teaching of reading and writing:

> When we read, we comprehend by putting together our impressions of the text with our personal, cultural, and contextual models of reality. When we write, we compose by making meaning from available information, our personal knowledge, and the cultural and contextual frames we happen to find ourselves in. Our theoretical understandings of these processes are converging . . . around the central role of human understanding—be it of texts or of the world—as a process of composition. (p. 26)

This convergence has serious implications not only for the classroom but for the profession of English at large.

In *The State of the Discipline, 1970s–1980s* (1979), half a dozen distinguished writers considered the literature-composition polarity and challenged the profession to counteract it. In "The Function of Rhetorical Study at the Present Time," J. Hillis Miller wrote that "the development of integrated programs in reading and writing" forms "the major challenge to our profession" (p. 12). Richard A. Lanham (1979) called for a "post-Darwinian humanism" that embraces the practicalities of composition and the play of literature alike. E. D. Hirsch, one of the first literary theorists to take a strong interest in composition, in "Remarks on Composition to the Yale English Department" (1979), commented that "our recent experiment at being exclusively professors of literature has been a rather short-lived and unsuccessful one, with unfortunate practical consequences" (p. 64). To counter this specialization, Hirsch reminded his listeners that in 1762, when Hugh Blair assumed the first chair of English at the University of Edinburgh, it was as professor of rhetoric and *belles lettres*; that is, as professor of composition and literature.

Although the literature-composition debate continues apace in professional journals, an anthology edited by Winifred Bryan Horner, *Composition and Literature* (1983), promises to bridge the gap. The collection includes Lanham's essay "One, Two, Three" (an argument that "teaching literature and teaching composition form different parts of the same activity"), Miller's "Composition and Decomposition," Booth's "LITCOMP," and Hirsch's "Reading, Writing, and Cultural Literacy." Josephine Miles, Walter J. Ong, Frederick Crews, and Edward P. J. Corbett are also among the contributors.

Literature, Discourse Theory, and the English Department

Anyone who sets out to define *literature* in classic Aristotelian fashion will do well to recall what Aristotle himself observed early in the *Nichomachean Ethics*: "The educated man looks for as much precision in each subject as the nature of the subject allows" (I.iii.4). Not surprisingly, the protean nature of literature has allowed literary theorists little real precision. In two essays, "Literature and Its Cognates" (1973) and "What Is Literature?" (1978), René Wellek surveyed how the concept of literature has evolved from antiquity to the present. The Latin word *littera* ("letter") was linked with the Greek *grammatiké*, the knowledge of reading and writing, Quintilian noted in his *Institutio Oratoria* (II.i.4). But even in classical times, this broad definition of *literature* as *all* writing coexisted with a second, qualitative, definition. In his second *Phillipic*, Cicero used the word *litterae* (xlv.116) not to indicate that Caesar was merely literate but to stress his "letters" or erudition. It is not until the second century A.D., however, that either *litterae* or *literatura* comes to be identified with a specific canon of literary works. At that time the Christian writers Tertullian and Cassian began using *literatura* to indicate secular pagan writing in contrast to *scripta*, the Holy Writ.

These broad and narrow meanings continue their permutations in later times. In the Middle Ages, the term *literatus* again indicates the ability to read and write, the words *litterae* and *literatura* having fallen into disuse. With the advent of Renaissance humanism, the *bonae litterae* of Cicero, indicating good writing, and the *humana literatura* of the church fathers, indicating secular writing, regain prominence. The term *les belles lettres*, denoting artistic writing, arises with French neo-classicism. Its adaptation into English soon followed, as revealed by Blair's title, professor of rhetoric and *belles lettres*. At the same time, with the rise of eighteenth-century aesthetics, the English word *literature* begins more and more to indicate a particular body of writing, specifically poetry and prose fiction.

In his "Literature and Its Cognates" (1973) essay, Wellek concluded that the term *literature* is used in three principal ways: "First, literature signifies the totality of literary production: everything in print; secondly, literature refers to great books, books of whatever subject, of historical impact; thirdly, literature may be more or less rigidly limited to imaginative fiction" (p. 85). The first definition is so broad as to make *literature* synonymous with *cultural history*; the second one restricts the term to an arbitrary canon of works that changes from age to age; the third definition, literature as imaginative fiction, excludes much "art" writing, including essays, from critical consideration.

Although none of these definitions is ultimately satisfactory, in modern literary theory, particularly that bearing the stamp of the New Criticism, the third definition has prevailed. It is this definition of "imaginative literature" that Wellek and Austin Warren adopted in their *Theory of Literature* (1956), along with an escape clause, "Perspectivism" (p. 43), that allows them to consider works historically as well as aesthetically. Even Northrop Frye, whose *Anatomy of Criticism* (1957) ranges far beyond the formalism of the New Critics, insisted on "hypothetical intention" (p. 326) as the hallmark of literature, this supplemented by "autonomous verbal structure" (pp. 71–74), a stylistic criterion.

During the 1970s, with the decline of New Critical formalism and a growing interest in the processes by which literature is created and understood, the fictionality criterion has come under steady fire. The Autumn 1973 issue of *New Literary History* is devoted entirely to the question "What Is Literature?" and includes valuable articles by Tzvetan Todorov, Alvin B. Kernan, Stanley Fish, and others. In "The Notion of Literature" (1973) Todorov revealed how Wellek and Frye both sidled between two definitions of literature, one based on fictionality, the other based on style. Since neither criterion is satisfactory in itself and there is no necessary connection between the two, Todorov rejected both. He then proposed to replace the opposition between literature and non-literature with "a typology of the various types of discourse," which includes fiction and nonfiction alike (p. 16). Like Todorov, Stanley Fish argued in "How Ordinary Is Ordinary Language?" (1973) that "essentialistic" definitions of literature beg the question. He took a more radical approach, however, arguing that literature is defined not by features in the text but by attitudes in the reader. For him, literature is "an open category," one defined "by what we decide to put into it" (p. 52).

The attack on essentialism continues in E. D. Hirsch's "'Intrinsic' Criticism" (1974). Moreover, Hirsch concerned himself not only with literary theory but with the teaching of composition as well. "Intrinsic" definitions of literature, promulgated by the New Critics but derived from the Romantics and, ultimately, Aristotle, have not only "isolated the literary work of art from the continuum of discourse" but also led us "to separate the teaching of literature from what is humbly called the teaching of composition" (p. 457). To end this schism, he urged teachers of reading and writing to replace the ill-defined notion of literature as *les belles lettres* with a classical conception of *bonae litterae* that encompasses "everything worthy to be read" (p. 455).

A recent anthology entitled *What Is Literature?* (1978), edited by Paul Hernadi, contains not only Wellek's "What Is Literature?" but also a companion piece by Hirsch, "What Isn't Literature?" Along with these essays in definition, the book includes articles on canon-formation and literature as act, effect, and artifact. Richard Ohmann, Murray Krieger, Norman Holland, and Morse Peckham are among the contributors.

The attack on critical essentialism bears directly on the teaching of writing, as Burton Hatlen suggested in "Why Is *The Education of Henry Adams* 'Literature,' While *The Theory of the Leisure Class* Is Not?" (1979). "Rather than thinking of English as the study of *certain kinds of texts*," he wrote, "I am proposing that we should instead see it as the study of texts *in a certain way*" (p. 675). That way, he argued, is rhetorical. But this shift of attention from product to process has more general implications as well. First, it invites English teachers to bring their finest tools to bear not only on privileged texts but on any writing they choose—including student writing. Second, it invites teachers of literature to present their material not as "great books" but as meaning-in-the-making. Finally, it collapses any polarity between the study of writing and the teaching of writing, since both prove to be processes of composition.

As Todorov's mention of "a typology of the various types of discourse" suggests, the relationship between literature and composition is a long-standing issue in discourse theory. There is as yet no comprehensive history of this field, although Frank D'Angelo's bibliographic essay "Modes of Discourse" (1976) offers a valuable historical review. The chapter on "Rhetoric and Literature" in Peter Dixon's short study *Rhetoric* (1971) is concise and informative, as is Marvin T. Herrick's "Rhetoric and Poetics" in the *Princeton Encyclopedia of Poetry and Poetics* (1974).

The Greeks loosely distinguished between two major modes of discourse that today we might term *composition* and *literature*. The titles of Aristotle's two works on discourse theory, the *Rhetoric* and the *Poetics*, indicate this division. The cross-references between the two treatises suggest, however, that although rhetoric and poetics can be initially separated, practical criticism quickly draws on both. In Plato's *Phaedrus*, Socrates contrasted the reason of the true orator with the madness of the poet (265b, 277b). For Aristotle, however, the difference between rhetoric and poetry is a technical matter of persuasion versus imitation. In Roman times even this broad distinction steadily wore away. Thus in his *De Oratore* Cicero wrote that "the poet is a very near kinsman of the orator" (I.xvi.70). Moreover, in *De Optimo Genere Oratorum* he defined the master orator as the one "whose speech instructs, delights and moves the minds of his audience" (I.3), a formulation that anticipates Horace's definition, in the *Ars Poetica*, of the poet as one who aims to delight and instruct his auditors (lines 333–34). The nominal distinction between rhetoric and poetics fades in the *Institutio Oratoria* as well, where Quintilian drew examples of great oratory from Homer (II.xvii.8).

For a full discussion of classical discourse theory, including translations of representative texts, see Charles Sears Baldwin's *Ancient Rhetoric and Poetic* (1924). In William K. Wimsatt and Cleanth Brooks's *Literary Criticism* (1957), the fourth chapter, "The Verbal Medium: Plato and Aristotle," is useful. M. L. Clarke's *Rhetoric at Rome* (1962) is a standard history, although the "Survey of Rhetoric'' in Edward P. J. Corbett's *Classical Rhetoric for the Modern Student* (1971a) may be sufficient for the generalist. Aldo Scaglione's *Classical Theory of Composition* (1972), a linguistic study, is also relevant.

"In the Middle Ages," Dixon wrote in *Rhetoric* (1971), "the identity of rhetoric and poetry was virtually complete. Ciceronian doctrines could easily be converted into poetical theory, and most 'Arts of Poetry' in this period are in fact arts of rhetoric with additional material on versification" (p. 52). A good example of this is Geoffroi de Vinsauf's *Poetria Nova* (c. 1210), a discussion of poetry in terms of invention, arrangement, and the "colors" of rhetoric. On this period the standard work is *Medieval Rhetoric and Poetic* (1928) by C. S. Baldwin.

The tendency to discuss poetry in rhetorical terms continued during the Renaissance. In *The Arte of English Poesie* (1589), George Puttenham declared, "[t]he poet is of all other the most auncient Orator" (p. 196). At the same time, however, Neoplatonists like Sir Philip Sidney introduced a countervailing conception of literature as superior to other discourse. In his *Defence of Poesie* (1595), Sidney set poetry above rhetoric, history, and nature itself. This definition of *literature* as elite discourse anticipates the essentialistic definitions examined above. Most works on rhetoric and poetics published during the period make no such radical distinction, however. Instead, they concentrate on style, the place where poetry and prose have most in common.

There are many good studies of Renaissance discourse theory, including several by Donald Leman Clark. His *Rhetoric and Poetry in the Renaissance* (1922) is a comprehensive history, and two of his articles, "The Requirements of a Poet" (1918) and "Ancient Rhetoric and English Renaissance Literature" (1951a), reveal the free commingling of rhetoric and poetry during the period. For discussions of rhetoric and poetics apart from each other, see Wilbur Samuel Howell's *Logic and Rhetoric in England, 1500–1700* (1935) and C. S. Baldwin's *Renaissance Literary Theory and Practice* (1939). Sister Miriam Joseph's *Rhetoric in Shakespeare's Time* (1947) is especially valuable for its first chapter, "The General Theory of Composition and of Reading in Shakespeare's England."

No comprehensive history of eighteenth-century discourse theory yet exists. Nevertheless, there are several studies of major works from this period, during which the modern discipline of English studies began taking shape. John M. Lothian's edition of Adam Smith's *Lectures on Rhetoric and Belles Lettres* (1963) has a valuable historical introduction, as does James L. Golden and Edward P. J. Corbett's edition of *The Rhetoric of Blair, Campbell, and Whately* (1968). It is during the second half of the century that the belletristic and elocutionary movements begin, and Wilbur Samuel Howell discussed the latter in *Eighteenth Century British Logic and Rhetoric* (1971).

The nineteenth century remains a dark era in discourse theory, largely unexplored. Albert Kitzhaber's dissertation "Rhetoric in American Colleges, 1850–1900" (1953) focuses on pedagogy, but it marks a point of departure for broader studies. Fortunately, the most influential discourse theorist of the late nineteenth century, Alexander Bain, has received considerable attention recently. In *English Composition and Rhetoric* (first American edition 1866), Bain initially distinguished five "kinds of composition": "Those that have for their object to inform the understanding, fall under three heads—*Description, Narration,* and *Exposition.* The means of influencing the will are given under one head, *Persuasion.* The employing of language to excite pleasurable Feelings is one of the chief characteristics of *Poetry*" (p. 19). This radical separation of the "forms of discourse" represents a break with both classical and belletristic doctrine. When, later in the book, Bain wrote that consideration of poetry is actually irrelevant to his purposes, the polarity between literature and composition widens. In "The Rise and Fall of the Modes of Discourse" (1981), Robert J. Connors assessed Bain's influence on later pedagogy, and in "Alexander Bain's Contributions to Discourse Theory" (1982), Andrea A. Lunsford showed how Bain's growing interest in the psychology of composition led him to temper his doctrine of "forms" in subsequent editions of his textbook.

Work in discourse theory has continued steadily in our own century. Between 1925 and 1950, the New Critics strove to develop an intrinsic approach to literature, a methodology in which, as Brooks and Warren wrote in *Understanding Poetry* (1938), emphasis remains on "the poem as poem" (p. ix). Similarly, first in *Science and Poetry* (1926; rewritten as *Poetries and Sciences,* 1970) and later in *Speculative Instruments* (1955), I. A. Richards sought to differentiate the referential language of science, which contains "statements," from the expressive language of literature, which contains "pseudo-statements." But the New Critics' disjunction between literature and non-literature has come under attack with the decline of formalism. Thus in "'Expressive Language' and the Expressive Function of Poetry" (1955), Susanne Langer rejected the idea that poetry is a separate "form of discourse," and in *The Burning Fountain* (1968), Philip Wheelwright demonstrated that expressive and referential discourse are not true opposites (pp. 56–72).

Since the "revival of rhetoric" in the 1960s, several comprehensive theories of discourse have appeared. Leo Rockas's *Modes of Rhetoric* (1964) is notable for its complete synthesis of literary and rhetorical discourse within a framework of static, temporal, mimetic, and mental modes. In addition, Rockas illustrated his theory with sample passages from both student and professional writers. Likewise, in *Teaching the Universe of Discourse* (1968), James Moffett proposed a "spectrum of discourse" that links "Recording, the drama of what is happening" with plays; "Reporting, the narrative of what happened" with fiction; "Generalizing, the exposition of what happens" with essays; and poetry with all of these activities (p. 47).

In *A Theory of Discourse* (1971), however, James L. Kinneavy returned to more rigid distinctions among the "aims of discourse" (pp. 17–40, 58–68). He distinguished literary discourse from reference, persuasive, and expressive discourse by means of a twofold criterion. First, in literary discourse the text is "an object worthy of being appreciated in its own right"; second, "[s]uch appreciation gives pleasure to the beholder'' (p. 39). The first standard is at once qualitative and formalistic, reminiscent of Frye's ''autonomous verbal structure.'' The second is psychological and aesthetic, recalling Bain's ''pleasurable Feelings.'' The connection of either standard to ''aim'' is obscure, as is the link between the two. For reasons similar to these, in ''*A Theory of Discourse*'' (1982), John D. O'Banion judged the *Theory* to have been a ''limited success'' (p. 196).

In contrast to Kinneavy's four ''aims,'' the three ''function categories''—transactional, expressive, and poetic—defined by James Britton and his colleagues in *The Development of Writing Abilities* (11–18) (1975) represent a breakthrough in discourse theory. Like the ''interactive'' systems of Wheelwright, Rockas, and Moffett, Britton's schema is a sliding scale, not a set of fixed boxes. It thus readily accommodates the necessarily mixed ''aims'' of practicing writers. Moreover, Britton's study is inductive, based on some 2,000 writing samples. Although Britton stressed that the expressive function of writing is fundamental, he concluded that students need to practice writing of all sorts: ''what we need above all to develop is a recognition of writings along the whole spectrum from expressive to poetic—a recognition of the principles upon which the work of literature is constructed, and the application of those principles to less highly organized kinds of writing, the 'art-like''' (p. 83). For more of Britton's thinking, see his *Language and Learning* (1970) and ''The Composing Processes and the Functions of Writing'' (1978).

To summarize, in the past decade both the ''essentialistic'' definition of literature and the traditional ''forms of discourse'' have been seriously challenged. Ironically, however, during this same decade a new ''polarity'' between literature and composition has arisen within the profession of English.

As Philip Fisher observed in ''Questions of English'' (1979), ''The discipline of English studies is a strikingly recent innovation,'' one dating from the late nineteenth century (p. 727). Given today's literature-composition polarity, it is not surprising to find earlier schisms. Established in 1883, the Modern Language Association (MLA) was followed by the National Council of Teachers of English (NCTE) (1911), the Speech Communication Association (1914), the Linguistic Society of America (1924),the Conference on College Composition and Communication (CCCC) (1950), and still more specialized bodies like the Council of Writing Program Administrators (1977). In a valuable but loosely documented essay, ''Where Do English Departments Come From?'' (1967), William Riley Parker discussed this turbulent evolution. Two doctoral dissertations offer more substantial information: Kitzhaber's ''Rhetoric in American Colleges, 1850–1900'' (1953) and Walter Achtert's ''History of English Studies to 1883 Based on the Research of William Riley Parker'' (1972). Leonard A. Greenbaum's ''The Tradition of Complaint'' (1969), a lively if polemical history, appears in *Course X* (1970) by Greenbaum and Rudolf B. Schmerl. The most comprehensive history of pedagogy is Arthur N. Applebee's *Tradition and Reform in the Teach-*

ing of English (1974). For more specialized studies, consult the References at the end of this chapter.

As Wallace Douglas suggested in "Rhetoric for the Meritocracy" (1976), the teaching of English has been shaped by economic as well as pedagogical forces. Jasper P. Neel's *Options for the Teaching of English* (1978) surveys the wide range of current programs, and the following studies assess the socio-economic realities of the profession: Ray Kytle's "Slaves, Serfs, or Colleagues—Who Shall Teach College Composition?" (1971); Robbins Burling's "An Anthropological Glimpse of English as a Profession" (1977); Dennis Szilak's "Teachers of Composition" (1977); and Michael Holzman's "Writing as Technique" (1982). In a provocative essay, "Comp. vs Lit." (1978), Donald C. Steward discussed the results of a "quiz" he gave English teachers at the 1977 NCTE Convention.

Arguments for and against the separation of literature and composition have begun appearing so frequently that I can discuss but a few and relegate the remainder to the References. Two essays appearing side by side in the February 1977 issue of *CE* conveniently illustrate the basic positions in the literature-composition debate. In "Comp. vs. Lit.," George R. Bramer, a separatist, argued that "literary study often affects composition teaching in adverse ways" (p. 32) by distracting writing teachers from the work at hand. He therefore favored the training and hiring of composition specialists. In "Literature in the Composition Course," however, John J. Fenstermaker defended the "literature-based composition course" as "squarely in line with the major objective of the Liberal Studies curriculum" (p. 37). He stressed the many ways in which good reading can be a springboard for good writing.

The changes rung on these themes are many. In an earlier "Literature in the Composition Course" (1958), John A. Hart and others urged a cautious integration in which imaginative literature is treated as "fact." Taking much the same approach, S. Leonard Rubinstein in "Composition" (1966) observed that "such a course is imperiled by the teacher who forgets the difference between the use of literary material for literary purposes and the use of literary material for compositional purposes" (p. 273). James Knapton and Bertrand Evans proposed an ambitious synthesis in *Teaching a Literature-Based English Program* (1967). Although seven of their nine chapters deal exclusively with literature, the eighth, "What about Composition?" is surprisingly rich. More recent calls for integrated curricula include former MLA president Florence Howe's "Literacy and Literature" (1974); S. M. Halloran's "On the Ends of Rhetoric, Classical and Modern" (1975); Alan M. Hollingsworth's "Beyond Survival" (1977); Dean Memering's "The Reading/Writing Heresy" (1977); J. N. Hook's "College English Departments" (1978); Thomas N. Smith's "Literature" (1981); and Robert Shenk's "The Self Enlarged" (1981); as well as the articles by Booth, Hirsch, Miller, and Lanham cited above.

Although no outstanding separatist manifesto has yet appeared, cautionary essays abound. In "How Critics Write and How Students Write" (1976), David

Carkeet argued that published criticism makes a poor model for student writers to imitate. John T. Gage voiced cogent reservations about recent critical theory in "Conflicting Assumptions about Intention in Teaching Reading and Composition" (1978). William Harmon execrated "composition specialists" in "So Many Words" (1980), but Frank D'Angelo offered a reasoned defense of specialized studies in "Regaining Our Composure" (1980). Helen Vendler's MLA "Presidential Address 1980" (1981), a lament over "the divorce of composition from the reading of powerful imaginative literature" (p. 345), seems to have fanned rather than cooled the fires in both camps.

What, finally, is one to conclude from this torrent of opinion? In "Teaching Writing; Teaching Literature" (1981), William E. Coles concluded that the current hostilities arise from oversimplified conceptions of reading and writing alike. Polemics aside, classical and modern discourse theory and practical pedagogy suggest that like rhetoric and poetics, composition and literature remain integrally connected. To return to Aristotle, "the nature of the subject" of English as yet allows no separation of the two without loss to both.

Recent Critical Theories and the Teaching of Composition

For the foreseeable future, as Max Schulz and Michael Holzman reasoned in "English Departments—Writing Programs" (1981), "The rhetoric and literature people in English departments . . . must learn to live together in loving amity" (p. 28). Fortunately, recent developments in critical theory and in the teaching of composition suggest that a reconciliation is in the works. Both John Warnock in "The Relation of Critical Perspectives to Teaching Methods in Composition" (1973) and Richard Fulkerson in "Four Philosophies of Composition" (1979) reveal ways in which literary theories—mimetic, pragmatic, expressive, or objective—already inform the teaching of composition. What follows is at once a primer for composition teachers seeking to learn what lies "beyond formalism" and an attempt to connect recent critical theories with the teaching of writing.

For a history of critical theory up to and including the New Criticism, see Wimsatt and Brook's *Literary Criticism* (1957; rpt. 1967). René Wellek's *A History of Modern Criticism* (1955–1965) covers the period of 1750–1950 in four volumes, and Frank Lentricchia's *After the New Criticism* (1980) concentrates on the years 1957–1977. Valuable appraisals of recent criticism can also be found in Gerald Graff's *Literature Against Itself* (1979), Wayne Booth's *Critical Understanding* (1979), Jonathan Culler's *Pursuit of Signs* (1981), and Denis Donoghue's *Ferocious Alphabets* (1981). Useful articles include Vincent B. Leitch's "Primer of Recent Critical Theories" (1977), James J. Sosinski's "The Use of the Word 'Text' in Critical Discourse" (1977), and Michael Fisher's "Why Realism Seems So Naive" (1979). Guest editor Raymond E. Fitch devoted the Winter 1981 issue of *Focus* to "Literary Theory in the English Classroom." Helpful review articles also appear regularly in *New Literary History* (1969–   ), *Diacritics* (1970–), and *Critical Inquiry* (1974–).

Before moving "beyond formalism," however, we should assess in what ways formalism, specifically the formalism of the New Critics, has affected the teaching of composition. Given shape by T. S. Eliot and I. A. Richards, defined (negatively) by John Crowe Ransom, the New Criticism was most widely promulgated by Brooks and Warren, whose *Understanding Poetry* (1938), like what is in many ways its companion volume, *Modern Rhetoric* (1949), became a college standard. Essentialists in their definition of *literature*, Brooks and Warren stressed that literary discourse is, in its organic integrity, unlike other forms of composition. This assumption allies them not only with Richards and other New Critics but also with Alexander Bain, whose "forms of discourse" become the categories of their *Modern Rhetoric*. The split between rhetoric and poetics thus widens as students study literature but practice composition. Brooks and Warren approached both their subjects formalistically, emphasizing the written product over the writing process, but a great difference in "authority" separates the student from the professional writer. When Wimsatt and Monroe E. Beardsley added "The Intentional Fallacy" (1946) and "The Affective Fallacy" (1949), both reprinted in *The Verbal Icon* (1954), to the New Critical vocabulary, the formalist classroom is complete: no authorial intentions, no affective responses to writing, only form. *Form*, although "organic" in literary discourse, becomes, in student writing, synonymous with *correctness*.

This sketch is a caricature, but in broad outline it describes the way in which radical formalism can distort the teaching of composition. Fortunately, not all associated with the New Criticism were strict formalists. In both *Principles of Literary Criticism* (1925) and *Practical Criticism* (1929), I. A. Richards, whom John Ransom in *The New Criticism* (1941) labeled "the Psychological Critic," explored the affective dimension of writing. Moreover, his later work on "Poetry as an Instrument of Research" in *Speculative Instruments* (1955) has been the springboard for Ann E. Berthoff's writing on "the composing imagination." See her essay "From Problem-Solving to a Theory of the Imagination" (1972), as well as her textbook *Forming, Thinking, Writing* (1978) and her collected papers on teaching, *The Making of Meaning* (1981).

A second New Critic whose work has widely influenced the teaching of composition is Kenneth Burke. His "dramatistic" theory of communication as well as his "pentad" of act, scene, agent, agency, and purpose, both presented in *A Grammar of Motives* (1945), are incorporated into a number of recent textbooks, including William F. Irmscher's *Holt Guide to English* (1981). Nearly all of Burke's books from *Counter-Statement* (1931) and *Permanence and Change* (1935) to *Language as Symbolic Action* (1966) and *A Rhetoric of Motives* (1969) bear on the teaching of writing, as do his essays "Rhetoric—Old and New" (1951), "Dramatism" (1968), and "Questions and Answers about the Pentad" (1978). Studies of him include Linda M. Turner's "On First Reading Burke's 'A Rhetoric of Motives'" (1973), Wayne Booth's "Kenneth Burke's Way of Knowing" (1974), Philip M. Keith's "Burke for the Composition Class" (1977), and Joseph Comprone's "Kenneth Burke and the Teaching of Writing" (1979).

Moving beyond the New Criticism, we encounter first the so-called "Chicago Critics": Ronald S. Crane, Elder Olson, and the other contributors to *Critics and Criticism* (1952), edited by Crane. These writers are notable for their critical pluralism and for their neo-Aristotelian interest in rhetoric and poetics. The most recent spokesman for this position has been Wayne Booth, whose MLA address "The Revival of Rhetoric" (1965) cleared the way for Kenneth Burke, Francis Christensen, and others whose work appears in Martin Steinmann's *New Rhetorics* (1967). Booth's essay "The Rhetorical Stance" (1963) remains a standard for teachers of composition, and his rhetorical criticism of literature in *The Rhetoric of Fiction* (1961) and *A Rhetoric of Irony* (1974) extends the Chicago tradition. For more on rhetorical criticism, see Alexander Scharbach's "Rhetoric and Literary Criticism" (1972), Jim W. Corder's bibliographic essay "Rhetorical Analysis of Writing" (1976), and Corder's "Rhetoric and Literary Study" (1981).

Northrop Frye's "synoptic" *Anatomy of Criticism* (1957) remains a milestone in modern criticism, pointing the way beyond New Critical formalism. "Rhetorical Criticism," the fourth essay in the *Anatomy*, includes the discussion "The Rhetoric of Non-Literary Prose" (pp. 326–37), and in "The Rhetoric of Doodle" (1978) Leo Rockas brought Frye's ideas to bear on the teaching of composition. Furthermore, Frye's essay "Elementary Teaching and Elemental Scholarship" in *The Stubborn Structure* (1970) has had a strong influence on Marie Ponsot and Rosemary Deen. Their *Beat Not the Poor Desk* (1982) is addressed to instructors who seek to teach the true "basics" of good writing, the "elemental skills."

With the waning of formalism, many scholars have laid aside "The Intentional Fallacy" and undertaken genetic studies of literature. In "Getting a Little Help from Our (Literary) Friends" (1982), Linda Peterson revealed how these studies can help the teacher of composition. Moreover, Paula Johnson's "Writing Programs and the English Department" (1979) argues that recent genetic and intentionalist criticism should prompt composition teachers to treat their students' work as "real writing" rather than as *pro forma* exercises. A genetic study like Charles L. Ross's work on Lawrence, *The Composition of "The Rainbow" and "Women in Love"* (1979), or Michael Grodin's *Ulysses in Progress* (1980) reveals much about the composing processes of master writers. In "Revision Strategies of Student Writers and Experienced Adult Writers" (1980), Nancy Sommers lamented that "current dicta on revising blind our students to what is actually involved in revision" (p. 387). Genetic studies of literature may therefore provide a healthy corrective to composition textbooks.

In much the same way, by rejecting "The Affective Fallacy," scholars examining reader response have established close connections between writing and reading. Jane P. Tompkins's anthology *Reader-Response Criticism* (1980) traces the development of this approach, as does *The Reader in the Text* (1980), edited by Susan Sulieman and Inge Crossman. Although Louise M. Rosenblatt's "transactional theory of the literary work" set forth in *The Reader, the Text, the Poem* (1978) is important, the farthest-reaching work on reader response has come from two camps, the one psychoanalytical and associated with Norman Holland, the other sociological and associated with Stanley Fish.

Holland's work from *The Dynamics of Literary Response* (1968) through *Five Readers Reading* (1975) has explored the ways in which readers' personal identities shape their responses to texts. In "The Delphi Seminar" (1975) Holland and Murray Schwartz revealed how largely *writing* in respose to reading figures in their classes—a lesson for composition and literature teachers alike. David Bleich's *Readings and Feelings* (1975), the manifesto of "subjective criticism," speaks to the teacher, as does his essay "The Identity of Pedagogy and Research in the Study of Response to Literature" (1980).

Fish's collection of essays, *Is There a Text in This Class?* (1980), reveals how his theory of "Literature in the Reader" (the title of the book's first part) has evolved over a decade. At times, Fish leaned toward what appears as critical solipsism, but his discussion of "the authority of interpretive communities" in "Interpreting the *Variorum*" (chapter 6) bears on the classroom, particularly on teachers' responses to students' own "texts." Cautious assessments of Fish's work include Eugene Regis's "Literature by the Reader" (1976), Alan C. Purves's "Putting Readers in Their Places" (1980), and Nancy and Peter Rabinowitz's "The Critical Balance" (1980). Susan Miller's "Is There a Text in This Class?" (1982) reaches provocative conclusions about composition textbooks that are "used," not read.

As Steven Mailloux argued, reader-response criticism and recent work in composition have proved highly compatible. In "Reader Response Criticism and Teaching Composition" (1982), he concluded that "a rapprochement may be taking place between literary and composition theory; shared paradigms are emerging" (p. 208). See also Marilyn Samuels's "Norman Holland's 'New Paradigm' and the Teaching of Writing" (1978); Peter Parisi's "Close Reading, Creative Writing, and Cognitive Development" (1979); and Bruce T. Peterson's "Writing about Responses" (1982). Lil Brannon and C. H. Knoblauch's "Teacher Commentary on Student Writing" (1981) is a valuable review essay, and in "On Students' Rights to Their Own Texts" (1982) these writers use reader-response theory to propose a fruitful approach to the marking of students' compositions.

Another major critical movement that may interest the teacher of writing is structuralism. Structuralism arose from the union of linguistics and anthropology, two disciplines with obvious links to the teaching of composition, and its vocabulary of sign, signifier, and signified; deep versus surface structures; and language (*langue*) versus speech (*parole*) seems highly compatible with analysis of students' writing. Moreover, its conception of writing (*écriture*) as an amalgam of personal and cultural "codes" draws no sharp distinction between literature and composition. For introductory remarks, see Jonathan Culler's "Structuralism" (1974), Dorothy B. Selz's "Structuralism for the Non-Specialist" (1975), and Ian Smithson's "Structuralism as a Method of Literary Criticism" (1975). John Sturrock's anthology *Structuralism and Since* (1979) is comprehensive, as is Edith Kurzweil's *The Age of Structuralism* (1980). Critical applications include

Robert Scholes's *Structuralism in Literature* (1974) and Culler's *Structuralist Poetics* (1975).

Roland Barthes, sometimes a structuralist, sometimes a semiologist, and most recently a connoisseur of textual erotics, has always been a brilliant student of "writing itself." His provocative books *Writing Degree Zero* (1953), *S/Z* (1970), *The Pleasure of the Text* (1973), and his final collection of essays in *Image-Music-Text* (1977) all challenge conventional notions of authorship, textuality, reading, and writing. Indeed, Barthes is guaranteed to disturb any teacher's dogmatic slumbers. Susan Sontag's *A Barthes Reader* (1982) includes a comprehensive introduction to the man and his work, and Peggy Rosenthal's "Deciphering *S/Z*" (1975) clarifies many of Barthes's unconventional terms.

"Post-structuralism," particularly "deconstruction" as practiced by Jacques Derrida and his faithful at Yale, seems at first glance to have nothing to offer the teacher of composition. In *Of Grammatology* (1976), *Positions* (1981), and related writings, Derrida undermined nearly every assumption upon which the typical composition course rests. Drawing on the "deconstruction of metaphysics" pioneered by Nietzsche, he assailed the "logocentricism" of Western culture and its faith in a godlike authorial voice at the center and origin of every text. It is this "metaphysics of presence," Derrida argued, that prompts readers to seek one authoritative meaning in a work rather than an infinite play of possible interpretations, none definitive.

Derrida's manifestoes, gleefully abstruse as they may seem, pose serious challenges to the "current-traditional" paradigms in both literature and composition. As Sharon Crowley revealed in "Of Gorgias and Grammatology" (1979), the typical writing class is shot through with "metaphysical" notions of voice, presence, and unequivocal meaning. Moreover, as J. Hillis Miller stressed in "The Function of Rhetorical Study" (1979), deconstruction is not mere nihilism. Instead, it is an acknowledgement of "the irreducibly figurative nature of language" (p. 13). Its relevance to the teaching of writing may thus be greater than one might suppose. For more on post-structuralism, see Josué Harari's anthology *Textual Strategies* (1979) and Philip Lewis's review essay "The Post-structuralist Condition" (1982). On deconstruction, see William Cain's "Deconstruction in America" (1979) and Denis Donoghue's "Deconstructing Deconstruction" (1980), a review of *Deconstruction and Criticism* (1979) by Harold Bloom and others.

These works, then, are the principal varieties of criticism in the wilderness of the 1970s–1980s. In addition, the work of two scholars not identifiable with any single movement also speaks to the teacher of writing. First, in both *Validity in Interpretation* (1967) and *The Aims of Interpretation* (1976), E. D. Hirsch has assailed the relativism of recent literary theory. It is not surprising, therefore, to find him in *The Philosophy of Composition* (1977) proposing a "scientific" method for analyzing nonfiction prose. William E. Cain reviewed Hirsch's literary theory in "Authority, 'Cognitive Atheism,' and the Aims of Interpretation" (1977), and in "Hirsch's *Philosophy of Composition*" (1982), and Paul C.

Doherty reassessed Hirsch's case for "relative readability" as the measure of effective writing. Second, in *The Presence of the Word* (1967), *Rhetoric, Romance, and Technology* (1971), and *Interfaces of the Word* (1977), Walter J. Ong, S.J., studied the interaction between culture and expression. Ong's essay "Literacy and Orality in Our Times" (1978) challenges the popular "'back-to-basics'" argument, and in "Literacy, the Basics, and All That Jazz" (1977) as well as "Developing Literacy" (1978), Thomas J. Farrell brought Ong's ideas to bear directly on the teaching of composition. As a final illustration of the diverse ways in which literary theory can serve a teacher of writing, one can turn to Louise Yelin's "Deciphering the Academic Hieroglyph" (1978). There, Yelin drew on Raymond William's *Marxism and Literature* (1977) to define her approach to basic writing.

Curricula and Teaching Techniques

A number of curricula and courses integrate the teaching of literature and composition. The most ambitious of them is James Moffett's *Student-Centered Language Arts and Reading* (1976). Both this and Moffett's *Active Voice* (1981), a writing program across-the-curriculum, combine fictional and non-fictional writing assignments based on reading and experience. Like Knapton and Evans's *Teaching a Literature-Based English Program* (1967), Edward P. J. Corbett's "Composition Course Based on Literature" (1970) is addressed to high school teachers but speaks to college teachers as well. Donald A. Daiker's ERIC essay "Integrating Composition and Literature" (1979) describes a second-semester freshman course "which carefully integrates the teaching of literature with the teaching of composition so that the secondary goal of heightened literary understanding does not overwhelm the primary goal of improved expository writing" (p. 1). During 1981–1982, working at Miami University (Ohio) under a National Endowment for the Humanities (NEH) grant, Daiker, Frank Jordan, and Jack E. Wallace developed further courses in literature and composition. Their textbook *Literature* is forthcoming. Finally, in "Combining Literature and Composition" (1982), Peter Conn described a special program for teaching assistants at the University of Pennsylvania.

Literature and composition were fully integrated in the classical curriculum. The *progymnasmata* or elementary exercises included themes in "pre-literary" forms such as the fable, tale, proverb, eulogy, and character sketch. For a dozen of these basic assignments, see *"The Progymnasmata of Aphthonius* in Translation" (1952) by Ray Nadeau. Donald Leman Clark's *Rhetoric in Greco-Roman Education* (1957) includes the chapters "Imitation" and "The Elementary Exercises." See also his *John Milton at St. Paul's School* (1948) and "The Rise and Fall of Progymnasmata in Sixteenth Century and Seventeenth Century Grammar Schools" (1952), as well as William H. Woodward's *Studies in Education During the Age of the Renaissance, 1400–1600* (1965). Frank D'Angelo adapted parts of the progymnasmata to the modern classroom in "Some Uses of Proverbs'' (1977), "Fables in the Composition Classroom" (1978), "The Art of Paraphrase" (1979), and "The Dialogue" (1982). Richard L. Harp took a similar approach in "Using Elementary Literary Forms in the Composition Class" (1978). The most comprehensive treatise on teaching these "elemental skills" is Ponsot and Deen's *Beat Not the Poor Desk* (1982), which aims to cultivate "the growth of expository writing as a literary skill through assignments designed as literary structures" (p. vii).

In addition to composing in literary forms, students in classical times regularly wrote translations, paraphrases, and imitations of master authors. The imitation of prose models is discussed by Dionysius of Halicarnassus in *On Imitation*, by Quintilian in *Institutio Oratoria* (X.ii), and by "Longinus" in *On the Sublime*. See also Richard McKeon's "Literary Criticism and the Concept of Imitation in Antiquity" (1936), Donald Leman Clark's "Imitation" (1951b), and Edward P. J. Corbett's "Theory and Practice of Imitation in Classical Rhetoric" (1971b). D. G. Kehl's "Composition in the Mimetic Mode" (1979) discusses *imitatio* in the context of *lectio* (reading) and *exercitatio* (practice), a triad Sir Philip Sidney championed in his *Defence* (1595) as "art, imitation, and exercise."

Nearly every writer from the Renaissance through the neo-classical period takes imitation as one of the cornerstones of literary training. But with the appearance of Edward Young's pre-romantic manifesto, *Conjectures on Original Composition* (1759), the modern controversy over imitation versus originality begins. For a recent defense of "creative imitation," see Frank D'Angelo's "Imitation and Style" (1973), as well as William E. Gruber's " 'Servile Copying' and the Teaching of English Composition" (1977). In "The Prose Models Approach" (1980), Paul A. Eschholz assessed the arguments on both sides of the imitation-originality debate and outlined "an introductory writing course in which prose models have been successfully integrated with the process approach" (p. 27). Arguments against the prose models approach include James Moffett's "Learning to Write by Writing" (1970), Robert M. Pirsig's denunciation of "calculated mimicry" (p. 170) in *Zen and the Art of Motorcycle Maintenance* (1974), and Max Morenberg's review of *The Norton Sampler* (1980). Cynthia Ozick's "The Lesson of the Master" (1982) is also provocative.

To review the dozens of "prose models" anthologies now on the market is beyond my scope. Laurence Behrens offers a comprehensive survey in "Meditations, Reminiscences, Polemics" (1980). Perhaps the most original approach to imitation in recent years is *An Alternative Style* (1980) by Winston Weathers, who urged teachers to supplement the usual models of clarity, consistency, and coherence ("Grammar A") with examples of "variegation, synchronicity, discontinuity and the like" gathered from Lawrence Stern, Gertrude Stein, and other masters of "Grammar B" (p. 8).

Although some teachers argue that, like literature and composition, "creative writing" and "expository writing" must be strictly separated, a number of authors maintain that *all* composition is creative writing and should be taught as such, using a workshop method. A classic of this approach is Roger H.

Garrison's *A Creative Approach to Composition* (1951). More recent arguments to this effect include Alvin D. Alley's "Guiding Principles for the Teaching of Rhetoric" (1974), Kenneth J. Kantor's "Creative Expression in the English Curriculum" (1975), and Randall Freisinger's "Creative Writing and Creative Composition" (1978). In "The Story Workshop Method" (1977), John Schultz eschewed the term *creative writing* but argued that all composition begins with storytelling; see also his textbook *Writing from Start to Finish* (1982).

In addition to these curricula and teaching methods, a number of teaching techniques use literature to teach style. They include the once "new" generative rhetoric of Francis Christensen described in *Notes Toward a New Rhetoric* (1978) by Franics and Bonniejean Christensen. Sentence combining, too, has linked composition and literature by asking students to recombine professional writing and thus study style from the inside out. For exercises of this sort, see Philip Arrington's "Sentence Combining, Literature, and the Composing Process" (1982) and William L. Stull's *Combining and Creating* (1983).

Whatever one judges the proper literature-composition quotient in a writing course to be, most teachers would agree that literature courses at every level could profit from a greater infusion of composition. Indeed, recent articles to this effect are a heartening sign that English teachers still consider reading and writing to be complementary arts. On integrating composition into literature courses, see Gayle E. Whittier's "The World We Never Made" (1972), Charles Moran's "Teaching Writing/Teaching Literature" (1981), and Patrick Scott's "Diverse Journeys" (1982). In this regard, exploratory essays like Russell A. Hunt's "Toward a Process-Intervention Model in Literature Teaching" (1982) suggest that a reunification of reading and writing within English studies has already begun. If this is in fact the case, the "fake polarity" between literature and composition will prove to be as short-lived as it has been shortsighted.

References

Achtert, Walter S. "A History of English Studies to 1883 Based on the Research of William Riley Parker." Diss. New York University, 1972.

Alley, Alvin D. "Guiding Principles for the Teaching of Rhetoric." *CCC*, 25 (1974), 374–81.

Aphthonius. "*The Progymnasmata of Aphthonius* in Translation." Trans. Ray Nadeau. *Speech Mon*, 19 (1952), 264–85.

Applebee, Arthur N. *Tradition and Reform in the Teaching of English*. Urbana, Ill.: NCTE, 1974.

————. *Poetics*. Trans. Gerald F. Else. Ann Arbor: University of Michigan Press, 1967.

Aristotle. *The Rhetoric of Aristotle*. Trans. and ed. Lane Cooper. New York: Appleton-Century-Crofts, 1932.

Arrington, Philip. "Sentence Combining, Literature, and the Composing Process." *JETT*, 11, No. 2 (1982), 64–74.

Bain, Alexander. *English Composition and Rhetoric*. New York: Appleton, 1866.

Baldwin, Charles Sears. *Ancient Rhetoric and Poetic*. New York: Macmillan, 1924.

————. *Medieval Rhetoric and Poetic*. New York: Macmillan, 1928.

————. *Renaissance Literary Theory and Practice*. New York: Columbia University Press, 1939.

Barthes, Roland. *S/Z* [1970]. Trans. Richard Miller, New York: Hill, Wang, 1974.

————. *The Pleasure of the Text*. [1973]. Trans. Richard Miller. New York: Hill, Wang, 1975.

————. *Image-Music-Text*. Trans. Stephen Heath. New York: Hill, Wang, 1977a.

————. *Writing Degree Zero*. [1953]. Trans. Annette Lavers and Colin Smith. New York: Hill, Wang, 1977b.

————. *A Barthes Reader*. Ed. and introd. Susan Sontag. New York: Hill, Wang, 1982.

Behrens, Lawrence. "Meditations, Reminiscences, Polemics: Composition Readers and the Service Course." *CE*, 41 (1980), 561–70.

Berthoff, Ann E. "From Problem-Solving to a Theory of the Imagination." *CE*, 33 (1972), 636–50.

————. *Forming, Thinking, Writing: The Composing Imagination*. Rochelle Park, N.J.: Hayden, 1978.

————. *The Making of Meaning: Metaphors, Models, and Maxims for Writing Teachers*. Montclair, N.J.: Boynton/Cook, 1981.

Bleich, David. *Readings and Feelings: An Introduction to Subjective Criticism*. Urbana, Ill.: NCTE, 1975.

————. "The Identity of Pedagogy and Research in the Study of Response to Literature." *CE*, 42 (1980), 350–66.

Bloom, Harold, et al. *Deconstruction and Criticism*. New York: Seabury, 1979.

Booth, Wayne C. *The Rhetoric of Fiction*. Chicago: University of Chicago Press, 1961.

————. "The Rhetorical Stance." *CCC*, 14 (1963), 139–45.

————. "The Revival of Rhetoric." *PMLA*, 80 (1965), 8–12.

————. "Kenneth Burke's Way of Knowing." *Crit I*, 1 (1974a), 1–22.

————. *A Rhetoric of Irony*. Chicago: University of Chicago Press, 1974b.

————. *Critical Understanding: The Powers and Limits of Pluralism*. Chicago: University of Chicago Press, 1979.

————. "The Common Aims That Divide Us; or, Is There a 'Profession 1981'?" *ADE Bul*, No. 69 (1981), 1–5.

Bramer, George R. "Comp. vs Lit.—What's the Score?" *CCC*, 28 (1977), 30–33.

Brannon, Lil, and C. H. Knoblauch. "Teacher Commentary on Student Writing: The State of the Art." *FEN*, 10, No. 2 (1981), 1–4.

————. "On Students' Rights to Their Own Texts: A Model of Teacher Response." *CCC*, 33 (1982), 157–66.

Britton, James. *Language and Learning*. Middlesex, England: Penguin, 1970.

————. "The Composing Processes and the Functions of Writing." In *Research on Composing: Points of Departure*. Ed. Charles R. Cooper and Lee Odell. Urbana, Ill.: NCTE, 1978, pp. 13–28.

————, et al. *The Development of Writing Abilities (11–18)*. London: Macmillan, 1975.

Brooks, Cleanth, and Robert Penn Warren. *Understanding Poetry*. New York: Holt, 1938.

————. *Modern Rhetoric*. New York: Harcourt, Brace, 1949.

Burke, Kenneth. *Permanence and Change: An Anatomy of Purpose*. New York: New Republic, 1935.

————. *A Grammar of Motives*. New York: Prentice-Hall, 1945.

————. "Rhetoric—Old and New." *J Gen Ed*, 5 (1951), 202–9.

————. *Language as Symbolic Action: Essays on Life, Literature, and Method*. Berkeley: University of California Press, 1966.

————. *Counter-Statement* [1931]. Rev. ed. Berkeley: University of California Press, 1967.

————. "Dramatism." *International Encyclopedia of the Social Sciences* (1968).

————. *A Rhetoric of Motives*. Berkeley: University of California Press, 1969.

————. "Questions and Answers about the Pentad." *CCC*, 29 (1978), 330–35.

Burling, Robbins, "An Anthropological Glimpse of English as a Profession." *CE*, 39 (1977), 18–24.

Cain, William E. "Authority, 'Cognitive Atheism,' and the Aims of Interpretation: The Literary Theory of E. D. Hirsch." *CE*, 39 (1977), 333–45.

————. "Deconstruction in America: The Recent Literary Criticism of J. Hillis Miller." *CE*, 41 (1979), 367–82.

Carkeet, David. "How Critics Write and How Students Write." *CE*, 37 (1976), 599–604.

Christensen, Francis, and Bonniejean Christensen. *Notes Toward a New Rhetoric: Nine Essays for Teachers*. 2nd ed. New York: Harper, Row, 1978.

Cicero. *Phillipics*. Trans. Walter C. A. Ker. Cambridge, Mass.: Harvard University Press, 1926.

————. *De Oratore*. Vol. 1. Trans. E. W. Sutton and H. Rackham. Cambridge, Mass.: Harvard University Press, 1948.

————. *De Inventione, De Optimo Genere Oratorum, and Topica*. Trans. H. M. Hubbell. Cambridge, Mass.: Harvard University Press, 1949.

Clark, Donald L. "The Requirements of a Poet." *MP*, 16 (1918), 413–29.

————. *Rhetoric and Poetry in the Renaissance*. New York: Columbia University Press, 1922.

————. *John Milton at St. Paul's School*. New York: Columbia University Press, 1948.

————. "Ancient Rhetoric and English Renaissance Literature." *SQ*, 2 (1951a), 195–204.

————. "Imitation: Theory and Practice in Roman Rhetoric." *QJS*, 37 (1951b), 11–22.

————. "The Rise and Fall of Progymasmata in Sixteenth and Seventeenth Century Grammar Schools. *Speech Mon*, 19 (1952), 259–63.

————. *Rhetoric in Greco-Roman Education*. New York: Columbia University Press, 1957.

Clarke, M. L. *Rhetoric at Rome: A Historical Survey*. London: Barnes, Noble, 1962.

Coles, William E., Jr. "Teaching Writing; Teaching Literature: The Plague on Both Houses." *FEN*, 9, No. 3 (1981), 3–4, 13–16.

Comprone Joseph. "Kenneth Burke and the Teaching of Writing." *CCC*, 29 (1979), 336–40.

Conn, Peter. "Combining Literature and Composition: English 886." *ADE Bul*, No. 72 (1982), 4–6.

Connors, Robert J. "The Rise and Fall of the Modes of Discourse." *CCC*, 31 (1981), 444–55.

Corbett, Edward P. J. "A Composition Course Based on Literature." In *Teaching High School Composition*. Ed. Gary Tate and Edward P. J. Corbett. New York: Oxford University Press, 1970, pp. 195–204.

————. *Classical Rhetoric for the Modern Student*. 2nd ed. New York: Oxford University Press, 1971a.

————. "The Theory and Practice of Imitation in Classical Rhetoric." *CCC*, 22 (1971b), 243–50.

Corder, Jim W. "Rhetorical Analysis of Writing." In *Teaching Composition: 10 Bibliographic Essays*. Ed. Gary Tate. Fort Worth: Texas Christian University Press, 1976, pp. 233–40.

————. "Rhetoric and Literary Study: Some Lines of Inquiry." *CCC*, 32 (1981), 13–20.

Crane, Ronald S., ed. *Critics and Criticism: Ancient and Modern*. Chicago: University of Chicago Press, 1952.

Crowley, Sharon. "Of Gorgias and Grammatology." *CCC*, 30 (1979), 279–84.

Culler, Jonathan. "Structuralism." *Princeton Encyclopedia of Poetry and Poetics* (1974).

————. *Structuralist Poetics: Structuralism, Linguistics, and the Study of Literature*. Ithaca, N.Y.: Cornell University Press, 1975.

————. *The Pursuit of Signs: Semiotics, Literature, Deconstruction*. Ithaca, N.Y.: Cornell University Press, 1981.

Daiker, Donald A. "Integrating Composition and Literature: Some Practical Suggestions." 1979. ERIC ED 177 587.

————, Frank Jordan, Jr., and Jack E. Wallace. *Literature: Options for Reading and Writing*. New York: Harper, Row, forthcoming.

D'Angelo, Frank. "Imitation and Style." *CCC*, 24 (1973), 283–90.

————. "Modes of Discourse." In *Teaching Composition: 10 Bibliographic Essays*. Ed. Gary Tate. Fort Worth: Texas Christian University Press, 1976, pp. 111–35.

————. "Some Uses of Proverbs." *CCC*, 28 (1977), 365–69.

————. "Fables in the Composition Classroom." *AEB*, 20 (1978), 21–24.

————. "The Art of Paraphrase." *CCC*, 30 (1979), 255–59.

————. "Regaining Our Composure." *CCC*, 31 (1980), 420–26.

————. "The Dialogue." *RR*, 1 (1982), 72–82.

Derrida, Jacques. *Of Grammatology*. Trans. G. C. Spivak. Baltimore: Johns Hopkins University Press, 1976.

————. *Positions*. Trans. Alan Bass. Chicago: University of Chicago Press, 1981.

Dixon, Peter. *Rhetoric: The Critical Idiom 19*. London: Methuen, 1971.

Doherty, Paul C. "Hirsch's *Philosophy of Composition:* An Evaluation of the Argument." *CCC*, 33 (1982), 184–95.

Donoghue, Denis. "Deconstructing Deconstruction." NY R B, 12 (1980), 37–41.

————. *Ferocious Alphabets*. Boston: Little, Brown, 1981.

Douglas, Wallace. "Rhetoric for the Meritocracy: The Creation of Composition at Harvard." In *English in America: A Radical View of the Profession*. By Richard Ohmann. New York: Oxford University Press, 1976, pp. 97–132.

Eschholz, Paul A. "The Prose Models Approach: Using Products in the Process." In *Eight Approaches to Teaching Composition*. Ed. Timothy R. Donovan and Ben W. McClelland. Urbana, Ill.: NCTE, 1980, pp. 21–36.

Farrell, Thomas J. "Literacy, the Basics, and All That Jazz." *CE*, 38 (1977), 443–60.

————. "Developing Literacy: Walter J. Ong and Basic Writing." *JBW*, 2 (1978), 30–51.

Fenstermaker, John J. "Literature in the Composition Class." *CCC*, 28 (1977), 34–37.

Fischer, Michael. "Why Realism Seems So Naive: Romanticism, Professionalism, and Contemporary Critical Theory." *CE*, 40 (1979), 740–50.

Fish, Stanley. "How Ordinary Is Ordinary Language?" *NLH*, 5 (1973), 41–54.

———. *Is There a Text in This Class? The Authority of Interpretive Communities*. Cambridge, Mass.: Harvard University Press, 1980.

Fisher, Philip. "Questions of English." *CE*, 40 (1979), 727–39.

Fitch, Raymond E., ed. "Literary Theory in the English Classroom." *Focus: Teach Eng Lang Arts*, 7, No. 2 (1981).

Freisinger, Randall. "Creative Writing and Creative Composition." *CE*, 40 (1978), 283–87.

Frye, Northrop. *Anatomy of Criticism: Four Essays*. Princeton, N.J.: Princeton University Press, 1957.

———. *The Stubborn Structure: Essays on Criticism and Society*. Ithaca, N.Y.: Cornell University Press, 1970.

Fulkerson, Richard. "Four Philosophies of Composition." *CCC*, 30 (1979), 343–47.

Gage, John T. "Conflicting Assumptions about Intention in Teaching Reading and Composition." *CE*, 40 (1978), 255–63.

Garrison, Roger H. *A Creative Approach to Composition*. New York: Holt, 1951.

Golden, James L., and Edward P. J. Corbett, ed. *The Rhetoric of Blair, Campbell, and Whately*. New York: Holt, Rinehart, Winston, 1968.

Gorrell, Robert M. "Like a Crab Backward: Has the CCCC Been Worth It?" *CCC*, 30 (1979), 32–36.

Graff, Gerald. *Literature Against Itself: Literary Ideas in Modern Society*. Chicago: University of Chicago Press. 1979.

Greenbaum, Leonard A. "The Tradition of Complaint." *CE*, 31 (1969), 174–78.

———, and Rudolf B. Schmerl. *Course X: A Left Field Guide to Freshman English*. New York: Lippincott, 1970.

Grodin, Michael. *Ulysses in Progress*. Princeton, N.J.: Princeton University Press, 1980.

Gruber, William E. " 'Servile Copying' and the Teaching of English Composition." *CE*, 39 (1977), 491–97.

Hairston, Maxine. "The Winds of Change: Thomas Kuhn and the Revolution in the Teaching of Writing." *CCC*, 33 (1982), 76–88.

Halloran, S. M. "On the End of Rhetoric, Classical and Modern." *CE*, 36 (1975), 621–31.

Harari, Josué, ed. *Textual Strategies: Perspectives in Post-Structuralist Criticism*. Ithaca, N.Y.: Cornell University Press, 1979.

Harmon, William. "So Many Words: An Epistle to the Laodiceans." *ADE Bul*, No. 54 (1980), 11–14.

Harp, Richard L. "Using Elementary Literary Forms in the Composition Class." *CCC*, 29 (1978), 158–61.

Hart, John A., et al. "Literature in the Composition Course." *CCC*, 9 (1958), 236–41.

Hartman, Geoffrey H. *Beyond Formalism: Literary Essays 1958–1970*. New Haven: Yale University Press, 1970.

———. *Criticism in the Wilderness: The Study of Literature Today*. New Haven: Yale University Press, 1980.

Hatlen, Burton. "Why Is *The Education of Henry Adams* 'Literature,' While *The Theory of the Leisure Class* Is Not?" *CE*, 40 (1979), 665–76.

Hernadi, Paul, ed. *What Is Literature*? Bloomington: Indiana University Press, 1978.

Herrick Marvin T. "Rhetoric and Poetics." *Princeton Encyclopedia of Poetry and Poetics* (1974).

Hirsch, E. D., Jr. *Validity in Interpretation*. New Haven: Yale University Press, 1967.

———. " 'Intrinsic' Criticism." *CE*, 36 (1974), 446–57.

———. *The Aims of Interpretation*. Chicago: University of Chicago Press, 1976.

———. *The Philosophy of Composition*. Chicago: University of Chicago Press, 1977.

———. "What Isn't Literature?" In *What Is Literature?* Ed. Paul Hernadi. Bloomington: Indiana University Press, 1978, pp. 24–34.

———. "Remarks on Composition to the Yale English Department." In *The State of the Discipline, 1970s–1980s*. Ed. Jasper P. Neel. *ADE Bul*, No. 62 (1979), 63–65.

Holland, Norman N. *The Dynamics of Literary Response*. New York: Norton, 1968.

———. *Five Readers Reading*. New Haven: Yale University Press, 1975.

———, and Murray Schwartz. "The Delphi Seminar." *CE*, 36 (1975), 789–800.

Hollingsworth, Alan M. "Beyond Survival." *ADE Bul*, No. 54 (1977), 1–5.

Holzman, Michael. "Writing as Technique." *CE*, 44 (1982), 129–34.

Hook, J. N. "College English Departments: We May Be Present at Their Birth." *CE*, 40 (1978), 269–73.

———. *A Long Way Together: A Personal View of NCTE's First Sixty-Seven Years*. Urbana, Ill.: NCTE, 1979.

Horace. *Satires, Epistles, and Ars Poetica*. Rev. ed. Trans. H. Rushton Fairclough. Cambridge, Mass.: Harvard University Press, 1929.

Horner, Winifred Bryan, ed. *Composition and Literature: Bridging the Gap*. Chicago: University of Chicago Press, 1983.

Howe, Florence. "Literacy and Literature." *PMLA*, 89 (1974), 433–41.

Howell, Wilbur Samuel. *Logic and Rhetoric in England, 1500–1700*. Princeton, N.J.: Princeton University Press, 1935.

———. *Eighteenth Century British Logic and Rhetoric*. Princeton, N.J.: Princeton University Press, 1971.

Hunt, Russell A. "Toward a Process-Intervention Model in Literature Teaching." *CE*, 44 (1982), 345–57.

Irmscher, William F. *The Holt Guide to English*. 3rd ed. New York: Holt, Rinehart, Winston, 1981.

Johnson, Paula. "The Politics of 'Back to Basics.' " *ADE Bul*, No. 53 (1977), 1–4.

———. "Writing Programs and the English Department." In *The State of the Discipline, 1970s–1980s*. Ed. Jasper P. Neel. *ADE Bul*, No. 62 (1979), 46–52.

Joseph, Sister Miriam. *Rhetoric in Shakespeare's Time: Literary Theory of Renaissance Europe*. 1947; rpt. New York: Harcourt, Brace, World, 1962.

Kantor, Kenneth J. "Creative Expression in the English Curriculum: An Historical Perspective." *RTE*, 9 (1975), 5–29.

Kehl, D. G. "Composition in the Mimetic Mode: *Imitatio* and *Exercitatio*." In *Linguistics, Stylistics, and the Teaching of Composition*. Ed. Donald McQuade. Akron, Ohio: University of Akron Department of English, 1979, pp. 135–42.

Keith, Philip M. "Burke for the Composition Class." *CCC*, 28 (1977), 348–51.

Kinneavy, James L. *A Theory of Discourse: The Aims of Discourse*. Englewood Cliffs, N.J.: Prentice-Hall, 1971.

Kitzhaber, Albert R. "Rhetoric in American Colleges, 1850–1900." Diss. University of Washington, 1953.

Knapton, James, and Bertrand Evans. *Teaching a Literature-Based English Program*. New York: Random House, 1967.

Kurzweil, Edith. *The Age of Structuralism: Lévi-Strauss to Foucault*. New York: Columbia University Press, 1980.

Kytle, Ray. "Slaves, Serfs, or Colleagues—Who Shall Teach College Composition?" *CCC*, 22 (1971), 339–41.

Langer, Susanne. " 'Expressive Language' and the Expressive Function of Poetry." In *On Expressive Language*. Ed. Heinz Werner. Worcester, Mass.: Clark University Press, 1955, pp. 3–9.

Lanham, Richard A. "Post-Darwinian Humanism." In *The State of the Discipline, 1970s–1980s*. Ed. Jasper P. Neel. *ADE Bul*, No. 62 (1979), 53–62.

Leitch, Vincent B. "A Primer of Recent Critical Theories." *CE*, 39 (1977), 138–52.

Lentricchia, Frank. *After the New Criticism*. Chicago: University of Chicago Press, 1980.

Lewis, Philip. "The Post-structuralist Condition." *Diacritics*, 12 (1982), 2–24.

Lunsford, Andrea A. "Alexander Bain's Contributions to Discourse Theory." *CE*, 44 (1982), 290–300.

Mailloux, Steven. "Reader Response Criticism and Teaching Composition." In *Interpretive Conventions: The Reader in the Study of American Fiction*. Ithaca, N.Y.: Cornell University Press, 1982, pp. 208–16.

Malone, Kemp. "The Rise of Modern Philology." *Bull Mod Hum Res Assoc*, 30 (1958), 19–31.

Marrou, Henri I. *A History of Education in Antiquity*. Trans. George Lamb. New York: Sheed, Ward, 1956.

McKeon, Richard. "Literary Criticism and the Concept of Imitation in Antiquity." *MP*, 34 (1936), 1–35.

Meikkle, Henry W. "The Chair of Rhetoric and Belles Lettres." *Univ of Edinburgh J*, 13 (1945), 89–103.

Memering, Dean. "The Reading/Writing Heresy." *CCC*, 28 (1977), 223–26.

Miller, J. Hillis. "The Function of Rhetorical Study at the Present Time." In *The State of the Discipline, 1970s–1980s*. Ed. Jasper P. Neel. *ADE Bul*, No. 62 (1979), 10–18.

Miller, Susan. "Is There a Text in This Class?" *FEN*, 2, No. 1 (1982), 20–24.

Moffett, James. *Teaching the Universe of Discourse*. Boston: Houghton Mifflin, 1968.

———. "Learning to Write by Writing." In *Teaching High School Composition*. Ed. Gary Tate and Edward P. J. Corbett. New York: Oxford University Press, 1970, pp. 43–60.

———. *Active Voice: A Writing Program Across the Curriculum*. Montclair, N.J.: Boynton/Cook, 1981.

———, and Betty Jane Wagner. *Student-Centered Language Arts and Reading: A Handbook for Teachers*. 2nd ed. Boston: Houghton Mifflin, 1976.

Moran, Charles. "Teaching Writing/Teaching Literature." *CCC*, 32 (1981), 21–29.

Morenberg, Max. Review of *The Norton Sampler*, ed. Thomas Cooley. *CCC*, 31 (1980), 100–102.

Nadeau, Ray. "*The Progymnasmata of Aphthonius* in Translation." *Common Man*, 19 (1952), 264–85.

Neel, Japser P., ed. *Options for the Teaching of English: Freshman Composition*. New York: Modern Language Association, 1978.

———, ed. *The State of the Discipline, 1970s–1980s*. *ADE Bul*, No. 62 (1979).

O'Banion, John D. "*A Theory of Discourse*: A Retrospective." *CCC*, 33 (1982), 196–201.

Ong, Walter J., S.J. *The Presence of the Word: Some Prolegomena for Cultural and Religious History*. New Haven: Yale University Press, 1967.

———. *Rhetoric, Romance, and Technology: Studies in the Interaction of Expression and Culture*. Ithaca, N.Y.: Cornell University Press, 1971.

———. *Interfaces of the Word: Studies in the Evolution of Consciousness and Culture*. Ithaca, N.Y.: Cornell University Press, 1977.

———. "Literacy and Orality in Our Times." *ADE Bul*, No. 58 (1978), 1–7.

Ozick, Cynthia. "The Lesson of the Master." *NY R B*, 12 August 1982, pp. 20–21.

Parisi, Peter. "Close Reading, Creative Writing, and Cognitive Development." *CE*, 41 (1979), 57–67.

Parker, William Riley. "Where Do English Departments Come From?" *CE*, 28 (1967), 339–51.

Perl, Sondra. "The State of the Art in Composition." *ADE Bul*, No. 63 (1980), 44–46.

Peterson, Bruce T. "Writing about Responses: A Unified Model of Reading, Interpretation, and Composition." *CE*, 44 (1982), 459–69.

Peterson, Linda. "Getting a Little Help from Our (Literary) Friends." *WPA*, 5, No. 3 (1982), 15–20.

Petrosky, Anthony. "From Story to Essay: Reading and Writing." *CCC*, 33 (1982), 19–36.

Pirsig, Robert. *Zen and the Art of Motorcycle Maintenance*. New York: Bantam, 1974.

Plato. *The Collected Dialogues of Plato*. Ed. Edith Hamilton and Huntington Cairns. Bollingen Series 71. Princeton, N.J.: Princeton University Press, 1963.

Ponsot, Marie, and Rosemary Deen. *Beat Not the Poor Desk: Writing: What to Teach, How to Teach It and Why*. Montclair, N.J.: Boynton/Cook, 1982.

Purves, Alan C. "Putting Readers in Their Places: Some Alternatives to Cloning Stanley Fish." *CE*, 42 (1980), 228–36.

Puttenham, George. *The Arte of English Poesie* [1589]. Ed. Gladys D. Willcock and Alice Walker. Cambridge: Cambridge University Press, 1936.

Quintilian. *Institutio Oratoria*. 4 vols. Trans. H. E. Butler. Cambridge, Mass.: Harvard University Press, 1920–1922.

Rabinowitz, Nancy and Peter. "The Critical Balance: Reader, Text, and Meaning." *CE*, 41 (1980), 924–32.

Ransom, John Crowe. *The New Criticism*. Norfolk, Conn.: New Directions, 1941.

Regis, Eugene, Jr. "Literature by the Reader: The Affective Theory of Stanley Fish." *CE*, 38 (1976), 263–80.

Richards, I. A. *Principles of Literary Criticism*. New York: Harcourt, Brace, World, 1925.

———. *Practical Criticism: A Study of Literary Judgment*. New York: Harcourt, Brace, World, 1929.

———. *Speculative Instruments*. Chicago: University of Chicago Press, 1955.

———. *Poetries and Sciences: A Reissue of Science and Poetry (1926, 1935)*. New York: Norton, 1970.

Rockas, Leo. *Modes of Rhetoric*. New York: St. Martin's, 1964.

———. "The Rhetoric of Doodle." *CE*, 40 (1978), 139–44.

Rosenblatt, Louise M. *The Reader, the Text, the Poem: The Transactional Theory of the Literary Work*. Carbondale: Southern Illinois University Press, 1978.

Rosenthal, Peggy. "Deciphering *S/Z*." *CE*, 37 (1975), 125–44.

Ross, Charles L. *The Composition of "The Rainbow" and "Women in Love."* Charlottesville: University Press of Virginia, 1979.

Rubinstein, S. Leonard. "Composition: A Collision with Literature." *CE*, 27 (1966), 273–77.

Rudolph, Frederick. *Curriculum: A History of the American Undergraduate Course of Study since 1636.* San Francisco: Jossey-Bass, 1977.

Samuels, Marilyn Schauer. "Norman Holland's 'New Paradigm' and the Teaching of Writing." *JBW*, 2 (1978), 52–61.

Savereid, Jay. "The Impermanent and Unbeautiful Rhetoric." *CCC*, 24 (1973), 31–35.

Scaglione, Aldo D. *The Classical Theory of Composition: From Its Origins to the Present.* Chapel Hill: University of North Carolina Press, 1972.

Scharbach, Alexander. "Rhetoric and Literary Criticism: Why Their Separation?" *CCC*, 23 (1972), 185–88.

Scholes, Robert. *Structuralism in Literature: An Introduction.* New Haven: Yale University Press, 1974.

Schultz, John. "The Story Workshop Method: Writing from Start to Finish." *CE*, 39 (1977), 411–36.

————. *Writing from Start to Finish.* Montclair, N.J.: Boynton/Cook, 1982.

Schulz, Max, and Michael Holzman. "English Departments—Writing Programs: Marriage or Divorce?" *ADE Bul*, No. 70 (1981), 26–29.

Scott, Patrick. "Diverse Journeys: Free-Writing, John Keats, and the Teaching of Poetry." *JETT*, 11 (1982), 28–38.

Selz, Dorothy B. "Structuralism for the Non-Specialist: A Glossary and a Bibliography." *CE*, 37 (1975), 160–66.

Shenk, Robert. "The Self Enlarged: The Case for Good Literature in the Composition Class." *E Rec*, 32, No. 4 (1981), 9–12.

Sidney, Sir Philip. *Defence of Poesy* [1595]. Ed. Dorothy M. Macardle. New York: St. Martin's, 1966.

Smith, Adam. *Lectures on Rhetoric and Belles Lettres.* Ed. and introd. John M. Lothian. Camden, N.J.: Nelson, 1963.

Smith, Thomas N. "Literature: The Fundamental Art." *The Leaflet* [New England Association of Teachers of English NEATE], 80 (1981), 4–6.

Smithson, Ian. "Structuralism as a Method of Literary Criticism." *CE*, 37 (1975), 145–59.

Sommers, Nancy. "Revision Strategies of Student Writers and Experienced Adult Writers." *CCC*, 31 (1980), 378–88.

Sontag, Susan. *A Barthes Reader.* New York: Hill, Wang, 1982.

Sosinski, James J. "The Use of the Word 'Text' in Critical Discourse." *CE*, 39 (1977), 121–36.

A Statement on the Preparation of Teachers of English and Language Arts. Urbana, Ill.: NCTE, 1976.

Steinmann, Martin, Jr., ed. *New Rhetorics.* New York: Scribner's, 1967.

Stewart, Donald C. "Comp. vs. Lit.: Which Is Your Job and Which Is Your Strength?" *CE*, 40 (1978), 65–69.

Stull, William L. *Combining and Creating: Sentence Combining and Generative Rhetoric.* New York: Holt, Rinehart, Winston, 1983.

Sturrock, John, ed. *Structuralism and Since: From Lévi-Strauss to Derrida*. New York: Oxford University Press, 1979.

Sulieman, Susan, and Inge Crossman, ed. *The Reader in the Text: Essays on Audience and Interpretation*. Princeton, N.J.: Princeton University Press, 1980.

Szilak, Dennis. "Teachers of Composition: A Re-Niggering." *CE*, 39 (1977), 25–32.

Tate, Gary, ed. *Teaching Composition: 10 Bibliographic Essays*. Fort Worth: Texas Christian University Press, 1976.

Todorov, Tzvetan. "The Notion of Literature." *NLH*, 5 (1973), 5–16.

Tompkins, Jane P., ed. *Reader-Response Criticism: From Formalism to Post-Structuralism*. Baltimore: Johns Hopkins University Press, 1980.

Turner, Linda M. "On First Reading Burke's 'A Rhetoric of Motives.' " *CCC*, 24 (1973), 22–30.

Veilh, Donald P. "An Historical Analysis of the Relations between 'English' and 'Speech' since 1910." Diss. Teachers College, Columbia University, 1952.

Vendler, Helen. "Presidential Address 1980." *PMLA*, 96 (1981), 344–50.

Wallace, Karl R. "Rhetorical Exercises in Tudor Education." *QJS*, 22 (1936), 28–51.

Warnock, John. "The Relation of Critical Perspectives to Teaching Methods in Composition." *CE*, 34 (1973), 690–700.

Weathers, Winston. *An Alternate Style: Options in Composition*. Rochelle Park, N.J.: Hayden, 1980.

Wellek, René. *A History of Modern Criticism, 1750–1950*. 4 vols. New Haven: Yale University Press, 1955–1965.

———. "Literature and Its Cognates." *Dictionary of the History of Ideas* (1973).

———. "What Is Literature." In *Rhetoric, Philosophy, and Literature: An Exploration*. Ed. Don M. Butts. West Lafayette, IN: Purdue University Press, 1978, pp. 16–23.

———, and Austin Warren. *Theory of Literature*. 3rd ed. New York: Harcourt, Brace, World, 1956.

Wheelwright, Philip. *The Burning Fountain: A Study in the Language of Symbolism*. Rev. ed. Bloomington: Indiana University Press, 1968.

Whittier, Gayle, E. "The World We Never Made: Teaching Writing in a Literature Course." *CCC*, 23 (1972), 175–84.

Williams, Raymond. *Marxism and Literature*. New York: Oxford University Press, 1977.

Wimsatt, William K., Jr. *The Verbal Icon: Studies in the Meaning of Poetry*. Louisville: University Press of Kentucky, 1954.

———, and Monroe E. Beardsley. "The Intentional Fallacy." *Sewanee R*, 54 (1946), 468–88.

———, and Monroe E. Beardsley. "The Affective Fallacy." *Swanee R*, 57 (1949), 31–55.

———, and Cleanth Brooks. *Literary Criticism: A Short History*. 1957; rpt. New York: Vintage, 1967.

Winterowd, W. Ross. "Getting It Together in the English Department." *ADE Bull*, No. 55 (1977), 28–31.

Woodward, William H. *Studies in Education During the Age of the Renaissance, 1400–1600*. New York: Russell, 1965.

Yelin, Louise. "Deciphering the Academic Hieroglyph: Marxist Literary Theory and the Practice of Basic Writing." *JBW*, 2 (1978), 13–29.

Young, Edward. *Conjectures on Original Composition* [1759]. Ed. Edith J. Morley. New York: Longmans, Green, 1918.
Zeilonka, Alfred Walter. ''The Modern Language Association of America, 1883–1960.'' Diss. State University of New York at Buffalo, 1964.

Reading and Writing: A Survey of the Questions about Texts

JASPER NEEL

Until 25 years ago, the phenomenon of reading was commonly construed as one person's attempt to extract from a text the meaning another person had put in it. Most literate people were no more concerned with how they read than ambulatory people were with how they walked. Even today the actual process of reading remains largely a mystery, much more so than walking, which neurophysiology has explained in the minutest detail. Astonishingly, those working in composition have remained innocent of and uninterested in theories of the reading process, even though the inextricable connection between writing and reading is self-evident.

There are good reasons for the split between writing and reading theories. Training in writing has been a college-level activity (albeit a grudging one until the last few years) ever since there have been colleges in North America. Arthur Applebee (*Tradition and Reform in the Teaching of English* [1974]) gave a detailed history of the emergence of English as a discipline in America, and Jasper Neel ("Vicissitudo Non Est" [1977]) explained the political history of composition in college English departments. Reading, on the other hand, has always been regarded as an elementary school activity. In addition, most serious research about the process of reading has been done by educationists or psychologists whose behavioral biases and social science jargon are off-putting to humanists. In the realm of language theory, the ascendency of New Criticism and archetypal criticism during the middle part of this century left theoretical speculation about the nature of texts to philosophers, who, because they distrust words, write in a manner even more inscrutable than psychologists.

Even today there are very few who specialize in composition from the angle of reading or textual theory. The three-part discussion in this chapter provides for the composition specialist an introduction to reading, or decoding, theory; to the philosophical, linguistic, and psychoanalytic theory upon which modern textual theory depends and without which it is incomprehensible; and to current textual theory and its influence on theories about the process of reading.

Current Theories of Reading

Decoding is the term used in this section to mean reading at the most basic level. Reading as decoding is an enormous industry in America—much larger than composition. The International Reading Association (IRA) has 61,000 members. It is more than twice the size of the Modern Language Association (MLA) and the Conference on College Composition and Communication (CCCC) combined. In a chapter like this, it would be impossible to provide even a selective bibliography of all publications in decoding theory. It is, however, possible to choose a few texts that have immediate relevance to composition. The common theme of all sources in this section is that the reader is far more important in the transaction between writer and reader than had been thought formerly. There is a revolution afoot among decoding theorists, with the revolutionaries arguing that as much information is put into a text by the decoder as by the encoder. Alan Hollingsworth (''Beyond Literacy'' [1973] and ''Beyond Survival'' [1977]) provided brief explanations of the changes occurring in decoding theory, of how disastrous the effects of the predominantly stimulus-response model of reading used during the mid-twentieth century has been, and of how decoding theories affect college English departments.

The idea that meaning resides as much in the brain of the reader as in the inscription of the writer is not a product of the 1970s. In 1908 E. B. Huey published *The Psychology and Pedagogy of Reading*, a book that was six decades ahead of its time. It was republished in 1968 and serves as a theoretical foundation for recent decoding theorists. Also, John Dewey's *Art as Experience* (1934), deals in part with decoding. He argued that each individual has a unique reading experience, and ''creates something new, something previously not existing'' (p. 108).

Psychology and psycho-linguistics have provided the impetus for changes in the conception of the decoding process. Eleanor Gibson and Harry Levin offered a good introduction to the psychology of decoding (*The Psychology of Reading* [1975]). Different decoders, they argued, decode in very different ways. Mature decoders tend to use highly ''economical'' strategies, which process very little of the vocabulary and punctuation in a text and which rely on careful selection and continuous synthesis. The image that Gibson and Levin gave of an adept decoder is of someone who moves exceedingly quickly across the surface of a text using highly idiosyncratic and entirely unconscious strategies for verifying that the meaning being imposed conforms to that intended by the encoder.

The best, most influential introduction to the psycho-linguistics of reading is the work of Frank Smith (*Understanding Reading* [1971] and *Psycholinguistics and Reading* [1973]). The process of reading, Smith argued, is the reduction of uncertainty. The brain and the decoder's prior knowledge of the world contribute much more than does what is on the page. Decoding is a sort of oscillation between prediction and confirmation: the brain tells the eye what it expects to see on the page; the eye in turn confirms the prediction; thus a good decoder can operate at a rapid rate. Some of Smith's experiments imply that 90 percent of the information necessary for decoding comes from the brain. Smith explained his ideas about the psychological aspects of writing in *Writing and the Writer* (1982).

Psychological and psycho-linguistic theories that reading depends more on the decoder than on the encoder and that reading is a transaction with, not an extraction from, a text began to influence reading specialists in the late 1960s. Two collections of essays, *The Psycholinguistic Nature of the Reading Process* (Kenneth Goodman, ed. [1968]) and *Basic Studies in Reading* (Harry Levin and Joanna Williams, eds. [1970]), are based on psycho-linguistic research. The authors of these essays contended that word recognition and *phonics* (the ability to pronounce words correctly and to associate aural and visual word images) have little to do with comprehension. In general, they argued that reading comprehension is only superficially different from speech comprehension, and they pointed out that every other letter, or about one word in five, can be omitted and a fluent reader can still comprehend. The model of reading projected by these essayists involves word recognition only slightly and letter identification not at all. A good reader skips directly from distinctive features to comprehension as if letter and word shapes were merely slight clues. Moreover, there is no evidence that the beginning reader moves in stages through letter identification and word recognition. Readers seem to make the leap to comprehension right away, and at no point in the development of decoding ability does letter or word identification play any sort of conscious role.

In the 1970s Kenneth and Yetta Goodman developed a strategy for measuring reading comprehension, which they called "reading miscue inventory." Using this technique, they have been able to show that readers comprehend texts in dialects and with vocabularies that the readers themselves have not mastered. In 1976 David Allen and Dorothy Watson edited *Findings of Research in Miscue Analysis*, a collection of essays on the effect that reading miscue inventory has on decoding instruction.

Two essays by Kenneth Goodman, both published in 1976, are important to an understanding of psycho-linguistic theory of the decoding process. In Goodman's "What Do We Know about Reading?" (see Allen and Watson, *Findings of Research in Miscue Analysis* [1976], pp. 54–65) he argued that the message produced by the writer depends very much on what the *reader* brings to the text. In his "Reading" (1976) he explained the sequence of and strategies for telling a text what it says and the risks of reading caused by the fluent reader's need to anticipate what a text will say. For a complete, annotated bibliography of psycho-linguistics and reading, see Kenneth and Yetta Goodman, *Linguistics, Psycholinguistics, and the Teaching of Reading* (1980).

For the composition specialist, the most useful recent development in the decoding theory of the last five years is called the "schema," or "schemata-theoretic," view of reading. The following sources are accessible to someone who is not a reading specialist and offer a comprehensive introduction: Robert Anderson, "The Notion of Schemata and the Educational Enterprise" (1977); Roger Schank and Robert Abelson, *Scripts, Plans, Goals, and Understanding* (1977); Marilyn J. Adams and Allan Collins, *A Schema-Theoretic View of Reading* (1977); David Rumelhart, "Schemata" (1980); and Robert de Beaugrande, "Design Criteria for Process Models of Reading" (1981). Following the work of Smith and Goodman, these writers argued that a text does not so much carry meaning as it provides directions for readers to construct meaning from their own prior knowledge and experiences. Reading is not merely the retrieval of information stored in a text by an author. In fact, if the text does not provide enough directions fitting into the "schema" of decoding in the reader's brain, the reader will be unable to read. Anthony Petrosky, "From Story to Essay" (1982), offers a good introduction to the relationship between "schema" theory and the composing process.

The idea that much, perhaps most, of the information in the decoding process comes from the mind of the reader and therefore that a reader will be unable to decode a text that does not fit his pre-existing "schema" of decoding is the most interesting in current decoding theory and has the most immediate consequences for the composition teacher. There is, however, another "school" of decoding theorists whose ideas are important. American educators have paid very little attention to this school because it is located in Third World countries with Marxist leanings and the base theory of the school is that literacy occurs only when the decoding process becomes political. The founder of this school is Brazilian educator Paulo Freire: *Pedagogy of the Oppressed* (1970b), *Cultural Action for Freedom* (1970a), and *Pedagogy in Process* (1978). Freire, who has designed astonishingly successful literacy campaigns in Brazil and Cuba, argued that reading and learning to read are highly political acts. Since literacy is the human equivalent of controlling external reality, only those who believe they can control their circumstances can learn to read. Literacy campaigns in capitalist countries are always doomed, because the illiterate (Freire would say "oppressed") must internalize the reduced, oppressed self-image implied by their teachers ("oppressors"). However, when reading is made an act of revolution, when it is joined with the act of destroying the oppressor, illiterate people learn to read quickly. One's ability to read depends on the self-conception that an encounter with a text creates. Education, said Freire, is never neutral; it serves for domestication or oppression. Those alienated from the master class cannot overcome their dependency by being incorporated into the system that excludes them. They must overthrow and remake it.

Jonathan Kozol, "A New Look at the Literacy Campaign in Cuba" (1978), offered an account of the 1961 Cuban literacy campaign, which was inspired by Freire's theories. In 11 months 16 percent of the Cuban population learned to read. The whole program was associated with the Castro revolution. The act of reading became synonymous with revolutionary warfare, and the first words the peasants learned to read were the names of the enemy: United States and Organization of American States. Nan Elsasser and Kyle Fiore, " 'Strangers No More' " (1982), described an American literacy program based on a softened Freirean theory. They, too, suggested that the self-conception of readers is shaped by their relationship with the text. They cause the text to exist, and the text cannot exist for them if it carries with it an unacceptable self-image.

The Background of Modern Textual Theory

Most college English professors are aware that literary criticism is undergoing a radical change. Although there is a great deal of controversy not only about the nature of that change but also about its value, the general drift is away from extracting meaning from a text and toward answering one or more of the following questions: How does a reader read? What is the nature of a text? What is the relationship between reader and writer? The general assumption behind all of these questions is that no definitive reading of a text is possible.

One of the problems with recent critical and textual theory is that it is jargon-ridden. It depends on familiarity with a hodgepodge of mostly European linguists, philosophers, psychoanalysts, and anthropologists. Since most English professors are unfamiliar with this background, they simply dismiss its modern proponents whose writings seem opaque. The purpose of this section is to introduce a highly selective bibliography that is accessible in English and that provides a solid background to current textual theory. The trail begins with the Swiss linguist Ferdinand de Saussure and the Harvard philosopher Charles Sanders Peirce and ends with the French philosopher Jacques Derrida.

Although de Saussure did not publish his theories, after his death the lecture notes of his students were compiled and published as *Cours de linguistique générale* (translated by Wade Baskin as *Course in General Linguistics* [1959]). De Saussure defined six terms that are widely used by modern textual theorists: *semiology*; the triad of *signifier, signified*, and *sign*; and the pair, *value* and *difference*.

Semiology (or *semiotics*) is de Saussure's term for "a science that studies the life of signs within society" (p. 16). The founding assumptions of semiology are: (1) almost every aspect of human culture—including not only language but food, medicine, religion, etc.—results from a system of signs whose operation is governed by laws of representation that make the signs comprehensible; (2) all sign systems, and thus almost all of human culture, are linguistic in origin.

An individual 'sign' is the result of a union between a 'signifier' and a 'signified.' This union is much more than conjoining a thing with a name; it is the temporary, arbitrary association of a concept with a sound image. De Saussure argued that both thought and sound are floating, amorphous masses. Each mass is permanently separated from the other; thus, any concept ('signified') can be linked temporarily with any sound image ('signifier'). When such a link occurs, the result is a 'sign.' A 'sign' is *always* a psychological phenomenon, occurring only in the mind of someone who operates within the semiological system that allows the link between 'signifier' and 'signified.' No 'signifier' has a natural connection with a 'signified'; the link is always arbitrary. De Saussure used two diagrams to demonstrate his idea:

1. $S \rightarrow \frac{s}{s'}$

   S = sign $\rightarrow$ = rewrite

   s = signifier $-$ = both the permanent gap and the

   s' = signified   temporary link between s and s'

2. | Signifier | Signified |
   |:---------:|:---------:|
   | Sign | |

According to Saussure, each 'sign' achieves its value from the differences within the system. A 'sign' *occurs* when a 'signifier' and 'signified' are linked, as in $s \rightarrow \frac{s}{s'}$. But a 'sign' *achieves value* solely from the simultaneous presence of all of the other signs in the system, as in $V \rightarrow \frac{s}{s'} \equiv \frac{s}{s'} \equiv \frac{s}{s'}$ (V = value; $\rightarrow$ = rewrite; $\equiv$ = not equal to but may be substituted for). The content of a 'sign' ''is really fixed only by the concurrence of everything that exists outside it'' (p. 115). The most precise characteristic of a 'sign' is in being what the others are not (difference); ''whatever distinguishes one sign from the others constitutes it'' (value) (p. 121).

Although de Saussure is a linguist, concerned primarily with speech, he is also a semiotician, concerned with any type of transaction of meaning. He explained briefly the relationship between speech and writing. Writing, which he called ''graphic representation,'' usurps and tyrannizes language, even though it exists for the sole purpose of representing language. This is true because: (1) Writing seems more ''permanent and stable.'' Although this appearance is a fiction, people prefer superficial representation to the real thing—speech. (2) The graphic forces itself on the perceiver, because visual impressions last longer than aural ones. (3) The literary language of school, grammars, and dictionaries assumes the primary place, and people forget they spoke before writing. (4) In a disagreement between speech and orthography, books are used to settle the dispute. The upshot of such conceptions of writing is that texts are more ephemeral and less trustworthy than speech. Moreover, they are deceitful, because they seem so precise and permanent.

Peirce, like de Saussure, left most of his works unpublished. They are, however, available through the *Collected Papers of Charles Sanders Peirce* (1931–1960), published after his death. This is an enormous collection, consisting of eight volumes; thus no bibliographic summary can do it justice. There are, however, a few ideas that can be extracted from Peirce's writing that are important to composition theory and clarify the ideas of Roland Barthes and Jacques Derrida.

Peirce, like de Saussure, was a semiologist, a student of the science of signs, and also like de Saussure, he tended to operate through a sort of tripartite analysis.

Peirce argued that the existence of a sign requires not only a signifier (vehicle) and signified (concept) but an interpretant—another sign or body of signs that is either concurrent with the sign in question or present in memory. For Peirce, the meaning of a sign is another sign that can translate it. Peirce's term *interpretant* corresponds roughly to de Saussure's term *value*.

Peirce contended that all signs have a dual nature: the sign itself and the context of signs from which it stands out and by which it is invested with meaning. Even humans are a sign embedded in a historical continuum. The mind, as it encounters other signs, creates an interpretation based on past experience. Thus no two minds ever produce identical interpretations. In reverse, through all of its interpretations of signs, the mind embodies itself to itself, thus becoming a sign (Vol. 2, Section 94).

Peirce divided signs into three types—icons, indexes, and symbols (Vol. 4, Section 572). Icons substitute for their object by having a quality similar enough to allow for substitution. Icons help to obtain information, but do not carry it. An example of an icon is a geometric figure representing a mathematical hypothesis. Indexes represent their object because some aspect of the object causes the sign. For example, a weathercock is an index for the direction of the wind. But indexes can be mendacious. If, for instance, the wind ceases blowing or blows only lightly in a different direction, the weathercock lies. Symbols represent their objects by appealing to law or habit. A reasoned argument, for example, is a symbol for a conclusion. A good argument will appeal to the laws of argument or logic.

Peircean semiological analysis is a powerful tool. Two recent examples (both 1982) of the effects of such analysis are Peter Salus's "What Is Evidence Evidence Of?" and Bruce Thompson's "The Application of Peircean Semiotic to Logic." Salus called into question the whole idea of evidence and argued that even the "pure sciences" are largely a combination of linguistic imposition of taxonomy on the one hand and artificial arrangement of highly random phenomena on the other hand. Thompson contended that the supposed dichotomy between induction and deduction that appears in many composition texts (and elsewhere) is false. He showed that *all* empirical study is based on a premise of some type and can be no better than the founding premise.

The next stage on what might be called the "road to Derrida" is another pair of language theorists. This pair also consists of a linguist, Roman Jakobson, and a philosopher, John Austin.

In "Concluding Statement" (1960) Jakobson provided a diagram for locating a text. Reading cannot occur until the text's relative place on the diagram is identified. W. Ross Winterowd explained this diagram's significance to the composing process in the introduction to *Contemporary Rhetoric* (1975). Jakobson argued that for reading to occur, an addresser (writer) must send a message to an addressee (reader). For the message to be operative, there must be a "context" (a situation in which the two can come together), a "code" common to both writer and reader, and a "contact" (a physical channel and psychological contact that keeps the reader's attention focused on the message). The verbal structure of the message depends largely on which of the six functions is primary. Messages focusing on the writer are *emotive*, the expression of the writer's emotion for its own sake. Messages focusing on the reader tend towards the vocative or imperative and are not liable to a truth test. One would not, for example, respond to "attach rod A to fender B" with "is it true or not true?" Jakobson called messages focusing on the reader *conative*. Messages focused on the context between reader and writer are *referential*. Those intended to establish, prolong, or test the validity of the contact between reader and writer are *phatic*. Those intended to study or check the commonality of the code in use are *metalingual*. A message focused on itself is *poetic*. Hence all texts are situated at some point on a dual axis, something like the following:

context
(referential)

message
(poetic)

writer   reader
(emotive) ─────────────────────────────────────── (conative)
contact
(phatic)

code
(metalingual)

A reader who cannot intuitively locate the text will receive a garbled message. A writer and reader without a context for relating to each other, without a common code, or without a channel for physical *and* psychological contact cannot generate a message at all.

The English philosopher J. L. Austin developed another mode of "locating" a text so that the transmission of meaning can occur. His theory is called "speech act" theory and is articulated in *How to Do Things with Words* (1962). (For a full introduction to speech act theory see also William Alston, *Philosophy of Language* [1964]; John Searle, *Speech Acts* [1968]; and Seymour Chatman, "The Structure of Narrative Transmission" [1975]). According to Austin, texts consist of sentences, and sentences have three separate forces: grammar, intention, and effect. Grammar Austin named the "locutionary force." This is somewhat like Jakobson's "code." Both the encoder and the decoder must operate in a common grammar, or a *locution*—a saying or writing—cannot exist. Intention of the encoder, he named "illocution." Effect on the decoder he named "perlocution." The locution, illocution, perlocution triad is an elegant, powerful way of studying a text. Once a locutionary base is established, both writer and reader attempt to achieve a match between illocution—what the writer wishes to effect—and per-locution—the effect actually achieved.

Although de Saussure, Peirce, Jakobson, and Austin do not constitute light reading, their major works are easily found in English and are, with patience and persistence, not too difficult to comprehend. That simply cannot be said about French psychoanalyst Jacques Lacan, who is the next major figure in the background to modern textual theory. Much of Lacan's work has not been translated. What has been translated is undeniably difficult to read not only because Lacan writes primarily for other psychoanalysts but because his style is willfully mysterious, elliptical, and vague. In places it is allusive and impressionistic to the point of appearing nothing more than a tease. Before reading Lacan, it is essential to read de Saussure's *Course in General Linguistics* (1959); at least volumes 4, 5, 18, and 23 of Freud's *Works* (1971–1972a, b, and c); and Claude Lévi-Strauss's *Elementary Structures of Kinship* (1969) and *Structural Anthropology* (1963). See above for de Saussure. The volumes from Freud provide an introduction to his ideas about dreams, pleasure, and psychoanalytic method. Lévi-Strauss, founder of structural anthropology, described a methodology for analyzing human culture. His purpose was to discover those universal social and mental processes that manifest themselves in cultural institutions.

As a psychoanalyst, Lacan operated from a double base: the Freudian theory of personality and the de Saussurean theory of language. Lacan made one fundamentally important change in de Saussurean analysis. Rather than focusing on the *sign*, the conjunction of signifier and signified, he focused on the *split*, or impenetrable line, between signifier and signified. Whereas de Saussure (and Peirce) focused analysis on signs, Lacan focused analysis more on the play between signifier and signified and on the hypothesis that what would make a sign (for example, contact between signifier and signified) is really a gap, or an uncrossable line. Signs, in Lacanian analysis, do not really occur; they merely seem to.

Language, Lacan argued, operates on two axes: metaphor, which requires one thing to stand for another, and metonymy, which requires that the part stand for the whole. Metaphor can be said to operate vertically, metonymy linearly, as in this sketch:

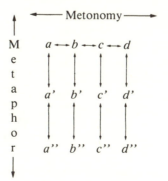

Any term must be extracted from this matrix; thus exact signification is impossible, because these two axes authorize substitutions of signifiers thereby making the meaning appear to "float" somewhere without being literally contained anywhere. Because metaphor and metonymy allow signification to be different from what is being said or written, they make language autonomous from meaning. Signifiers do signify, but the signified occurs in the commonality of shared experience and through the situation of signifiers in the code. Pure signifiers could appear only outside the code and would be intelligible to no one, because they would be situated in no code. There is an impenetrable line between the network of signifiers and the network of signifieds. Signification floats out of the balance between these networks.

All discourse, said Lacan, is multiple. It consists at least of what is said, what is implied but not said, and what is not said but could have been said. This multiplicity is complicated in academic discourse, which pretends to bring itself to closure in a self-contained, controlled presentation of truth. Indeed, Lacan argued that the very essence of academic discourse is to make a fiction out of an author, of the history of thought, or of scientific method and then pretend that the discourse is the closure of truth.

Lacan did not, however, believe that meaning is impossible. In the spiral of the play of signifiers and signifieds there are "anchoring points" where signification is apprehended, "even if the sentence completes its signification only with its last term, each term being anticipated in the construction of others, and inversely, sealing their meaning by its retroactive effect" (*Ecrits* (1977), p. 805). But discourse cannot lead to truth or reality, because signification can never be pinned down. Although words have meaning in sentences, the meaning is not stable. There is, in fact, no common measure between what exists through language and what exists outside language, for language operates through metaphor and metonymy, and the substitution of symbol for symbol is not real.

Lacan spent so much time explaining the linguistic split between signifier and signified because he saw this split as the foundation of human personality. To Lacan, the split between unconscious and conscious selves corresponds to the split between signifier and signified. The person's birth into language separates the person from lived experience and destroys any possibility of the integral unity of the womb. Language, or discourse, requires a split and is thus the root of human lack, the beginning of unfulfilled and unfulfillable desire. Birth into language is a movement out of lived experience (or reality) into a symbolic system in which reality is forever after mediated by language. People distance themselves from reality and thus situate themselves as individuals distinct from their surroundings. They objectify themselves to themselves, thus creating an unconscious, a self-dialogue, a split. The ego is the conscious, fictional self; it begins the moment the unconscious is repressed, and it begins as language.

The linguistic code is, then, supreme over humans who enter this code and immediately find themselves subjected to it. The code becomes the intermediary between humans and their world, between one human and another, and between self and the manifestation of self. This intermediary is necessary for culture, but it also creates, through repression, the unconscious. The person who enters this multifaceted symbolic order will be fashioned by it, indelibly marked by it, and unaware of it.

In effect, Lacan concluded, the person is lost in his or her own discourse; the person's language is a rebus. In submitting to the order of the linguistic code, the self is lost. As a result, Lacanian analysis is a reading of the signifier that the person has become. It brings out the contexts that underlie statements and shows the unconscious structural patterns in which repressed signification occurs. The unconscious is analyzed like a text. By going back in analytic time—layer to layer, chain to chain—the reader encounters the original text of the unconscious. But even this is a text, consisting of a bridge between signifier and signified. If one could reach behind the first text to "reality," one would have reached either before or beyond the human condition. Lacan argued finally that the split that allows personality to arise is also the reason for an individual's radical inability to find anything satisfying.

Admittedly, Lacan is difficult to follow. The place to begin is Anika Lemaire's indispensable book *Jacques Lacan* (revised and translated in 1977). This book, on which the above summary is largely based and from which the Lacan translations above were taken, lists a complete bibliography of Lacan. In addition, there are currently four good translations of parts of Lacan's works available in English. *The Four Fundamental Concepts of Psycho-Analysis* (1981a) is a translation of six lectures delivered by Lacan at the École Pratique des Hautes Études in 1964. The core of Lacanian thought, including his ideas about the unconscious, transference, and the "other," is presented in these lectures. *The Language of the Self* (1975) includes Lacan's argument that the unconscious is a linguistic phenomenon; it also includes an excellent set of notes by the translator Anthony Wilden. He also translated *Speech and Language in Psychoanalysis* (1981b). For those who read French, Éditions du Seuil has published *Le Seminaire de Jacques Lacan* (1973); and *Écrits* (1966). Alan Sheridan translated selections from *Écrits* (1977), and his book includes a helpful index to Lacan's major concepts as well as an explanation of Lacan's numerous graphs, or schemes, for representing his ideas.

Four other books are very useful in understanding Lacanian reading. Sherry Turkle's *Psychoanalytic Politics* (1978) explains Lacanian psychoanalytic theory and the politics of professional dominance. The Epilogue to Turkle's book is a good introduction to the way Lacanian thought has appeared in America. *The Talking Cure* (ed. Colin McCabe [1981]) is a collection of essays on Freudian theory as recast by Lacan. Also, it includes a good bibliography of Lacanian analysis. *The Fictional Father* (1981) (edited by Robert C. Davis), consists of six demonstrations of Lacanian reading, as well as an introduction and an epilogue that introduce and explain Lacanian thought. One of Lacan's most important followers, Jean Laplanche, working with J. B. Pontalis, complied a dictionary of psychoanalytical terms entitled *The Language of Psychoanalysis* (1973) which is a very useful aid to reading Lacan and his followers.

The next stage in the evolution of modern textual theory is called "structuralism." It is a movement based on Saussurean linguistics and Lévi-Straussean anthropology. A great deal has been written about structuralism, but an excellent introduction to and solid grounding in structuralist textual theory is available through two books by American English professors and the writings of Frenchman Roland Barthes, who called himself a professor of "the sociology of signs, symbols, and collective representations."

Robert Scholes's *Structuralism in Literature* (1974) is a primer for reading from a structuralist perspective and is based heavily on Lévi-Strauss. Any text, Scholes argued, is part of a system. The system has a linguistic base and a cultural facade. Structural analysts look at the text and perceive the metaphoric, metonymic, and narrative patterns. Next they look for the sign system and cultural pattern of which the text is a part. Finally, they write the grammar that brought the text into being. Because all products of human consciousness must fit into the structural patterns that create consciousness—patterns that are at base linguistic—it is possible for the analyst to create a grid that can be laid over any text to reveal the structural laws that brought the text into existence. Thus texts that are both intelligible and unique are impossible. The only part of Scholes's book that can be troublesome is the conclusion, where he argued for structuralism as a sort of religion in which belief in God is replaced by belief in the universal structuring patterns of human consciousness, a sort of universal grammar of everything.

Roland Barthes's theories are now available in excellent English translations. Barthes, unlike Lacan (see above) and Derrida (see below), is a delight to read. By reading five of his books, published between 1953 and 1973, one can trace the evolution of his thought and understand the theoretical frame for one of the most influential and widely practiced current schools of textual theory.

Writing Degree Zero (1967b) is a response to Sartre's *What Is Literature?* (1949) and is an early Barthian history of the structural and phenomenological aspects of writing. First, Barthes accepted the symbolist, surrealist, and anti-realistic conceptions of writing embodied in the works of Jorge Louis Borges and Alain Robbe-Grillet. "Realistic" writing, he argued, is the most unrealistic of all, because it falsifies human existence by providing a constructed, reduced world. This world is "supplied" by liars and "consumed" by dupes; it is "security born of a credible fabrication which is yet constantly held up as false" (p. 35).

Second, Barthes saw writing and reading as political acts. He assumed that all of his readers occupy a sort of left-wing, neo-Marxist stance. From this position he attacked the Sartrean-Camusean idea that literature must be socially committed. In the wake of Saussurean and Lacanian theories that language is a split, not a unity, Barthes concluded that a writer simply cannot use writing to embody meaning, because language always faces in two directions. Any text that requires its own pre-determined reading is police-state writing.

Finally, Barthes offered his own history of writing. He defined *bourgeois writing*, which occurred between 1650 and 1850, as "instrumental." In this sort of writing the author obtains some "meaning" and uses inscription to set the "meaning" in relief. Since 1850, however, writing has increasingly become the problematics of language. Obviously, when writing ceases to be an instrument and becomes a problem in itself, everything changes. The zero degree of writing would amount to a language stripped of history and of metaphor, a pure instrument that does not exist. If the problematics of language could be erased and a pure algebra created, if writing were merely the "equal" sign in a set of equations, the problematics of humans could be presented without elaboration and without complexity. But this zero degree is not possible; thus the conscious writer must battle "against ancestral and all-powerful signs which, from a past foreign to him, impose Literature on him like some ritual, not like a reconciliation" (p. 86).

In *Mythologies* (1972), Barthes explained how myths come to be read not as myth but as truth. Using de Saussure's triad of signifier, signified, sign, Barthes argued that in myth the linguistic code itself becomes a signifier. Myth, therefore, is a second order semiological system. As in

Language	Signifier	Signified		
	Sign/Signifier		Signified	Myth
	Sign			

Barthes gave as an example the Latin sentence "quia ego nominor leo" (my name is lion). At the level of language, the sentence names the lion. Placed in a twentieth-century Latin grammar book, however, the sentence signifies not the naming of the lion but Latin grammar's system of agreement and concord.

At the level of myth, in other words, language is impoverished and then usurped. The signifier of myth is full on one side as sign and empty on the other as signifier. In myth the prior system is distorted. Thus there are three ways of reading myth: focusing on the full sign of language, on the empty signifier of myth, or on the full sign of myth. What allows myth consumers to read innocently is that they do not see myth as a semiological system but as an inductive one. In myth things lose the memory that they were once made. Myth passes from history to nature; thus, things that are in fact historical seem natural. The world of meaning has no contradictions because the awareness that meaning is historical is lost. There is a blissful clarity where things seem to mean something by themselves. Because reading can occur only as a part of some sort of whole, as a playing out of a preconceived system, the structural analyst must look not at the sign in myth, but at the signifier, the thing that has been robbed or hollowed out.

Elements of Semiology (1967) is Barthes's most theoretical book. Its purpose is to extract from linguistics analytical concepts that would actually begin semi-nology. Working within the Saussurean *langue-parole* split, Barthes showed how to read clothes, food, cars, and furniture as both the individual (parole) and the system (langue). He also provided a history of the Saussurean-Peircean triad. It begins in Saussure as

sr	sd
sign	

Louis Hjelmslev (*Essais Linguistiques*, [1959]) modified this to REC: relation (R) between expression (E) and the plane of content (C). Lacan, with his followers Laplanche and Leclaire, reassumes the split ($\frac{sr}{sd}$) but focuses not on the resulting sign but on the line between the floating bodies of signifiers and signifieds. Finally, Barthes proposed $Sr = Sd$, where $=$ is equivalance but not identity. In other words, *Elements* is a contextualization of Saussure, which concludes that the sign, operating on the dual axes of metaphor and metonymy, draws its value from setting and difference and occurs only in the mind.

With *S/Z* (1974) Barthes moved away from the position that all texts are enabled by a universal grammar, or universal structure. Here he argued that a text does not have a single structure assigned to it by a writing system or super code. Instead, there are several possible grammars of meaning. The text has a plurality of meanings, because it involves the reader in producing meaning by using a variety of appropriate procedures. Barthes's strategy in *S/Z* was to analyze the plurality of meanings in Balzac's *Sarrasine*, the story of a man who falls in love with a castrated female impersonator. Barthes attempted to open, not repress, reading, and he concluded that what is being told is the telling. He attacked the idea of denotative writing, saying the quest for denotative writing is really a desire to shut off Western discourse entirely. Denotation is not first meaning; it is nothing more than the last of the connotations, which pretends to be first meaning. Because the ''I'' who reads the text is itself a text, reading can be nothing more than finding meanings. Thus the text encloses not definitive meaning but infinite structure. Finally Barthes showed that in *Sarrasine*, as in any text, it is the reader's voice that speaks in the text. There is no purely denotative inside to a text, only interstices. In *Sarrasine* the legal substitution upon which meaning is based is banished by endless metonymy: ''*Sarrasine* represents the very confusion of representation, the unbridled (pandemic) circulation of signs, of sexes, of fortunes'' (p. 216).

The purpose of Barthes's *Pleasure of the Text* (1975) is to explore the way people read. Because *Pleasure* is highly impressionistic, almost aphoristic, any report is apt to seem jerky. The principles Barthes enunciated are these: (1) There are two edges to language—one is conformist and appears in grammar and composition books, and the other is wild and incomprehensible. Reading occurs at the seam of these two edges. (2) *Tmesis* is the actual strategy of reading. It consists of alternating patterns of slow, contemplative reading and quick, impatient reading, skipping what seems unnecessary and even daydreaming while continuing to read. (3) All texts include *abrasions*, blank spaces that the reader must fill. (4) Readers open the text and watch the play of signifiers. They do not close the text with a reading. Conversely, authors are not the parents of a text. They are lost in it, needing the reading as badly as the reader needs them.

Near the end of *Pleasure* Barthes described a text as follows: "There is not, behind the text, someone active (the writer) and out front someone passive (the reader); there is not a subject and an object. The text supersedes grammatical attitudes: it is the undifferentiated eye . . . the eye by which I see God is the same eye by which He sees me" (p. 16).

Jonathan Culler's *Structuralist Poetics* (1975) is an excellent introduction to both structuralism and post-structuralism. It is a bridge between the structuralism of Barthes and the *Tel Quel* group, or Derridean post-structuralists. Culler began by explaining the linguistics-based theories of reading extrapolated from structural linguists such as de Saussure, Jakobson, and A. J. Greimas. He then developed his own theory of "literary competence,'" which is built on structural linguistics but comes primarily from Chomsky's idea of "linguistic competence." Culler argued that the competent reader has mastered enough of the semiotic system of a given text for the text to be comprehensible. The job of the reading theorist is to explain how this competence occurs and what structural patterns existing in the text trigger this competence. In effect, the structural semiologist studies the implicit rules that allow a reader to comprehend a text and that define the range of acceptable interpretations.

By reading Scholes, the five books by Barthes, and Culler, one can get a thorough grounding in structuralist theory. Those who want a broader background should look at the works of four Europeans: Vladimir Propp, Claude Bremond, A. J. Greimas, and Tzvetan Todorov. Propp's *Morphology of the Folk Tale* (1968) describes the structure of Russian folktales. Propp explained that there are 4 laws governing folktales and 31 functions of character appearing in them. All extant tales obey the 4 laws, and although no folktale has all 31 functions of character, whichever functions do appear *always* appear in the same order. Greimas's most influential works, *Du Sens* (1970), *Sémantique structurale* (1966), and *Essais de sémiotique poétique* (1971), are not available in English. For a bibliography of Todorov, who has been influential, see Scholes's *Structuralism in Literature* (1974, pp. 209–10), which lists Todorov's most important works and the essays that were translated into English before 1974. In addition, see "Reading as Construction" (Susan Suleiman and Inge Crosman, *The Reader in the Text* [1980], pp. 67–82), which is an excellent introduction to Todorov's ideas about the reader's contribution to the construction of a text, and Todorov's *Poetics of Prose* (1977). Claude Bremond's *Logique de récit* (1973) explains how texts work in sequential patterns. In effect, the sequences are to linear composition what gravity is to water. The sequences pull the writing in a specific direction on a course that can be pre-determined by the reader before reading the entire text.

Finally, those who can read French should read Victor Chklovski's *Sur la théorie de la prose* (1973). Chklovski described a process of reading called "defamiliarization." This strategy makes familiar things seem unfamiliar so that the reader can see them with heightened perception, with renewed intensity. The whole point is to make familiar things obscure so that they must be re-encountered, restudied. Habitualization, Chklovski contended, destroys reading.

The final stage in the background to modern textual theory is the work of Jacques Derrida. Before taking up Derrida, however, two brief asides are necessary. The first covers an area known as "phenomenology of reading." The second is a brief bibliography of traditional philosophers whose works are an essential background to an understanding of Derrida and what has come to be called "deconstruction."

The phenomenology of reading is associated with the "Geneva School," which includes Marcel Raymond, Jean Starobinski, and Georges Poulet. By focusing on Poulet alone, one can grasp the phenomenological strategy of reading. (For an excellent introduction to the Geneva School as well as a bibliography of works by and about Poulet, see J. Hillis Miller's "Geneva or Paris" [1970].) Poulet's strategy was to relive from within the specific quality of inner experience expressed by an author. He believes that in any worthwhile text there is a moment at which the self is revealed. This amounts to a supreme act of self-consciousness in which the mind separates itself from everything that can enter from the outside. In other words, Poulet believes the mind can come to rest on nothing but itself, and this is the moment he sought in literature. Through reading, Poulet wanted to re-create the mind of the author at the moment of composition. Readers must empty their own minds of all of their personal qualities so that their consciousness can become coincidental with the writer's. Poulet's ideas, as well as demonstrations of those ideas, are available in three books that have been translated into English: *Studies in Human Time* (1979), *The Metamorphoses of the Circle* (1967), and *Proustian Space* (1977). A briefer introduction is available in "Criticism and the Experience of Interiority" (see Jane Tompkins, *Reader-Response Criticism* [1980], pp. 41–49).

This chapter is not an essay about philosophy, but since Jacques Derrida is the single most important theorist whose work is discussed here, it is essential to provide a brief, sketchy background of the philosophical texts that have influenced him. What follows is a historical preface to Derridean analysis. It is not intended to be comprehensive. All of the texts mentioned are English translations and are available.

Heidegger's *Being and Time* (1962a), *The Question of Being* (1929), and *Kant and the Question of Metaphysics* (1962b) are the most important backgrounds to Derridean analysis. Heidegger, believing that Western philosophy had lost both the truths discovered by ancient great thinkers and the ability to penetrate to the real origins of consciousness, sought a "destructive" analysis of Western metaphysics to clear the way for a radical reinvestigation of human existence. Derrida studied Heidegger's idea of "transcendence," and it is from Heidegger that Derrida got his terms *empiricity* and *historicity*. Heidegger suggested that what empirical science must hide in order to exist is that it is really historical. Derrida generalized this strategy for analysis and argued that any method claiming to reveal ultimate truth or any statement or assumption claiming to be ultimate truth must hide its founding metaphor to exist. Because the method or claim exists only through language and because language operates through metaphor and metonymy, the method or claim must hide its origin in order to seem non-metaphysical.

From Heidegger's effort to mount a "destructive analysis" of Western metaphysics came Derrida's effort to mount a "deconstruction" of Western metaphysics. Heidegger seems to have argued that by destroying the wrongheaded, post-Aristotelian metaphysical tradition, a valid philosophical method could be regained. Derrida modified this position and attempted to show that by deconstructing this tradition, its essentially linguistic, metaphorical nature is revealed. No pure, revealing system could then be *re*constructed unless the system could exist outside language.

There is a long list of philosophers who lead up to Heidegger. To designate any philosopher before whom there is no one of importance is arbitrary. Even so, it is possible to begin with John Locke's *Essay on Human Understanding* (1952), which triggered a series of speculations about epistemology. Several post-Lockean philosophers are important to Derrida and are clear antecedents both to Heideggerian "destruction" and Derridean "deconstruction." The first is Leibnitz, who, in *Theodicy* (1952), made a distinction between what he called "the Book" and "books," which is a distinction between the "divine" and the "human." For God, who is not limited to the world, thought and action are one univocal event. But humans, who are in the world, are split between their thoughts, which are not limited, and their actions, which are. Because humans are finite, they must always choose among imperfect alternatives. Derrida analyzed Leibnitz, finding the constant juxtaposition of alternatives in fact a gap, an indication of an absence. Derrida was also stimulated by Leibnitz's idea that the universe is constructed from "monads"—spiritual building blocks, each representing the form of God's entire, preordained universe. To Derrida, these monads are invisible traces, an "always already absent presence." Finally, Derrida studied the idea of "the Book," which is pure, univocal meaning and which does not exist in the world, and "books," which are incomplete attempts to re-create "the Book."

Étienne Condillac's *Essay on the Origin of Human Knowledge* (1756, 1971) and *Treatise on the Sensations* (1930) are interesting to Derrida because of the way Condillac explained understanding as little more than comparison of multiple sensations. In Hegel's *Phenomenology of the Mind* (1931), Derrida studied the "voyage of discovery." For Hegel, the phenomenon of perception is always circular, the point of departure and the point of return being inseparable. Hegel argued that the distance between the perceiver and the perceived does not exist. Derrida linked these two Hegelian ideas to his own idea of "différance," the gap that both exists and does not exist.

It is difficult to single out specific works from Nietzsche and Husserl, because both are essential background reading for Derrida. The four most useful works from Nietzsche are *Beyond Good and Evil* (1966), *On the Geneology of Morals* (1969), *Ecce Homo* (1974), and *The Will to Power* (1968b). The most useful books by Husserl are *Logical Investigations* (1970) and *Ideas* (1931), where he described the nature of language by making a group of "essential distinctions" that demonstrate how meaning is embodied in language. Husserl argued that meaning comes through language in one of two ways: (1) *indication*, which means empirical association where something stands for something else; in Saussurean terms this amounts to a signifier that has been filled by a signified; and (2) *expression*, where meaning coexists with expression. For Husserl, expression only is real, and it is real internally, inside an immediate, self-present consciousness. Husserl called this the "solitary mental life" and the "transcendental consciousness." His phenomenology depends ultimately on the Western metaphysical assumption of the existence of presence—he called it self-presence—which Derrida attempted to prove as unprovable.

The final background to Derrida consists of the volumes from Freud's *Works* cited above in my discussion of Lacan.

Anyone familiar with the above background material can read and understand Derrida's writings. Someone who is not familiar with this background will probably experience only frustration, anger, and disgust when reading Derrida, who is hard to read. His style, which is a logical result of his beliefs about the nature of language, is difficult. Also, he assumed familiarity with the texts mentioned above. For some reason, *Of Grammatology* (1974a) has received more "hype" than Derrida's other works. Most English professors who have attempted to explore Derrida have done so by trying to read this book. Such an attempt, with no background in the philosophical and linguistic tradition on which the book rests and no introduction to Derridean method, can end only in confusion and hostility. Gayatri Spivak's Introduction to *Of Grammatology*, which is harder to follow than the Derrida text itself, is useless to someone who knows nothing about Derrida. Derrida published two other books in 1967 (see Derrida 1973 and 1978). Both have been translated, and both should be read before *Grammatology*. These three books present the core of Derridean thought and demonstrate his method. The point of entry consists of Newton Garver's excellent Preface to *Speech and Phenomena* (1973), which sets Derrida's thought against the philosophical background from which it emerges; David Allison's Translator's Introduction to *Speech and Phenomena*, which shows how Derrida rewrote and played off Husserl; and Alan Bass's Translator's Introduction to *Writing and Difference* (1978).

The Derridean lexicon is dense. In part, Derrida is hard to read because his style is both intentionally elusive and densely allusive, reaching across the whole spectrum of Western thought. He is, however, also hard to read because he wants to challenge the *way* we read. One of the inevitable by-products of Derridean analysis is that the reader's attitude toward a text is skeptical, even antagonistic. The reader asks not what the text "says" but where it "originated," not which questions the text answers but which questions the text denies existence to. Some of the terms that Derrida uses require a bit of "introducing" for the reader who is new to or exasperated by post-structuralist thought. *Signifier* and *signified* both come from Saussure, through Lacan. Derrida, like Lacan, is not, however, much concerned with "signs." He believes that language is the unlimited play of signifiers. In effect, there is no "sign" in the sense of original meaning. In denying its existence, Derrida usually termed this non-existent sign the "transcendental signified." Derrida used the term *abyss* (especially in *Of Grammatology*) to indicate the region where the readers fall when they give up belief in a transcendental signified and enter the realm of the free play of signifiers.

Deconstruction is the most famous Derridean term. Its antecedents in the history of philosophy are Nietzsche's "reversal" and Heidegger's "destruction." Deconstruction is an attempt to take apart the tradition of Western metaphysics in order to reveal the axiomatic and theoretical foundations upon which the tradition exists. For any discourse to exist, Derrida argued, it must begin with (be founded on) an assumption, an axiom, or a theory. If this foundation is a metaphor, everything built on it is also a metaphor. If it is a falsification in which many questions are ignored in order for discourse to begin by focusing on only one of many questions, everything built upon the falsification is also a falsification. All discourses, said Derrida, must hide their original metaphor or falsification to appear real. Derridean discourses, in other words, are like Lacanian people. There is, said Lacan, never one person, always two—the conscious, public, fictional self and the unconscious, repressed, denied self. There is, Derrida added, never one discourse, always two—the apparent, empirical discourse that sets itself up as real and the repressed discourse that consists of all things hidden in the first falsification or metaphor that allowed the empirical discourse to begin. In philosophy, for example, Derrida demonstrated that all philosophical texts from Plato onwards begin by excluding the nature of writing. Were philosophers to study the nature of writing, the nature of the play of written signifiers, they would never get to philosophizing. Derrida's point is not to show the limits of metaphysical speculation. Rather, it is to disassemble the structure of metaphysics to show that metaphysical discourse, like all other discourses, is built on paradox and contradiction, because something had to be repressed in order for something else to be said. Once the metaphoric, fake nature of discourse has been exposed, the way will be clear for a new kind of meditation, one not founded on the metaphysics of "presence."

The idea of "presence," Derrida argued, is what invests the Western metaphysical tradition with meaning. The thing that gives order and structure to Western discourse is something transcendent to that order. A foundation cannot be part of the structure that stands on it, and the foundation of Western discourse is an assumed presence: a divine, a one, a unity, a belief in intelligibility, a faith in right reason, a faith in progress, and so on. Derrida's analytic method shows that the origin of discourse is not presence but absence. Discourse occurs as an irreconcilable split between signifier and signified, between speaker and hearer. Derrida used several terms for this split: an *absence*, a *gap*, an *abyss*, an always already *absent presence*, a *trace*, and so on. The deconstructive method searches not for the meaning of a text but for what the text has hidden, forbidden, or repressed in order to seem whole and true.

Derrida used the term *différance* to describe how language works. (The term is kin to Saussure's *value*.) *Différance* means both waiting (deferral) and not-the-same (difference). Meaning exists only through a complex system of differences, each signifier coming to life by being what other signifiers are not. Because texts are founded on what they exclude, they are founded on the deferral of the need for an absolute foundation.

The first Derridean texts one should attempt to read are 8 of the 11 chapters in *Writing and Difference* (1978); the book is really a collection of essays; thus each chapter is a whole argument. In Chapter 1, "Force and Signification" Derrida explained his intention to develop a new way of reading, which begins with the assumption that language is not reducible to meaning. The "presence" of any meaning is a "hiding," for no thing can appear without hiding something else; no thing can be said without not-saying or unsaying the "Other." Writing and reading are acts of conversion, which require breaking off from the world and which cannot directly manifest experience. Writing only indicates experience through metaphor, which also cannot be reduced to an origin but only to a first saying. Thus writing begins with absence, the absence of the thing it first represents, and writing is always and only the play of absences.

In "Edmond Jabès and the Question of the Book" Derrida used the Lacanian concept of self-being in which the conscious self must repress the unconscious self to exist. Language emerges from this split. Writing must, therefore, be the presence of absence. Thus writing exists only through what it excludes; if it were complete, it would embody total unity, and total unity precludes discourse. Derrida explained again that in writing there is no way back to a beginning, an origin, because the origin itself is a split, an original loss. Writing is continual displacement through metaphor and metonymy, and displacement is not a place. It is a split or an empty space. The writer must hide something to make the text's foundation appear to be outside the text. In effect, writing is a process of hiding doubt and uncertainty. The more positive the conclusion, the more deeply the doubt is hidden.

"Violence and Metaphysics" explains that questions never appear independently but always in a symbiosis where the answer has begun to determine the question. Unmotivated questions cannot occur.

With "'Genesis and Structure' and Phenomenology" Derrida began to explain his strategy for reading, which is to inhabit a position by "putting it in question."

Since a structure requires a base, a genesis, or an origin, Derrida asked the text, "Where is the absence?" and "What is being hidden?" This essay, which is an explication of Husserlean phenomenology, shows how to expose assumptions hidden in a text. For example, what is the foundation of objectivity? What does objectivity hide in order to exist? Another example: Reason unveils itself by appearing to itself, speaking to itself, and operating on the assumption that since it cannot remember not being, it always has been. Reason denies its origin, emerging "from itself in order to take hold of itself within itself" (p. 166).

In "La parole soufflée" (1965) Derrida attempted a deconstruction of the accepted nature of reading. Any time a reader attempts to explain the meaning of a text, the explanation begins by ignoring that the text itself began as a split, a kind of erased trace. The reader refuses to remember that the language of the text is a metaphoric-metonymic string leading back to a lack, an absence, a covering up. Derrida called both writing and reading "theft." The writer "steals" meaning by pretending that everything that needs saying has been said. The reader "steals" meaning by pretending that the text is founded on reality, not language.

"Freud and the Scene of Writing" is Derrida's effort to demonstrate an alternative to the Western tradition of metaphysics. Because he conceived of logocentrism as hiding, Derrida did not write like other writers. In this chapter he explained that "presence" must be either the unity of the classical God in which everything is contained, from which nothing is missing, and where discourse is impossible; or the hiding of absence where something is missing and where discourse is the covering over of what is missing. All writing, Derrida argued, is a trace of what is missing. If pure, univocal meaning were possible, writing, indeed language itself, would be unnecessary. In exploring Freudian theory, Derrida argued that the conscious is not a transcription of the unconscious. Presence affects everything. There has never been an unconscious text of which the conscious text is a trace: "There is no present text in general . . . .The unconscious text is already a weave of traces" (p. 211).

In "Structure, Sign, and Play in the Discourse of the Human Sciences" (1966), Derrida asserted his theory of epistemology by attacking structuralism for the assumption that every structure has a center or foundation. He accused structuralists of naive blindness when they argue both that the center is part of the structure because it is the origin of the patterns and that the center is not part of the structure because it is the pre-existing, independent foundation upon which the structure exists. Structuralists, Derrida charged, use this center not only to orient and balance the structure but to limit the play of possible meanings in the structure. "Thus," Derrida concluded, "it has always been thought that the center . . . constituted that very thing within a structure which while governing structure escapes structurality" (pp. 278–79). This center allows for coherence, certitude, mastery of anxiety; it is full presence and fundamental immobility, which is beyond play.

But, Derrida argued, this central presence was never itself. Instead of a center, there is a substitute for a center, a substitute that does not take the place of anything that had existed before it. "In the absence of a center or origin," Derrida concluded, "everything became discourse . . . a system in which the central signified, the original . . . signified is never absolutely present." This absence in the place of presence "extends the domain and play of signification infinitely" (pp. 280–81).

With "Ellipsis" Derrida concluded his speculations about writing. In the place of first origin, the center is an abyss. Falling into the abyss is losing center and gaining play. Instead of bemoaning the loss of center, he suggested that one affirm play.

Speech and Phenomena (1973) is an analysis of Husserlean phenomenology. Here Derrida took up the idea of a "sign," and he elaborated his ideas about meaning, structure, origin, and différance. The reader who cannot obtain *Writing and Difference* would do well to begin with the two essays appended to *Speech and Phenomena*—"Form and Meaning" and "Différance."

Of Grammatology (1974a) is really two books. The first, "Writing Before the Letter," is an extended explanation of the nature of written language. The second, "Nature, Culture, Writing," is a "deconstruction" of Rousseau and what Derrida called the "Age of Rousseau." In Part 1 Derrida argued that no writer ever manages to write exactly what he means. Writing always occurs *sous rature*, under erasure. Writing is a trace of what wants to be said and a covering over of what the writer does not know or does not know how to say. "At each step," Derrida said of his own writing, "I was obliged to proceed by ellipses, corrections of corrections, letting go of each concept at the very moment I needed to use it" (p. xviii). Of course, if no writer succeeds at saying what he means, definitive readings make of a text what it cannot be.

In Part 2 of *Grammatology* Derrida exposed what he considered to be the inappropriate response to the abyss of free-playing signifiers. He called this response Rousseauistic and described it as a negative, saddened, nostalgic, guilty effort to escape play. He juxtaposed Rousseauistic negativism with Nietzschean affirmation.

In "White Mythology" (1974b) Derrida offered an extended demonstration both of deconstruction and of pedagogy (the essay began as a classroom lecture). In effect, he showed how to study metaphor by demonstrating that each metaphor has a whole history (a history that *began* as metaphor, not as presence) and a whole system (within whose differences the metaphor draws life). He also showed the metaphoric nature of any discourse by explaining that every discourse must begin with a metaphor that is accepted as presence: "If we wanted to conceive and classify all the metaphorical possibilities of philosophy, there would always be at least one metaphor which would always be excluded and remain outside the system: that one, at least, which was needed to construct the concept of metaphor, or, to cut the argument short, the metaphor of metaphor" (p. 18).

Derrida used "Living On" • "Border Lines" (see Bloom and others, *Deconstruction and Criticism* [1979], pp. 75–176) to demonstrate the nature of textuality. This essay, which consists of parallel texts and is either two essays or an essay and a commentary on an essay, shows that meaning never resides solely in one source. A text is a sort of infinitely expanding hendiadys that always embeds other texts. Any text expands metonymically because only part of the author appears and metaphorically because all other texts that went before made it possible and are embedded in it.

Modern Textual Theory

Structuralism and post-structuralism have caused a profound change in literary theory during the last decade. The purpose of this section is to provide an introduction to structuralist and post-structuralist literary theory. All of the authors in this section write about literary, not expository, texts; thus the link with composition theory is indirect. But the link exists, and it offers profound insight into the nature of textuality. In part, post-structuralist critics have refrained from dealing with non-literary texts, because they teach in prestigious literature departments and are wary of frightening their colleagues, who fear that composition will consume literary study and relegate it to the unimportant position. On the literary side, J. Hillis Miller, in "The Function of Rhetorical Study at the Present Time" (1979), suggested that English departments become rhetoric departments so that both literature and composition specialists will be engaged in the same enterprise. On the composition side, W. Ross Winterowd suggested the same thing in "Getting It Together in the English Department" (1977). In "A Dramatic Essay Not in Defense of Teaching Poesy" (1980) Jasper Neel explained why the two sides are still far apart.

Exploration of textuality and the reading process did not suddenly begin in 1970. Both enterprises have been underway at least since Aristotle. There are, however, four particular books that were published long before 1970 and that anticipate the sort of speculation that is so widespread today.

The first book is William Empson's *Seven Types of Ambiguity* (1930, 1966), which shows that any written statement gives room for a variety of alternative reactions. The second book is Ezra Pound's *ABC of Reading* (1934, 1960). Pound explained his own iconoclastic approach to reading, which includes several modern ideas. He explored the psychological effect of encountering language as sight instead of sound. Then he showed that meaning is present in a text in the same way melody is present in notes on a musical staff, that words operate both metaphorically and metonymically, and that a text exists as much by gaps as by presences. The third book is Roman Ingarden's *Cognition of the Literary Work of Art* (1973) in which he explained how reader, author, and text are bound together as a sort of single entity. According to Ingarden, reading depends on the participation of the reader and on the reader's ability to fill in places of indeterminacy in a text. Wolfgang Iser, in *The Implied Reader* (1974), offered a good introduction to Ingarden, who has been largely ignored in this country. The fourth book is Louise Rosenblatt's *Literature as Exploration* (1938, 1976).

This excellent book explores the relationship between reader and text, arguing that this relationship is a transaction in which both the reader *and* the text are modified.

Perhaps the best method of offering an introduction to modern textual theory is to divide the theorists into groups. It should be noted, however, that the divisions are arbitrary and that they overlap. The first group, concerned with textual wholeness, is not a group at all, but a question around which a group of writers can be gathered. The members of the other three groups—Yale school, reader-response group, and anti-post-structuralists—have much in common, even though the individual members may not believe so.

How whole is a written text? How does the reader discover beginning, center, and end? These questions are fundamental to reading theory. Grouped around this question are several famous critics. The first, Walter Ong, is a rhetorician who focused on the history of writing as a technology and on the effect writing has on human beings. In *The Presence of the Word* (1967, 1970), Ong explained the difference between oral and literate culture and traced the history and psychological effects of writing. The alphabet, Ong pointed out, was extremely hard to invent; it was, in fact, invented only once in history, about 1500 B.C. The effect of alphabetic writing is to spatialize language and thought, imputing to language a kind of consistency and control that is wholly fictional. Unfortunately, Ong continued, alphabetic writing is like Newtonian physics: it does not work when the writer gets down to details. The alphabet gives rise to the illusion, or delusion, of literal meaning.

In *Rhetoric, Romance, and Technology* (1971), Ong explained how rhetoric and literacy have re-formed modern consciousness. He explained again the difference between oral and written culture and showed the gradual triumph of written culture. In *Interfaces of the Word* (1977) Ong said, "With writing the earlier noetic [for example, pre-literate] state undergoes a kind of cleavage, separating the knower from the external universe and then from himself" (p. 18). Writing allows for art and science, "but it does so at the price of splitting up the original unity of consciousness," thus alienating man both from himself and from his world (p. 18). So powerful is writing, Ong argued, that it presumes priority over spoken language, so the written language of professional writers becomes the standard against which speakers are judged. Writing, which Ong called "permanent unreality," is more plausible and comforting than speech, which he called "transient reality." Chirographic and typographic biases actually redefine the psyche, creating artificial but extremely powerful graphocentrism. Ong's conclusion is that both the writer and the reader are masks: "For writing is itself an indirection. Direct communication by script is impossible" (p. 80). For writing to occur at all, the writer "has to make his readers up" (p. 59). First, writers must construct in their imagination an audience cast in some sort of role. Then they must provide clues about how the audience is to fictionalize itself and present the clues in such a way that the audience will agree.

In "Literacy and Orality in Our Times" (1979), Ong explained how a "secondary" oral culture has emerged and how it affects today's student writers. In "Literacy, Basics, and All That Jazz" (1977), Thomas Farrell treated the same subject. For an anticipation of Ong's theory about writing and alienation, see Eric Havelock's *Preface to Plato* (1963) where Havelock explained the cultural effect of writing: it allowed individuals to separate the knower from the known, and knowledge from memory.

In "Authors, Speakers, Readers, and Mock Readers" (1950) Walker Gibson, like Ong, argued that the reader is a function of the text; that, in other words, the writer makes up the reader. For the text to exist, Gibson said, the writer must create a "mock reader," "whose existence is entirely a function of the text." "A bad book," Gibson explained, "is a book in whose mock reader we find a person we refuse to become" (pp. 268–69).

Wayne Booth, in *The Rhetoric of Fiction* (1961), agreed with Ong by describing the other side of the transaction, the writer, also as a function of the text. All prose, Booth contended, is the product of a fictional writer created in the imagination of the author. This fictional writer, who both is and is not the author, lives and dies with the prose that gives him life. While writing, Booth explained, the real author "creates not simply an ideal, impersonal 'man in general' but an implied version of 'himself' that is different from the implied authors we meet in other men's works. . . . Whether we call him implied author or an 'official scribe,' or . . . the author's second self—it is clear that the picture the reader gets of this presence is one of the author's most important effects" (pp. 70–71).

Although Ong and Gibson argued that readers are a fiction and Booth argued that writers are a fiction, other textual theorists argued that texts themselves are a kind of trickery. In *Beginnings* (1975), Edward Said showed how the beginning of a text is faked and then assumed as real. In "Sensing Endings" (1978) Frank Kermode contended that the end of every text must be "faked," because it is impossible to stop a metonymic or metaphoric sequence. In his *Sense of an Ending* (1967), Kermode showed how writers since the Renaissance have used textuality to deal with a world whose beginning and ending are no longer certain; of course, the beginnings and endings of texts in this world are also uncertain.

Not only are authors and readers fictional, and beginnings and endings faked, but even the reality of middles and wholeness is questioned. In "The Figure in the Carpet" (1980a), J. Hillis Miller explained how an author creates a text that is not whole, yet appears to be. The strategy, said Miller, is to give the text an edge or border like the edge on a circular rug. All of the loose strings appear tied up. There appears to be nothing left out of the circle and nothing of value beyond it. In "Exigencies of Composition and Publication" (1978), Hershel Parker and Henry Binder showed how the growth of *Billy Budd* from a ballad to a long prose narrative caused real problems of sequence and reference to creep into the text, problems that Melville never resolved. They also showed how

Clemens extracted *Pudd'nhead Wilson* from a long manuscript and then tacked on a gaudy conclusion that "does not bear much thinking about in relation to the rest of the published story" (p. 142).

All of these studies question the positivistic techniques of teaching composition that dominate pedagogy. Readers and writers, beginnings and endings, middles and wholeness, are always illusions. Because no text can say everything that could be said, good writers learn how to give the illusion of completeness.

The Yale school is "led" by Harold Bloom, Paul de Man, Geoffrey Hartman, and J. Hillis Miller. The best introduction to Bloom is his *Anxiety of Influence* (1973) and "The Breaking of Form" in *Deconstruction and Criticism* (1979) edited by Bloom and others. In *The Anxiety of Influence*, Bloom argued that writers are enabled to write by those writers who preceded them; Tennyson can write because of Keats, Milton because of Spenser. But the relationship is Freudian in that the writer must "kill" his predecessor in order to have space for himself. The writer must have another writer who demonstrates how to write; but then the new writer must misread the teacher in order not to rewrite what the teacher has already written. The pattern is nourishment, apprenticeship, and then *misprison* (Bloom's word for "misreading"). Each new strong writer repeats the pattern by destroying the strong writer who preceded.

In "The Breaking of Form" (see Bloom, *Deconstruction and Criticism* [1979], pp. 1–38), Bloom explained his theory of reading. For Bloom, reading is "combat." A strong reading is a sort of misreading in which the reader takes over the text. Reading well, said Bloom, is not necessarily polite and may well not meet the academy's standards of civility. Bloom concluded that there are no texts, only interpretations. He named his readings "transgressive" and "aggressive" but not deconstructive.

The most difficult of the four Yale school writers is Paul de Man. This is true probably because the objects of his analysis are usually Continental rather than British or American. The best, most comprehensive, introduction to de Man is his *Allegories of Reading* (1979), which is a presentation of de Man's admittedly "deconstructive" theory of reading. The strategy de Man presented is to expose the rhetorical schemes through which a text hides its essentially rhetorical nature. He called this reading strategy "the undoing of a system of tropological transformations" (p. ix). De Man's famous book *Blindness and Insight* (1971) also presents his theory of reading, but it is much harder to read and less satisfying than *Allegories*.

The book by Geoffrey Hartman that bears most directly on composition theory is *The Fate of Reading* (1975), in which he studied both reading and writing. Writing, he contended, is a kind of "forgery," because metaphors and metonymies pretend to be what they are not. It is also an act of "violation," because something is stolen when it is inscribed. Hartman also analyzed the writing mode he called "managerial social science" (a phrase meaning something like "expository prose"). First, he exposed the history of the growth of faith in the communicative ability of this managerial prose, and then he suggested that such prose is almost entirely illusion. Finally, he gave an analysis of the human psyche and its relation to writing.

Reading, like writing, Hartman argued, is theft. The reader must master the text, and that requires stealing it from the writer. Chapter 1 of *Fate of Reading* is a self-analysis of the interpreter-thief. The cogito (or pretense of one), Hartman concluded, is the Archimedean point that allows the reader to displace the text and master it. In other words, the reader creates a fictional version of himself to get distance from a text and master it.

In "A Touching Compulsion" (1977), Hartman again explained his idea of writing as theft, forgery, trespass, *and* self-exposure. Representation, he said, is deceit; thus the deceitful medium—writing—invests itself with ultimate value. In the Preface to *Deconstruction and Criticism* (see Bloom and associates, *Deconstruction and Criticism* [1979], pp. vii–ix), Hartman explained that "deconstructors" refuse to identify a text with "embodied meaning." Although most readers assume that the presence of written words is equivalent to embodied meaning, Hartman and his colleagues urged the opposite, that written words carry with them a certain absence or indeterminacy of meaning. Chapter 7 of Hartman's book *Criticism in the Wilderness* (1980) elaborates and expands these theories of reading as theft and texts as indeterminate.

J. Hillis Miller's ideas about both reading and writing are available in *Fiction and Repetition* (1982). He explained that reading a book is somewhat like pulling a thread through a maze. Once the thread is through the maze, the thread and the maze shape each other. The thread defines the maze while the maze shapes the thread. Readers and texts are like thread and the maze; they "create" each other.

In "The Figure in the Carpet" (1980a), Miller gave a definition of what is meant when a deconstructive analyst uses the terms *unreadability* or *impossibility* of definitive reading. *Unreadability* does not mean ambiguity, plurisignificance, or richness of meaning; nor does it mean that since each reader brings something different to the text, the text means something different for each reader. Unreadability is an effect of the text's rhetoric, of its play of metaphor and metonymy. Unreadability "names the presence in a text of two or more incompatible or contradictory meanings which imply one another or are intertwined with one another, but which may by no means be felt or named as a unified totality" (p. 113). Unreadability, Miller concluded, is a name for the discomfort caused by the reader's inability to bring a text to closure. In a different manner, Miller dealt with the inability to close a text in "*Wuthering Heights* and the Ellipses of Interpretation" (1980b); here he shows that Heathcliff, Cathy, and critics alike are frustrated because they cannot achieve a dreamed-of lost unity that could exist only in a pre-linguistic state. Miller also gave an interesting response to recent attempts at deconstruction in "Deconstructing the Deconstructors" (1975a) and showed how the perspective of the perceiver gives a delusionary order to random phenomena in "Optic and Semiotic in *Middlemarch*" (1975b).

A "fifth" member of the Yale school is Barbara Johnson, whose *Critical*

Difference (1980) is a fine extended example of deconstructive reading. The last chapter of the book, "The Frame of Reference," focuses on Poe's "The Purloined Letter," Lacan's reading of Poe, Derrida's reading of Lacan, and, obliquely, on Johnson's reading of all three. The chapter is a brilliant demonstration of how a text "performs" its reader and of how exceedingly difficult it is to fix meaning in a text.

Reader-response criticism designates an approach to reading that can be described generally as follows: a text can be neither more nor less than what the reader reads there. The three most prominent and influential reader response critics are Norman Holland, Stanley Fish, and David Bleich. Reader-response pedagogy is not new with Holland, Fish, and Bleich. It is clearly anticipated in Louise Rosenblatt's *Literature as Exploration* (1976) as well as in several books aimed at public school teachers: J. W. Patrick Creber's *Sense and Sensitivity* (1965), Frank Whitehead's *The Disappearing Dais* (1966), and especially Alan Purves's *How Porcupines Make Love* (1972), where the authors make clear that the student's conception of and response to reading should be at the center of the English curriculum. Purves, writing with Richard Beach, summarized the growth of reader-centered pedagogy in *Literature and the Reader* (1972). James Hoetker, in "A Theory of Talking about Theories of Reading" (1982), explained the somewhat bemused response of English education specialists to the new concerns with readers and reading processes that are receiving so much attention at places like Yale, Johns Hopkins, and Chicago.

For the beginnings and evolution of reader response criticism, the starting point is Norman Holland's *Dynamics of Literary Response* (1968, 1975a), *5 Readers Reading* (1975b), "Literature as Transaction" (1978a), and "Poem Opening" (1978b). These four works show how Holland has modified his theory from the *analysis*, or psychoanalysis, of a reader's response to an *exploration* of reading as a transaction between reader and text. Holland's current position is that the reader constructs meaning. It is not something "in" the text waiting to be discovered. To explain the meaning "in" a text would be to "close" it, and the point of transactive reading is to open the text, thus allowing a sort of meditation that replenishes the text rather than getting something out of it.

Stanley Fish's *Is There a Text in This Class?* (1980) is a record of his constantly changing conception of the reading process. The book disagrees with (Fish would say "unwrites and then rewrites") itself. Among other things, Fish questioned the fixity of the text, the distinction between ordinary and literary language, and the nature of evidence. A text, Fish argued, without a context and a reader is no text at all. What is in the text can change, because the text can never be independent of or prior to interpretation. Definitive readings are tricks, because the "evidence" upon which they are based "is always a function of what it is to be evidence for, and is never independently available. That is, the interpretation determines what will count as evidence for it, and the evidence is able to be picked out only because the interpretation has *already* been assumed" (p. 272).

In "The Identity of Pedagogy and Research in the Study of Response to

Literature" (1980), David Bleich gave a brief history of reader-response criticism and then argued that English teachers should "authorize" their students to provide unique response statements to, not analyses of, their reading. Then, as a demonstration, Bleich provided his own response statement to Kafka's "A Country Doctor." The theory upon which this demonstration is based is articulated in *Subjective Criticism* (1978), where Bleich argued that English teachers' conceptions of reading need to undergo a "paradigm shift." All perception, said Bleich, comes through a paradigm, "a shared mental structure, a set of beliefs about the nature of reality subscribed to by a group of thinkers large enough to exercise leadership" over the entire society (p. 10). Until now, the paradigm for reading has imitated the procedures of science. The text is made into an object and is then explicated. With a paradigm shift to subjective criticism, the explanation of a symbolic object would become a subjective reconstruction of our own perceptions of the object. Bleich's idea of paradigm comes from T. S. Kuhn's *The Structure of Scientific Revolutions* (1962).

Two collections of essays dealing with reader response criticism appeared in 1980: *Reader-Response Criticism*, edited by Jane Tompkins, and *The Reader in the Text*, edited by Susan Suleiman and Inge Crosman. Both books include an excellent introduction to the subject as well as judiciously chosen essays by the major reader-response critics and bibliographies of modern textual theory and its background. Jasper Neel's "Writing about Literature" (1982) provides an introduction to the critical practices advocated by both the Yale school and the reader-response group.

Finally, three journals bear mentioning. *New Literary History*, begun in Autumn 1969; *Diacritics*, begun in Autumn 1971; and *Critical Inquiry*, begun in Autumn 1974, have stimulated and published most of the essays that have caused the re-thinking of the reading process. By leafing through the issues of these journals and reading selectively, one could discover all of the important issues in textual theory being argued today. A fourth important periodical is the eight issues of *Glyph* published by the Hopkins Press from 1977 to 1980. *Glyph*'s editor, Samuel Weber, announced in the inaugural issue a "Program," which focused *Glyph* on "the problems of representation and textuality." *Glyph* also set out to cause a confrontation between American and Continental critical theory. *Glyph* carried several of Derrida's first essays to appear in America, and from 1977 to 1980 was, more than any other single periodical, associated with Derridean analysis and deconstruction.

Not surprisingly, deconstruction and reader-response criticism are controversial. Many, perhaps most, English professors find both theories troublesome. Both have been called everything from silly and faddish to dangerous and immoral. The most famous attacks have been mounted by E. D. Hirsch, Jr. (*Validity in Interpretation* [1967], and *The Aims of Interpretation* [1976]) and Gerald Graff (*Literature Against Itself* [1979]). For a full account of the questions about and objections to post-structuralist criticism, the following are also both entertaining and useful: Murray Krieger's *Theory of Criticism* (1976) and "The Recent

Revolution in Theory and the Survival of the Literary Disciplines'' (1979); Frank Lentricchia's *After the New Criticism* (1980); Hayden White's ''The Absurdist Moment in Contemporary Literary Theory'' (1977); and M. H. Abrams's''The Deconstructing Angel'' (1977).

Conclusion

Some of the sources in this chapter have a connection with composition only at the remotest, most theoretical level. Perhaps none of them can be used directly in the composition classroom. The premise of this chapter is that it is foolish to study the teaching of writing without ever considering what happens to the writing once it is written. Moreover, these sources imply three very important points: (1) Communication in writing depends much more on the decoder than the encoder. (2) Language is at the base of human consciousness. It is a very problematic medium. Some students' ineffectiveness with and fear of writing may stem from their inability to enter a system that seems real and is not. (3) Almost every text is an illusion of completeness, with a faked beginning, middle, and end. Every aspect of every text is rhetorical, extending infinitely through metaphor and metonymy. Writing is a scary, uncertain playing out of multiple meanings through infinite combinations and transformations. The composition teacher who is unaware of this frightening uncertainty is apt to attempt a pedagogy that oversimplifies the most complex technology that humankind has ever invented—writing.

References

Abrams, Meyer H. ''The Deconstructing Angel.'' *Crit I,* 3 (1977), 425–39.

Adams, Marilyn J., and Allan Collins. *A Schema-Theoretic View of Reading.* Urbana, Ill.: Center for the Study of Reading, 1977.

Allen, P. David, and Dorothy J. Watson, eds. *Findings of Research in Miscue Analysis: Classroom Implications.* Urbana, Ill.: NCTE Press, 1976.

Alston, William. *Philosophy of Language.* Englewood Cliffs, N.J.: Prentice-Hall, 1964.

Anderson, Robert. ''The Notion of Schemata and the Educational Enterprise.'' In *Schooling and the Acquisition of Knowledge.* Ed. Robert Anderson et al. Hillsdale, N.J.: Erlbaum, 1977.

Applebee, Arthur. *Tradition and Reform in the Teaching of English.* Urbana, Ill.: NCTE Press, 1974.

Austin, John L. *How to Do Things with Words.* New York: Oxford University Press, 1962.

Barthes, Roland. *Elements of Semiology.* Trans. Annette Lavers and Colin Smith. New York: Hill, Wang, 1967a.

———. *Writing Degree Zero.* Trans. Annette Lavers and Colin Smith. New York: Hill, Wang, 1967b.

———. *Mythologies.* Trans. Annette Lavers. New York: Hill, Wang, 1972.

———. *S/Z.* Trans. Richard Miller. New York: Hill, Wang, 1974.

————. *The Pleasure of the Text*. Trans. Richard Miller. New York: Hill, Wang, 1975.

Bleich, David. *Subjective Criticism*. Baltimore: Johns Hopkins University Press, 1978.

————. "The Identity of Pedagogy and Research in the Study of Response to Literature." *CE*, 42 (1980), 350–66.

Bloom, Harold. *The Anxiety of Influence*. New York: Oxford University Press, 1973.

————, et al., ed. *Deconstruction and Criticism*. New York: Seabury, 1979.

Booth, Wayne C. *The Rhetoric of Fiction*. Chicago: University of Chicago Press, 1961.

Bremond, Claude. *Logique du récit*. Paris: Éditions du Seuil, 1973.

Chatman, Seymour. "The Structure of Narrative Transmission." In *Style and Structure in Literature: Essays in the New Stylistics*. Ed. Roger Fowler. Ithaca, N.Y.: Cornell University Press, 1975.

Chklovski, Victor. *Sur la théorie de la prose*. Lausanne: L'Age d'Homme, 1973.

Chomsky, Noam. *Aspects of the Theory of Syntax*. Cambridge: M.I.T. Press, 1965.

Condillac, Étienne. *Condillac's Treatise on the Sensations*. Trans. Geraldine Carr. Los Angeles: University of Southern California School of Philosophy, 1930.

————. *An Essay on the Origin of Human Knowledge: Being a Supplement to Mr. Locke's "Essay on the Human Understanding."* Trans. Thomas Nugent. 1756; rpt. Gainesville, Fla.: Scholars' Facsimiles & Reprints, 1971.

Creber, J. W. Patrick. *Sense and Sensitivity: The Philosophy and Practice of English Teaching*. London: University of London Press, 1965.

Critical Inquiry. Vols. 1–5. Ed. Sheldon Sacks. Vols. 6 and subsequent. Ed. W.J.T. Mitchell. Chicago: University of Chicago Press, journal published quarterly since Fall 1974.

Culler, Jonathan. *Structuralist Poetics: Structuralism, Linguistics and the Study of Literature*. Ithaca, N.Y.: Cornell University Press, 1975.

Davis, Robert Con, ed. *The Fictional Father: Lacanian Readings of the Text*. Amherst: University of Massachusetts Press, 1981.

de Beaugrande, Robert. "Design Criteria for Process Models of Reading." *Read Res Q*, 16 (1981), 261–315.

de Man, Paul. *Blindness and Insight: Essays in the Rhetoric of Contemporary Criticism*. New York: Oxford University Press, 1971.

————. *Allegories of Reading: Figural Language in Rousseau, Nietzsche, Rilke, and Proust*. New Haven: Yale University Press, 1979.

de Saussure, Ferdinand. *Course in General Linguistics*. Trans. Wade Baskin. New York: McGraw-Hill, 1959.

Dewey, John. *Art as Experience*. New York: Minton Balch, 1934.

Derrida, Jacques. *Speech and Phenomena: And Other Essays on Husserl's Theory of Signs*. Trans. David B. Allison. Evanston, Ill.: Northwestern University Press, 1973.

————. *Of Grammatology*. Trans. Gayatri Chakravorty Spivak. Baltimore: Johns Hopkins University Press, 1974a.

————. "White Mythology: Metaphor in the Text of Philosophy." Trans. F.C.T. Moore. *NLH*, 6 (1974b), 7–74.

————. *Writing and Difference*. Trans. Alan Bass. Chicago: University of Chicago Press, 1978.

Diacritics: A Review of Contemporary Criticism. Ed. Department of Romance Studies, Cornell University. Baltimore: Johns Hopkins University Press, journal published quarterly since Fall 1971.

Elsasser, Nan, and Kyle Fiore. " 'Strangers No More': A Libertory Literacy Curriculum." *CE*, 44 (1982), 115–28.

Empson, William. *Seven Types of Ambiguity*. 1930; rpt. New York: New Directions, 1966.

Farrell, Thomas J. "Literacy, Basics, and All That Jazz." *CE*, 39 (1977), 443–59.

Fish, Stanley. *Is There a Text in This Class? The Authority of Interpretive Communities*. Cambridge, Mass.: Harvard University Press, 1980.

Freire, Paulo. *Pedagogy in Process*. New York: Seabury, 1978.

———. *Cultural Action for Freedom*. *Harvard Educational Review* and Center for the Study of Development and Social Change, No. 1. Cambridge, Mass.: Harvard Educational Review, 1970a.

———. *Pedagogy of the Oppressed*. New York: Seabury, 1970b.

Freud, Sigmund. *Beyond the Pleasure Principle*. Vol. 18 in *The Standard Edition of the Complete Psychological Works of Sigmund Freud*. Trans. James Strachey et al. London: Hogarth, 1971–72a.

———. *The Interpretation of Dreams*. Vols. 4 and 5 in *The Standard Edition of the Complete Psychological Works of Sigmund Freud*. Trans. James Strachey et al. London: Hogarth, 1971–72b.

———. *An Outline of Psychoanalysis*. Vol. 23 in *The Standard Edition of the Complete Psychological Works of Sigmund Freud*. Trans. James Strachey et al. London: Hogarth, 1971–72c.

Gibson, Eleanor J., and Harry Levin. *The Psychology of Reading*. Cambridge, Mass.: M.I.T. Press, 1975.

Gibson, Walker. "Authors, Speakers, Readers, and Mock Readers." *CE*, 11 (1950), 265–69.

Glyph. Vols. 1–8. Ed. Samuel Weber. Baltimore: Johns Hopkins University Press, journal published semi-annually 1977–1980.

Goodman, Kenneth. "Reading: A Psycholinguistic Guessing Game." In *Current Topics in Language*. Ed. Nancy Ainsworth Johnson. Cambridge, Mass.: Winthrop, 1976, pp. 370–83.

———, ed. *The Psycholinguistic Nature of the Reading Process*. Detroit: Wayne State University Press, 1968.

———, and Yetta Goodman, eds. *Linguistics, Psycholinguistics, and the Teaching of Reading*. Newark, Delaware: International Reading Association, 1980.

Graff, Gerald. *Literature Against Itself: Literary Ideas in Modern Society*. Chicago: University of Chicago Press, 1979.

Greimas, A. J. *Sémantique structurale*. Paris: Larousse, 1966.

———. *Du Sens*. Paris: Éditions du Seuil, 1970.

———. *Essais de sémiotique poétique*. Paris: Larousse, 1971.

Hartman, Geoffrey H. *The Fate of Reading*. Chicago: University of Chicago Press, 1975.

———. "A Touching Compulsion: Wordsworth and the Problem of Literary Representation." *Ga R*, 31 (1977), 345–61.

———. *Criticism in the Wilderness: The Study of Literature Today*. New Haven: Yale University Press, 1980.

Havelock, Eric. *Preface to Plato*. Cambridge, Mass.: Harvard University Press, 1963.

Hegel, Georg Wilhelm Friedrich. *Phenomenology of the Mind*. Trans. J. B. Baillie. London: Allen, Unwin, 1931.

Heidegger, Martin. *The Question of Being*. Trans. William Kluback and Jean T. Wilde. New York: Twayne, 1958.

———. *Being and Time*. Trans. John Macquarrie and Edward Robinson. Evanston, Ill.: Northwestern University Press, 1962a.

———. *Kant and the Question of Metaphysics*. Trans. James S. Churchill. Bloomington: Indiana University Press, 1962b.

Hirsch, Eric D., Jr. *Validity in Interpretation*. New Haven: Yale University Press, 1967.

———. *The Aims of Interpretation*. Chicago: University of Chicago Press, 1976.

Hjelmslev, Louis. *Essais Linguistiques*. Travaux du Cercle Linguistique de Copenhaque, vol. 13. Copenhagen: Nordisk Sprog-og Kulturforlag, 1959.

———. *Prolegomena to a Theory of Language*. Trans. Francis J. Whitfield. Madison: University of Wisconsin Press, 1961.

———. *Language: An Introduction*. Trans. Francis J. Whitfield. Madison: University of Wisconsin Press, 1970.

Hoetker, James. "A Theory of Talking about Theories of Reading." *CE*, 44 (1982), 175–82.

Holland, Norman N. *The Dynamics of Literary Response*. 1968; rpt. New York: Norton, 1975a.

———. *5 Readers Reading*. New Haven: Yale University Press, 1975b.

———. "Literature as Transaction." In *What Is Literature?* Ed. Paul Hernadi. Bloomington: Indiana University Press, 1978a, pp. 206–18.

———, et al. "Poem Opening: An Invitation to Transactive Criticism." *CE*, 40 (1978b), 2–16.

Hollingsworth, Alan. "Beyond Literacy." In *Prospects for the 70's: English Departments and Multidisciplinary Study*. Ed. Harry Finestone and Michael F. Shugrue. New York: Modern Language Association Press, 1973, pp. 78–89.

———. "Beyond Survival." *ADE Bul*, 54 (1977), 1–5.

Huey, E. B. *The Psychology and Pedagogy of Reading*. 1908; rpt. Cambridge, Mass.: M.I.T. Press, 1968.

Husserl, Edmund. *Ideas: General Introduction to Pure Phenomenology*. Trans. W. R. Boyce Gibson. New York: Humanities, 1931.

———. *Logical Investigations*. 2 vols. Trans. J. N. Findlay. New York: Humanities, 1970.

Ingarden, Roman. *The Cognition of the Literary Work of Art*. Trans. Ruth Ann Crowley and Kenneth R. Olson. Evanston, Ill.: Northwestern University Press, 1973.

Iser, Wolfgang. *The Implied Reader: Patterns of Communication in Prose Fiction from Bunyan to Beckett*. Baltimore: Johns Hopkins University Press, 1974.

Jakobson, Roman. "Concluding Statement: Linguistics and Poetics." In *Style in Language*. Ed. Thomas A. Sebeok. Cambridge, Mass.: M.I.T. Press, 1960, pp. 350–78.

Johnson, Barbara. *The Critical Difference: Essays in the Contemporary Rhetoric of Reading*. Baltimore: Johns Hopkins University Press, 1980.

Kermode, Frank. *The Sense of an Ending: Studies in the Theory of Fiction*. London: Oxford University Press, 1967.

———. "Sensing Endings." *NCF*, 33 (1978), 144–58.

Kozol, Jonathan. "A New Look at the Literacy Campaign in Cuba." *Harvard Educ Rev*, 48 (1978), 341–77.

Krieger, Murray. *Theory of Criticism: A Tradition and Its System*. Baltimore: Johns Hopkins University Press, 1976.

————. "The Recent Revolution in Theory and the Survival of the Literary Disciplines." *ADE Bul* 62 (1979), 27–34.

Kuhn, T. S. *The Structure of Scientific Revolutions*. Chicago: University of Chicago Press, 1962.

Lacan, Jacques. *Écrits*. Paris: Éditions du Seuil, 1966.

————. *Le Seminaire de Jacques Lacan*. Paris: Éditions du Seuil, 1973.

————. *The Language of the Self*. Trans. Anthony Wilden. Baltimore: Johns Hopkins University Press, 1975.

————. *Écrits: A Selection*. Trans. Alan Sheridan. London: Tavistock, 1977.

————. *The Four Fundamental Concepts of Psycho-Analysis*. Trans. Alan Sheridan. Ed. Alain Miller. New York: Norton, 1981a.

————. *Speech and Language in Psychoanalysis*. Trans. Anthony Wilden. Baltimore: Johns Hopkins University Press, 1981b.

Laplanche, Jean, and J.-B. Pontalis. *The Language of Psychoanalysis*. Trans. Donald Nicholson-Smith. London: Hogarth, 1973.

Leibnitz, Gottfried Wilhelm von. *Theodicy: Essays on the Goodness of God, the Freedom of Man, and the Origin of Evil*. Trans. E. M. Huggard. New Haven: Yale University Press, 1952.

Lemaire, Anika. *Jacques Lacan*. Trans. David Macey. London: Routledge, Kegan Paul, 1977.

Lentricchia, Frank. *After the New Criticism*. Chicago, University of Chicago Press, 1980.

Levin, Harry, and Joanna Williams, eds. *Basic Studies in Reading*. New York: Harper, Row, 1970.

Lévi-Strauss, Claude. *Structural Anthropology*. Trans. Claire Jacobson and Brooke Grundfest Schoepf. New York: Basic, 1963.

————. *The Elementary Structures of Kinship*. Trans. James Harle Bell, John Richard von Sturmer, and Rodney Needham. Boston: Beacon, 1969.

Locke, John. *An Essay on Human Understanding*. Vol. 35 in *Great Books of the Western World*. Ed. Robert M. Hutchins et al. Chicago: Encyclopaedia Britannica, 1952, pp. 85–402.

McCabe, Colin, ed. *The Talking Cure: Essays in Psychoanalysis and Language*. New York: St. Martin's, 1981.

Miller, Joseph Hillis. "Geneva or Paris? The Recent Work of Georges Poulet." *UTQ*, 39 (1970), 212–28.

————. "Deconstructing the Deconstructors." *Diacritics*, 4 (1975a), 24–31.

————. "Optic and Semiotic in *Middlemarch*." In *The Worlds of Victorian Fiction*. Ed. Jerome H. Buckley. Cambridge, Mass.: Harvard University Press, 1975b, pp. 125–45.

————. "The Function of Rhetorical Study at the Present Time." In *The State of the Discipline: 1970s–1980s*. Ed. Jasper P. Neel. New York: Modern Language Association Press, 1979, pp. 10–18.

————. "The Figure in the Carpet." *Po T*, 1 (1980a), 107–18.

————. "*Wuthering Heights* and the Ellipses of Interpretation." *NDEJ* (1980b), 85–100.

————. *Fiction and Repetition: Seven English Novels*. Cambridge, Mass.: Harvard University Press, 1982.

Neel, Jasper P. "Vicissitudo Non Est." *CEAF*, 8 (1977), 1–5.

———. "A Dramatic Essay Not in Defense of Teaching Poesy." *FEN*, 9 (1980), 13–17.

———. "Writing about Literature (Or, Country Ham)." In *Publishing in English Education*. Ed. Stephen N. Judy. Montclair, N.J.: Boynton/Cook, 1982, pp. 53–72.

New Literary History: A Journal of Theory and Interpretation. Ed. Ralph Cohen. Baltimore: Johns Hopkins University Press, journal published tri-annually since Fall 1969.

Nietzsche, Friedrich, *Beyond Good and Evil*. New York: Vantage, 1966.

———. *On the Geneology of Morals*. New York: Vantage, 1969.

———. *Ecce Homo*. New York: Gordon, 1974.

———. *Basic Writings of Nietzsche*. Trans. Walter Kaufman. New York: Modern Library, 1968a.

———. *The Will to Power*. Trans. Walter Kaufman and R. J. Hollingdale. New York: Vintage, 1968b.

Ong, Walter. *The Presence of the Word: Some Prolegomena for Cultural and Religious History*. 1967; rpt. New York: Simon, Schuster, 1970.

———. *Rhetoric, Romance, and Technology: Studies in the Interaction of Expression and Culture*. Ithaca, N.Y.: Cornell University Press, 1971.

———. *Interfaces of the Word: Studies in the Evolution of Consciousness and Culture*. Ithaca, N.Y.: Cornell University Press, 1977.

———. "Literacy and Orality in Our Times." In *Profession 79*. Ed. Jasper P. Neel and Richard I. Brod. New York: Modern Language Association Press, 1979, pp. 1–7.

Parker, Hershel, and Henry Binder. "Exigencies of Composition and Publication: *Billy Budd, Sailor* and *Pudd'nhead Wilson*." *NCF*, 33 (1978), 131–43.

Peirce, Charles Sanders. *Collected Papers of Charles Sanders Peirce*. 4 vols. Ed. Charles Hartshorne and Paul Weiss. 1931–1960; rpt. Cambridge, Mass.: Belknap Press of Harvard University Press, 1965.

Petrosky, Anthony R. "From Story to Essay: Reading and Writing." *CCC*, 33 (1982), 19–36.

Poulet, Georges. *The Metamorphoses of the Circle*. Trans. Carley Dawson and Elliott Coleman. Baltimore: Johns Hopkins University Press, 1967.

———. *Proustian Space*. Trans. Elliott Coleman. Baltimore: Johns Hopkins University Press, 1977.

———. *Studies in Human Time*. Trans. Elliott Coleman. 1956; rpt. New York: Greenwood, 1979.

Pound, Ezra. *ABC of Reading*. 1934; rpt. New York: New Directions, 1960.

Propp, Vladimir. *Morphology of the Folktale*. Trans. Laurence Scott. 2nd ed., rev. and ed. Louis A. Wagner. Austin: University of Texas Press, 1968.

Purves, Alan, ed. *How Porcupines Make Love: Notes on a Response-Centered Curriculum*. Lexington, Mass.: Xerox College Publishing, 1972.

Purves, Alan C., and Richard Beach. *Literature and the Reader: Research in Response to Literature, Reading Interests, and the Teaching of Literature*. Urbana, Ill.: NCTE Press, 1972.

Rosenblatt, Louise M. *Literature as Exploration*. 1938; rpt. New York: Noble, 1976.

Rumelhart, David. "Schemata: The Building Blocks of Cognition." In *Theoretical Issues in Reading and Comprehension.* Ed. R. Spiro, B. Bruce, and W. Brewer. Hillsdale, N.J.: Erlbaum, 1980.

Said, Edward W. *Beginnings: Intention and Method.* New York: Basic, 1975.

Salus, Peter H. "What Is Evidence Evidence of?" In *Semiotics 1980.* Comp. Michael Herzfeld and Margot D. Lenhart, New York: Plenum, 1982, pp. 455–67.

Sartre, Jean-Paul. *What Is Literature?* Trans. Bernard Frechtman. New York: Philosophical Library, 1949.

Schank, Roger, and Robert Abelson. *Scripts, Plans, Goals, and Understanding: An Inquiry into Human Knowledge Structures.* Hillsdale, N.J.: Erlbaum, 1977.

Scholes, Robert. *Structuralism in Literature: An Introduction.* New Haven: Yale University Press, 1974.

Searle, John R. *Speech Acts.* London: Cambridge University Press, 1968.

Smith, Frank. *Understanding Reading: A Psycholinguistic Analysis of Reading and Learning to Read.* New York: Holt, Rinehart, Winston, 1971.

———. *Psycholinguistics and Reading.* New York: Holt, Rinehart, Winston, 1973.

———. *Writing and the Writer.* New York: Holt, Rinehart, Winston, 1982.

Starobinski, Jean. "Considérations sur l'état présent de la critique littéraire." *Diogène,* 74 (1971), 62–95.

Suleiman, Susan R., and Inge Crosman, ed. *The Reader in the Text: Essays on Audience and Interpretation.* Princeton, N.J.: Princeton University Press, 1980.

Tel Quel. Paris: Éditions du Seuil, journal published quarterly since Spring 1960.

Thompson, Bruce E. R. "The Application of Peircean Semiotic to Logic." In *Semiotics 1980.* Comp. Michael Herzfeld and Margot D. Lenhart. New York: Plenum, 1982, pp. 513–22.

Todorov, Tzvetan. *The Poetics of Prose.* Trans. Richard Howard. Ithaca, N.Y.: Cornell University Press, 1977.

Tompkins, Jane P., ed. *Reader-Response Criticism: From Formalism to Post-Structuralism.* Baltimore: Johns Hopkins University Press, 1980.

Turkle, Sherry. *Psychoanalytic Politics: Freud's French Revolution.* New York: Basic, 1978.

White, Hayden. "The Absurdist Moment in Contemporary Literary Theory." In *Directions for Criticism: Structuralism and Its Alternatives.* Ed. Murray Krieger and L. S. Dembo. Madison: University of Wisconsin Press, 1977, pp. 85–110.

Whitehead, Frank S. *The Disappearing Dais: A Study of the Principles and Practices of English Teaching.* London: Chatto, Windus, 1966.

Winterowd, W. Ross, ed. *Contemporary Rhetoric: A Conceptual Background with Readings.* New York: Harcourt, 1975.

———. "Getting It Together in the English Department." *ADE Bul,* 5 (1977), 28–32.

Part II
Major Issues

Research Methods in Composition

CHRISTOPHER C. BURNHAM

Rhetoric has never enjoyed a secure disciplinary identity. In the *Rhetoric* (Cooper, 1932), Aristotle named the "enthymeme" the most effective means of argument available to an orator. However, he derived his definition of the *enthymeme* by comparing it to the syllogism of dialectic. The enthymeme is flawed since the speaker omits one or more of the premises, trusting the audience to supply what is missing. Such an omission causes the enthymeme, and by inference rhetoric itself, to be found wanting. Edward Corbett in the "Survey of Rhetoric" in *Classical Rhetoric for the Modern Student* (1971) showed how rhetoric has had to weather debates about its nature as an art or a science, endure exclusion from its central position in the medieval liberal arts curriculum, and survive its reduction to a set of algorithmic formulae and language etiquettes. Today, in rhetoric and its descendant composition studies, disputes continue over theoretical models of the composing process, taxonomies of writing, and paradigms to guide research. These historical and contemporary controversies make a discussion of research methods difficult and complicated. Indeed, rhetoric endures, but it cannot claim a dominant research methodology any more than it can claim a stable disciplinary identity through time.

As its history suggests, the variety of disciplines involved in composition research today also suggests complexity. One of the several specialized bibliographies published by the *Rhetoric Society Quarterly*, "Heuristic Procedures and the Composing Process," compiled by R. L. Enos and colleagues (1982), although limiting itself through its title and including work completed primarily between 1970 and 1980, lists more than 70 periodicals representing five distinct disciplines. Psychology, including subdisciplines like behavioral, cognitive, and experimental psychology, as well as topical permutations like human-factors design and artificial intelligence, accounts for more than 31 journal titles. English discipline journals, including those concerned with administration and classroom practices as well as with research per se, account for 14. Education and educational research journals contribute 11. Speech and communication journals and journals devoted exclusively to rhetoric add 2 more each. Other journals included in the bibliography defy categorization. This sample alone describes a range from highly empirical methodologies like those used in experimental psychology to the traditional speculative inquiry of the Royal Society of the Arts.

The quantity as well as the diversity of disciplines involved in composition contributes to the complexity. The "Annotated Bibliography of Research in the Teaching of English," which appears each May and December in *RTE*, divides into four major categories—language, literature and media, writing, and teacher education—and subclassifies these four into preschool and elementary, secondary, and college and adult-interest areas and adds a section on research reviews. The bibliography for January through June 1981 lists more than 241 books, articles, ERIC/RCS monographs and studies, and dissertations. "Writing" accounts for 142 separate citations including 18 research reviews with one of them annotating more than 800 books and articles. So many journals publish composition research that William Woods edited a compilation, *A Directory of Publishing Opportunities for Teachers of Writing* (1979), with crossed ink quills, a heraldic bird, and the command "Publish or Perish" adorning its red and white cover.

The breadth and mass of research in rhetoric and composition cause two distinct problems. The first involves domain and definition. What is the province of rhetoric and composition? What should be included in a review of research methods? The composition researcher may make reference to the neuro-physiological journal *Brain*, but does using such information require extensive familiarity with that discipline's research methodologies?

Second, in realistic terms the mass of research precludes comprehensiveness. Each article reporting composition research depends implicitly or explicitly on a theory that applies particular research methods. Cataloguing articles according to research type would be as monumental as Sisyphus's task and equally absurd. The highly interdisciplinary and synthetic nature of composition as a discipline could not be adequately discussed in less than an encyclopedia. Even establishing criteria to determine inclusion and exclusion is problematic at best.

Comprehensiveness is not an aim here. The purpose is to provide an overview establishing the modern historical context of research in rhetoric and composition and to trace the evolution of the various principles important to researchers. These are the principles working in particularly effective models of various research methods. Within the discussion, a review of aids and handbooks directs researchers to helpful resources. My aim is to provide researchers an understanding of the context in which they work—how the discipline grew from chaos into an order encouraging a healthful diversity—and inform them of the principles that should guide their various projects.

Up from Chaos

Although as old as Aristotelian rhetoric, the problem of disciplinary identity has caused a series of crises in recent composition research, each culminating in the publication of a book serving as a manifesto addressing the issues of discipline definition and purpose and suggesting a program of research using a particular research methodology. Before the early 1960s, composition research had been a part of the classical humanistic tradition dating from the Renaissance. Although this tradition produced remarkable treatises like those of the eighteenth-century English rhetoricians Campbell, Blair, and Whateley, it was characterized by individual analyses of problems and speculations unharnessed by the rigor of an investigative system.

With the early 1960s in the wake of Sputnik and its influence on American science and education came a general concern for establishng discipline identities and directions for systematic investigation. Even the Modern Language Association (MLA) participates in this movement toward definition. James Thorpe edited *The Aims and Methods of Scholarship in Modern Languages and Literature* (1963), addressing the ''students into whose hands the future of American scholarship will in due course fall'' (p. vii). Concentrating its concerns on literary criticism, literary history, textual criticism, and linguistics, the MLA, through Thorpe, excludes composition research from its concerns. The section of the linguistics essay dealing with applied linguistics admits that its purview includes ''spelling reform and literacy campaigns'' but directs its ''few remarks'' only to ''literature, foreign language teaching, and international languages'' (p. 18).

That the MLA has consciously excluded the development of language skills by native English speakers from its concerns both explains and intensifies the disciplinary insecurity of researchers in composition, most of whom have been trained by and work in English departments affiliated with the MLA.

Although the MLA excludes composition research and denies its legitimacy as scholarship, composition studies is working to establish its own identity. Between 1963 and 1975, we see the establishment of the ''scientifically based'' program of experimental research announced by Richard Braddock and his colleagues in *Research in Written Composition* (1963). The appropriateness of the experimental methodology's application to the fundamentally humanistic activity of writing comes into question with J. Stephen Sherwin's *Four Problems in Teaching English* (1969). The cycle of establishing and then evaluating methodological principles culminates with W. Ross Winterowd's *Contemporary Rhetoric* (1975), which aims at establishing a disciplinary identity synthesizing scientific methodologies and humanistic concerns.

An awareness of the need for establishing a coherent theoretical and methodological base characterizes each of these books. Through such a base, the discipline can move from the chaos in which all ideas carry equal authority towards a tradition in which ideas carry merit only after they have been evaluated against a standard. These books and the professional activity they report trace progress towards a secure disciplinary identity unavailable to those without an articulated research tradition.

The publication of the *Handbook of Research on Teaching*, edited by N. L. Gage (1963a), reflects the general concern for methodology. A project of the National Education Association, the *Handbook* asserts that teaching deserves scientific attention. It places educational research in the social science tradition emphasizing empiricism and tightly controlled experimentation. For the composition researcher, the value of the *Handbook* is in its careful explanation of the procedures of empirical research.

Gage's "Paradigms for Research on Teaching" (1963b) discusses the relation of theories to research while introducing several research paradigms from the social sciences with relevance to teaching. The purpose is to establish a theory of teaching that will guide subsequent research. The crucial chapter for composition researchers, however, is Donald Campbell and Julian Stanley's "Experimental and Quasi-Experimental Designs for Research in Teaching" (1966). Their purpose is to establish a concern for *internal validity*, which monitors the internal consistency of an experiment so that the result it advertises is indeed a consequence of the experiment and nothing else; and *external validity*, which concerns the generalizability of an experiment so that it can be replicated with similar results. Validity thus results from the strict control of variables. They list variables including maturation, statistical regression, and the interactions between sample selection and experimental variables and discuss means of controlling them. They include rationales and descriptions of three "pre-experimental" designs including the one-shot case study, the one-group pretest-posttest design, and the static group design. Three "true experimental designs" include the pretest-posttest control group, Solomon four-group design, and the posttest-only control group design. These experimental designs are presented as processes with controls for internal validity explained, jeopardizing factors discussed, statistical tests of significance prescribed, and further references provided in an extensive bibliography. The *Handbook* establishes a context for educational research within the scientifically based social science tradition.

The *Handbook* devotes one chapter specifically to research in English disciplines. Henry C. Meckel's "Research on Teaching Composition and Literature" includes an extensive bibliography of the relevant studies completed up to that time. Topics treated in the chapter include objectives for composition instruction, comparative methods for teaching writing, relations between grammar teaching and composition skill, assignment making, and evaluation of writing. The summaries of research address the methodological problems in particular studies and end with evaluations that still retain historical interest for composition researchers. Testifying to the effectiveness of the volume, the final assertions of the chapter seem today like platitudes. In terms of general educational research, the *Handbook* established a sense of professional and disciplinary identity, joined the fragments, and established base-line data, both substantive and methodological, from which progress could begin.

Meckel addressed the problem of disciplinary identity in the introduction to his chapter. Noting the changing nature of American education, especially the increased opportunity for Americans to attend college, he called for a revised "interdependent" curriculum sequencing and integrating teaching efforts from the elementary and secondary schools through the colleges and universities. He credited the National Council of Teachers of English (NCTE) for providing much of the impetus for this integration. It was the NCTE that moved to provide a specific identity and purpose for the English teaching profession through the publication of *Research in Written Composition* (1963) by Braddock and his colleagues.

The purpose of the project was to review all that was known about teaching writing and present a "scientifically based" evaluation of the state of the art of composition research. The authors immediately eliminated all research that did not employ scientific methods, including controlled experimentation and textual analysis of written products. That this resulted in the elimination of a great deal of existing research is suggested by an early description of the status of composition research, which "taken as a whole may be compared to chemical research as it emerged from the state of alchemy...the field as a whole is laced with dreams, prejudices and makeshift operations" (p. 5).

To help move composition research beyond the alchemical stage Braddock reviewed existing research to find principles and practices that would guide new research. The concern for scientific respectabilty is evident throughout. A discussion of rating compositions breaks into considerations of the many variables involved, including the writer, assignment, rater, and colleagues. Such an involved discussion makes researchers aware of the range of variables potentially confounding an experiment. These variables must be controlled to allow for legitimate research claims to be made. "Suggested Methods of Research" lists and explains general considerations including planning procedures, controlling variables, and reporting results. Writing to an audience of research novices, the advice is appropriately clear and uncomplicated by jargon. The text includes an extensive review of research reminding researchers that they do not work in isolation but as a part of a community of inquiry guided by a tradition. The review ends with a list of 24 questions that existing research either ignores or answers inadequately. Among them are questions like "How does a person go about starting a paper? What questions must he answer for himself?" as well as other questions whose answers the profession continues to debate 20 years later (p. 53).

The penultimate chapter provides summaries of five selected research studies adhering to the criteria for valid research that have been amassing through the volume. These criteria state that:

1) "the investigation must involve *direct observation of actual writing*;

2) "the sample studied must be significant in number or controlled in selection to guarantee *generalizability of results*;

3) "the *procedures* of the controlled experiment and the *features of writing studied through textual analysis* are sufficient to determine the particular variable and effect examined;

4) "the *significance* of the results are to be *statistically tested* to validate but not obscure the data collected;

5) "the investigator will maintain objectivity by removing himself from the study, if possible, and control and report salient variables to insure *replicability*." (pp. 55–56)

These principles should guide the design and execution of research in the scientific mode.

The volume ends with "References for Further Research," which includes listings of valuable summaries and bibliographies of research, a guide to indices and abstracts, and a 500–item selected bibliography still valuable today.

The "scientifically based" program forwarded by Braddock provoked an interest in the nature of measuring growth in writing. Objective tests of writing based on multiple-choice items, regardless of their statistical reliability, violated the direct-observation principle announced by Braddock. Moreover, if the purpose of research was to advertise the advantage of certain methods over others, reliable pretest-posttest measures were crucial. Although only tangentially involved in the dispute over research methods in composition, Fred Godshalk and others in *The Measurement of Writing Ability* (1966) described the elaborate procedures and statistical tests used to validate the College Entrance Examination Board's English Composition Test. In addition, they concluded that the indirect measurement of writing through an accurate objective test coupled with direct although somewhat inaccurate measurement through a short essay is the most reliable measure of writing ability. The College Board with its intense concern with psychometric validity developed a testing procedure in line with the scientific method advanced in the *Handbook*. That the conclusions drawn from this method contradict a principle established by Braddock foreshadows the rift between the social science-based empiricists and many of the humanities-based researchers in composition.

Also concerned with the issue of measuring the growth of writing skills through testing is Paul B. Diederich's *Measuring Growth in English* (1974). Based on the Educational Testing Service (ETS)/College Board testing research and experience, Diederich described the complexity involved both in the learning of writing and in the evaluation of writing growth through testing. He advised reducing the time and energy teachers devote to evaluating writing, since evaluation per se does not lead to growth in writing. He presented a system of staff grading aimed at freeing teachers from the chore of constant evaluation, thus allowing more time for instruction. The book makes a sound distinction between testing and teaching.

Whether the NCTE accomplished its aim of establishing a tradition of "scientifically based" research in the early 1960s seems partially answered by J. Stephen Sherwin's *Four Problems in Teaching English* (1969). On one level Sherwin exposed a failure of progress because his concern duplicated that of Braddock. He reviewed past research and questioned its value. Admitting the importance of individual interpretation of research conclusions and encouraging eclecticism in application, he nevertheless stressed "objective inquiry," which established standards making practitioners accountable for their applications of research. Thus he argued against the "because it works" tradition of teaching in which teachers know neither what it is nor how it works. At the same time, Sherwin claimed his experience as a practitioner to be the source of his authority. He knew the research and its application. The NCTE began the decade trying to train researchers and ended with an attempt to prepare practitioners to take advantage of the fruits of its earlier labor.

Sherwin's book focuses on four specific topics: Latin and English teaching; spelling; traditional grammar, linguistics research, and skills practice in developing writing ability; and sentence diagraming. In the text and bibliography, Sherwin offered what he claimed to be a comprehensive listing of all research done in these areas up to 1966 to supplement Braddock and associates' *Research in Written Composition*. Throughout the text, Sherwin complained about the self-serving nature of much of the research he reported. Collecting and comparing findings of studies in these specific areas, he found contradictions and methodological inconsistencies that illustrate the failure of rigor typical of the research. Although his critique is primarily an indictment of research methods, he ended remarking about a change, an evolution towards professionalism. But he admitted a discomfort with this evolution, especially with the scientific principles advertised by Braddock. He questioned the value of hard research, since "laboratory conditions" don't exist in classrooms. Furthermore, he questioned the ethics behind scientifically based educational research, which depends so much on control groups and variably treated experimental groups: "A class of students cannot be treated like a swarm of fruit flies" (p. 189).

Sherwin's critique closed the first decade of discipline-identity development. Questioning the ethics of the scientific methodology serving as the basis for development, however, signals that the discipline is still far from enjoying a secure identity and an accepted research tradition.

Convergence and Divergence

Despite Sherwin's objections, a concern for scientific methodology influenced the discipline, moving it beyond the alchemical stage earlier noted in Braddock (1963). The discipline, however, still lacked a framework, a theory that could serve as a starting place for the training of new researchers and practitioners. Winterowd's *Contemporary Rhetoric* (1975) provides such a framework by collecting significant composition research completed in the wake of the call for professionalism in the 1960s. Prominent researchers in the scientific mode like Francis Christensen, Janet Emig, Richard Young, and Alton Becker are represented as well as rhetorical theoreticians like Kenneth Burke and Wayne Booth. Including researchers in the scientific tradition and theoreticians in the humanistic tradition enabled Winterowd to tap the great reservoir of ideas available through the classical rhetorical tradition. *Contemporary Rhetoric*, then, begins a synthesis of old and new, of speculation and experimentation, which characterizes the next period of growth in composition studies. But the center of the book and the source of its importance to this discussion is Winterowd's editorial commentary. His introductory comments, "Some Remarks on Pedagogy," discuss the function of and necessity for a unified conceptual framework in a discipline. That he directed his comments towards teachers suggests that they are without this framework and reinforces the claims made earlier by Braddock and Sherwin. That *Contemporary Rhetoric* collects materials published and readily available in books and professional journals implies that teachers are not aware of their own literature.

Winterowd's aim is to unify the profession through a conceptual framework rather than through a research methodology. Already the research tradition of Braddock had been questioned. Winterowd remarked: "There can be no 'Skinner box' studies of the composing process, for isolating the composer and limiting his or her activity to one segment of the process simply falsifies what goes on" (p. 17). The conceptual framework Winterowd called for is based in great part upon Roman Jakobson's schema for discourse analysis presented in "Linguistics and Politics," in *Style in Language* (1960). The purpose of the conceptual framework is to guide inquiry; it "allows one to organize a subject and it automatically becomes an inventive heuristic for the discovery of subject matter" (p. 1). Winterowd's framework uses the categories of classical rhetoric—invention, arrangement, and style. His contribution is even more fundamental than that of those concerned exclusively with research methodologies, since the conceptual framework provides the theoretical foundation from which researchers can derive principles to determine their methods.

Contemporary Rhetoric establishes a comprehensive disciplinary identity with a conceptual framework precluding dependence upon any one research methodology. Thus it begins to repair the split between the humanists and the empiricists. William Fagan and colleagues' *Measures for Research and Evaluation in the English Language Arts* (1975) marks further progress in establishing the tools for research in composition. It answers *The Measurement of Writing Ability* (1966) by Fred Godshalk and others by collecting all existing measurement instruments in English language arts and analyzing them in terms of their purpose, validity, and reliability. It also examines the theoretical framework supported by the use of the tests. Each test is discussed in terms of its ability to support specific types of research. This analysis encourages divergent research directions by establishing the principle that researchers must choose appropriate designs and measurement instruments from the many available. The design and measurement instruments must support the purpose of the research. There is no one way to conduct composition research; researchers must choose from a variety of methods to support particular research purposes and experimental objectives. The authors aimed "to alert the reader to new and better ways of measuring phenomena chosen as the focus of the study" (p. x). They cited *The Mental Measurements Yearbook* (the current edition is the *Eighth* [1978] by Oscar Buros), with its critical reviews of test instruments and extensive bibliographies, as one of their sources. The authors included ten suggestions for those constructing tests that today still serve the apprentice researcher, although the reviews of specific tests are generally out of date.

The concern with disciplinary identity and research tradition peaks with *Teaching Composition*, edited by Gary Tate (1976). Tate emphasized the need for the past to inform ongoing research. He explained that *Teaching Composition* is to supplement the yearly bibliographies that Richard Larson had published in *CCC*. In all, five Larson bibliographies were published in *CCC*, covering research published between 1973 and 1978. The bibliographies appear in the May issues from 1975 to 1979. (See Larson [1979b], for example.)

Stating that *Teaching Composition* would be concerned primarily with work done before 1973, Tate divided all composition into ten areas. Each area was the topic for an essay including annotations and evaluations of the research reviewed. Highlights include Young's chapter on invention, Mina Shaughnessy's on basic writing, and Winterowd's on linguistics and composition. All of the essays merit reading, since they provide a comprehensive overview of what was known about composition before 1976 and suggest areas still needing investigation.

Unfortunately, the volume is hard to use, since the essays are without itemized bibliographies. Recently, Barbara McDaniels published an *Index to Teaching Composition* (1982), making the volume more accessible as a reference text. But *Teaching Composition* makes no mention of Braddock and associates' *Research in Written Composition* as a forbearer. In fact, the volume pays little attention to research methods or the procedures and problems of research in composition, and it is the first book of its kind to take the existence of a research tradition as a given.

Rhetoric and Composition, edited by Richard Graves (1976), also collects essays reporting research in composition. Unlike Winterowd's text and Tate's bibliography, this collection is aimed at practioners in the hope that research discoveries can begin to inform practice. Three principles run throughout the Graves collection. First, writing is a complicated and idiosyncratic process whose end is the writer's discovery of meaning and the learning associated with such a discovery. Second, English teachers are not prepared adequately by their predominantly literary education to teach composition; yet composition teaching generally amounts to the greatest part of an English teacher's job. Third, recent composition research suggests that there are things known about writing and that teachers *can* help students learn to write. The practical bent of *Rhetoric and Composition* is evident in the subsections, which include motivating students, the sentence, the paragraph, and composition pedagogy. Important researcher-theoreticians like A. L. Becker, Charles Cooper, Frank D'Angelo, and Kellogg Hunt are represented in the collection, but there is little concern with the methodology underlying their discoveries. Emphasis is on applications. Like *Teaching Composition*, Graves's *Rhetoric and Composition* assumes a research tradition and the integrity of the discipline.

While one set of scholars was at work amassing and applying the work completed under the newly established "scientifically based" tradition, another was evaluating their claims and finding them less than satisfying. Previously, the research had been condemned for its lack of methodological principles. Now researchers and theoreticians began to complain about the experimental methodologies developed to answer the earlier complaints. Charles Cooper and Lee Odell in *Research on Composing* (1978) indicted the research tradition the profession had been developing for 15 years. Research that had been completed had been primarily pedagogical, aiming to discover what materials and methods would improve student writing the most with the least effort in the shortest period. Cooper and Odell questioned the assumption beneath such pedagogical research. They pointed out that research like Emig's *Composing Process of Twelfth Graders* (1971), a naturalistic case study and model of its kind, and James Britton and his colleagues' *Development of Writing Abilities (11–18)* (1975), a report of the grand failure of an empirically based study whose purpose was to determine the relationship of function and audience in the writing of British schoolchildren, illustrate that the knowledge that informs existing textbook and curricular practice does not reflect the way either professionals or students write. Moreover, they claimed that the discipline's interests should go deeper than the analysis of products to the making of texts—to the composing process itself. In this they called for a major shift in research emphasis.

Cooper and Odell, knowing they were questioning the precepts established in Braddock and associates' *Research in Written Composition*, addressed the issue specifically. They saw two differences between *Research on Composing* and *Research in Written Composition*. First, the latter summarizes existing research and advances "exemplary comparison-group research studies" in order to establish a research tradition, and the former is oppposed to conventional research methodology and suggests new areas and means of inquiry through which researchers might "begin to lift ourselves out of our own ignorance" (p. xiii). Second, Cooper and Odell emphasized basic theoretical research over pedagogical research. "Ultimately, comparison-group research may enable us to improve instruction in writing, but the research must be informed by carefully tested theory and by descriptions of written discourse and the processes by which that discourse comes into being" (p. xiv). Like Winterowd, Cooper and Odell saw the discipline's immediate need to be establishing a theoretical basis for research. Thus they called for a research of discovery rather than a research of confirmation ruled by narrow-minded empiricism.

Richard Young's "Paradigms and Problems" (1978) focuses on the importance of research tradition. Using Thomas Kuhn's *Structure of Scientific Revolutions* (1963), he defined *paradigm* as the system of values, beliefs, and methods shared within a discipline that ultimately determines what is or is not a part of the discipline, what deserves study and what does not. Young viewed the "current-traditional" paradigm in composition as dominated by "vitalists," descendants of the Romantics who emphasize composed product rather than composing process, who section discourse into discrete subparts like the sentence and paragraph, and who teach conventions of usage and style. In sum, vitalism's "stress on the natural powers of the mind and the uniqueness of the creative act lead to a repudiation of teaching the composing process'' (p. 31). Such an emphasis on product leads to research on problems of application and pedagogical practice while ignoring theory.

Young's particular interest is reincluding invention among the research interests of composition. Invention's nature as the finding and shaping of ideas for expression, a process that goes unnoticed if completed successfully, excluded it from the product centered current-traditional paradigm. Despite its exclusion from composition studies, rhetoricians and psychologists have developed four theories of invention, including the classical with its *topoi*, Kenneth Burke's dramatism, Gordon Rohman's prewriting, and Kenneth L. Pike's tagmemic invention. All of these theories posit a process view of composing and provide the discipline opportunities to understand better the nature of composition. Young emphasized the failure of the current-traditional paradigm to allow the testing of theories of invention *or* to understand its discipline completely. He then suggested several areas of inquiry in invention as part of the larger project of building a newer, more adequate paradigm for the discipline.

Richard Young set the tone for the whole of Cooper and Odell's *Research on Composing*. Other articles implicitly criticize the current-traditional paradigm by noting the discipline's inability to move forward in many areas. Suggesting new problems and new sources for answers to these problems, the contributors united in calling for multidisciplinary investigations characterized by synthesized research methods. Many of these methods, like the case study that is frequently mentioned as an effective method of investigating individual processes of composing, are borrowed from other disciplines like psychology. *Research on Composing*, in addition to mapping the concern of composition research for the foreseeable future, calls for the establishment of a disciplinary paradigm in composition studies. Although Braddock (1963) implied that disciplinary security is available through a particular research methodology, Cooper and Odell and their contributors (1978) argued that a secure identity comes only from developing a paradigm including a theory of composing. Theory-building must precede confirmation.

Supporting the call for divergence and discovery at the heart of *Research on Composing* and continuing the discipline's concern for developing appropriate tests and measures to support research ends, Cooper and Odell included in *Evaluating Writing* (1977) six essays discussing methods and purposes of evaluating writing. They include holistic scoring, Primary Trait Scoring, computer-assisted methods of assessing writing maturity through word choice, measures of syntactic maturity, measuring cognitive process through writing, and a broad range of evaluation strategies useful for teaching. In most essays, attention is given to how certain of these procedures grow out of and support particular types of research. As a handbook of evaluation purposes and procedures, *Evaluating Writing* is the standard.

Disciplinary interest in the research applications of testing continued, culminating in Regina Hoover's "Annotated Bibliography on Testing" (1979). Designed as a handbook and primer on testing, it includes citations of general treatments of the issues in testing writing as well as reviews of specific tests and testing efforts. More recently, Miles Myers of the Bay Area Writing Project in *A Procedure for Writing Assessment and Holistic Scoring* (1980) provided alternative evaluation methods for programs confronted by the standardized testing hysteria of the current back-to-basics movement.

The 1970s ended with *Linguistics, Stylistics, and the Teaching of Composition*, edited by Donald McQuade (1979), a collection of 14 articles whose aim is to "create a convenient and concentrated forum for enriching the writing teacher's understanding of the assumptions, methods, and the results of the thinking and research in linguistics and stylistics as they apply to composition classes" (p. xii). The contributors are all noteworthy in their field, including the familiar names of Frank D'Angelo, James Kinneavy, Richard Larson, and W. Ross Winterowd. Despite Lester Faigley's complaint in a review in *CCC* (1982) that much of the theoretical information in the text was obsolete at publication, most of the essays are interesting and valuable. Larson's "Language Studies and Composing Processes" (1979a) is an effective primer on transformational grammar research studies, although it ends with a reiteration of the complaint that we really do not know very much about how writers write but that psychology and psycho-linguistics with their interest in process may provide the methodologies needed for fruitful research. Winterowd's "Brain, Rhetoric, and Style" (1979) presents interesting speculations about brain hemisphericity, dominant writing style, and developing a program for teaching writing based on brain dominance. His synthesis and application of research in neuro-physiology to writing provides a fertile model for researchers. David Bartholomae's review of Shaughnessy's *Errors and Expectations* (1977) calls attention to the naturalistic, context-bound, research methodology that she pioneered. His review is especially interesting in the light of his own application of the methods in "The Study of Error" (1980) for which he won the Richard Braddock research award.

McQuade's *Linguistics, Stylistics and the Teaching of Composition* (1979) does not encourage the establishment of a new research tradition as much as it echoes Cooper and Odell's *Research on Composing*'s (1978) indictment of the scientific methodology celebrated by Braddock. As such it prepares the way for the 1980s in which attention is turned specifically to the creation and legitimization of a methodology able to test theories built and synthesized in the 1970s.

Healthful Multiplicity

Establishing a discipline paradigm is the major preoccupation of researchers in the 1980s. The first book to discuss the issue is the collection *Reinventing the Rhetorical Tradition* (1980), edited by Aviva Freedman and Jan Pringle, who saw their collection unified by a "commonality" signalling "the emergence of a new paradigm revealed in the shared assumptions and values of those at the forefront of the discipline" (p. 173). What these leaders—the contributors to the volume—share is a rejection of the immediate past, the current-traditional paradigm described by Young in Cooper and Odell's *Research on Composing* (1978). What is common is their view that the tradition must be reinvented, or at least reinvigorated. These leaders questioned the research methodologies used to validate the assertions of the current-traditional paradigm and argued "against the hegemony of the experimental method" (p. 176).

The essays making up the Freedman and Pringle collection are well worth examining. Susan Miller's "Rhetorical Maturity" (1980) applies L. Kohlberg's (1971) six-stage model of growth from childhood through maturity to the development of writing abilities and makes applications to teaching. Kinneavy's "A Pluralistic Synthesis of Four Contemporary Models for Teaching Composition" (1980) relates his own *Theory of Discourse* (1971) to the theories of Moffett (1968), Britton and colleagues (1975), and D'Angelo (1975), creating a "metasystem" incorporating all important principles of each theory. They include a concern with the functions of discourse, the modes of discourse, the effect of audience and the different cognitive demands made by writing to different audiences in various modes, and an emphasis on the holistic teaching of writing rather than the isolated teaching of the parts of the theme. Moreover, the synthesis he derived seems plausible and ready for testing.

Emig's "Tacit Tradition" (1980), the central essay of the collection, announces the source from which the new paradigm grows. Calling it "the tacit tradition" because it has previously served as an unstated foundation, she traced its roots to the works of the modern thinkers Kelly, John Dewey, Michael Polanyi, Thomas Kuhn, Suzanne Langer, Jean Piaget, Lev Vygotsky, A. R. Luria, and E. H. Lenneberg (p. 12). They are all "transactionalists" who view "the learner/writer, therefore, as an active construer of meaning in her transactions with experience" (p. 15). "Concerned with the centrality of processes...most would agree that the knower, the person herself, is a process" (p. 16). Emig saw these thinkers as humanists who were driven by the need to find final answers for their questions to the sciences. They are "multidisciplinarians." Emig ended her discussion by announcing the creed to guide participants in the tacit tradition: "almost all persons can write and want to write; not writing or not wanting to write is unnatural; if neither occurs, something major has been subverted in a mind, in a life; as teachers and researchers we must try to make writing natural again, and necessary" (p. 17).

In the end, however, we are left with beliefs—something short of a program. Although the old methodologies are inadequate, new ones have yet to take their place. Ironically, the current-traditional paradigm employed a method without a theory, and the tacit tradition has a multitude of theories without a research method.

Interest continues in the relation between theory and methodology. Lee Gregg and Erwin Steinberg edited *Cognitive Processes in Writing* (1980), which announces a unified view of writing based largely on the work of Linda Flower and John Hayes, collaborators from composition and psychology. The text is complete in a paradigmatic sense; it announces a theory and model of the composing process based on cognitive psychology and uses protocol analysis, a naturalistic research method developed to study problem-solving processes. In "Identifying the Organization of Writing Process" (1981), Flower and Hayes engaged the problem of methodology from the beginning by describing protocol analysis as a scientific method. A *protocol* is "a description of the activities ordered in time which a subject engages in while performing a task" (p. 4). They used a verbal protocol in which a writer speaks into a tape recorder while composing. The recording is the subject thinking aloud while composing. They made no claim for the protocol's completeness; at best the protocol is a trace of mental activity. "Analyzing a protocol is like following the tracks of a porpoise, which occasionally reveals itself by breaking the surface of the sea. Its brief surfacings are like the glimpses that the protocol affords us of the underlying mental processes" (p. 9). The experimenters' task is interpreting this incomplete record in the light of their understanding of the task being considered and of human capabilities to *infer* from these a model of the underlying processes. To introduce the theory so that novice researchers can understand the method and its application, Flower and Hayes presented and analyzed a model protocol.

The contributions of Flower and Hayes in *Cognitive Processes in Writing* (1980) represent theory-making while the balance of the text is devoted to elaboration of the theory's implications and experiments based on the theory. This text is the culmination of research that had been appearing in professional journals since Flower and Hayes's "Problem-Solving Strategies and the Writing Process" (1977). Their "Cognitive Process Theory of Writing" (1981) presents the various principles of their theory and its relation to existing composition research. Focusing there on theory-making, they paid little attention to the methodology. Two new books, *Writing* by C. Frederiksen and others (in press) and *Research on Writing*, edited by Peter Mosenthal and others (1983) will further elaborate the cognitive process model and the protocol methodology.

Although not a book per se, an entire issue of *RTE* devotes itself to a description and analysis of a particularly promising research method. Ethnographic research methods oppose the empirical tradition repudiated in Cooper and Odell's *Research on Composing* (1978) and offer a flexibility valuable in the theory-building stage of a discipline. Kenneth Kantor, Dan Kirby, and Judith Goetz in "Research in Context" (1981) illustrated the principles and benefits of this naturalistic research method. After announcing the roots of the method in educational sociology and anthropology, they cited numerous examples of English educators applying these methods successfully to language studies.

Ethnographic research contradicts the principles and methods of experimental research. Experimental inquiry, the tradition earlier advertised by Braddock (1963), "emphasizes hypothesis testing, control of variables, 'stripping' of contexts, educational outcomes, generalizability, reductionism, and researcher detachment from objects of study; while naturalistic inquiry is concerned with hypothesis generating, grounded theory, educational process, unique and multidimensional features of contexts, and the involvement of researcher with subject required by participant observation'' (Kantor, Kirby, and Goetz [1981], p. 294). Such concerns are surely more in line with the humanistic tradition of English studies than is the experimental tradition. Moreover, the findings of ethnographic studies are ''descriptive, qualitative, naturalistic and holistic.'' What ethnographic methods offer is an alternative to the previously unsatisfactory experimental empiricism, by allowing researchers opportunities to ''choose methods appropriate to the purposes of their studies, rather than arbitrarily restricting themselves to methods that seem to be required by a particular paradigm'' (p. 295).

Ethnographic inquiry offers five particular benefits to the researcher in writing. First, its purpose is hypothesis generating rather than hypothesis testing, allowing researchers to enter inquiry with the purpose of discovering rather than confirming. Given that composition research is in large part an examination of process, the ethnographic methods allow researchers to address a variety of questions and propose various answers and alternate explanations for phenomena. Tentative conclusions drawn from such studies are subject to rigorous debate and ''intensive reexamination and reevaluation'' (p. 295). Such a posture helps in the building and elaboration of a theory, which must take place at the current stage of composition research. Second, ethnographic methods emphasize the importance of context. Given that writing involves at its base the relation between the writer and an audience, the importance of context-bound research is evident. ''Language derives meaning from social context—the discourse topic, setting and audience—and cultural values of language users'' (p. 296). Ethnographic methods permit ''explication of a dynamic interplay among elements in the physical, natural, and socio-cultural environments'' (p. 296).

Third, the data amassed by the ethnographic researcher who is a witness to activity within an environment allows for ''thick description.'' The raw data include field notes, recorded or transcribed interviews, and explicit descriptions of process ultimately reduced to a verbal picture of the scene to allow the recreation of the scene by other researchers. Some of the language may be metaphoric and thereby encourage the formulation of new meanings. Such ''thick description'' leads to increased perception and a wealth of opportunities for interpretation.

Fourth, ethnographic inquiry depends on the active participation of the researcher. As the source of the eventual hypothesis or conclusion, the researcher must become involved since that involvement ends with interpretation, the purpose of the research. Controls like collaboration and comparative investigation requiring ''verifications and challenges to insights and recognition of other evidence'' offset any bias introduced through researcher participation (p. 298). Finally, ethnographic inquiry has ''meaning-making'' as one of its primary purposes. Thus the method is particularly relevant to composition research, since it is "concerned with ways in which individuals connect personal knowledge to their social awareness through language" (p. 298).

As they reviewed the literature, Kantor, Kirby, and Goetz pointed out the potential that ethnographic inquiry has for answering questions as yet unanswered by composition research. Acting in concert with experimental inquiry, ethnographic studies can document developmental processes and examine the relationship of teacher intentions to practices in the classroom. An extensive bibliography addresses both theoretical and practical concerns.

Within the *RTE* issue itself is a model application of ethnographic inquiry to the teaching of writing. Joan Pettigrew, Robert Shaw, and A. D. Van Nostrand in "Collaborative Analysis of Writing Instruction" described a method through which eight teachers and eight researchers compared the described behavior and actual behavior of teachers during writing instruction. The comparison indicated an alarming dissonance between assumptions about teaching writing and institutional support for writing teaching. In short, they found that managing interactions between students and between the teacher and students in a normal classroom environment created demands that precluded the application of what research has shown us about the learning of writing. Through such ethnographic investigation teachers can be made aware of the contradictions between their instructional theory and instructional practice and the environmental influences—especially lack of support—that cause the contradictions. Once such contradictions are evident, adjustments to solve the problems become possible. The legitimization of ethnographic inquiry offers composition researchers a new methodology with great potential. But it does not solve our indentity problem.

In fact, controversy over paradigms and discipline identity continues in the professional literature. *CCC* devoted a cluster of essays to the problem of paradigm in February 1982. In "The Winds of Change" (1982), Maxine Hairston reviewed Young's definition of the *current-traditional paradigm* and discussed the difference in emphasis in the new "emerging paradigm." Citing the existence of specialists who have completed research requiring attention, including that of Flower and Hayes, she briefly summarized the trends in new research and listed 12 precepts of the new paradigm, ending with an exhortation "to refine the new paradigm for teaching composition so that it provides a rewarding, productive, and feasible way of teaching writing for the non-specialists who do most of the composition teaching in our universities and colleges" (p. 88).

But Hairston hit hardest when she argued that the discipline as a whole lags far behind in its consideration of the relation between paradigm and methodology. She discussed who it is that retards progress including administrators and teachers who are not conversant with the new research and who resist change and textbook companies with a vested interest in maintaining the paradigm that their writing texts espouse.

In the same cluster, Janet Emig's "Inquiry Paradigms and Writing" (1982) illustrates some of the dangers rife in a paradigm shift. Defining a *paradigm* as an "explanatory matrix for any systematic investigation of phenomena" (p. 64), she summarized the commentary of Egon Guba (1978), Patricia Carini (1975), and Elliot Mishler (1979), as well as Thomas Kuhn. An inquiry paradigm has five characteristics: "(1) a governing gaze; (2) an acknowledged, or at least conscious, set of assumptions; (3) a coherent theory or theories; (4) an allegiance to an explicit or at least tacit intellectual tradition; and (5) an adequate methodology including an indigenous logic consonant with all of the above" (p. 65).

Reviewing composition studies, Emig found three existing governing gazes. The "positivists" emphasize empirical, experimental studies much in the manner of the program established by Braddock (1963). The positivists are the descendents of the vitalists noted by Young (1978) as practitioners in the current traditional paradigm. Emig's second group, the "phenomenologists," emphasizes the context and relativity of research and employs the methodology of ethnographic inquiry discussed by Kantor, Kirby, and Goetz (1981). A third group, the "transactional-constructivists" represent a middle road between the oppositions described by the positivists and phenomenologists. These synthesizers are the participants in the tacit tradition earlier described in Miller's *Reinventing the Rhetorical Tradition* (1980).

Emig's point is that contemporary composition research includes several paradigms, or pseudo-paradigms, which allow researchers a variety of purposes and methods. But she complained that the discipline is generally unaware of this variety and ignorant of the importance of a paradigm to ongoing research. Moreover, in political terms the positivists dominate, retarding the progress of research by either of the other two governing gazes. The evaluators who control the purse strings "do not know that more than the positivist paradigm exists" and therefore "cannot acknowledge the legitimacy of the other world views" (p. 73).

Emig's purpose was to make the discipline aware of the variety of legitimate research methods available to composition researchers. Although she feared the domination of the positivists, her argument illustrates the health and vitality of contemporary composition research. That three world views, each with a supporting methodology, exist suggests a fullness within the discipline. The three world views are not mutually exclusive. In fact, as the ethnographers insist, they are complementary. Each has a role in the process of observing and gathering data, forming hypothesis, testing and validating or adapting them, and designing applications for practitioners. In its struggle toward a secure disciplinary identity, composition research has defined, developed, questioned, and redefined itself to be large enough to contain multitudes and admit contradictions, since that is the nature of the task of understanding and teaching the process of writing. Richard Lloyd-Jones, a colleague of Braddock with whom so much activity began, reminded us in "What We May Become" (1982): "we must picture ourselves as humanistic scholars building on discoveries of the long past refined by traditional methods, elaborated by new techniques, but still concerned with the largest questions of the nature of humanity" (p. 203).

Given the disciplinary identity evolved through decades of controversy, Lloyd-

Jones offered the composition researcher no less a challenge than we have been prepared to meet.

References

Bartholomae, David. "The Study of Error." *CCC*, 31 (1980), 253–69.

Braddock, Richard, et al. *Research in Written Composition*. Champaign, Ill.: NCTE, 1963.

Britton, James, et al. *The Development of Writing Abilities (11–18)*. London: Macmillan, 1975.

Buros, Oscar. *The Eighth Mental Measurements Yearbook*. Highland Park, N.J.: Gryphon, 1978.

Campbell, Donald, and Julian Stanley. "Experimental and Quasi-Experimental Designs for Research in Teaching." In *Handbook of Educational Research*. Ed N. L. Gage. Chicago: Rand McNally, 1963, pp. 171–246. Also Chicago: Rand McNally, 1966.

Carini, Patricia. *Observation and Description: An Alternative Methodology for the Investigation of Human Phenomena*. North Dakota Study Group on Evaluation Monographs, Grand Forks: University of North Dakota Press, 1975.

Cooper, Charles, and Lee Odell, eds. *Evaluating Writing: Describing, Measuring, Judging*. Urbana, Ill.: NCTE, 1977.

———, eds. *Research on Composing: Points of Departure*. Urbana, Ill.: NCTE, 1978.

Cooper, Lane, trans. *The Rhetoric of Aristotle*. Englewood-Cliffs, N.J.: Prentice-Hall, 1932.

Corbett, Edward P. J. *Classical Rhetoric for the Modern Student*. 2nd ed. New York: Oxford University Press, 1971.

D'Angelo, Frank. *A Conceptual Theory of Rhetoric*. Cambridge, Mass.: Winthrop, 1975.

Diederich, Paul B. *Measuring Growth in English*, Urbana, Ill.: NCTE, 1974.

Dieterich, David, and Richard Behm. "Annotated Bibliography of Research in the Teaching of English: January through June 1981." *RTE*, 15 (1981), 355–88.

Emig, Janet. *The Composing Process of Twelfth Graders*. Urbana, Ill.: NCTE, 1971.

———. "The Tacit Tradition: The Inevitability of a Multi-Disciplinary Approach to Writing Research." In *Reinventing the Rhetorical Tradition*. Ed. Aviva Freedman and Ian Pringle. Conway, Ark.: L and S, 1980, pp. 9–18.

———. "Inquiry Paradigms and Writing." *CCC*, 33 (1982), 64–75.

Enos, R. L., et al. "Heuristic Procedures and the Composing Process: A Selected Bibliography." *RSQ*, Special Issue No. 1 (1982).

Fagan, William T., et al. *Measures for Research and Evaluation in the English Language Arts*. Urbana, Ill.: NCTE, 1975.

Faigley, Lester. Review of *Linguistics, Stylistics, and the Teaching of Composition*, ed. Donald McQuade. *CCC*, 33 (1982), 96–98.

Flower, Linda, and John Hayes. "Problem-Solving Strategies and the Writing Process." *CE*, 39 (1977), 449–61.

———. "A Cognitive Process Theory of Writing." *CCC*, 32 (1981), 365–87.

Frederiksen, C., et al., eds. *Writing: The Nature, Development, and Teaching of Written Communication*. Hillsdale, N.J.: Erlbaum, in press.

Freedman, Aviva, and Ian Pringle, eds. *Reinventing the Rhetorical Tradition*. Conway, Ark.: L and S, 1980.

Gage, N. L., ed. *Handbook of Research on Teaching*. Chicago: Rand McNally, 1963a.
———. "Paradigms for Research on Teaching." In *Handbook of Research on Teaching*. Ed. N. L. Gage. Chicago: Rand McNally, 1963b, pp. 94–141.

Godshalk, Fred, et al. *The Measurement of Writing Ability*. New York: College Entrance Examination Board, 1966.

Graves, Richard. *Rhetoric and Composition: A Sourcebook for Teachers*. Rochelle Park, N.J.: Hayden, 1976.

Gregg, Lee, and Erwin Steinberg, eds. *Cognitive Processes in Writing*. Hillsdale, N.J.: Erlbaum, 1980.

Guba, Egon. *Toward a Methodology of Naturalistic Inquiry in Education Evaluation*. UCLA Graduate School of Education Monograph Series, No. 8. Los Angeles: University of California, 1978.

Hairston, Maxine. "The Winds of Change: Thomas Kuhn and the Revolution in the Teaching of Writing." *CCC*, 33 (1982), 76–88.

Hayes, John, and Linda Flower. "Identifying the Organization of Writing Processes." In *Cognitive Processes in Writing*. Ed. Lee Grigg and Irwin Steinberg. Hillsdale, N.J.: Erlbaum, 1980, pp. 3–30.

Hoover, Regina. "An Annotated Bibliography on Testing." *CCC*, 30 (1979), 384–92.

Jakobson, Roman. "Linguistics and Poetics." In *Style in Language*. Ed. Thomas Sebeok. Cambridge, Mass.: The M.I.T. Press, 1960, pp. 350–77.

Kantor, Kenneth, Dan Kirby, and Judith Goetz. "Research in Context: Ethnographic Studies in English Education." *RTE*, 15 (1981), 293–309.

Kinneavy, James. *A Theory of Discourse*. Englewood Cliffs, N.J.: Prentice-Hall, 1971.
———. "A Pluralistic Synthesis of Four Contemporary Models for Teaching Composition." In *Reinventing the Rhetorical Tradition*. Ed. Aviva Freedman and Jan Pringle. Conway, Ark.: L and S, 1980.

Kohlberg, L. "From Is to Ought: How to Commit the Naturalistic Fallacy and Get Away with It in the Study of Moral Development." In *Cognitive Development and Epistemology*. Ed. T. Mishel. New York: Academic, 1971, pp. 151–235.

Kuhn, Thomas. *Structure of Scientific Revolutions*. Chicago: University of Chicago Press, 1963.

Larson, Richard. "Language Studies and Composing Processes." In *Linguistics, Stylistics, and the Teaching of Composition*. Ed. Donald McQuade. Akron, Ohio: L & S, 1979a, pp. 182–90.
———. "Selected Bibliography of Research and Writing About the Teaching of Composition, 1978." *CCC* 30 (1979b), 196–213.

Lloyd-Jones, Richard. "What We May Become." *CCC*, 33 (1982), 202–7.

McDaniels, Barbara. *An Index to Teaching Composition*. Ed. Gary Tate. Blaine, Wash.: Verlaine Books, 1982.

McQuade, Donald, ed. *Linguistics, Stylistics, and the Teaching of Composition*. Akron, Ohio: L & S, 1979.

Meckel, Henry C. "Research on Teaching Composition and Literature." In *Handbook of Educational Research*. Ed. N. L. Gage. Chicago: Rand McNally, 1963, pp. 966–1006.

Miller, Susan. "Rhetorical Maturity: Definition and Development." In *Reinventing the Rhetorical Tradition*. Ed. Aviva Freedman and Ian Pringle. Conway, Ark.: L & S, 1980, pp. 119–28.

Mishler, Elliot. "Meaning in Context: Is There Any Other Kind?" *Harvard Educ Rev*, 49 (1979), 1–19.

Moffett, James. *Teaching the Universe of Discourse*. Boston: Houghton Mifflin, 1968.

Mosenthal, Peter, et al., eds. *Research on Writing: Principles and Methods*. New York: Longman, 1983.

Myers, Miles. *A Procedure for Writing Assessment and Holistic Scoring*. Urbana, Ill.: ERIC/NCTE, 1980.

Pettigrew, Joan, Robert Shaw, and A. D. Van Nostrand. "Collaborative Analysis of Writing Instruction." *RTE*, 15 (1981), 329–41.

Shaughnessy, Mina. *Errors and Expectations*. New York: Oxford University Press, 1977.

Sherwin, J. Stephen. *Four Problems in Teaching English: A Critique of Research*. Scranton, Pa.: International Textbook, 1969.

Tate, Gary, ed. *Teaching Composition: Ten Bibliographical Essays*. Fort Worth, Tex.: Texas Christian University Press, 1976.

Thorpe, James, ed. *The Aims and Methods of Scholarship in Modern Language and Literatures*. New York: Modern Language Association, 1963.

Winterowd, W. Ross. *Contemporary Rhetoric: A Conceptual Background with Readings*. New York: Harcourt, 1975.

————. "Brain, Rhetoric, and Style." In *Linguistics, Stylistics, and the Teaching of Composition*. Ed. Donald McQuade. Akron, Ohio: L & S, 1979, pp. 151–81.

Woods, William, ed. *A Directory of Publishing Opportunities for Teachers of Writing*. Charlottesville, Va.: Community Collaborators, 1979.

Young, Richard. "Paradigms and Problems: Needed Research in Rhetorical Invention." In *Research on Composing: Points of Departure*. Ed. Charles Cooper and Lee Odell. Urbana, Ill.: NCTE, 1978, pp. 29–47.

Grading and Evaluation

ROBERT W. REISING AND BENJAMIN J. STEWART

In recent decades, writing has become increasingly important in the nation's schools, colleges, and universities. Accompanying the emphasis on writing has been a growing interest in grading and evaluation. Researchers have joined teachers in creating, validating, clarifying, and expanding procedures that are applicable to individual writers, small groups, large groups, or all three. Consequently, the profession now has access to more tools and techniques for assessing composition than ever before.

Yet breakthroughs have not eliminated controversy. No facet or subdiscipline of composition continues to invite more heated debate than grading and evaluation. Who should be graded or evaluated? When? Under what circumstances? By what means? For what purposes? Such questions have proven as unsettling within the profession as "Why Johnny Can't Write" articles have proven popular outside of it. Clearly, expertise and enlightenment have not outdistanced emotionalism, subjective preference, and administrative convenience. Grading and evaluation, as a result, stand as important and exciting concerns—but, simultaneously, as challenging ones.

At the outset of any discussion of those concerns, it is crucial to note that the title of this chapter contains no redundancy. *Grading* and *evaluation* are related but not synonymous terms. The latter is the broader of the two. Often evaluation takes the form of assertions designed to encourage or reward learning, some of them global ("Your writing is improving"), some of them specific ("Your semicolons are effective"). Always, however, evaluation alerts writers to strengths and weaknesses in their work.

The authors of this chapter are indebted to the Pembroke State University Research Council for a grant to support their research; to Pembroke State undergraduates Karen Deese, Toni Goodyear, Sue Loving, and Jacqueline McDonald for assistance with that research; and to Glenn Ellen Jones and Rue Stewart for manuscript typing.

In contrast, grading is ranking. It results from a judgment of how well a given piece of written discourse conforms to pre-determined, but not necessarily publicly delineated, achievement or proficiency standards. Those standards identify levels of success to which a reader, or group of readers, subscribes. Usually more than two, those levels invariably appear as numerical or other public marks (for example, *A, C, F*). When employed judiciously, or when subsumed under helpful and supportive evaluation, grading provides enlightened insight into students' growth in writing.

Both grading and evaluation, therefore, function as important pedagogical tools, not merely as popular assessment instruments. Grading delineates strata or rungs of accomplishments—information invaluable to any teacher of writing. Similarly, diagnostic evaluation represents an opportunity to illuminate the strengths and weaknesses of an individual student, a class of students, or a program of instruction and hence can initiate or guide curriculum reform. Progress evaluation supplies critical information for an ongoing writing program, in addition to providing feedback on the skill development of individual students. Follow-up or final assessment reveals both the extent to which a program has reached its objective and the ability of each student in that program.

The Evaluation of Composition Instruction (1981) by Barbara Gross Davis, Michael Scriven, and Susan Thomas clarifies the distinction between "grading" and "evaluation." The latter represents the principal focus of that volume, but "grading"is cogently treated in two valuable subsections: "Student Grades in Composition Courses" and "Glossary."

The surge of interest in the two concepts has brought with it a short but issue- and material-filled history, five procedures for grading and evaluation, and at least six promising directions warranting investigation in the years ahead.

The History, Issues and Purposes of Grading and Evaluation

The history of composition teaching is centuries old, as Thomas Rodd, Jr., outlined in "Before the Flood" (1983); but research into and measurement of writing are comparatively new. Only in the last half of the twentieth century has an "explosion" occurred in the "research activity in the field" of English in general, Dwight Burton noted in 1973 in *Research in the Teaching of English*, and it has been in even more recent years that writing research and measurement have surfaced as legitimate and pressing responsibilities of the profession. *Measures for Research and Evaluation in the English Language Arts* (1975) by William T. Fagan, Charles R. Cooper, and Julie M. Jensen provides a brief but useful history of research and measurement in English, as well as analyses of 14 measures of writing developed between 1960 and 1973. *Research in Written Composition* by Richard Braddock, Richard Lloyd-Jones, and Lowell Schoer (1963) and *The Measurement of Writing Ability* by Fred I. Godshalk, Francis Swineford, and William E. Coffman (1966) also assist in charting the history of writing research and measurement.

More recent treatments of that history include two essays with unusually complete bibliographies: Carl Bereiter's "Development in Writing," appearing in *Testing, Teaching and Learning* (1979), and Stanley B. Straw's "Assessment and Evaluation in Written Composition" (1981). The May and October 1982 issues of *College Composition and Communication*, both devoted to the subject "Responding to and Evaluating Writing," update developments in writing research and measurement. Especially enlightening in the earlier issue are "Evaluating Instruction in Writing," representing "materials from the Committee on Teaching and Its Evaluation in Composition, several years in preparation...offered for testing by teachers and administrators," and Richard Lloyd-Jones's "What We May Become," delineating directions for the future (p. 139). Of comparable worth in the October number is C. W. Griffin's "Theory of Responding to Student Writing," an evaluation of methods of responding to student writing studied or employed since 1972. *Notes* from the National Testing Network in Writing, the first issue of which appeared in October 1982, supplies current information on writing assessment, as do the broader-focused publications like *CAPTRENDS*, appearing regularly from the Center for Performance Assessment, a unit of the Portland-based Northwest Regional Educational Laboratory.

Any treatment of writing research and measurement invariably overlaps discussions of, and perhaps even presupposes commitments to, particular goals of writing assessment. In *Introduction to Common Sense and Testing in English* (1975), John C. Maxwell proclaimed that key among those goals is teacher enlightenment: "Teachers of English and the language arts have always wanted to know the results of their teachings, to see if their efforts have done someone good" (p. iv). In the Introduction to *Evaluating Writing* (1977), Charles R. Cooper and Lee Odell divided "writing evaluations" more broadly. Three "uses" are paramount, they argued: administrative, instructional, and evaluation and research. Like many other theorists and teachers, they conceded that predicting student grades, placing students, and assigning grades are administratively necessary. Instructional needs include diagnosis of writing proficiency and student feedback and guidance. Evaluation and research involve "measuring growth, determining writing performances, and identifying variables affecting writing performances" (p. lx). Approaches for reaching the four objectives obviously vary, and writing can be measured by either direct or indirect methods. Direct methods use student writing samples, and indirect ones rely on objective tests. Both methods can be employed to assess general writing proficiency as well as specific performance features. In addition, each method is useful for obtaining administrative data providing grades.

Direct-assessment methods, those that employ actual writing samples, evaluate not only conventions of composition but also less quantifiable skills. In a direct measurement, writers can be asked to present an expository essay, complete with formal thesis statement, several well-developed supportive paragraphs with topic sentences, and an effective concluding paragraph; or they can be asked to address writing tasks requiring more specific decisions about purpose and audience. Cooper and Odell recommended evaluating "several different kinds of writing performances" (*Nature and Measurement of Competency in English* [1981], p. 115). Students should be able, they suggested, to determine if their purpose is to persuade, inform, or express, and they should know their audience. Direct-assessment methods are accurate, because the writing experiences are authentic.

Yet the disadvantages of direct assessment are sizable. The cost in time and money for evaluating the results can be astronomical—far greater than the costs of initial development and testing of prompts. Such disadvantages are administrative, but another is not. Since writers responding to a prompt must make decisions about their composition, they may decide to avoid writing features and/or forms desired for evaluation. A person writing to a direct-assessment prompt may, for example, refuse to employ complex sentences and thus may limit the range of skills expected for measurement. The evaluator has little control over the writer's response.

Advantages and disadvantages are no less conspicuous, however, in the alternate approach. Although inexpensive, indirect assessment suffers from measurement by proxy. Examinees produce no prose. Commonly, they are asked to select or identify "correct" constructions or features that in their own writing they are incapable of producing or controlling. Although their responses may be the desired ones, they demonstrate their abilities not through creation but through recognition—a vastly different process that may produce vastly different results. Similarly, indirect assessment spawns few and feeble opportunities to test the writer's abilities with the larger elements of discourse—organization and development, for instance. It also offers even fewer opportunities for assessments of those characteristics of writing that dominate all exciting, engaging prose— honesty, vigor, and authority. As Cooper indicated in "Measuring Growth in Writing" (1975), "we might as well give up wishing for an early-scored multiple-choice growth measure of writing ability" (p. 117). That conviction governs subsequent pages of this chapter, most of which treat direct assessment.

Yet it would be unfair to suggest that all professionals concur with Cooper. An exchange in *The Chronicle of Higher Education* illustrates the controversy that surrounds this subject. Arnold Agee maligned indirect assessment in the September 2, 1981, issue of that publication ("The Real Victim of the Testers' Creeping Hegemony"). A few weeks later, Robert W. Lissitz countered by alleging that "The use of written samples is largely to calm the public" ("In Defense of Standardized Tests" [1981], pp. 27–28), a contention that Edward M. White and Ruth Mitchell, in separate responses, vigorously denied ("Correcting Old Errors with New Ones" [1981]). Perhaps the most striking point to emerge from the debate appears in the final response. Mitchell commented, "Of course, scores from multiple-choice usage tests and writing samples can correlate positively—but only if the writing samples are read for the same features. If writing samples are read for content, as we normally read, then the curves do not coincide" (p. 27).

But no disagreement appears in any discussion of two terms crucial to eval-uation: *reliability* and *validity*. The former reflects measurement stability over time and across raters. Reliability is weakened or lost in direct assessment with the appearance of inappropriate or inadequate prompts, inferior monitoring of readers, and inconsistent scoring procedures. Validity, in contrast, identifies three related concerns. *Content validity* refers to the ability of an evaluating procedure to measure the mastery of the properties of good writing that examinees have been asked to learn. *Criterion validity* denotes the ability of an assessment instrument to be directly translated into specific and clearly cited characteristics of writing proficiency at every level of any grading scale. *Construct validity* results when "explanatory concepts account for the evaluation of a perfor-mance. . . . Construct validity can be established, therefore, only when the prin-cipal factor of a construct can be identified and defined" (Collett Dilworth and Robert Reising, "Validity in Composition Evaluation" [1979], p. 44). Clearly, it is naïve to believe that evaluation is effective without adequate provision for reliability and validity; unless both are present, assessment results are certain to be skewed and useless.

Clearly, too, writing is a subjective discipline, unlike mathematics, chemistry, and those areas of study that require strict adherence to prescribed methods and procedures. It possesses none of the rigidity and precision of an equation or a formula. Its components include style, form, and substance. It follows certain syntactic, linguistic and usage/mechanics conventions. It has definition, but it cannot be defined. In fact, there is little agreement in the profession about what constitutes effective discursive writing. Likewise, there is little agreement about what constitutes appropriate evaluation and grading of such writing. Theorists, testing services, and teachers have long attempted to formulate substantive state-ments of evaluative criteria. Although all of the resulting proclamations share many common elements, no unchallenged definitive statement has emerged— this while evaluation and grading have continued to gain ever-greater attention from educators and lay people alike. Although discrimination of writing-profi-ciency levels determines instructional goals, research strategies, and student placement and admissions criteria, "the theoretical basis of evaluation remains unarticulated," Anne Ruggles Gere noted ("Written Composition" [1980], p. 44).

A distinction also remains to be made between the two general kinds of evaluation—summative evaluation and formative evaluation. *Summative eval-uation* provides data for "*an external client or audience*, and its main purpose is not to improve an ongoing enterprise but to report on the *quality of a project for purposes other than improvement*" (Barbara Davis, Michael Scriven, and Susan Thomas, *The Evaluation of Composition Instruction* [1981], p. 7). In composition instruction, such reports prove useful for certain administrative purposes connected with developing a writing program. Determinations of meth-ods of program instruction and evaluation, adoption of materials, and selection of personnel, both teacher and student, are key among those concerns. The decisions to implement an advanced or a remedial program and the criteria for placing students are often crucial to the success of such programs. Other purposes for summative evaluation include selecting students to receive citations for achievement or to benefit from remedial assistance (Davis, Scriven, and Thomas [1981]). Although program improvement is not the primary aim of summative evaluation, it may eventually result as a by-product and advantage of such evaluation.

Sources and Procedures of Grading and Evaluation

Among the several important sources that treat assessment procedures is Vickie Spandel and Richard J. Stiggins's *Direct Measures of Writing Skill* (1980). Dealing specifically with direct assessment, the Spandel and Stiggins monograph provides information pioneered principally by Educational Testing Service (ETS) and the National Assessment of Educational Progress (NAEP). Strategies for planning and conducting writing assessment are described, and resources for additional and more precise information on how to assess skills are provided, along with information on the general status of writing assessment methods.

Chapter 1, "A Status Report on Writing Assessment," reviews results of the National Assessment of Educational Progress studies of 1969 and 1974, as well as those of other national surveys. The authors concluded that there is no definitive way to assess writing skills and asserted that educators should be careful to select a measurement that meets the unique problem of "each individual educational assessment and writing circumstance" (p. 5).

Spandel and Stiggins presented an excellent discussion of the developmental state of procedures for measuring writing proficiency and the accompanying measurement issues of such an assessment. Additionally, their monograph provides both a detailed comparison of scoring methods for direct writing assessments and procedures for adapting evaluation to specific purposes (for example, diagnosis, placement, and program evaluation). It also has a functional bibliography.

Another comprehensive summary of current information on measuring growth in writing is Charles R. Cooper and Lee Odell's *Evaluating Writing* (1977). The publication provides a collection of papers prepared for a conference on writing and evaluation held before the 1975 Annual Convention of the National Council of Teachers of English. The contributors, recognizing that standardized tests of writing measure only editorial skills, called for direct methods that assess students' ability to write for different purposes and audiences. The measures described in the publication serve administrative, instructional, evaluation, and research purposes, as well as other, more limited, specialized ones.

Cooper's essay in their book reviews various types of holistic scoring and discusses, at length, analytic scales. The proposed refinements in analytic scoring that he presented can be used for prediction, placement, exemption, or growth measurement. He suggested methods of maintaining rater reliability and pointed out the time-saving factors of grading holistically.

Other essays in the Cooper and Odell book analyze more specialized methods for assessing composition. Odell's piece, "Measuring Changes in Intellectual Processes as One Dimension of Growth in Writing," identifies processes by which students formulate the idea or attitudes expressed in their writing. Patrick J. Finn discussed how the computer can give precise characterizations of the maturity of word choice and, thus, how that characterization can be facilitated when writing assessment addresses judgments about diction. Richard Lloyd-Jones contrasted atomistic and holistic scoring methods and defined Primary Trait Scoring as a tool for rhetorically evaluating discourse. Kellogg W. Hunt's essay provides an analysis of his research with T-unit measurement, which assesses the syntactic maturity of writing. Mary H. Beaven supplied a rationale for student participation in the process of evaluation.

Cooper and Odell's *Evaluating Writing* identifies uses of writing assessment and supports the proposition that evaluators should know "*why* they are evaluating before they choose measures and procedures" (p. ix). The authors' methods demonstrate validity and reliability in both limited and particular uses, as well as in more general and traditional ways.

Paul B. Diederich's monograph *Measuring Growth in English* (1974), another innovative source, presents ways to improve the reliability and validity of writing assessment and to reduce the time spent in grading. Diederich outlined a system for evaluation that reduces a majority of the grading that traditionally goes on day after day in almost every classroom. He reasoned that by using fewer and better measures teachers can devote more time and energy to teaching and learning.

Diederich's research reveals the following factors of quality writing: ideas, mechanics, organization, wording, and flavor. The measurement methods he illustrated present opportunities for assessing these five factors, determined by an ETS factor analysis of judgments of writing ability conducted by Diederich, John French, and Sydell Carlton. Appendix A of his monograph demonstrates an application of the five factors to papers rated high, middle, and low in quality.

Following a procedure for avoiding bias in grading papers, Diederich discussed a method for measuring improvement in writing and contrasted personal and staff grading. Factors such as computing the reliability of essay and objective tests, designing an examination in English/Language Arts, and initiating staff grading of test essays receive his scrutiny. The appendices are enlightening features of *Measuring Growth in English*. The author provided topics for test essays, as well as objective items based on a central theme. A broad view of what students need to learn about writing concludes this important measurement resource.

Another early and important book on composition assessment is *A Guide for Evaluating Student Composition* (1965), edited by Sister M. Judine, IMH. This collection of essays by "semanticists, structural linguists, philosophers and 'pure critics' '' discusses the relationship of writer to audience, problems and solutions in evaluations, and the total writing process (p. v). Although each section of the book is engaging and competent, attention here is limited to those that discuss grading and evaluation.

Several of the essays not only address procedures for composition assessment but also provide detailed evaluation guides and graded student writing samples. They reveal Irwin Berger's principles for examining writing for logic and clarity, Isidore Levine's breakdown of postulates of writing and correction, and Edwin L. Peterson's analysis of addressing assignment intentions. Perhaps more innovative are the essays by S. I. Hayakawa and Alfred H. Gromman, which cite the need for students to develop an ability to write for specific audiences outside the classroom and the need for teachers to improve students' critical thinking by relating writing to literature courses and by emphasizing discourse that grows from logical thinking.

Lou L. LaBrant, Paul Diederich, Sarah I. Roody, and William J. Dusal addressed the concerns of the evaluator—"which standards does he meet, and how, with large paper loads?" LaBrant applied standards for meeting college writing requirements as she discusses instructors' comments on student papers. Diederich suggested that by focusing on one error at a time, rather than drowning errors in a sea of red ink, teachers will help improve student writing. Dusal supported this belief with observations based on research in California schools indicating that students are not enlightened but are confused by over-marked papers. Roody's paper-management suggestions advocate student involvement, under teacher guidance and direction, in the evaluation process.

Lois Arnold's illuminating piece "Writer's Cramp and Eyestrain—Are They Paying Off?" is an apt conclusion to any discussion of the Judine *Guide*. Originally carried in the January 1964 *English Journal*, it precedes research that later has supported her contention that intensive grading does not improve writing proficiency. Her concerns are really the concerns of all teachers and evaluators of student writing—"a thorough understanding of what written composition actually is, what prompts students to write, and what methods of evaluation are most effective" (p. 88). *A Guide for Evaluating Student Composition* successfully addresses these fundamental concerns.

Many of the strategies tested in the earlier Judine collection are elaborated in *How to Handle the Paper Load*, edited by Gene Stanford and others (1979). The emergence of the National Writing Project and the growing popularity of the process-centered writing curriculum have generated several of the classroom practices discussed in this more recent collection of articles for using writing assessment as an instructional tool and an evaluative instrument.

Stanford and his associates organized the 27 articles under six headings: "Ungraded Writing," "Teacher Involvement—Not Evaluation," "Student Self-Editing," "Practice with Parts," "Focused Feedback," and "Alternative Audiences." The volume seeks to reexamine the methodologies traditionally used for teaching writing and to examine those newer strategies derived from more current research. As former sufferers of the "Assign-Assess Syndrome," the contributors attempted to dispel the myth that intensive grading of frequently assigned compositions will improve student writing.

All of the contributors have discovered "that by questioning various components of this myth they can foster growth in composition even more successfully than through the 'assign-assess' approach and at the same time save themselves from an avalanche of papers to grade" (p. xiv). Building upon the belief that every word written need not be graded, some contributors suggested a number of non-graded activities that provide practice and experimentation. Using the revision stage of the writing process, many stressed teacher involvement as consultants. Still others teach their students to edit their own papers and those of their peers and thus provide feedback. Many teachers concentrate on a few skills and/or a few errors as an effective way to stimulate growth in student writing. The theories developed in these articles provide sound instructional strategies.

Among these strategies are suggestions for ungraded writing. Freewriting activities, fluency-writing opportunities, and writing journals are some of the ways for students to write for pleasure without fearing evaluation. Some of these strategies motivate students by offering them avenues for publication. Although assessment is not imposed on each product, the freedom to grow through written expression usually results in greater proficiency in those products that are evaluated.

The student's role in editing and proofreading is undeniably important in such an approach to evaluation. Students who can recognize flaws in their own writing and that of peers are less likely to submit papers with those errors. Such products present fewer problems for evaluators, as do products resulting from focused feedback. One of the most important evaluation concepts offered in *How to Handle the Paper Load* is teacher involvement in the writing process. Teachers who write with their students are more likely to recognize and respond to student writing problems than those who do not write. By sharing the results of the stages of the process with students, teachers are able to demonstrate the skills needed for revision and/or editing and proofreading. This evaluative concern can lead to greater writing proficiency among students and thus make more selective the features to be assessed.

How to Handle the Paper Load demonstrates effective strategies and procedures used by experienced teachers. The practical application of these methods would seem certain to strengthen writing instruction and to make this book, like the other major sources, valuable for all teachers interested in improving writing proficiency and its evaluation.

Valuable also to those teachers are the five grading and evaluation procedures outlined in this chapter: analytic scoring, holistic scoring, Primary Trait Scoring, Focused Holistic Scoring, and T-unit analysis. Viewed individually, the five provide a variety of methods for a variety of assessment situations. None of these procedures meets all needs, but each, used with one or more of the others, can become an effective tool for strengthening assessment in any writing program and for assessing student proficiency.

Users of these tools must define the goals of each particular evaluation, determine how the information derived from the assessment will be used, and ascertain the resources that will be available for the evaluation and scoring procedures. Since financial resources are often a necessary concern, it is valid to point out that the intricacy of some methods makes them less cost-efficient than others.

As the name implies, *analytic scoring* analyzes the specific composition components that characterize a successful piece of writing. As Vickie Spandel and Richard Stiggins pointed out in *Direct Measures of Writing Skill* (1980), this evaluation method is most appropriate if the rater wants to measure student proficiency in using specific conventions of writing. These writing conventions must be isolated and scored individually as the rater examines the parts of a composition to assess its merits.

The key to the success of analytic scoring is the identification and relative weighing of factors to be assessed. Criteria must be clearly defined, as Paul Diederich explained in *Measuring Growth in English* (1974). The Diederich, or ETS, Composition Scale, is typical of analytic scales for expository writing. It focuses on ideas, organization, wording, style, and mechanics; it accords greatest assessment value to ideas and organization. For additional discussion of criteria, see *Measure for Measure*, edited by Norman C. Najimy (1981).

William Fagan, Charles Cooper, and Julie Jensen discussed other analytic scales that are useful for a variety of writers and writing assignments. These scales include the Glazer Narrative Composition Scale and the Schroeder Composition Scale, for narrative writing; the Sager Writing Scale, for use with intermediate and junior high students; and the Literary Rating Scale, for fictional stories. Additional scales and a discussion of analytic or linear measurement are found in R. W. Reising's "Basics of Evaluation," in *Writing in the Wild Young Spring*, edited by Denny T. Wolfe, Jr., and others (1978).

The several advantages of analytic scoring are inherent in its design. By identifying the specific factors of writing to be assessed, this method lends itself to both content validity and rater reliability. The adaptability of analytic scoring is equally advantageous because scoring can be tailored to fit the characteristics of every type of writing (for example, narration, exposition, biography). Since it provides a trait-by-trait analysis, analytic scoring is useful for formative evaluation—to provide feedback data for the purpose of improving an ongoing program or a student's proficiency. Additionally, the concentration on isolated features of a composition should negate any possible holistic bias caused by the rater's over-reacting to some unusual or outstanding feature of a particular writing sample. Analytic scoring is effective as a general guide for reacting to composition; however, it is not without its limitations.

Legitimate concerns are raised by Spandel and Stiggins. Can an assessment procedure that rates only selected features of a piece of writing accurately reflect the proficiency of a student writer? Likewise, are enough traits selected and are they significant in that they actually contribute to good writing? In addition, there is the danger of assigning excessive point value to a factor that does not merit such significance. Similarly, raters may allow a ''halo'' effect to influence their scoring of other features of the scale.

Analytic scoring, also, is more time-consuming than some of the other methods, such as holistic scoring; therefore, it may be less cost-efficient when applied to a large number of papers. Cooper pointed out, additionally, that by narrowly focusing on selected criteria, the rater ''may not be sensitive to variations in purpose, speaker role, and conception of audience'' (*Evaluating Writing* [1977], edited by Charles Cooper and Lee Odell, p. 14). The positive aspects of analytic scoring, however, recommend it for a variety of uses, as do discussions provided in the following: Charles C. Nash, ''The Cotter Grade and Comment Sheet'' (1981); M. E. Fowles, *Manual for Scoring the Writing Sample* (1978); and Richard Lloyd-Jones, ''Grading Compositions,'' in his *Student's Right to Write* (1976).

Another direct-assessment method, *holistic scoring*, differs dramatically from analytic scoring, which evaluates a piece of writing by assessing selected composition features. Holistic scoring is based on the premise that the measure of the effectiveness of a piece of writing is *not* reducible to the tally of its various components. The rationale of holistic scoring contends that the various elements of writing contribute to the effectiveness of the total piece. Effective writing occurs, therefore, when its various components (that is, voice, mood, tone, style, rhythm, juxtaposition of ideas, awareness of audience) interact with factors such as syntax, usage, and mechanics. If such interaction is undeniable, it would be incomprehensible to devise a separate scale to measure every possible combination of these features with every mode of written discourse. Holistic scoring, therefore, presents an opportunity for the rater to assess the merits of the *complete* composition.

In holistic scoring, the rater's impression or judgment in response to the total effectiveness of the writing sample determines the rating. In his essay ''Holistic Evaluation of Writing,'' in *Evaluating Writing* (1977), edited by Cooper and Odell, Cooper explained that ''a piece of writing communicates a whole message with a particular tone to a known audience for some purpose: information, argument, amusement, ridicule, titillation. At present, holistic evaluation by a human respondent gets us closer to what is essential in such communication'' (p. 3). Since holistic scoring does not enumerate the rhetorical, linguistic, or informational features of a composition but instead evaluates the piece as a whole, it has certain advantages.

High reliability emerges as one of those advantages, as John C. Mellon reported in *National Assessment and the Teaching of English* (1975). Diederich (1974) also attested that reliability is strengthened with appropriate scorer training. Such training develops a rater who matches one piece with another in a series of graded samples (essay scales) or who is assisted by a scoring guide to determine selected features important to a particular mode of discourse (general impression scoring).

Essay scales used in holistic scoring show the range of quality for writing tasks and set the standards of adequacy for each task. Writing samples are matched with comparable ones. The California Essay Scale is a popular example of this assessment method. This essay scale was developed for expository writing by a committee of the California Association for Teachers of English and is illustrated in *A Scale for Evaluation of High School Student Essays* (1960) by Pat Nail and others. Another useful booklet that also provides samples is *Assessing Composition* (1965) by Nancy C. Martin and colleagues. For a discussion of the Smith Scale, a composition scale for elementary school writing, see "Measuring Teacher Judgment in the Evaluation of Written Composition" (1969) by Vernon H. Smith.

The essay scale has both advantages and disadvantages. One advantage is its appropriateness as an instructional tool. The model essays that serve as qualitative examples in the scale become standards for the teacher and the student. Instruction coupled with discussion of these standards can lead to an awareness of the features that increase the values of the models. Creating and using the models, however, raise questions about reliability and time efficiency. Are the models universal? Does the procedure justify the expenditure of time involved in comparing a writing sample with each essay on the scale?

More reliable and efficient than essay scales is general-impression scoring, "the simplest of the procedures in...holistic evaluation," asserted Cooper in "Holistic Evaluation of Writing" (1977), because "the rater simply scores the paper by deciding where the paper fits within the range of papers produced for that assignment or occasion" (pp. 11–12). Using this method, the rater ranks papers according to their compliance with certain rubrics, or scoring guides. Rubrics identify criteria for each level of the grading scale (for example, 1–4, 1–7, or 1–9). R. W. Reising argued for this method in "More Than a Test" (1982).

General-impression scoring was designed for rating large numbers of papers and has been refined for that purpose by ETS and the College Entrance Examination Board. Two superior publications elaborate its application: *How the Essay in the CEEB English Test Is Scored* (1976) by Gertrude Conlan and *Grading the Advanced Placement Examination in English* (1980) by Paul Smith. Additionally, the National Assessment of Educational Progress uses general-impression scoring among other methods to measure writing achievement; samples are available in *Writing Achievement, 1969–79* (1980) by the National Assessment of Educational Progress. Further explanation of the design and rationale of such scoring is presented in Catherine Keech's paper "An Examination of Procedures and Implications of Holistic Assessment of Writing," in *Moving Between Practice and Research in Writing* (1981), edited by Ann Humes and others.

John Mellon (1975) also reviewed general-impression scoring in his discussion of the National Assessment results, as did Najimy in *Measure for Measure*

(1981). A practical illustration including samples is provided in *A Procedure for Writing Assessment and Holistic Scoring* (1980) by Miles Myers. For additional discussion of how such holistic scoring works and what its scores show, Judith Horner's "How Do We Know How Well Kids Write" (1978) is informative.

It should be evident that an advantage of holistic scoring is the time-efficiency factor. Holistic scoring allows a rater to score a large number of papers in a relatively short time. It also permits an instructor to return a graded paper quickly to a student writer and, thus, to take advantage of the rapid reinforcement a grade may provide. If such reinforcement is coupled with a review of the rubrics employed, other instructional possibilities, such as conferencing and revision, can make holistic scoring an effective teaching tool. It allows the teacher and the student to explore the writing process, not merely the writing product.

The many uses of holistic scoring make it widely applicable. As illustrated by the earlier reference to the Educational Testing Service (ETS) and the College Entrance Examination Board (CEEB), it is highly desirable with a large collection of writing samples. Additionally, it can easily be adapted for use with an individual class to order-rank papers reacting to a particular prompt. In other words, holistic-evaluation principles may be applied to varied writing activities such as creating a resumé, making an application, answering an essay question, and producing a term paper. Administrative uses include rank-ordering students for placement, grouping, or exempting.

But holistic scoring is not without disadvantages. Since it does not analyze the rhetorical, linguistic, or informational features of a composition, this assessment method cannot provide data on the development of the skills that contribute to increased proficiency. It produces a rating without isolating the criteria responsible for that rating and, therefore, is limited as an instructional aid.

As Richard Lloyd-Jones argues in "Primary Trait Scoring," holistic scoring, as described above, evaluates every piece of writing as "representative of all discourse" (Cooper and Odell [1977], p. 33). But holistic principles have also been applied to a measurement that isolates a particular type of discourse and evaluates it as an example of its class. This measurement, developed by the National Assessment of Educational Progress, is *Primary Trait Scoring*; it has the capability of being more informative than any of its holistic precursors.

As proponents of process-centered writing point out, people write for many reasons. Writing is not just an academic exercise for the classroom; writers attempt to instruct, entertain, persuade, reveal, request, and perform many other tasks. Primary Trait Scoring measures a particular type of discourse against the goal of that rhetorical task (for example, does the writing sample fulfill its aim?) As Lloyd-Jones explained in "Primary Trait Scoring" (1977), "The chief steps in using the Primary Trait Scoring System are to define the universe of discourse, to devise exercises which sample that universe precisely, to ensure cooperation of the writers, to devise workable scoring guides, and to use the guides" (p. 37).

By isolating only those features of a rhetorical task that are essential to its success, Primary Trait Scoring can serve as an instructional tool. The information it reveals can help to identify performance levels for particular writing skills. Possessing high degrees of validity and reliability, Primary Trait Scoring can also measure changes in performance over time. This evaluative procedure can help students learn to write in a world of discourse not limited by academic boundaries (for example, to write for different personal and social situations). By analyzing the strengths and weaknesses that Primary Trait Scoring reveals, an instructor can place emphasis on rhetorical- and situational-specific features such as speaker role, audience, and purpose.

Research on Composing (1978), edited by Charles R. Cooper and Lee Odell, devotes two chapters to the discussion of the theory and functions of the universe of discourse that Primary Trait Scoring was designed to measure. The first, "Discourse Theory," by Odell, Cooper, and Cynthia Courts, presents assumptions in current discourse theory, as well as questions about those assumptions. The second, James Britton's "Composing Process and the Functions of Writing," deals with the concerns of speaker, subject, and audience in the "three principal categories of writing functions—transactional, expressive, and poetic" (p. 16). James Moffett in *Teaching the Universe of Discourse* (1968b) elaborated this theory of discourse and such discourse models.

Another excellent discussion of the universe of discourse and Primary Trait Scoring is Ruth Windhover's chapter "A Holistic Pedagogy for Freshman Composition," in *Revising*, (1982), edited by Ronald A. Sudol. Windhover discussed the need for new paradigms in the study and teaching of writing that fit the process- and skills-oriented discipline of writing. She cited Linda Flower and John R. Hayes (see their "Cognition of Discovery" [1980]), who posited that writers solve a writing problem with stored information that includes definitions of *situation, audience*, and *purpose*, in addition to details related to solution, tone, and diction. Windhover reviewed work done by James Kinneavy (see Kinneavy's *Theory of Discourse* [1971]), which addresses those concerns. She concluded with a discussion of Lloyd-Jones's use of Primary Trait Scoring with the National Assessment of Educational Progress, which Mellon (1975) and *Writing Achievement* (1980) by the National Assessment of Educational Progress also documented with samples.

The criteria for Primary Trait Scoring are also discussed in Allen A. Glatthorn's useful monograph *Writing in the Schools* (1981). Glatthorn recommended Primary Trait Scoring for small groups and holistic scoring for larger groups, because Primary Trait Scoring is more time-consuming and expensive. Primary Trait Scoring yields more specific information about student achievement, Glatthorn reaffirmed, because it assesses the primary, and often the secondary, traits of a writing task. By doing so, Primary Trait Scoring isolates the subcategories that are crucial to the success of a writing task.

The application of Primary Trait Scoring to writing instruction offers exciting possibilities. As a research tool, Primary Trait Scoring allows a sharper view of the complexities of particular skills required for a particular writing task and, therefore, increases the likelihood that the assessor will be able to identify strengths and weaknesses precisely. Such information increases the writer's and the teacher's awareness of the subject, audience, and discourser essential for each mode of discourse. It also isolates the primary traits that each mode must possess to be effective, and thus it provides opportunities for developing proficiency in those particular traits.

Yet the rhetorically and situationally specific qualities of Primary Trait Scoring may contribute to certain disadvantages. Primary Trait Scoring requires a sufficient expenditure in time and money to determine the traits essential to success for each mode of discourse assessed. Testing of sample papers is often required to determine weights and to define criteria. Spandel and Stiggins (1980) suggested that evaluators use "a day of trial and error, discussion and debate for each trait to be defined" (p. 110). They also pointed out, however, that "the quality and clarity of the final definitions, and the ease with which they can be applied, will readily justify the time spent" (p. 112).

A similar, but less specialized direct-assessment method has been developed for the use in the Texas Assessment of Basic Skills (TABS). This method, *Focused Holistic Scoring*, combines features of Primary Trait Scoring with the ETS holistic scoring method. The totality of a piece of writing is evaluated; however, the assessment focuses on the precisely defined purposes of a particular mode of discourse. TABS identified two specific objectives: organization of ideas and appropriate response to purpose and audience. A possible advantage of this criterion-referenced assessment procedure over classical holistic scoring is the rating of compositions in terms of pre-defined criteria, instead of ranking them against each other, as is often done with general holistic scoring. It not only retains the holistic feature of responding impressionistically to all aspects of a composition but also provides opportunities for a rater to focus on the specifics that can be easily isolated for future instruction. Lacking the sophistication of Primary Trait Scoring and analytic scoring, Focused Holistic Scoring methods are nonetheless easier both to design and to use. Understandably, the varied details of information that the two other methods provide are unavailable through this method.

Assessing student performance on the writing sample of TABS was the designed purpose of Focused Holistic Scoring; as such, it is a valid means of rating a large number of papers. An innovative teacher, however, can adapt it to many classroom uses, including pretesting and posttesting. As with holistic scoring, this method allows the teacher to discuss rubrics and possibly to generate motivation for revision. Additionally, uses of Focused Holistic Scoring include self-evaluation and peer evaluation with students knowledgeable of the composing process.

Information concerning this relatively new scoring method is readily available—see *Texas Assessment of Basic Skills* (1980). This publication is not copyrighted, and its contents may be duplicated. Glencoe Publishing Co. also has focused holistic materials that it has recently developed for several textbooks designed for use in the schools. Carol Greenhalgh and Donna Townsend's article ''Evaluating Students' Writing Holistically—An Alternative Approach'' (1981) identifies the sources from which the criteria used in Focused Holistic Scoring are derived. In addition, they provided a sample writing exercise, the rationale for the exercise, descriptions of score points, sample papers, and implications for instruction. This article is valuable for those interested in Focused Holistic Scoring.

The methods of evaluation examined thus far can be charted on a scale or continuum, with analytic scoring at one extreme and holistic scoring at the other. Analytic scoring rates a number of specific skills common to the degree of proficiency necessary in a well-organized expository composition. Holistic scoring, on the other hand, does not specify the skills being assessed but impressionistically evaluates the overall effectiveness of a writing sample. In varying degrees, Primary Trait Scoring and Focused Holistic Scoring represent compromises of the two extremes. The common factors of all four assessment procedures are that they directly rate a piece of writing, as opposed to indirect methods, which attempt to measure writing proficiency by having writers respond to objective tests based on other writers' products; all four, moreover, are concerned with the ideas, message, and motives of composition.

Another popular assessment method does not fall on the aforementioned scale. In fact, it measures neither the sum of the parts of a composition nor its overall effectiveness. *T-unit analysis* addresses the syntactic maturity of a writer. Developed by Kellogg W. Hunt, such analysis evolves from the belief that the more mature writer uses more sophisticated sentence patterns. The minimal terminable unit, or T-unit, is an independent clause, with all of its modifying elements. The analysis results from dividing the number of words in a composition by the number of T-units present in that composition. In his chapter ''Early Blooming and Late Blooming Syntactic Structures'' (Cooper and Odell, eds., *Evaluating Writing* [1977]), Hunt reported recent research that supports his findings from work begun in the 1960s. Those early studies in 1964, 1965, 1967, 1970, and 1974 suggest that ''successively older students can consolidate a successively larger number of simple sentences into a single T-unit'' (p. 97). According to Hunt, research indicates that syntactic maturity can be enhanced by a sentence-combining curriculum. These findings are supported by John C. Mellon in *Transformational Sentence-Combining* (1969).

Other reports attest to the potential of T-unit analysis. Its effectiveness as a measure of syntactic complexity for different age and ability levels is shown in Stephen P. Witte and Anne S. Davis's study ''The Stability of T-unit Length in the Written Discourse of College Freshmen'' (1982). A comprehensive review of research on the syntactic development of students is reported by Collett B. Dilworth, Jr., Robert W. Reising, and Denny T. Wolfe (''Language Structure and Thought in Written Composition'' [1978]). These findings show that teachers tend to give higher ratings to papers in which some statements are at higher levels of ideation or abstraction.

Discussions of the validity of T-unit analysis as a measure of syntactic fluency include the following: Walter Loban, *Language Development* (1979); Roy C. O'Donnell, "A Critique of Some Indices of Syntactic Maturity" (1976); and O'Donnell and colleagues, *Syntax of Kindergarten and Elementary School Children* (1967). In addition, Marion Crowhurst reviewed the acceptance of sentence-combining instruction as a means for developing syntactic maturity and of T-unit analysis as a measure of that maturity; see her "Sentence Combining" (1983). Crowhurst also examined the relationship between T-unit length and writing quality and concluded that teachers should value variety in both T-unit length and structure.

The advantages and disadvantages of T-unit analysis are apparent. This assessment procedure is easy to construct and easy to administer, and little time is needed for either. It does appear limited as an instructional tool, however, since it fails to measure any feature of writing other than sentence structure.

Yet one popular application is in pretests and posttests. An instructor can measure the progress made by a student throughout a term or a year. Studies have indicated that sentence-combining or sentence-embedding practices invariably accelerate syntactic complexity. When a student writer becomes aware of a method of evaluation, he normally strives to meet its expectations. The opportunities and the internal motivation for revision of one's work are primary stages in the process of writing. T-unit analysis, therefore, has potential for contributing to writing improvement.

Promising Directions in Grading and Evaluation

Six thrusts are discernible as grading and evaluation reach unprecedented maturity in the final decades of the twentieth century. Although each of the six has obvious ties to the other five, none is so indebted or dependent that its uniqueness fades. Thus it is wise to treat each of the six separately.

One thrust has already received attention. Technology has married grading and evaluation, as Patrick Finn illustrated in "Computer-Aided Description of Mature Word Choices in Writing," in Cooper and Odell's *Evaluating Writing* (1977). Several advantages accrue to such a marriage, Finn indicated, all of them dictated by a major premise of the article: "The computer is not making judgments or evaluating anything; it is simply a tool." As a tool, however, it provides a unique advantage: It "may help a classroom teacher, a language arts diagnostician, a researcher in language development, or a school evaluating institution like the National Assessment to isolate, analyze, and organize one component of writing, *word choices*, in order to respond to that component more consciously, more intelligently, and with heightened sensitivity" (p. 88).

Finn's essay is helpful, moreover, because of its sub-section "Earlier Exploration into Using the Computer to Evaluate Writing,'' a several-page history of the computer's ties with writing assessment. This history dates from 1966 with Ellis B. Page's article "The Imminence of Grading Essays by Computer" (1966). The history, too, features another article by Page, published two years later in *International Review of Education*: "The Use of the Computer in Analyzing Student Essays" (1968b). It also includes two articles by Henry B. Slotnick, the earlier one a collaboration with John V. Knapp, "Essay Grading by Computer" (1971), and the later one published in 1972, "Toward a Theory of Computer Essay Grading."

Still other works focusing on technology's potential in writing assessment include a third contribution by Page, "The Analysis of Essay" (1968a); and two essays published more recently: Jim Bencivenga's "Electronic Editing as a Tool" (1982) and Charles Moran's "Word Processing and the Teaching of Writing" (1983). Also important, but emerging from studies of technology at work in the elementary school, is "Syntactic Density and the Computer" (1974) by Lester Golub and C. Kidder.

A second promising direction emerges in the seminal work by James Britton, Tony Burgess, Nancy Martin, Alex McLeod, and Harold Rosen: *The Development of Writing Abilities (11–18)*, a 1978 volume from the Schools Council Project on Written Language of 11–18 Year Olds, based at the University of London Institute, in Great Britain, from 1966 until 1971. Later distributed in paperback by the National Council of Teachers of English, the volume is a storehouse of information and insights from an assessment of writing based on not "the time-honoured text-book categories of narrative, descriptive, expository and argumentative" but on "eight assorted tasks which acted, so to speak, as landmarks but certainly did not attempt to map out the field" of writing (pp. 1– 2). Britton and his associates also achieve the objective that they identify in the first chapter of their book, "The Background to the Project": "to describe stages in the development of writing abilites" (p. 3). Thirty-four tables, three figures, and a fold-out sheet of "audience categories" and "function categories" reinforce the principal conclusions of the authors (1) that "candidates who chose the more difficult [writing] tasks gained examination marks that compared less favorably with their all-around assessment marks than did those of the rest of the sample" (p. 2), which provided 2,122 "scripts" (p. 101); and (2) that "the talk by which children will govern their lives will require mental abilities that will best be developed by the practice of writing" (p. 201).

The scope of the study, the thoroughness of the assessors, and the insistence on "finding satisfactory means of classifying writings according to the nature of the task and the nature of the demands made upon the writer" combine to make the report invaluable, a scrupulously conceived and monitored approach to program evaluation (p. 3). It stands as exemplary, furthermore, because of its attention to "the writing process itself," a process that, as later commentary reveals, demands evaluation instruments different from those traditionally employed (p. 3).

Building upon Britton's *Development of Writing Abilities* are three works authored by individuals who contributed to the Schools Council Project: Nancy Martin's *Writing and Learning Across the Curriculum (11–16)* (1982), completed with Pat D'Arcy, Bryan Newton, and Robert Parker; Martin's *Selected Essays* (1981); and Britton's *Prospect and Retrospect* (1981). Equally valuable, and equally indebted to the Schools Council Project, is Andrew Stibb's *Assessing Children's Language* (1979).

Britton's *Development of Writing Abilities (11–18)* acknowledges indebtedness to M.A.K. Halliday, whose work in writing assessment has emerged as so distinctive that it merits identification as a separate, and third, promising direction. Borrowing from linguistics and anthropology, Halliday declared that communication intention is central to meaning and that it must be the source of any defensible theory of writing evaluation. Halliday's *Language as Social Semiotic* (1978) outlines his reliance on the beliefs of Malinowski and his own contention that child language is mono-functional; adult language, multi-functional. In Halliday's *Explorations in the Functions of Language* (1977), he amplified the three functions of adult language: ideational, interpersonal, and textual. The *ideational* function he defined as the context of what language expresses: the writer's experience, thought, and knowledge; the *interpersonal* function, as the writer's relationship to audience and subject; and the *textual* function, as the features that produce a coherent and cohesive text. A system of evaluation, he concluded, must consider all three of these functions.

The role of the textual function—interrelating the ideational and the interpersonal and deriving largely from cohesion—can most fully be appreciated through *Cohesion in English* (1976), co-authored by Halliday with Ruqaiya Hasan. In that book, the pair defined *cohesion* as a product of grammar and *vocabulary* and as semantic, non-structural, text-forming relationships. They maintained, too, that "the continuity supplied by cohesion enables the reader to supply all the missing pieces, all the components of the picture which are not present in the text but necessary to its interpretation" (p. 299).

Anne Ruggles Gere provided uncommon insight into the content and potential of Halliday's work. In "Written Composition" (1980), she agreed that "communication intention constitutes an important dimension of meaning" and proclaimed that "M.A.K. Halliday's linguistic theory suggests a fruitful way of conceptualizing evaluation of writing." Although conceding that "none of Halliday's three functions include formal semantics or surface structures, despite their prominence in current evaluation systems," she argued that

Halliday does not eschew this dimension of a comprehensive definition of meaning: He explains structure as an integrated expression of all three functions. In other words, the features which preoccupy many evaluators of writing success, or lack of it, incorporate all three language functions. Examining formal semantics for their own sake cannot provide effective evaluation, but considering surface features as manifestations of communication intention can lead to new insights about student writing (p. 58).

In praising Halliday's perceptions of writing evaluation, Gere minimized those of several other theorists, including E. D. Hirsch. Yet because Hirsch's attempt to assess writing on the basis of "relative readability" will doubtless continue to influence the profession, his system warrants consideration in this chapter as a fourth promising direction. Hirsch explained this system in his *Philosophy of Composition* (1977). Central to the system are assumptions about and provisions for "intrinsic" and "extrinsic" evaluations. Acknowledging the usefulness of the latter, which he equated with the quality of a writer's ideas or content, Hirsch favored, and thus built his system upon, "the intrinsic quality of presentation" (p. 187). "Relative readability," he alleged, mandates reader attention to a single fundamental question: Does the writing communicate its meaning "without hindrance from the author's carelessness, ineptitude, or lack of craft?" (p. 85). Hirsch recommended, moreover, that, to qualify to assess via his method, candidates earn certification through procedures described in his mimeographed "Method for Forming Tests to Certify Assessors of Writing Ability" (1976).

A cursory examination of "relative readability" should not prove misleading. The method is well conceived; its creator is a provocative thinker, and Hirsch's *Philosophy of Composition* is a rich volume. In "Written Composition" (1980), Gere revealed respect for all three. So, too, did Odell and Cooper in "Procedures for Evaluating Writing: Assumptions and Needed Research" (1980). Although no panacea, "relative readability" is not easily dismissed.

Also not easily set aside is the method prompted by the work of Andrew Wilkinson and his colleagues at the University of Essex. Outlined in "Assessing Language Development" (1979), the Wilkinson model delineates four levels, or subcategories, of cognitive development: Describing, Interpreting, Generalizing, and Speculating. Believing the Wilkinson model for cognitive measures to be a useful means of assessing the cognitive level of development, and desiring to test its effectiveness as an instrument for placing composition students in appropriate sections of freshman English at Indiana University, Marilyn S. Sternglass "designed a preliminary [writing] task that would direct students to participate in the processes of analysis and synthesis," two challenges basic to Generalizing (p. 271). Described in her "Assessing Reading, Writing, and Reasoning" (1981), the results of her study, Sternglass maintained, validated the Wilkinson model as a catalyst and context for writing assessment. Conceding that "other criteria may need to be considered," she concluded that "it may be possible to classify students' levels of cognitive development using the Wilkinson model as a basis of assessment" (p. 270). In "Applications of the Wilkinson Model of Writing Maturity to College Writing" (1982), Sternglass added still more evidence in support of the Wilkinson model as an evaluation instrument, in this article focusing her attention on two student papers, both written by freshmen in a Basic Skills class at Indiana University. Clearly, as Sternglass suggested, the Wilkinson model possesses potential not yet exploited in writing assessment.

Exploitation of that potential may well lie with, and be encouraged by, the markedly altered writing pedagogy springing up in every nation of the English-speaking world. The product teaching of writing is disappearing. In its stead is process teaching. With its increasing popularity in classrooms will come pressures to reduce dependence upon, or to eliminate entirely, those evaluation devices designed for scoring large numbers of papers (that is, holistic, analytic, Focused Holistic, Primary Trait, and T-unit), all assuming, and seemingly mandating, first-draft writing. Although product must at times be evaluated, a sixth new direction promises to incorporate *both* the use of these five methods on something other than product writing (for example, the 20–minute writing sample) *and* the development of valid, reliable, and efficient scoring instruments that presuppose and accommodate process writing. The former alternative demands a different orientation toward the five instruments mentioned, a realization and an exploitation of their potential for assessing 2nd, 3rd, and even 55th drafts. The latter is obviously a call for instruments that arise directly out of a respect for writing as a process. That new commitment accepts a distinction between formative and summative grading and evaluation and is built upon peer evaluation, group evaluation, self-evaluation, and the pupil-teacher conference.

Methodology determines the form(s) of summative evaluation and is extremely sensitive to those formative strategies that accompany process: (1) peer evaluation, (2) group evaluation, (3) self-evaluation, and (4) one-on-one teacher-pupil conferencing. If unsupervised and unpracticed, these strategies are chaos; the teacher as organizer, coordinator, and reassurer is key. The instruments, shaped wisely by the teachers, are equally essential. The teacher's role in peer, group, and self-evaluation is to train the evaluators, to provide opportunities to practice, and to monitor the activities, with the evaluations moving sequentially from the unthreatening to the threatening. By training students in the skills of composition evaluation, a teacher also provides instruction in the skills of writing that are necessary to the task being evaluated. The role of evaluator facilitates a greater awareness of writing techniques. By using strategies that move the student from unthreatening to threatening evaluation situations, the teacher provides opportunities for the student to grow in confidence and proficiency. The conference as a formative evaluation tool also looms as an effective strategy in the process-centered writing curriculum. The effective use of such a pedagogy develops revision skills and thus aids the growth of the student as writer.

The rise in the use of these writer-oriented strategies parallels the ascendency of process-centered writing instruction. Theorists, researchers, and practitioners of process writing have documented their effectiveness. Among the more successful programs that use peer evaluation are the peer tutor-training courses at Brooklyn College, Nassau Community College, and the University of California at Berkeley. Studies of these programs are reported by Paula Beck, Thom Hawkins, and Marcia Silver in "Training and Using Peer Tutors" (1978). Cited are the principles of collaborative learning and the benefits of peer evaluation (for example, criticism and tutoring) for the student writer. This research finds multiple peer feedback from carefully trained student-evaluators often more "influential than the single opinion of a teacher" (p. 435).

Similar research by Mary H. Beaven further enunciates the advantages of peer evaluation. Beaven's chapter "Individualized Goal Setting, Self-Evaluation, and Peer Evaluation" (1977) is an excellent discussion. She found that peer evaluation facilitates the opportunities for students to develop confidence in their ability to communicate through writing. The result of this structured confidence-building includes exploration of "feelings, ideas, and perceptions through writing" as students find security within their audience of peers (p. 138).

Several techniques of assessment have been employed for peer evaluation. Although the most obvious is the analytic scale, John O. White reported effective and interesting results with holistic scoring (see his "Students Learn by Doing Holistic Scoring" [1982]). Frank O'Hare advocated the use of an editing sheet in his booklet *How to Cut Hours Off the Time You Spend Marking Papers* (1981). Additional sources addressing the concerns of criteria and tutor training include Stephen M. North's "Training Tutors to Talk about Writing" (1982) and Beth Neman's text *Teaching Students to Write* (1980).

Many of the principles and applications of peer evaluation are, of course, pertinent to group evaluation, also a significant part of the Brooklyn College program and those modeled after it. Group assessment can be adapted for purposes other than final evaluation. Critique, editing, and proofreading groups are frequently used with process-centered writing programs. The former serve specifically to provide oral or written feedback from each critic to each writer. Assignments may be tailored to meet the needs of each group as the teacher serves as resource person by designing tasks and ensuring that feedback has a positive focus. Analysis of organization, rhetoric, and style at the rough draft or final manuscript stage—or in any draft in between—is the frequent objective of those groups. Such feedback suggests a variety of editing skills and promotes revision strategies. Proofreading groups, in contrast, focus on skills such as usage, mechanics, and spelling, each essential to a polished "public draft." Participants in such groups develop those skills needed to polish a piece of writing. *How to Handle the Paper Load*, edited by Gene Stanford and others (1979), includes six chapters dealing with peer and group evaluation. In addition, the pedagogical soundness of group evaluation has been documented through its use in the Bay Area Writing Project (see M. K. Healy's *Using Student Writing Response Groups in the Classroom* [1980]) and in college writing programs (see T. Hawkins's *Group Inquiry Techniques for Writing* [1976]).

Self-evaluation is also an important formative assessment method. Like peer evaluation, it requires specific guidance in identifying the assessment and in instructing the students in its application. A remarkable feature of self-appraisal is the opportunity it provides for writers to become self-motivated. Since they possess the knowledge of their past accomplishments, they are in "a good position to comment on their own growth" and to feel satisfaction with their writing performance (Davis and others, *The Evaluation of Composition Instruction* [1981], p. 94). If weaknesses are discovered, student evaluators have immediate feedback that they can understand (having identified it themselves) and use. Concern for overgrading is unfounded, as Barbara Newman pointed out in "Peer Evaluating in Teaching Composition" (1980), when she reported that self-consciousness and false modesty often make students undergrade themselves. Beaven's essay (1977) and three chapters in Stanford's *How to Handle the Paper Load* (1979) also elaborate on self-evaluation methods.

A key to successful writing is revision—the stage in the process that prompts the writer to re-think, and perhaps to experiment with, shifts in point of view, focus, approach, tone, and other refining and honing skills necessary to editing. Revision is not necessarily rewriting, nor is it merely proofreading. In *A Writer Teaches Writing* (1968), Murray called revision "the process of seeing what you've said to discover what you have to say" (p. 56). Peer evaluation, group evaluation, and self-evaluation each generates feedback useful in revision strategies. An additional evaluation technique that promotes revision opportunities is the focused writer-teacher conference.

Key to such a conference is the focus. Murray (1968) saw the role of the teacher in the focused five-minute or less conference as coach or advisor. Murray's instructions for that conference emphasize the importance of identifying and solving one writing problem in each conference. Those instructions also suggest that the conference be initiated by the student and that the teacher not try to identify every problem in the paper but simply lead the student a step at a time. Murray's basic questions for a conference are "What's your problem in this paper?" and "How do you think you can solve it?" (1968, pp. 150–51). These questions reveal his conference strategy (that is, "to allow the student to make a tentative diagnosis of his own writing problem...and to prescribe a tentative treatment," which the teacher either confirms or nullifies) (p. 151). Through the use of conferencing, a teacher helps students to teach themselves.

It must be evident that an effective writing program would adapt not one grading or evaluation method but several. Even peer-, group-, and self-assessment procedures range from analytic scales to holistic feedback according to instructional needs. Final ranking and grading, similarly, can be determined by a variety of methods and thus can discourage "writing to the test," a bent known to hamper the authenticity of "student-owned writing." Adaptability to any writing contingency emerges as a common factor in any assessment method. Perhaps paramount to any effective writing program is the ability of the writing instructor to effect strategies that result in a positive evaluation and grade not only for the student and the program but for the teacher and the profession.

References

Agee, Arnold. "The Real Victim of the Testers' Creeping Hegemony." *Chron Higher Educ*, 2 (1981), 33.

Beach, R. "Self-evaluation Strategies of Extensive Revisers and Nonrevisers." *CCC*, 27 (1976), 160–64.

Beaven, Mary H. "Individualized Goal Setting, Self-Evaluation, and Peer Evaluation." In *Evaluating Writing: Describing, Measuring, Judging*. Urbana, Ill.: NCTE, 1977, pp. 135–56.

Beck, Paula, Thom Hawkins, and Marcia Silver. "Training and Using Peer Tutors." *CE*, 40 (1978), 432–49.

Bencivenga, Jim. "Electronic Editing as a Tool." *EJ*, 71 (1982), 91–92.

Bereiter, Carl. "Development in Writing." In Conference on Research on Testing. *Testing, Teaching, and Learning: Report of a Conference on Research on Testing, Aug. 17–26, 1979*. Ralph W. Tyler and Sheldon H. White, chairmen. Washington, D.C.: National Institute of Education, 1979, pp. 146–66.

Braddock, Richard, Richard Lloyd-Jones, and Lowell Schoer. *Research in Written Composition*. Champaign, Ill.: NCTE, 1963.

Britton, James. *Language and Learning*. Coral Gables, Fla.: University of Miami Press, 1970.

————. *Prospect and Retrospect: Selected Essays of James Britton*, ed. Gordon Pradle. Montclair, N.J.: Boynton/Cook, 1982.

————, Nancy C. Martin, and Harold Rosen. *Multiple Marking of Compositions*. London: Her Majesty's Stationery Office, 1966.

————, Tony Burgess, Nancy Martin, Alex McLeod, and Harold Rosen. *The Development of Writing Abilities (11–18)*. London: Macmillan, 1978.

Bruffee, Kenneth A. *A Short Course in Writing: Practical Rhetoric for Composition Courses, Writing Workshops and Tutor Training Programs*. Englewood Cliffs, N.J.: Winthrop Publishing Co., 1980.

Burton, Dwight. "Research in the Teaching of English: The Troubled Dream." *Research in the Teaching of English*, 7 (Fall 1973), 160–89.

Conlan, Gertrude. *How the Essay in the CEEB English Test is Scored*. Princeton, N.J.: Educational Testing Service, 1976.

Cooper, Charles R. "Measuring Growth in Writing." *EJ*, 64 (1975), 111–20.

————. "Holistic Evaluation of Writing." In *Evaluating Writing: Describing, Measuring, Judging*. Ed. Charles R. Cooper and Lee Odell. Urbana, Ill.: NCTE, 1977, pp. 3–32.

————, ed. *Nature and Measurement of Competency in English*. Urbana, Ill.: NCTE, 1981.

————, and Lee Odell, eds. *Evaluating Writing: Describing, Measuring, Judging*. Urbana, Ill.: NCTE, 1977.

————, and Lee Odell, eds. *Research on Composing*. Urbana, Ill.: NCTE, 1978.

Crowhurst, Marion. "Sentence Combining: Realistic Expectations." *CCC*, 34 (1983), 62–72.

Davis, Barbara G., Michael Scriven, and Susan Thomas. *The Evaluation of Composition Instruction*. Inverness, Calif.: Edgepress, 1981.

Diederich, Paul B. *Measuring Growth in English*. Urbana, Ill.: NCTE, 1974.

Dilworth, Collett, Jr., and Robert W. Reising. "Validity in Composition Evaluation: Practicing What You Preach." *Clear H*, 53 (1979), 43–46.

————, and Denny T. Wolfe. "Language Structure and Thought in Written Composition: Certain Relationships." *RTE*, 12 (1978), 97–106.

Doherty, Paul C. "Hirsch's Philosophy of Composition: an Evaluation of the Argument."
     CCC, 33 (1982), 184–95.
Elbow, Peter. *Writing without Teachers*. New York: Oxford University Press, 1973.
"Evaluating Instruction in Writing." *CCC*, 33 (1982), 213–29.
Fagan, William T., Charles R. Cooper, and Julie M. Jensen. *Measures for Research and
     Evaluation in the English Language Arts*. Urbana, Ill.: NCTE, 1975.
Finn, Patrick J. "Computer-Aided Description of Mature Word Choices in Writing." In
     Evaluating Writing: Describing, Measuring, Judging. Ed. Charles R. Cooper and
     Lee Odell. Urbana, Ill.: NCTE, 1977, pp. 69–90.
Flower, Linda, and John R. Hayes. "The Cognition of Discovery." *CCC*, 31 (1980),
     22–35.
Follman, John C., and James A. Anderson. "An Investigation of the Reliability of Five
     Procedures for Grading English Themes." *RTE*, 1 (1967), 190–200.
Ford, Bob Wayne. "The Effects of Peer Editing/Grading on the Grammar-Usage and
     Theme-Composition Ability of College Freshmen." Diss. University of Okla-
     homa, 1973. *DAI*, 33–A (1973), no. 6687–A (University of Oklahoma).
Fowles, M. E. *Manual for Scoring the Writing Sample: Analytic Scoring, Holistic Scoring*.
     Princeton, N.J.: Educational Testing Service, 1978.
Froese, Victor, and Stanley B. Straw, eds. *Research in the Language Arts: Language
     and Schooling*. Baltimore: University Park Press, 1981.
Gere, Anne Ruggles. "Written Composition: Toward a Theory of Composition." *CE*,
     42 (1980), 44–58.
Glatthorn, Allan A. *Writing in the Schools*. Reston, Va.: National Association of Sec-
     ondary School Principals, 1981.
Godshalk, Fred I., Frances Swineford, and William E. Coffman. *The Measurement of
     Writing Ability*. New York: College Entrance Examination Board, 1966.
Golub, Lester, and C. Kidder. "Syntactic Density and the Computer." *Elem Eng*, 51
     (1974), 1128–31.
Greenhalgh, Carol, and Donna Townsend. "Evaluating Students' Writing Holistically—
     An Alternative Approach." *Lang Arts*, 58 (1981), 811–22.
Griffin, C. W. "Theory of Responding to Student Writing: The State of the Art." *CCC*,
     33 (1982), 296–301.
Grigsby, Lucy, and the Conference on College Composition and Communication (CCCC)
     Committee on Teaching and its Evaluation in Composition. "Evaluating Instruc-
     tion in Writing: Approaches and Instruments." *CCC*, 33 (1982), 213–29.
Halliday, M.A.K. *Explorations in the Functions of Language*. New York: Elsevier, 1977.
———. *Language as a Social Semiotic*. Baltimore: University Park Press, 1978.
———, and Ruqaiya Hasan. *Cohesion in English*. London: Longman, 1976.
Harris, Murial. "Evaluation: The Process for Revision." *JBW*, 1 (1978), 82–90.
Hawkins, T. *Group Inquiry Techniques for Teaching Writing*. Urbana, Ill.: NCTE, 1976.
Healy, M. K. *Using Student Writing Response Groups in the Classroom*. Berkeley, Calif.:
     Bay Area Writing Project, School of Education, University of California, 1980.
Hirsch, E. D. "A Method for Forming Tests to Certify Assessors of Writing Ability."
     TS, 1976.
———. *The Philosophy of Composition*. Chicago: University of Chicago Press, 1977.
Horner, Judith. "How Do We Know How Well Kids Write?" *EJ*, 67 (1978), 60–61.
Humes, Ann, et al. *Moving Between Practice and Research in Writing*. Los Alamitos,
     Calif.: SWRL Educational Research and Development, 1981.

Hunt, Kellogg W. "Early Blooming and Late Blooming Syntactic Structures." In *Evaluating Writing: Describing, Measuring, Judging*. Ed. Charles R. Cooper and Lee Odell. Urbana, Ill.: NCTE, 1977, pp. 91–106.

Judine, Sister M., IHM, ed. *A Guide for Evaluating Student Composition*. Champaign, Ill.: NCTE, 1965.

Keech, Catherine. "An Examination of Procedures and Implications of Holistic Assessment of Writing." In *Moving Between Practice and Research in Writing*. Ed. Ann Humes et al. Los Alamitos, Calif.: SWRL Educational Research and Development, 1981.

Kinneavy, James. *A Theory of Discourse*. Englewood Cliffs, N.J.: Prentice-Hall, 1971.

Krupa, Gene H. "Primary Trait Scoring in the Classroom." *CCC*, 30 (1970), 214–15.

Lamberg, William. "Self-Provided and Peer-Provided Feedback." *CCC*, 31 (1980), 63.

Lissitz, Robert W. "In Defense of Standardized Tests." *Chron Higher Educ*, 23 (1981), 27–28.

Lloyd-Jones, Richard. *The Students' Right to Write*. Urbana, Ill.: NCTE, 1976.

———. "Primary Trait Scoring." In *Evaluating Writing: Describing, Measuring, Judging*. Ed. Charles R. Cooper and Lee Odell. Urbana, Ill.: NCTE, 1977, pp. 33–68.

———. "What We May Become." *CCC*, 33(1982), 202–7.

Loban, Walter. *Language Development: Kindergarten through Grade Twelve*. Urbana, Ill.: NCTE, 1979.

Macrorie, Ken. *Telling Writing*. Rochelle Park, N.J.: Hayden, 1980.

Martin, Nancy C. *Selected Essays*. Montclair, N.J.: Boynton/Cook, 1981.

———, Pat D'Arcy, Bryan Newton, and Robert Parker. *Writing and Learning Across the Curriculum (11–16)*. Montclair, N.J.: Boynton/Cook, 1982.

———, et al. *Assessing Composition: A Discussion*. London: Blackie, 1965.

Maxwell, John C. *Introduction to Common Sense and Testing in English*. Urbana, Ill.: NCTE, 1975.

McColly, William. "What Does Educational Research Say about the Judging of Writing Ability?" *J Educ Res*, 64 (1970), 148–56.

Mellon, John C. *Transformational Sentence-Combining: A Method for Enhancing the Development of Syntactic Fluency in English Composition*. Urbana, Ill.: NCTE, 1969.

———. *National Assessment and the Teaching of English*. Urbana, Ill.: NCTE, 1975.

Moffett, James. *A Student-Centered Language Arts Curriculum, Grades K–13: A Handbook for Teachers*. Boston: Houghton Mifflin, 1968a.

———. *Teaching the Universe of Discourse*. Boston: Houghton Mifflin, 1968b.

Moran, Charles. "Word Processing and the Teaching of Writing." *EJ*, 72 (1983), 113–15.

Murray, Donald M. *A Writer Teaches Writing*. New York: Houghton Mifflin, 1968.

———. *Learning by Teaching*. Montclair, N.J.: Boynton/Cook, 1982.

Myers, Miles. *A Procedure for Writing Assessment and Holistic Scoring*. Urbana, Ill.: NCTE, 1980.

Nail, Pat, Rodney Fitch, John Halvertson, Phil Grant, and N. Field Winn. *A Scale for Evaluation of High School Student Essays*. Urbana, Ill.: NCTE, 1960.

Najimy, Norman C., ed. *Measure for Measure: A Guidebook for Evaluating Students' Expository Writing*. Urbana, Ill.: NCTE, 1981.

Nash, Charles C. "The Cotter Grade and Comment Sheet." *TETYC*, 7 (1981), 113–19.

National Assessment of Educational Progress. *Writing Achievement, 1969–79: Results from the Third National Writing Assessment.* Denver: Education Commission of the States, 1980.

———. *Writing Mechanics, 1969–74: A Capsule Description of Changes in Writing Mechanics.* Denver: National Assessment of Educational Progress, 1975.

Neman, Beth. *Teaching Students to Write.* Columbus, Ohio: Merrill, 1980.

Newman, Barbara J. "Peer Evaluation in Teaching Composition." *Ohio Eng Lang Arts Bul* (1980), 61–64.

North, Stephen. "Training Tutors to Talk about Writing." *CCC*, 33 (1982), 434–41.

Odell, Lee. "Defining and Assessing Competence in Writing." In *Nature and Measurement of Competency in English.* Charles R. Cooper, ed. Urbana, Ill.: NCTE, 1981.

———. "Measuring Changes in Intellectual Processes as One Dimension of Growth in Writing." In *Evaluating Writing: Describing, Measuring, Judging.* Ed. Charles R. Cooper and Lee Odell. Urbana, Ill.: NCTE, 1977, pp. 107–34.

———, and Charles R. Cooper. "Procedures for Evaluating Writing: Assumptions and Needed Research." *CE*, 42 (1980), 35–42.

———, Charles R. Cooper, and Cynthia Courts. "Discourse Theory: Implication for Research in Composition." In *Research on Composing.* Charles R. Cooper and Lee Odell, eds. Urbana, Ill.: NCTE, 1978.

O'Donnell, Roy C. "A Critique of Some Indices of Syntactic Maturity." *RTE*, 10 (1976), 31–38.

———, et al. *Syntax of Kindergarten and Elementary School Children: A Transformational Analysis.* Urbana, Ill.: NCTE, 1976.

O'Hare, Frank. *How to Cut Hours Off the Time You Spend Marking Papers.* Englewood Cliffs, N.J.: Scholastic, 1981.

Page, Ellis B. "The Imminence of Grading Essays by Computer." *Phi Del Kap*, 47 (1966), 238–43.

———. "The Analysis of Essay: By Computer." U.S. Office of Education Project 6–1318. 1968a.

———. "The Use of the Computer in Analyzing Student Essays." *Int Rev Educ*, 14 (1968b), 210–25.

Pechham, Irvin. "Peer Evaluation: Close-Up: Evaluating and Revising Composition." *EJ*, 67 (1978), 61–63.

Pradl, Gordon M., ed. *Prospect and Retrospect: Selected Essays of James Britton.* Montclair, N.J.: Boynton/Cook, 1982.

Reising, Robert W. "The Basics of Evaluation." In *Writing in the Wild Young Spring: Teaching Composition, 4–12.* Ed. Denny T. Wolfe, Jr., C. C. Lipscomb, Mary Sexton, and M. Lawrence Tucker. Raleigh, N.C.: Division of Languages, State Department of Public Instruction, 1978, pp. 25–38.

———. "More Than a Test: AP English and Evaluation." In *Rich and Enriching.* Ed. Mary Ann Weathers. Raleigh, N.C.: North Carolina Department of Public Instruction, 1982, pp. 183–89.

Rodd, Thomas, Jr. "Before the Flood." *EJ*, 72 (1983), 62–69.

Segar, C. *Improving the Quality of Written Composition through Pupil Use of Rating Scale.* Ann Arbor, Mich.: University Microfilms International, 1973. Order no. 72-23 605.

Shaughnessy, Mina P. *Errors and Expectation*. New York: Oxford University Press, 1977.

Shuman, R. Baird. "What about Revision?" *EJ*, 64 (1975), 41–43.

Slotnick, Henry B. "Toward a Theory of Computer Essay Grading." *J Educ Method*, 9 (1972), 253–63.

———, and John V. Knapp. "Essay Grading by Computer: A Laboratory Phenomenon?" *EJ*, 60 (1971), 75–87.

Smith, Paul. *Grading the Advanced Placement Examination in English: Language and Composition*. Princeton, N.J.: College Board Publications, 1980.

Smith, Vernon H. "Measuring Teacher Judgment in the Evaluation of Written Composition." *RTE*, 3 (1969), 181–95.

Spandel, Vickie, and Richard J. Stiggins. *Direct Measures of Writing Skill: Issues and Applications*. Portland, Oreg.: Northwest Regional Educational Laboratory, 1980.

Stanford, Gene, et al., ed. *How to Handle the Paper Load*. Urbana, Ill.: NCTE, 1979.

Sternglass, Marilyn S. "Assessing Reading, Writing and Reasoning." *CE*, 43 (1981), 269–75.

———. "Applications of the Wilkinson Model of Writing Maturity to College Writing." *CCC*, 33 (1982), 167–75.

Stibbs, Andrew. *Assessing Children's Language*. London: Ward Lock Educational, 1979.

Stiggins, Richard J. *Report on Performance Assessment: Analysis of Direct and Indirect Writing Assessment Procedures*. Portland, Oreg.: Clearinghouse for Applied Performance Testing. Northwest Regional Educational Laboratory, 1981.

Straw, Stanley B. "Assessment and Evaluation in Written Composition: A Commonsense Perspective." *Research in the Language Arts*. Ed. Victor Froese and Stanley B. Straw. Baltimore, Md.: University Park Press, 1981, pp. 181–202.

Sudol, Ronald, ed. *Revising: New Essays for Teachers of Writing*. Urbana, Ill.: NCTE, 1982.

Texas Assessment of Basic Skills: Focused Holistic Scoring of TABS Writing Samples: Exit Level. Austin: Texas Education Agency, Division of Curriculum Development, 1980.

White, Edward M., and Ruth Mitchell. "Correcting Old Errors with New Ones." *Chron Higher Educ*, 23 (1981), 27.

White, John O. "Students Learn by Doing Holistic Scoring." *EJ*, 71 (1982), 50–51.

Wilkinson, Andrew. "Assessing Language Development: The Crediton Project." *Lang L*, 1 (1979), 60–77.

Windhover, Ruth. "A Holistic Pedagogy for Freshman Composition." In *Revising*. Ed. Ronald A. Sudol. Urbana, Ill.: NCTE, 1982, pp. 87–99.

Witte, Stephen P., and Anne S. Davis. "The Stability of T-unit Length in the Written Discourse of College Freshmen: A Second Study." *RTE*, 16 (1982), 71–84.

Wolfe, Denny T., C. C. Lipscomb, Mary Sexton, and M. Lawrence Tucker, eds. *Writing in the Wild Young Spring: Teaching Composition, 4–12*. Raleigh, N.C.: Division of Languages, State Department of Public Instruction, 1978.

Assignment Making

LYNN DIANE BEENE

Many composition specialists agree that one of the most important tasks writing teachers perform is making and evaluating writing assignments. But this function does not always receive the attention it deserves. In faculty seminars, in composition pedagogy classes, in professional journals, and, most often, in the faculty lounge over a hurried cup of coffee, writing teachers share stories, encouragement, and advice on evaluating their students' essays. However, many do not approach creating assignments with the same interest. True, topics that produced for one teacher a set of passable themes are frequently collected in a file or exchanged, complete with instructions on how the teacher "gave" the assignment and warnings on how the topics may not "work" in all classes. But just as often topics are created at the last minute, before or during classes, with teachers giving themselves a stern reprimand that the next time more care will go into the assignments. Less frequently, teachers will carefully design not just one writing assignment but an entire sequence, refining and rewriting individual assignments based on their students' responses.

For most writing teachers, making writing assignments is a skill learned not through careful instruction but by trial and error. Armed with their critical knowledge of literature—and perhaps some background in linguistics and composition theory—teachers try to create assignments that will prompt students to write well and interestingly.

Although much of this practical, hard-won knowledge has found its way into print, articles on writing assignments are both limited and varied. It is in their theoretical backgrounds that most of these articles display their limitations. Composition specialists have generally offered a limited set of frequently repeated guidelines for things such as creating writing assignments, determining aspects of writing that need to be considered, isolating linguistic criteria necessary for a good writing assignment, helping students see and relate ideas, and developing methods to get students to complete writing assignments successfully. If teachers will study James Kinneavy's *Theory of Discourse* (1971) and James Moffett's *Teaching the Universe of Discourse* (1968), they can derive many of these guidelines, in their more theoretical forms, for themselves.

On the other hand, if writing teachers want to find specific assignments for basic writing, freshman composition, or advanced composition students, they will find a rich variety in the literature. Although no one has yet integrated specific assignments with all stages in the writing process, many articles detail assignments for prewriting, revision, the various modes of writing (for example, narration, description, argumentation), and various formats (for example, formal reports, research or library papers).

The articles on writing assignments tend to fall into one or two "schools" concerning the planning of writing exercises. These schools develop on the sides of a frequently mentioned issue: whether the content or the form of a student essay is more important. The schools that develop on the content side of the issue generally promote practical, non-academic writing topics designed to benefit students in their extra-curricula or, at least, non-literary endeavors. These authors assume that the subject matter of writing assignments is at least as important as the formal properties of the writings. Thus the articles on this side of the issue often express the view that the students' process of writing the assignment, insofar as the preparation includes research and analysis, is as important as the product.

The schools on the form side of the issue generally ignore the subject matter of the writing assignments. These authors adhere to the view that good writing is primarily the result of the manipulation of formal or conventional properties (for example, sentence-level mechanics, paragraph development, rhetorical modes). Their tacit assumption is that mastery of discrete, practical subjects is the concern of teachers of other subjects. Interestingly, many of these authors promote daily writing exercises as a means to make students fluent with the use of formal properties. Thus for different reasons, the authors on the formal side of the issue also advance the process of writing as an important element in teaching writing.

Guidelines and Criteria

Most composition theorists see two basic problems inherent in assignment making. First, it is the nature of writing classes to establish stilted situations that students find divorced from both their other classes and their post-academic goals. Ken Macrorie noted in *Telling Writing* (1976) that the situation in a writing class is an artificial one that must be overcome: "No one outside school ever writes anything called *themes*. Apparently they are teachers' exercises, not really a kind of communication" (p. 2). Therefore, to make writing assignments that succeed, teachers must identify "real world" purposes and audiences.

Second, according to the theorists, writing teachers spend too little time creating writing assignments and too much time evaluating the products—student themes. Therefore, the product takes precedence over the process. Erika Linde-mann's chapter "Making and Evaluating Writing Assignments" in *A Rhetoric for Writing Teachers* (1982) is typical of this second complaint. In a brief section, she pointed out that the traditional and unproductive way to assign writing is to make an assignment quickly (usually at the end of the class period), to put little thought into the criteria for or the anticipated results of the assignment, and to evaluate the resulting papers from the first words of their first sentences rather than from how well the papers as texts respond to a given topic. Although she devoted most of her chapter to the evaluation of student themes, Lindemann did provide some general guidelines for making writing assignments: assignments should be sequenced; they should be complete and written, rather than oral; and they should provide for pre-writing, writing, and revision.

Sara R. Farley in "Constructing Composition Assignments" (1982) argued that for the student as well as the teacher the product (the theme) becomes more important than the process. For Farley students can become attuned to the writing process only if the assignment includes several basic principles that Kinneavy and Moffett stressed: a purpose; a recognizable audience other than just the teacher; and, as Harvey S. Wiener has put it in "Making and Carrying Out Assignments" in his *Writing Room* (1981), a "crystalline" set of criteria for the assignment. These principles appear again and again throughout the literature. For example, Gilbert Tierney and Stephen N. Judy discussed in "The Assignment Makers" (1972) nine assignments that didn't work and explained that the assignments lacked either a recognizable audience or a purpose or a set of options for the students. Tierney and Judy identified a set of criteria for assignment making (for example, include complete directions, be appropriate to the students' educational level, and allow for various responses) and a set of criteria for the audience (for example, allow for various points of view, designate a specific audience, and provide for audience response).

Edmund J. Farrell in "The Beginning Begets" (1969) also thought audience and a sense of purpose are vital, because these elements allow students to experiment with different points of view. In a seven-point checklist, Farrell advised teachers not to give assignments (1) that elicit true/false or yes/no answers, (2) that elicit fragmentary responses, (3) that call for undirected speculation, (4) that require knowledge students don't yet have, (5) that involve numerous questions, (6) that use very personal information about the student as support, or (7) that require the students to write in a style identical to the professional essays they are studying.

William Irmscher in *Teaching Expository Writing* (1979) identified purpose, audience, and clarity as his criteria for a good writing assignment; however, he believes that "in most instances, the purpose, mode, and audience will be implicit in the nature and wording of the topic" (p. 76). Teachers should establish at the beginning of the course, rather than for each assignment, the length, purpose, mode, and audience (that is, the class) for all writing assignments. If the students take the purposes of a writing class seriously, teachers can individualize writing assignments within these initial standards. Irmscher also offered a set of writing assignments that, in the main, do not follow his own advice.

Richard L. Larson systematized ways to prepare assignments, to draft the accompanying instructions, and to give the assignments to students in "Training New Teachers of Composition in Administering Theme Assignments" (1968). When preparing assignments, instructors should: (1) have a structure for the course in mind so that the assignments develop that structure, (2) order the assignments in a sequence so the students' progress can be charted, (3) make assignments relative to students' interests and experiences, (4) give assignments that make students form a thesis from their observations and thinking, (5) understand exactly what their assignments ask of the students, (6) give assignments that students can do, and (7) clearly specify what constitutes successful completion of an assignment. When teachers draft instructions for an assignment, they must (1) define the subject matter and scope of the assignment, (2) define the intended audience, (3) use directive verbs, (4) limit injunctions, and (5) write clearly. Rather than giving an assignment to the students at the end of the class period, teachers should: (1) write out or discuss the assignment fully, (2) allow for discussion before writing, (3) explore options to the topics, and (4) indicate the grading standards.

Eleanor M. Hoffman and John P. Schifsky, Cheryl S. Jenkins, William E. Gruber, B. Bernard Cohen, and Helen Throckmorton addressed in separate articles why writing assignments fail and what teachers can do to keep them from failing. Hoffman and Schifsky in "Designing Writing Assignments" (1977) deplored loose, unstructured essay assignments and argued that vague assignments with unspecified audiences and unclear aims can be graded only for mechanics and not for content or form. Jenkins in "The Writing Assignment" (1980) noted that the wording of an assignment frequently creates barriers for students. She suggested four criteria for a good writing assignment: clear instructions, room for speculation on the topic, no presuppositions regarding students' knowledge, and options for various points of view. For Gruber in " 'Servile Copying' and the Teaching of English Composition" (1977) writing assignments go wrong when teachers assume "that content is most important, and that if only [they] can produce an 'interesting' topic, the writing will magically improve" (p. 495). He structured his writing assignments on the premise that, after a discussion of linguistic and stylistic aspects of a text, students can learn to write well by imitation.

Cohen in "Writing Assignments in a Course with Readings in Imaginative Literature" (1968) argued that teachers' attitudes toward their departments' stated goals for composition courses, toward the textbooks they must use, and/or toward the students can adversely affect writing assignments. Cohen advised that teachers use a planned sequence of assignments based around a theme (for example, war); the sequence should include discussion questions for the literature, discussion questions for class time, and written assignments from the literature. Throckmorton in "Do Your Writing Assignments Work?" (1980) argued that assignments fail when teachers don't specify what they want or forget to build into an assignment opportunities to teach their students different aspects of writing. Synthesizing material from several other theorists (for example, E. J. Farrell, "The Beginning Begets" [1969], and R. L. Larson, "Teaching Before We Judge" [1967]), she recommended that assignments be appropriate to the students' educational level and course development, stimulating, instructive, purposeful, and measurable. Using three sample analysis/argumentative assignments, based on Jack London's short story "To Build a Fire," she detailed how every good writing assignment meets at least four of the five recommendations she makes.

Purpose, audience, and clarity are further refined in Timothy R. Donovan's article "Seeing Students as Writers" (1978). Donovan rightly believes that teachers do students a disservice "when the emphasis falls on 'assignment' rather than writing" (p. 13). Not only do assignments need to specify an audience, but they need to help students develop a persona, or voice, in their writing. Such specification helps students gain a sense of self that, in turn, gives students a perspective from which they can successfully finish any writing project in any class.

Although audience, aim, and clarity are important in making assignments, not all theorists think they must be precisely stated in each assignment. John E. Jordan noted in "Theme Assignments" (1963) that "channeling students into writing good essays is practically tantamount to writing them ourselves" (p. 51). If writing teachers do all of the initial work for their students, these students' imaginative abilities will be stifled and their expectations regarding writing assignments in other fields will be unrealistic. Although some controlled assignments are good to build students' confidence, Jordan argued that providing too many details on how to accomplish an assignment shifts the emphasis from writing to merely doing what the teacher wants on an assignment. Jordan, like Irmscher, believes that students should be given more credit for what they can do and not be led step-by-step through each writing assignment.

Margot K. Soven in "Helping Students Generalize, Specify, Clarify" (1982) also gave students credit for their abilities, although she believes that current teaching techniques don't give sufficient emphasis to the writing skills of generalizing, specifying, and clarifying. Soven argued that students can think abstractly as well as concretely, can improve their writing by themselves, and can learn effective writing skills best by practice with sequential writing assignments.

Instead of sequential writing assignments, Sharon Feaster argued in "Structuring for Composition" (1982) that, to help students practice their writing skills, teachers should give them writing assignments that parallel the writing process: prewriting, which includes reading, summarizing, and thinking; writing or drafting a text; re-writing or revising their texts; and post-writing, or presenting their texts to an audience. Other theorists agree. For example, Barbara King in "The Waiting Game" (1982) suggested that, as the emphasis in composition shifts from product to process, teachers must use prewriting activities such as journal writing, talking and questioning, and researching to help students with other writing assignments.

Still other theorists argued that writing assignments arise not from a sequence of processes but a sequence of products. James M. McCrimmon argued in "A Cumulative Sequence in Composition" (1966) that if students are to be successful at writing they must receive a sequence of writing assignments that escalate in difficulty, for example, from specification to comparison-contrast to classification. Richard L. Graves, believing form can potentially generate ideas, detailed in "CEHAE" (1972) a teaching sequence (concept, example, highlighting, activity, evaluation) that helps students understand and use rhetorical principles. Richard L. Larson, using many of his criteria described in his "Training New Teachers" (1968), argued in "Teaching Before We Judge" (1967) that since the purpose of a writing assignment is to teach students to think and to use their thinking in their writing, these assignments should be a sequenced part of a sequenced course. Larson offered 11 steps in writing assignments and using a sequenced course: (1) plan the course; (2) analyze each assignment; (3) consider the students' level of knowledge; (4) identify principles for the assignments; (5) specify purpose, mode, and audience; (6) set criteria for evaluation; (7) explain the assignments; (8) allow for questions; (9) evaluate the essays with positive criticism; (10) discuss the products; and (11) demand revision.

Another specific approach to making assignments is the case approach found in the work of Robert H. Weiss, John P. Field, David Tedlock, and Paul Jarvie. In an early research work, *Assignments That Succeed* (1978), Weiss summarized many of the objections others have made to hackneyed topics such as "How I Spent My Summer Vacation." (See Richard Braddock and his colleagues' *Research in Written Composition* [1963] for information on such topics.) These assignments are often done in haste and are thus superficial; they are not derived from the teaching; they do not reflect audience, aim, purpose, or practical considerations; thus they seem useless to students. Weiss thought cases, "carefully structured and high focused writing situations of applied rhetoric," provide realism and a sense of audience, help students establish a persona, and are adaptable both to students' educational levels (fifth grade through college senior) and to various writing tasks (p. 8). Weiss and Field, in a later research document *Cases for Composition* (1979), further justified the case approach as a way to teach writing that is based not on textbook readings but on situations that students must analyze and imitate. Weiss and Field argued that to teach writing well, teachers need to use readings not for their content but for their leads into writing. This is because students learn best not from writing assignments placed almost like afterthoughts at the end of a textbook reading but from carefully crafted, realistic assignments.

David Tedlock summarized much of the information on the case approach in his article "The Case Approach to Composition" (1981). Students are presented with a case that does not prescribe a writing assignment but allows the teacher to suggest several assignments based on the class discussion of the case. Because the assignments grow from the case and its discussion, Tedlock believes that the assignments develop students' analytic abilities by having them use problem-solving techniques with realistic situations. Tedlock noted that traditionalists object to the case approach because it does not use professional materials (that is, the standard textbook readings' approach) and ignores rhetorical modes and methods of development in favor of a combination of modes and methods. (See Richard E. Young's article "Paradigms and Problems" [1978] for a further discussion of current-traditional rhetoric and its influence on textbooks.) Two textbooks of cases and possible writing assignments have been published: John P. Field and Robert H. Weiss's *Cases for Composition* (1979) and David Tedlock and Paul Jarvie's *Casebook Rhetoric* (1981).

Several researchers have used more than their insights or particular approaches to discuss assignment making. Dan Donlan in the survey *Textbook Writing Assignments in Three Content Areas* (1976) found that although math, science, and social studies all assign writing, social science textbooks assign more and more varied types of writing than the others. Overall, the writing assignments in these three fields are of four broad types: reporting, exposition, narration, and argumentation—modes of writing usually emphasized in college freshman courses. Ann Raines detailed in *Writing and Learning Across the Curriculum* (1979) the findings of an interdisciplinary faculty seminar in which seminar members wrote and critiqued writing assignments and evaluated students' papers. The participants concluded that basic writing skills are similar across college curricula and that students gain knowledge of a subject—the content material—by writing about it, a distinct contrast to Weiss and Field's position that content interferes with composition. The participants recommended that academic writing (analysis, argumentation, and so on) should be taught sooner in composition classes because of its importance in college, that writing assignments should come from key ideas in the students' major fields and not from textbook readings, that basic skills ought to be taught by trained personnel in English departments, and that writing teachers should create good writing assignments using topics that allow students to learn while they write.

Nancy Arapoff-Cramer, using ESL students taking English as a second language as her base, reported in "A Survey of University Writing Assignments" (1971) that teachers in the sciences, liberal arts, and combination fields (for example, architecture) are more interested in students' abilities to handle content than in students' accuracy with written forms. In other words, teachers across the curricula want their students to communicate a clear understanding of the material and will tolerate some sentence-level errors (even from native speakers). Arapoff-Cramer also found, like Donlan, that writing assignments generally fall into three categories: reporting, which uses specific information; exposition, which uses evaluation; and pragmatic assignments, which require a creative synthesis of course material. Her most important conclusion for writing teachers surprised even her: English teachers should assign research or term papers both because there is a recognized form for them across the curricula and because they are so frequently required in other fields.

Perhaps the strongest statement on assignment making comes in a series of guidelines from the Commission on English's *Freedom and Discipline in English* (1975). The commission presented an argument that making writing assignments is the most important aspect of a writing teacher's job. Good writing assignments, carefully thought out and planned, should give students a chance to do their best work; should be a learning tool; should provide information on audience, mode, and purpose; should be phrased as propositions; should limit the content or form or both; should clearly identify the audience; and should be varied even within a sequence. In the following section of specific assignments, one can see how many of these guidelines are met.

Pre-Writing

For many instructors, pre-writing activities include anything a class or a student does before writing: games, discussion, thinking, analyzing previously written texts, or taking notes. (See James Britton's article "The Composing Process and the Functions of Writing" [1978] for a discussion of what *prewriting* is.) Several of these methods have been adopted by teachers to help their students before the students put pen to paper. Philip C. Kilin, finding in "Some Way of Teaching Unity" (1970) that the textbook advice about writing doesn't help students, devised an exercise on unity using a seven-sentence paragraph where four sentences don't fit. After a discussion of this paragraph, his students wrote a 60-70-word paragraph on a whimsical subject, such as the pleasures of a sneeze. Ken Davis in "The Circle Game" (1978) invented a classroom game that shows students that they are members of several groups and that, as communicators, they must use different tactics depending upon the group they are addressing. Davis's prewriting activity, therefore, is an effort to help students gain a sense of audience. Lynne Shackelford in "A Switch in Point of View" (1981) used role playing in a variation on audience perception. Using mostly class discussion, she gave a pair of exercises: first, the students described the class from the teacher's point of view; second, the class, divided into five groups, described a football game from five points of view (for example, the quarterback's, the coach's).

Pre-writing exercises frequently take the form of a discussion of another text before the students write their own essays. Fern Kupfer described in "Ruining Perfectly Good Writing" (1981) a variation on this tactic that she used to teach revision. She took a text of good writing and deleted the details, color, and emphasis; made specifics in the text abstractions; overworked the endings; and added clichés. Using the exercise as a discussion, Kupfer thought she could encourage students to develop a critical ability they could transfer to their own writing.

Other pre-writing exercises use writing to get the students started. Kristen M. Figg, for example, described an invention heuristic in "Introducing Invention Techniques" (1980). She prepared and had students respond to a series of questions on a topic they would be writing about (for example, a trip to the dentist). Mary Bigler in "Creative Writing Ideas" (1980) used ten writing assignments, varying from one sentence to one paragraph, to start students writing.

Other composition teachers use structured pre-writing assignments primarily to get students over the fear of writing. Baird R. Shuman, for one, detailed in "They Only Think They Have Nothing to Write About!" (1977) a sequence that he believes helps limber students up. The students write for three minutes (a project similar to ones Peter Elbow described in *Writing Without Teachers* [1973]). They then exchange papers and write for four more minutes, taking their cues from what the first writer started. This exchange process goes on for four or five more times, each time with the student taking the previous writer's work as the starting place. Thomas J. Morrissey in "The Five-Minute Entry" (1982) believes that students who write daily become better writers and that there is no need for teachers to read and grade all papers carefully, particularly not short writing exercises. Instead he suggested that a five-minute exercise, written in response to questions from a reading assignment, both provides the needed writing practice and gives the teachers writing samples that can be quickly checked.

Realizing that students are facing essay examinations in other classes and that they frequently "freeze" when faced with such examinations, Ronald E. Smith suggested in "A Twenty-Minute Exercise for In-Class Essays" (1981) a writing exercise that shows students that the planning for a paper does not always go on exclusively in a writer's mind. Students are given a list of topics; they go through a timed sequence of pre-writing exercises designed to develop a thesis statement and a sketchy outline. It is Smith's hope that this sequence of exercises is a tool students can use in other classes, relieving them from the tension they feel as they stare, sometimes for 20 minutes, at an assignment sheet.

Frequently, journal writing is used as a pre-writing tool—to overcome fear, to encourage invention, and to give students writing practice. Barbara L. Warren in "Journal Writing—The Quiet Time" (1982) argued that weekly, scheduled journal writing gets students quieted down for class quicker and makes them more accustomed to writing by alleviating the fear they have of a blank page of paper. Warren wrote with her students, thus creating a chronicle of the term. Dawn M. Wilson in "Steppingstones to Success" (1982) indicated that having students keep a journal that combines weekly freewriting and prescribed writing provides the students with an initial source of ideas for graded compositions. To make the project work, Wilson blended the journal writing with composition topics by annotating journal entries to push students for more detail and assigning topics that allow students to use journal ideas and prompted development.

Michael D. Platt's article "Writing Journals in Courses" (1975) presents the argument that journal writing is a good exercise in any course, because it makes students prepare for class as the teacher does, it provides the writing exercise that students at all levels need, it is perceived by students as a less formal form of writing (and therefore less forbidding), and it develops in the students a will to write. Because students feel they have nothing to say, don't see the necessity of writing, and aren't ready to correct their own mistakes, Patrick E. Kilburn in "Every Man His Own Pedagogue" (1962) argued that students should write in a journal 15 minutes a day, 7 days a week. He graded his students' journal entries on quantity only, not quality or grammar. Kilburn works from the theory that a person can correct errors only when he or she realizes them; daily writing, he believes, forces students to recognize their own errors while alleviating their fear of writing.

Narration and Description

Many teachers have become discouraged with narration and description assignments; all too often the themes they receive from such assignments are little more than sketchy outlines of a student's day, an event in a student's life, or an object that the student hasn't successfully described. Nonetheless, several writing teachers have found ways to use these two modes of writing to produce not only good essays but also good preparation for other, more academic forms of writing.

James S. Mulligan in " 'A Short Vision' " (1971) used the film *A Short Vision*, without sound, as the topic for a narrative essay. He expanded on this narrative topic by using the same film (this time with sound) later in the semester for an analytic assignment: is the film art or is it propaganda? Given the opinions they have formed from the first narration assignment, the students are less willing to classify the film as art or propaganda without careful support. Joseph Ciciotte's "The Sense Image in *A Death in the Family*" (1980) used the chapter "Knoxville 1915" as a stimulus for a descriptive essay. Unlike traditional textbook approaches, Ciciotte's approach uses the chapter as the incentive for the essay, not as a model to be imitated.

Lisa S. Ede's article "Oral History" (1977) also uses narrative to teach other writing skills. Using Studs Terkel's book *Hard Times* (1970), Ede taught her students interviewing techniques to use in collecting information for their own versions of oral histories. Ede considered this assignment one that uses narration to teach editing skills. Phillip Snyder in "Working 1-002" (1982) used another of Terkel's books, *Working* (1974), as the thematic base for a series of assignments that involved the topic of working and its importance to students in their futures. Students completed assignments such as personal-experience narratives, letters of application, resumés, and research papers on the theme of working.

Using Richard D. Kepes's ideas from "Write Your Own Obituary" (1976), R. C. Wess explained in "Written Logodrama" (1982) how he had students look at themselves from a future rather than a historical perspective. Students wrote their own obituaries, modeling their work on obituaries in the *New York*

Times. Moving even further away from students' own histories, Krystan V. Douglas detailed in "Yet Another Reason Not to Write a 500 Word Essay" (forthcoming) the steps in a six-week writing project in which students created (fictional) characters and their accompanying biographies. Not only did Douglas's sequence teach narration, but it also encouraged students to put more detail into their other writing assignments.

Putting details into student writing is one of the goals of descriptive assignments. Lynn Z. Bloom in "Intruder in the Classroom" (1971) taught the value of observation by having someone interrupt her class. Instead of a writing assignment per se, Bloom had the students respond to specific questions about the interruption. Robert C. Rosen suggested in "Teaching the Thesis Statement Through Description" (1981) that thesis statements can be effectively taught through descriptive writing. Like Bloom, Rosen taught part of the writing process, shaping the thesis statement, rather than a complete writing assignment.

Other teachers have used description to focus students' attention on a concept of audience. Lois Rubin's article "Moving from Prewriting to Composing" (1981) explains how to use Richard E. Young, Alton L. Becker, and Kenneth Pike's *Rhetoric* (1970) to teach description. Setting up a specific audience for this in-class exercise, Rubin had her students describe a tea bag by particle, wave, and field. Class discussion focused on how to revise the description from the point of view of the intended audience. H. C. Brashers in "Teaching Descriptive Style" (1968) proposed an exercise in which students describe a building three ways using three persona. The different persona enabled Brashers to teach five categories that describe style from the perspective of audience: features of pronunciation, features of vocabulary, features of grammar (that is, syntax), features of organization, and features of aesthetic patterns (a compilation of the first four features). Carol M. Jacko's article "Small-Group Triad" (1978), promoting multiple responses, advocates a triad approach to teaching writing. Three students work in a triad of reader-critic, writer-author, and observer-reporter, changing among the roles for each paper. David H. Karrfalt in "Writing Teams" (1971) used a similar triad approach. Students were put into three-person teams for the first three papers in the course; one student wrote the draft while the other students supplied suggested revisions. All three students received the same grade. Karrfalt's assignment, like Jacko's, emphasized the social situation of writing rather than the individual situation, thus giving greater emphasis to communication and to audience.

Analysis, Argumentation, Persuasion

Most writing courses include some analysis of literature. In "The Rhetoric of Satire" (1982), Betty J. Proctor suggested that satire is a good way to teach analysis, because its intent (that is, persuasion) is obvious, its manipulation of language is easy to teach, its audience identification is calculated, and its use of humor makes it easy for non-literature majors to understand. Proctor used cartoons and Jonathan Swift's "Modest Proposal" as the bases for two similar writing assignments: analyses of the cartoons and Swift's essay on the basis of criteria identified by the teacher. Robert M. Esch explained in "A Method of Teaching the Critical Essay" (1968) how, after giving the students introductory lectures on critical analysis of literature, he had the students write short analyses first. His goal was to have the students look at literary analysis as a problem to be solved rather than an academic paper to be written for the teacher. Esch found two drawbacks to his method: slow students find it a very difficult task and good students tend to overinterpret the work of literature.

Realizing what a difficult play *Hamlet* can be, M. J. Francoz in "The Logic of Question and Answer" (1979) gave students a three-part assignment to increase their understanding of the play. Students first wrote three or four questions they would ask Shakespeare about Hamlet, then developed one of these questions into a dialogue with Shakespeare, and finally revised the dialogue into an essay. Francoz believes that a writing assignment works well only if it is a topic the students can feel is important to them—an opinion frequently voiced by other composition teachers and specialists. To Francoz, the question-and-answer format provides this sense of purpose. Edward Proffitt in "Writing for Reading" (1978) also complained that asking students to write assignments without a clear purpose is wrong, because it avoids non-academic writing situations. Arguing that assignments directed at students' experiences are childish, Proffitt detailed two writing assignments that ask students to write a paragraph in answer to a pointed question and to write a paragraph of response to a literary text. These assignments, to Proffitt, are "natural" in that they are immediately purposeful to the class.

Many teachers have developed analytical assignments that do not refer to literature but focus on students' experiences and understanding of those experiences in practical situations. Several teachers contributed ideas that meet these criteria to a column called "Our Readers Write" (1980). Most of these assignments use events students have faced or will someday have to face: how to report the details of a traffic accident, how to write a letter of complaint, how to be a good parent. Fred Kroeger in "A Freshman Paper Based on the Words of Popular Songs" (1968) used two songs, "The Eve of Destruction" and "The Dawn of Correction," as the bases for an analytic-argumentative writing assignment. He had his students analyze these two songs not for their subject matter but for their efficacy as arguments. In "Choice for a First-Essay Topic" (1976), Marilyn S. Samuels reported the results she found when she gave a topic derived from Joseph C. Pattison's NCTE pamphlet "How to Write an F Paper" (1963). The students revealed, both in content and in form, their strengths and weaknesses, their attitudes toward writing, and their ability to diagnose their own errors. Some of Samuels' students identified a point writing teachers frequently stress: writing is communication. According to her students, there can be no such thing as an F paper, because even the worst paper communicates something.

Richard M. Coe and Kris Gutierrez in "Using Problem-Solving Procedures and Process Analysis to Help Students with Writing Problems'' (1981) took Samuels's idea one step further. Coe and Gutierrez detailed three writing assignments and accompanying classroom discussion designed to help students see what their writing problems are and strategies to resolve them. The authors based their assignments on five assumptions: that one can change writing quality by changing the processes of production; that active learning (that is, student motivated) is better than passive learning (that is, teacher motivated); that a precise statement of a writing problem leads to successful solutions to that problem; and that success comes with a strategy, a schedule, and an evaluative procedure. Coe and Gutierrez built these five assumptions into their writing assignments.

Lynn Z. Bloom argued in ''Milieus, Modes, and Messages'' (1976) that the study of verbal and non-verbal communication facilitates composition skills, because it increases students' awareness of themselves as both reactors and as judgment makers. Bloom suggested writing assignments that use standard methods of linguistic investigation as the bases for an assignment on verbal communication and standard methods of psychological observation as the bases for an assignment on non-verbal communication.

Terry Dean in ''Causal, Not Casual'' (1982) explained that students not only understand themselves, but they also understand causal relationships from their past experiences; however, they don't understand how to write about them. Dean developed a series of exercises to illustrate cause-effect relationships and to help students see how to organize a cause-effect essay. Dean stressed that, to make such exercises work, teachers must make sure that the audience is clear and that they have provided the students with complete information about the topic.

Using Bruno Bettelheim's *The Informed Heart* (1960) to discuss points of view of an opponent, Kathleen Kelly in ''Persuasion for Survival'' (1982) explained how she had her students write a letter on a topic from a point of view contrary to their own. This fusion of audience, persuasiveness, and argumentation is central to Pat E. Taylor's article ''Teaching Creativity in Argumentation'' (1977). Taylor thought the problem with writing assignments is how to get students motivated to think creatively on a controversial subject. After clearly defining the audience, Taylor had the students complete opinion sheets on a controversial topic; she then collected and redistributed the sheets to other students. The students interviewed one another, making sure they unearthed why the interviewees felt the way they did. The students then wrote an essay contradicting the opinion sheet they received. Richard A. Strugala in ''Values Clarification Through Writing'' (1982) also tried to include thinking about values. Students rated ten values. After class discussion, they wrote a definition of the word *value*, how they knew when a concept was a value, and how society transmitted its values. Much of Strugala's assignment depends upon class discussion. The same is true of Richard B. Larsen's argumentative essay assignment found in ''Back to the Board'' (1978). Larsen detailed a writing assignment done by the teacher on the board and the class at their desks; its benefit, he said, is that one can teach by immediate example.

David Schwab in "Writing as Thinking" (1981) and Julia C. Dietrich in "Giving Evidence" (1978) both used mystery and deduction as a means to teach analysis and persuasion. Schwab's assignment was a murder mystery with three suspects. The evidence he presented gave the students a reasonably clear solution to the crime based on motive, opportunity, and means. Students successfully completed the writing assignment by persuading the reader of their conclusions—whodunit. Dietrich's mystery is somewhat less bloody: with a fact sheet provided by the teacher, students must identify who stole a manuscript. Both exercises support information Dietrich found in her poll of faculty and students: the abilities to evaluate and draw conclusions are the primary skills students need from a writing class.

Writing Assignments as Sequences

As noted earlier, most theorists maintain that along with audience, aim, and purpose, writing teachers should arrange their writing assignments in a sequence. The feeling is that a sequence of assignments, increasing in difficulty or building one skill on another, is the most effective way for students to become more efficient writers. Sequencing assignments is particularly important for Basic Writing (BW) students who not only fear writing but are most in need of developing their skills in writing. Ann Petrie in "Teaching the Thinking Process in Essay Writing" (1976) detailed three techniques she used to teach BW students writing: constant writing assignments, frequent conferences, and various in-class writing exercises. Petrie used a tightly structured sequence of writing assignments beginning with personal writing and extending through critical essays. The process concentrates on using personal experience, rather than reading material, to help students develop analytic thinking. Marc Glasser in "Food for Thought— And Writing" (1982) also used students' personal experience—their love of and knowledge about food—as the subject of four essays of illustration that develop in a sequence.

In "Controlled Composition for Basic Writers" (1981) Donna Gorrell argued that writing assignments should not only be in a sequence, but they should also be controlled. Her controlled, or guided, writing assignments, similar to sentence-combining exercises but with tighter controls, are used to increase syntactic fluency, to promote control of sentence-level errors, and to build student confidence. The ordered exercises move from copying texts verbatim to replacement exercises (for example, past for a present tense in a paragraph) to minimal sentence-combining to full sentence-combining essays. Gorrell admitted that the exercises have aspects of behaviorism; however, the exercises do help build confidence that, in turn, promotes error-free prose. Susan V. Wall in *A Sequence of Assignments for Basic Writing* (1980) explained a set of assignments she used with BW students to help them see that writers write differently on the same topic, that writing is involved with other life experiences (for example, decision making), that students' behavior can be classified, and that language used to describe an event is not the same as the event. Wall encouraged students to criticize their own work, to see specific purpose to the assignments, and to increase their ability to generalize.

The ability to generalize is an important skill for writers, because it is at the heart of academic writing. In her research document *Respecting the Learner's Expertise* (1979), Elaine O. Lees detailed a sequence of five writing assignments that move students from narration to generalization to abstract thinking, using the students' experiences with and feelings about writing as the subject matter. Like Marilyn Samuels (1976), Lees recognized that BW students have marked opinions about writing that can be tapped as a ready source for subject matter. Lees's goals with these exercises were to make BW students realize that good writing doesn't spring from some writers unbidden and to move the students from an ability to narrate specific events to the ability to make generalizations about events and, eventually, ideas.

BW students are not the only students who can benefit from sequentially ordered assignments. In his article "The Sense and Nonsense as a Design for Sequential Writing Assignments" (1970), William E. Coles, Jr., detailed a sequence of 35 writing assignments designed to help students discover themselves. Coles wanted his students to see language "as the basis of experience and identity" (p. 28); therefore, his assignments, although chronological, are individual to each student. The student, not the instructor, provides continuity within the sequence. Coles used much the same approach in describing a writing course for science majors in *The Plural I* (1978).

Marilyn Katz in "From Self-Analysis to Academic Analysis" (1978) reported on a technique that Petrie, Lees, Coles, and others have also used: assignments that use students' personal experience to develop analytic thinking and, ultimately, academic writing skills. Katz complained that creative writing assignments are perceived as more interesting than expository writing assignments; therefore, she sought to elicit creativeness and self-expression in a sequence of expository assignments. The five-essay sequence includes a description of a place and its meaning to the student, a description and analysis of a relationship to another person, a description and analysis of an internal conflict, an analysis of an experience that resulted in the formation of a strong opinion, and a term paper with a topic of the student's own choice.

In "Teaching Creative Business Letters and Memos" (1982), Joan T. Knapp created an interesting variation on the sequence idea. Instead of a sequence of writing assignments, she gave each class member a different letter to write. When put together, the letters form a sequence, a narrative of some realistic situation such as applying for several jobs, being offered two jobs, accepting one and rejecting the other, losing the job one accepted, trying to get back the job one has rejected, and so on. Knapp argued, sometimes implicitly, that assignments must be realistic and must address three aspects mentioned in the literature: audience, mode, and purpose. Letters of application are the bases for at least two other writing-assignment sequences, one described by Michael E.

Walsh in "Teaching the Letter of Application" (1977) and one by Karen L. Pelz in "A Business Writing Sequence for a General Writing Course" (1981). Pelz based her assignments on a model used by James Britton in *The Development of Writing Abilities, 11–18* (1975), which emphasizes a variety of modes and potential audiences.

In "Student as Staff Writer, Instructor as Editor" (1981), Jack E. Tohtz and John L. Marsh are concerned with how "a writing course can be presented so that the student's performance is centered in the writer's reality" (p. 327). Tohtz and Marsh, to get their students to write detailed, audience-directed essays, set up a situation where the students are reporters for an in-class newspaper. Their sequential writing assignments, therefore, not only have a clear audience and establish a clear need for information, but they also support the key elements of the communication process: the writer, the writing, the editorial function, and the reader.

Peter M. Schiff used a variation on this situational context for writing in "Revising the Writing Conference" (1978). He described seven assignments he used in writing conferences to help students create, write, and revise their essays. Focusing on shared activities, the assignments include sharing journal entries; revising one another's five-minute freewriting exercises; watching the teacher compose; talking out a topic; jotting down the key ideas, writing the topic out; discussing values; rearranging sentences from a published text; and conferring with more than one student at a time. Schiff's exercises, like Tohtz and Marsh's, are designed to show students that writing not only is essentially communication, but it is also a process that everyone can learn to do better.

Several writing teachers have expanded the idea of sequential writing assignments into complete course descriptions. In "A Journalistic Approach to Composition" (1970), Marilyn M. Kennedy argued that writing from models in an anthology of readings is inadequate because 17- and 18-year-old BW students have little sense of involvement in these readings. A writing course needs to develop the students' abilities to communicate an idea to an audience. She, therefore, described a writing course that uses a variety of exercises, some written and some oral, to encourage students' abilities to observe and report details. Robert Perrin's position in "Rhetoric of the Printed Media" (1982), in many ways, complements Kennedy's. Noting that students tend to think printed essays are sacred and cannot be criticized, Perrin set up a thematic focus for his class and all of his writing assignments that did not depend upon an anthology of various essays. By using the book *Mass Media and the Popular Arts* (1971) by F. Rissover and D. C. Buch, Perrin claimed that he could give exercises that avoid the problem faced by many writing teachers: their classes talk about the different essays, but the content of the course is writing. Michael P. Orth outlined in "An Advanced Composition Course Aimed at Publication" (1976) a ten-week course for students who are not professional writers. Allowing the students to write on any subject or field, Orth had them produce 1,000- to 2,000-word essays, filled with facts and details and directed to particular publications. All of the articles were sent off for consideration by these publications, with about a 20 percent success rate. What the course does for the assignments is to make very clear the audience and the purpose.

Ruth Thaler in "Art and the Written Word" (1980) and Robert DiYanni in "Sound and Sense" (1980) described unique courses they have tried that use art and music, respectively, as the material and method for class. Thaler noted that at the New School of Liberal Arts (CUNY) each course is used to teach writing. Although the goal of her assignments is not the formal essay, Thaler's five-assignment sequence requires written exposition as well as three-dimensional presentations. The students begin writing without words, writing an autobiography in Quipa knots. Next, they complete self-portraits and self-descriptions to develop their skills in observation and understanding. Third, they write and describe a drawing of a hand on a wall. Then they create in clay a contemporary fertility figure, sketching the figure from three viewpoints and writing about the figure. Finally, they make a clay pot dedicated to a personality from the ancient world; their writing assignment is to explain the pot. Thus Thaler tries to fuse art and writing in one course. DiYanni described a more traditional writing course that uses music as its subject matter. He speculated that there are four important connections between writing and music: both center on an impulse to express; both must have shape (form) to create sense (meaning); both "play" (music with themes; writing with words); and both are shared acts (performer-listener; writer-reader).

Although not designed as a sequence of assignments or a complete course description, Littleton Long's anthology *Writing Exercises from Exercise Exchange* (1976) covers most phases and types of writing (for example, pre-writing, diction, essays, style, research papers, re-writing). Of the 56 articles in this text, several merit specific mention. Henry Person's "Pertinence in the Outline" describes an exercise that requires students to restate or dismiss various supporting statements from an outline he supplied the class. Walker Gibson's "How Do You Define 'Ceiling'?" is an exercise in diction using different points of view to define *ceiling*. James Stronks's "Coherence in the Paragraph" asks students to unscramble a paragraph comparing Mark Twain and Abraham Lincoln. Richard P. Benton presented students with a rhetorical form that they might not have encountered before, "The Chinese Eight-Legged Essay." After explaining the form and giving the students an example of an essay written to conform with it, Benton had the students write a Chinese eight-legged essay. Donald M. Murray's "Description" detailed several exercises Murray characterized as "finger exercises" to help students learn how to add descriptive details to their writing. Elmer F. Suderman's "Doing Research on Words" is a prototype assignment in word history.

Research Papers and Library Papers

As reported earlier, Arapoff-Cramer (1971) found in her survey of university professors that research papers are an important form of academic writing for students to learn. Nonetheless, many composition teachers have steered away from research papers, preferring instead to teach analytic skills through argumentation and analysis. Several instructors, however, have taught research papers and library papers with some success. Many vary the method and/or the amount of control over the materials that the students use; nevertheless, the authors implicitedly or explicitly give a format for research papers that matches Arapoff-Cramer's findings: an introduction that states the paper's purpose, a review of the literature, a summary or statement of findings, and a bibliography.

Bryant Mangum in "The Whole Is Not Equal to the Sum of the Parts" (1982) explained a sequence of biography assignments to develop research skills. He encouraged students to make research a science and appreciate the blending of research material as an art. Ann Rayne discussed in "Précis Writing" (1976) a controlled assignment that links careful reading to précis writing, a skill required in most research papers.

Two composition teachers in separate articles also used controlled exercises to teach the library paper. George R. Bramer in "Freedom and Control in the Research Paper" (1969) realized that different students will have different levels of ability with research materials. Therefore, he developed research paper topics from basic texts in the class and assigned students to different levels for their research; the higher the level, the less control the teacher exerts. Bramer argued that students consistently move to higher levels with their increasing confidence. Peter L. Paulson described in "Seven Methods for Helping Students Find Theme Topics" (1982) seven specific methods that help students not only find research paper topics but also diverse topics for other themes: the library browsing table, student observation, mass media, library browsing hour, classroom browsing hour, mock argument, and ambiguous stimulus.

H. O. Brogan in "The Freshman Research Paper" (1960) argued against controlled materials, because they don't teach research skills completely. He then detailed the six traditional stages commonly found in research-paper assignments that he believes form a better basis to teach this form of writing: approving the topic, checking the preliminary bibliography cards, reviewing the note cards, approving the sentence outline, examining the rough draft, and grading the final draft.

Believing that a research paper is essentially an opinion paper, Colleen Marshall in "A System for Teaching College Freshmen to Write a Research Paper" (1978) detailed eight steps plus writing assignments that demonstrate how to write a research paper: the instructor teaches reading skills, the students select a "universal" topic (for example, family, education), the instructor assigns the topic in a question form, the students write an opinion paper on the question, the students revise the opinion paper to tighten its logic, the students list questions implicit in the opinion paper, the instructor introduces the students to the library material and research techniques, and finally, the students write their assigned research paper from the opinion paper's topic. Marshall noted three problems with this method: students are reluctant to reveal much about themselves, particularly their opinions; a few students have difficulty grasping how reasons lead to conclusions; and students have a tendency to ignore research materials that don't support their theses.

Other composition teachers have discussed research topics that they feel are successful. Louise Flavin in "Investigating Birthdays" (1982) found that by writing a research paper on what happened the day they were born, the students learn to use the library, to limit their topics, and to formulate a clear thesis statement. William P. Woods, in the detailed research document *Freshman Histories* (1977), also used the topic of what happened on the students' birthdays; however, he provided additional information about the results of the topic. Students have to demonstrate the importance of their birthdays; thus they must address the problem of purpose in their reports. They must also consider themselves as historians; therefore, they must develop a voice or persona. Furthermore, the students realize that they are writing a paper that will be presented to their peers; as a result, they must develop a clear sense of audience and how to convey information to that audience.

Noting that some of his colleagues believe his assignment is unscholarly and lacks "high moral seriousness," Keith W. Kraus detailed his version of a research-paper topic in "The Research Paper Revisited" (1971). In freshman English, the typical research-paper topic, a discussion of a novel such as *Moby Dick*, tends to end up in patchwork essays that are uninteresting to both the students and the instructors. Therefore, Kraus initially gave his students the assignment to find out, in the *New York Times*, what happened on the day they were born. He then asked them to find out, again from the *Times*, the circumstances surrounding the death of a famous person such as Red Cassidy, Al Capone, or William Guldensuppe "Whose dismembered body was found over a course of three weeks, except the head" (p. 18). His students quickly discovered that doing research is not just a matter of finding an article and copying down its main points; they had to make determinations about what material is valuable and what material is superficial, about who is telling the truth and who is not in a report, and about how to blend material when they had an abundance of information and potentially conflicting research. Perhaps the most inventive of the research-paper topics, Kraus's article again unites the criteria necessary for a good writing assignment: audience, purpose, and a clear statement of mode.

References

Arapoff-Cramer, Nancy. "A Survey of University Writing Assignments." *CCC*, 22 (1971), 161–68.

Bettelheim, Bruno. *The Informed Heart: Autonomy in a Mass Age*. New York: Macmillan, 1960.

Bigler, Mary. "Creative Writing Ideas." *EJ*, 69, No. 9 (1980), 91–92.

Bloom, Lynn Z. "Intruder in the Classroom: The Remembrance of Things Present." *JETT*, 4, No. 2 (1971), 29–31.

————. "Milieus, Modes, and Messages: Writing about Verbal and Non-Verbal Communication." *JETT*, 9, No. 1-2 (1976), 23–29.

Braddock, Richard, Richard Lloyd-Jones, and Lowell Schoer. *Research in Written Composition*. Urbana, Ill.: NCTE, 1963.

Bramer, George R. "Freedom and Control in the Research Paper." *CCC*, 2 (1969), 352–59.

Brashers, H. C. "Teaching Descriptive Style." *JETT*, 1, No. 2 (1968), 1–12.

Britton, James. "The Composing Processes and the Functions of Writing." In *Research on Composing*. Ed. Charles R. Cooper and Lee Odell. Urbana, Ill.: NCTE, 1978, pp. 13–28.

————, et al. *The Development of Writing Abilities, 11–18*. London: Macmillan, 1975.

Brogan, H. O. "The Freshman Research Paper." *CCC*, 9 (1960), 224–26.

Burton, Dwight, et al. "Assigning Writing." In *Teaching English Today*. Boston: Houghton Mifflin, 1975, pp. 140–42.

Ciciotte, Joseph. "The Sense Image in *A Death in the Family*: A Unit on Creative Writing." *EJ*, 69, No. 9 (1980), 26–28.

Coe, Richard M., and Kris Gutierrez. "Using Problem-Solving Procedures and Process Analysis to Help Students with Writing Problems" *CCC*, 32 (1981), 262–71.

Cohen, B. Bernard. "Writing Assignments in a Course with Readings in Imaginative Literature." *CCC*, 19 (1968), 225–29.

Coles, William E., Jr. "The Sense of Nonsense as a Design for Sequential Writing Assignments." *CCC*, 21 (1970), 27–34.

————. *The Plural I: The Teaching of Writing*. New York: Holt, Rinehart, Winston, 1978.

Commission on English. *Freedom and Discipline in English: Report of the Commission on English*. New York: College Entrance Examination Board, 1975.

Davis, Ken. "The Circle Game: A Heuristic for Discovering Rhetorical Situations." *CCC*, 29 (1978), 285–87.

Dean, Terry. "Causal, Not Casual: An Advance Organizer for Cause-and-Effect Compositions." In *Structuring for Success in the English Classroom*. Ed. Candy Carter. Urbana, Ill.: NCTE, 1982, pp. 92–97.

Dietrich, Julia C. "Giving Evidence: A Framework for Student Writers." *EX E*, 23 No. 1 (1978), 17–19.

DiYanni, Robert. "Sound and Sense: Writing about Music." *JBW*, 2 (1980), 62–71.

Donlan, Dan. *Textbook Writing Assignments in Three Content Areas*. 1976. ERIC ED 123 635.

Donovan, Timothy R. "Seeing Students as Writers." *C&T*, 1 (1978), 13–16. Rpt. in *The Writing Teacher's Sourcebook*. Ed. Gary Tate and Edward P. J. Corbett. New York: Oxford University Press, 1981, pp. 220–23.

Douglas, Krystan V. "Yet Another Reason Not to Write a 500 Word Essay: A Biography Is Better." *CCC*, forthcoming.

Ede, Lisa S. "Oral History: One Way Out of the Slough of Despair." *CCC*, 28 (1977), 380–82.

Elbow, Peter. *Writing without Teachers*. New York: Oxford University Press, 1973.

Esch, Robert M. "A Method of Teaching the Critical Essay." *JETT*, 1, No. 1 (1968), 16–18.

Farley, Sara R. "Constructing Composition Assignments." In *Structuring for Success in the English Classroom*. Ed. Candy Carter. Urbana, Ill.: NCTE, 1982, pp. 98–101.

Farrell, Edmund J. "The Beginning Begets: Making Composition Assignments." *EJ*, 58, No. 3 (1969), 428–31. Rpt. in *Rhetoric and Composition: A Sourcebook for Teachers*. Ed. Richard L. Graves. Rochelle Park, N.J.: Hayden, 1976, pp. 220–24.

Feaster, Sharon. "Structuring for Composition." In *Structuring for Success in the English Classroom*. Ed. Candy Carter. Urbana, Ill.: NCTE, 1982, pp. 73–78.

Field, John P., and Robert H. Weiss. *Cases for Composition*. Boston: Little, Brown, 1979.

Figg, Kristen M., "Introducing Invention Techniques: A Middle School Writing Assignment." *EJ*, 69, No. 8 (1980), 60–61.

Fisher, Charles F. "Being There Vicariously by Case Studies." In *On College Teaching*. Ed. Ohmer Milton and Associates. San Francisco: Jossey-Bass, 1978, pp. 258–85.

Flavin, Louise. "Investigating Birthdays: A Library Research Project." *EX E*, 27, No. 1 (1982), 26–27.

Francoz, M. J. "The Logic of Question and Answer: Writing as Inquiry." *CE*, 41 (1979), 336–39.

Glasser, Marc. "Food for Thought—And Writing." *EJ*, 71, No. 7 (1982), 56–57.

Gorrell, Donna. "Controlled Composition for Basic Writers." *CCC*, 32 (1981), 308–16.

Graves, Richard L. "CEHAE: Five Steps for Teaching Writing." *EJ*, 61, No. 5 (1972), 696–701. Rpt. in *Rhetoric and Composition: A Sourcebook for Teachers*. Ed. Richard L. Graves. Rochelle Park, N.J.: Hayden, 1976, pp. 239–45.

Gruber, William E. " 'Servile Copying' and the Teaching of English Composition." *CE*, 39 (1977), 491–97.

Hoffman, Eleanor M., and John P. Schifsky. "Designing Writing Assignments." *EJ*, 66, No. 9 (1977), 41–45.

Irmscher, William F. *Teaching Expository Writing*. New York: Holt, Rinehart, Winston, 1979.

Jacko, Carol M. "Small-Group Triad: An Instructional Mode for the Teaching of Writing." *CCC*, 29 (1978), 290–92.

Jenkins, Cheryl S. "The Writing Assignment: An Obstacle or a Vehicle?" *EJ*, 69, No. 9 (1980), 66–69.

Jordan, John E. "Theme Assignments: Servants or Masters?" *CCC*, 14 (1963), 51–53. Rpt. in *Teaching Freshman Composition*. Ed. Gary Tate and Edward P. J. Corbett. New York: Oxford University Press, 1967, pp. 227–30.

Judy, Stephen M. "The Assignment Makers." In *Explorations in the Teaching of Secondary English*. By Stephen N. Judy. New York: Dodd Mead, 1974, pp. 96–99.

Karrfalt, David H. "Writing Teams: From Generating Composition to Generating Communication." *CCC*, 22 (1971), 377–78.

Katz, Marilyn. "From Self-Analysis to Academic Analysis: An Approach to Expository Writing." *CE*, 40 (1978), 288–92.

Keech, Catharine, and Susan Thomas. *Compendium of Promising Practices in Composition Instruction. Evaluation of the Bay Area Writing Project*. 1979. ERIC ED 191 058.

Kelly, Kathleen. "Persuasion for Survival." *EX E*, 27, No. 1 (1982), 23–26.

Kennedy, Marilyn M. "A Journalistic Approach to Composition." *CCC*, 21 (1970), 386–90.

Kepes, Richard D. "Write Your Own Obituary." In *Writing Exercises from Exercise Exchange*. Ed. Littleton Long. Urbana, Ill.: NCTE, 1976, pp. 88–89.

Kilburn, Patrick E. "Every Man His Own Pedagogue: A Project in the Teaching of Freshman Composition." *JHE*, 32 (1962), 89–95. Rpt. in *Teaching Freshman Composition*. Ed. Gary Tate and Edward P. J. Corbett. New York: Oxford University Press, 1967, pp. 238–44.

King, Barbara. "The Waiting Game: Structuring the English Class for Prewriting." In *Structuring for Success in the English Classroom*. Ed. Candy Carter. Urbana, Ill.: NCTE, 1982, pp. 84–87.

Kinneavy, James L. *A Theory of Discourse*. Englewood Cliffs, N.J.: Prentice-Hall, 1971; rpt. New York: Norton, 1980.

Kitzhaber, Albert R. *Themes, Theories, and Therapies: The Teaching of Writing in College*. New York: McGraw-Hill, 1963.

Knapp, Joan T. "Teaching Creative Business Letters and Memos." In *Structuring for Success in the English Classroom*. Ed. Candy Carter. Urbana, Ill.: NCTE, 1982, pp. 88–91.

Kilin, Phillip C. "Some Ways of Teaching Unity." *JETT*, 3, No. 3 (1970), 1–3.

Kraus, W. Keith. "The Research Paper Revisited." *JETT*, 4, No. 3 (1971), 16–21.

Kroeger, Fred. "A Freshman Paper Based on the Words of Popular Songs." *CCC*, 19 (1968), 337–40.

Kupfer, Fern. "Ruining Perfectly Good Writing." *CCC*, 32 (1981), 329–33.

Larsen, Richard B. "Back to the Board." *CCC*, 29 (1978), 292–94.

Larson, Richard L. "Teaching Before We Judge: Planning Assignments in Composition." *The Leaflet*, 66, No. 1 (1967), 3–15. Rpt. in *Teaching High School English*. Ed. Gary Tate and Edward P. J. Corbett. New York: Oxford University Press, 1970, pp. 207–18. Rpt. in *The Writing Teacher's Sourcebook*. Ed. Gary Tate and Edward P. J. Corbett. New York: Oxford University Press, 1981, pp. 208–19.

———. "Training New Teachers of Composition in Administering Theme Assignments." *JETT*, 1, No. 2 (1968), 1–5.

Ledger, Marshall. "Analogy: A Lesson in Composition." *EX E*, 21, No. 2 (1977), 8–12.

Lees, Elaine O. *Respecting the Learner's Expertise: Assignments That Ask Students to Write about Composing*. 1979. ERIC ED 184 129.

Lindemann, Erika. "Making and Evaluating Writing Assignments." In *A Rhetoric for Writing Teachers*. By Erika Lindemann. New York: Oxford University Press, 1982, pp. 203–35.

Long, Littleton, ed. *Writing Exercises from Exercise Exchange*. Urbana, Ill.: NCTE, 1976.

Macrorie, Ken. *Telling Writing*. 2nd ed. Rochelle Park, N.J.: Hayden, 1976.

Mangum, Bryant. "The Whole Is Not Equal to the Sum of the Parts: An Approach to Teaching the Research Paper." *EX E*, 27, No. 1 (1982), 17–20.

Marshall, Colleen. "A System for Teaching College Freshmen to Write a Research Paper." *CE*, 40 (1978), 87–89.

McCrimmon, James M. "A Cumulative Sequence in Composition." *EJ*, 55, No. 4 (1966), 425–34. Rpt. in *Rhetoric and Composition: A Sourcebook for Teachers*. Ed. Richard L. Graves. Rochelle Park, N.J.: Hayden, 1976, pp. 225–38.

Moffett, James. *Teaching the Universe of Discourse*. New York: Houghton Mifflin, 1968.

Morrissey, Thomas J. "The Five-Minute Entry: A Writing Exercise for Large Classes in All Disciplines." *EX E*, 27, No. 1 (1982), 41–42.

Mulligan, James S. " 'A Short Vision': Stimulus for Writing." *CCC*, 22 (1971), 260–61.

Orth, Michael P. "An Advanced Composition Course Aimed at Publication." *CCC*, 27 (1976), 210–12.

"Our Readers Write: What's a Sure-Fire Composition Assignment for Non-Sure-Fire Students?" *EJ*, 69, No. 8 (1980), 62–69.

Pattison, Joseph. "How to Write an F Paper." *CE*, 25 (1963), 38–39. Rpt. Urbana, Ill.: National Council of Teachers of English, 1963.

Paulson, Peter L. "Seven Methods for Helping Students Find Theme Topics." *TETYC*, 9, No. 1 (1982), 31–34.

Pelz, Karen L. "A Business Writing Sequence for a General Writing Course." *EX E*, 25, No. 2 (1981), 31–32.

Perrin, Robert. "Rhetoric of the Printed Media: An Approach to Composition." *EX E*, 26, No. 2 (1982), 15–18.

Petrie, Ann. "Teaching the Thinking Process in Essay Writing." *JBW*, 1, No. 2 (1976), 60–67.

Platt, Michael D. "Writing Journals in Courses." *CE*, 37 (1975), 408–11.

Proctor, Betty Jane. "The Rhetoric of Satire: Analyzing in Freshman English." *EX E*, 26, No. 2 (1982), 18–20.

Proffitt, Edward. "Writing for Reading." *EE*, 23, No. 1 (1978), 3–9.

Raines, Ann. *Writing and Learning Across the Curriculum: The Experience of a Faculty Seminar*. 1979. ERIC ED 176 327.

Rayne, Ann. "Précis Writing: An Approach to Basic Composition." *CCC*, 27 (1976), 403–16.

Rissover, F. and D. C. Buch. *Mass Media and the Popular Arts*. New York: McGraw-Hill, 1971.

Rosen, Robert C. "Teaching the Thesis Statement Through Description." *EX E*, 25, No. 2 (1981), 5–6.

Rubin, Lois. "Moving from Prewriting into Composing." *EX E*, 25, No. 2 (1981), 12–17.

Samuels, Marilyn S. "Choice for a First-Essay Topic." *CCC*, 27 (1976), 395–96.

Schiff, Peter M. "Revising the Writing Conference." *CCC*, 29 (1978), 294–96.

Schwab, David. "Writing as Thinking: Solving the Mystery of Deduction." *EX E*, 25, No. 2 (1981), 18–21.

Shackelford, Lynne. "A Switch in Point of View." *EX E*, 26, No. 2 (1981), 31–32.

Shuman, R. Baird. "They Only Think They Have Nothing to Write About!" *EX E*, 21, No. 2 (1977), 38–45.

Smith, Ronald L. "A Twenty-Minute Exercise for in-Class Essays." *EX E*, 25, No. 2 (1981), 33–34.

Snyder, Philip. "Working 1-002: A Theme Course for Freshman Composition." *CCC*, 33 (1982), 315–17.

Soven, Margot K. "Helping Students Generalize, Specify, Clarify: A Sequence for Writing Assignments." In *Structuring for Success in the English Classroom*. Ed. Candy Carter. Urbana, Ill.: NCTE, 1982, pp. 102–16.

Stewart, Donald C. "Practical Work for Advanced Composition Students." *CCC*, 31 (1980), 81–83.

Strugala, Richard A. "Values Clarification Through Writing." *EX E*, 27, No. 1 (1982), 37–39.

Tate, Gary, and Edward P. J. Corbett. *Teaching Freshman Composition*. New York: Oxford University Press, 1967.

Taylor, Pat E. "Teaching Creativity in Argumentation." *CE*, 39 (1977), 507–19.

Tedlock, David. "The Case Approach to Composition." *CCC*, 32 (1981), 253–61.

———, and Paul Jarvie. *Casebook Rhetoric: A Problem-Solving Approach to Composition*. New York: Holt, Rinehart, Winston, 1981.

Terkel, Studs. *Hard Times*. New York: Pantheon, 1970.

———. *Working*. New York: Pantheon, 1974.

Thaler, Ruth. "Art and the Written Word." *JBW*, 2, No. 4 (1980), 72–81.

Throckmorton, Helen J. "Do Your Writing Assignments Work? Checklist for a Good Writing Assignment." *EJ*, 69, No. 8 (1980), 56–59.

Tierney, Gilbert, and Stephen N. Judy. "The Assignment Makers." *EJ*, 61, No. 2 (1972), 265–69.

Tohtz, Jack E., and John L. Marsh. "Student as Staff Writer, Instructor as Editor: A Situational Context for Teaching Writing." *CCC*, 32 (1981), 327–29.

Wall, Susan V. *A Sequence of Assignments for Basic Writing: Teaching to Problems 'Beyond the Sentence'*. 1980. ERIC ED 186 937.

Walsh, E. Michael. "Teaching the Letter of Application." *CCC*, 28 (1977), 374–76.

Warren, Barbara L. "Journal Writing—The Quiet Time." In *Structuring for Success in the English Classroom*. Ed. Candy Carter. Urbana, Ill.: NCTE, 1982, pp. 107–10.

Weiss, Robert H. *Assignments That Succeed: A Case Approach to Composition*. 1978. ERIC ED 161 060.

———, and John P. Field. *Cases for Composition: A Theoretical Model for Writing Instruction*. 1979. ERIC ED 172 194.

Wess, Robert C. "Written Logodrama: The Projected Experience Essay." *EX E*, 26, No. 1 (1982), 3–5.

Wiener, Harvey S. "Making and Carrying Out Assignments." In *The Writing Room: A Resource Book for Teachers of English*. By Harvey S. Wiener. New York: Oxford University Press, 1981, pp. 11–58.

Wilson, Dawn M. "Steppingstones to Success: A Journal-Based Composition Course." In *Structuring for Success in the English Classroom*. Ed. Candy Carter. Urbana, Ill.: NCTE, 1982, pp. 67–72.

Woods, William P. *Freshman Histories: A Basic Research Assignment*. 1977. ERIC ED 155 689.

Young, Richard E. "Paradigms and Problems: Needed Research in Rhetorical Invention." In *Research in Composing*. Ed. Charles R. Cooper and Lee Odell. Urbana, Ill.: NCTE, 1978, pp. 29–47.

———, Alton L. Becker, and Kenneth Pike. *Rhetoric: Discovery and Change*. New York: Harcourt, Brace, World, 1970.

Part III

The Basics

Basic Writing

GLYNDA A. HULL AND DAVID J. BARTHOLOMAE

Mina Shaughnessy spoke of basic writing as a frontier, a territory for the most part uncharted, through which teachers must clear their own paths and for which they must devise their own maps.[1] Shaughnessy offered *Errors and Expectations* (1977) as a guide for teachers who took up this "frontier challenge," warning that the book was "certain to have the shortcomings of other frontier maps, with doubtless a few rivers in the wrong place and some trails that end nowhere" (p. 4).

In this chapter we survey other "frontier maps" for teaching and research in basic writing, work conducted mostly during the last ten years, but particularly that done since Shaughnessy compiled the first bibliography on basic writing for Gary Tate's *Teaching Composition* (1976).

The guides we offer in this chapter are still frontier maps that are apt to include some misplaced rivers and deadends. This is true for a number of reasons, perhaps the most important being that we don't yet know whom basic writers are, and thus we are not sure that we are all studying the same phenomenon. Not only do basic writers vary from school to school, as Mina Shaughnessy noted, but we can be sure that they vary from research project to research project as well, for there is no general agreement on the particular aspects of writing that indicate a basic writer. There are also distinctions yet to be sorted out between basic *writing* and basic *writers*, the problem here involving the extent to which we are justified in assigning students particular traits based on an analysis of their essays.

Given the complexities that characterize the study of our population, it is not likely that there will soon be a universally accepted definition of basic writers

1. We have followed Shaughnessy (1976; 1977) in calling students who arrive at college less proficient than is desirable for their age and educational level "basic writers," and their instruction, "basic writing."

and their prose. What we can achieve more quickly, however, is an understanding of the range of writing and writers we now call "basic," and we can assess the methods we use for gathering such information.

If more were known about what we refer to as "developmental" issues—about other factors besides instruction that affect the process of becoming a proficient writer and how we view it—we would be in a better position to teach inexperienced adult writers. However, with developmental issues, even more so than with descriptions of population, we stand at a frontier's edge. We do not yet know, for example, when it is profitable to view the difficulties our basic writers experience with composing solely in terms of writing, as writing problems, or when they should be viewed in conjunction with something else, with, say, the processes of intellectual maturation. In fact, connections between such issues of development and basic writers and their instruction have just recently begun to be posited. We trust these explorations will continue—many consider them crucial for curriculum planning—but continue with the caution due any application of one discipline's research findings to another.

The greatest part of the literature on basic writing is pedagogical: it consists of program descriptions, suggestions for curriculum planning, and teaching techniques. This may seem peculiar, given the little we say is known about whom basic writers are and what influences writing development. It may seem more peculiar still, since we aren't really certain about the extent to which basic writers actually require instructional methods that are different from those used to teach other writers, or what those methods should be. In another way, however, the abundance of literature on basic writing pedagogy is not peculiar at all: although attempts are being made to study the population and the prose, teachers still must teach. Nor is it surprising that these articles on programs and pedagogy vary widely, for they are borne of the same diversity as descriptions of population.

We may in the future direct our efforts toward determining which approaches to the teaching of basic writing are successful, identifying methods best suited for our particular purposes and students, or perhaps creating new and better methods. These processes can best take place, however, when we achieve more certainty about whom basic writers are and how writing skills develop and when we better understand and begin to assess the range of approaches that are now before us.

Population/Prose

There is a large and growing body of literature on students who have greater-than-average difficulty with college tasks. It details their racial and socio-economic backgrounds, describes their educational and career interests, and isolates their characteristics as learners. In this literature, students are given different names—"underprepared," "non-traditional," "underachiever"—and these labels, to an extent, refer to different populations with academic woes caused by different factors. The best overview of such literature is a recent book by Martha Maxwell, *Improving Student Learning Skills* (1979), for in order to place her text among the many already written about low-achieving college students, Maxwell is careful to synthesize a great deal of research. As she pointed out, psychologists have for a long time taken an interest in why students fail in college. For an example of this early research, see the extensive anthology by M. Kornrich, *Underachievement* (1965).

The more recent literature on high-risk college students, however, has grown out of the open admissions era of the 1960s and 1970s, when schools began to welcome large numbers of students who formerly had had no expectations of higher education and little preparation for it. One of the best known chroniclers of the open admissions era has been Patricia Cross, who in *Beyond the Open Door* (1971) described "non-traditional" or "new" students and argued that we can't teach them by "handing down the old education of traditional students" (p. 158). Among the learner characteristics shared by many non-traditional students, Cross noted poor study habits, poor basic skills, and low academic ability in general. These students feel less comfortable with risk-taking and less confident in their abilities than do traditional students; they are motivated by pragmatic aims and are fearful of academic failure. Although they come, for the most part, from impoverished backgrounds, financially as well as educationally, they include many whose fathers have attended college. The majority are Caucasian, but ethnic minority groups are well represented in their ranks.

For related discussions by Cross, see *Accent on Learning* (1976) and *Adults as Learners* (1981). For related discussions by other researchers, we recommend R. W. Pitcher and B. Blaushild's *Why College Students Fail* (1970) and John Roueche and Jerry Snow's *Overcoming Learning Problems* (1977). Lawrence Kasden provided a useful summary of the findings of Cross and others in "An Introduction to Basic Writing" (1980).

We further recommend the following works that describe the educational experiences of younger, "non-traditional" students. John Holt wrote a set of brief sketches on elementary schoolchildren based on his patient and respectful observations of their learning; his *How Children Fail* (1964) ought to make teachers at any level more perceptive about their students' fears and rationalizations. *Letter to a Teacher [by] Schoolboys of Barbiana* (1970) is a set of vignettes on middle-class-oriented Italian schools composed from the point of jview of country schoolchildren. Poet-writer David Holbrook in *English for the Rejected* (1964) described "backward" children—those in the bottom of their secondary school classes in Britain—and told how he helped with their literacy training.

Beginning in 1953 with 338 American students who represented a cross-section of the population in an urban setting, Walter Loban studied their writing, listening, and speaking skills for 13 years, from kindergarten to high school graduation or age 18. His research report *Language Development* (1976) should be of particular interest to basic writing teachers, for it asked, as one of its major research questions, "What are the differences between pupils who rank high in proficiency with language and those who rank low?" (p. 2).

There have been a few surveys that polled students in college writing classes rather than the larger populations of underprepared or non-traditional students. To our knowledge, the earliest one that pertains to basic writing is William D. Baker's "Investigation of Characteristics of Poor Writers" (1954), followed by J. Woodward and A. Phillips's "Profile of the Poor Writer" (1967). More recently, Susan Wall and Anthony Petrosky reported the results of the survey "Freshmen Students and Revision" (1981), which included responses from two levels of basic writers on their attitudes toward and their practice of revision.

Augmenting this survey research on basic writing is a small corpus of articles on "cases"—descriptive portraits of representative student writers and their backgrounds and attitudes toward writing. Lynn Quitman Troyka in "Perspectives on Legacies and Literacy in the 1980s" (1982) wrote help-fully about the non-traditional students who made up her developmental writing classes at an urban community college. Troyka first offered writing samples and brief portraits and then explained the four "legacies" or resources these students brought with them to college. For her dissertation "Revision in a Rhetorical Context" (1982), Susan Wall followed three first-year college students, two of whom had been required to enroll in basic writing classes, through a semester of composition instruction, conducting bi-weekly inter-views on their written work. Although Wall found each student to have as much difficulty learning to use revision as invention, she thought the basic writers were more receptive to discovery writing than the better writers. Two teachers have given us portraits of individual students they consider repre-sentative of larger subgroups of writers: Bill Linn in "Psychological Variants of Success" (1978) and Joan Bolker in "Teaching Griselda to Write" (1979). Michael Kressy enabled us in "The Community College Student" (1971) to appreciate the particular virtues of that population.

Most of the information we have about basic writers comes not from demo-graphic studies or group portraits but from text analysis: we study the papers of our students and describe the texts we see in order to infer our writers' strengths and weaknesses. Mina Shaughnessy in "Basic Writing" (1976) provided the first list of features that characterize basic writers' texts:

First, they tend to produce, whether in impromptu or home assignments, small numbers of words with large numbers of errors (roughly from 15 to 35 errors per 300 words) that puzzle and alarm college teachers when they see them for the first time, errors with the so-called regular features of standard English (the past tense of regular verbs, for example, or the plural inflections of nouns), misspellings that appear highly idiosyncratic, syntactic snarls that often seem to defy analysis, and punctuation errors that reflect an unstable understanding of the conventions for marking off the boundaries of sentences and little or no acquaintance with the uses of colons, semi-colons, parentheses, or quotations marks. (p. 139)

Of other accounts that seem close kin to Shaughnessy's, which describe, that is, writing severely troubled by uncommon sentence-level error, David Bartholomae's description of a basic writer whose 200-word essay contained 40 errors stands out ("The Study of Error" [1980]), as does Patricia Lawrence's description of errors resulting from perceptual confusion ("Error's Endless Train" [1975]). What appears in many other accounts, however, is a sense of basic writing papers that aren't so bothered by error. Richard C. Gebhardt explained that his students at Findlay College are best characterized "by their lack of academic confidence and motivation, and by difficulties abstracting and generalizing from written materials" ("Training Basic Writing Teachers at a Liberal Arts College" [1981], p. 48). One can infer also from various descriptions of programs that many students begin basic writing as more accomplished writers than were Shaughnessy's students, although it should be noted that basic writing courses sometimes proceed using the same curricula as other writing courses— despite an assumed difference in students.

In view of our diverse definitions of *basic writing*, it is helpful to have an essay like Barbara Quint Gray and Virginia B. Slaughter's "Writing" (1980), which describes three levels of writing skills with reference to sample essays. For descriptions of the writing skills of particular groups of students, one can consult several dissertations. Andrea Lunsford ("An Historical, Descriptive, and Evaluative Study of Remedial English in American Colleges and Universities" [1977]) isolated a number of characteristics shared by her basic writers at Ohio State, including poor reading ability. For further discussion of this reading-writing connection, see M. A. Tang's "Study of the Relationships between the Reading and Writing Abilities of Underprepared College Students" (1979). Karen Hjelmervic in "Trends in the Written Products of General Writers, Basic Writers, and Basic Readers and Writers Across Four Points in Time" (1982) compared at several points during a term the syntax, error, and holistically determined quality of essays written by basic and non-basic writers at the University of Pittsburgh.

Shaughnessy's *Errors and Expectations* (1977) remains the most comprehensive description of basic writing error, particularly the varieties that flaw the texts of the most severely unprepared writers. Her most important contribution was method: she classified error not according to grammatical types (which are conveniently common labels but far removed from students' processes of making errors) but according to cause, or why writers make errors. This book, with its many examples, has the effect of bringing us as close as descriptions of texts can come to viewing the activity of writing from the position of basic writers. For an assessment of *Errors and Expectations*, see David Bartholomae's review (1979a).

Other studies that analyze error in order to describe writers include Dona Kagan's research on sentence-boundary errors, "Run-on and Fragment Sentences" (1980), and Collette Daiute's article "Psycholinguistic Foundations of the Writing Process" (1981). Daiute suggested, based on her application of a psycho-linguistic model of speech to writing, that there are connections to be made between error and memory.

A few studies on basic writing have taken syntax as their measure. Some of this research causes us to question the efficacy of using T-unit and clause length as parameters for separating basic writers and non-basic writers. See, for example, the ERIC report by Elizabeth House and William House, *Some Similarities and Differences between Compositions Written by Remedial and Non-remedial College Freshmen* (1980), and the essay by Ann Gebhard, "Writing Quality and Syntax" (1978). In "Oral and Written Discourse of Basic Writers" (1979), Roger Cayer and Renee Sacks analyzed syntax to determine whether basic writers rely on an oral repertoire in their writing. In part, they found that basic writers elaborated the predicates of discourse much more than the subjects, which they interpreted as a reliance on what Lev Vygotsky (1962) called "inner speech." Studies of syntax that include a fluency measure, or a tabulation of how many words writers produce, generally have found that basic writers write less than do other students. Glynda Hull showed, however, that basic writers' fluency can be easily increased by means of self-monitoring and goal-setting techniques; see her article "The Effects of Self-Management Strategies on Journal Writing by College Freshmen" (1981).

Treatments of cohesion pertinent to a discussion of basic writing include a paper by Stephen Witte and Lester Faigley, "Coherence, Cohesion, and Writing Quality" (1981). Tabulating cohesive ties in the 5 highest and 5 lowest rated essays from a pool of 90, Witte and Faigley found fewer ties in general and fewer types of ties in the poorer papers. In a dissertation study that had cohesion analysis at its center, "The Evolution of Text" (1981), Margaret Atwell studied the effects of "blind writing"—of not being able to see what one has written—on basic writers and traditional freshmen. By means of propositional analysis, she was able to conclude that traditional writers could access alternate strategies, like planning ahead, to compensate for blind writing, whereas basic writers could not. Hull and William Smith used the similar technology of having students write essays in invisible ink to describe the effects of not being able to re-read on basic writers' essays compared to graduate students' essays; see their ERIC report *Examining the Function of Visual Feedback in Text Production* (1982).

We know of three content analyses of basic writers' essays. First was Marie Lederman's "Comparison of Student Projections" (1973), a study of students' responses to a placement exam that asked them to write about what they would choose to be were they reincarnated. Lederman reported that many basic writers chose "something smaller and less powerful than a human being" (p. 685). Andrea Lunsford ("The Content of Basic Writers' Essays" [1980]) reported how her basic writers, in response to an essay topic on advertising, "presented themselves as more or less helpless victims" (pp. 279–80). In several interesting experimental manipulations, all a part of the same dissertation research study

("Addressing an Audience" [1979]), Marshall Atlas investigated the degree to which basic writers, compared to non-basic writers, were able to consider the requirements of an audience when writing letters. For a description of other discourse flaws likely to mar basic writers' papers, we recommend the final chapter of Shaughnessy's *Errors and Expectations* (1977), "Beyond the Sentence." Shaughnessy discussed "the absence of 'play' upon ideas, the restriction to oral strategies for elaboration, [and] the difficulty with framing and holding on to a central or organizing idea" (p. 236).

There has been a recent trend in composition research to analyze process apart from, or at least in conjunction with, written products. These analyses, several of which pertain to basic writing, have commonly taken the form of *protocols*, where writers verbalize their thoughts as they write, or *process observations*, where writers are observed as they write. Charles Stallard in "An Analysis of the Writing Behavior of Good Student Writers" (1974) found that better writers spent more time writing and pre-writing and stopped more frequently to re-read than did a comparison group. Stallard's findings are complemented by Sharon Pianko's research, reported in "A Description of the Composing Processes of College Freshmen Writers" (1979a) and in "Reflection" (1979b). Pianko thought it especially significant that her remedial writers did not appear to reflect as long or as often upon what they wrote as did traditional students; she concluded that their composing processes were underdeveloped.

Sondra Perl in "The Composing Processes of Unskilled College Writers" (1979) and "A Look at Basic Writers in the Process of Composing" (1980) found that the basic writers who took part in her case studies had internalized writing processes that were "highly elaborated" and "deeply embedded" (1979, p. 334), including recursive behaviors like editing that actually impeded composing rhythms. Likewise, Mike Rose found that students suffer from writing block at the hands of self-imposed, inappropriate or rigid rules and plans. See his "Rigid Rules, Inflexible Plans, and the Stifling of Language" (1980), and for other composing process studies, see the unpublished dissertations by Eleanor Stiles (1977), E. A. Metzger (1977), and J. J. Sweeder (1981).

Most of the research we have surveyed in this section has focused on describing basic writers and their prose at one or a few points in time—typically, at the beginning of a basic writing course or, more rarely, across a term. There are other approaches to definition, however, that take a larger view; they attempt, for example, not only to describe students' writing within a period of months but to understand how students' writing skills at age 18 reflect levels of intellectual maturity. In other words, they investigate how writing development can be informed by other kinds of development. Such approaches to definition may finally bring us to a richer understanding of why basic writers are basic writers and how we can best help their writing skills to progress. However, since researchers and scholars are only beginning to study writing from such perspectives, we cannot speak now with much authority about the place basic writing holds in overall writing development, but we can offer a survey of research that seems to afford reasonable starting places for those interested in thinking of basic writers and their prose in developmental terms.

Developmental Issues

The best-known developmental theory that provides a way of thinking about writing growth and that has, in fact, already been associated with basic writers was developed by Jean Piaget. In more than 30 books and 100 articles, Piaget reported his research on how children progress through a fixed sequence of stages during which the nature of their thinking changes in predictable ways. We suggest Herbert Ginsburg and Sylvia Opper's *Piaget's Theory of Intellectual Development* (1978) as a brief and readable introduction to basic concepts. Piaget's *Language and Thought of the Child* (1926) is a likely starting place for those interested in his perspectives on language growth. Those who want to make connections between adolescents' cognitive growth and writing should see some of the recent attempts to redefine Piaget's stage of formal operations, including articles by Piaget, "Intellectual Evolution from Adolescence to Adulthood" (1972); Everett Dulit, "Adolescent Thinking à la Piaget" (1972); and P. K. Arlin, "Cognitive Development in Adulthood" (1975).

There's a great deal of literature assessing both Piagetian theory and attempts to apply it to education. We recommend particularly Margaret Donaldson's *Children's Minds* (1979), a readable critique of aspects of Piagetian theory (she claimed, for example, that children can do more than their performance on Piagetian tasks implies) and a sensitively reasoned theory of why children fail in school (she assigned part of the cause to the trouble children have acquiring skills abstractly, divorced from everyday life). Deanna Kuhn provided a historical review and evaluation of educational programs based on Piagetian theory: "The Application of Piaget's Theory of Cognitive Development to Education" (1979). See also the collection of essays edited by L. S. Siegel and C. J. Brainerd, *Alternatives to Piaget* (1978), which reassesses Piagetian theory in light of new research; and Rainer Kluwe and Hans Spada, *Developmental Models of Thinking* (1980), which presents research on "state-of-the-art" developmental models, including Piaget's. These two collections are technical discussions; to benefit from them one would need to be acquainted generally with Piagetian theory.

Loren Barritt and Barry Kroll suggested some applications of Piagetian theory to writing in "Some Implications of Cognitive-Developmental Psychology for Research in Composing" (1978). For an example of the kind of research that might be generated from this perspective, see Barry Kroll's "Cognitive Egocentrism and the Problem of Audience Awareness in Written Discourse" (1978).

Andrea Lunsford, in "Cognitive Development and the Basic Writer" (1979), wrote about the relationship she saw between cognitive development and certain characteristics of basic writers that she inferred from their essays. Drawing primarily on Piaget and Vygotsky (1962), Lunsford suggested that the difficulty her remedial students experience with those writing assignments that require analysis and synthesis, or drawing inferences and forming concepts, is an indication that basic writers "have not attained that level of cognitive development which would allow them to form abstractions or conceptions" (p. 38). This idea that basic writers have yet to mature as thinkers—to reach the stage of cognitive growth Piaget labeled "formal operations"—has caught the attention of not a few teachers, enough so that some ground their thinking about pedagogy on cognitive stage theory. See, as an example of how Piagetian concepts have informed pedagogy, Robert Holland's "Piagetian Theory and the Design of Composing Assignments" (1976).

Another aspect of stage-model developmental theory treats ethical development. Piaget studied judgment in children by analyzing their attitudes toward game rules and identified three broad stages of development in relation to the practice of rules (*The Moral Judgment of the Child* [1932]). Lawrence Kohlberg, complementing and expanding Piaget's work, identified six stages of moral development by interviewing subjects about their reasons for choosing particular solutions to moral dilemmas ("Moral Development" [1968]). Ronald Duska and Mariellen Whelan explicated Piaget's and Kohlberg's theories in the brief, readable text *Moral Development* (1975). The appendices to this text reproduce the stories used by Piaget and the situations used by Kohlberg to evaluate and codify moral judgment. Susan Miller applied the Kohlberg model to writing in "Rhetorical Maturity" (1980). Miller told how she discovered that her students' unsuccessful struggle to write essays directed toward a universal audience, on a universal topic, might be explained by their present stage of intellectual and/ or moral development, as defined by Kohlberg.

In a developmental-stage model concerned with the intellectual and ethical development of college students, W. G. Perry, Jr., suggested a sequence of "perspectives" through which students pass as they move from viewing the world in polar terms of "we-right-good" versus "other-wrong-bad" to perceiving all knowledge and values as contextual and relativistic. Perry wrote that "at each step in this development the student sees himself, his instructors and even truth itself in very different terms" (*Forms of Intellectual and Ethical Development in the College Years* [1968], p. 214). C. Widick in "The Perry Scheme" (1977) applied Perry's nine stages to counseling, but we know of no applications to composition.

For a useful critique of stage-model developmental theory, see D. C. Phillips and Mavis Kelly's "Hierarchical Theories of Development in Education and Psychology" (1975). These authors claimed that hierarchical theories—including those associated with Piaget and Kohlberg—have not been scrutinized rigorously, and they specified some particular problems. Although writing teachers may not be interested in Phillips and Kelly's arguments about whether stages of growth are truly invariant, they are likely to find the article a healthy antidote to any uncritical applications of developmental theory to writing.

The theories of development we have mentioned thus far are primarily psychological rather than educational. For a discussion of the differences between descriptive as opposed to prescriptive theories of development, see Jerome Bruner, *Toward a Theory of Instruction* (1966). See also Kieran Egan, *Educational Development* (1979), who attempted to define a theory of development that is specifically educational rather than psychological and therefore of immediate practical value to teachers.

Some recent research conducted under the rubric of "instructional psychology" joins a penchant for studying psychological development with an interest in the instructional process. Robert Glaser described this new field in "Toward a Psychology of Instruction" (1978), the introductory essay to a series designed specifically to foster such work. One area in which this brand of research is being done, an area that seems to be of particular relevance to basic writing instructors, involves what is called "task analysis," whereby one attempts to understand the knowledge and skills needed to perform complex tasks, like playing chess or writing an essay. There's an interest, then, in describing the distinctions between experts and novices at a given point in time and across time developmentally. An example of task analysis can be found in Michelene Chi, Paul Feltovich, and Robert Glaser's essay about how students and professors solve physics problems, "Categorization and Representation of Physics Problems by Experts and Novices" (1981). In an essay from the second volume of Glaser's series, "From Conversation to Composition" (1982), Carl Bereiter and Marlene Scardamalia recounted a variety of resourceful experiments carried out over two years that led them to believe that a major part of writing development is the transition from a language system that is dependent on feedback to a system able to function autonomously. Their research technique of "procedural facilitation" might prove, when adapted, a useful methodology for researchers in basic writing.

These last two papers also represent the newest school of research on cognitive development. Called the "informational-processing approach," such research will be recognized most readily by its use of computers to create models of cognitive activity. For an excellent and thorough review of related literature, see Robert Siegler's "Information Processing Approaches to Development" (1983). For other examples of how an information-processing approach can guide research on composing, we suggest the work of Linda Flower and John Hayes, such as "Identifying the Organization of Writing Processes" (1980) and "Problem-Solving Strategies and the Writing Process" (1977). Their approach might profitably be applied to the study of basic writing.

As a final example of work being done on cognition that may prove useful in understanding basic writers, we mention what are called by psychologists "cognitive styles"—the habitual modes a person uses to solve problems, to remember, to think. Martha Maxwell offered a readable introduction to cognitive styles in *Improving Student Learning Skills* (1979). See H. A. Witkin and associates for a thorough review of research on two cognitive styles, "Field-Dependent and Field-Independent Cognitive Styles and Their Educational Implications" (1977). Patricia Cross in *Accent on Learning* (1976) noted the similarities between field-dependent thinkers and her "new students," pointing out, for example, that they are people-oriented and sensitive to social situations. In "Perspectives on Legacies and Literacy in the 1980s" (1982), Lynn Quitman Troyka suggested that instructors might accommodate their teaching styles to match the field-dependent learning styles of their basic writers.

For other applications to writing, see Susan Kaufman, who argued in her dissertation "Cognitive Styles and Writing" (1981) that cognitive style offers a way to understand why students respond differently to instruction, specifically composition. In another dissertation study, "The Relationship Between Errors in Standard Usage in Written Compositions of College Students and the Students' Cognitive Styles" (1980), Grace Cooper compared errors in essays written by black college students who tended toward field dependence or field independence; she found partial support for the hypothesis that cognitive styles manifest themselves in written language.

A second broad way to think about possible influences on the development of a basic writer is to consider the ways in which language learning is a socially influenced and, some would argue, socially controlled phenomenon. From this perspective, development is less usefully considered in terms of universal stage models and better thought of as context-dependent growth. In education circles, the sociologist who has been most recently influential is Basil Bernstein; his research on the relationship between speech "codes" and social classes has been interpreted and misinterpreted as an explanation for why working-class children fail to do as well in school as middle-class children. A good introduction to Bernstein's work is *Class, Codes, and Control* (Vol. 1, 1971), a series of essays recording the evolution of his ideas on restricted and elaborated speech codes. Basic writing teachers may find his chapter "A Critique of the Concept of Compensatory Education" of special interest.

Millicent Poole reviewed Bernstein's work, as well as presenting her own research on social classes and language functions in an Australian school, in *Social Class Contrasts in Linguistic, Cognitive, and Verbal Domains* (1975). Richard Ohmann in "Reflections on Class and Language" (1982) argued against Bernstein's explanation of the relationship between social class and speech codes. John Rouse in "The Politics of Composition" (1979) argued against what he saw as methods used to maintain the political and social status quo in Shaughnessy's *Errors and Expectations* (1977) and in so doing used Bernstein's speech codes to interpret the difficulties basic writers experience in composition classrooms.

Although Bernstein claimed not to consider the restricted speech code inherently inferior, some linguists are willing to make a connection between particular language varieties and cognitive ability; see, for example, John Nist, who in *Handicapped English* (1974) discussed the consequences of speaking what he called a "basilect." Nist's book was reviewed by Virginia M. Burke (1975).

Bernstein and Nist described language "codes" and "lects" as broad categories that do not necessarily correspond to social-class dialects. To teachers of English, however, the sociology of language has most often meant the study of dialects. For a thorough bibliography on dialects, we recommend Jenefer M. Giannasi's "Dialects and Composition" (1976) and limit our own references to highlights and recent publications.

The Center for Applied Linguistics recently made available a set of five booklets entitled *Dialects and Educational Equity* (1979) by Donna Christian and Walt Wolfram, each addressing, through a question-answer format, some of the social and educational issues surrounding language diversity and each providing brief bibliographies on its particular topics. The series can be ordered through NCTE.

The best-known essay on dialects, and probably the most recently influential, is William Labov's *Study of Nonstandard English* (1970). Available in a monograph published by NCTE, the essay argues that non-standard English is a language variety worthy of study in its own right. In this essay and in "The Logic of Nonstandard English," a chapter from his *Language in the Inner City* (1972), Labov did much to challenge long-guarded beliefs about non-standard speech, illustrating forcefully that non-standard dialects have their own internal logic and structure, rather than being linguistically inferior mutilations of standard speech. In the same tradition is the recent book by Nicholas Anastasiow and Michael Hanes *Language Patterns of Poverty Children* (1976), which aims to correct misconceptions about lower socio-economic children's language and learning potential. We found particularly interesting the authors' discussion of how children who speak non-standard dialects "reconstruct" or translate standard speech into their own vernacular, a process that these researchers take as evidence not of deficient language skills but "rapid mental functioning" (p. 3). This book begins with a readable introduction to research on language acquisition and development and language-deficit theories.

For an introductory anthology on how speaking relates to writing, see *Exploring Speaking-Writing Relationships* (1981), edited by Barry Kroll and Roberta Vann. In this anthology John C. Schafer offered a wide-ranging review of linguistic approaches to the study of oral and written language relationships, including the work of Ferdinand de Saussure, Leonard Bloomfield, Noam Chomsky, M.A.K. Halliday and R. Hasan, and Basil Bernstein; he drew also upon the theories of Walter Ong, David Olson, and P. Greenfield for other perspectives on how speaking and writing differ. In the same volume, we suggest Barry Kroll's essay for a developmental perspective on how the relationship between speaking and writing may change as children become more experienced language users and the paper by Kenneth Kantor and Donald Rubin for abundant illustrations—drawn from grades 4 through 12—of students' learning to differentiate between speech and writing. See Kroll, "Developmental Relationships between Speaking and Writing" (1981) and Kantor and Rubin, "Between Speaking and Writing" (1981).

Some works deal with socialization in a broader way—for example, they treat the effects of literacy training on cognitive development. Jack Goody and Ian Watt (1963) wrote a seminal essay about the historical consequences of literacy, their aim being to shed "light not only upon the nature of the Greek achievement but also upon the intellectual differences between simple and complex societies" (p. 345). In discussing the invention of an alphabetic system, for example, they suggested that "logic" is a function of writing, for writing made it possible to segment speech, to manipulate the order of words and invent syllogistic reasoning. See their "Consequences of Literacy" (1963) and also the later volume edited by Goody, *Literacy in Traditional Societies* (1968). We further recommend Goody's most recent book *The Domestication of the Savage Mind* (1977), in which he continued his analysis of the differences between literate and non-literate societies and of the effect of writing on thought processes. Goody would raise the status of writing from the low place Bloomfield assigned it, as speech written down, claiming that writing "encourages special forms of linguistic activity associated with developments in particular kinds of problem-raising and problem-solving" (1977, p. 162). For an assessment of *The Domestication of the Savage Mind* in light of composition, see John Trimbur's review (1982).

In "Developing Literacy" (1978a), Thomas J. Farrell used Walter Ong's taxonomy of orality versus literacy to describe basic writers, claiming that individuals go through the same development of communication skills as do races of people. For an essay-length account of Ong's perspective, see his "Literacy and Orality in our Times" (1978).

David Olson argued that literacy and education push cognitive growth. See his essays "From Utterance to Text" (1977); "Writing" (1981); and "Culture, Technology, and Intellect" (1976). For a discussion of the thesis that writing promotes cognitive development, see the essay by P. Greenfield and J. Bruner, "Culture and Cognitive Growth" (1966). Bruner also speculated that language transforms thought only at a stage he called "analytic competence," when there is "movement toward context-free elaboration" ("Language as an Instrument of Thought" [1975], p. 70).

In "A Cultural Perspective on Talking and Writing" (1981), Ann Ruggles Gere questioned the high value we set on literacy, partly to engender a broader view of literacy training. For a recent attempt to assess the effects of literacy apart from the effects of schooling, see Sylvia Scribner and Michael Cole's *Psychology of Literacy* (1981). Their book was reviewed from a writing teacher's perspective by Kenneth Dowst (1982). In a thorough but readable assessment of literacy theory, Michael Stubbs reviewed long-standing controversies over how to teach reading and also argued for the place of written language in any literacy theory. Stubbs synthesized diverse work such as that of Goody, Bernstein, and Labov. His *Language and Literacy* (1980) is an excellent overview of many of the issues introduced in this section.

Those interested in historical studies of the consequences of literacy should also find provocative A. R. Luria's documentation of the changes that accompanied the introduction of literacy training (and socialist collectivism) to peasants living in a remote part of Russia—*Cognitive Development* (1976). Employing clever interview techniques, like the hypothetical contradiction ("But one man told me..."), Luria was able to induce reticent subjects to engage in verbal problem-solving tasks, like syllogisms. On the basis of such tasks, Luria demonstrated sharp changes, from practical to theoretical thinking, among adults exposed to minimal levels of education and different work contexts.

Michael Cole wrote the foreword to Luria's *Cognitive Development* (1976); in it he praised Luria's accomplishments but also differed in his interpretation of Luria's findings: "What Luria interprets as the acquisition of new modes of thought, I am more inclined to interpret as changes in the application of previously available modes to the particular problems and contexts of discourse represented by the experimental setting" (p. xv). In his own work, Cole exercised the caution he advised others to have in interpreting the findings of cross-cultural research. In *Culture and Thought* (1974) Cole and Sylvia Scribner reviewed cross-cultural studies from the perspective that "it will be more productive to direct our criticism at the deficiencies of our science rather than at the alleged deficiencies of the people we study" (pp. 172–73). In *Comparative Studies of How People Think* (1981), Cole and Barbara Means gave us an entire book on the problems inherent in comparative research—the study of the intellectual activity of special groups of subjects—and the strategies available for coping with those problems. They explained their concern over the "sweeping generalizations" too often drawn from such research in the following passage:

Of greatest concern to us is the frequency with which the poor performance of a special group on some experimental task is taken as evidence that its members lack a specific ability or process: not just that they do not show it in performing *that* task under *those* circumstances but that they lack it completely. This "finding" then becomes the basis either for restricting our aspirations for the group (for example, "preoperational children can't be taught science") or for focusing our attention almost exclusively on the presumed deficit ("poor children lack conceptual abilities and need to be taught to talk") when there may not be any such general inability (pp. 143–44).

Their concerns should also be the concerns of those who study basic writers and their prose. See Alan Purves's review (1982) of *Comparative Studies of How People Think* for a discussion of its relevance to the teaching of composition.

We have ventured in this section far afield of the basic writing classroom. Most of the research we have cited cannot easily or confidently be translated into pedagogical practice. We expect, however, that studies of writing that consider such developmental perspectives will eventually provide teachers with something more than interesting vantage points from which to speculate about students and their prose. This "something more" might consist, for example, of detailed and insightful descriptions of writers at various stages of development, with concomitant descriptions of the writing skills and tasks that ought to be encouraged during a particular stage. Whatever form such findings take, however, they must in the end be joined to—and in some measure transformed by—existing pedagogical theory and practice.

Pedagogies/Programs/Curricula

Traditionally, basic writing has been considered remedial, a designation that implies the intensive study of things already learned, but learned unsatisfactorily; the connotation, then, has been one of deficiencies that need making up. See Iva Hunter Unglesby's report "Remedial Writing Programs" (1953) for a firsthand survey of these courses as they existed during the 1950s. Martha Maxwell commented upon the history of remedial writing instruction (*Improving Student Learning Skills* [1979]), as did Andrea Lunsford, who observed in her dissertation that "the courses [as they existed at the turn of the century] offered no college credit and were clearly punitive in nature. They emphasized mechanical correctness and relied heavily on drills and exercises; ill-prepared students were often thought of as either lazy or stupid—or both" ("An Historical, Descriptive, and Evaluative Study of Remedial English in American Colleges and Universities" [1977], p. 41). In another dissertation, "Educational Misfits" (1973), S. J. Zehm analyzed the assumptions held by teachers of English from 1825 to 1925 concerning poorly performing high school students. Poor performance in English (and in other subjects) was attributed to moral deficiency.

It appears, however, that there have been recent changes of heart. The term *remedial* has been supplanted at least partially by newer labels, as words like *basic* and *developmental* become the descriptors for writing courses. In part, this change simply reflects discomfort with the more pejorative connotations of *remedial* and *compensatory*. More significantly, it signals a turnabout in attitude and approach, a movement toward viewing basic writing as a course for developing writing abilities that, for whatever reason, haven't been nurtured before; for teaching student writers who are, in a sense, beginners, because they lack experience using written language. Shaughnessy made this point and discussed it at length in *Errors and Expectations* (1977) and "Basic Writing" (1976). John Roueche and C. L. Wheeler commented on the distinctions between remedial and developmental education in "Instructional Procedures for the Disadvantaged" (1973), as did Patricia Cross in *Accent on Learning* (1976). Lawrence Kasden summarized their distinctions in "An Introduction to Basic Writing" (1980).

Although we see evidence all around of changes in attitude and in approach towards the teaching of basic writing, no dominant pedagogy has come to the fore. That is, there is as yet no generally accepted definition of what a "developmental" basic writing course or even a "non-remedial" one should be. Although we know of almost no comprehensive instructional theories designed specifically to guide the operation of a basic writing course—these theories are just in the making—we can cite here several designed for other writing courses that have been adapted to, or have offered insights for, the teaching of basic writing.

Possibly the best-known pedagogical theory of English is found in James Moffett's *Teaching the Universe of Discourse* (1968b), the set of essays written by Moffett to accompany his *Student-Centered Language Arts Curriculum, Grades K–13* (1968a). Moffett stated that, to him, "the most sensible strategy for determining a proper learning order in English. . .is to look for the main lines of child development and to assimilate to them, when fitting, the various formulations that scholars make about language and literature" (p. 14). Central to his theory is the notion of *abstraction*, or the process of "selecting and ranking the elements of experience" (p. 23). Moffett would propose an English curriculum that teaches students how to "abstract" along the entire hierarchy of levels of discourse, from recording to reporting to generalizing and theorizing.

For a description of an assignment sequence for a basic writing course based in part on Moffett's notion of abstraction, see Elaine O. Lees's "Building Thought on Paper with Adult Basic Writers" (in press). Lees explained how she had asked students to write about a nominal subject throughout a course—like "Changing and Preserving"—first by reporting their own experiences with change and preservation, then by generalizing about those experiences, and finally by theorizing about patterns of change and preservation they had discovered as a class.

We recommend also William Coles's assignment sequences *Teaching Composing* (1974), *The Plural I* (1978), and *Composing II* (1981) as embodiments of an approach toward the teaching of composition that could well be adapted to basic writing classes. Unlike Moffett, Coles did not concern himself with a theory of child language development: he wrote his assignments for college students, and he drew the ideas that control his sequences from his own experience with what writing can mean intellectually and personally, ideas developed under the tutelage of Theodore Baird at Amherst College and shared also with Walker Gibson. Kenneth Dowst wrote a useful explication of Coles's pedagogy, christening it "The Epistemic Approach" (1980) and contrasting this view of teaching writing with other current theories. As stated by Dowst, "The principle goals of the epistemic approach are enabling students to see the extent to which their 'worlds' are determined by their language, and helping students to manipulate language—especially written English—in ways conducive to discovery and learning" (p. 74). For examples of basic writing courses that reflect the influence of Coles's approach, see David Bartholomae's "Teaching Basic Writing" (1979b) and Susan Wall's ERIC report *A Sequence of Assignments for Basic Writing* (1980).

One of the hallmarks of a "Colesian" composition course is a certain seriousness born of the belief that to control one's writing is in some sense to order one's world. A complementary kind of seriousness and belief in the power of language is found in adult literacy training as conceived and practiced by Paulo Freire. There is little doubt that some readers will be taken aback by the frankly political, Third World, specifically Marxist orientation that underpins Freire's work; nevertheless, many will also be struck, and perhaps more forcefully, by Freire's broad vision of what being literate should mean. Including but going beyond the skills of reading and writing, Freire would have learners develop a "critical consciousness...from their intervention in the world as transformers of that world" (*Pedagogy of the Oppressed* [1968], p. 60). In such a program, Freire claimed, "as people learn to read and write words, they simultaneously learn to 'read' and to 're-write' reality" ("The People Speak Their Word" [1981], p. 29).

The best-known of Freire's works is *Pedagogy of the Oppressed* (1968), a presentation of his theory of literacy that makes worthwhile the effort required to come to terms with his text. We also recommend Freire's record of his correspondence to colleagues, *The Letters to Guinea-Bissau* (1978). This book seems more accessible than previous works, for in it Freire attempted to deal with some of the practical problems involved in carrying out his theories. For two descriptions of how Freire's theories have guided literacy struggles in Third World countries, see Fernando Cardenal and Valerie Miller's "Nicaragua 1980" (1981) and Jonathan Kozol's "A New Look at the Literacy Campaign in Cuba" (1978). We also recommend, as an introduction to Third World literacy theory and practice, the proceedings from an international symposium, *A Turning Point for Literacy* (1976), edited by Leon Bataille. For an example of how Freire's ideas have begun to influence basic writing pedagogy, see "An Interactionist Approach to Advancing Literacy" (1977), in which Nan Elsasser and Vera P. John-Steiner described how they joined Freire's theory to Lev Vygotsky's (1962) description of inner speech to create a literacy program for basic writers in an open-admissions college.

A recent textbook on the teaching of writing has the provocative name (a quotation from Ben Jonson) *Beat Not the Poor Desk* (1982). Its literary title hints of its authors' special bias: Marie Ponsot and Rosemary Deen believe that teachers can best teach writing, be it basic or advanced, by calling upon their own expertise as writers and readers of literature. A central way Ponsot and Deen would require teachers to rely on such knowledge is to work out structural "models" from oral literature—fables, sermons, proverbs—and have their students discover their own versions of these models inductively. The skill of "beginning writing for others with the whole structure" is one of five elemental skills Ponsot and Deen considered central for writers, the others being prolific writing, making observations and distinguishing them from inferences, writing both abstractly and concretely, and rewriting (p. 4). Marie Ponsot presented some of these principles in an article describing a writing course, "Total Immersion" (1976).

For a theory of composition designed specifically for basic writers, see a recent dissertation by Larry G. Mapp, "A Theory of Composition for Undergraduate Basic Writers" (1981), which proposes that we consider writing a heuristic process. Mapp recommended that a composition program emphasize writing as a means of self-discovery and learning; allow for the creation of a range of writing, from concrete to abstract; and provide for individual differences in writing development.

There are many descriptions available of basic writing programs and courses. Although these reports reveal much diversity in pedagogy and program organization from one university to another, they also stand as evidence that teachers and administrators are increasingly committed to creating basic writing programs that accommodate their own students. Those interested in discussions of the range of basic writing programs may consult two recent dissertations: "A Survey of College-Level Remedial Writing Programs at Selected State-Supported Institutions Currently Admitting the Underprepared" (1980) by A. Wilson; and "Developmental Composition in College (1976) by G. N. Vik. A set of guidelines for basic-skills writing programs, written by an NCTE panel commissioned by the U.S. Office of Education, was published in *CE*: "Standards for Basic Skills Writing Programs" (1970).

We cite, as representing a range of basic writing philosophies and pedagogies, the following descriptions of individual programs and courses, beginning with Sabina Thorne Johnson's early and detailed description-rationale for a remedial writing course at Berkeley: "Remedial English" (1972). The Fall/Winter 1976 issue of the *Journal of Basic Writing* published several varied perspectives on what a basic writing course should be. See, for example, the essays by Dianna S. Campbell and Terry Ryan, "A Design for a Developmental Writing Course for Academically Underprepared Black Students," and Jeanne Desy, "Reasoned Writing for Basic Students."

Vernon Lattin in "A Program for Basic Writing" (1978) looked at three approaches typically employed by English departments to deal with remedial writers and told why they typically fail. Lattin proposed and described "a regimented competency-based program in which each instructor and student knows what must be accomplished from week to week" (p. 314). For a contrast to traditional competency-based programs, see David Bartholomae's essay "Teaching Basic Writing" (1979b). Bartholomae argued for an alternative to basic skills in his description of the basic writing program at the University of Pittsburgh, where "the only text for the course . . . is the students' own writing and if there is a theory of instruction, it is embodied in the kinds of conversations we have in class about that writing" (p. 90).

Two recent books contain program descriptions: *Basic Writing* (1980), edited by Lawrence Kasden and Daniel Hoeber, and *Teaching Basic Skills in College* (1980), edited by Alice Trillin and colleagues. There exist in abundance reports of specific basic writing programs prepared in the context of program assessment. See particularly the ERIC files, where many such assessments are reported—for example, Mary Epes and colleagues' *COMP-LAB Project* (1979). Other program descriptions and assessments take the form of dissertation studies, such as R. A. Shine's "Remediation Conundrum" (1979).

A recent instructional phenomenon that has gained popularity as an aid to, and sometimes a substitute for, the traditional writing classroom is the variously named "writing laboratory," "writing workshop," or "writing center." Although the characteristics and services of these facilities vary from school to school, they all employ some version of what once was called "conferencing"— one writer (or teacher) working individually with another writer (or student). Because individual attention seems intuitively an excellent procedure for helping any writer progress quickly, but especially for dealing with idiosyncratic or severe problems, it is not surprising that writing labs often appear in conjunction with basic writing programs or that the number of these labs appears to be increasing. Two new publications attest to their growth: the *Writing Lab Newsletter*, begun in 1977 and edited by Muriel Harris; and the *Writing Center Journal*, begun in 1980 and co-edited by Lil Brannon and Stephen M. North. Muriel Harris has perhaps written most widely about writing labs. We recommend particularly her essay "Individualized Diagnosis" (1978) for its discussion of the importance of assessment in tutorials. The essay is reprinted in *Tutoring Writing* (1982), a sourcebook edited by Harris that contains a bibliography of further readings on writing centers.

Some research, most commonly in the form of dissertations, has begun to compare traditional instructional techniques with those methods usually characteristic of writing labs. Results are mixed. See the dissertation studies by W. V. Rakaukas, "A Comparative Study of a Laboratory Approach versus a Conventional Approach to Teaching Developmental Freshman Composition at the University of Scranton" (1973); B. J. Overton, "An Analysis of the Effects of Two Methods of Teaching Remedial Composition" (1981); Clare M. Silva, "A Comparative Study of the Needs and Concepts of Individual Students in a Post-Secondary Remedial Writing Program" (1977); and an article by Doris Sutton and Daniel Arnold, "The Effects of Two Methods of Compensatory Freshman English" (1974).

For an overview of the issues involved in evaluating the effectiveness of a basic writing program, we recommend a book chapter by Geoffrey Akst and Miriam Hecht, "Program Evaluation," in Alice Trillin and associates' *Teaching Basic Skills in College* (1980). These authors provided a surprisingly readable survey of possible research designs for evaluation and warned of biases to guard against—ostensible gains in students' performance that aren't attributable to instruction. In "Writing," another chapter from this anthology, Barbara Gray and Virginia Slaughter illustrated in useful detail another kind of evaluation that most basic writing teachers must deal with—placement exams. They described the placement procedures used to assign writers to three levels in the CUNY writing programs and reproduced some helpful tools—a rubric for holistic evaluation and a sample atomistic rating scale. Harvey Wiener also provided sample writing tests along with student responses and commentary in his guide for the teaching of basic writing, *The Writing Room* (1981b). In "Assessing Reading, Writing, and Reasoning" (1981), Marilyn Sternglass recommended an instrument for evaluating student writing "that will distinguish students who need fundamental exercises in basic cognitive training from those who do not" (p. 269). James Ford and Gregory Larkin described a university-wide writing evaluation whereby at least one teacher besides a student's instructor reads, and marks pass or fail, a representative sample of the student's work. See their "Portfolio System" (1978). The December 1982 issue of *CCC* contains several essays on testing proficiency in writing, including cautionary comments by James C. Raymond concerning the impossibility of "pure objectivity" in this enterprise—"What We Don't Know about the Evaluation of Writing" (1982).

In reviewing publications of teaching techniques designed to address particular pedagogical issues, we found a variety so wide and numerous as to require as many omissions in this chapter as inclusions. We include citations on the "back-to-basics" movement, computer-assisted instruction, dialects and standard English, sentence-combining, second-language learning, error, and teacher training. To make up for our selectivity, particularly our omissions on more general issues of writing pedagogy, we refer readers to Daniel Hoeber's "Selected Bibliography" (1980); Theodore F. Sheckel's "Annotated Bibliography" (1981) for basic writing; Bruce Peterson's "Select Bibliography" (1982) on writing across the curriculum; and to the annotated citations on writing taken from *Resources in Education* and published by ERIC, *Especially for Teachers* (1982).

There has been, recently, a popular mandate to "get back to the basics" in education—to return in writing, for example, to teaching "fundamental" and "basic" skills, often interpreted to mean punctuation and spelling. By virtue of its very name, *basic* writing would seem especially vulnerable to the influence of the mandate. Thus we cite several essays that reassess the hoped-for consequences of literacy in light of back to basics. In "The Nature of Literacy" (1977), Daniel Resnick and Lauren Resnick provided an interesting history of what literacy meant in previous times and places—during the Revolution in France, for example—and in so doing demonstrated how different our present social conditions and educational aims are from past models.

Thomas J. Farrell reviewed the consequences of literacy and orality, commenting for example on the effects of television, to assess the merits of back-to-basics tenets. He concluded: "Just as the conventions of regularized spelling, punctuation, and grammar were late historical developments, so too the perfection of these matters should be late in the teaching of writing process" ("Literacy, the Basics, and All That Jazz" [1977], p. 454). Other essays that have contributed to a redefinition of back to basics in language studies are Dale Adams's "Not Back to the Pedagogic Basics" (1976); Jim Corder's "Outhouses, Weather Changes, and the Return to Basics in English Education" (1977); Dean Memering's "Forward to the Basics" (1978); and Lorenz Boehm's "Human Values and the Basics" (1979). We also recommend two anthologies: *Educating All*

Our Children (1979), edited by Doxey Wilkerson and billed as the first serious challenge to the back-to-basics movement; and *The English Curriculum Under Fire* (1982), edited by George Hillocks, Jr., and dedicated to setting forth what is truly most basic to the study of English. In every instance, educators express concern that the popular movement to return to a mythic past in education not be allowed to subvert educational practice into a preoccupation with the mastery of sub-skills.

If going back to the basics in education signals in some sense a desire to return to a simpler past, there is a forward-looking movement to recompense—computer-assisted instruction. Robert Shostak reviewed promising computer programs that now exist for writing instruction in "Computer-Assisted Composition Instruction" (1982). Included among these programs are several that appear helpful for basic writing classes, such as K. Anandam's *RSVP* (1979). This program frees teachers from writing lengthy explanations of grammatical errors on students' papers. For other computerized sentence-level helps, see Michael Southwell's "Using Computer-Assisted Instruction for Developmental Writers" (1982). For examples of computer programs that model invention, the best-known references are Hugh Burns's ERIC report *A Writer's Tool* (1980) and an article by Ellen Nold, "Fear and Trembling" (1975).

For an interesting overview of the kind of research that can be done on how students learn to write with computer assistance, we recommend an essay by James Levin, Marcia Boruta, and Mary Vasconcellos, "Microcomputer-based Environments for Writing" (1983). These researchers' work should be of particular interest to writing teachers, for it involves using a computer as a teaching technique to help novice writers become more expert at their tasks. Those interested in this use of computers should also consult a recent article by John Seely Brown and Richard R. Burton, "Diagnostic Models for Procedural Bugs in Basic Mathematical Science" (1978). Brown and Burton used the computer to diagnose *math bugs*, the errors math students make because they consistently use an erroneous rule, and described a computer-based tutoring system that can teach students and student-teachers how to diagnose bugs. John Black and colleagues pointed out (in the context of an essay on using computer modeling methods to investigate tacit knowledge in writing) that Brown and Burton's technique might foretell the development of a similar program for diagnosing writing bugs. See "What Writers Need to Know That They Don't Know They Need to Know" (1982).

There is some research to suggest that non-standard dialect features are no respectors of race or ethnic group. See the articles by Marilyn Sternglass, "Dialect Features in the Compositions of Black and White College Students" (1974), and Samuel Kirschner and G. Howard Poteet, "Non-Standard English Usage in the Writing of Black, White, and Hispanic Remedial English Students in an Urban Community College" (1973). In the review paper "Dialect Interference in Writing" (1980), Patrick Hartwell argued that this interference, "in and of itself," does not exist. Such evidence does not, however, appear to have stilled the controversy over whether standard English should be taught as a part of writing classes, although the balance seems to have tilted toward carefully qualified pro-standard English proposals. This stance exists despite a recent Conference on College Composition and Communication resolution, "Students' Rights to Their Own Language" (1974). For responses to the resolution, see Milton Baxter, "Educating Teachers about Educating the Oppressed" (1976), and Thomas J. Farrell, "Differentiating Writing from Talking" (1978b).

David E. Eskey argued for the teaching of standard English not by "pouncing on every nonstandard form or making absurdly inflated claims for the beauties and virtues of standard English" but by acknowledging the role of dialects and style shifting and by presenting standard English as the language of educated speakers everywhere (p. 770). See his "Case for the Standard Language" (1974) and "Standard/Nonstandard English" (1976). Dennis E. Baron in "Non-Standard Academic English, Composition, and the Academic Establishment" (1975) argued that teachers ought to give more weight to what he called "intelligibility": "the arbitrary standards of correctness must be ignored, the relative means of effectiveness must be stressed, the student must develop a self-confident attitude toward his language" (p. 182).

Other related articles include Mary Bruder and Luddy Hayden, "Teaching Composition" (1973); Lou Kelly, "Is Competent Copyreading a Violation of the Students' Rights to Their Own Language?" (1974); Barbara Quint Gray, "Dialect Interference in Writing" (1975); Barbara Nauer, "Soundscript" (1975); James L. Collins, "Dialect Variation and Writing" (1979); and P. A. Ramsey, "Teaching the Teachers to Teach Black-Dialect Writers" (1979).

There also exists in abundance research on sentence-combining as an instructional tool. Much of it is reviewed by Sandra Stotsky in "Sentence-Combining as a Curricular Activity" (1975). Another bibliography can be found in a book of essays on sentence-combining edited by Donald Daiker, Andrew Kerek, and Max Morenberg, *Sentence Combining and the Teaching of Writing* (1979). But despite a great deal of research, there is still much disagreement concerning the effectiveness of this tool for improving writing skills. For contrasting opinions on the efficacy of sentence-combining, see William Strong, "Back to Basics and Beyond" (1976), and R. J. Marzano, "The Sentence Combining Myth" (1976). We recommend, as a brief and readable assessment of the uses of sentence-combining, William L. Smith's article "The Potential and Problems of Sentence-Combining" (1981). For an example of research designed to sort out the effects of sentence-combining lessons on writing, see William L. Smith and Warren Combs's "Effects of Overt and Covert Cues on Written Syntax" (1980). For a discussion of the theoretical basis for rhetorical sentence-combining practice, see Stephen Harris and Stephen Witte, "Sentence Combining in a Rhetorical Framework" (1980).

There are beginning to appear studies of whether sentence-combining will improve basic writers' prose and, if so, how. Marilyn Sternglass in "Creating the Memory of Unheard Sentences" (1980) hypothesized that basic writers may have trouble holding sentence "chunks" in memory. She reasoned that they may therefore profit from individualized sentence-combining activities designed to help them internalize the shapes of written sentences. In a dissertation Clarence Waterfall (1977) found that sentence-combining did not significantly affect the syntactic fluency of his remedial writers, although this experimental group did write essays judged better in overall quality than those of the control group. However, D. S. Menendez (1979), also in a dissertation, found that her remedial writers gained on two measures of syntactic complexity and one measure of punctuation after sentence-combining practice. Thus results on how sentence-combining exercises can help basic writers are as yet inconclusive.

Teachers of basic writing whose students include non-native speakers of English are most likely acquainted with the literature on teaching English as a second language (ESL). However, even those teachers who don't have non-native speakers among their basic writers may find ESL theory a helpful resource. For a useful summary of the four major approaches that have influenced foreign language teaching, see David Bensaler and Renate Schulz's "Methodological Trends in College Foreign Language Instruction" (1980). Helmut Esau and Michael L. Keene demonstrated how principles that are central to ESL models also apply to the teaching of writing, their claim being that "learning to write—at college age—may be more like learning a second language than has hitherto been granted" ("A TESOL Model for Native-Language Writing Instruction" [1981], p. 696). For a comprehensive review of articles on error correction in foreign language instruction—when and how a teacher should correct which errors of which students—see James M. Hendrickson's "Error Correction in Foreign Language Teaching" (1978).

The best-known second-language learning theory to influence writing pedagogy is called "error analysis." It is based on the premise that all language, even that which is incorrect, is rule-governed, and that, like children who acquire a first language, adults who learn a second one create temporary, often erroneous, rule systems to sort out the language data to which they are exposed. Frances Gorbet developed and illustrated this connection in " 'To Err is Human' " (1979). Error analysts typically collect a corpus of language data (speech and writing samples), locate the errors in these samples and classify them into patterns, and then assign "causes" for various error types. We recommend here three anthologies as introductions to error analysis as well as to second-language learning theory and practice: *Focus on the Learner* (1973), edited by John W. Oller; *Error Analysis* (1977), edited by Jack C. Richards; and *Second Language Acquisition Research* (1978), edited by William C. Ritchie.

The first researchers to recognize how error analysis might be applied to composition were Barry Kroll and John Schafer; their essay "Error Analysis and the Teaching of Composition" (1978) provides a readable introduction to ESL theory and a new, positive perspective on the role of error in writing. For related discussions, see Julia S. Falk's "Language Acquisition and the Teaching and Learning of Writing" (1979); Janet K. Black's "Those 'Mistakes' Tell Us a Lot'' (1980); and Constance Weaver's "Welcoming Errors as Signs of Growth" (1982). Those teachers interested in conducting research using error-analysis methods should also consult the cautionary article by Jacquelyn Schachter and C. M. Murcia, "Some Reservations Concerning Error Analysis" (1977).

David Bartholomae's "Study of Error" (1980) can also be read as a critique of error analysis. Drawing on research from second-language learning and reading-miscue studies, Bartholomae identified several categories of error in writing based on why the errors occur, and he demonstrated the complexities involved in inexperienced writers' attempts to edit their essays. In the tradition of Shaughnessy's *Errors and Expectations* (1977), Bartholomae's essay is an attempt to rescue the study of sentence-level error from its absorption with student writers' carelessness and/or stupidity and to promote a more humane view of the process of error analysis as a reader's interpretative act.

The most comprehensive account of basic writing error, within and beyond the sentence, is Shaughnessy's *Errors and Expectations* (1977), where, after describing and illustrating common types of error, she gave usefully detailed suggestions for helping writers overcome them. She would have her basic writers approach composition analytically, studying the rules governing written language and comparing them with those rules governing their own dialects. Besides outlining specific exercises for the errors she classified as punctuation, syntax, inflections, vocabulary, and spelling, Shaughnessy commented on several discourse flaws. She suggested some ways to help writers generate ideas and develop them, including training in perceiving the structure of discourse and in recognizing the basic thought patterns that cross disciplines. She commented briefly on the shape a whole basic writing course might take, listing where in the sequence she would place certain errors and the time she would allot to them. For another example of Shaughnessy's views on writing pedagogy, see the transcript of her informal discussion with high school teachers, "Helping Inexperienced Writers" (1980), edited by Jeanne Halpern and Dale Mathews.

Many other teachers of writing have employed some version of error analysis to study their students' sentence-level mistakes and to propose treatments in the form of exercises or editing practices. Elaine Chaika, in an early article on syntax and basic writers, "Who Can Be Taught?" (1974), defined how learning to write can be said to be learning a new dialect, claiming that "many of the students who fail to achieve proficiency in English comp actually do not know the syntax of the written language" (p. 761) and illustrating her own lessons on syntax. Valerie Krishna, on the other hand, would have teachers concentrate not on syntax errors themselves, which she believes are too varied for useful classification, but on the sentences in which these errors appear, which she believes to be of a particular structural type. See her "Syntax of Writing" (1975) and, for another example of syntax error analysis, David Carkeet's "Understanding Syntactic Errors in Remedial Writing" (1977).

Sarah D'Eloia reviewed the role of grammar instruction in eliminating inflectional errors; the title of her paper suggests her perspective: "The Uses—and

Limits—of Grammar'' (1977). Suzette Elgin more enthusiastically recommended the merits of transformational grammar for teaching writing in ''Don't No Revolutions Hardly *Ever* Come by Here'' (1978). For instructions on teaching students the concept of the sentence, see Jacqueline Griffin's report ''Remedial Composition at an Open Door College'' (1969).

Those who suspect that their students' spelling problems are akin to language disabilities, specifically dyslexia, may want to consult two brief articles, ''Spelling Demonology Revisited'' (1976) by Shirley Partoll and ''Remediation Techniques for the Dyslexic Speller'' (1981) by Jean Wykis. More traditional approaches for dealing with spelling difficulty can be found in the articles by James Conley, ''Speling'' (1974), and Jean Buck, ''A New Look at Teaching Spelling'' (1977). Leonard Cahen, Marlys Craun, and Susan Johnson reviewed attempts to find out what makes a word hard to spell in ''Spelling Difficulty'' (1971). W. J. Valmont provided a brief, negative review of studies on spelling in ''Active Pupil Involvement in Learning to Spell'' (1972).

The Fall/Winter 1979 issue of the *Journal of Basic Writing* treats vocabulary instruction. There, Anne Eisenberg in ''The Trouble with Teaching Vocabulary'' reviewed common techniques for teaching vocabulary and some of what is known about how children acquire new words. Drawing on the work of James Britton, she advised context-based learning rather than isolated skill mastery. In the same issue Sandra Stotsky described academic language, or ''the formal English of college-level textbooks'' (p. 15), and went over some of the issues surrounding the selection of vocabulary and instructional techniques in ''Teaching the Vocabulary of Academic Discourse.''

For those who are interested in reassessing the significance of sentence-level errors, we recommend Maxine Hairston's survey of how laypersons respond to errors in usage, ''Not All Errors Are Created Equal'' (1981), and Joseph Williams's argument that errors exist differently for writers, readers, and grammarians in ''The Phenomenology of Error'' (1981). See as well the literature from the study of English as a second language, such as Kenneth Chastain's article ''Native Speaker Evaluation of Student Composition Errors'' (1981), where an error's gravity is determined according to how seriously it impedes communication. John Butler in ''Remedial Writers'' (1980) cautioned teachers that it is impossible for marginal notations and textual underlinings of error to mean to the student what they mean to the teacher. For a theory of editing's place in composing, we recommend highly Ann Berthoff's ''Writing and Editing'' in her book *The Making of Meaning* (1981).

Among the small and varied group of articles that address basic writing problems we roughly designate ''beyond the sentence'' in a paper by Jeffrey Youdelman, ''Limiting Students'' (1978). Youdelman wrote about teachers' and colleges' failure to have students write to learn about the social issues that affect them. Dean R. Baldwin in ''Introducing Rhetoric in Remedial Writing Courses'' (1978) suggested a way to ensure that basic writers stay aware of rhetorical elements when they write. ''Teaching the Grammar of Discourse'' (1980) by

Janice Hays draws on Pitkin's system of discourse analysis and Christensen's generative rhetoric of the sentence to suggest how we might teach students to develop and relate assertions. Lewis Meyers took a critical look at textbooks in "Texts and Teaching Basic Writing" (1978); he categorized current texts by the method they use for eliciting and improving student writing. Linda Flower enumerated and explained the skills one needs to revise reader-based prose; she suggested four teaching techniques to foster this kind of revision. See "Revising Writer-Based Prose" (1981), and for her earlier, theoretical discussion of the same topic, see "Writer-Based Prose" (1979).

Perhaps the most hopeful sign that pioneering efforts are underway in basic writing pedagogy is a movement toward specialized teacher training. There have been published several outlines of specific programs of study for prospective basic writing instructors. In "Training Teachers of Basic Writing" (1980), Constance Gefvert described a new graduate course at Virginia Tech by providing its week-by-week syllabus complete with readings and commentary. A 1981 issue of the *Journal of Basic Writing* is devoted solely to teacher training and is useful for the range of contrasting views it provides. Harvey Wiener ("Preparing the Teacher of Writing" [1981a]), for example, favors belletristic training, and Joseph Comprone ("Graduate Programs for Teachers of Basic Writing" [1981]) would have prospective teachers study cognitive psychology, among other "non-literary" pursuits. Comprone's paper and the essay by Richard Gebhardt, "Training Basic Writing Teachers at a Liberal Arts College" (1981), provide reading lists.

In "Teaching Ourselves to Teach Basic Writing" (1977), David Bartholomae contrasted some conventional postures toward dealing with basic writing with the proposal to "teach writing as a way of knowing, as a process of inquiry and discovery" (p. 14). This article doesn't deal directly with teacher training; its pertinence lies in demonstrating how teachers might best imagine basic writing in order to teach it. We also suggest the essay by William E. Coles, Jr., "Teacher Training and the Composing Process" (1980). Coles described a way of training teachers of writing by providing them (as students) with an analogue of what they will be expected to teach their own students. A well-known in-service training program similar to Coles's in that it, too, calls on teachers to write is described by J. Gray and M. Myers in "The Bay Area Writing Project" (1978).

The range of research we have cited may lead one to conclude that the time has come for selecting a new metaphor to describe the study of basic writing, one that reflects a great progress made since Shaughnessy invited us to join her in exploring a new frontier. We believe, however, that such a conclusion would at this time be premature. Despite new research and promising scholarship on basic writers and their prose, what we still need to learn dwarfs what we can claim to know. Rather than settling too quickly, and mistaking an increased familiarity with our students' writing problems for a true understanding of how best to teach them, we would encourage basic writing teachers and researchers to accept Shaughnessy's frontier challenge anew. This chapter, we hope, has helped identify some promising points of departure.

References

Adams, Dale T. "Not Back to the Pedagogic Basics." *CCC*, 27 (1976), 264–67.

Akst, Geoffrey, and Miriam Hecht. "Program Evaluation." In *Teaching Basic Skills in College*. Ed. Alice Stewart Trillin and Associates. San Francisco: Jossey-Bass, 1980, 261–96.

Anandam, K. *RSVP: Feedback Program for Individualized Analysis of Writing*. Miami: Miami-Dade Junior College, 1979. ERIC ED 191 511.

Anastasiow, Nicholas J., and Michael L. Hanes. *Language Patterns of Poverty Children*. Springfield, Ill.: Thomas, 1976.

Arlin, P. K. "Cognitive Development in Adulthood: A Fifth Stage." *Develop Psychol*, 11 (1975), 602–6.

Atlas, Marshall. "Addressing an Audience: A Study of Expert-Novice Differences in Writing." Diss. Carnegie-Mellon, 1979.

Atwell, Margaret. "The Evolution of Text: The Interrelationship of Reading and Writing in the Composing Process." Diss. Indiana University, 1981.

Baker, William D. "An Investigation of Characteristics of Poor Writers." *CCC*, 5 (1954), 23–27.

Baldwin, Dean R. "Introducing Rhetoric in Remedial Writing Courses." *CCC*, 29 (1978), 392–94.

Baron, Dennis E. "Non-Standard Academic English, Composition, and the Academic Establishment." *CE*, 37 (1975), 176–83.

Barritt, Loren S., and Barry M. Kroll. "Some Implications of Cognitive-Developmental Psychology for Research in Composing." In *Research on Composing: Points of Departure*. Ed. Charles Cooper and Lee Odell. Urbana, Ill.: NCTE, 1978, pp. 49–57.

Bartholomae, David. "Teaching Ourselves to Teach Basic Writing." *PCTE*, No. 35 (1977), 9–21.

———. Review of *Errors and Expectations: A Guide for the Teacher of Basic Writing*, by Mina Shaughnessy. In *Linguistics, Stylistics, and the Teaching of Composition*. Ed. Donald McQuade. Akron, Ohio: L and S, 1979a, pp. 209–20.

———. "Teaching Basic Writing: An Alternative to Basic Skills." *JBW*, 2 (1979b), 85–109.

———. "The Study of Error." *CCC*, 31 (1980), 253–69.

Bataille, Leon, ed. *A Turning Point for Literacy: Adult Education for Development; The Spirit and Declaration of Persepolis*. Proc. of the International Symposium for Literacy. Oxford: Pergamon, 1976.

Baxter, Milton. "Educating Teachers about Educating the Oppressed." *CE*, 37 (1976), 677–81.

Benseler, David P., and Renate A. Schulz. "Methodological Trends in College Foreign Language Instruction." *Mod Lang J*, 64 (1980), 88–96.

Bereiter, Carl, and Marlene Scardamalia. "From Conversation to Composition: The Role of Instruction in a Developmental Process." In *Advances in Instructional Psychology*. Vol. 2. Ed. Robert Glaser. Hillsdale, N.J.: Erlbaum, 1982, pp. 1–64.

Bernstein, Basil. *Class, Codes, and Control*. Vol. 1 in *Theoretical Studies towards a Sociology of Language*. London: Routledge, Kegan Paul, 1971.

Berthoff, Ann E. *The Making of Meaning: Metaphors, Models, and Maxims for Writing Teachers*. Montclair, N.J.: Boynton/Cook, 1981.

Black, Janet K. "Those 'Mistakes' Tell Us a Lot." *Lang Arts*, 57 (1980), 508–13.

Black, John B., Deanna Wilkes-Gibbs, and Raymond W. Gibbs. "What Writers Need to Know That They Don't Know They Need to Know." In *What Writers Know: The Language, Process, and Structure of Written Discourse*. Ed. Martin Nystrand. New York: Academic, 1982, pp. 325–43.

Boehm, Lorenz. "Human Values and the Basics: Is There Any Choice?" *CE*, 40 (1979), 505–11.

Bolker, Joan. "Teaching Griselda to Write." *CE*, 40 (1979), 906–8.

Brown, John Seely, and Richard R. Burton. "Diagnostic Models for Procedural Bugs in Basic Mathematical Skills." *Cog Sci*, 2 (1978), 155–92.

Bruder, Mary Newton, and Luddy Hayden. "Teaching Composition: A Report on a Bidialectal Approach." *Lang L*, 23 (1973), 1–15.

Bruner, Jerome S. "Language as an Instrument of Thought." In *Problems in Language and Learning*. Ed. Alan Davies. London: Heinemann, 1975, pp. 61–81.

———. *Toward a Theory of Instruction*. Cambridge, Mass.: Harvard University Press, 1966.

Buck, Jean L. "A New Look at Teaching Spelling." *CE*, 38 (1977), 703–6.

Burke, Virginia M. Review of *Handicapped English*, by John Nist. *CCC*, 26 (1975), 102–6.

Burns, Hugh. *A Writer's Tool: Computing as a Mode of Inventing*. 1980. ERIC ED 193 693.

Butler, John F. "Remedial Writers: The Teacher's Job as Corrector of Papers." *CCC*, 31 (1980), 270–77.

Cahen, Leonard S., Marlys J. Craun, and Susan K. Johnson. "Spelling Difficulty: A Survey of the Research." *Rev Educ Res*, 41 (1971), 281–301.

Campbell, Dianna S., and Terry Ryan Meier. "A Design for a Developmental Writing Course for Academically Underprepared Black Students." *JBW*, 1 (1976), 20–30.

Cardenal, Fernando, and Valerie Miller. "Nicaragua 1980: The Battle of the ABC's." *Harvard Educ Rev*, 51 (1981), 1–26.

Carkeet, David. "Understanding Syntactic Errors in Remedial Writing." *CE*, 38 (1977), 682–86.

Cayer, Roger L., and Renee K. Sacks. "Oral and Written Discourse of Basic Writers." *RTE*, 13 (1979), 121–28.

Chaika, Elaine. "Who Can Be Taught?" *CE*, 35 (1974), 575–83.

Chastain, Kenneth. "Native Speaker Evaluation of Student Composition Errors." *Mod Lang J*, 65 (1981), 288–94.

Chi, Michelene T. H., Paul J. Feltovich, and Robert Glaser. "Categorization and Representation of Physics Problems by Experts and Novices." *Cog Sci*, 5 (1981), 121–52.

Christian, Donna, and Walt Wolfram. *Dialects and Educational Equity*. Arlington, Va.: Center for Applied Linguistics, 1979.

Cole, Michael, and Barbara Means. *Comparative Studies of How People Think: An Introduction.* Cambridge, Mass.: Harvard University Press, 1981.

Cole, Michael, and Sylvia Scribner. *Culture and Thought: A Psychological Introduction.* New York: Wiley, 1974.

Coles, William E., Jr. *Teaching Composing: A Guide to Teaching Writing as a Self-Creating Process.* Rochelle Park, N.J.: Hayden, 1974.

———. *The Plural I: The Teaching of Writing.* New York: Holt, Rinehart, Winston, 1978.

———. "Teacher Training and the Composing Process: The Demand for Structure as a Shaper of Styles." *C&T,* 2 (1980), 23–31.

———. *Composing II: Writing as a Self-Creating Process.* Rochelle Park, N.J.: Hayden, 1981.

Collins, James L. "Dialect Variation and Writing: One Problem at a Time." *EJ,* 68 (1979), 49–51.

Comprone, Joseph. "Graduate Programs for Teachers of Basic Writing: The University of Louisville's Ph.D. in Rhetoric and Composition." *JBN,* 3 (1981), 23–45.

Conley, James. "Speling." *CCC,* 25 (1974), 243–46.

Cooper, Grace C. W. "The Relationship Between Errors in Standard Usage in Written Compositions of College Students and the Students' Cognitive Styles." *DAI,* 40 (1980), 6257A (Howard University).

Corder, Jim W. "Outhouses, Weather Changes, and the Return to Basics in English Education." *CE,* 38 (1977), 474–82.

Cross, K. Patricia. *Beyond the Open Door.* San Francisco: Jossey-Bass, 1971.

———. *Accent on Learning: Improving Instruction and Reshaping the Curriculum.* San Francisco: Jossey-Bass, 1976.

———. *Adults as Learners.* San Francisco: Jossey-Bass, 1981.

Daiker, Donald A., Andrew Kerek, and Max Morenberg, eds. *Sentence-Combining and the Teaching of Writing: Selected Papers from the Miami University Conference.* Conway, Ark.: L and S, 1979.

Daiute, Collette A. "Psycholinguistic Foundations of the Writing Process." *RTE,* 15 (1981), 5–22.

D'Eloia, Sarah. "The Uses—and Limits—of Grammar." *JBW,* 1 (1977), 1–48.

Desy, Jeanne. "Reasoned Writing for Basic Students: A Course Design." *JBW,* 1 (1976), 4–19.

Donaldson, Margaret. *Children's Minds.* New York: Norton, 1979.

Dowst, Kenneth. "The Epistemic Approach: Writing, Knowing, and Learning." In *Eight Approaches to Teaching Composition.* Ed. Timothy R. Donovan and Ben W. McClelland. Urbana, Ill.: NCTE, 1980, pp. 65–85.

———. Review of *The Psychology of Literacy,* by Sylvia Scribner and Michael Cole. *CCC,* 33 (1982), 332–33.

Dulit, Everett. "Adolescent Thinking à la Piaget: The Formal Stage." *J Youth Ado,* 1 (1972), 281–301.

Duska, Ronald, and Mariellen Whelan. *Moral Development: A Guide to Piaget and Kohlberg.* New York: Paulist, 1975.

Egan, Kieran. *Educational Development.* New York: Oxford University Press, 1979.

Eisenberg, Anne. "The Trouble with Teaching Vocabulary." *JBW,* 2 (1979), 5–14.

Elgin, Suzette Haden. "Don't No Revolutions Hardly *Ever* Come by Here." *CE,* 39 (1978), 784–89.

Elsasser, Nan, and Vera P. John-Steiner. "An Interactionist Approach to Advancing Literacy." *Harvard Educ Rev*, 47 (1977), 355–69.

Epes, Mary, et al. *The COMP-LAB Project: Assessing the Effectiveness of a Laboratory-Centered Basic Writing Course on the College Level.* 1979. ERIC ED 194 908.

Esau, Helmut, and Michael L. Keene. "A TESOL Model for Native-Language Writing Instruction: In Search of a Model for the Teaching of Writing." *CE*, 43 (1981), 694–710.

Eskey, David E. "The Case for the Standard Language." *CE*, 35 (1974), 769–74.

———. "Standard/Nonstandard English: Toward a Balanced View." *EJ*, 65 (1976), 28–31.

Especially for Teachers: ERIC Documents on the Teaching of Writing 1966–1981. Urbana, Ill.: ERIC Clearinghouse on Reading and Communication Skills, 1982.

Falk, Julia S. "Language Acquisition and the Teaching and Learning of Writing." *CE*, 41 (1979), 436–47.

Farrell, Thomas J. "Literacy, the Basics, and All That Jazz." *CE*, 38 (1977), 443–59.

———. "Developing Literacy: Walter J. Ong and Basic Writing." *JBW*, 2 (1978a), 30–51.

———. "Differentiating Writing from Talking." *CCC*, 29 (1978b), 346–50.

Flower, Linda. "Writer-Based Prose: A Cognitive Basis for Problems in Writing." *CE*, 41 (1979), 19–37.

———. "Revising Writer-Based Prose." *JBW*, 3, No. 3 (1981), 62–74.

———, and John Hayes. "Identifying the Organization of Writing Processes." In *Cognitive Processes in Writing*. Ed. L. Gregg and E. R. Steinberg. Hillsdale, N.J.: Erlbaum, 1980, pp. 3–30.

———. "Problem-Solving Strategies and the Writing Process." *CE*, 39 (1977), 449–61.

Ford, James E., and Gregory Larkin. "The Portfolio System: An End to Backsliding Writing Standards." *CE*, 39 (1978), 950–55.

Friere, Paulo. *Pedagogy of the Oppressed.* Trans. Myra Bergman Ramos. New York: Seabury, 1968.

———. *The Letters to Guinea-Bissau.* Trans. Carman St. John Hunter. New York: Seabury, 1978.

———. "The People Speak Their Word: Learning to Read and Write in São Tomé and Principé." Trans. Loretta Porto Slover. *Harvard Educ Rev*, 51 (1981), 27–30.

Gebhard, Ann O. "Writing Quality and Syntax: A Transformational Analysis of Three Prose Samples." *RTE*, (1978), 211–31.

Gebhardt, Richard C. "Training Basic Writing Teachers at a Liberal Arts College." *JBW*, 3 (1981), 46–63.

Gefvert, Constance J. "Training Teachers of Basic Writing." In *Basic Writing: Essays for Teachers, Researchers, and Administrators*. Ed. Lawrence N. Kasden and Daniel R. Hoeber. Urbana, Ill.: NCTE, 1980, pp. 119–40.

Gere, Anne Ruggles. "A Cultural Perspective on Talking and Writing." In *Exploring Speaking-Writing Relationships: Connections and Contrasts*. Ed. Barry M. Kroll and Roberta J. Vann. Urbana, Ill.: NCTE, 1981, pp. 111–23.

Giannasi, Jenefer M. "Dialects and Composition." In *Teaching Composition: Ten Bibliographic Essays*. Ed. Gary Tate. Fort Worth: Texas Christian University Press, 1976, pp. 275–304.

Ginsburg, Herbert, and Sylvia Opper. *Piaget's Theory of Intellectual Development.* 2nd ed. Englewood Cliffs, N.J.: Prentice-Hall, 1978.

Glaser, Robert. "Introduction: Toward a Psychology of Instruction." In *Advances of Instructional Psychology.* Vol. 1. Ed. Robert Glaser. Hillsdale, N.J.: Erlbaum, 1978, pp. 1–12.

Goody, Jack. *The Domestication of the Savage Mind.* New York: Cambridge University Press, 1977.

———, ed. *Literacy in Traditional Societies.* Cambridge: Cambridge University Press, 1968.

———, and I. Watt. "The Consequences of Literacy." *Comp Stud Hist & Soc*, 5 (1963), 304–45.

Gorbert, Frances. "'To Err is Human': Error Analysis and Child Language Acquisition." *Engl Lang Teach J*, 34 (1979), 22–28.

Gray, Barbara Quint. "Dialect Interference in Writing: A Tripartite Analysis." *JBW*, 1 (1975), 14–22.

———, and Virginia B. Slaughter. "Writing." In *Teaching Basic Skills in College.* Ed. Alice Stewart Trillin and Associates. San Francisco: Jossey-Bass, 1980, pp. 12–90.

Gray, J., and M. Myers. "The Bay Area Writing Project." *Phi Del Kap*, 59 (1978), 410–13.

Greenfield, P., and J. Bruner. "Culture and Cognitive Growth." *Int J Psychol*, 1 (1966), 89–107.

Griffin, Jacqueline. "Remedial Composition at an Open Door College." *CCC*, 20 (1969), 360–63.

Hairston, Maxine. "Not All Errors Are Created Equal: Nonacademic Readers in the Professions Respond to Lapses in Usage." *CE*, 43 (1981), 794–806.

Halpern, Jeanne W., and Dale Mathews. "Helping Inexperienced Writers: An Informal Discussion with Mina Shaughnessy." *EJ*, 69 (1980), 32–37.

Halsted, Isabella. "Putting Error in Its Place." *JBW*, 1 (1975), 72–86.

Harris, Muriel. "Individualized Diagnosis: Searching for Causes, Not Symptoms of Writing Deficiencies." *CE*, 40 (1978), 318–23.

———, ed. *Tutoring Writing: A Sourcebook for Writing Labs.* Glenview, Ill.: Scott, Foresman, 1982.

Harris, Stephen, and Stephen P. Witte. "Sentence Combining in a Rhetorical Framework: Directions for Further Research." In *Reinventing the Rhetorical Tradition.* Ed. Aviva Freedman and Ian Pringle. Conway, Ark.: L and S, 1980, pp. 89–98.

Hartwell, Patrick. "Dialect Interference in Writing: A Critical View." *RTE*, 14 (1980), 101–18.

Hays, Janice N. "Teaching the Grammar of Discourse." In *Reinventing the Rhetorical Tradition.* Ed. Aviva Freedman and Ian Pringle. Conway, Arkansas: L and S, 1980, pp. 145–55.

Hendrickson, James M. "Error Correction in Foreign Language Teaching: Recent Theory, Research, and Practice; an Historical Perspective." *Mod Lang J*, 62 (1978), 387–98.

Hillocks, George, Jr., ed. *The English Curriculum Under Fire: What Are the Real Basics?* Urbana, Ill.: NCTE, 1982.

Hjelmervic, Karen. "Trends in the Written Products of General Writers, Basic Writers, and Basic Readers and Writers Across Four Points in Time.'' Diss. University of Pittsburgh, 1982.

Hoeber, Daniel R. ''Selected Bibliography: Composition and Basic Writing.'' In *Basic Writing: Essays for Teachers, Researchers, Administrators*. Ed. Lawrence N. Kasden and Daniel R. Hoeber. Urbana, Ill.: NCTE, 1980, pp. 164–73.

Holbrook, David. *English for the Rejected: Training Literacy in the Lower Streams of the Secondary School*. London: Cambridge University Press, 1964.

Holland, Robert M. ''Piagetian Theory and the Design of Composing Assignments.'' *AEB*, 19 (1976), 17–22.

Holt, John. *How Children Fail*. New York: Pitman, 1964.

House, Elizabeth B., and William B. House. *Some Similarities and Differences between Compositions Written by Remedial and Non-remedial College Freshmen*. 1980. ERIC ED 186 931.

Hull, Glynda A. ''The Effects of Self-Management Strategies on Journal Writing by College Freshmen.'' *RTE*, 15 (1981), 135–48.

———, and William L. Smith. *Examining the Function of Visual Feedback in Text Production*. 1982. ERIC ED 213 255.

Johnson, Sabina Thome. ''Remedial English: The Anglocentric Albatross?'' *CE*, 33 (1972), 670–85.

Kagan, Dona M. ''Run-on and Fragment Sentences: An Error Analysis.'' *RTE*, 14 (1980), 127–38.

Kantor, Kenneth J., and Donald L. Rubin. ''Between Speaking and Writing: Processes of Differentiation.'' In *Exploring Speaking-Writing Relationships: Connections and Contrasts*. Ed. Barry M. Kroll and Roberta J. Vann. Urbana, Ill.: NCTE, 1981, pp. 55–81.

Kasden, Lawrence N. ''An Introduction to Basic Writing.'' In *Basic Writing: Essays for Teachers, Researchers, and Administrators*. Ed. Lawrence N. Kasden and Daniel R. Hoeber. Urbana, Ill.: NCTE, 1980, pp. 1–9.

———, and Daniel R. Hoeber, eds. *Basic Writing: Essays for Teachers, Researchers, and Administrators*. Urbana, Ill.: NCTE, 1980.

Kaufman, Susan DeFord Sumners. ''Cognitive Style and Writing: An Inquiry.'' Diss. Rutgers University, 1981.

Kelly, Lou. ''Is Competent Copyreading a Violation of the Students' Right to Their Own Language?'' *CCC*, 25 (1974), 254–58.

Kirschner, Samuel, and G. Howard Poteet. ''Non-Standard English Usage in the Writing of Black, White, and Hispanic Remedial English Students in an Urban Community College.'' *RTE*, 7 (1973), 351–55.

Kluwe, Rainer H., and Hans Spada, eds. *Developmental Models of Thinking*. New York: Academic, 1980.

Kohlberg, Lawrence. ''Moral Development.'' In *Int Encycl Social Sc*. Vol. 10. Ed. David L. Sills. New York: Macmillan and the Free Press, 1968, pp. 483–94.

Kornrich, M., ed. *Underachievement*. Springfield, Ill.: Thomas, 1965.

Kozol, Jonathan. ''A New Look at the Literary Campaign in Cuba.'' *Harvard Educ Rev*, 48 (1978), 341–77.

Kressy, Michael. ''The Community College Student: A Lesson in Humility.'' *CE*, 32 (1971), 772–77.

Krishna, Valerie. ''The Syntax of Error.'' *JBW*, 1 (1975), 43–49.

Kroll, B. "Cognitive Egocentricism and the Problem of Audience Awareness in Written Discourse." *RTE*, 12 (1978), 269–81.

———. "Developmental Relationships between Speaking and Writing." In *Exploring Speaking-Writing Relationships: Connections and Contrasts*. Ed. Barry M. Kroll and Roberta J. Vann. Urbana, Ill.: NCTE, 1981, pp. 32–54.

———, and John C. Schafer. "Error Analysis and the Teaching of Composition." *CCC*, 29 (1978), 243–48.

———, and Roberta J. Vann, eds. *Exploring Speaking-Writing Relationships: Connections and Contrasts*. Urbana, Ill.: NCTE, 1981.

Kuhn, Deanna. "The Application of Piaget's Theory of Cognitive Development to Education." *Harvard Educ Rev*, 49 (1979), 340–60.

Labov, William. *The Study of Nonstandard English*. Urbana, Ill.: NCTE, 1970.

———. *Language in the Inner City: Studies in the Black English Vernacular*. Philadelphia: University of Pennsylvania Press, 1972.

Lattin, Vernon E. "A Program for Basic Writing." *CE*, 40 (1978), 312–17.

Lawrence, Patricia. "Error's Endless Train: Why Students Don't Perceive Errors." *JBW*, 1 (1975), 23–43.

Lederman, Marie Jean. "A Comparison of Student Projections: Magic and the Teaching of Writing." *CE*, 34 (1973), 674–89.

Lees, Elaine. "Building Thought on Paper with Adult Basic Writers." In *The Writer's Mind*. Ed. Phyllis Roth et al. Urbana, Ill.: NCTE, 1983, pp. 145–51.

Letter to a Teacher [by] Schoolboys of Barbiana. Trans. Nora Rossi and Tom Cole. New York: Random House, 1970.

Levin, James A., Marcia J. Boruta, and Mary T. Vasconcellos. "Microcomputer-based Environments for Writing: A Writer's Assistant." In *Classroom Computers and Cognitive Science*. Ed. A. C. Wilkinson. New York: Academic, 1983.

Linn, Bill. "Psychological Variants of Success: Four In-Depth Case Studies of Freshmen in a Composition Course." *CE*, 39 (1978), 903–17.

Linn, Michael D. "Black Rhetorical Patterns and the Teaching of Composition." *CCC*, 26 (1975), 149–53.

Loban, Walter. *Language Development: Kindergarten Through Grade Twelve*. NCTE Research Report No. 18. Urbana, Ill.: NCTE, 1976.

Lunsford, Andrea A. "An Historical, Descriptive, and Evaluative Study of Remedial English in American Colleges and Universities." Diss. Ohio State University, 1977.

———. "Cognitive Development and the Basic Writer." *CE*, 41 (1979), 38–46.

———. "The Content of Basic Writers' Essays." *CCC*, 31 (1980), 278–90.

Luria, A. R. *Cognitive Development: Its Cultural and Social Foundations*. Trans. Martin Lopez-Marillas and Lynn Solotaroff. Ed. Michael Cole. Cambridge, Mass.: Harvard University Press, 1976.

Mandel, Barrett J. "Losing One's Mind: Learning to Write and Edit." *CCC*, 29 (1978), 362–68.

Mapp, L. G. "A Theory of Composition for Undergraduate Basic Writers." *DAI*, 42 (1981), 1464A (George Peabody College for Teachers).

Marzano, R. J. "The Sentence Combining Myth." *EJ*, 65 (1976), 57–59.

Maxwell, Martha. *Improving Student Learning Skills: A Comprehensive Guide to Successful Practices and Programs for Increasing the Performance of Underprepared Students*. San Francisco: Jossey-Bass, 1979.

Memering, Dean. "Forward to the Basics." *CE*, 39 (1978), 553–61.

Menendez, D. S. "The Effect of Sentence-Combining Practice on Remedial College Students' Syntactic Maturity, Punctuation Skills and Reading Ability." *DAI*, 39 (1979), 6599A (Indiana University).

Metzger, E. A. "Causes of Failure to Learn to Write: Exploratory Case Studies at Grade Seven, Grade Ten, and College Level." *DAI*, 38 (1977), 3346A (University of New York at Buffalo).

Meyers, Lewis. "Texts and Teaching Basic Writing." *CE*, 39 (1978), 918–33.

Miller, Susan. "Rhetorical Maturity: Definition and Development." *Reinventing the Rhetorical Tradition*. Ed. Aviva Freedman and Ian Pringle. Conway, Ark.: L and S, 1980, pp. 119–27.

Moffett, James. *A Student-Centered Language Arts Curriculum: Grades K–13*. Boston: Houghton Mifflin, 1968a.

————. *Teaching the Universe of Discourse*. Boston: Houghton Mifflin, 1968b.

Nauer, Barbara. "Soundscript: A Way to Help Black Students to Write Standard English." *CE*, 36 (1975), 586–88.

Nist, John. *Handicapped English*. Springfield, Ill.: Thomas, 1974.

Nold, Ellen. "Fear and Trembling: The Humanist Approaches the Computer." *CCC*, 26 (1975), 269–73.

Ohmann, Richard. "Reflections on Class and Language." *CE*, 44 (1982), 1–17.

Oller, John W., ed. *Focus on the Learner: Pragmatic Perspectives for the Language Teacher*. Rowley, Mass.: Newbury, 1973.

Olson, David R. "Culture, Technology, and Intellect." In *The Nature of Intelligence*. Ed. Lauren B. Resnick. Hillsdale, N.J.: Erlbaum, 1976, pp. 189–202.

————. "From Utterance to Text: The Bias of Language in Speech and Writing." *Harvard Educ Rev*, 47 (1977), 257–81.

————. "Writing: The Divorce of the Author from the Text." In *Exploring Speaking-Writing Relationships: Connections and Contrasts*. Ed. Barry M. Kroll and Roberta J. Vann. Urbana, Ill.: NCTE, 1981, pp. 99–110.

Ong, Walter J. "Literacy and Orality in Our Times." *ADE Bul*, 58 (1978), 1–7.

Overton, B. J. "An Analysis of the Effects of two Methods of Teaching Remedial Composition." *DAI*, 42 (1981), 118A (George Peabody Teachers College).

Partoll, Shirley F. "Spelling Demonology Revisited." *Acad Ther*, 11 (1976), 339–48.

Perl, Sondra. "The Composing Processes of Unskilled College Writers" *RTE*, 13 (1979), 317–36.

————. "A Look at Basic Writers in the Process of Composing." In *Basic Writing: Essays for Teachers, Researchers, and Administrators*. Ed. Lawrence N. Kasden and Daniel R. Hoeber. Urbana, Ill.: NCTE, 1980, pp. 13–32.

Perry, W. G., Jr. *Forms of Intellectual and Ethical Development in the College Years*. New York: Holt, Rinehart, Winston, 1968.

Peterson, Bruce. "A Select Bibliography." In *Language Connections: Writing and Reading Across the Curriculum*. Ed. Toby Fulwiler and Art Young. Urbana, Ill.: NCTE, 1982, pp. 179–88.

Phillips, D. C., and Mavis E. Kelly. "Hierarchical Theories of Development in Education and Psychology." *Harvard Educ Rev*, 45 (1975), 351–75.

Piaget, Jean. *Language and Thought of the Child*. Trans. M. Gabain. London: Routledge, Kegan Paul, 1926.

————. *The Moral Judgment of the Child*. Trans. M. Gabain. New York: Harcourt, Brace, World, 1932.

————. "Intellectual Evolution from Adolescence to Adulthood." *Human Dev*, 15 (1972), 1–12.

Pianko, Sharon. "A Description of the Composing Processes of College Freshman Writers." *RTE*, 13 (1979a), 5–22.

————. "Reflection: A Critical Component of the Composing Process." *CCC*, 30 (1979b), 275–78.

Pitcher, R. W., and B. Blaushild. *Why College Students Fail*. New York: Funk, Wagnalls, 1970.

Pixton, William H. "A Contemporary Dilemma: The Question of Standard English." *CCC*, 25 (1974), 247–53.

Ponsot, Maire. "Total Immersion." *JBW*, 1 (1976), 31–43.

Ponsot, Marie, and Rosemary Deen. *Beat Not the Poor Desk; Writing; What to Teach, How to Teach it and Why*. Montclair, N.J.: Boynton/Cook, 1982.

Poole, Millicent. *Social Class Contrasts in Linguistic, Cognitive, and Verbal Domains*. Melbourne, Australia: La Trobe University, 1975.

Purves, Alan. Review of *Comparative Studies of How People Think: An Introduction*, by Michael Cole and Barbara Means. *CCC*, 33 (1982), 333–35.

Rakauskas, W. V. "A Comparative Study of a Laboratory Approach versus a Conventional Approach to Teaching Developmental Freshman Composition at the University of Scranton." *DAI*, 34 (1973), 1657A (Temple University).

Ramsey, P. A. "Teaching the Teachers to Teach Black-Dialect Writers." *CE*, 41 (1979), 197–201.

Raymond, James C. "What We Don't Know about the Evaluation of Writing." *CCC*, 33 (1982), 399–403.

Resnick, Daniel P., and Lauren B. Resnick. "The Nature of Literacy: An Historical Exploration." *Harvard Educ Rev*, 45 (1977), 370–85.

Richards, Jack C., ed. *Error Analysis: Perspectives on Second Language Acquisition*. London: Longman, 1977.

Ritchie, William C., ed. *Second Language Acquisition Research: Issues and Implications*. New York: Academic, 1978.

Rose, Mike. "Rigid Rules, Inflexible Plans, and the Stifling of Language: A Cognitivist Analysis of Writer's Block." *CCC*, 31 (1980), 389–401.

Roueche, John, and C. L. Wheeler. "Instructional Procedures for the Disadvantaged." *Improv Coll & Univ Teaching*, 21 (1973), 222–25.

Roueche, John, and Jerry J. Snow. *Overcoming Learning Problems*. San Francisco: Jossey-Bass, 1977.

Rouse, John. "The Politics of Composition." *CE*, 41 (1979), 1–12.

Schachter, J., and C.-M. Murcia. "Some Reservations Concerning Error Analysis." *TESOL Quarterly*, 11 (1977), 441–51.

Schafer, John C. "The Linguistic Analysis of Spoken and Written Texts." In *Exploring Speaking-Writing Relationships*. Ed. Barry M. Kroll and Roberta J. Vann. Urbana, Ill.: NCTE, 1981, pp. 1–31.

Scribner, Sylvia, and Michael Cole. *The Psychology of Literacy*. Cambridge, Mass.: Harvard University Press, 1981.

Shaughnessy, Mina. "Basic Writing." In *Teaching Composition: Ten Bibliographic*

Essays. Ed. Gary Tate. Fort Worth: Texas Christian University Press, 1976, pp. 137–67.

————. *Errors and Expectations: A Guide for the Teacher of Basic Writing*. New York: Oxford University Press, 1977.

Sheckel, Theodore F. "Annotated Bibliography." In *The Writing Room: A Resource Book for Teachers of English*. By Harvey S. Wiener. New York: Oxford University Press, 1981, pp. 293–325.

Shine, R. A. "The Remediation Conundrum: A Workshop/Tutorial Experiment in Developmental Writing." *DAI*, 40 (1979), 1439A (University of Massachusetts).

Shostak, Robert. "Computer-Assisted Composition Instruction: The State of the Art." In *Computers in Composition Instruction*. Ed. Joseph Lawlor. Los Alamitos, Calif.: Southwest Regional Laboratory for Educational Research and Development, 1982, pp. 5–18.

Siegel, L. S., and C. J. Brainerd, eds. *Alternatives to Piaget: Critical Essays on the Theory*. New York: Academic, 1978.

Siegler, Robert S. "Information Processing Approaches to Development." In *Manual of Child Psychology*. Ed. P. Mussen. New York: Wiley, 1983, pp. 1–88.

Silva, C. M. "A Comparative Study of the Needs and Concepts of Individual Students in a Post-Secondary Remedial Writing Program." *DAI*, 38 (1977), 2533A (Ohio State University).

Sloan, Gary. "The Subversive Effects of an Oral Culture on Student Writing." *CCC*, 30 (1979), 156–60.

Smith, William L. "The Potential and Problems of Sentence Combining." *EJ*, 70 (1981), 79–81.

————, and Warren E. Combs. "The Effects of Overt and Covert Cues on Written Syntax." *RTE*, 14 (1980), 19–38.

Southwell, Michael. "Using Computer-Assisted Instruction for Developmental Writers." *AEDS J*, 15 (1982), 80–91.

Stallard, Charles K. "An Analysis of the Writing Behavior of Good Student Writers." *RTE*, 8 (1974), 206–18.

"Standards for Basic Skills Writing Programs." *CE*, 41 (1979), 220–22.

Sternglass, Marilyn S. "Dialect Features in the Compositions of Black and White College Students: The Same or Different?" *CCC*, 25 (1974), 259–63.

————. "Creating the Memory of Unheard Sentences." In *Reinventing the Rhetorical Tradition*. Ed. Aviva Freedman and Ian Pringle. Conway, Ark.: L and S, 1980, pp. 113–18.

————. "Assessing Reading, Writing, and Reasoning." *CE*, 43 (1981), 269–75.

Stiles, Eleanor Elizabeth. "A Case Study of Remedial Writers in Selected Two-Year Colleges in East Tennessee." *DAI*, 37 (1977), 7004A (University of Tennessee).

Stotsky, Sandra L. "Sentence-Combining as a Curricular Activity: Its Effects on Written Language Development and Reading Comprehension." *RTE*, 9 (1975), 30–71.

————. "Teaching the Vocabulary of Academic Discourse." *JBW*, 2 (1979), 15–39.

Strong, William. "Back to Basics and Beyond." *EJ*, 65 (1976), 56, 60–64.

Stubbs, Michael. *Language and Literacy: The Sociolinguistics of Reading and Writing*. London: Routledge, Kegan Paul, 1980.

"Students' Rights to Their Own Language." *CCC*, 25 (1974), 1–18.

Sutton, Doris G., and Daniel S. Arnold. "The Effects of Two Methods of Compensatory Freshman English." *RTE*, 8 (1974), 241–49.

Sweeder, J. J. "A Descriptive Study of Six Adult Remedial Writers: Their Composing Processes and Heuristic Strategies." *DAI*, 42 (1981), 2004A (Temple University).

Tang, M. A. "A Study of the Relationships between the Reading and Writing Abilities of Underprepared College Students." *DAI*, 1979 (40), 3215A (University of Missouri).

Tate, Gary ed., *Teaching Composition*. Fort Worth, Tex.: Texas Christian University Press, 1976.

Trillin, Alice Stewart, and Colleagues, eds. *Teaching Basic Skills in College*. San Francisco: Jossey-Bass, 1980.

Trimbur, John. Review of *The Domestication of the Savage Mind*, by Jack Goody. *CCC*, 33 (1982), 461–63.

Troyka, Lynn Quitman. "Perspectives on Legacies and Literacy in the 1980s." *CCC*, 33 (1982), 252–62.

Unglesby, Iva Hunter. "Remedial Writing Programs." *Sch & Soc*, 78 (1953), 89–91.

Valmont, W. J. "Active Pupil Involvement in Learning to Spell." *Education*, 93 (1972), 189–91.

Vik, G. N. "Developmental Composition in College." *DAI*, 36 (1976), 8037A (University of Florida).

Vygotsky, Lev. *Thought and Language*. Ed. and trans. Eugenia Hanfmann and Gertrude Vakar. Cambridge: M.I.T. Press, 1962.

Wall, Susan V. *A Sequence of Assignments for Basic Writing: Problems "Beyond the Sentence."* 1980. ERIC ED 186 937.

———. "Revision in a Rhetorical Context: Case Studies of First Year College Writers." Diss. University of Pittsburgh, 1982.

———, and Anthony R. Petrosky. "Freshmen Students and Revision." *JBW*, 3, No. 3 (1981), 109–22.

Waterfall, Clarence Malan. "An Experimental Study of Sentence Combining as a Means of Increasing Syntactic Maturity and Writing Quality in the Compositions of College Age Students Enrolled in Remedial English Classes." Diss. Utah State University, 1977.

Weaver, Constance. "Welcoming Errors as Signs of Growth." *Lang Arts*, 59 (1982), 438–44.

Widick, C. "The Perry Scheme: A Foundation for Developmental Practice." *Couns Psychol*, 6 (1977), 35–38.

Wiener, Harvey S. "Basic Writing: First Days' Thoughts on Process and Detail." In *Eight Approaches to Teaching Composition*. Ed. Timothy R. Donovan and Ben W. McClelland. Urbana, Ill.: NCTE, 1980, pp. 87–99.

———. "Preparing the Teacher of Writing." *JBW*, 3 (1981a), 5–13.

———. *The Writing Room: A Resource Book for Teachers of English*. New York: Oxford University Press, 1981b.

Wilkerson, Doxey A. *Educating All Our Children*. Westport, Conn.: Mediax, 1979.

Williams, Joseph M. "The Phenomenology of Error." *CCC*, 32 (1981), 152–68.

Wilson, A. "A Survey of College-Level Remedial Writing Programs at Selected State-Supported Institutions Currently Admitting the Underprepared. *DAI*, 40 (1980), 4881A (Columbia University Teachers College).

Witkin, Herman A., et al. "Field Dependent and Field-Independent Cognitive Styles and Their Educational Implications." *Rev Educ Res*, 47 (1977), 1–64.

Witte, Stephen P., and Lester Faigley. "Coherence, Cohesion, and Writing Quality." *CCC*, 32 (1981), 189–204.

Woodward, J., and A. Phillips. "Profile of the Poor Writer." *RTE*, 1 (1967), 41–53.

Writing Center Journal. Ed. Lil Brannon and Stephen M. North. Albany: State University of New York at Albany.

Writing Lab Newsletter. Ed. Muriel Harris. West Lafayette, Ind.: Purdue University Department of English.

Wykis, Jean A. "Remediation Techniques for the Dyslexic Speller." *Acad Ther*, 16 (1981), 521–26.

Youdelman, Jeffrey. "Limiting Students: Remedial Writing and The Death of Open Admissions." *CE*, 39 (1978), 562–72.

Zehm, S. J. "Educational Misfits: A Study of Poor Performers in the English Class 1825–1925." *DAI*, 1973 (34), 3106A (Stanford University).

The Sentence

FRANK J. D'ANGELO

The word *sentence*, derived from the Latin word *sententia*, has a variety of meanings, most of them suggesting its origin in speech: for example, feeling, opinion, judgment, and saying. To pronounce "sentence" over the actions of men and women is to engage in a serious moral enterprise. Mindful of its primitive origins as an emotional utterance and echoing the grammarian Otto Jespersen, Herbert Read, in his book *English Prose Style* (1952), called the sentence "a single cry."

Rhetorically, the sentence is related to the aphorism and to the rhetorical commonplaces that were the repositories of subject matter and arguments in classical rhetoric. These *sententiae* were collections of moral sayings that students used for the proper construction of Latin sentences and for developing themes.

Despite the fact that the sentence is such a fundamental grammatical and rhetorical form, Richard Graves, in his book *Rhetoric and Composition* (1976b), complained that "the most neglected rhetorical unit in the teaching of composition is the sentence. Much current textbook treatment of the sentence," he remarked, "takes a negative slant, consisting largely of 'rules for salvaging misbegotten sentences.' In the composition course itself a disproportionate emphasis falls on broad global concerns and theme length efforts, with little attention given to the sentence" (p. 83). This chapter is an attempt to correct that neglect by presenting a bibliographic survey of the principal developments of the sentence from the nineteenth century to the present, with particular emphasis on the relationship of the sentence to composition theory and practice.

The Grammar of the Sentence

Any survey that deals with the grammar of the sentence must begin with the traditional division of sentence types into simple, compound, complex, and compound-complex. Francis Christensen, in his article "A Generative Rhetoric of the Sentence'' (1963a), criticized the traditional grammatical classification of sentences as being ''barren'' because it rests ''on a semantic confusion, equating complexity of structure with complexity of thought and vice versa'' (p. 3). James Sledd, in his article ''Coordination (Faulty) and Subordination (Upside-Down)'' (1956), demonstrated that the traditional theory of clauses is untenable, that main clauses can express subordinate ideas and coordinate clauses can express the same relations as the clauses in a complex sentence. Yet composition textbooks continue to present the traditional classification of sentences to students as a meaningful way of constructing sentences. Some textbooks relegate the traditional classification of sentences to the handbook section of the text under the assumption that the terminology of traditional grammar might at least provide a common vocabulary for students of composition.

Few of the nineteenth- and early twentieth-century composition textbooks that I have surveyed attempt to show a relationship between grammatical classification and rhetoric. Most of the texts proceed on the assumption, as Francis Christensen (1963a) pointed out, that ''we think naturally in primer sentences, progress naturally to compound sentences, and must be taught to combine the primer sentences into complex sentences—and that complex sentences are the mark of maturity'' (p. 4). One text that does point out the relationship between grammatical classification and rhetoric, William T. Brewster's *English Composition and Style* (1912), gives the kind of advice that both Christensen and Sledd found untenable. ''This customary, grammatical classification has much to do with rhetoric,'' he wrote. ''A succession of simple sentences . . . is likely to be jerky, to give the impression of haste, and simple sentences are, moreover, unfitted for expressing complex ideas'' (p. 228). Some typical examples of textbooks that use the traditional classification of sentence types to teach sentence structure are David J. Hill's *The Elements of Rhetoric and Composition* (1878); Henry W. Jameson's *Rhetorical Method* (1879); C. W. Bardeen's *A Shorter Course in Rhetoric* (1885); John Hays Gardiner and others' *Elements of English Composition* (1902); and Fred Newton Scott and Joseph Villiers Denney's *Elementary English Composition* (1908). All of these texts divide sentences into simple, complex, and compound sentences. I could not determine when the mixed category of compound-complex sentences first began to be used in composition textbooks, nor could I determine the earliest use of traditional grammar to teach the construction of sentences. Clearly, we need more detailed studies to investigate the earliest use of traditional grammar in composition textbooks, their methods of classification, the relationship between sentence type and rhetoric, and the kinds of advice given by textbook writers for constructing sentences.

In my survey of the late nineteenth- and early twentieth-century composition textbooks, I expected to find numerous texts that advocated using *functional sentence types*: declarative, interrogative, exclamatory, and imperative. But I did not. Perhaps the textbook writers of that time agreed with William T. Brewster who, in his text *English Composition and Style* (1912), asserted that ''the grammatical classifications of sentences into declarative, exclamative, and imperative have no special significance in rhetoric'' (p. 227). A. D. Hepburn's *Manual of English Rhetoric* (1875), however, divided sentences into two categories, the intellective and the volitive, which relate directly to the functional sentence types. Hepburn defined these categories so that the *intellective category* includes declarative and interrogative sentences and the *volitive category* includes exclamatory and imperative sentences. Hepburn apparently based his categories on the faculties of the mind, the intellect and will, and this relating of sentence types to faculty psychology suggests another possible area of scholarly investigation. I found almost no twentieth-century textbooks that asked students to construct sentences using these function categories. Richard Weaver's book *Composition* (1957) deals with them briefly in the handbook section of his text. One of his four categories—declarative, interrogative, imperative, and volitive— is identical to one of Hepburn's. One last point needs to be made about these functional sentence types. They seem to relate to the basic categories of *illocutionary acts* (assertives, directives, commissives, expressives, and declaratives); yet I could find no discussions of speech-act theory as it relates to sentence types in composition textbooks. The relationship between functional sentence types and speech-act theory may be another area of fruitful investigation.

Structural linguistics seems to have had little impact on the teaching of composition, except as it relates to the work of Francis Christensen. In the composition journals, I could find only two articles that directly relate structural grammar to composition: Sister Marie Aquin's ''Structural Approach to the Freshman Theme'' (1960), which advocates using structural grammar to teach sentence construction, and Michael Grady's ''Structured Structuralism'' (1965), which describes a composition course based on the structural analyses of English syntax using sentence patterns adapted from Paul Roberts's *English Sentences* (1962), a book that was an early attempt to bridge the gap between structural grammar and transformational grammar.

Perhaps the most successful attempt to bring structural linguistics to bear on the teaching of composition was made by Francis Christensen in his classic essay ''A Generative Rhetoric of the Sentence'' (1963a). Christensen began that essay by complaining that with the hundreds of handbooks and rhetorics available, he had never been able successfully to use the advice they give to teach the sentence. He saw little value in traditional grammar or in the rhetorical classification of sentences as loose, periodic, and balanced. Yet Christensen is insistent on the value of grammar as the foundation for rhetoric. The best grammar for his purposes, he said, is *immediate constituent analysis*. Christensen used immediate constituent analysis both as a means of analyzing sentences and as a means of getting students to construct sentences, using the sentence patterns described by Paul Roberts in *English Sentences* (1962). Christensen's method in analyzing sentences is to cut off the higher level immediate constituents, the free modifiers, from the base. To escape from the linearity of immediate constituent analysis, he devised a method of indenting the modifiers to reveal their grammatical relationships and of numbering the base clause and free modifiers. The kind of sentence Christensen was describing is the *cumulative*, a sentence that usually begins with a sentence base, consisting of a subject and a predicate together with any bound modifiers. Christensen's method in getting students to construct cumulative sentences is to have them begin with a sentence base and then support it with specific details in the form of free modifiers. To his discussion of grammatical principles Christensen added four rhetorical principles: addition, direction of modification or movement, levels of generality or abstraction, and texture.

Christensen extended his ideas about the sentence in a series of articles, some written before "A Generative Rhetoric of the Sentence" and others written about the same time. They include "In Defense of the Absolute" (1967a); "Restrictive and Non-Restrictive Modifiers Again" (1957); "Sentence Openers" (1963c); and "A Lesson from Hemingway" (1963b). All of these articles have been reprinted in *Notes Toward a New Rhetoric* (1967b). Another important article of Christensen's, "A Generative Rhetoric of the Paragraph" (1963a), is also included in that collection, and although its emphasis is on the paragraph, it deserves to be a part of a bibliography on the sentence, because Christensen bases his concept of the paragraph on an analogy with the cumulative sentence: the top sentence in a paragraph is parallel to the base clause, and the supporting sentences are parallel to the free modifiers. A second edition of *Notes Toward a New Rhetoric* appeared in 1978. Christensen's ideas were extended in *A New Rhetoric* (1976), a book written with the collaboration of his wife, Bonniejean Christensen.

Not everyone accepted Christensen's ideas uncritically. Sabina Thorne Johnson's essay "Some Tentative Strictures on Generative Rhetoric" (1969) argued that the concept of free modifiers says only a part of what there is to say about sentences. She concluded that teachers should welcome any method to counteract the emptiness of student writing. A. M. Tibbetts, in his article "On the Practical Uses of a Grammatical System" (1970), faulted Christensen for his excessive use of literary models, for presenting his ideas in absolute terms, and for his seeming lack of interest in getting students to define issues and make value judgments, but he commended him for providing understandable directions and suitable exercises for students to follow. Martha Solomon, in "Teaching the Nominative Absolute" (1975), extended Christensen's discussion of the absolute, and at least two studies, Charles Bond's "New Approach to Freshman Composition" (1972) and Lester Faigley's "Generative Rhetoric as a Way of Increasing Syntactic Fluency" (1979), have attempted to show that Christensen's generative method results in a quantitative and qualitative increase in the syntactic maturity of student writing.

Several years after Christensen's articles, the first articles advocating the use of *transformational grammar* as a method for teaching students to construct sentences appeared. Philip Cook's "Putting Grammar to Work" (1968) outlined a composition course that showed how transformational grammar could be used in the teaching of writing. Dorothy Petitt's "Rhetorical Absolute" (1969), claiming that Christensen's grammatical analysis of the absolute was incomplete, offered a transformational analysis of it. Janet Ross, in "A Transformational Approach to Teaching Composition" (1971), advocated reducing passages, taken from essays, to kernel sentences and then having students combine them and compare them to the original. Virginia Tufte, in her book *Grammar as Style* (1971) and in *Grammar as Style: Exercises in Creativity* (1971), written with the assistance of Garrett Stewart, demonstrated how transformational grammar might be used to teach prose style.

Closely related to those articles that advocate the use of transformational grammar in teaching writing are those articles dealing with *sentence-combining*. However, the scholarship in sentence-combining is so extensive that no useful purpose would be served merely in enumerating titles. The most important bibliographies, however, are those by Donald A. Daiker, Andrew Kerek, and Max Morenberg, particularly in Morenberg and Kerek's "Bibliography on Sentence Combining" (1979a) and in their book with Daiker, *Sentence Combining and the Teaching of Writing* (1979b). This book contains a collection of papers from the Miami University Conference on sentence-combining by almost every significant scholar in the field of sentence-combining. The book is divided into three sections: "Theory of Sentence Combining," "Research in Sentence Combining," and "Sentence Combining in the Classroom."

Of the articles in the composition journals that attempt to point out the value of transformational grammar in getting students to write sentences of greater structural variety and complexity, I would cite Charles Cooper's "Outline for Writing Sentence-Combining Problems" (1973); Harold Nugent and Darryl LeDuc's article "Creating Sentence Combining Activities" (1977); and Glenn Broadhead and James Berlin's "Twelve Steps to Using Generative Sentences and Sentence Combining in the Composition Classroom" (1981). An article of related interest is Marilyn Sternglass's "Sentence-Combining and the Reading of Sentences" (1980).

A number of textbooks have successfully incorporated sentence-combining techniques to teach composition. A few deal exclusively with sentence-combining. They include *The Writer's Options* (1982) by Donald Daiker and others; *Sentence Combining and Paragraph Building* (1981) by William Strong; *Connecting and Combining* (1982) by Helen Mills; and *Syntax and Style* (1974) by Clarence Schneider. The two books by Daiker and Strong offer exercises that extend the range of transformational sentence-combining beyond the sentence. In addition to those texts exclusively concerned with sentence-combining, there are a number of composition and rhetoric textbooks that contain at least one chapter on sentence-combining. Because they are so numerous, I'll mention only a few characteristic examples. Dean Memering and Frank O'Hare's text *The Writer's Work* (1980) contains a chapter with sections on "beyond the sentence" and "sentence chunks." *Four Worlds of Writing* (1981) by Janice Lauer and others has a brief section on sentence-combining in almost every chapter, so that the effect is cumulative. Finally, W. Ross Winterowd's text *The Contemporary Writer* (1981), in a section in the appendix, ties in sentence-combining with readability.

No composition textbook, as far as I can determine, has attempted to use *case grammar* in the teaching of English sentences. (Case grammar might be another fruitful area of scholarly investigation.) However, I did find an interesting article by Donald Mortland, "The Sentence" (1965), that describes the sentence as a two-scene drama, with the words as characters involved in the plot of making a sentence. In the *Essentials of English Grammar* (1970), Terence Langendoen described the semantic relationships in English sentences in similar terms.

It might seem anomalous to include a section on *sentence fragments* in this part of the bibliographical survey dealing with the grammar of the sentence, but more and more scholars are beginning to question the traditional handbook advice about avoiding the sentence fragment in writing. At least one modern grammar, tagmemic grammar, treats the sentence fragment as a minor sentence type. Walter Cook's *Introduction to Tagmemic Analysis* (1969) classified minor sentences by formal structure as being divided into sequential sentences, marginal sentences, and elliptical sentences. He classified minor sentences by *function* as consisting of addition sentences, response sentences, and exclamatory sentences. He included as types of the *nonclause minor sentence* calls, greetings, interjections, titles, mottoes, inscriptions, abbreviations, and the like. I know of no composition textbooks that have attempted to use these ideas to teach students the meaningful uses of sentence fragments.

In the composition journals, the earliest article I found that attempts to demonstrate the acceptability of the sentence fragment in writing is Kathryn McEuen's "Is the Sentence Disintegrating?" (1946). In their study of sentence fragments, reported in *Research in the Teaching of English* (1977), Charles Kline and W. Dean Memering reviewed the various positions taken by writers of composition textbooks on fragments and then compared these positions with actual practices in English formal writing. They differentiated between minor sentences and broken sentences (which are errors), and they presented a rule governing the use of minor sentences. They concluded that some fragments are acceptable rhetorical minor sentences. Muriel Harris, in her article "Mending the Fragmented Free Modifier" (1981), asserted that we ought not to treat fragmented free modifiers as serious errors. However, William Pixton, in the article "The Dangling Gerund" (1973), written before Muriel Harris's study, took a more traditional view of free modifiers and claimed that avoidance of dangling gerunds increases precision. Finally, Frank D'Angelo, in the handbook section of his text *Process and Thought in Composition* (1980), gave examples of fragments from professional writers and suggested that fragments can be effective in achieving certain rhetorical effects. He advised that in using fragments, the student writer should consider audience, purpose, and occasion. The sentence fragment is another area for scholarly inquiry.

The Rhetoric of the Sentence

There is a close relationship between the grammar of the sentence and the rhetoric of the sentence, as the work of Francis Christensen reveals. Christensen believed that the rhetoric of the sentence ought to be based on a solid grammatical foundation. Any discussion of the rhetoric of the sentence, therefore, is bound to overlap with a discussion of the grammar of the sentence. Christensen's work on the generative rhetoric of the sentence and with free modifiers could easily have been put into this section, but I wanted to emphasize his indebtedness to structural linguistics.

The rhetorical division of sentences into loose, periodic, balanced, and antithetical types ultimately derives from classical rhetoric and was ubiquitous in nineteenth-century rhetoric and composition textbooks. It is still being used in composition textbooks today. Christensen, you may recall, saw little use in getting students to write sentences based on the traditional rhetorical classification of sentences. Yet ironically, Christensen's concept of the cumulative sentence came to be closely aligned with the loose sentence, although the cumulative sentence, depending upon whether or not the free modifiers come before or after the base, can include both the periodic sentence and the loose sentence. (Whereas some cumulative sentences can be classified as loose or periodic, not all loose or periodic sentences, especially those with bound modifiers, are cumulative sentences.)

Richard Whately, in the *Elements of Rhetoric* (1832), classified sentences as loose, periodic, and antithetical. Whately, together with Hugh Blair and George Campbell, were transitional figures between classical rhetoric and nineteenth-century composition. The earliest composition textbook I could find that advocates using a rhetorical classification similar to Whately's was James Boyd's *Elements of English Composition* (1860), which divides sentences into periodic and non-periodic (that is, loose). John S. Hart in his text *A Manual of Composition and Rhetoric* (1876) classified sentences as period, loose, balanced, short, and long. Many nineteenth-century composition textbooks included long and short sentences as sentence types.

Some of the classifications of rhetorical sentence types found in nineteenth-century composition textbooks are interesting and amusing. For instance, Brainerd Kellogg's *Text-Book on Rhetoric* (1880) divides sentences into the loose sentence, the period, and the compromise. Kellogg's last category calls to mind Christensen's witty aside about the "loose" sentence. ("It sounds immoral.") The Rev. Charles Coppens, S.J., in his text *A Practical Introduction to English Rhetoric* (1880) divided sentences into periods, partial periods (that is, balanced), and loose. Other texts that classify sentences as being loose, periodic, and balanced are: John Genung's *Practical Elements of Rhetoric* (1891); John Hays Gardiner and others' *Elements of English Composition* (1902); Fred Newton

Scott and Joseph Villiers Denney's *Elementary English Composition* (1908); and William T. Brewster's *English Composition and Style* (1912).

No useful purpose would be served in enumerating the titles of all the twentieth-century textbooks that follow in this tradition. However, some typical examples of later texts that use the rhetorical classification of sentence types are Robert M. Gorrell and Charlton Laird's *Modern English Handbook* (1976) and William F. Irmscher's *Holt Guide to English* (1981). The classification and use of these rhetorical sentence types to teach students to construct sentences is another obvious area for scholarly investigation.

Closely related to the rhetorical division of sentences into loose, periodic, balanced, and antithetical is the classical rhetorical division of the figures of style into *schemes and tropes*. Because the classification of these figures can get confusing, I have adopted Edward P. J. Corbett's division in *Classical Rhetoric for the Modern Student* (1971) into schemes and tropes and have confined myself for the most part to a discussion of those schemes that deal with the patterning or arrangement of words. Richard Lanham's *Handlist of Rhetorical Terms* (1969) and Corbett's *Classical Rhetoric for the Modern Student* (1971) provide an easy access into the classification and use of the figures for English composition. Lanham's *Handlist* contains an alphabetical listing of the terms with copious examples. Corbett's strategy is to introduce students to figurative resources they may not be aware of. Of the schemes that have to do with word order, Corbett includes parallelism, antithesis, inversion, parenthesis, and apposition. Schemes of omission include ellipsis, asyndeton, and polysyndeton. Schemes of repetition include anaphora, epistrophe, epanalepsis, anadisplosis, climax, antimetabole, chiasmus, and polyptoton.

Nineteenth-century composition textbooks abound with chapters on the rhetorical figures that ultimately derive from classical rhetoric. James R. Boyd, however, in *Elements of English Composition* (1860), saw no useful reason for dividing the figures into figures of words and figures of thought or into schemes and tropes. In his discussion of the ''figures of expression,'' he includes categories such as antithesis and interrogation that have to do with the forms of sentences. Henry Day, in *The Art of Discourse* (1867), divided the figures into tropes, representative imagery, and the structure of the sentence. His sentence categories include inversion, anacoluthon, *aposiopesis* (''leaving a statement unfinished''), and sententiousness. In his text *Advanced Course in Composition and Rhetoric* (1873) George Payne Quackenbos divided the figures into figures of orthography, figures of etymology, figures of syntax, and figures of rhetoric. But much of what Quackenbos included in his discussion of figures of rhetoric have to do with sentence structure; the rest have to do with tropes. In the category labeled figures of rhetoric, Quackenbos included familiar tropes such as metaphor, simile, allegory, hyperbole, personification, metonymy, and synecdoche, but he also included interrogation and exclamation (functional sentence types) as well as antithesis and climax (rhetorical sentence types). Under figures of syntax he included ellipsis, *pleonasm* (needless repetition), syllepsis (which some rhetoricians treat as a pun), *enallage* (the substitution of one person, tense, gender, part of speech, and so on for another), and *hyperbaton* (departure from ordinary word order). These figures have importance for a bibliographical survey of this kind, but it is clear that some work is needed to sort them out.

At least two nineteenth-century composition textbooks attempt to reclassify the figures by basing them on associationist psychology. David J. Hill, in *The Science of Rhetoric* (1877), based the figures in his text on the primary laws of association: figures of resemblance (simile, metaphor, personification, allegory), figures of contiguity (synecdoche, metonymy, exclamation, hyperbole, apostrophe, vision), and figures of contrast (antithesis, contrast, epigram, interrogation, and irony). In Hill's scheme, the figures that have to do with sentence construction are mixed in with the tropes. In his text *The Principles of Written Discourse* (1884), Theodore Hunt divided figures of speech into figures of resemblance (simile, metaphor, allegory), of contrast (antithesis, epigram, irony), of contiguity (metonymy, synecdoche), and mixed figures (interrogation, exclamation, apostrophe, hyperbole, personification, and climax). Other texts that deal with the classical figures are John Genung's *Practical Elements of Rhetoric* (1891); Fred Newton Scott and Joseph Villiers Denney's *Elementary English Composition* (1908); and Henry Canby and John Opdycke's *Elements of Composition* (1927).

Few middle or late twentieth-century composition textbooks use these rhetorical categories except incidentally. Among those that do are Winston Weathers and Otis Winchester's *Copy and Compose* (1969) and *The New Strategy of Style* (1978) and J. Mitchell Morse's *Matters of Style* (1968). Nor could I find many articles in the composition journals that advocate the use of the schemes and tropes to teach sentence structure and matters of style. The exceptions are Richard Graves's "Primer for Teaching Style" (1974) and Frank D'Angelo's "Sacred Cows Make Great Hamburgers" (1974) and "Up Against the Wall, Mother!" (1982).

There are some articles in the journals that deal with individual schemes, such as parallelism and apposition. But there is no attempt by the authors to tie in the discussion of these categories to the classical schemes and tropes. There are other articles that deal with the rhetoric of the sentence in interesting ways. But I have not attempted to put them into a separate category. All can be subsumed under the rhetoric of the sentence. They include Robert Walker's article "The Common Writer" (1970), which argues that the parallel structure sentence, not the cumulative sentence, is the typical sentence of modern English; Orin Seright's "On Defining the Appositive" (1966); Tim Shopen's exploration of the grammar of ellipsis in his article "Some Contributions from Grammar to the Theory of Style" (1974); Winston Weathers's "Rhetoric of the Series" (1966); Leo Rockas's "Rhetoric of the Doodle" (1978), which argues that teachers ought to give some attention to teaching curt, precise, thought-provoking sentences; and Thomas

Kane's article "The Shape and Ring of Sentences" (1977), which asserts that teachers pay too little attention to showing students how to improve the rhythm of their sentences.

Sentence Structure and the Forms and Modes of Discourse

Unfortunately, the terms *forms* and *modes of discourse* have not been used with any precision by teachers of composition. Sometimes the terms are used as synonyms of each other. Sometimes the term *forms of discourse* refers to the categories of descriptions, narration, exposition, and argumentation used by nineteenth-century rhetoricians to classify kinds of writing. But because these rhetoricians mixed modes (descriptions and narration) with forms (exposition and argumentation), I refer to these nineteenth-century categories as the "forms"/ "modes of discourse." By *modes of discourse*, I mean what James Kinneavy in *A Theory of Discourse* (1971) referred to as "strategies" of discourse or what composition teachers mean when they talk about methods of development. Kinneavy's modes, which include description, narration, classification, and evaluation (he also called them the "hows" of discourse), subsume the methods of development (analysis, definition, comparison, contrast, exemplification, process, and cause and effect). These latter categories originated in the nineteenth-century as methods of developing paragraphs, but ultimately they derive from the classical *topoi*. Because of this close relationship between the *topoi* and the methods of development (that is, the modes) and sentence structure, I want to look at those articles that attempt to relate the teaching of the sentence to the forms and modes of discourse.

One of the earliest studies that attempts to relate sentence structure to the nineteenth-century concept of the forms/modes of discourse is J. C. Seegars's article "The Forms of Discourse and Sentence Structure" (1933). In this essay, Seegars argued that the techniques of discourse ought to be taught with regard to the form of discourse used. Seegars discovered that the form of discourse (description, narration, exposition, and argumentation) has a definite influence on the kind of clause structure used. In his essay "Abstract and Concrete Sentences" (1963), which later appeared as a chapter in his book *Modes of Rhetoric* (1964), Leo Rockas argued that the writer must consider how sentences communicate four orders of perception: static, temporal, mimetic, and mental. These orders of perception tie in with four modes of discourse: static, temporal, mimetic, and mental. The static modes include description, and definition; the temporal modes include narration and process; the mimetic modes, drama and dialogue; and the mental modes, reverie and persuasion. Richard Larson, in his article "Sentences in Action" (1967), proposed a method "that will reveal the contribution of each sentence and the interrelationship among sentences in a paragraph" (p. 16). Larson's method of analyzing sentences is to consider the sentence in terms of its various roles: state, restate, expand, particularize, exemplify, define, describe, narrate, qualify, concede, support, refute, evaluate, identify, compare or contrast, summarize, and conclude. Many of Larson's roles are identical to certain modes of discourse. Finally, Frank D'Angelo, in *A Conceptual Theory of Rhetoric* (1975), theorized that there is a close relationship among the classical topoi, the modes, and the schemes and tropes, and he suggested that in teaching writing these relationships need to be taken into consideration.

Sentence Structure and Classroom Activities

Many of the books and articles that I have referred to throughout this chapter have a more than passing interest in the process of teaching students to construct sentences. The following books and articles give more than ordinary attention to the process. For example, Robert Hume's "Sentence a Day" (1960), Jackson Burgess's "Sentence by Sentence" (1963), Marjorie Benton's "Reasonable Assignment" (1965), and Jane Walpole's "Vigorous Pursuit of Grace and Style" (1982) describe assignments in which students have to write one sentence every day. Richard Graves, in "A Strategy for Teaching Sentence Sense" (1976a), presented strategies for teaching students how to achieve a better understanding and command of sentence structure. In his text *Style* (1978), Richard Eastman presented three chapters on constructing sentences: basic placement, concentration, and higher organization. Erika Lindemann, in "Teaching about Sentences" in *A Rhetoric for Writing Teachers* (1982), described two techniques for teaching sentences in the context of composing: sentence-combining and the cumulative sentence. Finally, Joseph Williams, in his book *Style* (1981), categorized sentence problems and suggested ways of dealing with wordiness, sentence sprawl, and nominalizations. The book also contains chapters on sustaining the longer sentence, sentences in context, balance and symmetry, emphasis and rhythm, and sentence length and rhythm.

It should be apparent from this brief survey that we need to know much more about the grammar and rhetoric of the sentence as it relates to the teaching of composition. I have probably overlooked important books and articles, and I did not attempt to cover the extensive material on style in journals such as *Style* and *Language and Style*. Nor did I attempt to include the more specialized materials on the sentence found in linguistic journals. However, I sometimes included a more specialized reference to an article or book in linguistics or stylistics if that reference could be brought to bear on the teaching of writing. This chapter, then, only surveys the various aproaches to teaching the sentence, but it offers suggestions for further scholarly inquiry.

References

Aquin, Sister Marie. "A Structural Approach to the Freshman Theme." *CCC*, 11 (1960), 43–50.

Bardeen, C. W. *A Shorter Course in Rhetoric*. New York: Barnes, 1885.

Benton, Marjorie F. "A Reasonable Assignment: One Sentence." *EJ*, 54 (1965), 716–19.

Bond, Charles A. "A New Approach to Freshman Composition: A Trial of the Christensen Method." *CE*, 33 (1972), 623–27.

Boyd, James R. *Elements of English Composition.* New York: Barnes, Burr, 1860.

Brewster, William T. *English Composition and Style.* New York: Century, 1912.

Broadhead, Glenn J., and James A. Berlin. "Twelve Steps to Using Generative Sentences and Sentence Combining in the Composition Classroom." *CCC*, 32 (1981), 295–307.

Burgess, Jackson. "Sentence by Sentence." *CCC*, 14 (1963), 257–62.

Canby, Henry Seidel, and John Baker Opdycke. *The Elements of Composition.* Rev. ed. New York: Macmillan, 1927.

Christensen, Francis. "Restrictive and Non-Restrictive Modifiers Again." *CE*, 19 (1957), 27–28.

———. "A Generative Rhetoric of the Sentence." *CCC*, 14 (1963a), 155–61.

———. "A Lesson from Hemingway." *CE*, 25 (1963b), 12–18.

———. "Sentence Openers." *CE*, 25 (1963c), 7–11.

———. "In Defense of the Absolute." In *Notes Toward a New Rhetoric.* New York: Harper, Row, 1967a, pp. 82–94.

———. *Notes Toward a New Rhetoric.* New York: Harper, Row, 1967b.

———, and Bonniejean Christensen. *A New Rhetoric.* New York: Harper, Row, 1976.

———. *Notes Toward a New Rhetoric.* 2nd ed. New York: Harper, Row, 1978.

Cook, Philip H. "Putting Grammar to Work: The Generative Grammar in the Generative Rhetoric." *EJ*, 57 (1968), 1168–75.

Cook, Walter A., S.J. *Introduction to Tagmemic Analysis.* New York: Holt, Rinehart, Winston, 1969.

Cooper, Charles R. "An Outline for Writing Sentence-Combining Problems." *EJ*, 62 (1973), 96–102.

Coppens, Rev. Charles, S.J. *A Practical Introduction to English Rhetoric.* New York: Schwartz, Kirwin, Fauss, 1880.

Corbett, Edward P. J. *Classical Rhetoric for the Modern Student.* 2nd ed. New York: Oxford University Press, 1971.

Daiker, Donald A., Andrew Kerek, and Max Morenberg. *The Writer's Options: Combining to Composing.* 2nd ed. New York: Harper, Row, 1982.

———, eds. *Sentence Combining and the Teaching of Writing.* Conway, Ark.: L and S, 1979b.

D'Angelo, Frank J. "Sacred Cows Make Great Hamburgers: The Rhetoric of Graffiti." *CCC*, 25 (1974), 173–80.

———. *A Conceptual Theory of Rhetoric.* Cambridge, Mass.: Winthrop, 1975.

———. *Process and Thought in Composition.* Cambridge, Mass.: Winthrop, 1980.

———. "Up Against the Wall, Mother! The Rhetoric of Slogans, Catchphrases, and Graffiti." In *Rhetoric and Change.* Ed. William E. Tanner and J. Dean Bishop. Mesquite, Tex.: Ide House, 1982, pp. 104–14.

Day, Henry N. *The Art of Discourse.* New York: Scribner, 1867.

Eastman, Richard M. *Style: Writing and Reading as the Discovery of Outlook.* 2nd ed. New York: Oxford University Press, 1978.

Faigley, Lester L. "Generative Rhetoric as a Way of Increasing Syntactic Fluency." *CCC*, 30 (1979), 176–81.

Gardiner, John Hays, George Lyman Kittredge, and Sarah Louise Arnold. *Elements of English Composition*. Boston: Ginn, 1902.

Genung, John F. *The Practical Elements of Rhetoric*. Boston: Ginn, 1891.

Gorrell, Robert M., and Charlton Laird. *Modern English Handbook*. Englewood Cliffs, N.J.: Prentice-Hall, 1976.

Grady, Michael. "Structured Structuralism: Composition and Modern Linguistics." *EJ*, 54 (1965), 633–39.

Graves, Richard L. "A Primer for Teaching Style." *CCC*, 25 (1974), 186–90.

———. "A Strategy for Teaching Sentence Sense." In *Rhetoric and Composition*. Ed. Richard L. Graves. Rochelle Park, N.J.: Hayden, 1976a, pp. 86–94.

———, ed. *Rhetoric and Composition*. Rochelle Park, N.J.: Hayden, 1976b.

Harris, Muriel. "Mending the Fragmented Free Modifier." *CCC*, 32 (1981), 175–82.

Hart, John S. *A Manual of Composition and Rhetoric*. Philadelphia: Eldredge, 1876.

Hepburn, A. D. *Manual of English Rhetoric*. New York: Van Antwerp, 1875.

Hill, David J. *The Elements of Rhetoric and Composition*. New ed. New York and Chicago: Sheldon, 1884.

———. *The Science of Rhetoric*. New York: Sheldon, 1877.

Hume, Robert A. "A Sentence a Day." *CCC*, 11 (1960), 90–94.

Hunt, Theodore W. *The Principles of Written Discourse*. 2nd ed. New York: Armstrong, 1884.

Irmscher, William F. *The Holt Guide to English*. 3rd ed. New York: Holt, Rinehart, Winston, 1981.

Jameson, Henry W. *Rhetorical Method*. St. Louis: G. I. Jones, 1879.

Johnson, Sabina Thorne. "Some Tentative Strictures on Generative Rhetoric." *CE*, 31 (1969), 155–65.

Kane, Thomas S. " 'The Shape and Ring of Sentences': A Neglected Aspect of Composition." *CCC*, 28 (1977), 38–42.

Kellogg, Brainerd. *A Text-Book on Rhetoric*. New York: Clark, Maynard, 1880.

Kinneavy, James L. *A Theory of Discourse*. New York: Norton, 1971.

Kline, Charles R., Jr., and W. Dean Memering. "Formal Fragments: The English Minor Sentence." *RTE*, 11 (1977), 97–110.

Langendoen, D. Terence. *Essentials of English Grammar*. New York: Holt, Rinehart, Winston, 1970.

Lanham, Richard A. *A Handlist of Rhetorical Terms*. Berkeley and Los Angeles: University of California Press, 1969.

Larson, Richard L. "Sentences in Action: A Technique for Analyzing Paragraphs." *CCC*, 18 (1967), 16–22.

Lauer, Janice M., Gene Montague, Andrea Lunsford, and Janet Emig. *Four Worlds of Writing*. New York: Harper, Row, 1981.

Lindemann, Erika. "Teaching about Sentences." *A Rhetoric for Writing Teachers*. New York: Oxford University Press, 1982, pp. 138–48.

McEuen, Kathryn. "Is the Sentence Disintegrating?" *EJ*, 35 (1946), 433–38.

Memering, Dean, and Frank O'Hare. *The Writer's Work*. Englewood Cliffs, N.J.: Prentice-Hall, 1980.

Mills, Helen. *Connecting and Combining*. Glenview, Ill.: Scott, Foresman, 1982.

Morenberg, Max, and Andrew Kerek. "Bibliography on Sentence Combining: Theory and Teaching, 1964–1979." *RSQ*, 9 (1979), 97–111.

Morse, J. Mitchell. *Matters of Style*. New York: Bobbs-Merrill, 1968.

Mortland, Donald F. "The Sentence." *EJ*, 54 (1965), 95–100.

Nugent, Harold E., and Darryl LeDuc. "Creating Sentence Combining Activities." *Conn EJ*, 9 (1977), 106–16.

Petitt, Dorothy. "The Rhetorical Absolute: A Transformed Sentence." *CCC*, 20 (1969), 29–34.

Pixton, William H. "The Dangling Gerund: A Working Definition." *CCC*, 24 (1973), 193–99.

Quackenbos, George Payne. *Advanced Course in Composition and Rhetoric*. New York: Appleton, 1873.

Read, Herbert. *English Prose Style*. New York: Pantheon, 1952.

Roberts, Paul. *English Sentences*. New York: Harcourt, Brace, World, 1962.

Rockas, Leo. "Abstract and Concrete Sentences." *CCC*, 14 (1963), 97–101.

———. *Modes of Rhetoric*. New York: St. Martin's, 1964.

———. "The Rhetoric of Doodle." *CE*, 40 (1978), 139–44.

Ross, Janet. "A Transformational Approach to Teaching Composition." *CCC*, 22 (1971), 179–84.

Schneider, Clarence E. *Syntax and Style*. San Francisco: Chandler, Sharp, 1974.

Scott, Fred Newton, and Joseph Villiers Denney. *Elementary English Composition*. New ed. Boston: Allyn, Bacon, 1908.

Searle, John R. *Expression and Meaning*. Cambridge: Cambridge University Press, 1979.

Seegars, J. C. "The Form of Discourse and Sentence Structure." *Elem Eng*, 10 (1933), 51–54.

Seright, Orin D. "On Defining the Appositive." *CCC*, 17 (1966), 107–10.

Shopen, Tim. "Some Contributions from Grammar to the Theory of Style." *CE*, 35 (1974), 775–97.

Sledd, James. "Coordination (Faulty) and Subordination (Upside-Down)." *CCC*, 7 (1956), 181–87.

Solomon, Martha. "Teaching the Nominative Absolute." *CCC*, 26 (1975), 356–61.

Sternglass, Marilyn. "Sentence-Combining and the Reading of Sentences." *CCC*, 31 (1980), 325–28.

Strong, William. *Sentence Combining and Paragraph Building*. New York: Random House, 1981.

Tibbetts, A. M. "On the Practical Uses of a Grammatical System: A Note on Christensen and Johnson." *CE*, 31 (1970), 870–78.

Tufte, Virginia. *Grammar as Style*. With the Assistance of Garrett Stewart. New York: Holt, Rinehart, Winston, 1971.

———, and Garrett Stewart. *Grammar as Style: Exercises in Creativity*. New York: Holt, Rinehart, Winston, 1971.

Walker, Robert L., O.P. "The Common Writer: A Case for Parallel Structure." *CCC*, 21 (1970), 373–79.

Walpole, Jane R. "The Vigorous Pursuit of Grace and Style." *Writ Instr*, 1 (1982), 163–69.

Weathers, Winston. "The Rhetoric of the Series." *CCC*, 17 (1966), 217–22.

Weathers, Winston, and Otis Winchester. *Copy and Compose*. Englewood Cliffs, N.J.: Prentice-Hall, 1969.

———. *The New Strategy of Style*. New York: McGraw-Hill, 1978.

Weaver, Richard M. *Composition*. New York: Holt, Rinehart, Winston, 1957.

Whately, Richard. *Elements of Rhetoric*. Boston: Hilliard, Gray, 1832.

Williams, Joseph M. *Style: Ten Lessons in Clarity & Grace*. Glenview, Ill.: Scott, Foresman, 1981.

Winterowd, W. Ross. *The Contemporary Writer*. 2nd ed. New York: Harcourt, 1981.

The Role of Spelling in Composition for Older Students

JAMES S. BEGGS

The difficulties of spelling English words correctly and the importance of that proper sequencing of letters to the composition process have been much debated. Two extreme factions find the present system insupportable; one has, for 200 years, called for a greatly revamped spelling system, and the other thinks we should simply relax the current standard for spelling, which is, after all, perfection. Spelling Reform, which expresses the first of these views, has weakened recently after enjoying the endorsement in years past of men like Benjamin Franklin and George Bernard Shaw. Appeals to relax spelling standards have been more scattered. But these two extreme views on spelling have come to be less frequently represented in the literature. In the "middle ground," however, many and varied approaches, theoretical and practical, vie for acceptance. They are most commonly classified as the *traditional* methods, calling for teaching spelling through self-corrected tests on selective word lists and backed by an impressive body of research, and the newer *linguistic* methods, which seek to teach an understanding of the way the orthographic system works. Although still largely untested, these methods may provide important links between reading, spelling, and vocabulary curricula. Both concede that, at least for the time being, we must work within our present orthographic system and within society's standard of perfect spelling.

Spelling Reform versus Relaxation of Current Standards

The two extremes of the spelling spectrum deserve some mention. The crusade to reform English spelling has benefited from the advocacy of prominent men such as Ben Franklin and Noah Webster in the eighteenth century and, more recently, of Col. R. R. McCormick of *The Chicago Tribune* and George Bernard Shaw. But today, even those who most passionately believe that the seemingly illogical nature of English spelling is a real hindrance to the development of reading and communication skills acknowledge that our orthographic system is solidly entrenched and that the more radical spelling reform movements are in their death throes. The ITA, or International Teaching Alphabet, a highly phonetic system of representation for introducing children to spelling, has scored some successes on the elementary level, but as children mature, they are able to make more sophisticated connections between language and spelling, and the ITA can and should be discarded. A simplified spelling system that seeks permanent, widespread acceptance, albeit on a limited scale, is discussed by Alfred J. Mazurkiewicz and Charlotte L. Rath in "Affects on Adult Speaking Choices" (1976). Spelling Reform One, calling for spellings like *altho* and *thru*, they reported, has been adopted by the Australian Teacher Association and, with help from the media, is making inroads in America.

The influence of the harder line attitudes on spelling reform are still being felt as well. Arthur W. Heilman, in *Phonics in Proper Perspective* (1968), spoke for this view: "The present practice of attempting to teach *all* American youth to read and spell English is the foremost example of conspicuous consumption of a nation's resources since the building of the pyramids" (p. 112). A somewhat more conservative expression of the reformer's stance is John R. Malone's "Larger Aspects of Spelling Reform" (1962).

At the opposite end of the spectrum is a group of commentators who question the importance of spelling. To them, spelling has assumed too large a place in the whole of composition. Ken Macrorie was one of the first to speak against unduly high standards for spelling in student papers. In "The Hypocracy of Perfection" (1953), Macrorie maintained that society's standard of perfect spelling is dubiously upheld, citing numerous errors on signs, in professors' blackboard writing, and even in a professionally printed poster he himself put up advertising a campus function. Moreover, Macrorie scoffed at the standard line that "poor spelling inhibits communication." He conceded that numerous errors can distract a reader who is a proficient speller, but that an occasional slip does not, and he cited some informal proofreading tests in which a "glaring" error was missed repeatedly by educated readers. Macrorie's stance, then, is not an abandonment of spelling standards but a relaxation of them; we cannot, he said, "condemn a few mistakes so harshly that we make students feel like lepers among educated men" (p. 289). Robbins Burling agrees with Macrorie but is much more strident. Proclaiming himself a "liberated bad speller," Burling has written one article, "Poor Spellers of the World, Unite!" (1976), employing progressively poorer spelling, as an attempt to refute Noam Chomsky and Morris Halle's statement that English orthography is a near optimal system. An earlier article, "An Anthropologist Among the English Teachers" (1974), presents a more sensible case, although one that may shock or alienate many teachers of

English. Burling asked that his spelling be left uncorrected, arguing that "if anyone finds my spelling so distracting that it interferes with his understanding of my ideas, then that person is unqualified to be a teacher of composition" (p. 237). Too much attention on the mechanical competence of a student paper is as much a fallacy to Burling as what he called the "freedom fallacy," or asking only that a student "express himself." Penalizing poor spelling, said Burling, reveals an immature adherence to the "mechanical fallacy," and teachers insecure enough to feel this need should get out of the business.

As abrasive as he may seem, Burling should arouse, along with anger, feelings of guilt and embarrassment in those teachers guilty of what might be called "grading virtuosity." Sometimes in our zeal to help students correct every error in their papers, we are showing off our own proofreading ability more than helping students. Frank Whitehead, in *The Disappearing Dais* (1966), called "direct attack" on mechanics and spelling "time utterly wasted." Teachers must mark errors selectively, he said. He cited a 13-year-old's two-paragraph theme containing 13 misspellings: "to ask a pupil at this ability level to relearn all thirteen of them may only flummox him" (p. 214). Moreover, he asked, do we want to discourage a student like the 11-year-old who misspells *audience, miniature, fascinating,* and *applaud* from using these words? Peter Medway found student creativity and self-confidence similarly suffocated by England's rigid spelling standards. In "Let Down by Speling" (1976), Medway observed that "typists' bad spelling is on a par with mugging, drug-taking and long hair as a sign of national decadence" but that such high standards in schools and the business world are wasteful, irrelevant, and damaging. He thought that bad spellers are unfairly stigmatized as lazy or stupid and that insistence on perfect spelling alienates many who are intelligent, basically interested in learning, and otherwise competent in communication. Medway, perhaps in a moment of idealistic weakness, even suggested completely abandoning our insistence on consistent spelling, believing we could probably get used to the variant spellings.

The Middle Ground: Overviews and Syntheses of Research

In the very large middle ground of attitudes toward spelling, between the reformers and the anarchists, are those who seek to instill a sound theoretical understanding of English orthography and offer the best possible methods for teaching students to meet current spelling standards. Even these theorists, though, are split into two schools that are often at odds. One, loosely called the "old school," assumes that English spelling is essentially illogical, because the correspondence between English sounds and their alphabetic representations is low. Phonics, then, is an unreliable teaching technique, and since only a few spelling generalizations, for example the *y* to *i* suffixation rule, hold up with few enough exceptions to justify their use, most words must be memorized from lists and learned using a study-test-correction sequence. A newer theory is espoused by Paul Hanna, Noam Chomsky, Carol Chomsky, and Richard Venezky, although it has not been thoroughly tested in the classroom but seems basically sound. These proponents of the "linguistic school" argue that English spelling is not random but does exhibit logic. Paul Hanna and his colleagues (*Phoneme-Grapheme Correspondences as Cues to Spelling Improvement* [1966]) discovered that English spelling even makes phonetic sense when the position of the *graphemes* (letters or letter combinations) is considered. Their work refutes George Bernard Shaw's assertion that *ghoti* is a possible spelling of *fish*, since *gh* is never found to represent /f/ at the beginning of a word and *ti* is never found to represent /š/ at the end of a word. Other important consistencies in English spelling have been noted by the Chomskys, working independently, and Richard Venezky, who contended that orthography shouldn't be judged as a perfect phonetic representation of English but that it preserves the relatedness of words like *sane* and *sanity* in a way that pronounciation (long vowel versus short vowel) or a phonetic representation ([sɛyn] vs. [sænǝtɪy]) do not.

The "old school" is an arbitrary label and perhaps should be taken as a mere convenience, a designation for the many techniques for teaching spelling that largely ignore the generalizations made by the linguists. These methods have proven effective in the classroom and have received support from experimental research over the past half century. Such techniques include the teaching of certain spelling rules, the learning of spelling words from a prepared list rather than in context, and analysis and categorization of recurrent errors. Several sources in the field may provide helpful syntheses of this half-century or so of research. Thomas D. Horn's chapter on "Spelling" in the *Encyclopedia of Educational Research* (1969) is one of the first efforts at pulling together the massive body of twentieth-century spelling research. Ruel Allred's *Spelling* (1977) is another good survey of the field with an emphasis on teaching younger students to spell. Allred expressed suspicion of the new linguistic methods, which he believes have not undergone the rigors of practical testing and are more applicable to reading rather than spelling improvement. Another short book offering a survey of the field comes from Robert J. Fitzsimmons and Bradley M. Loomer. *Spelling Research and Practice* (1977), like Allred's booklet, laments the failure of teachers to apply conscientiously the findings of research to their classroom practices; teachers are especially stubborn in attempting to teach spelling words in context instead of from lists and in concentrating on the "hard spots" of words instead of using a holistic approach. Smaller, more manageable overviews of spelling research can be found in Loomer's *Educator's Guide to Spelling Research and Practice* (1978); in Timothy R. Blair and William H. Rupley's "New Trends in Spelling Instruction" (1980), which updates the earlier work and also suggests the means for obtaining materials through the ERIC system; and in Terry Johnson, Kenneth Langford, and Kerry Quorn's "Characteristics of an Effective Spelling Program" (1981). See also Patricia S. Geedy's, "What Research Tells Us about Spelling" (1975) and Walter Petty's, "The Teaching of Spelling" (1969). There have also been many book-length studies on the teaching of spelling, most of which report principles and techniques proven through years of research and classroom practice. Some of the most highly respected are *Spelling* (1971) by Paul Hanna, Richard Hodges, and Jean Hanna; *Better Spelling* (1960) by Edward W. Dolch; *Teaching Spelling* (1955) by Gertrude Hildreth; *Teaching Spelling* (1954) by Ernest Horn; and *The Teaching of Spelling* (1951) by James A. Fitzgerald.

Some of the recent overviews of the field give more acknowledgement to the emergence of linguistic defenses of English orthography, and some try to reconcile them with the "seat-of-the-pants" methods advocated by scholars like Allred, Loomer, and the Horns. Caryl Rivers's article "Its Tyme to Du Something" (1974) does not claim to be an exhaustive work but in a light, readable tone sensibly delineates the conflict between what she called the "look-say" or functionalist approach and the linguistic approach. This seven-page piece looks at the history of our orthography as well as reform movements and spelling research and, after investigating the conflict over methodology, takes a middle stance in the final section, diplomatically headed "More Research, More Compromise." Another "peacemaker" is Shane Templeton, author of many articles on spelling, frequently with a focus on the older student. In "The Circle Game of English Spelling" (1979a), Templeton sought a compromise between Noam Chomsky's "dignity" and optimality of English spelling and "the popular excesses of back-to-basics advocates" (p. 790). Templeton's discussion of popular theories, his observation that children make different use and have a changing understanding of English orthography as they mature, his advice to embed spelling consciousness into a broader program, such as vocabulary, and his concurrence with Hemingway that the writing act, done "in hot blood, like an argument," should be kept separate from the "cooler-tempered" concerns of proofreading all hit home and are especially salient for the needs of the older student with spelling problems. Robert L. Hillerich has also written a sage overview, "Let's Teach Spelling—Not Phonetic Misspelling" (1977), that is not as comprehensive as some but is full of thoughtful advice and well supported by research. Hillerich's views, however, are summarily dismissed as archaic in one of the most current overview articles, "On the Development of Spelling Ability" (1982) by Richard E. Hodges. Hodges argued that requiring a student to master a basic core of words typically used in written communication is a strategy that ignores the recent revelations of orthography's logic, but he did concede a conspicuously unresolved issue, that of a spelling curriculum based on those revelations. There seems to be an ongoing battle between Hillerich and Hodges, and their bickering in a 1982 issue of *Educational Leadership*, for example, demonstrates the head-on clash of two schools of thought.

Learning Principles and Research-Tested Methods

What then are some of the specific methods for teaching spelling, either proven effective or discounted by research and classroom practice? Most successful programs seem to work from some sort of prepared word list or from a list of the students' own errors or both. Whichever method or combination of methods is chosen, the words should be presented to students in list form, and the students should be asked only to reproduce that list to the teacher and not be required to write words in a meaningful context. This principle is born out by much research but, as Allred and others noted, is stubbornly ignored by many teachers. An early study by W. H. Winch, "Additional Researches on Learning to Spell" (1916), noted that a "direct" teaching method produced better spelling results than an "indirect" or context approach. Later studies by W. E. Hawley and Jackson Gallup ("The 'List' vs. the 'Sentence' Method of Teaching Spelling" [1922]) and Paul McKee ("Teaching Spelling by Column and Context Forms" [1927]) corroborate Winch's findings.

The use of the list method means that the student should be required to write only the word in question. It does not imply that the word cannot be clarified with context clues to help students distinguish homophones, nor does it suggest that there is not a correlation between knowledge of a word's meaning and the ability to spell it. John N. Mangieri and R. Scott Baldwin's "Meaning as a Factor in Predicting Spelling Difficulty" (1979), meticulously designed and evaluated, reports that "when subjects were unable to match words with appropriate meanings, they tended to misspell those words" (p. 286). Mangieri and Baldwin suggested that meaning is a factor that may help a student visualize a word and, like Templeton, advocated a coordinated spelling and vocabulary program. The role of meaning for determining which spelling words should be taught, in fact, should be one of the chief criteria for a word's selection from a prepared list. It makes no sense to offer words like *soliloquy* or *sacrilegious* which students would use infrequently; students should probably consult a dictionary for spelling such words. As a matter of fact, as Gertrude Hildreth (1955) noted, "A low meaning vocabulary is likely to be a cause of spelling deficiency. Children have a hard time even copying a word that is unknown to them in context" (p. 27).

There are scores of carefully prepared word lists for teachers to draw from. For most, frequency is the prime criterion, but words can be further evaluated by the conscientious teacher on the basis of their difficulty, degree of local interest and importance, permanency, and relevance to a particular student or group of students. One of the first such lists prepared, Ernest Horn's *Basic Writing Vocabulary* (1927), has retained its validity. Notably, the highly respected list of Edward L. Thorndike and Irving Lorge, *The Teacher's Word Book of 30,000 Words* (1944), contains only 170 words that did not appear on Horn's list of 5,000. Many of the lists based on the writing of elementary schoolchildren, such as James Fitzgerald's "Words Misspelled Most Frequently by Children of the Fourth, Fifth, and Sixth Grade Levels in Life Outside the School" (1932), Henry D. Rinsland's *Basic Vocabulary of Elementary School Children* (1945), and Edward Dolch's list in *Better Spelling* (1960), can be applied to the teaching of adults, but several compilations are geared specifically to older students. Among them are the lists amassed by Ernest Simmons and

Harold Bixler in *The New Standard High School Spelling Scale* (1940), by Fred C. Ayer in *A Study of High School Vocabulary* (1945), and by Henry Kučera and W. Nelson Francis in *Computational Analysis of Present-Day American English* (1967).

The work of Thomas Clark Pollock might also prove helpful to the teacher seeking to prepare meaningful spelling lists. Pollock conducted a survey, the results of which appear in "Spelling Report" (1954), calling for a tabulation of the words college teachers found most frequently misspelled in their students' papers. Of the 31,375 misspellings returned, Pollock found that only 9 percent of the words or word groups accounted for more than half of the misspellings. This finding greatly limits most words that, through frequency of use and misspelling, a teacher might deem important for students to know. Pollock also found that the intersection of the list of the 100 words most frequently misspelled by college students and the 100 most often misspelled by seventh and eighth graders yielded 31 words, which might prove a solid core for remedial college students. *The University Spelling Book* (1955), cowritten with Pollock by William D. Baker, presents six lists: the 10 words or word groups most often misspelled by college students, the 100 most frequent errors, and the third, fourth, fifth, and sixth "hundreds." College composition teachers will find these compilations so full of familiar misspellings that they may think they had prepared the lists themselves.

Although the aforementioned word lists have proved reliable over the years in providing words of importance to students, they should be supplemented by a personal word list, kept by the students, of the words they have misspelled in their work both for English class and other courses. Almost all of the self-help courses and most of the works covering a full spectrum of spelling education advocate this method; several writers have given it special attention. Jean L. Buck, a teacher of remedial spelling, wrote in "A New Look at Teaching Spelling" (1977) about requiring students to keep file cards on their misspellings. She gauged her teaching approach according to how general or individual the errors seemed; thus she could choose to spend class time on a recurring problem, group students according to similar errors, work individually with students making uncommon or unusual errors, or, if necessary, refer students to a specialist. Several writers have advocated the analysis and categorization of student errors as a corrective and preventative measure. Rochelle Ireland, in "A Proposal for Teaching English in the Virginia Community College System" (1980), described her successful use of a classification system devised by George Spache. Two of Spache's categories, omissions of letters or syllables and transpositions or partial reversals, were the most highly represented errors among Ireland's students. Spache's other groupings—additions and repetitions, substitutions, homonyms, incomplete renderings, and unrecognizable renderings—were about equally represented. Error analysis is also a large part of Mina Shaughnessy's program for teaching spelling to Basic Writers, as described in her book *Errors and Expectations* (1977). Although as a teacher she saw five broad causes for spelling error, among them unpredictabilities of English spelling, pronunciation discrepancies, and inability to remember or "see" words, she required her students to file errors under 1 of 12 categories, similar to Spache's divisions.

Each of these systems uses the important principle of self-correction, considered by several writers as the single most valuable concept in the teaching of spelling. Thomas Horn's "Effect of the Corrected Test on Learning to Spell" (1947), Ernest Horn's *Teaching Spelling* (1954), and Gerald C. Eicholz's "Spelling Improvement Through a Self-Check Device" (1964) all report good results from having students correct their own tests, and Ernest Horn particularly noted the system's efficiency. Feedback and correction should follow a student's use of a word as soon as possible. For older students especially, the best approach for coordinating testing and study of words, as observed particularly by Arthur T. Gates in "An Experimental Comparison of the Study-Test and Test-Study Methods in Spelling" (1931) and J. Stephen Sherwin in "Research and the Teaching of English" (1971), seems to be the test-study-test method, as opposed to the study-test pattern. Typical study methods used in this pattern, for example those recommended by Ernest Horn in *Teaching Spelling* (1954) and a somewhat simplified method devised by Robert Gilstrap ("Development of Independent Spelling Skills in the Intermediate Grades" [1962]), involve the discipline of saying the letters repeatedly in sequence, looking away and trying to visualize the word, and then writing the word and checking its spelling against the list.

Teachers must recognize, too, that students turning in papers containing misspellings may be suffering from a proofreading rather than a spelling problem. Proofreading skills can be taught, but often poor proofreading stems from a deeper motivational problem; a student may be simply too lazy to give the paper the necessary rereadings to discover careless errors. Some students prefer the security of the "I could have" attitude; rather than recognizing that their best proofreading efforts weren't good enough, they can excuse the errors, at least to themselves, as attributable to not having enough time or desire to perform such a menial task.

But for students willing to improve their proofreading, there are some sensible principles they can apply. Consensus seems to support Hemingway's belief in the separation of the cool, methodical chore of proofreading from the heat of invention. As Geneva Pilgrim wrote in *Learning and Teaching Practices in English* (1966), writers "become so engrossed in putting down whatever they are trying to say that they neglect the niceties of punctuation or spelling. There is no harm in this, provided that—after the glow of creative inspiration has subsided—the writer goes back and rereads the manuscript, correcting it until it conforms with the expected standards" (p. 109). Indeed, nothing seems more annoying to a teacher than to watch a student "break stride," fumbling for a dictionary every other line of an in-class composition.

Once instructors establish the distinction between creation and proofreading, they can teach some principles of the latter skill. Some of the more scholarly studies in the field seek insight into reading rather than composition and examine the proofing of printed material; nevertheless, some of their findings apply to spelling, composing, and proofreading handwritten papers. Ralph Haber and Robert Schindler's "Error in Proofreading" (1981) summarizes some of the important work in the field and notes that the many possible variables leading to proofreading error, such as word frequency, word type, word shape, and word length, are difficult to isolate. Nevertheless, Haber and Schindler observed that shape-changing misspellings (for example, *pad* written as *pag*) were detected more easily than those not influencing word shape (for example, *pad* rendered as *pab*). Both A. F. Healy, in "Proofreading Errors on the Word *the*" (1980), and M. B. Holbrook, in "Effect of Subjective Interletter Similarity, Perceived Word Similarity, and Contextual Variables on the Recognition of Letter Substitutions in a Proofreading Task" (1978), found that errors in long words escape the proofreader's scrutiny more easily than those in short words. Haber and Schindler (1981) and D.W.J. Corcoran and D. L. Weening ("Acoustic Factors in Visual Search" [1968]) found that word length was not the only significant variable, making an important distinction between "content" words (essentially nouns, verbs, non-demonstrative adjectives) and "function" words (articles, prepositions, conjunctions). Corcoran and Weening found that misprints were harder to detect in short, high-frequency words, particularly function words, than in larger words. Haber and Schindler observed that subjects had more difficulty finding errors in function words than in content words of the same length. Letter transpositions, identified by Ireland (1980) and Shaughnessy (1977) as typical errors in word representation, have been studied by both Healy (1980) and J. L. Sloboda ("The Effect of Item Position on the Likelihood of Identification by Inference in Prose Reading and Music Reading" [1976]). Each found what may seem intuitively obvious, that letters switched at the ends of words were more difficult to detect than initial transpositions, but that transposed letter pairs in medial positions were the hardest to detect.

Emerging from the esoteric to the more widely applicable, we find Shirley Wong's "Proofreading Pitfalls" (1975), which describes proofreading as a complex visual process that requires more fixations (single visual images) and faster saccades (rapid sideways movements of the eye) than regular reading. Significantly, Wong's subjects identified misspellings at a 98.98 percent rate but proofread at only a 93.5 percent rate. Even when instructed to proofread letter by letter (small fixations), they were unable to avoid making larger fixations, grouping letters and even words in a single fixation. Essentially, they became caught up in reading, which is done in word chunks, rather than proofreading, which should be performed, if not letter by letter, at least word by word. To avoid making the large word groupings typical of the reading process, students have often been instructed to proofread backwards, and Wong's study lends credibility to the method. This technique, of course, will not catch homophone errors, but a careful forward proofreading job, to supplement the backwards effort, should pick up the common (and usually careless) confusion of *their/there/they're*, *its/it's*, *your/you're*, and similar homophone groups. Mina Shaughnessy (1977) observed, as many teachers have, that students often perform well on proofreading exercises or fault-finding in classmates' papers but have difficulty "transferring the same disinterested watchfulness to their own words and sentences" (p. 182). Teachers must weigh the advantages of exchanging papers for proofreading against the possible disadvantages of students' not accepting responsibility for their own writing.

All of the above-mentioned techniques for good spelling—word lists, test-study-test, repetition, careful proofreading—although time-honored and proven effective, may seem to promote the rote droning of letters by bored students, and teachers and researchers have constantly sought other techniques and supplementary methods that might instill in students more interest and a broader understanding of English orthography. Unfortunately, few of the newer techniques have proven as reliable as the traditional methods. One typical supplement to the traditional methods is the teaching of spelling rules. At least one writer, Edmund Henderson ("Correct Spelling—An Inquiry" [1974]), debunked the use of spelling rules (as well as other spelling aids such as mnemonics) altogether: "good spellers do not know them, and bad spellers remember them incorrectly" (p. 177). But most of the research and the spelling programs and advice growing out of the research have advocated the teaching of some spelling rules. They can, however, be more trouble than they are worth, especially if they are complexly worded or if there are so many violations of the rules as to require mastering a long list of exceptions as well as the rule itself. In *Educator's Guide to Spelling Research and Practice* (1978), Bradley Loomer argued that the only spelling rules worth teaching are those that hold at least 80 percent of the time. Scores of sources list what their authors consider to be the most reliable and applicable spelling rules, but at the intersection of these lists stand only three. All are rules of affixation: droping the silent *e*, changing the *y* to *i*, and the consonant-doubling rule. The first calls for a deletion of a final silent *e* before a suffix beginning with a vowel, and the second says that a final *y*, except when preceded by a vowel, should be changed to *i* before any suffix except *-ing*. The third rule for adding a suffix is perhaps best expressed as a sequence of instructions, as Shaughnessy suggested, rather than a complex single statement: (1) Does the word end consonant-vowel-consonant? (2) Is the word accented on the final syllable? (3) Does the suffix begin with a vowel? If yes to all three, double the consonant.

The familiar "*i* before *e*, except after *c*" jingle has been omitted from many textbooks and self-help programs, probably because it requires a bulky list of exceptions or additional comment to account for words like *weird*, *deficient*, and *deity*. Most of the other English spelling rules (and some books list as many as 70) are even more limited in applicability for various reasons. Edwin Read, Ruel Allred, and Louise Baird added two rules for forming plurals, the substitution of *-ves* for a single final *f* and the addition of *-es* to works like *box* and *watch* ending with a hissing sound; the first of these rules, however, has very limited use and the second seems intuitively obvious to most native speakers. Several sources, including "Great Disasters of the Twentieth Century" (1979) by W. E.

Perkins and Melba Benson, offer rules to distinguish often-confused suffixes like *-able/-ible* and *-cede/-ceed/-sede*. The latter simply divides the 20 or so English words ending in *sid* into groups that must be memorized, and neither Perkins and Benson nor anyone else has come up with a reliable rule to differentiate *-able* and *-ible*. Words ending with these suffixes, as well as those ending in other problem suffixes like *-ant/-ent*, *-ize/-ise/-yze*, and *-er/-or/-ar*, would probably serve the weak speller best as part of a list pasted to the inside cover of his dictionary; learning a complicated rule or trying to memorize the list does not seem worth the effort.

Another group of spelling truisms are what Allred in *Spelling* (1977) called "linguistic generalizations." They grew largely out of the work of Paul Hanna and others, particularly in their work at Stanford, which sought, in part, to defend English orthography from charges of erratic phoneme to grapheme correspondence. (See their *Phoneme-Grapheme Correspondences as Cues to Spelling Improvement* [1966].) Although often of near 100 percent validity, many of these generalizations aid the speller negligibly. Granted, no English words end in *v* (as long as we discount *rev*), and *q* is always followed by *u* in common English words, but how helpful are these patterns to spellers? Allred is also skeptical of the pedagogical value of patterns such as *y*, *e*, or *i* following a *c* as a cue to its /s/ pronunciation. Such a generalization, as Allred noted, will not help one spell *sister* or *sit*, but he failed to note that it can eliminate as impossible spellings like *cilt* for *kilt* or *cept* for *kept*.

Reliable and easy-to-apply generalizations about English orthography are difficult to establish and should thus be used by teachers carefully and sparingly. Shaughnessy (1977), Thomas Horn (1969), Perkins and Benson (1979), and others also advised evaluating students on their ability to apply a given rule, not on their ability to state it. Many commentators have also affirmed the value of induction in the learning of spelling generalizations. Shaughnessy advocated inductive learning for the most regular spelling generalizations, as did C. Glennon Rowell in "Inductive Teaching as a Strategy for Instruction in Spelling" (1979). Rowell observed that when students must formulate their own rule from a large bank of words, they are not passive but active learners, assimilating data to make a significant conclusion. He found that students enjoy their active role and also retain knowledge longer. Rowell sorted the inductive methods into three divisions: experiential, investigatory, and pre-arranged data. In the *experiential* method, the data are supplied from the students' previous knowledge; thus the students supply words in class like *cake*, *make*, *black*, and *duck* to generalize the pattern for using *-ke* or *-ck*. In the *investigatory* process, the students find examples out of class, and in the *pre-arranged-data* method, the teacher supplies a list of words. Teachers must weigh the advantages of each; for example, the pre-arranged-data method may offer security for the teacher but keep the students passive in the initial stages. Other findings on induction and spelling can be found in *Generalization in Spelling* (1931) by Ina Craig Sartorius; "Some Spelling Facts" (1970) by Howard E. Blake and Robert Emans; and "The 'Hey,

What's This?' Approach to Spelling'' (1978) by Bill Hardin, Bonnie Bernstein, and Francis Shands, a sensible article suggesting an eclectic approach combining memory with induction and including a page (don't be put off by the pictures) of 24 of the most reliable and teachable spelling generalizations. Not all of them, of course, will be as reliable as the ''qu'' generalization or as practical as the consonant-doubling rule, but the benefit of inductive learning, the active role the student assumes, may offset any limitations in the derived rules.

Another device that might supplement the more basic approaches to spelling proficiency is the use of mnemonics, or memory tricks that, as Gertrude Hildreth (1955) reported, yield better results with adults than with children. We are all aware that jingles like ''Thirty days have September'' and ''*i* before *e*, except after *c*'' aid our memory through the use of rhyme. Other types of mnemonics may also facilitate the learning of a spelling rule or the spelling of a particular word or group of words. Murray Suid, in ''A Tricky Approach to Spelling'' (1980), outlined some guidelines for the construction and application of mnemonics. One byword is that ''anything goes''; whatever trick helps a student remember a spelling is the best one. Suid offered some examples; the two-in-one definition (for example, stati*ona*ry...st*and* in one place; stati*one*ry...*on* which you write *lette*rs); a built-in word (you *hear* with your *ear*); or a clue sentence, such as Suid's mnemonic for remembering the major exceptions to the ''*i* before *e*'' rule: ''Neither leisured foreigner could seize the weird heights without protein.'' This clue sentence has the advantage of conjuring up a bizarre image that, as the Greeks have told us, is a powerful aid to memorization. Bruce L. Hawkinson's sensible and humorously written self-help program, *Dispel Misspelling* (1978), makes at least implicit reference to this method. Said Hawkinson: ''If pretending that Betsy Ross's husband was A. C. Ross, and that she ran 13 stripes across the flag, but that she didn't put *a cross* on it because she was a Buddhist—if all this pretense helps you remember how to spell *across*, then pretend'' (p. 18). Don Ungaro's ''Imagineering the Spelling Process'' (1982) also advocates the use of nonsense sentences and bizarre images to help remember spellings. Barbara Parke's ''Quick Tricks for 'Cold' Spellers'' (1979) suggests mnemonics like syllable exaggeration (*man-AGE*, *def-I-NITE*, *go-vern-OR*) and scrutiny of roots (*ex-PORT*, *re-PORT-er*, *PORT-able*) as a revitalizing interlude between other spelling activities. Gary A. Negin extolled the virtues of mnemonics in ''Mnemonics and Demonic Words'' (1978). Of the 42 sixth graders Negin tested, one group learned spelling by writing ''demon'' words in context, and a second group devised their own mnemonic devices.

Visual training is another possible attack on spelling deficiency, particularly on errors in the spelling of the demons that don't respond to spelling rules or ''sound-it-out'' strategies. Poor spellers are often inexperienced readers who are unable to ''picture'' a word as it should correctly appear on the page. Several studies have sought to understand the correlation between skill in visual imagery and spelling ability, notably Homer Hendrickson's ''Spelling'' (1972) and J. B. Day and K. Wendell's ''Visual and Auditory Memory in Spelling'' (1972).

Some studies have attempted to explore the use of visual training methods to improve spelling; the results of these studies, however, are equivocal. A project by Leon D. Radaker, "The Effect of Visual Imagery upon Spelling Performance" (1963), asked children to visualize obscure or unfamiliar words (assuring pure visual memory) as though they were projected on a large outdoor theater screen. The experiment showed a fairly significant improvement in spelling over a long period. Donald J. Getz, in the introduction to his experiment ("Learning Enhancement Through Visual Training" [1980]), observed that some previous tests have shown a correlation between visual training and spelling improvement when a consulting optometrist was used to help design the program. Some other studies, he reported, have shown no correlation. Getz's own experiment resulted in a one-month growth in spelling achievement that was not significant at the 0.05 level of testing. An experiment by Juan P. Cabán and others ("Mental Imagery as an Approach to Spelling Instruction" [1978]) divided its subjects into three groups. One control group was given no directions, and the other was asked to learn its spelling words using a drill-and-practice approach. The experimental group used Malcolm Conway's *Imagetics*, which provides a stylus to record responses and a "magic slate" to offer immediate feedback on a correct or incorrect response. The experimenters' conclusion is qualified: "There was a *fairly* strong *trend* in the data to *suggest* that the mental imagery method was *somewhat* better at improving the quality of spelling instruction for the eighth grade students than the other two standard approaches for spelling instruction" [emphasis mine] (p. 21). Cabán's unconvincing results are typical of studies in visual training; it may be an aid to spelling ability, but the body of evidence is inconclusive. Researchers must further investigate its validity and practicality.

Visual imagery may or may not work, but phonics definitely does not. The "sound-it-out" strategy, or using pronunciation as a guide to correct spelling, seems to be a tenuous system at best. Paul Hanna's (1966) Stanford team did find that many consonantal phonemes were represented by their alphabetic counterparts nearly 100.0 percent of the time and that there was also a correspondence of more than 90.0 percent between three short-vowel phonemes (/a/, /e/, /o/) and their letter equivalents. But even if students were to spell the phoneme *l* with the letter *l* every time, they would still be incorrect, according to Hanna's figures, 9.2 percent of the time. Even if we assume the unassumable—a perfect rendering of the rest of the word in which the *l* occurred—the student is still spelling at a 90.8 percent accuracy rate, which does not approach the adult standard of perfection. Add to this the difficulty of representing the "schwa" sound, which has 30 possible letter representations; the "r-controlled vowel," which may be represented by *a* (*molar*), *e* (*feather*), *i* (*bird*), *o* (*doctor*), *u* (*Saturday*), *y* (*martyr*); or any number of vowel combinations; and all other phonemes that Hanna doesn't include on his high correspondence list, and the possibilities for error increase logarithmically. Vast differences in dialect also work against a phonetic approach to spelling. The recent paucity of articles on phonics indicates its relegation to a supporting role at best in the process of learning to spell. Two works to look at are Arthur Heilman's *Phonics in Proper Perspective* (1968) and Duane R. Tovey's " 'Sound-It-Out' " (1978).

A technique that seems to be on the upswing is what might be called the "imitation-of-error" method. Many of us have worked under the assumption that once an incorrect spelling is made, it must be exorcised and the correct spelling reinforced five or even ten times. But repetition of the correct form, as Bradley Loomer (*Educator's Guide to Spelling Research and Practice* [1978]) and others observed, does not help, and several writers have recently suggested that students, especially those with learning disabilities, can benefit from a repetition of their error before reinforcement of the correct form. J. M. Kauffman and colleagues, in "Imitating Children's Errors to Improve Their Spelling Performance" (1978), found that students gained faster acquisition of words when a monitoring teacher imitated their error and then corrected it as opposed to only presenting the correction. Elaine Yudkovitz designed a three-stage remedial program based on these findings. In "A Visual Error-Scanning Approach to Spelling Disorders" (1979), she called first for "interpersonal scanning for error," in which children must attain a proficiency in finding errors in written copy presented by a monitoring teacher. Upon achieving 90 percent recognition, the children move on to "intrapersonal" scanning, in which the teacher dictates to the students, provides options for their errors, and then invites the students to "approximate progressively" until three errors or the correct form has been produced. The final stage of correction requires the students to scan and judge their own work. According to Yudkovitz, these incorrect reproductions and visual images enable students to develop awareness of their own typical errors. Development of a critical eye and a proofreading sense seems to be another benefit of her system. To claim reproduction of error as an asset to spelling improvement would also redeem the much-maligned "bad speller's dictionary," which has heretofore been seen as a crutch rather than a tool for improvement. Most of those available today alphabetize possible misspellings, followed in each case by the correct spelling; conscientious students can compare their rendering with the correct one.

Several authors have suggested mechanical help such as computers to aid the teaching of spelling. Ted S. Hasselbring, in "Remediating Spelling Problems of Learning Handicapped Students through the Use of Microcomputers" (1982), asserted that the Computerized Spelling Remediation Program (CSRP) is an ideal complement to Kauffman's error-imitation and correction system. Hasselbring maintained that the CSRP provides all of the benefits of the Kauffman approach with the advantages of (1) a tireless tutor precluding the need for close monitoring by a teacher, (2) easy and constant updating of student progress, (3) easy maintenance of 40 student word lists on a single disk, and (4) the flexibility to change word lists at any time rather than being bound to commercially prepared lists. Hasselbring also lauded the varied uses of computers for diagnosis and instruction in spelling, especially for learning-disabled students, in "Using Microcomputers for Diagnosing Spelling Problems in Learning-Handicapped Children" (1981), co-written by Cathy L. Crossland, and in his "Comparison of Computer-Based versus Traditional Forms of Spelling Assessment" (1981). Hasselbring is by no means the first to find computer-assisted instruction (CAI) an ideal vehicle for individualization in spelling. As early as 1945, Donald D. Durrell and Helen Blair Sullivan used CAI effectively in teaching weaker and learning-disabled students (see their *Ready to Read* [1945]). Other studies in the field of spelling and computers are George M. Demshock and Alan C. Riedesel's "Use of C.A.I. to Teach Spelling to Sixth Graders" (1968) and Lydia Bubba and John Thorhallsson's "SPELLING CLUES Project at Red Deer College" (1974).

The typewriter has also been seen as a helpful spelling aid. Both Perkins and Benson (1979) and Rochelle Ireland (1980) saw benefits in the method; Ireland believes spelling at the typewriter precludes the carelessness of handwriting, forcing the student to concentrate on each letter as the key is punched. Lloyd W. Bartholome, in "Using the Typewriter for Learning" (1977), also promoted this method. There is even a text available for incorporating typing into a spelling program or vice versa: *Spelling Drills and Exercises* (1979) by LeRoy A. Brendel and Doris Near.

The Linguistic School

Recent research in linguistics has threatened much of the traditional thinking and practice in spelling. The "linguistic school" has perhaps been a reaction against what seemed the mindless discipline of accepted techniques and against the "unpatriotic" attacks on the inconsistency and illogic of our orthography. Many educators have an aversion to the discipline of rote learning or memorization of mathematical formulas, chemistry equations, and spelling principles. They want their students to understand, deep within themselves, the beauty, simplicity, and logic behind these profound inductions, so that perhaps students can duplicate the great derivational thinking that allowed men like Newton and Boyle to arrive at them. They believe they are not asking too much of their students to appreciate these revelations, and they also believe they may be insulting their students' scholarly sensibility to ask them to memorize rules or particular applications. Perhaps the Chomskys and Richard Venezky felt compelled to discover deep, underlying truths about English orthography in part to exorcise the awful vision of Johnny spelling out *soliloquy*, letter by letter, 20 times. Another motivation may have been that patriotic urge to defend the way we do things that prompted Arthur Linksz to record the "thirty-years' love affair of an immigrant with the English language" and glorify the beauty, subtlety, and logic of its spelling system in *On Writing, Reading, and Dyslexia* (1973, p. vii). For whatever reasons, the late 1960s seemed ripe for defenses of English orthography, and many noted linguists took up the challenge.

The above-mentioned work by Linksz is adapted from a lecture, which perhaps explains its digressive discussion of the language and learning to read and write it. The book will work best for those who can afford a complete read, but most of the material pertinent to spelling appears in the first six chapters. A much more systematic project, and one of the first comprehensive linguistic studies of English orthography with the end of improving spelling instruction, was the Stanford "Project 1991" conducted by Paul Hanna and others, recorded minutely in their 1,716-page government tome *Phoneme-Grapheme Correspondences as Cues to Spelling Improvement* (1966) and in a 20-page summary found in *Spelling* (1971) by Hanna, Richard E. Hodges, and Jean S. Hanna. In Project 1991, a computer that was programmed with an algorithm of some 200 phonological rules (incorporating the effects of phonetics, letter position, and syllable stress) managed to spell about half of 17,000 words correctly. Hanna, Hodges, and Hanna concluded that 50.0 percent accuracy is higher than most skeptics would have allowed and that the computer made only a single error in 37.0 percent of the words and only two in another 11.4 percent; thus the correspondence between sounds and letter representations is more consistent, the researchers concluded, than traditionally thought. The Stanford group also observed that a knowledge of *morphology*—how words have been created from roots—might have helped the computer (and might help a student) spell with greater accuracy. For instance, the computer spelled the first syllable of *playground* as *pla*; it lacked an understanding of morphology—in this case, the formulation of compound words—to supplement the strictly phonological principle of spelling the long *a* sound as *a* when it occurs at the end of syllables not ending words. Finally, the researchers concluded that the so-called "spelling demons," those words that defy phonetic or morphemic logic, comprise only about 3.0 percent of our core vocabulary, and of them, only certain parts, such as the initial vowel in *women*, violate the general principles of English spelling.

The work of the Hannas and Richard Hodges has come under fire from several quarters. In "Phoneme-Grapheme Correspondences as Cues to Spelling Improvement" (1978), Albert Mazurkiewicz refuted many of the findings of the Hanna group, suspecting the researchers of duplication and misclassification of the phonemes and "fitting the spelling patterns and the phonemes they represented to a procrustean bed of their own choosing" (p. 194). Mazurkiewicz also rejected the spelling programs that grew out of the phoneme-grapheme work (those outlined in Hanna and colleagues' *Spelling* [1971] and Hanna and others' *Power to Spell* series [1967]) because of their fallacious theoretical basis. Ruel Allred is similarly skeptical of spelling programs that follow too closely on the heels of linguistic research; he believes such research offers insight into the structure of the language but does not believe that it necessarily aids students in encoding that language. Nor does he believe that linguistic-based spelling programs have been sufficiently tested in the field. A final shortcoming of the Hanna studies is a failure to account for semantic factors as cues to correct spelling, and these are precisely the factors that Noam Chomsky and Morris Halle (1968), Richard Venezky (1970), and Carol Chomsky (1970) have investigated.

The work of Noam Chomsky and Morris Halle, *The Sound Pattern of English* (1968), is the earliest and most esoteric of the three. Modestly termed "an interim report of a work in progress" (p. vii), the book nevertheless offers a history of the English sound system and works toward a comprehensive theory of English phonology. The authors advertised the first part of the book as a general survey for the reader who seeks only general conclusions; Parts 2 to 4 are designed for more serious students of linguistics. Ironically, mention of English orthography is made only sporadically throughout the volume, but other remarks made "incidentally" have become the book's most oft-quoted and oft-debated statements by teachers and scholars of English spelling. "It is...noteworthy," said the authors, "but not too surprising, that English orthography, despite its often cited inconsistencies, comes remarkably close to being an optimal orthographic system for English" (p. 49). Orthography is not intended to be a phonetic aid for non-speakers, nor should it be called upon to represent the phonetic changes that occur when words undergo morphemic change, as when the suffix -ity is added to the word divine. To represent the vowel alternation from [ɛy] to [æ] with a new symbol to explain a rule that is easily described by a phonological rule intuitively understood by all native speakers, said Chomsky and Halle, is a redundancy that would only bog down a reader of English. Moreover, added the authors, orthography will hold its ground well against the caprices of history and against variation in dialects. Conventional orthography will remain closer to the underlying structure of language and "may have a very long useful life, for a wide range of phonetically divergent dialects" (p. 49).

Richard L. Venezky also sought to dispel the "purblind attitude that writing serves only to mirror speech" in The Structure of English Orthography (1970, p. 11). On the contrary, said Venezky, English orthography often preserves relationships in meaning, for example between bomb and bombard, that speech (or a phonetic representation of it) obscures. Venezky's work, written in a readable style and with little jargon, reviews historical attitudes toward spelling, from the grammarians to recent reformers and the ITA, then describes the present system, and, finally, offers conclusions and implications. One of the conclusions is that our current orthography is a complex system that marks phonological, morphological, and syntactical patterns; any spelling program must take all of them into account. Some spelling reform, conceded Venezky, might be in order, but it must be a rational, far-sighted approach that recognizes the connections of the patterns; regularizing orthography to conform with speech will destroy its connection with meaning and vice versa. Some changes, said Venezky, like eliminating the silent b in debt and doubt, would make the current system more systematic, but require different letters for the first vowel in both sane and sanity would undermine the current morphological pattern.[1]

The landmark effort in wedding such linguistic principles to spelling pedagogy was made by Carol Chomsky and reported in her "Reading, Writing, and Phonology" (1970). As was observed in Chomsky and Halle's Sound Pattern of English (1968), Chomsky noted that orthography is not a phonetic description, a characteristic that is one of its primary advantages for reading facility. It

---

1. Note, however, Venezky's contention that spelling helps preserve word relationships. The silent b's in debt and doubt help retain the kinship of these words in debit and dubious, respectively.

corresponds instead to an abstract underlying level of representation; thus English spelling allows the reader to get right from print to meaning, without having to "abstract [meaning] away from superficial and irrelevant phonetic detail" (p. 294). Strict phonetic transcription would obscure the relatedness of word pairs like *wide/width* and *medicine/medicate*; these are instances of vowel and consonant alternation, completely predictable by English phonological rules, and to represent the initial vowels in *wide* and *width* with two different letters would mask their morphological connection and make reading more tedious. Chomsky applied these concepts to the teaching and learning of spelling in her 1970 article; "If [a teacher] works on the assumption," she said, "that spelling corresponds to something real, *that it makes sense*, she will encourage the child to recognize and exploit the regularities that do exist" (pp. 302–3). More specifically, Chomsky contended that students can use a "clue word" to aid the spelling of a word with an unstressed syllable; hence the second syllable of *industry* must be spelled with a *u* upon analogy with the clue word *industrial*. But frequently, the necessary clue word is unknown to the student. In perhaps the classic statement of the linguists' thinking that correct spelling must be justified, Chomsky said that it is better to introduce a new word than an arbitrary spelling. She also offered some sample spelling lessons. One calls for students to fill in missing vowels in words from one column (for example, *dem cratic*) by filling in a related word in a second column (in this case, *democracy*). Another two-column exercise illustrates consonant shifts, as in *criticize/critical*, and a third asks students to account for the silent letters in words like *muscle, sign,* and *condemn* by supplying a related word. Chomsky did not pretend to outline an exhaustive spelling program; her exercises, moreover, make limited use of single-morpheme words and seem less to *teach* the spelling of words than to *justify* them. But her article makes good sense, and she has built the foundation for at least a combination vocabulary-spelling program for more advanced spellers.

Some recent work has been done on the relationship of linguistic principles to the teaching of spelling, and most of it touches back on the work of Chomsky and Halle (1968), Venezky (1970), and Carol Chomsky (1970). Several studies focus on stages in the acquisition of spelling ability. Carol Strickland Beers and James Wheelock Beers, in "Three Assumptions about Learning to Spell" (1981), identified an early stage, from first grade to third grade approximately, during which students use phonetic clues almost exclusively. Later, as children come to understand morphological and syntactic elements, they can easily cope with three phonemes for the same morpheme (/t/, /∂d/, /d/ for *-ed*) and different stress patterns within word groups (*photograph/photography*). Shane Templeton, in "The Circle Game of English Spelling" (1979a), found that students reach this stage earlier than we think; they can intuit the morphemic similarities between two phonemes, like the final sounds in *dogs* and *cats*, and thus don't need the one-symbol, one-sound correspondence of a system like the ITA. Templeton also noted that, later in their development (upper elementary, middle, and secondary school), students use spelling to aid pronunciation rather than the reverse:

"their knowledge of certain spelling patterns is more advanced than the ability to use the phonological rules that correspond to those patterns" (pp. 793–94). An experiment conducted by Templeton on proficient spellers from the sixth, eighth, and tenth grades and reported in his "Spelling First, Sound Later" (1979b) verified this conclusion and affirmed what Templeton called a truism, that "the more information concerning the logic of words to which students are sensitive, the more sophisticated and adaptive will be their interaction with printed language" (p. 263). Jerry Zuttell echoed this approach of interaction and experimentation with language but applied it more directly to the teaching of spelling in his "Some Psycholinguistic Perspectives on Children's Spelling" (1978). Learning to spell, he said, is not habit, but "the active, systematic and progressive formulation and testing of rules and strategies" (p. 847). Zuttell's article begins with the now-standard defense of orthography as not just a representation of sound, followed by the standard denouncement of phonics on those grounds, but it also offers helpful sections on psychological principles of language learning and practical suggestions for parents and teachers.

At least two articles further contend that an understanding of etymology can furnish spelling help for words that defy all other language clues. Both Shane Templeton's "Logic and Mnemonics for Demons and Curiosities" (1980) and John G. Barnitz's "Linguistic and Cultural Perspectives on Spelling Irregularity" (1980), however, speak in rather vague, idealistic terms of "language appreciation" and "cultural motivation," respectively; their probes into the history behind certain irregular spellings are interesting for most teachers but of questionable value for all but the most highly motivated of older students, who may in fact already have some proficiency in spelling. The poor speller would have little interest in and less practical use for studying how recent borrowings like *police* and *mesa* violate our standard vowel patterns determined by the Great Vowel Shift or how spelling fads and shortsightedness brought on strange spellings like *scent*. Although these articles admittedly present specialized techniques for a small body of students, they typify the "left wing" of spelling scholarship, which seeks to teach a deeper understanding of the mechanism of our language and its orthography, while eschewing all mention of drill or memorization. For further reading on linguistic and psycho-linguistic perspectives on the teaching of spelling, see Sandra M. Gould, "Spelling Isn't Reading Backwards" (1976); *Cognitive Processes in Spelling*, edited by Uta Frith (1980); and *Developmental and Cognitive Aspects of Learning to Spell* (1980), edited by Edmund Henderson and James Beers.

Special Cases: Motivational Problems, Learning Disabilities, Variant Dialects

Students must come to the task of learning to spell with a good attitude and the right language equipment, and teachers must watch for those who need incentive; have handicaps of mind, body, or speech apparatus; or have barriers of language and dialect. Motivational problems are "handicaps" that can be corrected. Carelessness, for example, is a common cause of poor spelling, according to Rochelle Ireland (1980) and Perkins and Benson (1979). It is a behavioral factor plaguing good spellers especially, whereas apathy, discouragement, laziness, and defiance hinder the poor speller. Thomas Horn, in "Spelling" in the *Encyclopedia of Educational Research* (1969), specified lack of motivation and bad work habits as two detractors from spelling competence, emphasizing that both are "correctable." The keys to improving the attitude of the speller seem not to be rigid demands for perfection, which we have seen Ken Macrorie (1953), Frank Whitehead (1966), Peter Medway (1976) and Robbins Burling (1974) denounce. In fact, Marlene and Robert McCracken (*Spelling* [1976]) and Joanne Yatvin ("How to Get Good Spelling from Poor Spellers" [1979]) have found them to be damaging. More effective methods suggest that teachers should empathize with the poor spellers' predicament, bolstering their confidence and convincing them of the importance and relevancy of correct spelling. Bertrand F. Richards addressed the first of these methods in his response to a question about spelling programs in secondary schools found in "What Is the Best Approach to Teaching Spelling to Secondary School Youngsters," in *Questions English Teachers Ask* (1977). Richards advocated a relaxed attitude toward spelling, at least at first, and warned teachers not to forget that they themselves weren't "sprung fully spelled from the forehead of Zeus" (p. 192).

Confidence may be the most important attitude a teacher can instill in students who have difficulty with spelling. Ward Mitchell Cates, in "Perhaps, Sorta, Kinda, Maybe" (1980), spoke of a generalized diffidence he observed in students, who circled warily around answers on essay exams or tried to read clues in the teacher's face when responding in class. This lack of assertiveness showed itself especially in spelling, and it worried Cates, who instituted an ingenious plan to combat it. In the first phase of his plan, students were allowed to circle all words whose spellings they questioned. Cates checked all circled words that were correct, corrected those that weren't, and deducted two points for any uncircled words spelled incorrectly. Cates noticed some improvement and instituted a more rigid second phase, in which students were docked two points for circled words spelled correctly as well as uncircled words spelled incorrectly. Cates was very pleased with the results of his experiment, finding increased spelling proficiency and receiving numerous reports in students' evaluations of newfound confidence in spelling and composition.

Gloria O. McGettigan reported in "Spelling" (1981) an encounter with another obstacle to learning. When she distributed a list of 500 spelling words that her tenth graders were required to know by year's end (her article includes the list), she found that "the first step was to change student attitude towards spelling and develop a sense of relevancy" (p. 404). This sense of relevancy is one of the "intrinsic" motivators that Thomas Horn ("Spelling," in the *Encyclopedia of Educational Research* [1969]) found much more effective than "extrinsic" motivators like grades or competition with classmates. Some older students may be motivated by the argument that learning spelling helps develop a generalized understanding of the workings of the language, and others may be able to see correct spelling as an important aspect of the written communication process, just as clear enunciation and projection are in speech. A final resort might be the motivational approach that almost every popular or business-oriented article or text takes, that poor spelling connotes to many a lack of scholarship, intelligence, or conscientiousness. Said Joanne Yatvin (1979), "Educated people are expected to spell correctly, just as they are expected to have good table manners. When they do not, others are shocked and inclined to lower their regard for the transgressor's education" (p. 128). Jack E. Hulbert's "Spelling" (1982) argued along the same lines: "In essence, issuing a message containing spelling errors is like sending a message with a hole in the paper, a coffee stain, a cigarette burn, or a poor typing correction—it connotes slovenliness and inconsideration" (p. 185). Using this approach to inculcate the importance of correct spelling is a delicate business, and teachers must be sure not to undermine the students' confidence.

"Uncorrectable" handicaps of mind and body can also hamper the speller. Most of the aforementioned books on spelling and the teaching of spelling (Fitzgerald [1951], Ernest Horn [1927], Hildreth [1955], Dolch [1960], and Hanna, Hodges, and Hanna [1971]) contain sections on psychological and sensori-motor skills and handicaps. A chapter in Hanna, Hodges, and Hanna, "A Psychology of Spelling," reported that speech, audition, vision, and haptics all take a role in the spelling process and that a spelling program that emphasizes all four mechanisms can help the student deficient in one or more to compensate. Besides going to general books on spelling, the teacher can seek out general sources on learning disabilities. The organization of many of them, however, is not exactly tailor-made for the spelling teacher: their indexes often reveal a scattering of references on spelling rather than a specific section on it. Janet W. Lerner's *Children with Learning Disabilities* (1976) is an exception. It treats spelling specifically, following the pattern suggested in the book's subtitle: *Theories, Diagnoses, Teaching Strategies* (pp. 260–66). Doris J. Johnson and Helmer R. Myklebust's *Learning Disabilities* (1967) is a little harder to work with but, as one of the most respected works in the field, should not be ignored. Chapter 6, dealing with disorders of written language, is of special interest to the teacher of spelling for its discussion of *dysgraphia*, an inability of a student to copy accurately, which results in some bizarre and illogical renderings. The chapter also deals with disabilities of revisualization, handicapping students who can read, speak, and copy well enough, but who have difficulty re-envisioning things they've seen. Johnson and Myklebust also offered the sensible suggestion of dividing spelling words into phonetic and non-phonetic lists, to be taught by oral and visual means, respectively. Another source, indexed thoroughly but not conveniently for spelling instructors, is Alexander Bannatyne's *Language, Reading, and Learning Disabilities* (1971), which contains some helpful but widely scattered information and may be difficult for all but those with a strong background in neuro-psychology. See also Louise Clarke's *Can't Read, Can't Write, Can't Takl too Good Either* (1975).

Two articles deal with specific dysfunctions. Amy Richards's "Writing Dysfunction" (1979) characterizes the "typical" dysgraphic as the one who "seems bright, but can't spell." Her definition of *dysgraphia*, although never stated, differs from Johnson and Myklebust's (1967) "can't copy" label; dysgraphia may be simply a mix-up between the message given the hand and inscribing that message on paper. The misspellings of dysgraphics often defy phonetic and morphemic logic; they may be reversals (*falut* for *fault*), variant spellings (*convines* for *convince*), or gross mutilations (*spargoat* for *scapegoat*). As a further aid for recognizing the disorder, Richards included photocopies of papers written by dysgraphics. Once dysgraphia is diagnosed, treatment can begin. Richards found the old-fashioned method of overlearning effective (case in point: all of her subjects could spell their own names). Unfortunately, dysgraphia is still a mystery and currently untreatable, and many of Richards's "treatments," such as focusing only on content in the papers of dysgraphics or allowing them to dictate their papers, do not solve the underlying problem. A technique she does not mention, but one that would bypass the manual letter formulation so tedious and frustrating to the dysgraphic, is spelling at the typewriter. Ilene Rothschild focused on dyslexia in "Spelling Instruction for the Dyslexic Child" (1982). Among the "ten timely tips" she offered are the "writing workout," a freewrite designed mostly to give the student kinesthetic feedback, evaluation and categorization of errors (for example, poor letter sequence as in *aminal*, poor visual imagery as in *enuff*), integration of spelling with other curricula, and manipulation of modalities, in which auditory input and the vocal student feedback might occur one day, auditory input and motor output the next, visual input and vocal output the next, and visual input and motor output the next. Rothschild noted also the memory deficiency common with dyslexics and suggested several standardized tests for diagnosis and evaluation, as well as numerous games and resources for learning. For more information on dyslexia and written language, see Arthur Linksz's *On Writing, Reading, and Dyslexia* (1973) and *Orthography, Reading, and Dyslexia* (1980), edited by James E. Kavanaugh and Richard L. Venezky.

Speech difficulties or dialects varying significantly from Standard English (SE) may also impede spelling performance, although some of the recent linguistic study seems to deny a very strong relationship between pronunciation and spelling. Patrick Groff, in "Speaking and Spelling" (1979), concluded that poor articulation has little effect on spelling competence. Groff did see some dialect-related misspellings in young speakers of Black English (BE) but also observed that misspellings decreased significantly by the middle grades and occurred less in written composition than in words spelled in isolation. In light of this work, Groff favored a phonic approach to instruction, while conceding its controversial nature. There is quite a bit of evidence, however, to refute Groff's assertion of a tenuous relationship between speaking and spelling. Mina Shaughnessy (1977) conceded that correct pronunciation cannot guarantee correct spelling but maintained that it can at least eliminate some choices as impossible (for example, *parell* for *parallel* and *imblance* for *imbalance*). Gertrude Hildreth, in *Teaching Spelling* (1955), saw accurate pronunciation as "such an asset in learning that children with speech articulation difficulties may be slow learners for that cause alone" (p. 28–29). Although students of spelling seem to rely less on pronunciation clues as they mature, there remains a connection between the way we say a word and the way we represent it on paper.

Studies on the spelling competence of speakers of variant dialects, particularly Black English, seem to bear this principle out. Bruce Cronnell's "Black English and Spelling" (1979) began with the assumption of 43 differences between BE and SE that might affect spelling and found that speakers of BE made twice the non-BE-related errors and seven times the BE-related spelling errors as their white counterparts. Cronnell concluded that BE speakers need special help with spelling from teachers who are conscientious enough not to try to change a student's dialect but to understand it and relate it to the English spelling system. More specifically, Cronnell observed that BE pronunciations affecting grammatical markers caused more problems in spelling than those not affecting grammatical markers. Thus the BE speaker is more likely to misspell *passed* than *last*. Although in BE pronunciation, the final consonant cluster of each is reduced, the former signifies an important grammatical concept, that of the past tense. Patrick Groff's "Children's Spelling Features of Black English" (1978), an extension of some of Cronnell's earlier work, concurs that only a few features of BE pronunciation "justify pedagogical concern." Only one of the four he cited does not mark a grammatical element, and that is the *I* phoneme, which is often mispronounced as a long e sound before *l*, resulting in a rendering of *steel* or *steal* for *still*. More typically misspelled are words with grammatical markers like the suffix *-ed*, the third person singular as in *goes*, and plural suffixes represented by /s/, /z/ and /iz/.

Other dialects may need special attention too. Richard T. Graham and E. Hugh Rudorf's "Dialect and Spelling" (1970) examines mostly vowel differences between students in Ohio, Massachusetts, and Georgia, and Carolyn Boiarsky's "Consistency of Spelling and Pronunciation Deviations of Appalachian Students" (1969) looks at mountain dialect pronunciation that strays from the standard. As in Black English, the *I* preceding *l* causes problems.

Foreign students have special spelling problems, too, and Muhammad H. Ibrahim provided a helpful treatment of them in "Patterns of Spelling Errors" (1978). A major difficulty is that many foreign sound systems are at odds with that of English. Arabs, for example, find the [ɔ] sound particularly troublesome, producing renderings like *coast* for *cost*. Most Arab tongues have no [g] and none have the [p] sound. We find, therefore, misspellings like *covernment* and *Jaban* as well as hypercorrected forms such as *distripution*. Foreign students may also make three kinds of inappropriate analogy: phonetic, as in *origional* (faulty analogy with *regional*); orthographic, as in *cann't* (analogous to *doesn't* or a similar contracted form); and grammatical, as in *heared* (likened to a standard inflection such as *played*). Other typical errors are confusion of American and British spelling conventions (resulting, for example, in *inflextional*), trouble with the schwa (*husbund, villigers*), and overgeneralization or ignorance of spelling rules. Ibraham noted, too, that the traditional approach to teaching English as a second language is rigidly compartmentalized, with hours set aside for spelling, punctuation, and so on, and advocated a more integrated method.

References

Allred, Ruel A. *Spelling: The Application of Research Findings*. Washington, D.C.: National Education Association, 1977.

Ayer, Fred C. *A Study of High School Spelling Vocabulary*. Austin, Tex.: Steck, 1945.

Bannatyne, Alexander. *Language, Reading, and Learning Disabilities: Psychology, Neuropsychology, Diagnosis, and Remediation*. Springfield, Ill.: Thomas, 1971.

Barnitz, John G. "Linguistic and Cultural Perspectives on Spelling Irregularity." *J Read*, 23 (1980), 320–26.

Bartholome, Lloyd W. "Using the Typewriter for Learning: Spelling." *Bal Sheet*, 58 (1977), 196–200.

Beers, Carol Strickland, and James Wheelock Beers. "Three Assumptions about Learning to Spell." *Lang Arts*, 58 (1981), 573–80.

Blair, Timothy R., and William H. Rupley. "New Trends in Spelling Instruction." *Read Teach*, 33 (1980), 760–63.

Blake, Howard E., and Robert Emans. "Some Spelling Facts." *Elem Eng*, 47 (1970), 241–49.

Boiarsky, Carolyn. "Consistency of Spelling and Pronunciation Deviations of Appalachian Students." *Mod Lang J*, 53 (1969), 347–50.

Brendel, LeRoy A., and Doris Near. *Spelling Drills and Exercises: Programmed for the Typewriter*. 3rd ed. New York: McGraw-Hill, 1979.

Brown, William E., Tyrone Payne, and Marcia Brown. "We Are Phloundering: Help Us." *J Read*, 22 (1979), 294–95.

Bubba, Lydia, and John Thorhallsson. "The SPELLING CLUES Project at Red Deer College: Dialogue with the Computer as an Approach toward Improving English Spelling." 1974. ERIC ED 086 247.

Buck, Jean L. "A New Look at Teaching Spelling." *CE*, 38 (1977), 703-6.

Burling, Robbins. "An Anthropologist Among the English Teachers." *CCC*, 25 (1974), 234–42.

———. "Poor Spellers of the World, Unite!" *Learning*, 4 (March 1976), 76–78.

Cabán, Juan P., et al. "Mental Imagery as an Approach to Spelling Instruction." *J Exp Educ*, 46 (Spring 1978), 15–21.

Cates, Ward Mitchell. "Perhaps, Sorta, Kinda, Maybe." *Clear H*, 54 (1980), 217–18.

Chomsky, Carol. "Reading, Writing, and Phonology." *Harvard Educ Rev*, 40 (1970), 287–307.

Chomsky, Noam, and Morris Halle. *The Sound Pattern of English*. New York: Harper, Row, 1968.

Clarke, Louise. *Can't Read, Can't Write, Can't Talk Too Good Either*. New York: Penguin, 1975.

Conely, James. "Spelling." *CCC*, 25 (1974), 243–46.

Corcoran, D.W.J., and D. L. Weening. "Acoustic Factors in Visual Search." *Q J Exp Psychol*, 20 (1968), 83–85.

Cronnell, Bruce. "Black English and Spelling." *RTE*, 13 (1979), 81–90.

Day, J. B., and K. Wedell. "Visual and Auditory Memory in Spelling." *Brit J Educ Psychol*, 42 (February 1972), 33–39.

Demshock, George M., and Alan Riedesel. "Use of C.A.I. to Teach Spelling to Sixth Graders: Final Report." State College: Pennsylvania State University, August, 1968.

Dolch, Edward W. *Better Spelling*. Champaign, Ill.: Garrard, 1960.

Durrell, Donald D., and Helen Blair Sullivan. *Ready to Read*. Yonkers-on-Hudson, N.Y.: World Book, 1945.

Eicholz, Gerald C. "Spelling Improvement through a Self-Check Device." *El Sch J*, 64 (1964), 373–76.

Fitzgerald, James A. "Words Misspelled Most Frequently by Children of the Fourth, Fifth, and Sixth Grade Levels in Life Outside the School." *J Educ Res*, 26 (1932), 213–18.

————. *The Teaching of Spelling*. Milwaukee: Bruce, 1951.

Fitzsimmons, Robert J., and Bradley M. Loomer, *Spelling Research and Practice*. Des Moines: Iowa State Department of Public Instruction and the University of Iowa, 1977.

Frith, Uta, ed. *Cognitive Processes in Spelling*. London: Academic, 1980.

Gates, Arthur T. "An Experimental Comparison of the Study-Test and Test-Study Methods in Spelling." *J Educ Psychol*, 22 (1931), 1–19.

Geedy, Patricia S. "What Research Tells Us about Spelling." *Elem Eng*, 52 (1975), 233–36.

Getz, Donald J. "Learning Enhancement Through Visual Training." *Acad Ther*, 15 (1980), 457–66.

Gilstrap, Robert. "Development of Independent Spelling Skills in the Intermediate Grades." *Elem Eng*, 39 (1962), 481–83.

Gould, Sandra M. "Spelling Isn't Reading Backwards." *J Read*, 20 (1976), 220–25.

Graham, Richard T., and E. Hugh Rudorf. "Dialect and Spelling." *Elem Eng*, 47 (1970), 363–76.

Groff, Patrick. "Children's Spelling of Features of Black English." *RTE*, 12 (1978), 21–28.

————. "Speaking and Spelling." *Lang Arts*, 56 (1979), 26–32.

Haber, Ralph Norman, and Robert M. Schindler. "Error in Proofreading: Evidence of Syntactic Control of Letter Processing?" *J Exp Psychol Hum Perc Perf*, 7 (1981), 573–79.

Hanna, Paul R., Richard E. Hodges, and Jean S. Hanna. *Spelling: Structure and Strategies*. Boston: Houghton Mifflin, 1971.

Hanna, Paul R., et al. *Phoneme-Grapheme Correspondences as Cues to Spelling Improvement*. OE-32008. Washington, D.C.: U.S. Department of Health, Education, and Welfare, 1966.

————. *Power to Spell*. Boston: Houghton Mifflin, 1967.

Hardin, Bill, Bonnie Bernstein, and Francis Shands. "The 'Hey, What's This?' Approach to Teaching Spelling." *Teacher*, 96 (November 1978), 64–67.

Hasselbring, Ted. "A Comparison of Computer-Based versus Traditional Forms of Spelling Assessment." Paper presented at the Institute on Microcomputers for Instruction and Research in Higher Education. Raleigh, N.C., October 1981.

———. "Remediating Spelling Problems of Learning and Handicapped Students Through the Use of Microcomputers." *Educ Tech*, 22 (April 1982), 31–32.

———, and Cathy L. Crossland. "Using Microcomputers for Diagnosing Spelling Problems in Learning-Handicapped Children." *Educ Tech*, 21 (April 1981), 37–39.

Hawkinson, Bruce L. *Dispel Misspelling: An Office Education Mini-Curriculum Manual on Spelling*. 1978. ERIC ED 146 328.

Hawley, W. E., and Jackson Gallup. "The 'List' vs. the 'Sentence' Method of Teaching Spelling." *J Educ Res*, 5 (1922), 306–10.

Healy, A. F. "Proofreading Errors on the Word *the*: New Evidence on Reading Units." *J Exp Psychol Hum Perc Perf*, 6 (1980), 45–57.

Heilman, Arthur W. *Phonics in Proper Perspective*. 2nd ed. Columbus, Ohio: Merrill, 1968.

Henderson, Edmund H. "Correct Spelling—an Inquiry." *Read Teach*, 28 (1974), 176–79.

———, and James W. Beers, eds. *Developmental and Cognitive Aspects of Learning to Spell: A Reflection of Word Knowledge*. 1981. ERIC ED 197 285.

Hendrickson, Homer. "Spelling: A Visual Skill. A Discussion of Visual Imagery and the Manipulation of Visual Symbols as Basic Skills in the Ability to Spell." 1972. ERIC ED 055 070.

Hildreth, Gertrude. *Teaching Spelling: A Guide to Basic Principles and Practices*. New York: Holt, Rinehart, Winston, 1955.

Hillerich, Robert L. "Let's Teach Spelling—Not Phonetic Misspelling." *Lang Arts*, 54 (1977), 301–7.

———. "Hillerich Replies." *Educ Lead*, 39 (1982), 633.

———. "That's Teaching Spelling???" *Educ Lead*, 39 (1982b), 615–17.

Hodges. Richard E. "Teaching Spelling: A Response to Hillerich." *Educ Lead*, 39 (1982), 617, 633.

———. "On the Development of Spelling Ability." *Lang Arts*, 59 (1982), 284–90.

Holbrook, Morris B. "Effect of Subjective Interletter Similarity, Perceived Word Similarity, and Contextual Variables on the Recognition of Letter Substitutions in a Proofreading Task." *Perc Motor Skills*, 47 (1978), 251–58.

Horn, Ernest. *A Basic Writing Vocabulary*. Iowa City: University of Iowa Press, 1927.

———. *Teaching Spelling*. Washington, D.C.: American Educational Research Association, 1954.

Horn, Thomas D. "The Effect of the Corrected Test on Learning to Spell." *El Sch J*, 47 (1947), 277–85.

———. "Spelling." In *Encyclopedia of Educational Research*. 4th ed. Ed. Robert C. Ebel. London: Macmillan, 1969.

Hulbert, Jack E. "Spelling: A Fundamental Skill for Effective Business Communication." *J Bus Ed*, 57 (February 1982), 185–87.

Ibrahim, Muhammad H. "Patterns in Spelling Errors." *Engl Lang Teach J*, 32 (1978), 207–12.

Ireland, Rochelle. "A Proposal for Teaching Spelling in the Virginia Community College System." 1980. ERIC ED 176 827.

Johnson, Doris J., and Helmer R. Myklebust. *Learning Disabilities: Educational Principles and Practices*. New York: Grune, Stratton, 1967.

Johnson, Terry D., Kenneth G. Langford, and Kerry C. Quorn. "Characteristics of an Effective Spelling Program." *Lang Arts*, 58 (1981), 581–88.

Kauffman, J. M., et al. "Imitating Children's Errors to Improve Their Spelling Performance." *J Learn Dis*, 11 (1978), 217–22.

Kavanaugh, James F., and Richard L. Venezky, eds. *Orthography, Reading, and Dyslexia*. Baltimore: University Park Press, 1980.

Kučera, Henry, and W. Nelson Francis. *Computational Analysis of Present-Day American English*. Providence: Brown University Press, 1967.

Lerner, Janet W. *Children with Learning Disabilities: Theories, Diagnosis, Teaching Strategies*. Boston: Houghton Mifflin, 1976.

Linksz, Arthur. *On Writing, Reading, and Dyslexia*. New York: Grune, Stratton, 1973.

Loomer, Bradley M. *Educator's Guide to Spelling Research and Practice*. Des Moines: Iowa State Department of Public Instruction, 1978.

Macrorie, Ken. "The Hypocracy of Perfection." *CE*, 15 (1953), 288–90.

Malone, John R. "The Larger Aspects of Spelling Reform." *Elem Eng*, 39 (1962), 435–45.

Mangieri, John N., and R. Scott Baldwin. "Meaning as a Factor in Predicting Spelling Difficulty." *J Educ Res*, 72 (1979), 285–87.

Mazurkiewicz, Albert J. "Phoneme-Grapheme Correspondences as Cues to Spelling Improvement: A Further Appraisal." *Read World*, 17 (1978), 190–96.

———, and Charlotte L. Rath. "Affects on Adult Spelling Choices." *Read World*, 16 (1976), 15–20.

McCracken, Marlene, and Robert McCracken. *Spelling*. Grand Forks, N. Dak.: Center for Teaching and Learning, 1976.

McGettigan, Gloria O. "Spelling: A Multi-Purpose Lesson." *Clear H*, 54 (1981), 404–10.

McKee, Paul. "Teaching Spelling by Column and Context Forms." *J Educ Res*, 15 (1927), 246–55.

Medway, Peter. "Let Down by Speling." *Times Educ Sup*, 28 May 1976, p. 19.

Negin, Gary A. "Mnemonics and Demonic Words." *Read Improv*, 15 (1978), 180–82.

Parke, Barbara W. "Quick Tricks for 'Cold' Spellers." *Teacher*, 96 (April 1979), 74–76.

Perkins, W. E., and Melba Benson. "Great Disasters of the Twentieth Century: The Hindenburg, the San Francisco Earthquake, the Chicago Fire, and Spelling." *J Bus Ed*, 55 (1979), 98–103.

Petty, Walter. "The Teaching of Spelling." *Bul Sch Ed, Indiana Univ*, 21 (November 1969), 79–98.

Pilgrim, Geneva Hanna. *Learning and Teaching Practices in English*. New York: The Center for Applied Research in Education, 1966.

Pollock, Thomas Clark. "Spelling Report." *CE*, 16 (1954), 102–9.

———, and William D. Baker. *The University Spelling Book*. Englewood Cliffs, N.J.: Prentice-Hall, 1955.

Radaker, Leon D. "The Effect of Visual Imagery upon Spelling Performance." *J Educ Res*, 56 (1963), 370–72.

Read, Edwin A., Ruel A. Allred, and Louise O. Baird. *Continuous Progress in Spelling: Intermediate Teacher's Manual*. Oklahoma City: Individualized Instruction (The Economy Company), 1972.

Richards, Amy. "Writing Dysfunction: A Problem in College Composition Courses."
    1979. ERIC ED 158 171.

Richards, Bertrand F. Answer to "What Is the Best Approach to Teaching Spelling to
    Secondary School Youngsters?" In *Questions English Teachers Ask*. Ed. R. Baird
    Shuman. Rochelle Park, N.J.: Hayden, 1977, pp. 190–92.

Rinsland, Henry D. *A Basic Vocabulary of Elementary School Children*. New York:
    Macmillan, 1945.

Rivers, Caryl. "Its Tyme to Du Somthing." *Learning*, 3 (November 1974), 72–78.

Rockas, Leo. "Teaching Literacy." *CCC*, 28 (1977), 273–75.

Rothschild, Ilene. "Spelling Instruction for the Dyslexic Child: Ten Timely Tips." *Acad
    Ther*, 17 (1982), 395–400.

Rowell, C. Glennon. "Inductive Teaching as a Strategy for Instruction in Spelling."
    1979. ERIC ED 169 542.

Sartorius, Ina Craig. *Generalization in Spelling*. New York: Columbia University, 1931.

Shaughnessy, Mina. *Errors and Expectations: A Guide for the Teacher of Basic Writing*.
    New York: Oxford University Press, 1977.

Sherwin, J. Stephen. "Research and the Teaching of English." 1971. ERIC ED 050
    082.

Simmons, Ernest P., and Harold H. Bixler. *The New Standard High School Spelling
    Scale*. Atlanta, Ga.: Smith, 1940.

Sloboda, J. A. "The Effect of Item Position on the Likelihood of Identification by
    Inference in Prose Reading and Music Reading." *Can J Psychol*, 30 (1976), 228–
    37.

Suid, Murray. "A Tricky Approach to Spelling." *Learning*, 8 (March 1980), 24–26.

Templeton, Shane. "The Circle Game of English Spelling: A Reappraisal for Teachers."
    Lang Arts, 56 (1979a), 789–97.

———. "Logic and Mnemonics for Demons and Curiosities: Spelling Awareness of
    Middle- and Secondary-Level Students." *Read World*, 20 (1980), 123–30.

———. "Spelling First, Sound Later: The Relationship between Orthography and Higher
    Order Phonological Knowledge in Older Students." *RTE*, 13 (1979b), 255-64.

Thorndike, Edward L., and Irving Lorge. *The Teacher's Word Book of 30,000 Words*.
    New York: Teacher's College Press, Columbia University, 1944.

Tovey, Duane R. " 'Sound-It-Out': A Reasonable Approach to Spelling?" *Read World*,
    17 (1978), 220–33.

Ungaro, Don. "Imagineering the Spelling Process." *Clear H*, 55 (1982), 400–405.

Venezky, Richard L. *The Structure of English Orthography*. The Hague: Mouton, 1970.

Whitehead, Frank. *The Disappearing Dais: A Study of the Principles and Practice of
    English Teaching*. London: Chatto, Windus, 1966.

Winch, W. H. "Additional Researches on Learning to Spell." *J Educ Psychol*, 7 (1916),
    109–10.

Wong, Shirley. "Proofreading Pitfalls." *Bus Educ Forum*, 29 (1975), 16–17.

Yatvin, Joanne. "How to Get Good Spelling from Poor Spellers." *Learning*, 8 (August/
    September 1979), 122–23.

Yudkovitz, Elaine. "A Visual Error-Scanning Approach for Spelling Disorders." *J Learn
    Dis*, 12 (1979), 553–57.

Zuttell, Jerry. "Some Psycholinguistic Perspectives on Children's Spelling." *Lang Arts*,
    55 (1978), 844–50.

Vocabulary Development

Americans have long believed that possession of an extensive, precise vocabulary is a valuable asset. The assumption that people's conceptual abilities are closely related to the quality and quantity of their stock of words was apparently confirmed in the early part of this century with the introduction of the Stanford-Binet I.Q. Test, which shows a high correlation between intelligence and vocabulary level. To a less egalitarian-minded era than our own, a good vocabulary was also the sign of superior breeding and education, and so upwardly mobile individuals strove to use "big" words. In 1934 an article published in the *Atlantic Monthly* provided Americans with yet another reason for desiring to increase their vocabularies: Johnson O'Connor, in "Vocabulary and Success," reported the results of a study conducted by the Human Engineering Laboratories that revealed that successful business executives have the largest vocabularies of all Americans. This discovery was no doubt one of the major causes behind the current plethora of commercial vocabulary workbooks promising financial and social success to their users.

Finally, the post-World War II increase in the number of high school students desiring a college education resulted in widespread use of standardized college entrance exams, the verbal section of which is in good part a vocabulary test. Particularly in the 1960s and 1970s, when the baby-boom generation was applying to college, the stiff competition meant that high school students desperately tried to increase their vocabularies in preparation for the tests. Many schools even offered crash courses to this end, and publishing houses churned out vocabulary workbooks with sample tests modeled on the SATs and ACTs.

Although the attitudes toward vocabulary development described above are somewhat misguided and naive, many educators have long held sound reasons for valuing a good vocabulary. Reading teachers claim that the main obstacle to comprehension of written material is an inadequate vocabulary. Content-area teachers recognize that if students do not understand the meaning of the terms used in a particular subject, they cannot comprehend the subject. Writing teachers know that without an adequate vocabulary students cannot express their ideas clearly or forcefully.

Nearly everyone, then, agrees on the desirability of developing one's vocabulary. The disagreement arises over the question of how this can most effectively be done. As the survey of works will show, there are basically two methods of teaching vocabulary, although many educators advocate a mixture of them. The *direct method* involves teaching specific word-attack skills and having students memorize definitions. The *indirect method* is patterned after the way people naturally learn new words—through reading, conversation, rich experience, and curiosity about language. Although the direct method remains the more popular of the two, the indirect method is receiving increasing attention today, because it conforms more closely to current semantic and language-acquisition theories.

In addition to the present study, two other major bibliographical surveys have been done in the twentieth century. In 1939 Edgar Dale published his first comprehensive *Bibliography of Vocabulary Studies*, an un-annotated listing of 1,145 books and articles published since the turn of the century on every conceivable aspect of vocabulary development. This list has been updated four times, in 1949, 1957, 1963, and 1973 (with 2,855 entries).

More immediately helpful to the English teacher, however, is the NCTE report published in 1968 by Walter T. Petty, Curtis P. Herold, and Earline Stoll, *The State of Knowledge about the Teaching of Vocabulary*. This monograph describes the ways vocabulary has been taught since the 1930s, discusses the shortcomings of many of these approaches, gives detailed reviews of 13 of the best works on vocabulary instruction, and points out that there is still much we do not know about how vocabulary is learned and can most effectively be taught. The authors included a list of 25 needed areas of investigation and explained how to go about scientifically structuring future vocabulary experiments. They concluded with a selected bibliography of approximately 350 entries, consisting of articles, books, and unpublished theses and papers.

The present study is more extensive than the NCTE monograph, reviewing the best and most representative works from the 1930s through mid-1982, and more selective than Dale's work, focusing primarily on works dealing with vocabulary pedagogy. The works constitute a continuum from the purely theoretical to the purely practical, with most situated somewhere in the middle range, describing a pedagogical approach that is based on a particular theory. Lack of space prevents my covering textbooks and workbooks, but the reader can gain insight into them from my description of the direct method, which such books are based on. Finally, although most vocabulary pedagogy works have implications for reading as well as writing instruction, those that are concerned exclusively with the former are not dealt with in this survey, since its intended audience is primarily composition teachers.

Theoretical Works

A frequent criticism of word-list drill, which is the most widespread of the direct approaches to vocabulary instruction, is that it is based on out-of-date semantic and psycho-linguistic theories. Briefly, critics claim that underlying this approach is a philosophy akin to eighteenth- and nineteenth-century associationism. Applied to semantics, this theory assumed that the meaning of a word inheres in the word itself, not in the context where it is found or in the mind of the person who encounters it, and, applied to psycho-linguistics, the theory assumed that by learning a new word people could master the concept it denoted and thereby increase their stock of ideas. However, twentieth-century semantic and psycho-linguistic philosophies depart from these mechanistic views, and the best articles on vocabulary pedagogy are based on modern theories. The following discussion covers works that illuminate these theories for the non-specialist reader and are therefore suited for teachers desiring a sound theoretical underpinning to their vocabulary instruction. Although these books are not directly applicable to the classroom, they raise issues—such as the relationship between words and thinking, how vocabulary is learned, and whether vocabulary can be taught—that a teacher should consider in planning a vocabulary unit.

Stephen Ullman's book *Semantics* (1962) provides an excellent overview of the field, including its historical development and its current theories. Ullman pointed out that modern linguistics stresses the contextual nature of words, arguing that the context provides the word with its meaning rather than that the meaning resides in the word itself. This view is in line with the current descriptive—in contrast to the older prescriptive—approach to language: contemporary linguists regard the dictionary as a source of information about the ways words have actually been used, whereas prescriptive linguists of the past saw the dictionary as the arbiter of usage.

A second tenet of modern semantics is that there is no such thing as complete synonymy. Ullman listed the various differences that can exist among supposed synonyms, such as one's being more general than another and one's having a more pejorative connotation than another. Since many students—and, unfortunately, some teachers—naively assume that one can improve one's writing merely by substituting a "fancy" synonym for a plain word, it is important that students and teachers alike become sophisticated about the nature of synonyms and connotations.

Modern semantics also holds that the meaning of a word is always in flux, and Ullman therefore included a discussion of the kinds and causes of semantic change. This section is informative for the teacher who wants to stress etymology and the history of the language, an approach to vocabulary instruction advocated by many contemporary educators.

Another important aspect of Ullman's book is his discussion of semantic fields. The author explained how, in keeping with the emphasis on structure that characterizes modern linguistics, linguists have invented a structuralist scheme whereby they can analyze the vocabulary of a language, just as they can do for the syntax. These structures, or fields, are constellations of words that are related to one another through an intricate network of associations, some formal and some semantic. Each field is divided up, classified, and organized so that every element (word) helps to delimit every other element. Thus the raw material of experience is analyzed and classified in a particular way for each language. As we shall see, some of the more innovative methods of teaching vocabulary involve examining words in their semantic fields. Again, the word-list technique is diametrically opposed to this method in that it presents words in isolation and implies that there is a fixed meaning for them, whereas the semantic-field approach stresses that a word's meaning is in part determined by other words in the field.

By logical extension, the semantic-field theory implies that our thinking is dependent upon our language. That is, a semantic field does not merely reflect the ideas and perceptions of a paticular culture; it also formulates and perpetuates them. This is where the field theory is related to another recent linguistic development: the Sapir-Whorf hypothesis. Framed by linguist-anthropologists Edward Sapir and Benjamin Lee Whorf, this hypothesis is most clearly articulated in Whorf's 1956 book *Language, Thought, and Reality*. Its basic propositions are that all higher levels of thinking are dependent on language and that the structure of the language one habitually uses determines the way one perceives, analyzes, and reasons about the world. Whorf argued that the *patternment* of a language—its syntactic structure—always overrides and controls the *lexation*— its name-giving aspect. Although he focused on syntax, his theory invites speculation about the effect of the lexicon of a language on its users' conceptualizations. That is, does the possession of a particular word affect one's thinking? For example, if people know the words *despondent*, *dejected*, and *depressed*, do they experience finer gradations of sadness than people who know only the word *sad*?

Familiarity with modern language-acquisition theories is important for teachers of vocabulary at all levels. In his classic work *Thought and Language* (1962), Lev Vygotsky charted the development of language use in children, stating that the egocentric speech characteristic of the young child until about age seven becomes inner speech, or verbal thinking, as the child grows older. The striking lexical feature of this inner speech is the preponderance of the sense of a word over its meaning. Vygotsky explained that the *sense* is "the sum of all the psychological events aroused in our consciousness by the word" (p. 146), whereas the *meaning* is the dictionary definition of the word. Sense accrues as one meets a word in a variety of contexts. Although Vygotsky did not discuss the practical implications his theory has for vocabulary instruction, it clearly suggests that one cannot truly learn a word merely by studying its dictionary definition.

Paula Menyuk, in *The Acquisition and Development of Language* (1971), discussed the kinds of words children can understand at various stages of their development. She explained that studies indicate a child first learns concrete nouns and verbs (that is, nouns referring to tangible items and verbs referring to animal or human movement) and that lexical items do not have meaning separate from the sentence contexts in which the child encounters them until after age ten. Younger children appear to "store the semantic properties of a phrase, rather than the properties of a word, in the lexicon" (p. 178). These observations suggest that elementary school teachers must take a different approach to vocabulary instruction from that taken by high school and college teachers. The teacher of young children should concentrate on concrete nouns and verbs, making sure to introduce them in context rather than in isolation, whereas the high school and college teacher can move on to abstract meanings of words.

Direct Method

Since the early decades of the twentieth century, when vocabulary instruction became a regular part of the elementary and high school language arts curriculum, the direct method has been by far the more commonly used of the two major approaches. The following survey will examine each of the four forms that this method generally takes. These are the word-list drill (which usually involves some teaching of dictionary skills), word analysis, context-clue study, and some of mixture of the above.

The *word-list drill* is the most popular kind of direct vocabulary teaching— and the most abused, according to the many authors of vocabulary articles who begin by decrying this method. With this approach the instructor provides students with weekly lists of words, the definitions of which are to be looked up and memorized. Follow-up multiple-choice tests are subsequently given, in which the student must choose the definition or synonym that best fits the given word.

The main advantage of the word-list approach is that teachers can control the kinds of words students learn. Although some teachers select their words on an arbitrary basis or on the basis of their obscurity, there are others whose choices spring from sound theories. One such theory, upheld by many of the authors surveyed but most fully explained by Edgar Dale, Joseph O'Rourke, and Henry Bamman in *Techniques of Teaching Vocabulary* (1971), is that students should be taught only those words on the threshold of their recognition—that is, those that they have a hazy notion of and can generally understand in meaningful contexts but that they never use in their own writing or speaking. The aim should be to draw words from the students' passive vocabularies into their active ones. Teachers can either devise their own ways of finding out what words constitute the passive category for their particular class of students or they can refer to one of the many works that list the words most students know at various levels. Of them, one of the best is Edgar Dale and Gerhard Eicholz's *Children's Knowledge of Words* (1960). This book contains lists of words known to children in grades 4, 6, 8, 10, and 12 and indicates the percentage of children tested who knew each word. It also provides the particular meaning known to the children if the word has more than one.

Another, and probably the most usual, criterion of selection is the frequency of a word's use. This information can be obtained from one of the numerous works listing words in order of their frequency of occurrence. The massive word-count approach was initiated by E. L. Thorndike in 1921 with his *Teacher's Word Book of 10,000 Words*, which he followed in 1931 with *A Teacher's Word Book of 20,000 Words* and in 1944 with *A Teacher's Word Book of 30,000 Words*. Examining 10.5 million words of reading material, Thorndike categorized them into the first 500 most frequently used words, the second 500, the second 1,000, and so forth. His approach has been imitated by many others, and these lists have been used in constructing readability formulas for elementary school vocabulary-controlled readers. In 1938 Thorndike also published, with Irving Lorge, a work that classifies the most common meanings of multiple-definition high-frequency words. Entitled *A Semantic Count of English Words*, it is the only book that takes this approach.

A third basis for word selection is *morphemic similarity*, that is, words that share the same roots or affixes. Edgar Dale, Joseph O'Rourke, and Henry Bamman (1971) urged teachers to use this as well as the recognition-threshold criterion in their construction of word lists. Many of the authors mentioned in the discussion of word analysis, below, argued that the word-list drill is a viable pedagogical technique only if the words presented belong to the same morphemic families.

Utility is yet another basis of selection upheld by some educators, with many suggesting an across-the-curriculum approach that would allow English teachers to teach terms that students would soon be discovering in their other subjects. Edward W. Dolch, one of the first to point out the need for this approach, published "The Vocabularies of Teaching Units" (1939), in which he explained that a study he did of elementary school teaching units revealed that the words symbolizing the central concepts of a topic were not always the ones most stressed by the teachers of these units. Instead, emphasis tended to be placed on words symbolizing picturesque or obscure aspects of the topic. Dolch's advice that teachers should concentrate on a subject's key terms has been echoed and expanded upon by many current educators. Richard A. Bruland, in "Learnin' Words" (1974), and Rexel E. Brown, in "A Three-Dimensional Approach to Teaching Vocabulary" (1975), suggested that in deciding what words to teach, instructors should be aware of their students' vocational and extra-curricular interests as well as the academic subjects they are studying.

Another criterion for word lists is the students' cognitive level, a particularly crucial consideration for elementary school teachers. In their classic 1932–1933 experiment with fourth graders, described in *The Development of Meaning Vocabularies in Reading* (1938), William S. Gray and Eleanor Holmes discovered that the words elementary school children have most difficulty comprehending are those symbolizing abstractions or generalizations, a fact that has been discussed in depth by child psychologists and language-acquisition experts. Many more recent educators, such as Sandra Thunander ("Increasing All Vocabularies" [1963]) and Anne Eisenberg ("The Trouble with Teaching Vocabulary" [1979]), emphasized the need for elementary school teachers to be aware of the sequence of the cognitive phases children go through: from concrete to functional to abstract. In pedagogical terms this means that until about age ten children should be taught only limited, concrete meanings of words.

Accordingly, teachers of older students should introduce them to abstract words as well as to unfamiliar meanings of familiar words. In an attempt to pinpoint exactly which words can most profitably be taught to high school students, Ward S. Miller ("A Plan for Teaching Vocabulary" [1938]) divided the 25,000 commonest words, which he garnered from Thorndike's lists and from a college dictionary, into six categories, including those words that the average elementary school graduate knows, those that students will no doubt learn on their own because they are in some way transparent, archaic and obsolete words, and so forth. He concluded that the best category to teach high school students is unfamiliar words having a non-transparent meaning, excluding those that pertain to some specialized hobby or skill.

Finally, college teachers as well as teachers of college-bound high school students would do well to consider the kinds of words that characterize academic writing. A few educators have attempted to tabulate and describe the lexical features of such writing. An early study of this sort was Marion Anderson's, reported in her article "The Quality of Adult Writing Vocabulary" (1934). Comparing the writings of ordinary adults (mainly their social and business correspondence) to those of literary people, the author discovered that some words are used much more frequently by one group than by the other.

Despite certain flaws in this study, it set a precedent for later, more effective versions. For example, in her chapter on vocabulary in *Errors and Expectations* (1977), Mina Shaughnessy did an excellent analysis of the lexical differences among the various levels of adult writing. Examining batches of freshman college essays, she categorized their authors into basic, intermediate, and advanced levels. *Basic writers* employ mainly vague nouns and basic verbs, with virtually no modifiers. *Intermediate writers* use more nouns, more specific verbs, some adverbs, and more informative adjectives and are able to alter the forms of words (for example, turn *existing* into *existence*). The writing of *advanced students* is characterized by a great gain in the use of relational words, phrases, and sentences, by the absence of vague terms like *thing* and *a lot*, by an increased use of modifiers and appositives, and by the possession of long Latinate words.

Sandra Stotsky's lexical tabulation and comparison studies also point to the preponderance of Latinate words in academic and expository writing. In "Teaching the Vocabulary of Academic Discourse" (1979) and "The Vocabulary of Essay Writing" (1981), Stotsky reported that a good number of the key words in academic and expository writing are abstract, multisyllabic, Latinate, and/or complex. The implication of her studies for teachers using the word-list approach is that words of Latin origin are the most profitable ones to teach to college or college-bound students.

An effective word-list approach not only takes into consideration the types of words to be learned but also includes some demonstration of usage. John R. Warner, in "A Test of Meaning" (1964), warned teachers about the misunderstandings that frequently occur when students are left on their own to learn a word's meaning. He cited two examples of the ludicrous ways students often use words learned in this manner: "*Abeyance* is a fear of the working man" (the dictionary had informed the student that "abeyance" means "temporary inactivity or suspension", and so the student took it to be a synonym for "layoff") and "The passing train caused the ground to *tremor*" (the student had failed to note the part-of-speech label in the dictionary entry). Warner suggested that teachers discuss the words on the list, pointing out their connotations, parts of speech, idiomatic usages, syntactic constraints, and so forth. Other educators who vouch for the effectiveness of the word-list approach if it is accompanied by some teacher demonstration of usage are Alvin C. Eurich ("Enlarging the Vocabularies of College Freshmen" [1932]), Arthur E. Traxler ("Improvement of Vocabulary Through Drill" [1938]), Philip R. V. Curoe ("An Experiment in Enriching the Active Vocabularies of College Seniors" [1939]), J. R. Shannon and Marian A. Kittle ("An Experiment in Teaching Vocabulary" [1942]), Gene Stanford ("Word Study That Works" [1971]), Charles Croll ("Teaching Vocabulary" [1971]), and Arthur G. Draper and Gerald H. Moeller ("We Think with Words" [1971]).

Misunderstandings of the type Warner cited often go uncorrected because of the nature of the follow-up tests typically used with word lists. Choosing the correct definition or synonym of a word on a multiple-choice test is no indication of whether students can use the word effectively in their writing or speaking. Indeed, the authors of both sentences quoted by Warner could easily have selected the correct definition on such a test. Further evidence of this phenomenon is provided by Sister M. Benigna Herbers's 1939 article "Comprehension Difficulties in a Third Grade Reader," describing the author's vocabulary experiment with a third-grade class: the written work and oral interviews following reading lessons indicated that the students did not really understand the meanings of those words whose definitions they had correctly chosen on the multiple-choice tests. Similarly, Barbara Brown Hillje ("Some Horsesense about Raising SAT Scores" [1980]) pointed out that students who have taken crash vocabulary courses to prepare for the SAT often use the newly acquired words inappropriately when they attempt to incorporate them into the essay-writing part of the test, even though they correctly identified them in the objective part.

Even when students use correctly the vocabulary words learned from word lists, the effect is often stilted. Fern Young, in "Vocabulary Work in the Third Form (Grades 6 and 7)" (1932), and Joseph Pecorino, in "Give Them Word Power!" (1970), cited as signs of success their middle-school pupils' ability to incorporate many of the weekly vocabulary words into their subsequent compositions, but to most readers attuned to current taste in prose style, the writing sounds pedantic and forced.

Such a showy use of vocabulary met with greater approval in the earlier decades of our century, when, as Bertha V. Nair explained in "Means of Developing Word Consciousness" (1934), the use of "big" words was considered proof of one's culture, character, and social standing. But even in those days there were certain enlightened educators who regarded this kind of language use as superficial. In "Veneer in Vocabulary Training" (1938), for example, H. Wayne Driggs recounted his extended study comparing junior high school children's out-of-school correspondence (mainly letters to friends who had moved to other cities) to their themes written for English teachers. He discovered that in the letters only 6.7 percent of the words were uncommon (that is, not found in Thorndike's first 1,000) compared with 10.5 percent in the themes, but that the uncommon words in the former were employed effectively and spontaneously whereas those in the latter were used in an awkward, stilted fashion. Observing that in the themes "the child is merely toying with big words he has met superficially" (p. 743), Driggs called this kind of vocabulary use "veneer."

Another early critic of the superficial approach to vocabulary instruction was Harold B. Dunkel ("Testing the Precise Use of Words" [1944]). He devised a vocabulary test that measured precision and depth of understanding and discovered that many students who had achieved high scores on the traditional vocabulary-range test did poorly on his test and vice versa. If the aim of vocabulary teaching is to help students use words effectively rather than merely use a wide variety of unusual words, the traditional vocabulary test is not an accurate measure of achievement. Dunkel argued not only that the tests should be changed but also that the word-list approach should be re-designed so as to teach a few words in depth rather than a large number superficially. Others who argued this point are the author of "Editorial: Recognition and Usage Vocabularies" (1934); Lawrence H. Conrad ("Intensive Vocabulary Study" [1940]); and Virgil E. Herrick and Miriam Howell ("Growth in the Maturity of Writing Vocabularies of Primary- and Middle-Grade Children" [1954]).

The second type of direct vocabulary instruction, *word analysis* (breaking a word into its morpheme components), is widely advocated because many educators believe it allows for greater "transferrability" than any other method: teaching students the meanings of morphemes found in familiar words can enable them to derive the meanings of unfamiliar words containing the same morphemes. This method is not only more efficient than random word lists but also more interesting, claimed Edgar Dale and Jerry L. Milligan ("Techniques in Vocabulary Development" [1970]), Justine Landry ("Say It With Flowers" [1973]), and H. Thompson Fillmer ("A Generative Vocabulary Program for Grades 4–6" [1977]). Many who argue for this approach provide lists of the most profitable morphemes to teach, namely those with invariant meanings and those appearing in a great many current words. See, for example, Lee C. Deighton, *Vocabulary Development in the Classroom* (1959); Ann F. Isaacs, "Vocabulary Enrichment for Which We Can Thank the Greeks'' (1971); and Edgar Dale, Joseph O'Rourke, and Henry A. Bamman, *Techniques of Teaching Vocabulary* (1971).

Sandra Stotsky, in "Teaching Prefixes" (1977), argued that the first step in vocabulary instruction for children should be to teach the meanings of common prefixes and how to recognize them. However, she warned that many workbooks define prefixes incorrectly, calling them simply initial sequences of letters and thus not distinguishing them from etymological elements. It is therefore important that teachers themselves be sophisticated about etymology and prefixation.

Stotsky's warning points to the flaw that many see in the word-analysis approach: the student must still ultimately refer to the dictionary to determine whether a sequence of letters is a true morpheme or merely an etymological element. Thus, they argue, this method is no more efficient than word lists. Other critics add that students can figure out whether a word contains a certain morpheme only if they already understand the meaning of the word, and so mopheme study does not help them to learn new words. Indeed, Lois M. Otterman, in "The Value of Teaching Prefixes and Word-Roots" (1955), and Gene Stanford, in "Word Study That Works" (1971), mentioned how far afield students sometimes are when they attempt to infer the meaning of an unfamiliar word from their knowledge of morpheme meanings, a problem in part created by semantic change, which causes a word gradually to take on a meaning different from the sum of its morphemic parts. Finally, some critics observe that memorizing lists of morphemes is just as difficult and tedious for students as memorizing lists of words.

Since about 50 percent of the morphemes in English words, especially in academic and scientific discourse, are of Latin origin, some educators, such as Sandra Stotsky ("Teaching the Vocabulary of Academic Discourse" [1979]), argued for Latin being reinstated in the high school curriculum. Although studies in the 1920s and 1930s, such as those surveyed by Frederick L. Pond ("Influence of the Study of Latin on Word Knowledge" [1938]) and Fran Lehr ("Latin Study" [1979]), indicated that knowledge of Latin does not significantly aid English vocabulary development, several recent studies contradict these findings. John D. Anderson ("Latin, English Vocabulary, and Declining SAT's" [1975]), Rudolph Masciantonio ("Tangible Benefits of the Study of Latin" [1977]), Nancy A. Mavrogenes ("Latin in the Elementary School" [1979]), and Jeremiah Reedy ("It's a Factoid, Tessa's in Italy" [1981]) all reported on experiments revealing that Latin study yields dramatic increases on SAT and other vocabulary test scores.

In addition to word lists and word analysis, a third popular way to teach vocabulary by the direct method is context analysis. Robert L. Crist, in "Learning Concepts from Contexts and Definitions" (1981), described a study in which college seniors who were exposed to new words solely through sentence contexts scored as high on multiple-choice tests of correct definitions as those who had been exposed solely to the definitions. Joan P. Gipe and Richard D. Arnold ("Teaching Vocabulary Through Familiar Associations and Contexts" [1979]) reported similar findings with elementary school pupils. Martha H. Bradley, Loretta A. Cahill, and Harry L. Tate ("Acquisition of a Reading Vocabulary" [1941]) pointed out that the value of the context approach is that students become familiar with the usage constraints of particular words, such as which prepositions, phrases, and so forth usually accompany them.

However, for this method to be effective, teachers must do more than simply urge the student to figure out a word's meaning from the context it appears in: they must describe the various kinds of context clues that exist. A number of vocabulary workbooks list these clues, which include example, apposition, definition, restatement, and modification. Particularly thorough explanations and illustrations are provided by Lee C. Deighton (*Vocabulary Development in the Classroom* [1959]) and Ann Humes ("Structures, Signals, and Cognitive Processes in Context Clues" [1978]). Roger J. Quealy ("Senior High School Students' Use of Contextual Aids in Reading" [1969]) observed that the ability to use context aids is positively correlated with intellectual ability and that further research is needed to determine which aids are most effective for which intellectual levels. A certain amount of such research has in fact been done. For example, Earl F. Rankin and Betsy M. Overholser ("Reaction of Intermediate Grade Children to Contextual Clues" [1969]) ran an experiment that revealed that the most helpful context clue for intermediate grade children is a series of familiar words related to the unfamiliar one and the least helpful clues are nonrestrictive clauses and appositives. Dorothy H. Cohen ("Word Meaning and the Literary Experience in Early Childhood" [1969]) listed the context clues good children's books contain. Deighton (*Vocabulary Development in the Classroom*) believes that there are four straightforward clues—definition, example, modification, and restatement—but that the other, less specific clues are difficult for the average high school student to identify without teacher guidance.

Some educators feel that students need more than simply a description of context clues; in addition, teachers should involve the class in in-depth discussion of the context the words appear in, for often a word's meaning can be determined only by examining the whole text. Lettie J. Austin ("Reading and Writing for Black Youth" [1972]) and Elaine M. Kaplan and Anita Tuchman ("Vocabulary Strategies Belong in the Hands of Learners" [1980]) explained how they took this approach with their college composition classes. Some teachers have discovered that certain fictional works particularly lend themselves to context-clue study both because they contain vocabulary words students need to learn and because their context clues are unusually helpful. James R. Sturdevant ("Shaw's *Don Juan in Hell*" [1968]) explained why the play *Don Juan in Hell* is a good vehicle for teaching high school students context analysis. Shirley Aaronson ("A 'Novel' Approach to Vocabulary Instruction" [1971]) made the same claim for *Slaughterhouse-Five* and college students.

The context-clue approach is not without its limitations, however. Gray and Holmes (*The Development of Meaning Vocabularies in Reading* [1938]) attempted to determine the extent to which context reveals meaning and discovered that it does so far less frequently than has commonly been supposed. They also discovered that children often form the wrong ideas about a word's meaning when they read it in context. Deighton (*Vocabulary Development in the Classroom* [1959]) found that in 500,000 running words of discourse fewer than 50 percent of the context clues were the straightforward kind understandable to the average reader. Deighton cited as another drawback to this method the fact that context reveals only one of the meanings of a word.

Because of the limitations of each of the direct methods, many educators, such as Holmes and Gray, advocate a mixture of these approaches. Helen M. Robinson, for example, argued in "Vocabulary" (1963) that direct vocabulary instruction yields greater gains than the indirect method and that a variety of direct methods is more effective than a single one. This view was also set forth by Ward S. Miller ("A Plan for Teaching Vocabulary" [1938]) and Samuel Weintraub ("Vocabulary Control" [1967]).

Most who advocate a mixture of direct methods want vocabulary to be taught in a systematic, comprehensive manner rather than in the haphazard way it is usually done. Dale, O'Rourke, and Bamman (*Techniques of Teaching Vocabulary* [1971]) argued that vocabulary instruction should hold a central place in the curriculum from elementary through high school. Each chapter of their book provides a theoretical discussion of a particular direct technique, suggests ways to teach it, and gives specific pedagogical exercises.

Dale D. Johnson and David P. Pearson's book *Teaching Reading Vocabulary* (1978), a teaching guide that advises a mixture of direct methods, has a similar format. The book also contains a bibliography of approximately 60 works done on vocabulary instruction from the 1950s through the mid-1970s.

In *Toward a Theory of Vocabulary Study* (1976), Joseph Patrick O'Rourke surveyed the state of vocabulary teaching and echoed others' complaints that it is done in a haphazard way. On the basis of key principles operating in language acquisition, which he discussed, the author proposed a theoretical framework for vocabulary instruction and then described a systematic, practical approach for implementing his theory, mainly by means of morpheme and context-clue work. His book includes a selected bibliography of works on language acquisition.

Others who urged teachers to use a mixture of direct methods are Wilhelmina T. Decock ("Words Words Words Words Words" [1970]), Rexel E. Brown ("A Three-Dimensional Approach to Teaching Vocabulary" [1975]), Richard C. Culyer III ("Guidelines for Skill Development" [1978]), Donald C. Cushenbery ("Effective Ways of Building Vocabulary in Every Content Area" [1978]), Carol J. Fisher ("Words Come First!" [1978]), and Donna E. Norton ("Vocabulary Development to Improve Writing Style" [1980]).

Indirect Method

The indirect method of vocabulary instruction cannot be as neatly defined as the direct. Any attempt to pattern vocabulary instruction after the way people naturally learn new words may be called an indirect method. Although this approach had a few champions in the early decades of the century, for the most part it is a more recent development than the direct method.

The indirect approach is a response both to a growing awareness on the part of English teachers of modern semantic and linguistic theories and to a recent shift in English and language arts programs from an emphasis on reading to an emphasis on writing. Basic Writing expert Mina Shaughnessy, an advocate of this approach, argued in her chapter on syntax in *Errors and Expectations* (1977) that a poor vocabulary is at the root of many more writing difficulties than has usually been realized. Wordiness, obscurity, and mixed syntax are often the result of writers' not having at their disposal the one apt word or phrase that would efficiently and clearly convey a thought. But Shaughnessy warned that word lists are not the solution. Instead, teachers must devise techniques based on the natural vocabulary-acquisition process, taking into consideration that there are limits to the rate at which we can acquire new words and that there are degrees of difficulty with words, depending on everything from their physical characteristics to the complexity of their referential meanings.

Advocates of the indirect approach believe that mastery of a word is achieved only when one can use it spontaneously and effectively in one's writing. Pointing out that the natural way such mastery occurs with adults is for a word to move gradually through one's four vocabularies, usually from reading to listening to writing to speaking, they urge teachers to devise pedagogical techniques to speed up this process. In "Developing Vocabulary" (1960), Lee C. Deighton argued that although it is natural for the four vocabularies to develop at different rates, the writing and speaking ones need not lag so far behind the reading and hearing ones. He suggested ways the gap can be narrowed, mainly by arranging for increased writing and discussion in the language arts classroom. But Deighton also warned that since word meanings can be learned only gradually, after repeated encounters with a word, the word-list approach is to be avoided.

Aware of the necessary time lag between a word's existence in one's reading vocabulary and its existence in one's writing vocabulary, Regina M. Hoover ("In the Beginning" [1979]) devised a teaching technique based on the natural word-acquisition sequence. When her students look up an unfamiliar word they have come across in their reading, they must re-write the original sentence in their own words, not using the new term. This helps them relate the new word to ones they already know, which is what one does in the natural process. Hoover then instructs her students to use the word in their own writing only after they have had more exposure to it, again simulating the natural process.

Robert K. Jackson ("Does the World Need Another Article on Vocabulary Development" [1973]) and Jeanette Harris and Lil Brannon ("Recognizing the Basic Writer's Vocabulary Acquisition Sequence" [1979]) pointed out that a child's vocabulary-acquisition sequence is different from an adult's and that this fact should be taken into account in designing pedagogical techniques for elementary school pupils. Because for children a new word moves from the speaking and listening vocabularies into first the reading and then the writing ones, they should be introduced to a word orally before they encounter it in their reading. Harris and Brannon believe that teachers of remedial college students should use this same approach, because, living in a primarily oral world, such students cannot understand enough of the content of a written text to be able to learn unfamiliar words that appear in it, as the average adult can.

Although these theorists believe it is wrong to use a word in writing before one has mastered its meaning, there are ways the process can be speeded up. In "Word Retrieval" (1977), Mary Culver described a technique to help college students activate their passive vocabularies. She had them read an essay containing several words they could understand but never used themselves. Pointing out to them that since they could recognize them, these—and many other—words were lying dormant in their own minds, she then had them do a group brainstorm session in which they tried to come up with the most precise words to describe a particular object or picture at the front of the classroom. This resulted in the students bringing to the surface of their minds words they had not realized they possessed, and it showed them that good writers do not seek out words in a dictionary or thesaurus but rather tap into their own passive vocabularies.

Another excellent method for activating students' passive vocabularies is described by Bruce T. Petersen in "An Emotional Lexicon" (1981). Basing his approach on psychologist John Gottman's technique for helping his clients better articulate their feelings, Petersen gave his college students a list of emotion-describing adjectives that they recognized but would not normally use. He then instructed them to write about situations in which they had experienced these feelings and to describe the physical sensations that accompanied them. As the students discovered how the words embodied emotions they had experienced, they added the words to their active vocabularies.

Those who advocate the indirect method usually observe that vocabulary instruction has mistakenly been called the study of words when it is actually the study of concepts. Edward W. Dolch ("Vocabulary Development" [1953]) pointed out that words are symbols of experience and that the only way to expand vocabulary is to expand experience. The direct method, continued Dolch, consists merely of substituting new words for old ones, without changing the learner's understanding. For example, a student who is taught that *nutrition* is a synonym for *food* thinks of the same meaning but merely hears a different word. This method, then, increases vocabulary without increasing meaning. But with the indirect method the teacher attempts to teach new meanings along with new words by building upon students' old concepts and by providing new experiences via field trips, class discussions, meaningful reading, and so forth.

Charles I. Glicksberg ("The Dynamics of Vocabulary Building" [1940]) argued along similar lines as Dolch. Pointing out that the "study of vocabulary has been simplified to an absurd degree," he said that "a new word that is learned does not simply move in and occupy new quarters as a total stranger; it does not actually become a member of the semantic community in the mind until it has become organically linked with the vast treasury of antecedent experiences and meanings'' (p. 200). He argued that people learn new words only when they are deeply and earnestly interested in the topic the words pertain to. The only way, then, to "teach" vocabulary is to provide students with experiences and with reading that relates to their interests; they will then naturally learn the new words involved.

Others who stressed that vocabulary building should rightly be experience and concept building are Mary C. Serra ("How to Develop Concepts and Their Verbal Representations" [1953]), Albert J. Kingston ("Vocabulary Development" [1964–1965]), and Anne Eisenberg ("The Trouble with Teaching Vocabulary" [1979]).

John B. Carroll ("Words, Meanings, and Concepts" [1964]) and John H. Langer ("Vocabulary and Concept Development" [1967]) described the intricate relationship between vocabulary acquisition and concept acquisition. Carroll, arguing that true meaning accrues to a word only when one has had experience with the concept it symbolizes, cited as an example a child who assumed that *tourist* and *immigrant* were interchangeable terms until he had exposure to what each denotes and then could differentiate their meanings. Langer explored the process of vocabulary acquisition, explaining that as one refines and discriminates a concept, one searches for new terms to symbolize it. Thus words facilitate the organization of experience for an individual by providing labels for systems of that experience.

Children in particular, because of the concrete, functional nature of their cognitive thinking, benefit from an experiential approach to vocabulary instruction. According to a study by Dorothy H. Cohen ("The Effect of Literature on Vocabulary and Reading Achievement" [1968]), the slower children are academically, the more difficult it is for them to deal with words in isolation, unrelated to meaningful experience. Others who stress the importance of using the experiential approach for elementary school children are Martha L. Addy ("Development of a Meaning Vocabulary in the Intermediate Grades" [1941]), Alan Muskopf ("Increasing All Vocabularies" [1963]), Ruth G. Strickland ("Vocabulary Development and Language Learning" [1972]), Carol Washburne ("Vocabulary Development" [1972]), and George A. Miller ("On Knowing the Right Word" [1978]).

Many educators who favor the indirect method talk about the crucial role played by "felt need" in vocabulary development. For example, John S. Mayher ("Another Journey Through the Looking-Glass" [1982]) observed that vocabulary development occurs when people feel the need for a word to articulate a new situation, emotion, or concept. It is at this point that they should be introduced to the new word rather than have it artificially imposed upon them. Thus the traditional practice of giving students a word and then having them use it meaningfully in an original sentence has reversed the natural order. A number of suggestions for teaching vocabulary in accordance with students' needs are suggested by Jay E. Greene ("Modernizing the Teaching of Vocabulary" [1945]), who observed that "the importance of 'felt need' has been universally acknowledged in every phase of teaching but vocabulary" (p. 344).

In "One Capsule a Week—a Painless Remedy for Vocabulary Ills" (1975), Barbara I. Crist described how she used students' "felt need" in teaching vocabulary to her college freshman composition class. She drew up each week's list of words on the basis of the topic of interest provided by her students. She then involved the class in discussions and writing assignments designed to create in them the need for certain words related to the topic at hand. Another excellent approach was taken by Ruby L. Thompson ("Word Power" [1971]), who had students in her college composition class bring in one word that they personally thought the rest of the class should know. The students had to defend the choice, explaining the word's meaning and importance and providing contexts for it. Then the rest of the class decided whether they wanted to add the word to the list they were compiling. Thompson discovered that once the list was drawn up, she could use traditional direct methods to reinforce students' understanding, because they already had an interest in and contexts for the words.

David J. Kahle took an approach similar to Thompson's in his junior high school English class. In "Student-Centered Vocabulary" (1972), he explained how he had his students compile their list of words on the basis of need and interest and then had them teach one another the words. The results were favorable: a good many students were able to use the new words effectively in their subsequent compositions.

Another indirect approach involves reinforcing vocabulary learning by presenting the words in media other than writing, since natural vocabulary mastery is usually achieved by encountering a word in a range of meaningful situations and contexts. "Courtesy of Network T.V." (1974) describes a method called "telestrating," in which the teacher super-imposes vocabulary words on a television screen to label the concepts, situations, and emotions that are being dramatized in a given show. (The teacher, of course, has viewed the program beforehand.) This is followed up by worksheet exercises and discussion.

Berenice B. Beggs ("Speak the Word Trippingly" [1951]) and Louis D. Perry, Jr. ("Teaching Vocabulary to Slow Learners" [1969]) included in their vocabulary instruction pictures illustrating the concepts and phenomena symbolized by the words. Ruth Beaumont Reuse ("All It Takes Is a Little Incentive" [1977]) and Frederick A. Duffelmeyer ("The Influence of Experience-based Vocabulary Instruction on Learning Word Meanings" [1980]) reported that having their respective high school and college students dramatize the concepts and phenomena being taught is much more effective than the direct methods of word analysis, context study, and dictionary usage.

Despite studies showing the limitations of context as an aid in understanding unfamiliar words (see my discussion of context clues in the section on direct methods, above), many believe that extensive reading is the most effective, most natural way to develop vocabulary. These advocates include George M. Usova

("Improving Vocabulary Through Wide Reading and Context" [1977]), Barbara Brown Hillje ("Some Horsesense about Raising SAT Scores" [1980]), and Bill Hardin ("Miles and Miles of Print, or the Better Way to Teach Vocabulary" [1980]). Isidore Levine ("Quantity Reading" [1972]) observed that one of the major differences between oral and written discourse is that the former contains far fewer uncommon words. Therefore, only through reading will people encounter and master certain kinds of words.

Some educators, however, warn that reading improves vocabulary only when the student is deeply involved in the story or subject matter. Robert E. Newman ("Increasing All Vocabularies" [1963]) argued that the best way for children to develop their vocabularies is to read widely in books that are exciting or personally meaningful to them. Teachers must therefore acquaint themselves with a large number of good children's and adolescents' books.

Georgia E. Miller ("Vocabulary Building Through Extensive Reading" [1941]) described a combined English-science-social studies junior high school study unit that inadvertently increased students' vocabularies by means of purposeful reading. The assignment—to write editorial essays proposing a plan for conservation—entailed students having to do extensive reading on the topic. Although the teachers never said anything about vocabulary, the resulting essays indicated an improvement in this area, with students effectively using words, such as *demolition* and *replenish*, that formerly had not been a part of their vocabularies.

Robert S. Burroughs ("Vocabulary Study and Context, or How I Learned to Stop Worrying about Word Lists" [1982]) also discussed the benefits of directed reading as a form of vocabulary instruction. Observing that the traditional word-list approach gives students the impression that the dictionary is the place to end their search, he designed an approach that would show them it is really just the place to begin. Students are provided with a list of words they will discover in their fiction reading that week and are instructed to learn the meanings by both context scrutiny and dictionary use. In the follow-up tests, they are given minimal points for merely repeating the dictionary definitions and maximum points for explaining effectively the meaning they have gleaned from the context. This method brings to bear their imaginations and powers of analysis, rather than simply their memories, and not only teaches them new words but helps them to learn about the crucial role played by context, to gain knowledge of literary devices, and to read more carefully.

A final form of indirect vocabulary teaching is based on the assumption that people are more receptive to learning about new words if they have a curiosity about and an awareness of how words evolve and function in our language. This approach involves teaching students about semantics and etymology. Sidney Shanker ("Is Your Vocabulary Teaching Obsolete?" [1964]) outlined the semantic principles he taught his high school students, and Robert J. Munnelly ("Teach That Word Meanings Are Open" [1972]) suggested a number of exercises teachers can use to make students aware of the semantic openness of words.

Joanna Channell ("Applying Semantic Theory to Vocabulary Teaching" [1981]) used semantic-field theory as the basis for teaching vocabulary. She had her students list several words in the same semantic field (such as *surprise*, *astonish*, *flabbergast*, and *amaze*) and then, by means of a grid or matrix, indicate the distinguishing features of each synonym. Others who used variations of the semantic-field approach are Susanna W. Pflaum ("Expansion of Meaning Vocabulary" [1973]), John E. Readence and Lyndon W. Searfoss ("Teaching Strategies for Vocabulary Development" [1980]), R. Scott Baldwin, Jeff C. Ford, and John E. Readence ("Teaching Word Connotations" [1981]), and Shirley Koeller ("Concept Building Through Vocabulary Development" [1981]). G. M. Fess ("Teaching Synonyms" [1938]), Milford A. Jeremiah ("Teaching Vocabulary in Social Context" [1981]), and Joanne Palmer ("A Lesson in Euphemisms" [1981]) emphasized the social factors that give rise to synonyms and euphemisms. Linda Shadiow ("A Short Recipe for 'Slang Concentrate' " [1981]) and James Park Hyde ("Rat Talk" [1982]) aroused their high school and college students' interest in semantics by analyzing the special vocabulary of teenagers and young adults.

Closely related to the semantic approach is the etymological approach, in which students are introduced to the histories of the particular words being studied. Most advocates of this method cite as its major advantage the fact that students are usually fascinated by the history of words. Martha E. Woundy ("A Project in Vocabulary Study" [1935]), for example, remarked that her students found this approach "less odious" than word lists (p. 759). Her view was shared by William Moir ("A World of Words" [1953]), Isabel R. Frizzell ("Historical Approach to Word Study" [1963]), and Charlton Laird ("Down Giantwife" [1970]). Laird noted an additional advantage: students usually have no trouble remembering the meaning of a word after they have examined its history in depth. Berenice B. Beggs ("Creating Excitement in Learning" [1973]) observed that one reason students like this approach is that they can all cite numerous examples of recently coined words and enjoy speculating about the causes behind their emergence. Finally, for teachers who would like to use this approach, a helpful list of etymological sourcebooks is provided by Rexel E. Brown in "A Three-Dimensional Approach to Teaching Vocabulary" (1975).

Although vocabulary instruction can be divided into two major theoretical schools and their respective methods, the direct and the indirect, in actuality the two methods are often used in conjunction. For example, many teachers who work with word lists also urge their students to read widely. Similarly, many advocates of the indirect method believe that direct approaches can be used once the student has experienced the concept being symbolized and has discovered the word in a variety of contexts. Furthermore, both schools of thought agree that vocabulary development should receive greater attention at all grade levels. Indeed, the fact that poor writers regard their under-developed vocabularies to be the main cause of their writing deficiencies (see Shaughnessy's "Vocabulary" in her *Errors and Expectations* [1977]) along with the fact that vocabulary level is the most significant factor in teachers' holistic quality ratings of student essays (Cary Grobe, "Syntactic Maturity, Mechanics, and Vocabulary as Predictors of Quality Ratings" [1981]) indicate that it is high time that vocabulary instruction be given the central place it warrants in the academic curriculum.

References

Aaronson, Shirley. "A 'Novel' Approach to Vocabulary Instruction." *J Read*, 14 (1971), 476–79.

Addy, Martha L. "Development of a Meaning Vocabulary in the Intermediate Grades." *Elem Eng*, 18 (1941), 22–26, 30.

Anderson, John D. "Latin, English Vocabulary, and Declining SAT's." *Class J*, 70, No. 3 (1975), 42–46.

Anderson, Marion. "The Quality of the Adult Writing Vocabulary." *Elem Eng*, 11 (1934), 135–38.

Austin, Lettie J. "Reading and Writing for Black Youth." *Read Improv*, 9, No. 2 (1972), 45–47.

Baldwin, R. Scott, Jeff C. Ford, and John E. Readence. "Teaching Word Connotations: An Alternative Strategy." *Read World*, 21 (1981), 103–8.

Beggs, Berenice B. "Speak the Word Trippingly." *EJ*, 40 (1951), 39–40.

———. "Creating Excitement in Learning." *Sch & Com*, 59, No. 5 (1973), 31, 44–45.

Bradley, Martha H., Loretta A. Cahill, and Harry L. Tate. "Acquisition of a Reading Vocabulary." *Elem Eng*, 18 (1941), 19–21, 32.

Brown, Rexel E. "A Three-Dimensional Approach to Teaching Vocabulary." *Ind Read Q*, 7, No. 2 (1975), 5–8, 31.

Bruland, Richard A. "Learnin' Words: Evaluating Vocabulary Development Efforts." *J. Read*, 18 (1974), 212-14.

Burroughs, Robert S. "Vocabulary Study and Context, or How I Learned to Stop Worrying about Word Lists." *EJ*, 71, No. 2 (1982), 53–55.

Carroll, John B. "Words, Meanings and Concepts." *Harvard Educ Rev*, 34 (1964), 178–202.

Channell, Joanna. "Applying Semantic Theory to Vocabulary Teaching." *Eng Lang Teach J*, 35 (1981), 115–22.

Cohen, Dorothy H. "The Effect of Literature on Vocabulary and Reading Achievement." *Elem Eng*, 45 (1968), 209–13.

———. "Word Meaning and the Literacy Experience in Early Childhood." *Elem Eng*, 46 (1969), 914–25.

Conrad, Lawrence H. "Intensive Vocabulary Study." *EJ*, 29 (1940), 794–99.

"Courtesy of Network T.V." *Nation's Sch & Coll*, 1 (1974), 24.

Crist, Barbara I. "One Capsule a Week—A Painless Remedy for Vocabulary Ills." *J Read*, 19 (1975), 147–49.

Crist, Robert L. "Learning Concepts from Contexts and Definitions: A Single Subject Replication." *J Read Behav*, 13 (1981), 271–77.

Croll, Charles. "Teaching Vocabulary." *CCC*, 22 (1971), 378–80.

Culver, Mary. "Word Retrieval." *Ex E*, 22 (1977), 15–17.

Culyer, Richard C., III. "Guidelines for Skill Development: Vocabulary." *Read Teach*, 32 (1978), 316–22.

Curoe, Philip R. V. "An Experiment in Enriching the Active Vocabularies of College Seniors." *Sch & Soc*, 49 (1939), 522–24.

Cushenbery, Donald C. "Effective Ways of Building Vocabulary in Every Content Area." *Read Horizons*, 18 (1978), 142–44.

Dale, Edgar. *Bibliography of Vocabulary Studies*. Columbus, Ohio: Bureau of Educational Research, Ohio State University, 1939.

————. *Bibliography of Vocabulary Studies*. Columbus, Ohio: Bureau of Educational Research, Ohio State University, 1949.

————, and Gerhard Eicholz. *Children's Knowledge of Words: An Interim Report*. Columbus, Ohio: Bureau of Educational Research, Ohio State University, 1960.

————, and Jerry L. Milligan. "Techniques in Vocabulary Development." *Read Improv*, 7, No. 1 (1970), 1–5, 13.

————, and Taher Razik. *Bibliography of Vocabulary Studies*. 2nd rev ed. Columbus, Ohio: Bureau of Educational Research, Ohio State University, 1963.

————, and Donald Reichert. *Bibliography of Vocabulary Studies*. Rev. ed. Columbus, Ohio: Bureau of Educational Research, Ohio State University, 1957.

————, Joseph O'Rourke, and Henry A. Bamman. *Techniques of Teaching Vocabulary*. Palo Alto, Calif.: Field Educational Publications, 1971.

————, Taher Razik, and Walter Petty. *Bibliography of Vocabulary Studies*. Columbus, Ohio: Ohio State University, 1973.

Decock, Wilhelmina T. "Words Words Words Words Words." *Penn Sch J*, 118 (1970), 182–83.

Deighton, Lee C. *Vocabulary Development in the Classroom*. New York: Teachers College Press, 1959.

————. "Developing Vocabulary: Another Look at the Problem." *EJ*, 49 (1960), 82–88.

Dolch, Edward W. "The Vocabularies of Teaching Units." *Elem Eng*, 16 (1939), 43–46, 57.

————. "Vocabulary Development." *Elem Eng*, 30 (1953), 70–75.

Draper, Arthur G., and Gerald H. Moeller. "We Think with Words." *Phi Del Kap*, 52 (1971), 482–84.

Driggs, H. Wayne. "Veneer in Vocabulary Training." *EJ*, 27 (1938), 740–46.

Duffelmeyer, Frederick A. "The Influence of Experience-based Vocabulary Instruction on Learning Word Meanings." *J Read*, 24 (1980), 35–40.

Dunkel, Harold B. "Testing the Precise Use of Words." *CE*, 5 (1944), 386–89.

"Editorial: Recognition and Usage Vocabularies." *Elem Eng*, 11 (1934), 147.

Eisenberg, Anne. "The Trouble with Teaching Vocabulary." *JBW*, 2, No. 3 (1979), 5–14.

Eurich, Alvin C. "Enlarging the Vocabularies of College Freshmen." *EJ* (College Edition), 21 (1932), 135–41.

Fess, G. M. "Teaching Synonyms." *EJ*, 27 (1938), 347–49.

Fillmer, H. Thompson. "A Generative Vocabulary Program for Grades 4–6." *El Sch J*, 78 (1977), 53–58.

Fisher, Carol J. "Words Come First!" *Instr*, 88, No. 2 (1978), 187–88.

Frizzell, Isabel R. "Historical Approach to Word Study." *EJ*, 52 (1963), 679–99.

Gipe, Joan P., and Richard D. Arnold. "Teaching Vocabulary Through Familiar Associations and Contexts." *J Read Behav*, 11 (1979), 281–85.

Glicksberg, Charles I. "The Dynamics of Vocabulary-Building." *EJ*, 29 (1940), 197–206.

Gray, William S., and Eleanor Holmes. *The Development of Meaning Vocabularies in Reading*. Publications of the Laboratory Schools of the University of Chicago, No. 6. Chicago: University of Chicago Press, 1938.

Greene, Jay E. "Modernizing the Teaching of Vocabulary." *EJ*, 34 (1945), 343–44.

Grobe, Cary. "Syntactic Maturity, Mechanics, and Vocabulary as Predictors of Quality Ratings." *RTE*, 15 (1981), 75–85.

Hardin, Bill. "Miles and Miles of Print, or the Better Way to Teach Vocabulary." *Teacher*, 97, No. 4 (1980), 46–48.

Harris, Jeanette, and Lil Brannon. "Recognizing the Basic Writer's Vocabulary Acquisition Sequence." *JBW*, 2, No. 3 (1979), 76-81.

Herbers, Sister M. Benigna. "Comprehension Difficulties in a Third Grade Reader." *Elem Eng*, 16 (1939), 53–57.

Herrick, Virgil E., and Miriam Howell. "Growth in the Maturity of Writing Vocabularies of Primary- and Middle-Grade Children." *El Sch J*, 54 (1954), 338–44.

Hillje, Barbara Brown. "Some Horsesense about Raising SAT Scores." *EJ*, 69, No. 6 (1980), 29–31.

Hoover, Regina M. "In the Beginning: The Word." *JBW*, 2, No. 3 (1979), 82–87.

Humes, Ann. "Structures, Signals, and Cognitive Processes in Context Clues." *RTE*, 12 (1978), 321–34.

Hyde, James Park. "Rat Talk: The Special Vocabulary of Some Teenagers." *EJ*, 71, No. 3 (1982), 98–101.

Isaacs, Ann F. "Vocabulary Enrichment for Which We Can Thank the Greeks." *Gifted Child Q*, 15 (1971), 311–12.

Jackson, Robert K. "Does the World Need Another Article on Vocabulary Development." *Read Improv*, 10, No. 1 (1973), 9–11.

Jeremiah, Milford A. "Teaching Vocabulary in Social Context." *J Read*, 25 (1981), 68–69.

Johnson, Dale D., and David P. Pearson. *Teaching Reading Vocabulary*. New York: Holt, Rinehart, Winston, 1978.

Kahle, David J. "Student-Centered Vocabulary." *EJ*, 61 (1972), 286–88.

Kaplan, Elaine M., and Anita Tuchman. "Vocabulary Strategies Belong in the Hands of Learners." *J Read*, 24 (1980), 32–34.

Kingston, Albert J. "Vocabulary Development." *J Read*, 8 (1964–1965), 265–71.

Koeller, Shirley. "Concept Building Through Vocabulary Development." *El Sch J*, 82 (1981), 136–41.

Laird, Charlton. "Down Giantwife: The Uses of Etymology." *EJ*, 59 (1970), 1106–12.

Landry, Justine. "Say It with Flowers." *Instr*, 83, No. 2 (1973), 162.

Langer, John H. "Vocabulary and Concept Development." *J Read*, 10 (1967), 448–56.

Lehr, Fran. "Latin Study: A Promising Practice in English Vocabulary Instruction?" *J Read*, 23 (1979), 76–79.

Levine, Isidore. "Quantity Reading: An Introduction." *J Read*, 15 (1972), 576–83.

Masciantonio, Rudolph. "Tangible Benefits of the Study of Latin: A Review of Research." *Foreign Language Annals*, 10 (1977), 375–82.

Mavrogenes, Nancy A. "Latin in the Elementary School: A Help for Reading and Language Arts." *Phi Del Kap*, 60 (1979), 675–77.

Mayher, John S. "Another Journey Through the Looking-Glass: New Lenses for Old Problems." *AEB*, 24, No. 3 (1982), 86–96.

Menyuk, Paula. *The Acquisition and Development of Language*. Prentice-Hall Current Research in Developmental Psychology Series. Englewood Cliffs, N.J.: Prentice-Hall, 1971.

Miller, George A. "On Knowing the Right Word." *Natl El Prin*, 57, No. 4 (1978), 36–40.

Miller, Georgia E. "Vocabulary Building Through Extensive Reading." *EJ*, 30 (1941), 664–66.

Miller, Ward S. "A Plan for Teaching Vocabulary." *EJ*, 27 (1938), 566–73.

Moir, William. "A World of Words." *EJ*, 42 (1953), 153–55.

Munnelly, Robert J. "Teach That Word Meanings Are Open." *Instr*, 81, No. 7 (1972), 57–58.

Muskopf, Alan. "Increasing All Vocabularies: In Grades Four Through Eight." In *Reading and the Language Arts*. Proceedings of the Annual Conference on Reading at the University of Chicago, Vol. 25, No. 93. Chicago: University of Chicago Press, 1963, pp. 182–85.

Nair, Bertha V. "Means of Developing Word Consciousness." *Elem Eng*, 11 (1934), 125–29, 146.

Newman, Robert E. "Increasing All Vocabularies: In Kindergarten Through Grade Three." In *Reading and the Language Arts*. Proceedings of the Annual Conference on Reading at the University of Chicago, Vol. 25, No. 93. Chicago: University of Chicago Press, 1963, pp. 177–81.

Norton, Donna E. "Vocabulary Development to Improve Writing Style." In *The Effective Teaching of Language Arts*. Columbus, Ohio: Merrill, 1980.

O'Connor, Johnson. "Vocabulary and Success." *Atlantic Monthly*, Feb. 1934, pp. 160–66.

O'Rourke, Joseph Patrick. *Toward a Theory of Vocabulary Development*. The Hague: Mouton, 1976.

Otterman, Lois M. "The Value of Teaching Prefixes and Word-Roots." *J Educ Res*, 48 (1955), 611–16.

Palmer, Joanne. "A Lesson on Euphemisms." *AEB*, 23, No. 3 (1981), 87.

Pecorino, Joseph. "Give Them Word Power!" *Instr*, 79, No. 8 (1970), 66–67.

Perry, Louis D., Jr. "Teaching Vocabulary to Slow Learners." *Clear H*, 44, No. 3 (1969), 164–65.

Petersen, Bruce T. "An Emotional Lexicon: Words for Feelings." *AEB*, 23, No. 2 (1981), 7–12.

Petty, Walter T., Curtis P. Herold, and Earline Stoll. *The State of Knowledge about the Teaching of Vocabulary*. Champaign, Ill.: NCTE, 1968.

Pflaum, Susanna W. "Expansion of Meaning Vocabulary: Strategies for Classroom Instruction." *Elem Eng*, 50 (1973), 89–93.

Pond, Frederick L. "Influence of the Study of Latin on Word Knowledge." *Sch Rev*, 46 (1938), 611–18.

Quealy, Roger J. "Senior High School Students' Use of Contextual Aids in Reading." *Read Res Q*, 4 (1969), 512–33.

Rankin, Earl F., and Betsy M. Overholser. "Reaction of Intermediate Grade Children to Contextual Clues." *J Read Behav*, 1, No. 3 (1969), 50–73.

Readence, John E., and Lyndon W. Searfoss. "Teaching Strategies for Vocabulary Development." *EJ*, 69, No. 7 (1980), 43–46.

Reedy, Jeremiah. " 'It's a Factoid, Tessa's in Italy:' Latin Is Asset in Which the Author Discusses 101 Ways to Enliven a Course in Vocabulary Building." *Class J*, 76 (1981), 259–65.

Reuse, Ruth Beaumont. "All It Takes Is a Little Incentive." *Media and Methods*, 13 (1977), 59.

Robinson, Helen M. "Vocabulary: Speaking, Listening, Reading, and Writing." In *Reading and the Language Arts*. Proceedings of the Annual Conference on Reading at the University of Chicago, Vol. 25, No. 93. Chicago: University of Chicago Press, 1963, pp. 167–76.

Serra, Mary C. "How to Develop Concepts and Their Verbal Representations." *El Sch J*, 53 (1953), 275–85.

Shadiow, Linda. "A Short Recipe for 'Slang Concentrate.' " *AEB*, 23, No. 2 (1981), 37–38.

Shanker, Sidney. "Is Your Vocabulary Teaching Obsolete?" *EJ*, 53 (1964), 422–27.

Shannon, J. R., and Marian A. Kittle. "An Experiment in Teaching Vocabulary." *Teach Col J*, 14 (1942), 1–6.

Shaughnessy, Mina P. *Errors and Expectations: A Guide for the Teacher of Basic Writing*. New York: Oxford University Press, 1977.

Stanford, Gene. "Word Study That Works." *EJ*, 60 (1971), 111–15.

Stotsky, Sandra. "Teaching Prefixes: Facts and Fallacies." *Lang Arts*, 54 (1977), 887–90.

———. "Teaching the Vocabulary of Academic Discourse." *JBW*, 2, No. 3 (1979), 15–39.

———. "The Vocabulary of Essay Writing: Can It Be Taught?" *CCC*, 32 (1981), 317–26.

Strickland, Ruth G. "Vocabulary Development and Language Learning." *Educ Horizons*, 50 (1972), 150–55.

Sturdevant, James R. "Shaw's *Don Juan in Hell*: A Study in Word Power." *EJ*, 57 (1968), 1002–4.

Thompson, Ruby L. "Word Power: How to Use What They Like to Give Them What They Need." *J Read*, 15 (1971), 13–15.

Thorndike, E. L. *A Teacher's Word Book of 10,000 Words*. New York: Teachers College, Columbia University, 1921.

———. *A Teacher's Word Book of 20,000 Words*. New York: Teachers College, Columbia University, 1931.

———. *A Teacher's Word Book of 30,000 Words*. New York: Teachers College, Columbia University, 1944.

———, and Irving Lorge. *A Semantic Count of English Words*. New York: New York Institute of Educational Research, Teachers College, Columbia University, 1938.

Thunander, Sandra. "Increasing All Vocabularies: In Corrective and Remedial Classes." In *Reading and the Language Arts*. Proceedings of the Annual Conference on Reading at the University of Chicago, Vol. 25, No. 93. Chicago: University of Chicago Press, 1963, pp. 190–94.

Traxler, Arthur E. "Improvement of Vocabulary Through Drill." *EJ*, 27 (1938), 491–94.

Ullman, Stephen. *Semantics: An Introduction to the Science of Meaning*. 1962; rpt. Oxford: Basil Blackwell, 1967.

Usova, George M. "Improving Vocabulary Through Wide Reading and Context." *Read Improv*, 14, No. 1 (1977), 62–64.

Vygotsky, Lev Semenovich. *Thought and Language*. Trans. and ed. Eugenia Hanfmann and Gertrude Vakar. Cambridge, Mass.: M.I.T. Press, 1962.

Warner, John R. "A Test of Meaning." *CEA*, 26 (1964), 4–5.

Washburne, Carol. "Vocabulary Development." *Elem Eng*, 49 (1972), 541–44.

Weintraub, Samuel. "Vocabulary Control." *Read Teach*, 20 (1967), 759, 761, 763, 765.

Whorf, Benjamin Lee. *Language, Thought, and Reality: Selected Writings of Benjamin Lee Whorf*. Ed. John B. Carroll. Cambridge, Mass.: M.I.T. Press, 1956.

Woundy, Martha E. "A Project in Vocabulary Study." *EJ*, 24 (1935), 759–60.

Young, Fern. "Vocabulary Work in Third Form (Grades 6 and 7)." *Sch*, 21 (1932), 312–15.

Punctuation

GRETA D. LITTLE

In spite of the fact that punctuation has been used for more than 2,000 years, it seems we are not yet sure what it is or why we need it. Although it is employed by both reader and writer, we have given the major portion of our attention to the role of punctuation in writing. On the one hand, we say it is governed by rules, but on the other hand, we claim that no two persons punctuate alike. All the while, we often delegate the task to printers and compositors. Why? For most of us punctuation is dull, a mere mechanical activity, not a part of the actual composing process. As in writing, the role of punctuation in reading has been addressed only erratically. It is not a regular feature of reading instruction or of investigation into the psychology of reading. Thus we find that punctuation has, by and large, been ignored by modern scholars. However, this was not always the case. Major controversies about punctuation and its nature raged for several centuries, and most of those arguments were never really settled. Consequently, when we look at punctuation today, we find a confusing picture.

The earliest punctuation served to separate words in ancient Greek and Latin manuscripts. A system attributed to Aristophanes of Byzantium appeared in some of the later manuscripts to indicate stops or pauses. However, the system was not widely adopted. Our punctuation had its true beginnings in the "pointing" of medieval scribes. Points, the punctuation marks, were inserted to indicate pauses and to assist in reading the text. Medieval punctuation thus was primarily elocutionary. With the coming of the printing press, order was brought to pointing by Aldus Manutius, an Italian printer who outlined the use of the comma, semicolon, colon, and period, laying the foundation for modern punctuation. In the sixteenth and seventeenth centuries, English printing followed the pattern of medieval elocutionary pointing, known today as the rhetorical tradition of punctuation. During the seventeenth century, the basis for pointing began to shift from pronunciation to grammar. By 1850 the dominant consideration in punctuation was grammatical structure. The rhetorical tradition, however, had not died and continued to command the attention of students of punctuation. During the nineteenth century, standardized conventions of punctuation began to appear, carefully nurtured by printers and compositors. Today's punctuation, therefore, is the product of three traditions: rhetorical, grammatical, and typographical.

I am not addressing the conventions of punctuation themselves in this chapter. Lists of rules are available in any handbook. I am concerned with punctuation for its own sake: its history, foundations, use, controversies. Rhetorical and grammatical punctuation are usually distinguished on the basis of definition and purpose. Because rhetorical punctuation is usually concerned with sound and emphasis, it is difficult to devise hard and fast rules for its use. On the other hand, grammatical punctuation, governed by sentence structure, can be described in terms of fairly rigid rules. In this chapter, I consider punctuation involving issues not subject to rigid rules as rhetorical. The typographical tradition includes the history and development of printing and the division of labor between author and printer in matters of punctuation. Despite the necessity for dividing punctuation into separate traditions, it is crucial to keep in mind that today's punctuation incorporates all of them.

Although a few good books on punctuation have appeared in this century, most modern scholars have contributed little new to our understanding of punctuation and its use. The only exception is George Summey, whose two books, *Modern Punctuation* (1919) and *American Punctuation* (1949), are the most informative sources available. Other useful books are Reginald Skelton's *Modern English Punctuation* (1949) and Eric Partridge's *You Have a Point There* (1953). For a somewhat different perspective, that of the printer, John Wilson's *Treatise on Punctuation* (1899) and Theodore L. Devinne's *Practice of Typography* (1921) are best; furthermore, both were influential in the evolution of current usage.

In addition to these few recent investigations of punctuation, there are also a number of older studies worthy of notice. Scholars whose primary focus is education, literary criticism, or communication have made notable contributions.

The Rhetorical Tradition

The rhetorical tradition of punctuation grew out of a concern for how written texts would be read aloud. Our earliest explanations for individual symbols addressed intonation and pauses. Emphasis, too, came to be a major consideration in determining punctuation. These issues dominated approaches to punctuation until the mid-nineteenth century when a desire for scientific explanation replaced rhetorical concerns as the guiding principle in assigning punctuation marks. Recently, however, the rhetorical tradition has begun to receive attention, primarily in the context of the relationship between reading and writing.

Studies of early punctuation reflect the concern for how a text is to be read. In his essay "Punctuation, or Pause and Effect" (1978), Malcolm B. Parkes looked at the rise of punctuation as used by medieval scribes writing Latin and Greek. He emphasized that they used punctuation not only to indicate the sound but to guide the interpretation of the reader. Elizabeth Zeeman's "Punctuation in an Early Manuscript of Love's Mirror" (1956) explained the pointing of a fifteenth-century manuscript in terms of rhetorical force for reading aloud. Further evidence of punctuation used for the purpose of guiding oral delivery can be found in Peter Clemoes's *Liturgical Influence on Punctuation in Late Old English and Early Middle English Manuscripts* (1952). Walter Ong outlined the continued influence of the medieval approach to punctuation during the sixteenth and seventeenth centuries in "Historical Backgrounds of Elizabethan and Jacobean Punctuation Theory" (1944). T. F. and M.F.A. Husband included summaries of several books that appeared on punctuation during the seventeenth, eighteenth, and nineteenth centuries in Chapter 4 of their *Punctuation* (1905). These summaries show evidence of this concern for reading aloud well into the eighteenth century. The persistence of the rhetorical tradition while the grammatical tradition began to assert itself is clearly demonstrated in Park Honan's excellent article "Eighteenth and Nineteenth Century Punctuation Theory" (1960).

An important source of information about rhetorical punctuation in English is the work of early writers such as Shakespeare, Jonson, Donne, and Milton. Several attempts to analyze and explain Shakespeare's punctuation have contributed to our understanding of the rhetorical tradition. Percy Simpson's classic *Shakespearian Punctuation* (1911) seeks a reason for the punctuation in Shakespeare instead of dismissing it as chaotic as previous scholars had done. He explained that the pointing of that era was flexible and designed to indicate the rhythm. His approach is endorsed by T. J. Cobden-Sanderson in his brief pamphlet *Shakespearian Punctuation* (1912), which was first published as a letter to the *London Times*. Simpson's work also raises important questions about the sources of the pointing in Shakespeare's published works. Alfred W. Pollard addressed these questions in his chapter "The Improvers of Shakespeare," in his *Shakespeare's Fight with the Pirates and the Problems of the Transmission of His Text* (1920), beginning a long series of scholarly investigations to verify the source of Shakespeare's punctuation. Although these issues are still being debated by textual scholars (see the typographical section, below), punctuation that was actually assigned in Shakespeare's time can inform us about the practices of that era. Useful observations about Shakespeare and Ben Jonson can be found in A. C. Partridge's *Orthography in Shakespeare and Elizabethan Drama* (1964), *The Accidence of Ben Jonson's Plays, Masques, and Entertainments* (1953a), and *Studies in the Syntax of Ben Jonson's Plays* (1953b). The last two are the subject of a lengthy, largely critical review by E. J. Dobson (1955). H.J.C. Grierson commented on Donne's compliance with contemporary punctuation practices in the introduction to volume 2 of his *Poems of John Donne* (1912). Because John Milton, who wrote during a time when usage was changing, exercised considerable control over the printed text of his works, his punctuation usage is especially interesting. Therefore, *Milton's Punctuation* (1970) by Mindele Treip is a valuable resource not only for Milton's style, but for punctuation practices of the period as well.

During the eighteenth and nineteenth centuries, the rhetorical tradition of punctuation was relegated to a secondary position. The grammatical tradition held sway and was the dominant consideration in pointing until rhetorical issues were raised again in this century.

In *Why We Punctuate* (1916), William L. Klein recognized the rhetorical role of punctuation when he claimed that punctuation conveys sense relationships that intonation conveys in spoken language. His desire to get away from rigid application of rules is clear in his choice of the subtitle *Reason versus Rule in the Use of Marks*. The major statement reasserting the value of the rhetorical tradition is George Summey's *Modern Punctuation* (1919), reviewed by R. L. Lasley in "Present-Day Punctuation" (1921). In the book, written as his dissertation under the direction of George P. Krapp, Summey included a survey and evaluation of the most recent works on punctuation as well as the presentation of his own views. He refused to accept a secondary rule for the rhetorical aspects of punctuation: "The fundamental truth is that *all structural punctuation marks in straight reading matter are rhetorical points, because they are at once grouping points and (intentionally or otherwise) emphasis points, with effects on movement*" (p. 25). In addition, Summey objected strongly to rigid rules and an arbitrary doctrine of correctness. He also pointed out the much overlooked fact that punctuation must be assigned with respect to larger units of discourse like the paragraph, not isolated sentences. Modern students of composition usually ignore punctuation except as one of the editing tasks performed when most of the actual business of the writing process is accomplished. Summey, however, viewed punctuation as a far more crucial factor in successful writing: "Punctuation is not a panacea for bad composition. Points may reveal the meaning of a badly constructed sentence, but in that case they will also reveal the badness of the structure. The remedy for faulty structure is revision" (p. 23). Summey's second book, *American Punctuation* (1949), is even stronger in its emphasis on punctuation as a part of the writing process: "Punctuation is not the mere routine business of inserting marks in words already composed. It is part of the process of writing good paragraphs and sentences and grouping them well by suitable paragraph breaks and punctuation marks and by the omission of useful marks. . . . Good punctuation is possible only in good writing" (p. 13). Despite the excellent advice he gave writers, neither of Summey's books can be described as a handbook. In fact, George Ives, author of *Text, Type, and Style* (1921), complained that *Modern Punctuation* shows "what punctuation *is*, rather than what it ought to be" (p. 7).

The Logic of Punctuation (1926) by William Chambers Morrow is didactic and more like a handbook; however, Morrow, too, recognized that rules are an insufficient guide to usage because the punctuation is frequently tied to meaning. He also pointed out that there are two standards of punctuation practice in the United States—one for newspapers and another for books and magazines.

Objections to an overly enthusiastic concentration on grammar and rules in punctuation were another factor in the revival of the rhetorical tradition. In "The

Rationale of Punctuation'' (1915), Constance Mayfield Rourke claimed that emphasis is the motivation for all punctuation. Her views were attacked by Sterling A. Leonard in his response, ''The Rationale of Punctuation'' (1916), and C. H. Ward in *What Is English?* (1917). E. L. Thorndike also advocated the rhetorical tradition in two enlightening articles on punctuation and its use. In ''The Psychology of Punctuation'' (1948a) he addressed the usage of several authors, paying special attention to the colon and the ellipsis. He also considered the usage of authors and printers in ''Punctuation'' (1948b), but his major focus was a summary of the development of punctuation and what he saw as the major myths of modern punctuation. In ''Professor Thorndike on Punctuation'' (1949), Eivion Owens charged Thorndike with oversimplification and argued that punctuation is incidental to sentence structure.

In his 1949 revision of *Modern English Punctuation*, Reginald Skelton attempted to integrate the rhetorical and grammatical traditions, citing difficulties for each. He combined the two approaches into a fundamental principle that ''our punctuation strives, not to represent, but to be consistent with a correct mode of speech'' (p. 167). In addition, he raised the question of the subconscious psychological effect of punctuation, a question that deserves a great deal more attention than it has received. A good overview of how modern punctuation usage came to be a reflection of both grammar and intonation can be found in Arthur F. Beringause's ''Punctuation'' (1964).

Eric Partridge, in *You Have a Point There* (1953), accepted the role of grammatical structure but claimed that the non-grammatical elements, the artistic elements—intonation, pause, emphasis—are also essential for good punctuation. For Partridge, ''Punctuation is both an art and a craft; predominantly, however, it is an art; a humble yet far from insignificant art for it forms a means to an end and is not in itself an end. The purpose it serves, the art it subserves, is the art of good writing'' (p. 183). Partridge advocated a flexible standard of usage that is typical of the British, who seem less concerned with rigor in matters of punctuation than their American counterparts. E. Dudley Parsons also saw no virtue in punctuation by absolute rule as he made clear in ''Bowing Down Before the God of Punctuation'' (1915).

Various modern scholars and teachers have found the rhetorical tradition of punctuation to be attractive. Because he recognized that punctuation must satisfy both the eye and ear, H. Sopher argued in ''The Problem of Punctuation'' (1977) that rhetorical punctuation is more natural and meaningful. Applications of the rhetorical perspective to teaching punctuation can be found in Ellen M. Johnson's ''Simpler Approach to Punctuation'' (1954). ''Has Punctuation Been Forgotten?'' (1979) by Chris Perkins called for a rhetorical focus for teaching English punctuation to speakers of German. In ''Learning from Our Mistakes'' (1973), Judith Stitzel argued that a key factor in teaching punctuation is the recognition of the causes for punctuation errors.

Twentieth century re-discoverers of the rhetorical tradition have often addressed the connection between punctuation and sound. In ''The Linguistic

Characteristics of Punctuation Symbols and the Teaching of Punctuation Skills'' (1963) Robert S. Zais found a connection between punctuation and the elements of structural linguistics such as juncture; however, tests indicate that the connection does not enhance instruction. The relationship of individual punctuation marks and intonation is examined in Edna L. Furness's "Pupils, Pedagogues, and Punctuation" (1960). Louis Foley emphasized the meaningful role of the hyphen by tying it to pronunciation in "The How of the Hyphen" (1943). Garland Cannon, in "Punctuation and Sentence Rhythm" (1957), and J. Esser, in "Contrastive Intonation of German and English" (1978), pointed out the significance of the connection between punctuation and intonation in teaching English to speakers of other languages. J. R. Held used intonation cues in "Teaching Punctuation in the Ninth Grade by Means of Intonation Cues" (1969). The connection can also be exploited in literary analysis. Sarah Simmons, for example, recognized punctuation's function as a foregrounding device in "Mukarovsky, Structuralism, and the Essay" (1977). Evelyn Scroth showed how punctuation is used to control rhythm, intonation, and repetition in "Dr. Seuss and Language Usage" (1978).

A number of studies emphasize the relationship of punctuation to reading. In "Tools and Terms in Recent Researches" (1946), Madison Bentley suggested that investigators examine punctuation from a psychological point of view, addressing the question of punctuation's role in reading. His suggestion did not touch off significant empirical research, and the question remains largely unexplored today. That punctuation guides the reader is widely accepted and has become a major assumption for several studies. Basically, they argue that punctuation is to serve the reader, not the writer. Rachel Salisbury wrote two articles focusing on meaning rather than grammar as the major consideration in punctuation: "The Psychology of Punctuation" (1939) and "Reading Road to Punctuation Skills" (1945). Paul Backschneider made the same point in his "Punctuation for the Reader" (1972). Attempts to test these assumptions about the effect of punctuation on reading have produced some interesting but inconclusive results. Wilbur Hatfield found that commas in sentences with restrictive and non-restrictive clauses actually slowed down the reading and reduced comprehension. A description of the study is given in "Objective Determination of Punctuation" (1933). A more sophisticated study comparing oral and silent reading with and without punctuation is reported in "The Effect of Reading Variation and Punctuation Condition upon Reading Comprehension (1970) by Wendell Weaver and others. The implications and application of the connection between punctuation and reading are the subject of Russell Long's "Common Features of Writing and Oral Reading" (1981) and Frances Alexander's "From a Teacher's Notebook–5" (1979).

Lucy M. Calkins reported the success of children learning to punctuate their own writing by reading it aloud to fellow students in "Research Update" (1980). This study is part of the exciting research on children's writing conducted by Donald Graves and the University of New Hampshire's Writing Process Laboratory. Marie Clay's observations of New Zealand children learning to write, *What Did I Write?* (1975), also include reference to children learning to punctuate by reading aloud.

Reader-response critics are beginning to recognize the usefulness of the rhetorical tradition of punctuation for their investigations. George Dillon established that some readers do respond to punctuation in "Clause, Pause, and Punctuation in Poetry" (1976). He examined punctuation especially as a clause boundary at some length in *Language Processing and the Reading of Literature* (1978). In "Interpreting *The Variorum*" (1980), Stanley Fish acknowledged the role played by punctuation in a reader's hypothesis about the meaning of what is read. How readers respond to punctuation has not been fully investigated by any means, and enlightening studies should appear in the future.

The twentieth-century re-discovery of rhetorical factors in punctuation has proved both interesting and valuable. Grammar certainly cannot be ignored as an important factor in punctuation; however, some scholars and grammarians have neglected the other, rhetorical duties performed by punctuation.

The Grammatical Tradition

Seeking scientific explanations and consistent rules for punctuation led to a heavy reliance on grammatical structure as the primary basis for assigning punctuation marks. The grammatical tradition that emerged to meet these needs was promoted by scholars, teachers, and printers who looked for external, logical tests of usage. They were convinced that the chief function of punctuation was to clarify the grammatical structure, and the major controversy concerned how much punctuation was necessary.

Exactly when or where the grammatical tradition of punctuation began is unclear. Some claim that Aldus Manutius, founder of the Aldine system of punctuation, recognized the importance of grammatical structure. Others say it was Ben Jonson who first emphasized structure over sound. Surveys of early grammars by Charles Fries and Park Honan proved that both grammatical and rhetorical considerations influenced punctuation well into the nineteenth century. In his study, Fries examined grammars published between 1589 and 1900, finding evidence that grammar governed the use of punctuation. This survey is included in his "Shakespearian Punctuation" (1925). The Honan study, "Eighteenth and Nineteenth Century English Punctuation Theory" (1960), deals with the period from 1700 to 1900 and concentrates more on the continuing mention of rhetorical considerations.

The debate about who was responsible for punctuation in the early editions of Shakespeare inspired more studies of seventeenth-century punctuation and its basis. Raymond Alden, in "The Punctuation of Shakespeare's Printers" (1924), found a grammatical explanation for some usage. Vivian Salmon reached a similar conclusion in "Early Seventeenth Century Punctuation as a Guide to Sentence Structure" (1962). In "A Note on the Punctuation in the Authorized

Version of the English Bible'' (1973), Samuel Hornsby suggested that Elizabethan punctuation was neither so rhetorical nor so haphazard as had been
believed. John Diekhoff and Albert C. Baugh saw evidence for both rhetorical
punctuation as described by Simpson and grammatical punctuation as described
by Fries. In his article ''The Punctuation of Comus'' (1936), Diekhoff suggested
that Milton's punctuation falls into three categories: rhetorical, grammatical, and
verse. Baugh, too, saw the influence of verse in Elizabethan punctuation in ''A
Medieval Survival'' (1959). After reviewing the major points discussed by advocates of the opposing views, he claimed that some pointing is the result of a
medieval practice that used punctuation at the end of lines for verse printed in
prose form.

As the eighteenth century and the Age of Reason began, there was an increasing
desire for order, which affected how punctuation was viewed. In *The True and
Genuine Art of Pointing* (1704), Robert Monteith declared that punctuation rests
on a knowlege of grammar. Joseph Robertson called for punctuation based on
the ''rational and determinate principles'' of grammatical structure in *An Essay
on Punctuation* (1785).

The call for order was taken up by printers, who are responsible for much of
what has been written about punctuation. John Wilson and Henry Beadnell in
the nineteenth century and Theodore Low Devinne in the twentieth century
published books intended for compositors or typesetters. Beadnell's manual for
printers, *Spelling and Punctuation* (1880), insists on a logical justification for
all punctuation. *Correct Composition* by Devinne (1921) is part of a series called
The Practice of Typography. In his view, pointing is governed by grammatical
construction, and ''points have small elocutionary value'' (p. 245). Yet despite
his emphasis on grammar, Devinne advised his readers:

A working knowledge of punctuation is not to be acquired merely by learning rules; the
understanding of an author's meaning should be the earliest study. Next comes a knowledge of the elements of grammar. Careful reading of standard editions of good authors
is always helpful. . . . The great object of punctuation is to make clear to the reader the
meaning of the author. Rules are of value, but the unfolding of obscured sense is the
object of most importance. (p. 293).

Adele M. Smith, *Proofreading and Punctuation* (1907), also for printers, advocated punctuation to indicate the grammatical structure and to make the meaning clear. A desire to establish uniform usage prompted Paul Allardyce's *Stops,
or How to Punctuate* (1884). He saw punctuation as a counterpart to grammatical
inflection in other languages, showing what goes together in a sentence. Horace
F. Teall claimed that punctuation is independent of elocution in *Punctuation*
(1897) and attempted to reconcile differences between rules and practice by
reducing the number of rules and increasing their grammatical explication. Harold
Whitehall described punctuation as making grammar ''graphic'' in *Structural
Essentials of English* (1956). Julian T. Brown accepted without question that

grammatical structure is the explanation for punctuation in his *Encyclopaedia Britannica* entry "Punctuation" (1980).

In many respects it is foolish to attempt to separate grammatical and rhetorical foundations for punctuation. Linguistic descriptions tell us that most pauses occur at structural junctures. But punctuation that is governed solely by grammatical structure is redundant and adds nothing to the meaning of the sentence. Consequently, students of punctuation have had to recognize that punctuation also has rhetorical purposes that do not necessarily conflict with its grammatical basis. John Wilson recognized this dual role of punctuation in his popular work *A Treatise on Grammatical Punctuation* (32 editions between 1826 and 1899). Although he strongly asserted, "it will be found that the art of Punctuation is founded rather on grammar than on rhetoric," Wilson accepted that rhetorical considerations do have a role in punctuation (p. 17). His answer is to divide the marks of punctuation into grammatical points and points that are both rhetorical and grammatical—the question mark, the exclamation point, parentheses, and the dash. A similar division was proposed by M. G. Lund in "Punctuation and Personality' (1953).

C. H. Ward extolled Wilson and his influence in "Punctuator Gingriens" (1915) and a subsequent review of that article, "John Wilson's Idea," in his book *What Is English*? (1917). Another chapter of the book, "What Is a Comma?" is a response to Constance Rourke, "The Rationale of Punctuation" (1915), arguing that sentence structure is more important to the use of commas than emphasis. Ward's view puts him very much within the grammatical tradition. Nevertheless, he recognized that the choice to punctuate or not involves an artistic process when the concern is meaning and a mechanical process once the decision has been made.

In the most recent book-length treatment of punctuation, *Punctuate It Right!* (1963), Harry Shaw saw all punctuation as serving one of four general purposes: to terminate, to introduce, to separate, or to enclose. Although he recognized that as much as one-fourth of punctuation may be a matter of taste, his chief purpose is to explain standard rules for correct punctuation by referring to grammatical structure.

Among those who argue that punctuation is to guide the mind through the grammatical structure of a sentence, the controversy lies in the question of how much punctuation should be used. In Chapter 4 of *The King's English* (1931), H. W. and F. G. Fowler warned against overstopping and in so doing highlighted the conflict between heavy and light punctuation. Heavy punctuation, the fashion at the end of the nineteenth century, is characterized by the use of punctuation wherever possible. Light punctuation uses as few points or stops as necessary. The Fowlers urged writers not to depend on punctuation to make meaning clear: "It may almost be said that what reads wrongly if the stops are removed is radically bad; stops are not to alter meaning, but merely to show it up" (p. 234).

This attitude toward punctuation is the one advocated in legal writing. Jesse L. Dilbert provided an appendix to Morrow's *Logic of Punctuation* (1921),

"Punctuation and the Law," explaining that courts usually disregard punctuation in reaching their decisions. Robert A. Hume found the same attitude in "The Supreme Court on the Commas" (1940). Punctuation is viewed as fallible and therefore not allowed to change the meaning of a statute or document. In a response to Hume, "Courts and Commas" (1940), Charles Roger Hicks defended the courts by pointing out the numerous opportunities for error in the transmission process.

Another advocate of light punctuation, J. D. Logan, claimed in his *Quantitative Punctuation* (1907) that three marks are sufficient. The book is an explanation and justification for his odd system of punctuation that employs only the comma, the period, and the question mark. *Mind the Stop* by G. V. Carey (1948) also presented a positive view of light punctuation. To Carey the "best punctuation is that which the reader is least aware of." R. F. McCoy's point in "Simplifying Punctuation" (1939) is that lighter punctuation and simpler rules will promote correct usage.

Simplicity in punctuation rules is one reason that many teachers strongly endorse the grammatical tradition. Julia Norton McCorkle claimed that punctuation is a more exact science than previously thought. In "Eliminating Guesswork from Sentence Punctuation" (1926), she used sentence structure to devise a simple table explaining the comma, period, and semicolon. Robert Odum called grammar essential in "Growth of a Language Skill" (1964). Gary Sloan, too, accepted the notion that punctuation is motivated by the grammar of a sentence in "The Subversive Effects of an Oral Culture on Student Writing" (1979). Elinor Yaggy's "Let's Take the Guesswork Out of Punctuation" (1953) is a call for simplified standardization.

John L. Presland's "In Search of an 'Early Teaching Grammar' " (1974) ties the question of when to teach punctuation to the grammatical tradition by arguing that students cannot punctuate correctly even one-half of the time until they are ten years old, because they must be able to identify sentences first. R. Scott Baldwin and James M. Coady, in "Psycholinguistic Approaches to a Theory of Punctuation" (1978), found that even fifth graders ignored critical (meaningful) punctuation in a study of reading cues. Both studies seem to indicate that punctuation skills are learned very late and should perhaps be compared to findings in Lucy Calkins's "Research Update" (1980).

In "The No-man's Land of Writing" (1924) Dora Davis Farrington examined 22 textbooks and 1,539 rules of punctuation, finding that standardization exists within punctuation since there are only six contradictory rules. The foundation of these rules is the grammatical tradition of punctuation. One of the four questions that Walter Meyers asked in his 1971 study of freshman textbooks, "Handbooks, Subhandbooks, and Non-handbooks," concerns punctuation. His findings reveal that only a few of the more recent texts have departed from purely grammatical discussions citing oral reading as a test of punctuation. The desire to see punctuation as a precise science remains strong, especially in textbooks and handbooks.

Although grammatical and rhetorical considerations have been important in the evolution of modern punctuation practices, it is impossible to ignore the influence exercised by printers. The importance of Wilson and Devinne amply demonstrates that the development of punctuation is tied to the growth and development of the printing industry.

The Typographical Tradition

Much of the development and history of punctuation has been directly tied to publishing practices. Thus punctuation must be seen as part of the printing craft. Printers have often accepted responsibility for punctuation as part of their task in the publishing process, and the extent of their role has raised thorny questions for textual scholars who determine authoritative texts written before publishers' styling began to dictate usage. The typographical tradition of punctuation also addresses the effect printing has had and continues to have on good style and modern punctuation conventions.

Punctuation existed before printing; in fact, many of the marks we use today originated in ancient Latin and Greek manuscripts that were copied by hand. Edward Maunde Thompson examined the origin and use of several in *An Introduction to Greek and Latin Palaeography* (1912). Punctuation of medieval Latin is the subject of Malcolm Parkes's study "Punctuation, or Pause and Effect" (1978). In a series of notes, "Punctuation in Mss. and Printed Books" (1904, 1905, 1907), F.W.G. Foat outlined the usage of punctuation in early documents both in English and in Latin or Greek. The Husbands introduced Old English manuscripts in their discussion of early punctuation in the first three chapters of *Punctuation* (1905). They also included a translation of Aldus Manutius's "Interpungendi Ratio" (1566). An Italian printer, Manutius is generally given credit for our present system of punctuation. Lengthy summaries of the origin of printing are included in Julian T. Brown's *Encyclopaedia Britannica* (1980) entry "Punctuation" and in the eighth appendix to A. C. Partridge's *Orthography in Shakespeare and Elizabethan Drama* (1964).

The only sources of information for early English practices are the manuscripts and publications of the sixteenth- and seventeenth-century presses. Until Joseph Moxon's *Mechanick Exercises on the Whole Art of Printing* (1683–1684), there were no printing manuals in English, and even Moxon did not include specific guidelines about punctuation. However, he did introduce the notion that compositors should take responsibility for punctuation:

by the Laws of Printing, a Composister [sic] is strictly to follow his Copy. . . . But the carelessness of some good Authors, and the ignorance of other Authors has forc'd Printers to introduce a Custom, which among them is look'd upon as a task and duty incumbent on the Composister [sic], viz. to discern and amend bad Spelling and Pointing. (p. 192)

Philip Luckombe's 1771 *History and Art of Printing* assigns the task of correcting wrong spelling and pointing to correctors who read the text even before the compositors set the copy. Unlike Moxon, Luckombe provided guidance about pointing for compositors and correctors. In *Proof-Reading in the Sixteenth, Seventeenth, and Eighteenth Centuries* (1935), Percy Simpson examined how the printing industry operated during that period and looked at early proof and copy, assessing the probability that the author had a hand in changes.

In the nineteenth century, compositors' manuals lament the deficient punctuation found in most works sent to press. John Johnson in *Typographia, or the Printers' Instructor* (1824) and Thomas Hansard in his own *Typographia* (1825) argued that pointing should be the responsibility of the printers. Although there are substantial differences in other parts of the books, the sections on points are identical and may well come from a third source. Since these views were the prevailing attitudes among printers of the time, the same information is available in most compositors' manuals of the period.

Conflicting approaches to the preparation of copy sent to printers have played an important role in textual scholarship. Ronald B. McKerrow, in *An Introduction to Bibliography for Literary Students* (1927), argued that early authors paid little attention to punctuation, because rules existed only for printers in the sixteenth and seventeenth centuries. Edwin Howard agreed in ''The Printer and Elizabethan Punctuation'' (1930). Hereward T. Price found that compositors were more likely to change spelling or punctuation than grammar in ''Grammar and the Compositor in the Sixteenth and Seventeenth Centuries'' (1939). D. F. McKenzie, in ''Shakespearian Punctuation—A New Beginning'' (1959), and Trevor H. Howard-Hill, in *Ralph Crane and Some Shakespeare First Folio Comedies* (1972), pointed out that printer changes usually lead to heavier punctuation than in the original. As a result of the view that compositorial changes were so frequent, Albert Howard Carter advised a cautious approach in ''On the Use of Spelling, Punctuation, and Typography to Determine the Dependence of Editions'' (1947). Some scholars see evidence of the author's hand in punctuation. Evelyn Simpson, in ''A Note on Donne's Punctuation'' (1928), examined Donne's work and found that compositors or correctors changed spelling and capitalization but not punctuation.

In 1950 W. W. Greg introduced a distinction between substantives and accidentals in an influential article ''The Rationale of Copy-Text'' (1950). *Substantives* are the elements of the text that affect the meaning or essence of the author's expression; *accidentals* are spelling, punctuation, and word division, which affect the formal presentation of a work. Greg advocated strict adherence to the earliest available text for determining accidentals. Fredson Bowers promoted Greg's views in ''Some Principles for Scholarly Editions of Nineteenth Century American Authors'' (1964), saying, ''if an author's habits of expression go beyond words and into the forms that these take, together with the punctuation that helps to shape the relationships of these, then one is foolish to prefer a printing-house style to the author's style'' (p. 226). In ''Regularizing Accidentals'' (1973) Hershel Parker argued against a practice employed by the editors of many nineteenth-century authors, who are trying to create consistency in spelling and punctuation. Parker pointed out that the desire for regularization is modern; thus to regularize is to modernize.

G. Thomas Tanselle endorsed strict preservation of the author's intention and defended it against critics in "Greg's Theory of Copy Text and the Editing of American Literature" (1975). The objection raised by one of those critics, Morse Peckham, is that Greg's rationale is valid only for early texts. In "Reflections on the Foundations of Modern Textual Editing" (1971), Peckham claimed that modern authors are involved in the revision of their texts, giving authenticity to changes even in punctuation. As Tanselle pointed out, Greg and Peckham were in basic agreement that punctuation is an important part of the author's message. James Thorpe, another of Greg's critics, is convinced that authors are rarely concerned about the accidentals of their texts. In "Watching the Ps and Qs" (1971) and *Principles of Textual Criticism* (1972), he argued that writers seldom showed any interest in punctuating their work and that printers accepted accidentals as their responsibility. John Bush Jones examined printers' manuals from Moxon to Devinne to test Thorpe's generalization in "Victorian 'Readers' and Modern Editors" (1977). Jones found considerable variation in the attitude of printers. After 1850 the more prevalent view, he claimed, is to preserve authorial accidentals. However, the charge that authors neglected punctuation persisted into the twentieth century as Frederick Hamilton's *Punctuation* published by the United Typothetae of America (1920) demonstrates.

At the end of the nineteenth century, house styling became a significant factor in publishing. In a study of the *Atlantic Monthly* entitled *Text, Type, and Style* (1921), George Ives explained the duties of a proofreader as "properly confined to making the type agree with the copy. She may correct errors as to which there is no possible question" (p. 28). However, in his later explanation of what happens to an article as it moves through the press, he revealed: "When proofs are sent to the author, they bear only such queries as relate to the substance of the article, such matters as punctuation, spelling, and the like being made to conform to the regular Atlantic style" (p. 38n).

The question of original punctuation is not limited to the period from 1500 to 1900. These issues concerning the form of a text have been subject to extensive study and debate. The research cited represents only a sample of the material available. Each includes numerous references for those who wish to pursue this aspect of punctuation further. Bruce Mitchell, in "Dangers of Disguise" (1980), advocated maintaining the original punctuation in Old English texts, and Oliver Farrar Emerson looked at the effect of changes in punctuation on the interpretation of *Beowulf* in "The Punctuation of *Beowulf* and Literary Interpretation" (1926).

Choice of punctuation is often an importannt factor in an author's development of distinctive style. "Punctuation and Style" (1977) by James R. Bennett and others is an annotated bibliography of books and articles addressing the role of punctuation in the style of authors including Chaucer, Blake, Sterne, Dickens, Twain, and Joyce to name only a few. Barry Menikoff's "Punctuation and Point of View in the Late Style of Henry James" (1970) and Frank Baldanza's "Faulkner and Stein'' (1959) are only examples of works listed. One article, published after the bibliography and worth attention, is Richard Kallan's analysis of Tom Wolfe, ''Style and the New Journalism'' (1979). He cited Wolfe's unconventional use of punctuation to attract a reader's attention.

The use of punctuation as a means of visual expression is a relatively new area of investigation, but one that is likely to grow. Rudolf Modley looked at future uses of graphic symbols in ''World Language without Words'' (1974). An exciting German article, ''Drucktypenwechsel'' (1974), by Harald Wentzlaff-Eggebert, calls for an extensive graphemic theory to detail how typeface, capitals, and punctuation can be used as a means of expression in written language. The journal *Visible Language* addresses this question and occasionally has articles such as ''Visual Components of the Reading Process'' (1981) by Ralph Norman Haber and Lyn R. Haber that include specific references to punctuation.

Another new area of investigation for students of punctuation concerns the impact of the computer age. There are now programs to style texts, and at least one study shows that they are more efficient than proofreaders. Starr D. Randall reported a study of typographical errors in the *Charlotte Observer* covering three one-year periods. In ''The Effect of Electronic Editing on Error Rate of a Newspaper'' (1979), he compared the error rate before the use of electronic equipment, after the terminals had been installed, but before the full corrective system was operative, and finally with the entire system operating. The results showed large reductions in all types of errors. The system, however, was least successful in eliminating punctuation errors. Problems of encoding literary texts and the use of punctuation symbols in various programming languages are also subjects of interest in the study of modern punctuation. The following are among the sources of information on punctuation and computers: ''Encoding Literary Texts'' (1976) by J. B. Smith, ''An Extended Character Set for Humanities Computer Printout'' (1970) by Phyllis Richmond, ''Computational Linguistics at Salford University'' (1973) by F. E. Knowles, ''SNAP—A Programming Language for Humanities'' (1970) by Michael P. Barnett, and ''COCOA as a Tool for the Analysis of Poetry'' (1975) by Wendy Rosslyn.

A discussion of the typographical tradition of punctuation would not be complete without mention of the primary guides to appropriate usage of modern printers. In the United States there are several representative sources: the *Associated Press Stylebook and Libel Manual* (1977), *The Chicago Manual of Style* (1982), and the *U.S. Government Printing Office Style Manual* (1973). Horace Hart's *Rules for Compositors and Readers at the University Press, Oxford* (1978) contains the rules for British usage. In spite of attempts to standardize usage, variation continues to persist.

A Host of Other Points

Although many studies of punctuation fall into one of the three traditions discussed above, some have a limited focus, addressing individual marks and the problems associated with them. Others are concerned with patterns of usage, with pedagogical questions related to punctuation, or with cross-linguistic comparisons of punctuation use. The symbols themselves have been remarkably standard since the seventeenth century. Modern efforts to introduce new symbols, such as the interabang cited in *The Visible Word* (1969) by Herbert Spencer or the specialized quotation marks used by I. A. Richards in *So Much Nearer* (1968), have not been successful. By most counts there are 13 symbols: the period (or full stop as it is known in Britain), the comma, the colon, the semicolon, the question mark, the exclamation point, the dash, parentheses, brackets, double and single quotation marks, the ellipsis, and the apostrophe. Many studies of punctuation concentrate on a single mark and its use. The apostrophe and comma have received the most attention by far.

Several serious investigations of the apostrophe have traced its history. Elizabeth S. Sklar examined the development and spread of the apostrophe as a marker of possession as well as the recent confusion over its appropriate use in "The Possessive Apostrophe" (1976). The early use of the apostrophe is the subject of a well-documented article by L. F. Brosnahan, "The Apostrophe in the Genitive Singular in the Seventeenth Century" (1961), and a brief note by N. E. Osselton, "The Apostrophe in the Genitive Singular in the Seventeenth and Eighteenth Centuries" (1962). Charles C. Fries pointed out the confusing and changing practices associated with the apostrophe in "Our Possessive Forms" (1927). In "Has Modern English a Genitive Plural?" (1941), M. H. Braaksma addressed the question of whether *s'* is a true possessive marker. "'The Possessive Apostrophe in Names" (1958) by Robert L. Coard is an interesting study surveying various names both with and without apostrophes. A lighter treatment of the apostrophe and its divided usage is to be found in L. H. Feigenbaum's "Rally 'Round the Apostrophe, Boys!" (1966).

Because of its inconsistent use and the problems they have in teaching it, some teachers have called for an end to the apostrophe. "Away with Apostrophes!" (1947) by Helen Rand Miller; a supportive response, "Amen!" (1947), by Gunnar Horn; and "Apostrophe to the Ocean—And Heave It In!" (1966) by Robert E. Moore point out difficulties with the apostrophe. In a more scholarly study, "Certain Fashions in Commas and Apostrophes" (1945), Steven T. Byington also urged abolishment of the apostrophe and favored light punctuation, advising writers to omit commas when in doubt.

The most common punctuation mark, and thus the most difficult to isolate and describe, is the comma. Alan Wycherly, in "A Pride of Commas" (1967), cited the importance of the comma to the meaning of a sentence. V. H. Collins, in "Vicious Fashion in Punctuation" (1942), and Josephine M. Burnham, in "A Problem in Punctuation" (1947), discussed the use of the comma with adverbial phrases and clauses. Additionally, parenthetical information and its punctuation receive attention in W. Paul Jones's "Punctuating Nonrestrictives" (1948) and J. H. McKee's "Two Commas or None" (1940).

Raymond Miller attempted to find order in the punctuation of coordinate sentences in "Coordination and the Comma" (1908). Subsequent studies address the question from the teacher's point of view: "In the Freshman English Stage of Punctuation" (1928) by Helen Rand, "A Small Plea for Conformity" (1939) by J. H. McKee, "Commas and Conformity" (1939) (a response to McKee) by James M. McCrimmon, "Punctuating the Compound Sentence" (1962) by J. C. Gray, and "A Few Good Words for the Comma Splice" (1976) by Irene T. Brosnahan. On the basis of research reported in "An Application of Error Analysis to Comma Splices and Fused Sentences" (1978), Mary Lamb claimed that students lack the experience to formulate the proper rules for punctuating: consequently, they are unable to apply them. Maurice Winter Moe, in "Teaching the Use of the Comma" (1913); Maxwell Nurnberg, in "Comedy of Commas" (1960); and Anna May Gertsmeyer, in "Teaching the Punctuation of the Appositive" (1950), offered instructional hints about the comma.

Hyphenation or word division raises questions that have plagued writing students, especially non-native speakers of English. Michael Pearce explained that hyphens are not decorative but an aid to understanding in "The Hyphen in English" (1978). Robert A. Hall, Jr., claimed that the hyphen should correlate to the pronunciation feature of juncture in "To Hyphenate or Not to Hyphenate" (1964). F. M. O'Hara, Jr., examined the subject in "The Use of the Hyphen in Printing to Indicate Divided Words" (1971). R. M. Hoover's "Principles of English Hyphenation" (1971) details five rules capable of instructing a computer to hyphenate correctly.

Other marks of punctuation have also been examined. A. P. Herbert, a regular contributor to *Punch*, questioned the use of periods in public announcements prepared by the King's Printers in "Fullstops" (1936). Tom Burns Haber lamented the loss of a minor punctuation mark in "The Decline and Near Demise of the Diaresis" (1962). J. T. Dillon published two articles on the colon as a sign of complexity: "Functions of the Colon" (1981) and "In Pursuit of the Colon" (1982). In a series called "Holiday Tasks" (1938), A. P. Herbert presented an entertaining explanation of the comma, fullstop (period), colon, semicolon, and hyphen.

In addition, almost all of the book-length studies of punctuation cited in this chapter include rules for the use of each mark of punctuation. Many also have a discussion of usage along with examples.

Another source of information about punctuation and its use can be found in publications about business education. Dorothy M. Johnson's "Ten Commandments for Practical Punctuation" (1944), Ted Stoddard's "Challenging the Great Punctuation Copout" (1977), and W. E. Perkins's "Programmed Materials Teach Punctuation" (1971) join the two series on punctuation prepared by Verne Ellis Waltimyer (1944a, 1944b, 1949a, 1949b, 1949c) on various punctuation marks for *Business Education World* as examples of the business view.

During the 1920s and 1930s a number of very useful language studies, many of which include information about punctuation, were conducted. According to R. L. Lyman, who reported on those conducted in the 1920s in *Summary of*

Investigations Relating to Grammar, Language, and Composition (1929), the studies generally follow one of two lines: "The first is the analysis of language activities most frequently needed in daily life; the second is the analysis of the language usages and difficulties of pupils at various grade levels and of adults" (p. 5). The first type of study took the form of usage surveys. Helen Ruhlen and S. L. Pressey examined business and professional letters and representatives of the best current publications noting the comparative frequency of various marks and the adequacy of current rules in accounting for the usage. Their findings appear in their "Statistical Study of Current Usage in Punctuation" (1924). Part 1 of Sterling A. Leonard's *Current English Usage* (1932) is a survey of 144 publishers asked to judge the punctuation of 81 sentences. It gives evidence of a strong preference for light punctuation motivated chiefly by concern for clarity. Harry A. Greene's comparison of the style books recommended by 26 publishers is briefly reported in "Researches in Contemporary Usage" (1931). The full-scale report appears in "A Criterion for the Course of Study in the Mechanics of Written Composition" (1933). Greene listed all rules found in these style books and indicated the degree to which they are uniform. Among studies of the second type are four of interest: S. L. Pressey, "A Statistical Study of Current Usage and of Children's Errors in Capitalization" (1924); W. S. Guiler, "Analysis of Children's Writings as a Basis for Instruction in English" (1926); Percival M. Symonds and Baldwin Lee, "Studies in the Learning of English Expression No. 1" (1929), and W. S. Guiler, "Analysis of Punctuation Errors" (1931). An extensive bibliography of various language studies before 1929 is available in the Lyman book.

Worth special attention are the usage surveys included in the two George Summey books (1919, 1949). Both surveys investigate the frequency of various punctuation marks and provide important diachronic information about changes in punctuation usage. Another excellent source of diachronic information about punctuation and our attitudes to it is *One Hundred Fifty Years of Grammar Textbooks* (1946) by Henry Lester Smith and others. It examines how punctuation was explained and taught in the United States from 1770 to 1944. The study includes information about standardization of the names for the punctuation marks, the number of pages in each text devoted to punctuation, and the growth and development of practice exercises.

More current usage studies should be possible using data from the Brown Corpus (available from TEXT RESEARCH, 196 Bowen Street, Providence, RI 02906) and its British counterpart, the Lancaster—Oslo/Bergen Corpus (available from The Norwegian Computing Centre for the Humanities, P.O. Box 53, N-5014 Bergen-University, Norway), both on computer tape.

For educators, testing and subsequent analysis of results are important sources of information about punctuation and pupils' mastery of it. By focusing on particular errors, they hope to be able to explain where pupils' problems lie. Data on the most common errors can be found in "The Persistency of Error in English Composition" (1917) by Roy Ivan Johnson and "Growth in Punctuation and Capitalization Abilities'' (1934) by J. H. Goodman. A study by S. L. Pressey and Pera Campbell, reported in their "Causes of Children's Errors in Capitalization" (1933), focuses on student explanations of errors, as does an extensive investigation by Philip L. Harriman, "Sources of Confusion in Punctuation and Capitalization Usages" (1934). Sterling A. Leonard demonstrated how tests can be used to help plan curriculum in "The Wisconsin Tests of Sentence Recognition" (1926). Nevertheless, when testing is complete, the results must be weighed in light of the doubts voiced by Gerald V. Lannholm, in "Measurement of Ability in Capitalization and Punctuation" (1939), that results are inconclusive because of the large number of variables.

How and when punctuation should enter school curricula is another topic of concern for educators. W. S. Guiler, in "Analysis of Children's Writing as a Basis for Instruction in English" (1926); L. J. O'Rourke, in *Rebuilding the English-Usage Curriculum to Insure Greater Mastery of Essentials* (1934); and Paul McKee, in Chapter 5 of *Language in the Elementary School* (1939), addressed the place of punctuation in the elementary school curriculum. In "Maturity Factor in the Grade Placement of Certain Punctuation Skills in Bibliographic Form" (1939) Norma Gillet warned that children may not be ready to learn certain punctuation skills until the fifth grade. Suggestions for curriculum structure can be found in M. A. Dawson, "Tools That Facilitate Expression" (1944); Martha E. Dallmann, "Capitalization and Punctuation" (1960); Robert Odum, "Sequence and Grade Placement of Punctuation Skills" (1962); and Rita Phipps, "An Example of Teaching Along Natural Lines" (1981). Larry A. Gentry pointed out the lack of consistency in textbooks for the elementary grades in his study "Punctuation Instruction in Elementary School Textbooks" (1981). A word of caution is offered to any curriculum by Greta D. Little in "Punctuation" (1983). Her point is that the punctuation that students see around them rarely conforms to the patterns they are taught in school.

The difficulty teachers have teaching punctuation has prompted a number of articles and notes about teaching students how to punctuate. J. Paul Leonard stressed the need for practice in *The Use of Practice Exercises in the Teaching of Capitalization and Punctuation* (1930a), summarized in his article by the same title in the *Journal of Educational Research* (1930b). Henrietta Holland also advocated practice in "Clarify Punctuation" (1947). Tristram P. Coffin offered a mathematical formula in "An Aid to the Teaching of Punctuation" (1951). Wilbur Hatfields's "Lesson Plan" (1926) used the etymology of *period* and *comma* to explain when they should be used. Innovative techniques demonstrating the use of punctuation through real world observations were suggested by Hardy R. Finch, in "Use Newspapers and Magazines to Teach Punctuation and Spelling" (1949); by Gertrude Overton, in "Discovering Who Makes the Rules" (1951); and by Ken Macrorie, in "Getting the Point," in his book *Searching Writing* (1980). John P. Milligan employed the language-experience technique for reading in introducing punctuation. He asserted the value of early learning even in the absence of complete mastery in his "Learning about Punctuation in the Primary Grades" (1941). His approach is not unlike that of Donald Graves: students find in their own writing a need to discover punctuation and how to use it. (See the 1980 report by Lucy McCormick Calkins.)

In 1906 Wendell P. Garrison suggested teaching punctuation to schoolchildren on the basis of function in "A Dissolving View of Punctuation." His call was ignored until recently. After recognizing that the rhetorical and grammatical considerations in punctuation are inextricably intertwined, Garland Cannon argued for the functional approach in "Handbooks, Dictionaries, and Punctuation" (1966). "Composition Is Speech Written Down" (1972) by Dorothy Burrus and Idella Lohmann advocates the language-experience technique coupled with an emphasis on the functional significance of the punctuation marks. Mina Shaughnessy's *Errors and Expectations* (1977) argues that students need to understand why punctuation is useful before they can learn it. Greta D. Little's "Toward Describing Punctuation" (1980) classifies punctuation according to function and introduces the level of formality as a factor in punctuation usage. Bruce Cronnell also stressed the idea of teaching function in his brief review of literature "Punctuation and Capitalization" (1982).

One point that has not yet received adequate attention is the difference in punctuation practices across languages. "Punctuation Problems for Speakers of Germanic Languages" (1962) by Ann Eljenholm Nichols is a contrastive analysis outlining the differences between English and German, Swedish, Danish, and Norwegian. *Dokumente zur Interpunktion Europäischer Sprachen*, a report from the Fifth International Congress of Linguists (1939), looks at the punctuation conventions of 14 European languages. It highlights the differences between rhetorical and grammatical traditions and provides contrasting versions of a text for each language. French scholars have recognized the need to investigate punctuation seriously. A special volume of *Langue Francaise* (No. 45, 1980), "La Ponctuation," edited by Nina Catach, is devoted entirely to research on punctuation. It includes a useful bibliography of additional sources as well as excellent articles on French punctuation.

Even within the English language, there are British and American conventions for punctuation. The split can be traced to the end of the nineteenth century when American printers and educators stopped looking to Great Britain and began to produce their own guidelines. John W. Clark contributed "A Chapter on American Practice" to Eric Partridge's *You Have A Point There* (1953) outlining where American punctuation does not conform to British practices. Canada holds an anomalous position as Lydia Barton's "In Search of a Canadian Style" (1982) points out.

Conclusion

In spite of the extensive material published, scholars on the whole have not taken punctuation seriously as an area of research. It is too often investigated as the means to an end rather than as the end itself. The textual scholars who have given us extensive useful information about earlier punctuation practices focus only a small portion of their attention on punctuation. The education researchers of the 1920s and the 1930s (Smith and his colleagues, Green, McKee, Leonard), who contributed some of our most enlightening pictures of modern usage in their surveys of textbooks, manuals, and publishers, are primarily interested in the possible implications their work might have for curriculum revision. In studies where the genuine focus of the research was indeed punctuation, the questions addressed involve acceptable usage conventions not basic issues of theory or principle.

By and large, composition specialists have ignored punctuation as anything more than a peripheral issue of correct usage. They have devoted their attention to the major stages of the writing process—pre-writing, composing, revising—considering punctuation when a finished manuscript is checked for mechanical flaws. Thus punctuation has become associated with the product, having little or no serious role in the writing process. The result is an understandable lack of interest in punctuation. However, such a view of punctuation and its role in writing is, I believe, shortsighted, because it obscures possible contributions to our understanding of writing that can come from viewing punctuation within expanding research on the relationship between written and oral languages.

For us to understand the nature and use of punctuation, we must accept the diverse approaches to punctuation scholarship and recognize that future advances must incorporate and synthesize the rhetorical, grammatical, and typographical traditions. The study of punctuation combines aspects of art, science, and craft. It is a complex topic, one that deserves more serious attention.

References

Alden, Raymond. "The Punctuation of Shakespeare's Printers." *PMLA*, 39 (1924), 557–80.

Alexander, Frances. "From a Teacher's Notebook-5: Punctuation—The Oral Way." *Use Engl*, 30 (1979), 43–50.

Allardyce, Paul. (George Paul MacDonnell). *Stops, or How to Punctuate: A Practical Handbook for Writers and Students*. London: Unwin, 1884.

Associated Press. *Associated Press Stylebook and Libel Manual*. Rev. ed. Dayton, Ohio: Lorenz, 1977.

Backscheider, Paul. "Punctuation for the Reader: A Teaching Approach." *EJ*, 61 (1972), 874–77.

Baldanza, Frank. "Faulkner and Stein: A Study in Stylistic Intransigence." *Ga R*, 13 (1959), 274–86.

Baldwin, R. Scott, and James M. Coady. "Psycholinguistic Approaches to a Theory of Punctuation." *J Read Behav*, 10 (1978), 363–75.

Banks, T. "Miltonic Rhythm: A Study of the Relation of the Full Stops to the Rhythm of Paradise Lost." *PMLA*, 42 (1927), 140–45.

Barnett, Michael P. "SNAP—A Programming Language for Humanities." *Comput Hum*, 4 (1970), 225–40.

Barton, Lydia. "In Search of a Canadian Style." *Sch P* 13 (1982), 347–54.

Baugh, Albert. "A Medieval Survival in Elizabethan Punctuation." In *Studies in English Renaissance Drama*, Ed. Josephine W. Bennett, Oscar Cargill, and Vernon Hall, Jr. New York: New York University Press, 1959, pp. 1–15.

Beadnell, Henry. *Spelling and Punctuation*. London: Beadnell, 1880.

Bennett, James R., Betty Brigham, Shirley Carson, John Fleischauer, Turner Kobler, Foster Park, and Allan Thies. "Punctuation and Style: An Annotated Bibliography." *Style*, 11 (1977), 119–35.

Bentley, Madison. "Tools and Terms in Recent Researches." *AJPs*, 59 (1946), 463–68.

Beringause, Arthur F. "Punctuation." *CEA*, 24, No. 5 (1964), 6–7.

Blayney, Glen. "Dramatic Pointing in the Yorkshire Tragedy." *N&Q*, 202 (1957), 191–92.

Bowers, Fredson. "Some Principles for Scholarly Editions of Nineteenth Century American Authors." *SB*, 17 (1964), 223–28.

Braaksma, M. H. "Has Modern English a Genitive Plural? A Study in Synchronous Grammar." *Engl Stud*, 23 (1941), 65–74.

Brooke, C. T. Review of *The Handwriting of the Renaissance*, by Samuel Aaron Tennenbaum. *JEGP*, 31 (1932), 148–50.

Brosnahan, Irene T. "A Few Good Words for the Comma Splice." *CE*, 38 (1976), 184–88.

Brosnahan, L. F. "The Apostrophe in Genitive Singular in the Seventeenth Century." *Engl Stud*, 42 (1961), 363–69.

Brown, Julian T. "Punctuation." *Encyclopaedia Britannica: Macropaedia,* 1980 ed.

Burnham, Josephine M. "A Problem in Punctuation." *EJ*, 35 (1947), 536–37.

Burrus, Dorothy, and Idella Lohmann. "Composition Is Speech Written Down." *Instr*, 81, No. 7 (1972), 55–56.

Byington, Steven T. "Certain Fashions in Commas and Apostrophes." *Am Sp*, 20 (1945), 22–27.

Calkins, Lucy McCormick. "Research Update: When Children Want to Punctuate: Basic Skills Belong in Context." *Lang Arts*, 57 (1980) 567–73.

Cannon, Garland H. "Punctuation and Sentence Rhythm." *CCC*, 8 (1957), 16–22.

————. "Handbooks, Dictionaries, and Punctuation." *CCC*, 17 (1966), 143–47.

Carey, Gordon Vero. *Mind the Stop*. Cambridge: Cambridge University Press, 1948.

————. *Punctuation*. Cambridge: Cambridge University Press, 1957.

Carter, Albert Howard. "On the Use of Spelling, Punctuation, and Typography to Determine the Dependence of Editions." *SP*, 44 (1947), 497–503.

Catach, Nina, Ed. "La Ponctuation." Special Issue of *LF*, No. 45, (1980), pp. 3–128.

Chicago Manual of Style, The. 13th ed. Chicago: University of Chicago Press, 1982.

Church, Frank C. "Stress-Terminal Patterns: Intonation Clues to Punctuation." *EJ*, 56 (1967), 426–34.

Clark, John W. "A Chapter on American Practice." In Eric Partridge, *You Have a Point There*. London: Hamish Hamilton, 1953, pp. 211–21.

Clay, Marie M. *What Did I Write?* Aukland: Heinemann, 1975.

Clemoes, Peter. *Liturgical Influence on Punctuation in Late Old English and Early Middle English Manuscripts*. Cambridge: University of Cambridge Department of Anglo-Saxon Occasional Papers, 1952.

Coard, Robert L. "The Possessive Apostrophe in Names." *Am Sp*, 33 (1958), 176–79.

Cobden-Sanderson, T. J. *Shakespearian Punctuation*. London, 1912; rpt. New York: Franklin, 1969.

Coffin, Tristram P. "Aid to the Teaching of Punctuation." *CE*, 12 (1951), 216–19.

Collins, V. H. "Vicious Fashion in Punctuation." *J Educ* (London), 74 (1942), 20.

Cronnell, Bruce. "Punctuation and Capitalization: A Review of Literature." National Institute of Education. 1982. ERIC 208 404.

Dallman, Martha E. "Capitalization and Punctuation." *Grade Teach*, 77 (1960), 24–25.

Dawson, M. A. "Tools That Facilitate Expression: Correct Usage Including Capitalization and Punctuation." *Nat Soc Study Ed Yrbk*, 43 (1944), Part 2, 164–71.

Devinne, Theodore Low. *The Practice of Typography: Correct Composition*. New York: Oswald, 1921.

Diekhoff, John S. "Punctuation of *Comus*." *PMLA*, 51 (1936), 757–68.

Dilbert, Jesse L. "Punctuation and the Law: How Courts View Punctuation." In William Chambers Morrow, *The Logic of Punctuation*. San Francisco: Hartland Law, 1921, pp. 237–39.

———. "Clause, Pause, and Punctuation in Poetry." *Linguistics*, 169 (1976), 5–20.

Dillon, George L. *Language Processing and the Reading of Literature*. Bloomington: Indiana University Press, 1978.

Dillon, J. T. "Functions of the Colon: An Empirical Test of Scholarly Character." *ERQ*, 5, No. 4 (1981), 71–75.

———. "In Pursuit of the Colon: A Century of Scholarly Progress: 1880–1980." *JHE*, 53, No. 1 (1982), 93–99.

Dobson, E. J. Review of *The Accidence of Ben Jonson's Plays* and *Studies in the Syntax of Ben Jonson's Plays*, by A. C. Partridge, *RES*, 6 (1955), 197–207.

Emerson, Oliver Farrar. "The Punctuation of *Beowulf* and Literary Interpretation." *MP*, 23 (1926), 393–405.

Esser, J. "Contrastive Intonation of German and English: Problems and Some Results." *Phonetica*, 35 (1978), 41–55.

Farrington, Dora Davis. "The No-Man's Land of Writing." *EJ*, 13 (1924), 264–67.

Feigenbaum, L. H. "Rally 'Round the Apostrophe, Boys!" *H Points*, 48, No. 1 (1966), 64–65.

Fifth International Congress of Linguistics. *Dokumente zur Interpunktion Europäischer Sprachen*. Goteborg: Elanders Boktryckeri Aktiebolag, 1939.

Finch, Hardy R. "Use Newspapers and Magazines to Teach Punctuation and Spelling." *EJ*, 38 (1949), 44.

Fish, Stanley. "Interpreting the *Variorum*." In *Is There a Text in This Class*? by Stanley Fish. Cambridge, Mass.: Harvard University Press, 1980, pp. 155–59.

Foat, F.W.G. "Punctuation in Mss. and Printed Books." *N&Q*, NS 2 (1904), 301–3, 462–63; 4 (1905), 144, 262; 8 (1907), 222–24.

Foley, Louis. "How of the Hyphen." *Mod Lang J*, 27 (1943), 443–46.

Fowler, H. W., and F. G. Fowler. *The King's English*. 3rd ed. London: Oxford University Press, 1931.

Fries, Charles C. "Shakespearian Punctuation." *Studies in Shakespeare, Milton, and Donne*. University of Michigan Publications in Language and Literature, 1. New York: Macmillan, 1925, pp. 65–86.

———. "Our Possessive Forms." *EJ*, 16 (1927), 693–97.

Furness, Edna L. "Pupils, Pedagogues, and Punctuation." *Elem Eng.*, 37 (1960), 184–89.

Garrison, Wendell P. "A Dissolving View of Punctuation." *AM*, 98 (1906), 233–39.

Gentry, Larry A. "Punctuation Instruction in Elementary School Textbooks." National Institute of Education, 1981. ERIC 199 757.

Gertsmeyer, Anna May. "Teaching the Punctuation of the Appositive." *EJ*, 39 (1950), 557–60.

Gillet, Norma. "Maturity Factor in the Grade Placement of Certain Punctuation Skills in Bibliographic Form." *J Educ Res*, 32 (1939), 449–55.

Goodman, J. H. "Growth in Punctuation and Capitalization Abilities." *J Educ Res*, 28 (1934), 195–202.

Gowers, Ernest. *The Complete Plain Words*. Rev. Sir Bruce Fraser. Harmondsworth, England: Penguin, 1973.

Gray, J. C. "Punctuating the Compound Sentence." *EJ*, 51 (1962), 573–74.

Greene, Harry Andrew. "Researches in Contemporary Usage." *EJ* (Coll Ed), 20 (1931), 316–20.

———. "A Criterion for the Course of Study in the Mechanics of Written Composition." University of Iowa: Studies in Education, 8, No. 4 (1933), 5–66.

Greg, Sir Walter Warren. "Jonson's Masques—Points of Editorial Principle and Practice." *RES*, 18 (1942), 144–66.

———. "The Rationale of Copy-Text." *SB*, 3 (1950), 19–36.

Grierson, H.J.C., ed. *The Poems of John Donne*. Oxford: Clarendon, 1912.

Guiler, W. S. "Analysis of Children's Writing as a Basis for Instruction in English." *J Educ Method*, 5 (1926), 259–64.

———. "Analysis of Punctuation Errors." *J Educ Method*, 10 (1931), 425–29.

Haber, Ralph Norman, and Lyn R. Haber. "Visual Components of the Reading Process." *Visibl Lang*, 15 (1981), 147–82.

Haber, Tom Burns. "The Decline and Near Demise of the Diaresis." *CEA*, 25, No. 3 (1962), 1, 3.

Hall, Robert A., Jr. "To Hyphenate or Not to Hyphenate." *EJ*, 53 (1964), 662–65.

Hamilton, Frederick W. *Punctuation*. Chicago: United Typothetae of America, 1920.

Hansard, Thomas Curson. *Typographia: An Historical Sketch*. 1825; rpt. London: Gregg, 1966.

Harriman, Philip L. "Sources of Confusion in Punctuation and Capitalization Usages." *PJE* 12 (1934), 31–35.

Hart, Horace. *Rules for Compositors and Readers at the University Press, Oxford*. 38th ed. Oxford: Oxford University Press, 1978.

Hatfield, W. Wilbur. "Lesson Plan: Tenth Grade Mechanics." *EJ*, 15 (1926), 706–7.

———. "Objective Determination of Punctuation." *J Educ Res*, 26 (1933), 569–71.

Held, J. R. "Teaching Punctuation in the Ninth Grade by Means of Intonation Cues." *RTE*, 3 (1969), 196–208.

Herbert, A. P. "Fullstops." *Punch*, 190 (1936), 488.

———. "Holiday Tasks: Punctuation." *Punch*, 195 (1938), 236–37, 262–63, 304–5, 318–19.

Hicks, Charles Roger. "Courts and Commas." *Sch & Soc*, 51 (1940) , 522–23.

Holland, Henrietta. "Clarify Punctuation." *Instr*, 56, No. 8 (1947), 16.

Honan, Park. "Eighteenth and Nineteenth Century Punctuation Theory." *ES*, 41 (1960), 92–102.

Hoover, R. M. "Principles of English Hyphenation." *CCC*, 22 (1971), 156–60.

Horn, Gunnar, "Amen!" *EJ*, 36 (1947), 493.

Hornsby, Samuel A. "A Note on the Punctuation in the Authorized Version of the English Bible." *Engl Stud*, 54 (1973), 566–68.

Howard, Edwin J. "The Printer and Elizabethan Punctuation." *SP*, 27 (1930), 220–29.

Howard-Hill, Trevor H. *Ralph Crane and Some Shakespeare First Folio Comedies*. Charlottesville: University Press of Virginia, 1972.

Hume, Robert A. "The Supreme Court on the Commas." *Sch & Soc*, 51 (1940), 278–79.

Husband, T. F., and M.F.A. Husband. *Punctuation: Its Principles and Practices*. London: Routledge, 1905.

Ives, George. *Text, Type, and Style: A Compendium of Atlantic Usage*. Boston: Atlantic Monthly Press, 1921.

Jenkinson, Hilary, "Notes on the Study of English Punctuation of the Sixteenth Century." *RES*, 2, No. 6 (1926), 152–58.

Johnson, Dorothy M. "Ten Commandments for Practical Punctuation." *Bus Educ World*, 24 (1944), 256–66.

Johnson, Ellen M. "A Simpler Approach to Punctuation." *CE*, 15 (1954), 399–404.

Johnson, John. *Typographia, or the Printers' Instructor*. 1824; rpt. London: Gregg, 1966.

Johnson, Roy Ivan. "The Persistency of Error in English Composition." *Sch Rev* 25 (1917), 555–80.

Jones, John Bush. "Victorian 'Readers' and Modern Editors: Attitudes and Accidentals Revisited." *PBSA*, 71 (1977), 49–59.

Jones, W. Paul. "Punctuating Nonrestrictives." *CE*, 10 (1948), 158–62.

Kallan, Richard. "Style and the New Journalism: A Rhetorical Analysis of Tom Wolfe." *Comm Mon*, 46 (1979), 56–62.

Klein, William Livingston. *Why We Punctuate: Reason versus Rule in the Use of Marks*. Minneapolis: Lancet, 1916.

Knowles, F. E. "Computational Linguistics at Salford University: Past, Present, and Future." *ALLC Bul*, 1 (1973), 10–13.

Lamb, Mary. "An Application of Error Analysis to Comma Splices and Fused Sentences." Resources in Education, 1978. ERIC 146 595.

Lannholm, Gerald V. "Measurement of Ability in Capitalization and Punctuation." *J Exp Educ*, 8 (1939), 55–86.

Lasley, R. L. "Present-Day Punctuation," Rev. of *Modern Punctuation*, by George Summey. *EJ*, 10 (1921), 235–36.

Leonard, J. Paul. *The Use of Practice Exercises in the Teaching of Capitalization and Punctuation*. New York: Teachers College, Columbia, 1930a.

———. "The Use of Practice Exercises in the Teaching of Capitalization and Punctuation." Summary in *J Educ Res*, 21 (1930b), 186–90.

Leonard, Sterling A. "The Rationale of Punctuation: A Criticism." *E Rec*, 51 (1916), 89–92.

———. "The Wisconsin Tests of Sentence Recognition." *EJ* 15 (1926), 348–57.

———. *Current English Usage*. English Monographs No. 1. Chicago: Inland, 1932.

Little, Greta D. "Toward Describing Punctuation." *SECOL B*, 4, No. 1 (1980), 1–9.

———. "Punctuation: Evidence of a Linguistic Credibility Gap." *NOTE*, 10, No. 2 (1983), 15–18.

Logan, John Daniel. *Quantitative Punctuation*. Toronto: Briggs, 1907.

Long, Russell C. "Common Features of Writing and Oral Reading: Implications and Applications." Resources in Education, 1981. ERIC 196 012.

Luckombe, Philip. *The History and Art of Printing.* 1771; rpt. London: Gregg, 1956.

Lund, M. G. "Punctuation and Personality." *Clear H*, 27 (1953), 541–43.

Lyman, R. L. *Summary of Investigation Relating to Grammar, Language, and Composition.* Chicago: University of Chicago Press, 1929.

Macrorie, Ken. "Getting the Point." In *Searching Writing: A Context Book.* Rochelle Park, N.J.: Hayden, 1980, pp. 212–215.

Manutius, Aldus. "Interpungendi Ratio." 1566. In *Punctuation: Its Principles and Practice.* Trans. T. F. and M.F.A. Husband, London: Routledge, 1905, Appendix B, pp. 130–36.

McCorkle, Julia Norton. "Eliminating Guesswork from Sentence Punctuation." *EJ*, 15 (1926), 673–80.

McCoy, R. F. "Simplifying Punctuation." *EJ*, 28 (1939), 576–78.

McCrimmon, James M. "Commas and Conformity." *CE*, 1 (1939), 68–70.

McKee, J. H. "A Small Plea for Conformity." *EJ* (Coll Ed), 28 (1939), 312–14.

———. "Two Commas or None." *CE*, 1 (1940), 538–41.

McKee, Paul. *Language in the Elementary School.* Boston: Houghton Mifflin, 1939.

McKenzie, D. F. "Shakespearian Punctuation—A New Beginning." *RES*, NS 10 (1959), 361–70.

McKerrow, Ronald B. *An Introduction to Bibliography for Literary Students.* Oxford: Clarendon, 1927.

Menikoff, Barry. "Punctuation and Point of View in the Late Style of Henry James." *Style*, 1 (1970), 29–47.

Meyers, Walter. "Books: Handbooks, Subhandbooks, and Non-Handbooks: Texts for Freshman English." *CE*, 32 (1971), 716–24.

Miller, Helen Rand. "Away with Apostrophes!" *EJ*, 36 (1947), 381.

Miller, Raymond. "Coordination and the Comma." *PMLA*, 23 (1908), 316–28.

Milligan, John P. "Learning about Punctuation in the Primary Grades." *EER*, 18 (1941), 96–98.

Mitchell, Bruce. Dangers of Disguise: Old English Texts in Modern Punctuation." *RES*, 31 (1980), 385–413.

Modley, Rudolf. "World Language without Words." *J Comm*, 24, No. 4 (1974), 59–66.

Moe, Maurice Winter. "Teaching the Use of the Comma." *EJ*, 2 (1913), 104–8.

Monteith, Robert. *The True and Genuine Art of Pointing.* Edinburgh: n.p., 1704.

Moore, Robert E. "Apostrophe to the Ocean—And Heave It In!" *EJ*, 55 (1966), 198–200.

Morrow, William Chambers. *The Logic of Punctuation.* San Francisco: Hartland Law, 1926.

Moxon, Joseph. *Mechanick Exercises on the Whole Art of Printing, 1683–84*; Ed. Herbert Davis and Harry Carter. 2nd ed. London: Oxford University Press, 1962.

Munsell, Joel. *The Typographical Miscellany.* Albany, N.Y.: Munsell, 1850.

Nichols, Ann Eljenholm. "Punctuation Problems for Speakers for Germanic Languages." *Lang L*, 12 (1962), 195–204.

Nurnberg, Maxwell. "Comedy of Commas." *H Points*, 42, No. 4 (1960), 47–50.

———. "Growth of a Language Skill: Punctuation." *Calif J Ed Res*, 15 (1964), 12–17.

Odum, Robert S. "Sequence and Grade Placement of Punctuation Skills." *Calif J Ed Res*, 13 (1962), 179–85.

O'Hara, F. M., Jr. "The Use of the Hyphen in Printing to Indicate Divided Words." *Visibl Lang*, 5 (1971), 111–24.

Ong, Walter. "Historical Backgrounds of Elizabethan and Jacobean Punctuation Theory." *PMLA*, 59 (1944), 349–60.

O'Rourke, L. J. *Rebuilding the English-Usage Curriculum to Insure Greater Mastery of Essentials*. Washington: Psychological Institute, 1934.

Osselton, N.E. "The Apostrophe in the Genitive Singular in the Seventeenth and Eighteenth Centuries." *Engl Stud*, 43 (1962), 107–8.

Overton, Gertrude H. "Discovering Who Makes the Rules." *EJ*, 40 (1951), 337–38.

Owens, Eivion. "Professor Thorndike on Punctuation." *TCR*, 50 (1949), 258–63.

Parker, Hershel. "Regularizing Accidentals." *Proof*, (1973), 1–20.

Parkes, Malcolm B. "Punctuation, or Pause and Effect." In *Medieval Eloquence*. Ed. James J. Murphy. Berkeley: University of California Press, 1978, pp. 127–42.

Parsons, E. Dudley. "Bowing Down Before the God of Punctuation." *EJ*, 4 (1915), 598–99.

Partridge, A. C. *The Accidence of Ben Jonson's Plays, Masques, and Entertainments*. Cambridge: Bowes, 1953a.

———. *Orthography in Shakespeare and Elizabethan Drama*. London: Edwin Arnold, 1964.

———. *Studies in the Syntax of Ben Jonson's Plays*. Cambridge: Bowes, 1953b.

Partridge, Eric. *You Have a Point There*. London: Hamish Hamilton, 1953.

Pearce, Michael. "The Hyphen in English." *Englisch* 13, No. 4 (1978), 146–48.

Peckham, Morse. "Reflections on the Foundations of Modern Textual Editing." *Proof*, 1 (1971), 122–55.

Perkins, Chris. "Has Punctuation Been Forgotten?" *Englisch*. 14, No. 2 (1979), 63–67.

Perkins, W. E. "Programmed Materials Teach Punctuation." *Bus Educ Forum*, 26, No. 1 (1971), 22–23.

Phipps, Rita. "An Example of Teaching Along Natural Lines: An Instructional Sequence on the Use of Commas in Lists Based on the Hierarchies of Piaget, Bloom, Krathwohl, and Harrow." Resources in Education, 1981. ERIC 204 784.

Pollard, Alfred W. *Shakespeare's Fight with the Pirates and the Problems of the Transmission of His Text*. 1920; rpt. Cambridge: Cambridge University Press, 1967.

Presland, John L. "In Search of an 'Early Teaching Grammar.' " *Ed Res* (Brit), 16 (1974), 112–20.

Pressey, S. L. "A Statistical Study of Current Usage and of Children's Errors in Capitalization." *EJ*. 13 (1924), 727–32.

———, and Pera Campbell. "The Cause of Children's Errors in Capitalization." *EJ*, 22 (1933), 197–201.

Price, Hereward T. "Grammar and the Compositor in the Sixteenth and Seventeenth Centuries." *JEGP*, 38 (1939), 540–48.

Rand, Helen. "In the Freshman Stage of Punctuation." *EJ*, 17 (1928), 160–61.

Randall, Starr D. "The Effect of Electronic Editing on Error Rate of a Newspaper." *JQ*, 56, No. 1 (1979), 161–65.

Richards, I. A. *So Much Nearer: Essays Toward a World English*. New York: Harcourt, Brace, World, 1968.

Richmond, Phyllis. "An Extended Character Set for Humanities Computer Printout." *Comput Hum*, 4 (1970), 247–50.

Robertson, Joseph. *An Essay on Punctuation*. 1785; rpt. Menston, England: Scholar Press Facsimile, 1969.

Rosslyn, Wendy. "COCOA as a Tool for the Analysis of Poetry." *ALLC Bul*, 3 (1975), 15–18.

Rourke, Constance Mayfield. "The Rationale of Punctuation." *ER*, 50 (1915), 246–58.

Ruhlen, H., and S. L. Pressey. "A Statistical Study of Current Usage in Punctuation." *EJ*, 13 (1924), 325–31.

Salisbury, Rachel. "The Psychology of Punctuation." *EJ*, 28 (1939), 794–806.

———. "Reading Road to Punctuation Skills." *EER*, 22 (1945), 117–23.

Salmon, Vivian. "Early Seventeenth Century Punctuation as a Guide to Sentence Structure." *RES*, NS 13 (1962), 347–60.

Schroth, Evelyn. "Dr. Seuss and Language Usage." *Read Teach*, 31 (1978), 748–50.

Shakes, C. T. "About Those Sentence Fragments." *EJ*, 58 (1969), 1223, 1232.

Shaughnessy, Mina. "Handwriting and Punctuation." In *Errors and Expectations*. New York: Oxford University Press, 1977, pp. 14–43.

Shaw, Harry. *Punctuate It Right!* New York: Barnes, Noble, 1963.

Simmons, Sarah. "Mukarovsky, Structuralism, and the Essay." *Semiotica*, 19 (1977), 335–40.

Simpson, Evelyn M. "A Note on Donne's Punctuation." *RES*, 4 (1928), 295–300.

Simpson, Percy. *Shakespearian Punctuation*. Oxford: Clarendon, 1911.

———. *Proof-Reading in the Sixteenth, Seventeenth, and Eighteenth Centuries*. 1935; rpt. London: Oxford University Press, 1970.

Singleton, Ralph H. "How to Teach Punctuation." *CE*, 6 (1944), 111–15.

Skelton, Reginald. *Modern English Punctuation*. 2nd ed. London: Pitman, 1949.

Sklar, Elizabeth S. "The Possessive Apostrophe: The Development and Decline of a Crooked Mark." *CE*, 38 (1976), 175–83.

Sloan, Gary. "The Subversive Effects of an Oral Culture on Student Writing." *CCC*, 30 (1979), 156–60.

Smith, Adele Millicent. *Proofreading and Punctuation*. Philadelphia: The Author, 1907.

Smith, Henry Lester, Katherine Dugdale, Beulah Faris Steele, and Robert Stewart McElhinney. *One Hundred Fifty Years of Grammar Textbooks*. Bulletin of School Education. Bloomington: Division of Research and Field Services, Indiana University, 1946.

Smith, J. B. "Encoding Literary Texts: Some Considerations." *ALLC Bul*, 4 (1976), 190–98.

Sopher, H. "The Problem of Punctuation." *Engl Lang Teach J*, 31 (1977), 304–13.

Spencer, Herbert. *The Visible Word*. 2nd ed. New York: Hastings House, 1969.

Stitzel, Judith. "Learning from Our Mistakes: Who's Learning? Whose Mistakes?" *JETT*, 6, No. 1 (1973), 12–17.

Stoddard, Ted. "Challenging the Great Punctuation Copout." Resources in Education, 1977. ERIC 136 283.

Summey, George. *Modern Punctuation: Its Utilities and Conventions*. New York: Oxford University Press, 1919.

———. *American Punctuation*. New York: Ronald, 1949.

Symonds, Percival M., and Baldwin Lee. "Studies in the Learning of English Expression No. 1: Punctuation." *TCR*, 30 (1929), 461–80.

Tannenbaum, Samuel Aaron. *The Handwriting of the Renaissance*. New York: Columbia University Press, 1930.

Tanselle, G. Thomas. "Greg's Theory of Copy-Text and the Editing of American Literature." *SB*, 28 (1975), 167–229.

Teall, Horace F. *Punctuation*. New York: Appleton, 1897.

Thompson, Sir Edward Maunde. *An Introduction to Greek and Latin Palaeography*, 1912; rpt. New York: Burt Franklin, n.d.

Thorndike, E. L. "The Psychology of Punctuation." *AJPs*, 61 (1948a), 224–28.

———. "Punctuation." *TCR*, 49 (1948b), 531–37.

Thorpe, James. *Watching the Ps and Qs: Editorial Treatment of Accidentals*. University of Kansas Publications Library Series, 38. Lawrence: University of Kansas, 1971.

———. *Principles of Textual Criticism*. San Marino: Huntington Library, 1972.

Treip, Mindele. *Milton's Punctuation and Changing English Usage, 1582–1676*. London: Methuen, 1970.

U.S. Government Printing Office Style Manual. Rev. ed. Washington: U.S. Government Printing Office, 1973.

Waltimyer, Verne Ellis. "Conquering the Capitals." *Bus Educ World*, 25 (1944a), 215.

———. "Conquering the Commas." *Bus Educ World*, 25 (1944b), 65–66.

———. "Colon or the Dash?" *Bus Educ World*, 30 (1949a), 37–38.

———. "Punctuation: Meanings and Marks: The Comma." *Bus Educ World*, 29 (1949b), 274–75.

———. "Semicolon, Good Brakes." *Bus Educ World*, 29 (1949c), 368.

Ward, C. H. "Punctuator Gingriens' " A Call to Arms." *EJ*, 4 (1915), 451–57.

———. *What Is English?* New York: Scott Foresman, 1917.

Weaver, Wendell W., et al. "The Effect of Reading Variation and Punctuation Conditions Upon Reading Comprehension." *J Read Behav*, 2 (1970), 75–84.

Wentzlaff-Eggebert, Harald. "Drucktypenwechsel: Ein Grezphanomen Der Sprachtheorie Im Dienst Der Leserforschung." *Li Li*, 4 (1974), 27–49.

Whitehall, Harold. *Structural Essentials of English*, New York: Harcourt, Brace, World, 1956.

Wilson, John, *A Treatise on Grammatical Punctuation*. 32nd ed. New York: American Book, 1899.

Wycherly, Alan. "A Pride of Commas." *CEA*, 29, No. 8 (1967), 1, 6.

Yaggy, Elinor. "Let's Take the Guesswork Out of Punctuation." *CCC*, 4 (1953), 128–31.

Zais, Robert S. "The Linguistic Characteristics of Punctuation Symbols and the Teaching of Punctuation Skills." *EJ*, 52 (1963), 677–81.

Zeeman, Elizabeth. "Punctuation in an Early Manuscript of Love's Mirror." *RES*, 7 (1956), 11–18.

Usage

MARVIN K. L. CHING

Usage is often distinguished from *grammar* by contemporary linguists when a technical distinction is made between the two. *Grammar*, according to linguists, is a study of the underlying syntactic structures in a language that enable a sentence to make sense. In English, word order largely constitutes the grammar of a sentence. *Grammar* is thus more related to the chapter on sentence structure in this book.

Usage, on the other hand, is a broad term for the study of the propriety or, more often, the lack of propriety in using various elements of language: the lack of propriety of (1) various locutions (for example, *to be because*); (2) less preferred words (for example, *aggravate* for *irritate*); (3) the wrong inflection or word form (for example, not using the *-s* marker for the third person singular verb or using wrong forms for the plurals of nouns and the principal parts of verbs); (4) incorrect word order (for example, the split infinitive, dangling modifiers, misplacement of the word *only*, the ending of a sentence with a preposition); (5) clichés; (6) jargon that makes comprehension difficult; and (7) socially improper diction (for example, sexist language and euphemisms that obfuscate political, social, or medical realities). Usage is most often the stuff of "grammar" books. Wrong usage rarely violates the basic meaning of the sentence (although popular and lay opinion claims that it does); instead, incorrect usage offends the audience because of convention, propriety, taste, or preference.

Because usage is a matter of choice, it is related to other topics in this book where the writer has alternatives: for example, the writing process, where the writer has a choice of behavior; punctuation, where choice of mark affects meaning; and spelling, where there are permissible variants.

Unfortunately, what is considered "good usage" is controversial, highly dependent upon the definer's basic assumptions on how language operates. The essays under "Standard English" in Part 2 of David L. Shores's anthology *Contemporary English* (1972) present a cursory view of the problems and complexities in discovering the myths and truths of usage. Philip B. Gove, the editor-in-chief of *Webster's Second New International Dictionary (Webster's II)*, described in the introduction to Part 2 of Shores's anthology what most linguists—not what popular pundits of language and literary stylists—assume to be standard English. Gove cited as satisfactory the third definition of *Webster's Third New International Dictionary (Webster's III)*, which acknowledges the relative uniformity of the standard but which at the same time recognizes not only some regional differences but also a great range as being standard: both the formal and informal speech and writing of the educated. Thus the standard is not limited to literary or formal English, which, he said, can sound foolish in situations requiring another variety.

Thomas Pyles's essay "English Usage" (1972), after Gove's introduction, reinforces Gove's idea that standard English cannot be equated with usage handbooks, because many reputable writers violate the rules of handbooks, as evidenced in the *Oxford English Dictionary (OED)*. John S. Kenyon's seminal essay "Cultural Levels and Functional Varieties of English" (1948), the next article, points out people's confusion of *levels* (good or bad, standard or substandard, language) with *functional varieties* (different language for different situations). The idea of levels—for example, literary, colloquial, and illiterate, in descending order of innate worth—is no longer considered tenable. Some varieties of speech and writing require the familiar or colloquial; others, the formal.

Patrick E. Kilburn's "Gentleman's Guide to Linguistic Etiquette" in the same section of Shore's anthology warns the reader against a simplistic acceptance of standard English, in particular the brand of standard English promulgated by the *American Heritage Dictionary*. Kilburn pointed to a cause for the ultraconservative or reactionary judgments of the dictionary's panel of experts: 70 or more of the 100 members were born in the nineteenth century. He also questioned the propriety of judging usage by percentage figures, of ascertaining right and wrong by a majority.

Martin Joos, in his "Standard in the Community Language" (1972), also dealt with the functional varieties of English. Joos emphasized that appropriateness of language depends upon social context—the desired formality or informality and the desired distance or intimacy between speaker and listener.

The last essay in Part 2 of Shores's anthology—David DeCamp's "Dimensions of English Usage"—warns of the chaos created by those who, in trying to be true to their fastidiousness about language and yet be enlightened with the new knowledge about language, vacillate schizophrenically between authoritarian rigidity of language rules and unenlightened anarchy of choice. In citing the changes in thinking about usage, he traced the objective studies—Sterling Leonard's *Current English Usage* (1932); C. C. Fries's *American English Grammar* (1940); Hans Kurath's *Linguistic Atlas of New England* (1939–1943); and Robert C. Pooley's pedagogical books in the 1930s and 1940s—showing the influence of the NCTE in many of these studies and Fries's influence in spreading the concept of usage as levels, from top to bottom, from formal to colloquial to illiterate. Porter Perrin, DeCamp stated, also fell prey to this incorrect view, although he did not label all language as dichotomous in scale: correct or incorrect, standard or substandard. According to DeCamp, John Kenyon, in his "Cultural Levels and Functional Varieties of English" (1948), did not make the mistake of offering a single scale, or even a two-dimensional one, contrasting written and spoken language. DeCamp asserted that Kenyon opened up new possibilities—multi-dimensional considerations in choosing correct and responsible usage: the considerations of functional variety or style; geographical use; time or historical period; age; cultural level, depending on social context; and responsibility.

Such complexity of considerations, however, is harder for teachers to grasp. Moreover, as twentieth-century styles have grown less formal and more conversational, the formal range has been relegated to specific and narrow uses: for example, the language of dissertations, eulogies, ceremonial occasions, law, and scientific discourse. The informal range, as James M. McCrimmon pointed out in *Writing with a Purpose* (1973), has the widest spectrum of usage of the three ranges he named: the colloquial, the informal, and the formal styles. Calling this informal style the "moderate range" in his seventh edition of his textbook (1980), McCrimmon said that it is the most usable style for all expository and argumentative writing. It is the prevailing style in non-technical books, magazines, newspapers, editorials, college lectures, and discussions. It is appropriate for all student writing except for fiction because of its wide range. At one extreme, the informal or moderate style, according to McCrimmon, is similar to the colloquial style, and at the other extreme, it sounds more like formal language. Therefore, informal prose, unlike the other two styles, fluctuates greatly.

But no doubt the seminal source for relativity is Martin Joos's *Five Clocks* (1967), a penetrating account naming various considerations in usage—age, style, breadth, and responsibility—and emphasizing the various styles (the five clocks) available to a speaker and a writer: intimate, informal, consultative, formal, and frozen. A peson chooses a style according to the requirements of a given situation: the language depending upon the degree of explicitness deemed necessary by the background information the audience already possesses, the degree to which the audience has an opportunity to question and participate in the discussion, the degree of distance or intimacy desired, the degree of planning demanded, and the degree to which the language should be memorable so that it can be repeated intact.

Although acknowledging, like the others above, the interrelation between speech and writing—that some writing sounds more like speech and some speech sounds more like writing—E. D. Hirsch in *The Philosophy of Composition* (1977), taking a minority view, emphasized the great chasm between speech, which he called "oral speech," and writing, which he called "written speech." Deploring the structural linguists' idea of the primacy of speech—that writing is just a record of oral language written down—Hirsch instead argued that in many instances the written language is primary, as for example in legal documents, where every matter is defined and made explicit to prevent misinterpretation. Such writing, he asserted, often is not vocalized or is only subvocalized, so oral speech is only a secondary representation of such writing. More like ideographs, the standard written language, he said, serves as a *lingua franca*, like Chinese characters, no matter what dialect a person speaks. Largely fixed and stable over time—not constantly evolving like speech—it is not elitist at all; rather, it allows all segments of society to use the same language. Hirsch thus lamented the NCTE's Conference on College Composition and Communication's adoption of the resolution "The Students' Right to Their Own Language."

However, facts of usage do not fully support Hirsch's position. There is a relationship between good usage in speech and good usage in writing. Furthermore, as mentioned earlier in our discussion of McCrimmon, the informal style—the predominant style of writing—incorporates both the colloquial and the formal styles. Moreover, where writing is so different from speech that it no longer accompanies the historical evolution of usage in speech so that it becomes wholly different from the written form of language, learning the written language is made much more difficult.

What is needed in disagreements about usage is a sound and enlightened view of how language really operates. As Robert C. Pooley advised, in his latest and updated book *The Teaching of English Usage* (1975), which adopts a multi-dimensional instead of a single scale of usage, the study of usage must *not* be based on cherished myths: the absolute and unchanging nature of language, the determination of good usage by reference to reputable and standard authors, the preservation of traditional rules because they are thought of as more elegant, and the identification of good usage with formal literary usage. Instead of following an authoritarian approach to language that incorporates the myths above, the prescriptive approach of most school textbooks, we must describe how language is really used by real people in different contexts. This descriptive study of language, which records the facts of usage, is difficult. The truth is not found in popular handbooks, or prescriptive dictionaries like the *American Heritage Dictionary* (*AHD*), or even in the most progressive dictionary, because by the time a dictionary has been printed, the language has changed. What is absolutely essential, Pooley maintained, is a healthy skepticism of all rules. Teachers must take into consideration the requirements of the social situation in judging what is good and bad usage.

To follow such a flexible approach, a scholar researching current English usage needs to be grounded in these areas of language: (1) a history of the English language, (2) semantic shifts and word formation, (3) lexicography, (4) language variation, (5) twentieth-century usage studies and the current thrust in usage study, and (6) linguistics and pedagogy.

A History of the English Language

To understand the roots of the conflict between the prescriptive and the descriptive approaches to language, the two approaches to language cited in the preceding section, one must understand the history of the English language—especially the literary scholars and grammarians' orientation toward grammar during the Restoration and the neo-classic periods, a perspective that caused a radical departure from the past uses of the language in England and that has dominated the thinking of literary stylists, popular pundits of language, the stuff of handbooks, and laymen's opinions and judgments about language, producing the insecurity of Americans about correct usage. A comparison with the previous period—Renaissance English—is helpful in understanding the late seventeenth and the eighteenth centuries' distinctive attitudes and motivation in not tolerating divided usage, in pressing for an academy of language like the French and the Italian academies, in desiring to fix and ascertain the language, and in searching for a monolithic standard—all resulting in a steady movement toward a prescriptive use of language with various proscriptions and prescriptions on a variety of matters. Many of today's rules about the incorrect use of language originate from this period. But to evaluate these rules from an enlightened view, one must weigh the arguments of the prescriptive and the descriptive approaches against each other.

An exemplar of the eighteenth century's prescriptivism is Bishop Robert Lowth's *Short Introduction to English Grammar* (1762); a model of the period's descriptivism is Joseph Priestley's *Rudiments of English Grammar* (1761). The present habit of fault finding, gleefully naming and ridiculing supposed infelicitous usage of language (even if a usage is common and current) of well-known writers, is manifestly evident in Lowth's work. Lowth not only pointed out the supposed "mistakes" of prominent writers during his time but also those before his era—including those in the King James Bible, Shakespeare, and Milton. Because of Lowth's simplistic viewpoint—that a given rule was innately right or wrong and to be followed forever and that any deviance was evidence of decadence—his work won the allegiance of most people, especially the rising middle class, whose linguistic insecurity caused them to seek the "correct" rules of usage, not the more accurate and complex usage derived from the theory that language changes so the rules of usage change. In attempting to hold on to much of the old, Lowth kept distinctions between principal parts of verbs, distinctions that were disappearing, thus retarding and even stopping many of the natural processes that were occurring.

In contrast, Priestley opposed legislation in language, defending the principle that language has an ability to take care of itself where there are controversies, so that legislative bodies on language—"synods" or academies—are not only unnecessary but also undesirable, because their decisions are "hasty" and "injudicious." According to Priestley, tampering with natural processes of language causes undesirable results. Largely consistent in faithfully describing the language as currently used, Priestley deviated from his principles only to a small extent.

To gain an understanding of the deviation of the late seventeenth century and the eighteenth century's practice from all previous periods in the English language, one should examine standard books on the history of the English language, which all show a great contrast between the flexibility, experimentation, and flowering of creativity in language and tolerance of divided usage preceding the neo-classic period and the rigidity, conformity to rules, and concentration on detection of error during that period. Albert C. Baugh and Thomas Cable's *History of the English Language* (1978); Thomas Pyles and John Algeo's *Origins and Development of the English Language* (1982) and its accompanying workbook, John Algeo's *Problems in the Origins and Development of the English Language* (1982); J. N. Hook's *History of the English Language* (1975); and L. M. Myers and Richard L. Hoffman's *Roots of Modern English* (1979) are informative works where this contrast can be seen. The huge influx of vocabulary (the adoption of many "inkhorn" terms, the revival of Chaucerisms, and the experimentation of compounding Old English words from the native stock and of switching parts of speech) and the characteristics of language now frowned upon but characteristic of Shakespearean English (the double negative, the double comparative and superlative, principal parts of verbs no longer used, the tolerance for divided usage, the indiscriminate use of case of pronouns, the *his*-genitive, and the differences in idiom of preposition) may be seen in the chapters on Renaissance English: Chapter 8 in Baugh and Cable (1978), Chapter 8 in Pyles and Algeo (1982) and the same chapter in the accompanying workbook by Algeo (1982), Chapter 6 in Hook (1975), and Chapter 6 in Myers and Hoffman (1979).

The socio-political, economic, religious, literary, and scientific background producing intolerance toward innovation and variation in language and the exact prescriptions and proscriptions of the language in the subsequent periods—the Restoration and the neo-classic periods of literature—may be found in Chapter 9 in Baugh and Cable (1978), Chapter 8 in Pyles and Algeo (1982) and the same chapter in the accompanying workbook by Algeo (1982), Chapter 7 in Hook (1975), and Chapter 7 in Myers and Hoffman (1979). Proscribed out of the language were constructions such as the double negative, the double comparative and the double superlative, and the comparison of incomparables because these constructions were considered either illogical or redundant. Prescribed as desirable was the maintenance of distinctions wherever possible for prosody, rhyme, or nuances: the distinction between principal parts of verbs that were collapsing and the distinction between *shall* and *will*. The great intolerance for innovation in diction is evident in Swift's condemnation of new words introduced into the language and terms considered slang because of their clipped forms. Intolerance against divided usage is found in many critics' pronouncements about which form was considered to be correct: *different from* or *different than*, *between* or *among*, *averse from* or *averse to*. In the same chapters named above on the neo-classic period may also be found the key figures (for example, Dryden, Swift, Addison, Steele, Pope, and Johnson) in their zealous passion for prescriptivism and their methods of resolving divided usage (etymology, analogy, and the example of Latin and Greek) and the opposing minority (for example, Joseph Priestley and George Campbell) in their advocacy of an objective, descriptive study of language. The reason that the prescriptivists won the battle is also given.

An especially fine account tracing the acrimonious battle between the two divergent views of language is Edward Finegan's most comprehensive, lucid, and yet succinct treatment of the spirited battle from the Age of Reason in England to present-day America in *Attitudes Towards English Usage* (1980). In his prologue and also in the first chapter, Finegan enabled us to comprehend the stances of the two opposing camps by using different names for prescriptivists and descriptivists. Thus the antagonists may be thought of as opponents in other terms: purists, traditionalists, and absolutists versus relativists and debunkers; those subscribing to a doctrine of innate correctness in certain forms of language versus those believing in the doctrine of usage, a factual and accurate account of how the language is actually used; language guardians who believe that change means decay and must be stopped versus language describers who believe that language has a natural way of taking care of unsettled usage without legislation by "experts"; and the verbal critics of language versus the grammarians of language.

Throughout, Finegan depicted the smugness, complacency, and self-righteousness of both sides. He not only discussed the attitudes toward usage held by eighteenth-century writers, rhetoricians, and grammarians but also demonstrated the difficulty in applying even the best criteria—for example, the subjectivity in employing Campbell's criteria for good usage: English that is present, reputable, and national. Furthermore, he treated in depth the developments in usage in America, in the work of Lindley Murray, Noah Webster, and others, through the influential role of usage studies in the twentieth century endorsed by the National Council of Teachers of English; the influence of the new linguistics; and the brouhaha over *Webster's III*. He appropriately ended with a significant chapter: some suggestions for solving the usage conflict.

Finegan, believing that both sides—the prescriptivists and the descriptivists—are to blame, saw a possibility of a cessation of hostilities between the two so that productive work on usage in composition might take place. Not only should the literary stylists, verbal critics, and self-appointed pundits of language understand and acknowledge linguistic truths, but the linguists, who pride themselves on an enlightened understanding of language, should also change in their attitudes regarding usage.

It is too often true that the traditionalists—the literary stylists, in prizing impeccable, elegant, and esthetic English—focus on the trivial: for example, the condemnation of *like* for *as* or of *finalize* because of the *-ize* suffix. Too often have these traditionalists, ignorant of natural processes in the language, complained about new words, lexical mergers, or familiar suffixes added to old words and falsely labeled any deviation from their standards as moral decadence and illogical thinking. There are more significant matters to consider: students should be studying real grammar, logic, rhetoric, dialects, and the origins and development of the English language. Popular pundits like Edwin Newman improve language when they expose opaque jargon, clichés, and euphemisms that obfuscate and mitigate the reality of a situation for sinister and political purposes. However, they are often ignorant when they engage in prissy matters of changes in vocabulary, word forms, constructions, or idioms already accepted in the language.

But the linguists are also to blame, according to Finegan. In believing that the spoken language is the language and that writing is a mere secondary representation of the oral mode, they have not prized the written form enough. Coming from a historical background of translating the language of American Indians into writing for the first time, structural linguists natually considered the oral form to be primary. However, for a study of usage in schools, Finegan argued, students come to school to learn how to write. Linguists should therefore be cognizant of the differences between speech and writing and describe precisely the various kinds of writing: what types of writing are more like conversational or informal speech and what types are more formal in character. Moreover, linguists have been derelict in providing for the needs of dictionary users, who many times use the dictionary for the written, not the oral, mode of communication, because the range of what is accepted in writing is often narrower.

If both sides will change from a stubborn attachment to their fixed positions and make some compromises true to the facts of usage in both speech and writing, there can be, Finegan believed, a reconciliation that will lead to more fruitful work.

The concluding sections of Finegan's book—the bibliography of references cited in his work and of suggested readings and the indexes—are most useful for the investigator of language. The bibliography is comprehensive in naming the significant works on English usage, and the index of names and topics and the index of selected usage items make specific information easy to find in the main text.

In contrast to a general sweep of the warring factions in the decision of what constitutes good usage, J. J. Lamberts's *Short Introduction to English Usage* (1972) explains how the history of the language has influenced specific items of usage and how certain forms, according to history, will move predictably in a certain direction or why a divided usage will be kept, namely, because it is functional. Lamberts is most illuminating in his discussion of foreign nouns that become naturalized in the language; the collapsing of verb forms; the reason for the lack of the third person singular inflectional ending in the present tense and the lack of an infinitival form of modals; the reason for adverbs without the *-ly* suffix, like *slow* and *hard*; and the development of sentential or dangling adverbs like *evidently, supposedly, regrettably,* and the much discussed *hopefully.*

Giving a historical perspective to usage, Lamberts's work is explanatory, not just descriptive of the development of preferred forms of usage, although some of his judgments are far too conservative because there are variants not mentioned or accepted by him that are cited as acceptable in today's dictionaries.

Clearly, an understanding of the history of the English language is essential in wise decisions about usage.

Semantic Shifts and Word Formation

Although the traditionalists ridicule current usage whereby old words acquire new meanings not found in dictionaries and words take on new prefixes or suffixes, these critics in many instances show ignorance of the systematic processes by which words acquire new meanings and the systematic methods of coining new words. Rather than condemning all such instances as evidence of slovenly, haphazard, and decadent usage, the traditionalists need to know the processes of word formation and semantic shifts to realize how a number of present-day words once scorned as vulgar or disreputable are now prefectly well accepted. Only the passage of time—not legislation by experts—decides how users regard the words' respectability and whether they will remain in the language.

In word formation, for example, clipping commonly occurs, producing a racy flavor to words that may at first be considered slang and thus are unacceptable in writing but that may later become acceptable: for example, *mob* for *mobile vulgus* and *stress* for *distress*. *Mob* was one of the words condemned by Swift as slang; on the other hand, *rep* for *reputation*, also condemned by Swift, is still considered slang. Most of these examples from Chapter 9 in Albert Baugh and Thomas Cable's *History of the English Language* (1978) illustrate that only actual usage by speakers of a language determines the future status of words.

Chapter 11, "New Words from Old," in Thomas Pyles and John Algeo's *Origins and Development of the English Language* (1982) and the same chapter in the accompanying workbook by Algeo, *Problems in the Origins and Development of the English Language* (1982), cite different processes of word formation: types of clipping—*aphesis* (clipping of the first and unaccented syllable of a word) and *back formation* (clipping of the back part of a word to produce a new word); *blending* or *telescoping* (creation of portmanteau words); acronyms; *folk etymology* (mispronunciation of foreign words, resulting in new word derivations unrelated to the meaning of the original foreign words); *eponymy* (common words from proper names); literary coinages; *functional shifts* (change of part of speech of a word without deleting or adding any new element); onomatopeia; compounding; *affixation* (prefixing and suffixing); and *root creations* (invention of words *ex nihilo*). Because most new words are not invented *ex nihilo* but result from new combinations of familiar roots or affixes, the innovative results may at first seem strange or slangy, but many times they gradually acquire respectability with time.

In Chapter 12, "Foreign Elements in the English Word Stock," Pyles and Algeo cited another source of new words: loan words or calques.

Other sources giving a detailed survey of processes in word formation are Appendix 1, "Word Formation," in Randolph Quirk and colleague's *Grammar of Contemporary English* (1972); Chapter 10, "What Happens to Words," in J. N. Hook's *History of the English Language* (1975); Chapter 13, "Recent Developments," in W. F. Bolton's *Living Language* (1982); and Chapter 12,

"Derivation," in J. J. Lamberts's *Short Introduction to English Usage* (1972). Good illustrative examples of the gradual settlement and usage of word forms and their meanings are cited in Hook and Bolton.

Rather than looking on innovation as decadence, inventions of new words or use of new word forms from old words can be seen from a positive perspective: the fertility, ingenuity, and inventive capacity of the human mind to combine and recombine various roots, inflections, and affixes in the language to express new ideas. Such an orientation is evident in the appendix of Harold Wentworth and Stuart Berg Flexner's *Dictionary of American Slang* (1975), where the same processes of word formation are found to be applied in the creation of slang. Slang, then, can be viewed as creativity and renewal. Current usage may reject newly created forms from more formal stylistic uses for a time, but users of the language will eventually decide what words will be accorded the dignity of being fully reputable members of the language.

The regularity of principles of word formation and their psychological reality are shown in Chapter 7, "Morphology," in Adrian Akmajian and colleague's *Linguistics* (1979), which demonstrates how speakers' intuitions of the underlying properties of suffixes and the underlying syntactic properties of certain verbs are so strong that even nonsense words based on certain linguistic verb patterns follow the same rules.

The same view of flexibility and creativity in word formation can be applied to the regular tendency of familiar or old words to acquire new meanings. Most often, the added meanings indicate a broadening of the original definition by metaphoric or metonymic interpretations of the original or older meanings of a word. This generalizing of well-established meanings of words is explained and illustrated well in the introduction to the appendix of Harold Wentworth and Stuart Berg Flexner's *Dictionary of American Slang* (1975), where a metaphoric interpretation is called *radiation* and where a metonymic interpretation is termed *concatenation*.

The variety of semantic processes evident in semantic shifts of words is also discussed and illustrated in detail in Chapter 10, "Words and Meanings," of Pyles and Algeo's *Origins and Development of the English Language* (1982) and the same chapter in the accompanying workbook by Algeo, where these shifts are named: generalization; specialization; transfer of meaning through metaphor, metonymy, synecdoche, synesthesia, reversal of abstract or concrete level, reversal of objective or subjective point of view, sound associations, and influence of meaning from a parallel word in another language; pejoration and amelioration; taboo and euphemism; palliation; popular use of words of learned origin; and the use of desexed language. The next best discussion after Pyles and Algeo's comprehensive treatment is Chapter 10, "What Happens to Words," is J. N. Hook's *History of the English Language* (1975).

No doubt, regularity of principles of word formation and semantic shifts indicates systematic and underlying application of rules. Too often, however, change is equated with quixotic corruption in language.

Lexicography

To judge fairly and intelligently the admonitions on various usage items advocated by various contemporary dictionaries, the evaluator must know the history of lexicography: the aims, assumptions, and achievements or results of various dictionaries in the past and their influence on current dictionaries. The reason is that new dictionaries are often produced not only by interleaving pages of old dictionaries with new words, but also by accepting and perpetrating the old word usages, even if they are outdated, inadequate, or erroneous. Pyles and Algeo's *Origins and Development of the English Language* (1982, pp. 207, 208) and especially the material in the accompanying workbook, Algeo's *Problems in the Origins and Development of the English Language* (1982, pp. 214–19), section 8.9, "The Early Dictionaries," present the evolution of the early dictionaries up to Samuel Johnson's dictionary of 1755.

To know how Johnson's 1755 *Dictionary of the English Language* embodied the ideals of his time—the neo-classic age's goals of ascertaining and fixing the language, of codifying the rules of the language, and of settling divided usage—one should understand that Johnson's work substituted for an academy of language in the area of vocabulary. (See the books on the history of the English language cited above in the history discussion in this chapter.) Whereas Bishop Lowth provided a prescriptive grammar, Johnson in his dictionary provided prescriptive judgments on the vocabulary of the language. But despite the follies of Johnson's work—its inaccurate and false etymologies; its foolish condemnation of certain items of usage, totally prescriptive and thus subsequently failing the test of time; and some definitions blatantly reflecting the author's prejudices—a student of usage should recognize its monumental accomplishments. Not only was there an attempt to list and treat all of the words of the language, but his definitions, for the most part, were not false and foolish. The majority of his definitions were surprisingly rational, citing illustrative quotations from actual authors to justify the various definitions of words, a practice followed by the nineteenth and the early twentieth centuries' *OED*, which is still lauded for basing its entries on actual historical data, as evidenced in the illustrative quotations for each definition.

Moreover, one should read the preface to Johnson's dictionary (for example, in *Major British Writers*, Vol. 1 [1959], pp. 928–37) to see not only Johnson's erroneous assumptions about language but also his true insight into the nature of usage from his work in lexicography. Although he considered change as evidence of decay in language and elegance as earlier language use—beliefs even held by today's traditionalists—he also recognized the folly of trying to make usage immutable: he understood correctly that he could not stop natural processes of evolution in usage, that all of the academies' efforts in other countries were in vain. From the evidence he discovered, he reduced his goal from freezing the language to retarding its decay. The great traditionalist and absolutist thus acknowledged the inevitability of change. James Sledd and Gwin J. Kolb's

Dr. Johnson's Dictionary (1955) discussed these shortcomings and strengths of Johnson's work and showed how subsequent landmark dictionaries also fulfilled the ideals of their age.

But perhaps no dictionary met such a violent fury against its merits as *Webster's III* of 1961. Raven I. McDavid, Jr.'s "False Scents and Cold Trails" (1971) cites ten basic factors on how the prepublication promotional releases goaded critics to think that the new dictionary degraded the language, destroying all that was good, true, and beautiful. Belletristic writers, popularizers of language, editorial writers, journalists, and professional book reviewers—in short, the self-appointed pundits of language—were horrified about the information in the early publicity releases of Merriam because of its emphasis on the novelty of the new dictionary. Rather than a work for scholars, the dictionary seemed to be for a mass audience, these legislators thought, as they read the publicity that emphasized the unconventionally popular sources of illustrative quotations—the celebrities of the sports and entertainment world and pedestrian literature, such as a TWA timetable for *no-show*, sources that constituted only a small fraction of the quotations. Such persons and literature were not deemed worthy as models and authorities on language by the reviewers. The press especially played up the dictionary's approval of the word *ain't*, ignoring the dictionary's careful caveat about its use. Many journalists took the dictionary's statement that "Ain't I?" was used by many cultivated speakers as wholesale endorsement for the use of *ain't*. Thus the first press releases of *Webster's III* provoked a rapid onslaught of vicious attacks against the dictionary even before it was available. Acknowledging its considerable accomplishments, which, McDavid said, override its faults, he then criticized the dictionary because of its paucity of status labels, single-phrase definitions, lack of a pronunciation line on each page, and typography.

But capitalizing on the supposed defects of *Webster's III*, the *American Heritage Dictionary*, McDavid pointed out, sought to rectify the alleged follies through a usage panel largely stacked with those against *Webster's III*, experts who could thus be trusted to produce prescriptive admonitions with many restrictions on certain matters of usage. McDavid cited Roy Copperud as the only one of the 105 panel members who approved of *Webster's III*.

In marked contrast to the popular pundits' attacks on *Webster's III* as a contributor to the erosion of good usage, reviews of the dictionary by scholars largely supported the dictionary as a landmark in faithfully following the science of descriptive linguistics and thought that its shortcomings did not vitiate the strengths of its scholarship. Robert G. Gunderson's "Webster's Third New International Dictionary" (1962) includes the reviews of respected linguists—Harold B. Allen; Margaret Bryant; Robert A. Hall, Jr.; Raven I. McDavid, Jr.; John B. Newman; Allen Walker Read; and Robert Sonkin. Of these scholars, only the last one is critical of the dictionary: Sonkin expressed dissatisfaction with the dictionary's handling of pronunciation.

A good casebook on lexicographical history and the exact comments of critics of *Webster's III* is James Sledd and Wilma R. Ebbitt's *Dictionaries and That Dictionary* (1962). Part 1, "Some Dictionaries," includes excerpts from the prefaces to Samuel Johnson's 1755 dictionary and Noah Webster's 1828 dictionary as well as Richard Chenevix Trench's 1857 report "On Some Deficiencies in Our English Dictionaries," which launched work on the *OED*. Part 2, "Materials for Judgment," reprints critical articles on both sides of the debate concerning the new dictionary: condemnation by various traditionalists like the American Bar Association, Wilson Follett, Dwight McDonald, and Mario Pei and commendation and justification from linguists like Philip B. Gove, James Sledd, and Patrick E. Kilburn.

The gross discrepancies among dictionaries are discussed in Thomas J. Creswell's "Usage in Contemporary American Dictionaries" (1977), which shows the alarming inconsistency of dictionaries and usage handbooks in their identification of problems of usage and their treatment or lack of treatment on various matters of usage. He showed the differences in results of the *American Heritage*'s admonitions when compared with the objective studies of Sterling A. Leonard's *Current English Usage* (1932), Albert H. Marckwardt and Fred Walcott's *Facts about Current English Usage* (1938), and Raymond D. Crisp's "Changes in Attitudes Toward English Usage" (1971). He accounted for the undue conservatism of the AHD panel in the dictionary's attempt to rectify *Webster III*'s supposed permissiveness and abrogation of authority and in its usage panel of older and more conservative critics, many of whom already had published articles highly critical of *Webster III*'s liberalism. Creswell deplored the prejudicial frames of the usage notes and the problems in reporting the usage panel votes: for example, irregularity in reporting the exact figure, unevenness in stating whether the judgment was made in reference to the written or oral medium, discrepancy between editorial application of restrictive labels and the data, and the problem of interpreting the data when a wide range of experts' opinions resulted. The article ends with an appendix listing the 318 locutions on which the ADH panel voted.

A cursory glance at the recently published second college edition of the *American Heritage Dictionary* (1982) indicates a new policy, a uniformity in not mentioning the exact percentage in the votes of the usage panel, and a growing movement toward liberalization of usage restrictions. Thus there is now no restrictive usage label or note for *balding, senior citizen, bimonthly* ("happening twice a month") and *biweekly* ("twice a week"); *enthuse* is still labeled as *informal* but now without any usage note disparaging its use. However, *finalize* and *contact* as verbs are still condemned.

Language Variation

Because effective writers adopt a *persona* (a speaking voice) or identity and shape their language for a certain purpose, audience, and occasion, the variety of language usage chosen should be appropriate to the rhetorical context. The composition teacher and the researcher should thus be aware of dialects—regional and social—and cultural and functional varieties or registers of English and the close relation between dialect and identity. The researcher needs to know, for example, of dialectal usage accepted only in informal speech, of those accepted in both speech and writing, of non-standard variants that affect the basic writing student's choices, of sexual and other social variations of language, and of the social and linguistic reasons that make it difficult for a person to be bidialectal.

A knowledge of linguistic diversity will enable teachers to be more tolerant toward divided usage and less prone to engage in dichotomous judgments of "correct" or "incorrect" when writers and speakers accept more than one form. But even though a teacher's goal is to move non-standard speakers toward standard English, cognizance of the systematic or rule-governed character of the non-standard modes should improve teachers' attitudes toward students, who are often judged inferior because their language is erroneously considered slovenly, haphazard, impoverished, non-logical, and deprived. But a linguistic analysis of dialects shows that even non-standard forms exhibit systematic rules, ingenuity, creativity, soundness of logic, and expressive power just as potent and effective as standard varieties of English. Non-standard dialects are stigmatized not because of linguistic inferiority but because of their association with class status: they are not spoken by the middle class or prestigious persons who wield power.

A good source for the beginner who wishes to explore the rich variety of information about dialects and registers of English is Harold B. Allen and Michael D. Linn's *Readings in Applied English Linguistics* (1982), Parts 4 and 5: "Regional and Social Variation" and "Linguistics and Usage." The introductory section to Part 4 gives succinct information on the roots of Hans Kurath's *Work Sheets for the Linguistic Atlas of the United States and Canada* (1931) in the accomplishments of the German, French, and Italian atlases; the range of publications and offshoots of the *Atlas* project (although out of date); important books and publications on dialectology, such as William Labov's groundbreaking dissertation *The Social Stratification of English in New York City* (1966), and important periodicals in the field; and Black speech, the rise of racial consciousness and pride in minority dialects, and bidialectalism and the reasons for the difficulty of mastering standard English.

In Part 4 Harold B. Allen's "*Linguistic Atlas of the Upper Midwest* [LAUM] as a Source of Sociolinguistic Information" (1982) presents information that teachers can use to predict the type of usage problems that will appear in student writing because of the way people speak in a certain region. The information is clearly representative of what can be found in LAUM: an amazing range of Type I (non-educated) forms extending to Types II (high school educated) and III (college-educated) speech. Some forms, such as the substitution of *laid* for *lay*, are used by as many as 47 percent of Type III speakers; and the pronunciation of *fists* as *fist* or *fis* is present in 46 percent of Type III speakers: a clear revelation to teachers of usage that even college students from middle-class homes in the

Upper Midwest may have problems with *lie* and *lay* and problems in writing the plural of *fist* for agreement of subject and verb because of the pronunciation of *fists* as *fist* or *fis*.

The relation between language variation and identity is established in the Allen and Linn anthology (1982) in the articles on sex—Mary Ritchie Key's "Linguistic Behavior of Male and Female" in Part 4 and Robin Lakoff's "Language in Context" in Part 5—and in the Part 4 articles on Black versus White speech—Bruce Fraser's "Some 'Unexpected' Reactions to Various American English Dialects," Robbins Burling's "Black English," and Roger D. Abrahams's "Black Talking on the Streets." These articles reveal that language variation and dialect are closely related to identity and culture. Therefore, one can surmise that any attempt to change someone's dialect or register has grave social consequences that may not always be desired by those learning another register or dialect.

But no substitute for a study of dialects is a thorough grounding in the linguistic atlas materials that have been published—*The Linguistic Atlas of New England* (1939–1943), edited by Hans Kurath; *The Linguistic Atlas of the Upper Midwest* (1973–1976), edited by Harold B. Allen; and *The Linguistic Atlas of the Gulf States*, (1981–1982), edited by Lee Pederson—and offshoots based on the atlas materials. Although the records of even the most recently published work have often been collected decades before publication and although the data are of the oral variety and not of the edited English of the written medium, the linguistic atlases, their offshoots, and the atlases yet to be published—such as Raven I. McDavid's *Linguistic Atlas of the North Central States* and *Linguistic Atlas of the Middle and Atlantic States*—present the best in scholarly procedures in systematic collection, elicitation, and control of results. Moreover, the written language of students—even of middle-class students—is often a reflection of their speech. Unfortunately, the actual field records and tapes of informants are not easily accessible to all but are most useful for validating the claims of usage experts.

Guy Bailey and Marvin Bassett, for example, field workers for the *Linguistic Atlas of the Gulf States*, reported in their presentation "Invariant *Be* in the South" (1981) at the conference "Language Variety in the South" in Columbia, South Carolina, that habitual *be*, once widely thought a mark of Black speech, was a prevalent form among certain old White speakers in various parts of the South.

Therefore, one must scrutinize critically Robbins Burling's *English in Black and White* (1973). This is a popular, readable book describing features of Black speech, their pedagogical implications, their stigmatic consequences, the verbal culture of Black speech and the two competing theories of the origins of Black speech—the earlier English hypothesis versus the creole hypothesis. However, a person must not, as Burling himself warned, label every feature as Black or of African or creole origin. Too often, when the speech of Blacks is thought of as exotic and foreign, teachers lower their expectations of this minority, thinking it is hopeless to change the dialectal errors in the writing of these students.

One should therefore be open to new empirical research. Ralph W. Fasold's

"Relation between Black and White Speech in the South" (1981) is one of the most up-to-date accounts scaling down the features once considered innate in Black speech to only a few selected features. Interestingly, the article still lists habitual *be* as present only in Black language, contrary to the later discovery by Bailey and Bassett from the *Linguistic Atlas of the Gulf States* field records. As Raven I. McDavid, Jr., and Virginia McDavid's "Relation of the Speech of American Negroes to the Speech of Whites" (1951) warns, researchers have used linguistic records naively without knowing what studies are necessary in judging what features are Black. Theories of Black dialect, McDavid stated, have ranged from the primitive ability of Africans to pronounce English to the retainment of the provincial dialects of Great Britain to genuine Africanisms. He cautioned that the data examined must be measured against features used by White persons from the same area from which the Blacks came. For example, Juanita Williamson's "Selected Features of Speech" (1971) demonstrates how features labeled as *Black* by some linguists from the literature of Black characters' speech are used by non-Black people when one looks in the prose of newspapers, fiction, learned scholars, and southern White speech. Thus caution is warranted.

To read linguistic works on dialect, one should be acquainted with how sounds are produced, the natural processes of sound change, and various methods of transcription. Chapter 2, "The Sounds and Spelling of Current English," in Thomas Pyles and John Algeo's *Origins and Development of the English Language* (1982) and the same chapter in Algeo's accompanying workbook (1982) are excellent sources for an introduction to phonology and the natural processes that occur, such as epenthesis, metathesis, assimilation, dissimilation, aphesis, and changes in stress and the resulting dialectal variants that are produced. Moreover, some problems in usage—for example, *ice tea* for *iced tea* and *can goods* for *canned goods*—have a phonological basis: consonant cluster simplification, in this instance. Another resource for information on the production and transcription of sounds is Harold Gleason's *Introduction to Descriptive Linguistics* (1961)—Chapter 2, "English Consonants," and Chapter 3, "The English Vowel System" and the accompanying chapters in the workbook.

Twentieth-Century Usage Studies and the Current Thrust

Twentieth-century usage studies have attempted to ascertain the facts of usage to replace the typical mythic admonitions and simplistic prescriptions in usage textbooks for students. Professional societies such as the National Council of Teachers of English, the Modern Language Association, and the American Dialect Society encouraged, endorsed, and funded such studies.

But with the rise of the great social movements and uprisings in the 1960s— the protest against Watergate and Vietnam, the civil rights battle for minorities, the women's movement and the Equal Rights Amendment, and cries for environmental protection—the investigation of usage took a social orientation: the discovery of deliberate obfuscation in euphemistic, hifalutin, and highly technical jargon by those in power to mask the unpleasant reality of a situation, to condone and justify immoral practices, and to keep those without power powerless. Work in current usage studies still reflects this thrust.

With the influx of non-traditional students in the 1960s, caused, in part, by open admissions and integration, there has been an equal emphasis on discovering the fastest methods of teaching correct usage and of placing as highest priority ways to overcome non-standard usage that stigmatized its users as unintelligent, socially unacceptable, and inferior. Less attention was paid to the hairsplitting niceties and nuances of belletrists. Instead of ridiculing errors, teachers and usage experts began to find the strengths and intelligence in the worst of errors to help minority students gain standard written English.

Finally, the current thrust has also questioned the more descriptive studies in this century and challenged their assumptions and practices.

The seminal study upon which most important twentieth-century work is based in discovering the facts of usage is Sterling Andrus Leonard's *Current English Usage* (1932). Part 1 consists of questions on punctuation, but Part 2 deals with items conventionally considered as usage. To determine whether the cherished rules of textbooks corresponded to reality or were arbitrary, Leonard used a wide variety of judges to decide the status of 230 items of usage. The judges came from different groups: linguistic experts (lexicographers, philologists, and grammarians), active members of the NCTE, well-known authors, editors of influential publications, leading businessmen, members of the Modern Language Association (MLA), and teachers of speech. They were asked to rank the items according to this system: 1—formally correct English, literary English; 2—fully acceptable English for informal conversation, that is, standard, colloquial cultivated usage; 3—technical terms; and 4—popular or illiterate speech not passing as cultivated, except for jocose use (often called "vulgar [common] English" with no disparagement meant). However, rank 3 proved unnecessary since there were few technical terms.

Items were rated "established" if they were approved as cultivated usage (rank of 1 or 2) by at least 75 percent of the judges and disapproved by not more than 25 percent; "disputable" if they were approved by fewer than 75 percent and disapproved by more than 25 percent; "illiterate" if they were disapproved by more than 75 percent and approved by fewer than 25 percent of the judges. The results of each item and the results according to the different judges are discussed. The results of the linguistic group, which serves as a touchstone for what usage results should be, are compared to the ranking of all other judges. There is also a ranking of items according to a per capita vote of all judges. Handily available is an index of items tested and discussed in the text.

Leonard thought it would be a waste of time if teachers drilled on what was listed as established. The finer points of style, he believed, should be taught only to those who have already mastered the more crucial usages that separated the cultivated from the illiterate. Items established as disputable should not be called to the attention of average students, he advocated.

Because the Leonard study reported only the opinions of judges and not what the judges employed in actual usage, Albert H. Marckwardt and Fred C. Walcott's *Facts about Current English Usage* (1938) studied recorded usage of the same 230 items, dividing the items according to those judged "established" by the linguists and the per capita vote of all judges; those voted "established" by the linguists and "disputable" by the per capita vote of all the judges in the pioneering study; and those judged "disputable" and "illiterate" in Leonard's seminal study. For empirical evidence, Marckwardt and Walcott used the *OED, Webster's II*, usage and grammar books by respected grammarians, and, in a few instances, scholarly journals. Because Leonard's study revealed a discrepancy between American and British English, this scheme of ranking was used: 1—Literary English; 2—American Literary English; 3—Colloquial English; 4—American Colloquial English; 5—Dialect; 6—Archaic.

Moreover, the two researchers scrutinized the illustrative citations of the items under study when there was no usage label to determine the status of the items. Scrupulously seeking for the facts of actual usage, they also adjusted the classification of items when there was a mismatch between the status label and the illustrative citations. The study revealed that Leonard's judges were far too conservative on all three types of usage examined.

Following this objective approach to discovering the facts of usage with painstaking care and scrupulous objectivity is Margaret M. Bryant's *Current English Usage* (1962). It is a respectable work, faithful in discriminating between speech and writing, standard and non-standard forms, and the citation of variant or alternate forms in percentages of frequency. For each of the 240 alphabetical entries, which are cross-referenced, there is a succinct summary before a fuller discussion. Collection of data and editing for the study, an outgrowth of the Committee on Current English Usage appointed by NCTE, occurred between 1952 and 1961. Other professional societies, such as the Modern Language Association, the American Dialect Society, and the Speech Association of America, endorsed this endeavor. Not only the usage committee of NCTE, but also dozens of distinguished specialists, such as Jean Malstrom, Raven I. McDavid, Jr., Virginia McDavid, John Algeo, James McMillan, and Harold B. Allen, and their advanced students took part in the study to supplement the information in Kurath's *Linguistic Atlas of New England* (1939–1943), which had already been published, and the materials from the files of the other atlases. Bryant's work is out of date, having been published two decades ago, reflecting past usage and lacking current information such as actual recorded usage in Pederson's *Linguistic Atlas of the Gulf States* (1981–1982). But it is a distinguished piece of scholarship.

Raymond Dwight Crisp's unpublished dissertation "Changes in Attitudes Toward English Usage" (1971) attempted to replicate the Leonard study to discover if the gap between actual recorded usage and opinions toward usage had been closed. Items where there was no dispute were excluded from the study, questions that had a quaint flavor were re-written, and new items deemed as problems, such as *finalize, ice tea, weather-wise*, and *contact* as a verb, were added. His new categories for ranking items were as follows: 1—Literary English; 2—Literary and Standard English; 3—Standard English; and 4—Non-standard English. However, there was a problem with these categories in that judges placed few items exclusively in number 1 and thought that many colloquial items were also used in literary English, depending upon the rhetorical context: thus the problems with 2 and 3. Therefore, the judges' complaints reflected the growing overlap between literary and colloquial English and the increasing sophistication in awareness that items of usage could be judged only within their rhetorical context. Crisp used 17 groups of judges, including the *American Heritage Dictionary* Usage Panel, but as in Leonard's survey, the group of "Language Specialists" was considered the touchstone in the analysis of the results. The language specialists proved the most liberal; the *American Heritage Dictionary* Usage Panel, the most conservative. Data for dialectal differences were analyzed by geographical regions but yielded no significant results.

Although judges' comments indicated a difficulty in separating their preference from actual usage, there was a clear movement toward liberalization. Although there were exceptions, many of Leonard's "disputable" items advanced to the "established" range, and many of Leonard's "illiterate" items were judged as "disputable" in the Crisp survey, showing that even opinions about usage, despite their conservative and subjective nature, liberalize with time.

Thomas J. Creswell's *Usage in Dictionaries and Dictionaries of Usage* (1975) takes ten books on usage, including the Leonard, Crisp, and Bryant studies, compares them with the 318 usage items of the *American Heritage Dictionary*'s Usage Panel, and comments on the disquieting lack of agreement on problematic usage items and the great inconsistency of usage handbooks and dictionaries in treating, accepting, or restricting various items. Creswell disparaged the constant reliance of various usage books on certain authors of usage, because their "incestuous practice," he maintained, produces "inbreeding" that magnifies inaccurate judgments, especially when little attention is paid to empirical data. Moreover, even when usage books, particularly the popular ones, try to be objective, they invariably render a decision based on the authors' own opinions despite the recorded facts of usage.

But since the 1960s, with the rise of the great social and political movements, the traditional content of usage study has turned from the typical matters listed under any glossary of usage in a handbook to a disclosure of the insidious uses of language to deceive, obscure, or palliate unethical practices—an orientation embodied in the NCTE's establishment of a Committee on Doublespeak and its annual award to the person who has used the most florid, jargonish, and Orwellian language for obfuscation. *Language and Public Policy* (1974), edited by Hugh Rank, is also concerned with the unethical misuses of language. It shows how the public was manipulated by the government and inured to the atrocities in Vietnam through euphemistic language; it also names phrases that made the immorality of Watergate palatable to its instigators and participants.

Some incisive analysis has resulted from examination of sexist language and women's use of language to show the supportive and subservient role women are expected to play in our society and their struggle to overcome language that fosters a lack of equality and power. The linguistic characteristics in our language militating against equality and the linguistic modes of expression thrust upon women prohibiting their treatment as peers of men are analyzed well in works such as Robin Lakoff's *Language and Woman's Place* (1975), Mary Ritchie Key's *Male/Female Language with a Comprehensive Bibliography* (1975), Barbara Westbrook Eakins and R. Gene Eakins's *Sex Differences in Human Communication* (1978), and Maxine S. Rose's "Sexism in Five Leading Collegiate Dictionaries" (1979).

Such social and political concerns are part of the current thrust in usage studies along with a discriminating examination of which types of errors are more serious than others, including cases where a label for a particular error does not reveal the gradations of severity. Some errors generally considered bad, moreover, may go unnoticed because of various factors, such as lack of confusion despite the errors, the general high quality of the prose, the arrangements of words making some errors less noticeable, the incorrect assessment of handbooks that such errors are grievous, or the rhetorical context.

Joseph M. Williams's "The Phenomenology of Error" (1981) trenchantly points out that some errors are worse than others and that not all errors are atrocious or clumsy, despite what handbooks say. The subjective reaction to errors in a passage should be measured, he advised. The effects of following or deviating from the rules of usage may be classified under these categories: (1) the violation of a rule that causes an unfavorable reaction; (2) the adherence to a rule that causes a favorable reaction; (3) the violation of a rule that causes a favorable reaction; and (4) the adherence to a rule that causes an unfavorable reaction. Thus there is a danger, he maintained, of engaging in error hunting and not considering the overall communicative power of an essay. Research should delve into discovering which rules do not bother readers, he said.

For example, the most admired stylists—such as E. B. White, H. W. Fowler, Jacques Barzun, and George Orwell—Williams pointed out, break their own admonitions and rules about writing without being detected by their readers. The subjective experience, he argued, of not being distracted by some errors is more reliable in judging a piece of work than the objective knowledge of the kinds and frequency of rules that are broken in a work. The most serious errors are those that are glaringly distracting to a reader upon first reading.

Williams made his point by saying that he purposely included 100 errors in his prose, which is quite readable, and wishes the readers of *College Composition and Communication* to name the errors that they noticed in his article upon first reading. Certainly Williams's classification of errors is more complex than previous research, such as the Leonard and the Crisp studies, which judged the acceptability of an item of usage only within a given sentence, often a short one where the error could be blatantly discovered, and always without a rhetorical context.

Other works on usage also challenge the basic assumptions of previous admonitions: Jane R. Walpole's "Why Must the Passive Be Damned?" (1979),

Dean Baldwin's "When Is the Second Person Appropriate in Writing?" (1981), and Martha Kolln's "Closing the Books on Alchemy" (1981), which points out the incorrect conclusion reached by past researchers that the teaching of grammar or usage may have a harmful effect on the improvement of writing. This conclusion, Kolln argued, is misleading, simplistic, and not true to the facts of the data of researchers who make such a claim.

But no doubt the thrust in pedagogy to concentrate on the most stigmatic errors and the consideration of error as a strength rather than as a liability arose from the influx of non-traditional student minorities in colleges. In particular, the seminal work of Mina P. Shaughnessy is discussed in the next section.

Linguistics and Pedagogy

Although the NCTE's resolution "Students' Right to Their Own Language" was passed by its members at the 1974 Spring Conference on College Composition and Communication, and this resolution and a statement of the theory and pragmatic consequences for the adoption of such a stance was printed in the *CCC* (1974), a position that affirmed students had a right to "the dialects of their nurture or whatever dialects in which they find their own identity and style," no school has taken such an extreme view that standard English should not be taught (p. 2). If certain leaders of the NCTE believed in the literal words of the resolution and the rationale as printed in the *CCC*, certainly the rank and file have understood otherwise: that standard English must be taught lest non-standard speakers be barred from the mainstream of society. The resolution and statement, however, have served to warn teachers against misjudging a student's abilities because of the student's non-standard dialect.

The resolution and statement were a culmination of a momentous proposal at the NCTE by James Sledd in the late 1960s to move from bidialectalism (the position held by language specialists as the most enlightened approach to teaching speakers of non-standard dialects) to the radical stance of allowing speakers to use non-standard dialects, as he stated in "Bi-Dialectalism" (1969). However, some who have heard Sledd speak on several occasions have tried to ascertain the degree to which he meant literally what he said—the extent to which he overstated his case to awaken middle-class teachers to the validity of all dialects and to the miniscule importance of prescriptive usage rules taught in the classroom when the results gained were few and disappointing.

Teachers were indeed frustrated by the lack of progress of their non-standard speaking students. There was a period of experimenting and floundering with Teaching English as a Second Language (TESL) methods to remedy gross errors in usage, as seen in the various essays in Part 3 of "Standard and Nonstandard English" in David L. Shores's *Contemporary English* (1972). Because the pattern drills and substitution exercises were mindless and lacked the challenge of communicative competence, students often went through the motion of their lessons without learning the rules or refused to comply with the teacher.

Progress was made, however, in the last decade and a half in defining more explicitly and carefully the grossest errors, in proposing a sequence and a methodology for teaching these items, and in citing what items of usage are merely niceties or nuances to be ignored for students struggling to master the standard dialect. Raven I. McDavid, Jr.'s "Checklist of Significant Features for Discriminating Social Dialects" (1973) and William Card and Virginia Glenn McDavid's "Problem Areas in Grammar" in A. L. Davis's *Culture, Class, and Language Variety* (1973), and Robert C. Pooley's *Teaching of English Usage* (1975) are examples of such work. Pooley, moreover, gave a sequence of usage items to be taught and accompanying teaching activities from the elementary grades through high school and presented diagnostic and evaluative measures.

But no doubt it is Mina Shaughnessy's *Errors and Expectations* (1977) that has become the bible for basic writing teachers to overcome stigmatic usage as well as other language errors. The pedagogical suggestions show how various matters can be taught in a thorough and systematic fashion through innovative and ingenious techniques, although hard work is required by both student and teacher. With the flood of open admissions at CUNY, Shaughnessy with insight and compassion recognized "the intelligence to all the errors," errors often revealing partial knowledge and often resulting from the misapplication of rules, because the rules taught did not cover all cases.

Her detailed sample lessons on teaching the *-s* marker for the third-person singular verb in the present tense, the possessive case, the plural noun, and words "born with an '*s*'" cleverly show how to relate neatly and clearly in one place items usually found in different parts of a usage handbook. Her comments on developing the idiomatic usage of prepositions, correct verb forms, and the correct forms of other parts of speech are also most helpful.

Although much advancement has taken place in theoretical and pedagogical research on usage, the average classroom teacher is often unaware of studies on usage, never having taken a course in linguistics, history of the English language, or modern grammars. Anne Ruggles Gere and Eugene Smith's *Attitudes, Language, and Change* (1979) gives some suggestions for changing the minds of professionals about judgments on usage, one of the most difficult tasks to achieve. Unlike researchers and the leaders of professional organizations on English, the rank and file of the teaching profession are often lamentably ignorant of the facts of usage and the dynamics of language.

References

Abrahams, Roger D. "Black Talking on the Streets." *Readings in Applied English Linguistics.* 3rd ed. Ed. Harold B.G. Allen and Michael D. Linn. New York: Knopf, 1982, pp. 259–80.

Akmajian, Adrian, et al. *Linguistics: An Introduction to Language and Communication.* Cambridge, Mass.: M.I.T. Press, 1979.

Algeo, John. *Problems in the Origins and Development of the English Language.* 3rd ed. New York: Harcourt, 1982.

Allen, Harold B. *The Linguistic Atlas of the Upper Midwest*. 3 vols. Minneapolis: University of Minnesota Press, 1973–1976.

———. "The *Linguistic Atlas of the Upper Midwest* as a Source of Sociolinguistic Information." *Readings in Applied English Linguistics*. 3rd ed. Ed. Harold B. Allen and Michael D. Linn. New York: Knopf, 1982, pp. 210–20.

———, and Michael D. Linn. *Readings in Applied English Linguistics*. 3rd ed. New York: Knopf, 1982.

American Heritage Dictionary (1982).

Bailey, Guy, and Marvin Bassett. "Invariant *Be* in the South." Language Variety in the South: Perspectives in Black and White, NEH Conference, Columbia, S.C. 2 Oct. 1981.

Baldwin, Dean. "When Is the Second Person Appropriate in Writing?" *CCC*, 32 (1981), 222–24.

Baugh, Albert C., and Thomas Cable. *A History of the English Language*. 3rd ed. Englewood Cliffs, N.J.: Prentice-Hall, 1978.

Bolton, W. F. *A Living Language: The History and Structure of English*. New York: Random House, 1982.

Bryant, Margaret M. *Current English Usage*. New York: Funk, Wagnalls, 1962.

Burling, Robbins. *English in Black and White*. New York: Holt, Rinehart, Winston, 1973.

———. "Black English." In *Readings in Applied English Linguistics*. 3rd ed. Ed. Harold B. Allen and Michael D. Linn. New York: Knopf, 1982, pp. 246–58.

Card, William, and Virginia Glenn McDavid. "Problem Areas in Grammar." In *Culture, Class, and Language Variety*. Ed. A. L. Davis. Urbana, Ill: NCTE, 1973, pp. 89–132.

Creswell, Thomas J. *Usage in Dictionaries and Dictionaries of Usage*. Publication of the American Dialect Society, Nos. 63–64. Tuscaloosa: University of Alabama Press, 1975.

———. "Usage in Contemporary American Dictionaries." *Babel*, 23 (1977), 23–28. Rpt. in *Readings in Applied English Linguistics*. 3rd ed. Ed. Harold B. Allen and Michael D. Linn. New York: Knopf, 1982, pp. 503–11.

Crisp, Raymond Dwight. "Changes in Attitudes Toward English Usage." Diss. University of Illinois at Urbana-Champaign, 1971.

Davis, A. L. *Culture, Class, and Language Variety*. Urbana, Ill.: NCTE, 1973.

DeCamp, David. "Dimensions of English Usage." In *Contemporary English: Change and Variation*. Ed. David L. Shores, New York: Lippincott, 1972, pp. 200–215.

Eakins, Barbara Westbrook, and R. Gene Eakins. *Sex Differences in Human Communication*. Boston: Houghton Mifflin, 1978.

Fasold, Ralph W. "The Relation between Black and White Speech in the South." *Am Sp*, 56 (1981), 163–89.

Finegan, Edward. *Attitudes Toward English Usage: The History of a War of Words*. New York: Teachers College Press, 1980.

Fraser, Bruce. "Some 'Unexpected' Reactions to Various American English Dialects." In *Readings in Applied English Linguistics*. 3rd ed. Ed. Harold B. Allen and Michael D. Linn. New York: Knopf, 1982, pp. 221–22.

Fries, C. C. *American English Grammar*. New York: Appleton-Century, 1940.

Gere, Anne Ruggles, and Eugene Smith. *Attitudes, Language, and Change*. Urbana: NCTE, 1979.

Gleason, H. A. *Workbook in Descriptive Linguistics*. New York: Holt, Rinehart, Winston, 1955.

————. *An Introduction to Descriptive Linguistics*. Rev. ed. New York: Holt, Rinehart, Winston, 1961.

Gove, Philip B. Introduction to Part 2, "Standard English: The Problem of Definition." In *Contemporary English: Change and Variation*. Ed. David L. Shores. New York: Lippincott, 1972, pp. 155–59.

Gunderson, Robert G., ed. "Webster's Third New International Dictionary: A Symposium." *QJS*, 48 (1962), 431–40.

Hirsch, Jr., E. D. *The Philosophy of Composition*. Chicago: University of Chicago Press, 1977.

Hook, J. N. *History of the English Language*. New York: Ronald, 1975.

Johnson, Samuel. "Preface to *A Dictionary of the English Language*." In *Major British Writers*. Vol. 1. Ed. G. B. Harrison. New York: Harcourt, Brace, World, 1959.

Joos, Martin. *The Five Clocks*. New York: Harcourt, Brace, World, 1967.

————. "Standards in the Community Language." In *Contemporary English: Change and Variation*. Ed. David L. Shores, New York: Lippincott, 1972, pp. 188–99.

Kenyon, John S. "Cultural Levels and Functional Varieties of English." *CE*, 10 (1948), 31–36.

Key, Mary Ritchie. *Male/Female Language with a Comprehensive Bibliography*. Metuchen, N.J.: Scarecrow, 1975.

————. "Lingusitic Behavior of Male and Female." In *Readings in Applied English Linguistics*. 3rd ed. Ed. Harold B. Allen and Michael D. Linn. New York: Knopf, 1982, pp. 281–94.

Kilburn, Patrick E. "The Gentleman's Guide to Linguistic Etiquette." In *Contemporary English: Change and Variation*. Ed. David L. Shores, New York: Lippincott, 1972, pp. 178–87.

Kolln, Martha. "Closing the Books on Alchemy." *CCC*, 32 (1981), 139–51.

Kurath, Hans. *The Linguistic Atlas of New England*. 3 vols. Providence, R.I.: Brown University, 1939–1943.

Kurath, Hans. *Work Sheets for the Linguistic Atlas of the United States and Canada*. Washington, D.C.: American Council of Learned Societies, 1931.

Labov, William. *The Social Stratification of English in New York City*. Washington, D.C.: Center for Applied Linguistics, 1966.

Lakoff, Robin. "Language in Context." In *Contemporary English: Change and Variation*. Ed. David L. Shores. New York: Lippincott, 1972, pp. 298–317.

————. *Language and Woman's Place*. New York: Harper, Row, 1975.

————. "Language in Context." In *Readings in Applied Linguistics*. 3rd ed. Ed. Harold B. Allen and Michael D. Linn. New York: Knopf, 1982, pp. 298–317.

Lamberts, J. J. *A Short Introduction to English Usage*. New York: McGraw-Hill, 1972.

Leonard, Sterling Andrus. *Current English Usage*. English Monographs, No. 1 [for NCTE]. Chicago: Inland, 1932.

Lowth, Robert. *A Short Introduction to English Grammar: 1762*. English Linguistics 1500–1800, No. 18. 1762; rpt. Menston, England: The Scholar Press Limited, 1967.

Major British Writers. Vol. 1. Ed. G. B. Harrison. New York: Harcourt, Brace, World, 1959.

Marckwardt, Albert H., and Fred G. Walcott. *Facts about Current English Usage*. New York: Appleton-Century-Crofts, 1938.

McCrimmon, James M. *Writing with a Purpose*. Short ed. Boston: Houghton Mifflin, 1973, pp. 161–69.

———. *Writing with a Purpose*. Short ed. Boston: Houghton Mifflin, 1980, 194–97.

McDavid, Jr., Raven I. "False Scents and Cold Trails: The Pre-Publication Criticism of the Merriam *Third*." *J Linguist*, 5 (1971), 101–21.

———. "A Checklist of Significant Features for Discriminating Social Dialects." In *Culture, Class and Language Variety*. By A. L. Davis, Urbana, Ill.: NCTE, 1973, pp. 133–39.

———, and Virginia McDavid. "The Relationship of the Speech of American Negroes to the Speech of Whites." *Am Sp*, 26 (1951), 3–17.

———, ed. *Linguistic Atlas of the Middle and Atlantic States* (forthcoming).

———, ed. *Linguistic Atlas of the North Central States* (forthcoming).

Myers, L. M., and Richard L. Hoffman. *The Roots of Modern English*. 2nd ed. Boston: Little, Brown, 1979.

Pederson, Lee. *The Linguistic Atlas of the Gulf States*. Ann Arbor: University Microfilms, 1981–1982.

Pooley, Robert C. *The Teaching of English Usage*. 2nd ed. Urbana: NCTE, 1975.

Priestley, Joseph. *The Rudiments of English Grammar: 1761*. English Linguistics 1500–1800, No. 210. 1761; rpt. Menston, England: The Scholar Press Limited, 1969.

Pyles, Thomas. "English Usage: The Views of the Literari." In *Contemporary English: Changes and Variation*. Ed. David L. Shores. New York: Lippincott, 1972, pp. 160–69.

———, and John Algeo. *The Origins and Development of the English Language*. 3rd ed. New York: Harcourt, 1982.

Quirk, Randolph, et al. *A Grammar of Contemporary English*. New York: Seminar, 1972.

Rank, Hugh, ed. *Language and Public Policy*. Urbana: NCTE, 1974.

Rose, Maxine S. "Sexism in Five Leading Collegiate Dictionaries." *CCC*, 30 (1979), 375–79.

Shaughnessy, Mina P. *Errors and Expectations: A Guide for the Teacher of Basic Writing*. New York: Oxford University Press, 1977.

Shores, David L., ed. *Contemporary English: Change and Variation*. New York: Lippincott, 1972.

Sledd, James. "Bi-Dialectalism: The Language of White Supremacy." *EJ*, 58 (1969), 1307–15.

———, and Wilma R. Ebbitt. *Dictionaries and That Dictionary: A Casebook on the Aims of Lexicographers and the Targets of Reviewers*. Chicago: Scott, Foresman, 1962.

———, and Gwin J. Kolb. *Dr. Johnson's Dictionary: Essays in the Biography of a Book*. Chicago: University of Chicago Press, 1955.

Students' Right to Their Own Language. CCC, 25, No. 3 (1974).

Walpole, Jane R. "Why Must the Passive Be Damned?" *CCC*, 30 (1979), 251–54.

Webster's Second New International Dictionary (1959).

Webster's Third New International Dictionary (1961).

Wentworth, Harold, and Stuart Berg Flexner. *Dictionary of American Slang*. 2nd suppl. ed. New York: Crowell, 1975.

Williams, Joseph M. "The Phenomenology of Error." *CCC*, 32 (1981), 152–68.

Williamson, Juanita V. "Selected Features of Speech: Black and White." In *A Various Language: Perspectives on American Dialects*. Ed. Juanita V. Williamson and Virginia M. Burke. New York: Holt, Rinehart, Winston, 1971, pp. 496–507.

———, and Virginia M. Burke, ed. *A Various Language: Perspectives on American Dialects*. New York: Holt, Rinehart, Winston, 1971.

The English Paragraph

MICHAEL G. MORAN

The word *paragraph* is derived from two Greek words, *para* meaning "beside," and *graph*, meaning "to write." In ancient Greek, the word means "to write beside," which gives a sense of the original concept of paragraphing: as ancient manuscripts show, scribes marked important passages with a marginal symbol to draw attention to their significance or to indicate some sort of break or shift. As E. G. Turner noted in *Greek Manuscripts of the Ancient World* (1971), the *paragraphus* appears in most ancient Greek manuscripts, and it serves a variety of functions and takes a variety of forms. It is used to separate verse from prose, to mark a change in speaker, to mark the end of a section of poetry, or to mark divisions within verse. Just as it serves many fuctions, the *paragraphus* took a myriad of forms, there being no single character to represent it in ancient manuscripts. In its earliest form it appeared as a single horizontal stroke, often with a dot over it. Edwin Herbert Lewis in *The History of the English Paragraph* (1894) traced the development of these marginal marks from the earliest to the modern reference mark (¶), which evolved, he speculated, from the Latin *P*. By the fifteenth century, however, the modern method of indenting the first sentence was fairly well established in English printing and prose.

Although the concept of the paragraph is ancient, scholars continue to debate its nature and function. Two major views have frequently appeared in various forms. One argues that the paragraph is a unit—either logical, rhetorical, linguistic, psychological, or a combination of them—that possesses an internal structure that can be described using a finite set of rules. The other view argues that the paragraph is a stretch of discourse that owes its existence to the larger requirements of the whole piece of prose. In this view, the paragraph does not exist as a separate entity but as a flexible and convenient method of marking some stage in a larger organic process. These two views appear in various forms throughout all periods of scholarly debate, although recently several scholars have attempted to synthesize the two.

As of this writing, only two major bibliographies on the paragraph are in print. The first is Richard L. Larson's "Structure and Form in Non-Fiction Discourse" (1976), which reviews much of the important current theoretical work. The second, which is more extensive but only lightly annotated, is James P. Bennett and colleagues' "Paragraph" (1977). This list is concerned mostly with literary stylistics, although it does cite many sources for the teacher and researcher of composition.

Nineteenth-Century Paragraph Theory

Although the two early grammarians Lindley Murray, in *An English Grammar* (1808), and Joseph Angus, in *Handbook of the English Tongue* (1862), sketch rules of paragraphing, the first rhetorician to discuss the device in detail is Alexander Bain in *English Composition and Rhetoric* (1867). He was the first to define the concept: "The division of discourse next higher than the sentence is the Paragraph: which is a collection of sentences with unity of purpose" (p. 142). This purpose, he noted, is to exhaust a particular subject, not to serve a communicative function.

Bain was also the first rhetorician to establish a set of rules for effective paragraphing. First, "the bearing of each sentence upon what precedes shall be explicit and unmistakable" (p. 142). Under this, he discussed a number of conjunctions and connectives that maintain coherence. Second, sentences illustrating or restating the same idea should be in the same, parallel structure. Third, the opening sentence should generally establish clearly the paragraph's subject. Fourth, each paragraph should "be consecutive, or free from dislocation" as dictated by the essay as a whole. Fifth, the paragraph should be unified and have a definite purpose that allows for no digressions. Sixth, the paragraph should maintain the proper relationship between ordinate and subordinate parts, to give it focus.

Contemporary writers have debated the validity of Bain's work. Paul C. Rodgers, Jr., in "Alexander Bain and the Rise of the Organic Paragraph" (1965), attacked Bain's notion of the topic sentence and his view that the paragraph is a logical unit. Rodgers argued that the rules grow from Bain's interest in logic and that writers do not always structure paragraphs that are logical units exhausting a single subject. Ned A. Shearer, however, in "Alexander Bain and the Genesis of Paragraph Theory" (1972), defended Bain by claiming that he was not the first to discuss the topic sentence and other paragraph rules (Murray and Angus preceded him) and that Bain's six rules grew not out of his study of logic but out of his interest in association psychology. Furthermore, the rules are consistent, useful, and psychologically valid.

Although Bain had introduced the concept, John G. R. McElroy introduced the term *topic sentence* to paragraph theory in *The Structure of English Prose* (1885). He was also the first to claim that the paragraph is "a whole composition in miniature," an assertion that continues to appear in modern textbooks (p. 196).

Another early writer who made new observations is John Earle. In his *English Prose* (1890), he observed that the paragraph developed in part because of the shortness of English sentences. More prescriptively, he introduced the still common assertion that a paragraph must consist of at least three sentences.

After Bain, the most influential—and most ideosyncratic—of the early theorists is Barrett Wendell. In his *English Composition* (1891), originally a set of popular lectures delivered at the Lowell Institute, he stated the sentence-paragraph analogy that Bain had implied: "A Paragraph is to a sentence what a sentence is to a word" (p. 119). Even though this greatly simplifies the complexity of paragraph structure, the idea continues to influence current paragraph pedagogy. Wendell also applied the same three principles—unity, mass, and coherence—to the sentence, the paragraph, and the essay, although the principles function differently in each. He claimed that paragraphs, unlike sentences, are the results of *prevision*, not revision, a view that most contemporary rhetoricians concerned with the writing process reject.

Wendell's major contribution to paragraph theory is his concept of mass, one of his three principles. *Mass* is concerned with where, physically, in the paragraph significant ideas appear. He noted that the opening sentence is not the only place for important ideas, since the eye tends to fall on the end as well as the beginning of a passage. Furthermore, as a rule of thumb, writers should give more physical space to principal rather than to subordinate ideas. Thus the concern becomes one of number of words and amount of space on the page rather than one of syntactic relationship alone.

Another early theorist who contributed to paragraph theory is John F. Genung. In his *Practical Elements of Rhetoric* (1892), he was one of the first to argue that the paragraph functions as a unit of invention, and he developed a heuristic of the paragraph. This consists of three functions that the writer can use to develop a subject: definition of the subject, establishment of the subject, and application of the subject. Under each function, Genung listed several strategies that the writer can combine in many ways. In his revision of *Elements* entitled *The Working Principles of Rhetoric* (1900), he fell under the influence of other theorists who argue for the tight sentence-paragraph analogy. He consequently did not develop his insight into the paragraph as a unit of invention any further. Instead, he viewed it as a stage of style, thus making his revised book more concerned with the mechanics of paragraphing.

Genung's second major contribution was to classify paragraph types. He discussed four: the *propositional*, which begins with an assertion that other sentences must prove; the *amplifying*, which has an implied assertion and is most often found in description and narration; the *preliminary*, which presents the general theme of a piece; and the *transitional*, which connects two larger pieces of discourse.

The first book devoted entirely to the paragraph is Fred N. Scott and Joseph V. Denney's textbook *Paragraph Writing* (3rd ed., 1893), which went through several editions. It is important for two major reasons. First, it establishes a method of teaching writing based on the progression from paragraphs to entire themes that is designed to help the weak writer. Second, it announces a theoretical position that views the paragraph as an organic unit within a larger piece of discourse.

Scott and Denney, observing that newspaper editorials of the time often consisted of a single paragraph, defined the *isolated paragraph*, which functions as an essay in miniature. They based their pedagogy, therefore, on the belief that students can be taught to write single paragraphs in order to learn principles that they can apply to entire compositions. To achieve this, they teach five laws, four of which grow out of Bain's work: unity, selection, sequence, and variety. The fifth idea, that of *proportion*, possesses two qualities. First, a paragraph must develop its subject fully enough to exhaust its purpose and idea. Thus there can be no single rule for paragraph length since this is tied to the breadth of the idea and the author's purpose in developing it. Second, details should be developed according to their relationship to the main idea. Subordinate ideas therefore cannot be developed as extensively as main ideas.

More important than the pedagogy, *Paragraph Writing* contains a significant theoretical discussion. Although the authors teach the isolated paragraph using modifications of Bain's rules, they defined the paragraph in relationship to the entire essay. They argued that the paragraph performs functions analogous to those of the composition, but the paragraph can be neither arbitrary nor accidental since it performs a given function within the organic essay, which is the record of the writer's movement of thought toward an achievable goal. Thinking, however, progresses in stages, or *stadia*, and paragraphs are articulations of thought within these arenas. Essays can be paragraphed in a number of ways, since one paragraph can contain several stadia or a stadium can be divided into several paragraphs, depending on the purpose of the writer and the needs of the reader. By emphasizing the dynamic nature of the paragraph, Scott and Denney escaped from the mechanistic, prescriptive approaches that mark most nineteenth-century discussions.

The only book-length, scholarly dicussion of the paragraph is Edwin Herbert Lewis's *History of the English Paragraph* (1894). Although dated, this work remains the most important single study of the subject and continues to influence current scholarship. Lewis discussed the paragraph as (1) a marginal character in ancient manuscripts used to mark significant passages; (2) a similar character placed within a text; (3) a division of discourse marked either by a symbol or an indentation; and (4) a rhetorical unit possessing an organic internal arrangement.

Although the book contains the only detailed discussion of ancient paragraph marks (an area needing further study), Lewis's most important contributions are his discussions of paragraph rhetoric. Building on L.A. Sherman's *Analytics of Literature* (1893), Lewis argued that there is a relationship between sentence length and paragraph rhetoric. By studying selected paragraphs from the earliest writers to his contemporaries, he discovered that the average number of words has doubled since Ascham. He attributed this to the decline of the long, Latin sentence that led to shorter sentences requiring other methods such as the paragraph to maintain cohesion and unity. He also noted that even early English writers thought in units larger than the sentence. They used the paragraph because they thought in larger, nebulous stages before thinking more accurately in short, precise steps. He was contemporary in his thinking, because he rejected the pedagogical school of theorists who viewed the paragraph as a group of related sentences. Instead, he argued that it is a logical or rhetorical stadium that performs a function within the whole composition. By rejecting logical structure as the only principle, he allowed for other reasons for paragraphing, including rhetorical and artistic concerns.

Lewis's study is marred by poor research methodology. His conclusions are based on simple word and sentence counts of randomly selected prose from a few English writers also randomly selected. Lewis, however, pointed the way for more focused and controlled work.

After the turn of the century, the paragraph receives little attention, although several articles appear that either support or modify earlier theory. L. W. Crawford, Jr., in "Paragraphs as Trains" (1912) and J. M. Grainger in " 'Paragraphs as Trains—The Caboose" (1913) discussed the importance of the topic sentence as controlling element. Herbert Winslow Smith argued in "Concerning Organization of Paragraphs" (1920) that students need work on topic sentences and logical development to help them think straight. Leon Mones, however, in "Teaching the Paragraph" (1921) argued that Bain and his followers teach only rules, not habits of writing. To counter this, Mones proposed a process-oriented pedagogy. Charles E. Whitmore in "A Doctrine of the Paragraph" (1923) also questioned key ideas about paragraphs including the notions of the topic sentence and logical development. He noted that all paragraphs do not have topic sentences; only expository and argumentative ones generally do. All paragraphs do, however, have *motive*, a unifying end or purpose, that may or may not be stated. Whitmore also questioned the concept of logical development and made a useful distinction between *support* and *development*. Many paragraphs have *support*, which consists of details or illustrations that make the motive concrete. Only paragraphs of a more logical kind possess *development*. In them, the writer must plan strategies—such as definition, enforcement, and other essentially logical processes to develop the motive. Finally, H. B. Lathrop in "Unity, Coherence, and Emphasis" (1918) attacked the three principles of sound paragraphing that grew out of Bain's and Wendell's work. In agreement with Scott and Denney and Lewis, Lathrop viewed the composition as a process of moving to an end. Coherence and emphasis, he argued, are actually parts of unity, the primary quality that good paragraphs and essays must possess, because a process is unified inasmuch as connections between parts are clear and the parts each receive proper emphasis.

A good evaluation of the early theorists is Virginia M. Burke's "Paragraph" (1968). She was critical of Bain and Wendell for being rule bound, but she found the ideas of Scott, Denney, Lewis, and Lathrop sounder since they recognized composition as a process. She also correctly noted that the early theories failed because they did not account for the complex semantic and syntactic relationships that function within and between paragraphs. Burke also edited *The Paragraph in Context* (1969), which contains selections from the work of Sherman, Lewis, Scott and Denny, and Lathrop as well as several essays by current theorists. Her introduction to the volume puts the nineteenth-century work in social and intellectual contexts.

Contemporary Paragraph Theory

Relatively little scholarship on the paragraph appeared during the first half of this century. Although virtually every textbook and handbook published covered the paragraph, little new information appeared. In 1958, the Conference on College Composition and Communication (CCCC) report "The Rhetoric of the Paragraph" (1958) concluded that new theories of the paragraph were needed. Several years later, the work of Francis Christensen, Alton Becker, and Paul C. Rodgers, Jr., appeared. This led to the NCTE monograph *The Sentence and the Paragraph* (1963), edited by Christensen, that reprints the most important articles on the paragraph as well as the "Symposium on the Paragraph" (1963) in which these three theorists and several others commented on one another's work.

In Christensen's "Generative Rhetoric of the Paragraph," which appears in his *Notes Toward a New Rhetoric* (1978), he developed a theory of the paragraph based on a structural analogy between the paragraph and the cumulative sentence: the top sentence of a paragraph is equivalent to the base clause of a cumulative sentence, and the supporting sentences are equivalent to the free modifiers of the sentence. He viewed the paragraph as a "macrosentence" or a "metasentence" and analyzed the paragraph's structure using the same techniques developed to describe the cumulative sentence: its levels of generality, direction of modification or movement, and its density of texture. Instead of being a logical unit, the Christensen paragraph is a sequence of sentences related by coordination—sentences that are structured alike and on the same level of generality—and subordination—sentences structured differently and on different, lower levels of generality. This theory is generative in that it can help students intuit these hierarchical relationships between sentences and assist them in making appropriate leaps of thought and corresponding syntactic connections between sentences. In "A New Approach to Freshman Composition" (1972), Charles A. Bond reported on an experiment suggesting that this rhetoric is more effective than a traditional course, and Michael Grady in "On Teaching Christensen Rhetoric" (1972) reported similar positive results and gave some helpful advice on using it.

Several theorists have qualified, modified, or expanded Christensen's work. David H. Karrfalt's papers question the concept of levels of generality. In the "Symposium on the Paragraph" (1963) he distinguished between *vertical structures* (modification and coordination) and *horizontal structures* (predication and complementation) of sentences and paragraphs, and he criticized Christensen for being concerned only with the vertical. He noted that parts of a sentence other than sentence modifiers, such as predication and complementation, may be more important than the modifiers themselves; he thus questioned the singular importance of the cumulative sentence. Likewise, paragraphs do not always have a vertical structure. Many have horizontal ones in which each sentence adds to the previous one without being subordinate to it. Karrfalt continued Christensen's analogy between the sentence and the paragraph, suggesting however that horizontal structuring is analogous to the relationship between the predicate and its subject, not the modifier and its head word. In a later article, "The Generation of Paragraphs and Larger Units" (1968), Karrfalt summed up his theory, demonstrating his essential relationship to Christensen, by arguing for three, not two, dimensions of generality: *coordination*, sentences at the same level of generality; *subordination*, those at a different level; and *completion*, those at a higher level of abstraction. This work suggests that some paragraphs advance in a series of ideas horizontally rather than develop and explore a single idea vertically. In a third essay, "Some Comments on the Principle of Rhythm in a Generative Rhetoric" (1969), Karrfalt argued that the concept of rhythm, working in conjunction with the concept of structure, helps students construct sound paragraphs.

Richard L. Larson also expanded on Christensen's paragraph theory in "Sentences in Action" (1967) by arguing that coordinate and subordinate relationships are not the only ones that function in prose. Each sentence acts to accomplish a particular task in conjunction with other sentences, and he presented a list of 17 roles that sentences can play in paragraphs.

Another theorist who has advanced Christensen's work is Willis L. Pitkin, Jr. In "Discourse Blocs" (1969), he argued that all language is hierarchically organized. He applied this concept to the sentence, the paragraph, and larger units of discourse. In place of the sentence and paragraph, he used the more general term *discourse bloc* to emphasize that the writer must establish junctures between blocs to maintain coherence. These blocs, functioning as a series of hierarchical units embedded in or added to larger blocs to form a continuum, should be discovered by their function in the overall discourse. This rhetorical emphasis is a departure from Christensen's theory, which is primarily concerned with structural relationships. Pitkin followed Karrfalt by recognizing the horizontal as well as vertical relationships between discourse blocs, but he attempted to clarify the exact nature of the relationships by emphasizing the function of each. In place of Christensen's coordination, he proposed *horizontal relation*, which includes simple coordination and Karrfalt's complementation, when two blocs are meaningful in terms of their own relationship (such as cause-effect). Instead of Christensen's subordination, Pitkin proposed *vertical relation*, including subordination, which is the logical movement from genus to species, and *superordination* (similar to Karrfalt's completion), from species to genus. He made an attempt, therefore, to avoid Christensen's problem of levels of generality by making the vertical relationships logical categories of inclusiveness so that smaller blocs are contained within larger ones, although he used the term *embedded*, which is confusing given its grammatical associations.

In a later article, "Hierarchies and the Discourse Hierarchy" (1977a), Pitkin attempted to clarify the essential ambiguity in the term *hierarchy* as applied to his own and Christensen's theories. He isolated three distinct uses of the term. The first refers to *grammatical or structural rank*, the traditional hierarchies of structuralism that range from the smallest elements of discourse to the largest ones. The second use of the term refers to *levels of semantic generality*, Christensen's concept, and this use also fails to recognize the operational nature of discourse, capturing only one relationship, that of specific-general, important in the encoding and decoding of discourse. The third and most appropriate use of the term *hierarchy* is *levels of functional inclusiveness,* an idea that grows out of his earlier notion of discourse blocs. Smaller blocs are included within larger ones, but the relationships are not logical or structural. In fact, structure and function are often at odds, and this creates a tension between the two. The same morpheme, for instance, can have one structural form but an entirely different hierarchical function, so analysis of the same unit will differ greatly depending on whether the analysis is structural or functional. This principle is important in teaching, since it suggests that structure cannot be taught separately from function. In a third article, "X/Y" (1977b), Pitkin developed in more detail some of the possible operational binary relationships that exist between functional units of discourse.

Several theorists have tried to apply Christensen's paragraph theory to the entire essay. Michael Grady in "A Conceptual Rhetoric of the Composition" (1971) discussed a method of teaching the freshman paper as a structure with an introductory sequence analogous to the top sentence, a series of body paragraphs related to it by coordination and subordination, and a concluding sequence that reiterates main ideas. Frank D'Angelo in "Arrangement" (1975) took a different approach by viewing the essay as a macroparagraph just as Christensen saw the paragraph as a macrosentence. The sentences within the essay are related to each other by coordination and subordination. Richard L. Larson in "Toward a Linear Rhetoric of the Essay" (1971) developed the notion of *linear analysis*, defined as a series of steps taken in a temporal sequence to reach a goal or conclusion, that complements Christensen's hierarchical model. The concept combines invention with arrangement, emphasizing the writer's need to identify the audience, the goal in writing, and the steps needed to achieve that end.

Some work has been done to develop pedagogies based on the Christensen paragraph. The most thorough treatment is Francis Christensen and Bonniejean Christensen's *New Rhetoric* (1976), which explains in detail Christensen's sentence and paragraph principles. R. Craig Hogan in "Self-Instructional Units Based on the Christensen Method" (1977) reported on a method of teaching Christensen rhetoric of the paragraph using short, self-instructional units that simplify the terminology. Stanley Archer in "Christensen's Rhetoric of the Paragraph Revisited" (1977) discusses how he applied the theory in the classroom.

For recent criticisms of Christensen's theory, see Joseph Williams's "Nuclear Structures of Discourse" (1981) and Rick Eden and Ruth Mitchell's "Paragraphing for the Reader" (in press).

The second major theorist is Alton L. Becker, whose interest in the paragraph grows in part out of Kenneth Pike's application of tagmemic theory in two early articles, "A Linguistic Contribution to Composition" (1964b) and "Beyond the Sentence" (1964a). The second paper is useful because it outlines how tagmemic theory can analyze larger linguistic structures.

In "A Tagmemic Approach to Paragraph Analysis" (1965), Becker established his basic theory, the fundamental notion of which is the *tagmeme*. This is both a grammatical slot and a slot filler, a composite of form and function. Expository paragraphs (the only kind he discussed) can be viewed as having slots and forms to fill them, and Becker isolated several major patterns common to many expository paragraphs. The first is the T (Topic) R (Restriction) I (Illustration) form. This type shares obvious similarities to the Christensen paragraph since the R slot is usually a statement of lower generality than the T slot. The second pattern, P (Problem) S (Solution), often follows the form of question-answer (QA). The S slot, however, often follows the TRI form, which can be embedded in it. One of the powerful components of Becker's theory is the notion that various operations can be performed on these basic patterns to make them flexible. These operations include deletion, reordering, addition, and combination. They offer teachers a potentially powerful instructional device: instruction can begin with the most common patterns and advance through various permutations.

There are, however, a limited number of formal signs that mark internal tagmemic structures of paragraphs despite the wide variation of slot orderings. The simplest of them, according to Becker, is the graphic marker *indentation*, a convention that signals the reader that the unit possesses internal structure. Two types of lexical markers also operate: (1) *equivalence classes,* commonly known as key terms with their synonyms and pronouns repeated throughout the structure; and (2) *lexical transitions,* transition words and phrases marking semantic concord. Changes in either of these marker systems often signal the beginning of a new slot. In "The Role of Lexical and Grammatical Cues in Paragraph Recognition" (1966), Richard Young and Becker reported an experiment that suggests readers can recognize these signs when reading paragraphs with their content words changed to nonsense syllables. Young, Becker, and Kenneth Pike, in Chapter 15 of *Rhetoric* (1970), emphasized even more the importance of chains of lexical items that run through sentences and bind them together into coherent and unified paragraphs. In Chapter 14 of the text, they developed a method of analyzing paragraphs that emphasize invention more than Becker's earlier articles do. They introduced the idea of the *plot*, a conventional sequence of slots that creates a structural framework for the paragraph. The TRI and PS slots are two of the most common, generalized plot structures for expository paragraphs, but the writer can invent others. The writer's job is to reveal the plot structure clearly to the reader and to insure that the plot conveys a sense of closure and completion after the topic sentence arouses reader expectation.

Becker also explored the paragraph as a psychological and grammatical unit, and this has led to experiments of interest to the composition teacher. The first, conducted by Frank Koen, Young, and Becker, "The Psychological Reality of the Paragraph" (1969), attempts to determine (1) the degree of agreement between subjects identifying paragraph boundaries in unindented prose passages; (2) the number of cues to paragraph structure that are formal; (3) the role semantic cues play in determining the structure; and (4) the role that age and experience play in the development of paragraph sense. The experimenters used ten prose passages of various modes and changed the content words into nonsense paralogs. In general, they found a high degree of interjudge agreement in the marking of paragraph breaks in the English passages, in the nonsense passages, and between the two. This suggests "that the paragraph is a psychologically real unit" (p. 52). Furthermore, they found that the youngest subjects, third graders, often placed the markers in mid-sentence, suggesting that these youngsters have not yet learned, either through direct teaching or through their reading, the concept of the paragraph. This experiment has been extended by Betty Cain in "Discourse Competence in Nonsense Paralogs" (1973).

Other scholars have used tagmemic theory to analyze extended discourse. Victor J. Vitanza in "A Tagmemic Heuristic for the Whole Composition" (1979) applied Becker's tagmemic slots TRI, PS, and QA to the essay. This system, he maintained, helps students generate entire compositions as well as the paragraphs within them. For an extensive application of tagmemic theory to Philippine languages, see Robert E. Longacre's *Discourse, Paragraph, and Sentence Structures in Selected Phillippine Languages* (1968).

The third major contemporary theorist is Paul C. Rodgers, Jr. who, as I mentioned earlier, attacked Bain's rule-bound theory of the paragraph. Instead of viewing the paragraph as an isolated unit, Rodgers argued in "A Discourse-Centered Rhetoric of the Paragraph" (1966) that paragraphs are actually not always logical breaks within a piece of discourse. To replace the paragraph as a basic unit of writing, he returned to the idea of the *stadium of discourse* introduced in the nineteenth century. This unit is a logical whole that is often a paragraph but not always. This, he claimed, represents the actual practice of modern writers, who indent their prose for a number of reasons other than for logical breaks. These reasons include structural, physical, rhythmical, formal, tonal, and rhetorical considerations. A stadium can be divided into several paragraphs or a single paragraph can include several stadia. Like Scott and Denney and Lewis of the nineteenth century, he viewed discourse as an organic process and allowed writers considerable flexibility when marking paragraph breaks.

Rodgers developed his theory more fully in "The Stadium of Discourse" (1967), in which he explored its rhetorical orientation in more detail. To determine the function of the paragraph, the reader must ask why it was written, what purpose the writer was trying to fulfill. The stadium usually has a topic sentence, but it is offered for its own sake, its own intrinsic value, not because it is attached to a paragraph, and the rest of the stadium justifies, clarifies, or emphasizes the major sentence—but not necessarily in a single paragraph. Paragraph structure, Rodgers argued, is an ineffable quality, "the web of argument, the pattern of thought flow, the system of alliances and tensions among associated statements" (p. 178).

Recent evidence supports Rodgers's contention that contemporary writers do not use topic sentences in all paragraphs. In "The Frequency and Placement of Topic Sentences in Expository Prose" (1974), Richard Braddock analyzed the paragraphs of 25 essays in major popular magazines published from 1964 to 1965 by breaking them down into T-units, identifying the topic sentences, and determining their forms. He discovered four major kinds of topic sentences plus two extra-paragraph types: (1) the *simple* topic sentence that is stated in one T-unit; (2) the *delayed-completion* topic sentence that begins in one T-unit and ends in a later one; (3) the *assembled* topic sentence found by combining phrases scattered throughout the paragraph; (4) the *inferred* topic sentence implied by the author; (5) the *major* topic sentence that controls a number of paragraphs; and (6) the *subtopic* sentence that states part of the main idea of a previous paragraph. Braddock found that only 45 percent of all topic sentences are simple, and almost as many, 39 percent, are assembled. The more text that a topic sentence controls, however, the more likely it is to be simple. Most topic sentences are implicit (55 percent), compared with 44 percent that are explicit. As for placement, only 13 percent of expository prose paragraphs begin with a topic sentence. Arther A. Stern in "When Is a Paragraph?" (1976) reported that students, when asked to mark paragraph breaks in passages, invariably place the breaks in different but equally justifiable places. This supports Braddock's findings that not all paragraphs begin with a simple topic sentence.

The theoretical work of Christensen, Becker, and Rodgers has not always been received enthusiastically. In "Further Comments on the Paragraph" (1966), Leo Rockas argued that these theories ask the wrong questions because they assume that paragraphs exist. A better approach, he argued, is to examine how sentences are connected in discourse, an argument he returned to in "The Rhetoric of Doodle" (1978). In "Response to Leo Rockas' 'Further Comments on the Paragraph' " (1967), Christensen answered these objections by noting that the basic unit of narration is the sentence, but the basic unit of exposition is the paragraph. In "The Persistent Ptolemy and the Paradox of the Paragraph" (1968), Rockas, in the manner of Sterne, poked fun at theorists for arguing over the nature of paragraphing, which is an art, not a science. Textbook and handbook authors have often ignored current work on the paragraph as J. Karl Nicholas showed in "Handbooks and Horsesense" (1973), an article in which he examined several popular texts for the influence of contemporary paragraph theory.

Although Christensen, Becker, and Rodgers have been the most influential theorists, other scholars have also written important essays on the subject. Herbert Read in *English Prose Style* (1952) rejected many traditional ideas about paragraphs, particularly the notion that they are logical structures. He viewed them as devices of punctuation that offer readers a breathing space. Paragraphs also help writers explore their subjects until relevant ideas are exhausted and therefore represent a psychological process of exploring all facets of a thought. One of Read's most innovative ideas is that paragraphs possess rhythmical unity, the paragraph in fact being the "first complete unit of prose rhythm" (p. 59). Rhythm, however, has less to do with words than with thoughts, so the paragraph became for Read the shape of thought, a gestalt that possesses its own unity and hierarchical organization. Paul Franklin Baum, in . . . *the other harmony of prose* . . . (1952) objected to Read's "mystical" notions and analyzed several paragraphs closely to show that rhythm is not always associated with their thought patterns in obvious ways.

Other contemporary theorists have been concerned about paragraph form. Josephine Miles in "What We Compose" (1963) suggested a tripartite system of function classes that help students compose meaningful sentences, paragraphs, and essays. The first is *assertive*, a subject and its predicate; the second is *development*, the addition of modification; and the third is *connective*, the use of prepositions, conjunctions, and other connectives. Robert Gorrell in "Not by Nature" (1966) developed another approach by discussing three other principles: addition, continuity, and selection. By *addition* he meant those techniques—predication, linkage, coordination, and subordination—by which writers add comments to topics in both sentences and paragraphs. By *continuity* he meant that every unit of coherent discourse must establish a kind of contract between reader and writer. The paragraph must establish a commitment to what follows it and function as a response to what precedes it. Finally, by *selection* he meant that writers must select from a limited set of discourse alternatives for each slot. Gorrell briefly discussed these concepts in the context of our need for a new rhetoric in "Very Like a Whale" (1965). Edna L. Furness in "New Dimensions in Paragraph Instruction" (1968) also proposed a new view of paragraph form based on structural and strategic sentences.

In "Aesthetic Form in Familiar Essays" (1971), Howard C. Brashers explained a series of organizational categories that apply to familiar essays that are artistically rather than logically organized. He viewed form as being comprised of the interaction of two principles, design and pattern. *Design,* which contributes variety to familiar prose, consists of four principles: contrast, gradation, theme and variation, and restraint. These principles are associated with structures of thought as well as paragraph organization. Of less importance to paragraph theory are Brasher's concepts of *pattern*, which are larger methods of organizing discourse into wholes. These concepts are linear, radical-circular, and mytho-literary. Although of limited use for teaching argument and exposition, this system can explain the organization of artistic, non-logical paragraphs and essays. Another writer who addressed this question is William F. Irmscher.

In *Teaching Expository Writing* (1979), he used the theories of artist Ben Shahn to discuss "the shape of content," arguing that in any writing, content comes first and then is shaped into appropriate form, not vice versa. He discussed "outer shape" and "inner parts." The *outer shape* sets the limits of the piece and the *inner parts*, which directly concern matters of paragraphing, determine the ways that discourse is made coherent and unified.

Richard Warner in "Teaching the Paragraph as a Structural Unit" (1979) used linguistic principles to teach paragraph structure by developing a set of generative-transformational, as well as rhetorical, rules to generate paragraphs, which he argued are recognizable units of linguistic structure. The *generative rules* consist of three sentence functions that can produce analytic paragraph structures. These rules are topic (T), limitor (L), and developer (D). Transformational rules can then delete and rearrange these functions, changing TLD structures to DLT, for instance. The third set of rules, the *rhetorical*, motivates the transformations. Another linguistic discussion of form is Jay Kyle Perrin's "Subject Isn't What It Seems" (1972) in which she noted that the main subject of a paragraph—generally the subject of the topic sentence—performs various grammatical functions in the body sentences.

A new, promising direction in paragraph research makes use of information from psycho-linguistic, linguistic, and reading research. Rick Eden and Ruth Mitchell's "Paragraphing for the Reader" (in press) used this research to develop a theory of paragraphing based on the premise that writers do not need to learn common paragraph patterns; instead, they need to learn how to use paragraph conventions to affect the reader's perception of prose discourse.

This view finds support in the empirical research in reading theory. Bonnie J. F. Meyer's work, reported in her "What Is Recalled After Hearing a Passage?" (1973), coauthored with G. W. McConkie, and in her *Organization of Prose and Its Effect on Memory* (1975), explored the effect of content structure of a paragraph on a reader's memory. Using Joseph E. Grime's *Tread of Discourse* (1975) as a theoretical base, she designed experiments suggesting that superordinate semantic content placed high in the content structure tended to be recalled more readily than subordinate information low in the structure. This phenomenon, known as top-down processing, suggests that readers need an abstract statement to orient them before they can make sense of following details. Perry Thorndyke in "Cognitive Structures in Comprehension and Memory of Narrative Discourse" (1977) and J. D. Bransford and M. K. Johnson in "Considerations of Some Problems of Comprehension" (1973) also explored this question.

Although Robert de Beaugrande's experiments reported in "Psychology and Composition" (1979) do not support this position, most work by reading specialists does. James Coomber in "Perceiving the Structure of Written Materials" (1975) reported that students cannot write paragraphs because they cannot read to distinguish main from subordinate material. William Wensch in the review article "What Reading Research Tells Us about Writing" (1979) argued that reading research supports the importance of traditional principles of paragraphing such as the beginning topic sentence. David E. Kieras in "Good and Bad Structure in Simple Paragraphs" (1978) found that subjects had more difficulty processing and remembering paragraphs that did not conform to the conventions of coherent development and opening topic sentences.

Studies also suggest that organization, context, and reader experience and belief-structures affect text processing. L. T. Frase in "Paragraph Organization of Written Materials" (1969) reported on an experiment suggesting that organizing sentence sequences so that they follow the conceptual structure inherent in the material facilitates learning. Marcie Waller and F. L. Durley in "The Influence of Context on the Auditory Comprehension of Paragraphs by Aphasic Subjects" (1978) found that establishing a verbal context for subjects before they read the paragraphs significantly improved recall. Richard C. Anderson and colleagues in "Frameworks for Comprehending Discourse" (1977) questioned the predominant belief that meaning resides in language and that readers merely need linguistic skills to process it. The authors demonstrated that readers interpret an ambiguous paragraph according to their knowledge of the world and their analysis of the paragraph's context. For writers, this suggests that paragraphs cannot be seen apart from the beliefs and general background and expectations of those reading them. Douglas Sjogren and W. Timpson in "Frameworks for Comprehending Discourse" (1979) replicated Anderson's study and reached similar conclusions.

Work in the area of readability also supports the need for traditionally sound paragraphing. In *The Philosophy of Composition* (1977), E. D. Hirsch, Jr., argued that psycho-linguistic research suggests that traditional techniques of paragraphing assist the memory and help maintain attention. Jack Selzer in "Another Look at Paragraphs in Technical Writing" (1980) questioned the validity of readability formulas that do not take the paragraph into consideration. Current work in rhetoric, linguistics, and cognitive psychology shows that meaning grows from the relationship between the parts of the paragraph, not just from the length of words and sentences. In "Readability of Expository Paragraphs with Identical or Related Sentence Topics" (1979), William J. Vande Kopple reported experimental findings about the relationship between readability and paragraphs. He demonstrated that most readers consider paragraphs more readable that present older material in the topic position and newer material in the predicate position that naturally receives more stress. This is known as the "Functional Sentence Perspective" (FSP). The most readable paragraph, he concluded, is the one that repeats the topic idea at the beginning of each sentence. In another study, "Readability of a Rhetorically Linked Expository Paragraph" (1980), Vande Kopple tested a second type of paragraph. This one links all of its sentences together by having new information in the stressed position of one sentence carry over to the non-stressed, topic position of the following one. Readers judged this paragraph more readable than a paragraph arranged in the opposite manner. Vande Kopple discussed the pedagogical implications of FSP in "Functional Sentence Perspective, Composition, and Reading" (1982). A. S. Fishman in "The Effect of Anaphoric References and Noun Phrase Organizers on Paragraph Comprehension" (1978) found that general nouns introduced in the topic sentences of paragraphs help readers organize and remember what they read. This "noun phrase organizer" names a category and is frequently repeated throughout the paragraph, and this leads to superior recall.

Coherence is another traditional principle of sound paragraphing that has received support from recent scholarship. The seminal work in the area is M.A.K. Halliday and R. Hasan's *Cohesion in English* (1976), which exhaustively explores the major cohesive devices of English. The study identifies cohesion as one of the most important qualities of a text, which is a semantic unit possessing *texture*, a rich interconnection between its parts. Halliday and Hasan discussed five devices that English uses to achieve coherence: reference, substitution, ellipses, conjunction, and lexical cohesion.

Although Halliday and Hasan's work has been widely read by composition specialists, the work of Edward J. Crothers, whose *Paragraph Inference Structures* (1979) extends Halliday and Hasan's *Cohesion in English* (1976), is not as well known. Unlike Halliday and Hasan, who are concerned mostly with syntactic and semantic relationships within a text, Crothers argued that cohesion also depends on psychological and logical patterns that are extra-linguistic. These patterns he called "inferences." Unstated assumptions, *inferences* are propositions not manifested in the text but assumed by it. Inferences contribute to cohesion by connecting statements much as mortar connects bricks.

Other theorists also discuss the importance of coherence in paragraphing. E. K. Lybbert and D. W. Cummings in "On Repetition and Coherence" (1969) argued that unity and coherence are two independent variables. Unity grows from the selection of related material, and coherence grows from fitting together parts to form a whole. Anita Brostoff in "Coherence" (1981) developed a program for teaching the concept based on the work of Piaget, Christensen, Hayakawa, Burke, and Young, Becker, and Pike. Dennis J. Packard in "From Logic to Composition and Reading" (1976) presented a method of using logic to help students achieve and maintain coherence in paragraphs. Stephen P. Witte and Lester Faigley in "Coherence, Cohesion, and Writing Quality" (1981) argued that coherence and cohesion are essential qualities found in good paragraphs. They analyzed high- and low-rated essays using Halliday and Hasan's classification and found that the better essays were richer in their use of cohesive devices. They attributed this to better writers possessing skills of invention that allow them to elaborate and extend concepts. Although cohesion is important, they concluded that coherence, the way a text fits into a larger world situation, may be even more so.

Although much of the research cited on the last few pages supports the importance of traditional paragraphing, not all scholars believe that form in the traditional sense is important to teach. Thomas W. Wilcox in "Composition Where None Is Apparent" (1965) argued that available rhetorics of the paragraph do not reflect the sense of formlessness found in serious contemporary literature. If teachers recognize that our best writers break all conventions to express their world views, why do they continue to insist that their students write unified paragraphs? Winston Weathers in "Grammars of Style" (1976) offered an alternative to traditional grammar and rhetoric in the form of *Grammar B*, which includes, among other innovations, the *crot*, which is a short, impressionistic alternative to the paragraph. In this essay and in his *Alternative Style* (1980), Weathers maintained that students should be exposed to Grammar B because it is as effective as the traditional Grammar A. Furthermore, it has a long list of practitioners, including Sterne, Whitman, Joyce, and the New Journalists. Jane R. Walpole in "Rhetorical Form" (1979) suggested that the crot has advantages over the traditional paragraph because it is more flexible and expressive.

Teaching the Paragraph

Although most of the theory discussed so far has implications for teaching, some articles have been written on the paragraph that are primarily pedagogical in intent. They include exercises, assignments, and textbooks. As would be expected, much of this material is designed for the basic writing classroom or can be used to meet the needs of basic writers.

Relatively little work has been done on teaching elementary students to paragraph. Jo Tagliente in "The Edible Paragraph" (1973) taught paragraph structure to young students by comparing it to a Dagwood sandwich, and Don M. Wolfe in "Crucial First Assignment" (1970) argued that young students should be introduced to the paragraph by means of a simple description assignment. R. W. Reising in "Turning the Corner" (1970) compared the walls of the classroom to the paragraphs of an essay. Turning corners while walking around the room is analogous to a writer's thinking while paragraphing each major unit of an essay. In the seminal article "Nobody Writes a Paragraph" (1972), O. S. Trosky and C. C. Wood described a method to teach young children that paragraphs are parts of larger discourse. The method grows out of research on brainstorming and problem-solving, and it requires students to complete the following five steps: (1) list ideas about a subject; (2) group them appropriately; (3) name each group to show how the ideas fit together; (4) number the ideas in each group systematically; and (5) write about the ideas of each group to form connected paragraphs. In a second article, "Paragraph Writing" (1975), Trosky and Wood described a method to help students group the ideas and name the groups more effectively. Finally, James Charnock in "Paragraphing Made Simple" (1978) discussed how to teach students to list information under a topic, organize it into categories, rank it in order of importance, and fashion paragraphs first in oral and then in written form.

Even less work has been done on teaching junior and senior high school students to paragraph. Ruth M. Barns in "Try Paragraph Writing" (1956) reported a step-by-step method for moving students from discussing a model paragraph to writing one of their own. Joseph P. Fotos in "Teaching the Paragraph in Junior High School" (1966) described a technique for evaluating student paragraphs by having the class develop its own criterion that the teacher can gradually expand. Finally, Leo M. Schell in "Paragraph Composition" (1969) explained a systematic procedure for teaching high school students by beginning with a topic sentence and working sentence by sentence to the conclusion.

More work has been done on teaching basic writers to paragraph. Harvey S. Wiener in "The Single Narrative Paragraph and College Remediation" (1972) argued that basic writers should be taught to write short narrative paragraphs rather than the more difficult expository ones, because the first, being short and personal, allows students to concentrate on structural elements. After mastering the narrative paragraph, students can then learn to write short expository pieces. Writing for teachers of English as a second language, Michael Donley in "The Paragraph in Advanced Composition" (1976) suggested a series of exercises that use paragraph models heuristically to teach students the role that reader expectation plays in paragraph development. He gives students parts of paragraphs—the topic sentence, for instance—and asks them to predict how the rest of the structure will unfold. William Jones in "A Little Pen and Pencil Magic" (1977) reported on a method for helping basic writers to fill out sparse, poorly developed paragraphs by adding sentences between sentences of the original. Dean R. Baldwin in "Introducing Rhetoric in Remedial Writing Courses" (1978) required his basic writers to answer questions on Pre-writing Sheets about the audience and the purpose of each paragraph. Linda Feldmeir in "Teaching Paragraph Coherence" (1979) taught coherence by giving basic writers a topic sentence followed by a series of related sentences that need to be reconstructed to form a paragraph. Finally, Beverly D. Stratton, John Charlton-Seifert, and Maurice G. Williams in "Reading and Writing Shapes" (1980) taught basic writers paragraph organization by showing geometric shapes to reinforce five general patterns of development.

Some work has also been done on teaching freshman writers to paragraph. Hermann C. Bowersox in "The Idea of the Freshman Composition Course" (1955) discussed a technique to make students more aware of paragraph rhetoric. After they analyzed the rhetorical strategies of paragraphs, he had students make grammatical and structural changes in particular sentences and then discuss the effects on the paragraph as a whole. Donald Cunningham in "Analyzing Paragraph Structure" (1971) explained a system to teach students three types of functional sentences operating in many paragraphs: topic, explanatory, and exemplification. Norma J. Engberg in "Pumpkin-Head Paragraphs" (1974) described how to teach style by presenting students with a short paragraph comprised only of simple sentences and having the class make and discuss a number of changes in sentence structure and diction. Carol Cohan in "Writing Effective Paragraphs" (1976) taught paragraphs by emphasizing that topic sentences must pose questions for the body sentences to answer. John H. Clarke in "Generating

Paragraphs in a Four-Part Formula'' (1978) taught his students to structure paragraphs according to four slots, each with its own question: (1) *leader* (What's true?); (2) *qualifier* (Why is it true); (3) *example* (Where or when with details?); and (4) *interpretation* (So what?). Finally, Laurie G. Kirszner in ''Supporting Topic Sentences'' (1978) described how to teach concrete support by providing groups of students with topic sentences that they can develop.

One method of teaching the paragraph that has received considerable attention is imitation, one of the oldest methods of writing instruction. It includes a cluster of techniques such as copying a passage, substituting new content while following the original's syntax and organization, paraphrasing the original, and loosely using it as a model. James W. Ney in ''On Not Practicing Errors'' (1963) based his entire semester on close imitation. Until mid-semester, he had his students imitate sentences; then he had them imitate paragraphs. C. D. Rogers in ''The Sedulous but Successful Ape'' (1967) described a similar program. J. F. McCampbell in ''Using Models for Improving Composition'' (1966) argued that imitation of paragraphs helps remedial students internalize syntactic structures, larger organizational patterns, and other structural conventions. Also working with basic writers, Phyllis Brooks in ''Memesis'' (1973) argued that *persona paraphrase*, a form of imitation, helps basic writers develop mature voices when writing. Frank D'Angelo in ''Imitation and Style'' (1973) noted that imitating a paragraph allows students to participate in archetypal forms. Like invention, imitation is generative, but it has the advantage of helping students develop sophisticated styles relatively quickly. D. G. Kehl in ''Composition and the Mimetic Mode'' (1975) articulated a broad system of invention based on imitation and Christensen paragraph theory. Finally, several textbooks use imitation to teach paragraph structure including Edward P. J. Corbett's *Classical Rhetoric for the Modern Student* (1971), which discusses the importance of imitation in classical rhetoric; M. E. Whitten's *Creative Pattern Practice* (1966); Winston Weathers and Otis Winchester's *Copy and Compose* (1969), a text devoted entirely to imitating models; and Frank D'Angelo's *Process and Thought in Composition* (1980).

Another method that has received considerable attention is the scrambled-sentence approach. James Stronks in ''Coherence in the Paragraph'' (1976) described an exercise in which students receive a scrambled paragraph that they must reconstruct and then compare with the original version. Suzanne F. Kistler in ''Scrambling the Unscramblable'' (1978) worked first with scrambled professional models and then turned to scrambled student models to help students find weaknesses in coherence. Michael G. Moran in ''An Inductive Method of Teaching the Paragraph'' (1981) described a learning game that has student groups compete to reconstruct scrambled paragraphs. Finally, Peter M. Schiff in ''Problem Solving and the Composition Model'' (1978) lent credence to the method by reporting experimental results suggesting that students taught to manipulate sentence strips of model paragraphs write statistically superior paragraphs compared to those in a control group. The problem-solving process, he concluded, leads to improvement.

Relatively little work has been done on opening and closing paragraphs. In "An Effective Opening" (1969), Thomas Stanko described how he gave his students the first sentence of professional openings and asked them to generate the rest of the paragraph. Lila Chaplin in "On Improving Opening Paragraphs" (1967) listed numerous effective techniques to begin essays. They include things such as beginning with a question, a quotation, or an anecdote. Robert M. Gassen in "A Sense of Audience and Commitment" (1975) described how he taught students that openings must interest the reader and express the writer's enthusiasm for the subject. Robert L. Baker in "Twelve Ways to End Your Article Gracefully" (1982) discussed effective ways to conclude popular essays.

Since almost every textbook and handbook published contains a section on paragraphing, I cannot discuss all of them. This is no great loss since most books approach paragraphing by means of the modes or patterns of discourse, a method that has been questioned by the work of Richard A. Meade and W. Geiger Ellis. In their "Paragraph Development in the Modern Age of Rhetoric" (1970), they described a study in which they examined 300 paragraphs from contemporary periodicals and found that more than half (56 percent) were not developed using a traditional pattern. Most were developed using additional comment, reasons, examples, or a combination of these three patterns. In "The Use in Writing of Textbook Methods of Paragraph Development" (1971), Meade and Ellis presented the statistics of the study and concluded that instruction should focus on methods of development other than the traditonal. Because of this, I will cite only textbooks that take novel approaches to paragraphing.

Chapter 4 of W. Ross Winterowd's *Contemporary Writer* (1976) not only reflects many of the findings from current paragraph research, but it also introduces several new, useful concepts. Winterowd assumed that conscious and unconscious imitation of models helps students develop as writers, so he provided numerous samples of interesting, well-written paragraphs throughout the chapter. He also discussed non-traditional methods of development such as the tagmemic slots, examples, images, facts, analogy, and others. Perhaps his most innovative idea is that of distance. Paragraphs fall along a spectrum from a private, intimate vision using intuitive methods of development to an impersonal presentation using formal chains of logic.

Other rhetorics with interesting sections on the paragraph include William F. Irmscher's *Holt Guide to English* (1981), which discusses nine function slots similar to tagmemic slots (TRIAC-SELD); Donald Daiker, Andrew Kerek, and Max Morenberg's *Writer's Options* (1982), which in Units 11–13 uses sentence-combining to teach principles of paragraphing; and Frederick Crews's *Random House Handbook* (1980), which discusses the development of direct, turnabout, and climactic paragraphs. In *Writing* (1984) Charles Bridges and Ronald Lunsford introduced a paragraphing scheme based on Kenneth Burke's Logological Analysis.

Several textbooks, many of them geared to freshmen and basic writers, treat the paragraph as the major unit of discourse. I will cite only two of them. The best remains John B. Lord's *Paragraph* (1964). This book views the paragraph as both a unit of structure and style, and Lord intelligently discussed questions of organization, development, movement, diction, rhythm, and tone. Less innovative but also good is Helen Mills's *Commanding Paragraphs* (1981), which is the best book available for teaching traditional paragraph theory. It also has an excellent instructor's manual with suggestions for using the text in various classroom contexts.

References

Anderson, Richard C., et al. "Frameworks for Comprehending Discourse." *Am Educ Res J*, 14 (1977), 367–81.

Angus, Joseph. *Hand-Book of the English Tongue*. London: Religious Tract Society, 1862.

Archer, Stanley. "Christensen's Rhetoric of the Paragraph Revisited." *Ex E*, 21 (1977), 22–27.

Bain, Alexander. *English Composition and Rhetoric: A Manual*. New York: Appleton, 1867.

Baker, Robert L. "Twelve Ways to End Your Article Gracefully." *Writer's Digest*, Oct. 1982, pp. 30–33.

Baldwin, Dean R. "Introducing Rhetoric in Remedial Writing Courses." *CCC*, 29 (1978), 392–94.

Barns, Ruth M. "Try Paragraph Writing." *EJ*, 45 (1956), 412–14.

Baum, Paul Franklin. . . . *the other harmony of prose* . . . Durham, N.C.: Duke University Press, 1952, pp. 61–74.

Becker, Alton L. "A Tagmemic Approach to Paragraph Analysis." *CCC*, 16 (1965), 237–42.

Bennett, James, et al. "The Paragraph: An Annotated Bibliography." *Style*, 11 (1977), 107–18.

Bond, Charles A. "A New Approach to Freshman Composition: A Trial of the Christensen Method." *CE*, 33 (1972), 623–27.

Bowersox, Hermann C. "The Idea of the Freshman Composition Course—A Polemical Discussion." *CCC*, 6 (1955), 38–44.

Braddock, Richard. "The Frequency and Placement of Topic Sentences in Expository Prose." *RTE*, 8 (1974), 287–302.

Bransford, J. D., and M. K. Johnson. "Consideration of Some Problems of Comprehension." In *Visual Information Processing*. Ed. W. D. Chase. New York: Academic, 1973.

Brashers, Howard C. "Aesthetic Form in Familiar Essays." *CCC*, 22 (1971), 147–55.

Bridges, Charles W., and Ronald Lunsford. *Writing: Discovering Form and Meaning*. San Francisco: Wadsworth, 1984.

Brooks, Phyllis. "Memesis: Grammar and the Echoing Voice." *CE*, 35 (1973), 161–68.

Brostoff, Anita. "Coherence: 'Next to' Is Not 'Connected to.' " *CCC*, 32 (1981), 278–94.

Burke, Virginia. "The Paragraph: Dancer in Chains." In *Rhetoric: Theories for Applications*. Ed. Robert Gorrell. Champaign, Ill.: NCTE, 1968. Shortened version:

"Continuity of the Paragraph." In *Prose Style: A Historical Approach Through Studies*. Ed. James R. Bennett. San Francisco: Chandler, 1971, pp. 18–23.

———, ed. *The Paragraph in Context*. Indianapolis: Bobbs-Merrill, 1969.

Cain, Betty. "Discourse Competence in Nonsense Paralogs." *CCC*, 24 (1973), 171–81.

Chaplin, Lila. "On Improving Opening Paragraphs." *CCC*, 18 (1967), 53–56.

Charnock, James. "Paragraphing Made Simple." *Teacher*, Jan. 1978, p. 90.

Christensen, Francis. "Response to Leo Rockas' 'Further Comments on the Paragraph.' " *CCC*, 18 (1967), 186–88.

———. "A Generative Rhetoric of the Paragraph." In *Notes Toward a New Rhetoric*. 2nd ed. New York: Harper, Row, 1978, pp. 74–103.

———, ed. *The Sentence and the Paragraph*. Champaign, Ill.: NCTE, 1963.

———, and Bonniejean Christensen. *A New Rhetoric*. New York: Harper, Row, 1976, pp. 83–192.

Clark, John R. "Paragraphs for Freshmen." *CE*, 32 (1970), 66–72.

Clarke, John H. "Generating Paragraphs in a Four-Part Formula." *Ex E*, 23 (1978), 28–30.

Cohan, Carol. "Writing Effective Paragraphs." *CCC*, 27 (1976), 363–65.

Coomber, James W. "Teaching Organizational Skills in Reading and Writing." *Minn Engl J*, 9 (1973), 37–41.

———. "Perceiving the Structure of Written Materials." *RTE*, 9 (1975), 263–66.

Corbett, Edward P. J. *Classical Rhetoric for the Modern Student*. 2nd ed. New York: Oxford University Press, 1971, pp. 496–538.

Crawford, L. W., Jr. "Paragraphs as Trains." *EJ*, 10 (1912), 644.

Crews, Frederick. *The Random House Handbook*. 3rd ed. New York: Random House, 1980, pp. 90–124.

Crothers, Edward J. *Paragraph Inference Structures*. Norwood, N.J.: Albex, 1979.

Cunningham, Donald. "Analyzing Paragraph Structure." *Elem Eng*, 16 (1971), 8–9. Also in *Writing Exercises from Exercise Exchange*. Ed. Littleton Long. Urbana, Ill.: NCTE, 1976, pp. 45–47.

Daiker, Donald, Andrew Kerek, and Max Morenberg. *The Writer's Options*. 2nd ed. New York: Harper, Row, 1982.

D'Angelo, Frank. "Imitation and Style." *CCC*, 24 (1973), 283–90.

———. "A Generative Rhetoric of the Essay." *CCC*, 25 (1974), 388–96.

———. "Arrangement." In *A Conceptual Theory of Rhetoric*. Cambridge, Mass.: Winthrop, 1975.

———. *Process and Thought in Composition*. 2nd ed. Cambridge, Mass.: Winthrop, 1980, pp. 317–74, 425–58.

de Beaugrande, Robert. "Generative Stylistics: Between Grammar and Rhetoric." *CCC*, 28 (1977), 240–46.

———. "Psychology and Composition." *CCC*, 30 (1979), 50–53.

Donley, Michael. "The Paragraph in Advanced Composition: A Heuristic Approach." *Engl Lang Teach J*, 30 (1976), 224–35.

Earle, John. *English Prose*. New York: Putnam's, 1890.

Eden, Rick, and Ruth Mitchell. "Paragraphing for the Reader." *CCC*, forthcoming.

Engberg, Norma J. "Pumpkin-Head Paragraphs." *FEN*, 3 (1974), 15–17.

Feldmeir, Linda. "Teaching Paragraph Coherence." *Ex E*, 24 (1979), 41–44.

Fishman, A. S. "The Effect of Anaphoric References and Noun Phrase Organizers on Paragraph Comprehension." *J Read Behav*, 10 (1978), 159–69.

Fotos, Joseph P. "Teaching the Paragraph in the Junior High School." *EJ*, 55 (1966), 1071–72.

Frase, L. T. "Paragraph Organization of Written Materials: The Influences of Conceptual Clustering Upon the Level and Organization of Recall." *Educ Psychol*, 60 (1969), 394–401.

Furness, Edna L. "New Dimensions in Paragraph Instruction." *Education*, 89 (1968), 105–10.

Gassen, Robert M. "A Sense of Audience and Commitment: An Approach to Teaching the Introductory Paragraph." *JETT*, 8 (1975), 25–27.

Genung, John F. *The Practical Elements of Rhetoric: With Illustrative Examples*. Boston: Ginn, 1892, pp. 193–214.

———. *The Working Principles of Rhetoric: Examined in Their Literary Relations and Illustrated with Examples*. Boston: Ginn, 1900, pp. 356–83.

Gorrell, Robert. "Very Like a Whale—A Report on Rhetoric." *CCC*, 16 (1965), 138–43.

———. "Not by Nature: Approaches to Rhetoric." *EJ* 55 (1966), 49, 409–16.

Grady, Michael. "A Conceptual Rhetoric of the Composition." *CCC*, 22 (1971), 348–54.

———. "On Teaching Christensen Rhetoric." *EJ*, 61 (1972), 77, 859–73.

Grainger, J. M. " 'Paragraphs as Trains'—The Caboose." *EJ*, 2 (1913), 126.

Grimes, Joseph E. *The Thread of Discourse*. The Hague: Mouton, 1975.

Gruber, William E. " 'Servile Copying' and the Teaching of English Composition." *CE*, 39 (1977), 491–97.

Halliday, M.A.K., and Ruqaiya Hasan. *Cohesion in English*. London: Longman, 1976.

Hirsch, E. D., Jr. *The Philosophy of Composition*. Chicago: University of Chicago Press, 1977.

Hogan, R. Craig. "Self-Instructional Units Based on the Christensen Method." *CCC*, 28 (1977), 275–77.

Irmscher, William F. *Teaching Expository Writing*. New York: Holt, Rinehart, Winston, 1979, pp. 94–106.

———. *The Holt Guide to English*. 3rd ed. New York: Holt, Rinehart, Winston, 1981, pp. 79–84.

Jones, William. "A Little Pen and Pencil Magic: Adapting an English-as-a-Second-Language Technique for Native Speakers of English." *Ex E*, 22 (1977), 21–26.

Karrfalt, David H. "Symposium on the Paragraph." In *The Sentence and the Paragraph*. Ed. Francis Christensen. Champaign, Ill.: NCTE,. 1963, pp. 71–76.

———. "The Generation of Paragraphs and Larger Units." *CCC*, 19 (1968), 211–17.

———. "Some Comments on the Principle of Rhythm in a Generative Rhetoric." *JETT*, 2 (1969), 4–15.

Kehl, D. G. "Composition and the Mimetic Mode: Imitation and Exertitiatio." In *Linguistics, Stylistics, and the Teaching of Composition*. Ed. Donald McQuade. Akron, Ohio: University of Akron, 1975, pp. 135–42.

Kieras, David E. "Good Structure and Bad Structure in Simple Paragraphs: Effects on Apparent Theme, Reading Time, and Recall." *J Verb Learn Verb Behav*, 17 (1978), 13–28.

Kirszner, Laurie G. "Supporting Topic Sentences: An Exercise for Composition Courses." *Ex E*, 22 (1978), 3–7.

Kistler, Suzanne F. "Scrambling the Unscramblable: Coherence in the Classroom." *CCC*, 29 (1978), 198–200.

Koen, Frank, Richard Young, and Alton Becker. "The Psychological Reality of the Paragraph." *Stud Lang & Lang Behav*, 3 (1967), Part 1, 526–38.

———. "The Psychological Reality of the Paragraph." *Stud Lang & Lang Behav*, 4 (1968), Part II, 482–98.

———. "The Psychological Reality of the Paragraph." *J Vrb Learn Verb Behav*, 8 (1969), 49–53.

Larson, Richard B. "Back to the Board." *CCC*, 29 (1978), 292–94.

Larson, Richard L. "Sentences in Action: A Technique for Analyzing Paragraphs." *CCC*, 18 (1967), 16–22.

———. "Toward a Linear Rhetoric of the Essay." *CCC,* 22 (1971), 140–46.

———. "Structure and Form in Non-Fiction Discourse." In *Teaching Composition: 10 Bibliographic Essays*. Ed. Gary Tate. Fort Worth: Texas Christian University Press, 1976, pp. 45–72.

Lathrop, H. B. "Unity, Coherence, and Emphasis." University of Wisconsin Studies in Language and Literature, No. 2. Madison: University of Wisconsin, 1918, pp. 77–98.

Lewis, Edwin Herbert. *The History of the English Paragraph*. Chicago, 1894; rpt. New York: AMS, 1970.

Longacre, Robert E. *Discourse, Paragraph, and Sentence Structure in Selected Phillippine Languages*. Part II, Santa Ana, Calif.: Summer Institute of Linguistics, 1968, pp. 53–192.

Lord, John B. *The Paragraph: Structure and Style*. New York: Holt, Rinehart, Winston, 1964.

Lybbert, E. K., and D. W. Cummings. "On Repetition and Coherence." *CCC*, 20 (1969), 35–38.

McCampbell, J. F. "Using Models for Improving Composition." *EJ*, 55 (1966), 772–76.

McElroy, John G. R. *The Structure of English Prose: A Manual of Composition and Rhetoric*. New York: Armstrong, 1885.

Meade, Richard A., and W. G. Ellis. "Paragraph Development in the Modern Age of Rhetoric." *EJ*, 59 (1970), 219–26; rpt. in *Rhetoric and Composition: A Sourcebook for Teachers*. Ed. Richard L. Graves. Rochelle Park, N.J.: Hayden, 1978, pp. 193–200.

———. "The Use in Writing of Textbook Methods of Paragraph Development." *J Educ Res*, 65 (1971), 74–76.

Meyer, Bonnie J. F. *The Organization of Prose and Its Effects on Memory*. Amsterdam: North-Holland, 1975.

———, and George W. McConkie. "What Is Recalled After Hearing a Passage?" *J Educ Psychol*, 65 (1973), 109–17.

Miles, Josephine. "What We Compose." *CCC*, 14 (1963), 146–54; rpt. in *Rhetoric and Composition,* Ed. Richard L. Graves. Rochelle Park, N.J.: Hayden, 1978, pp. 183–92.

Mills, Helen. *Commanding Paragraphs*. 2nd ed. Glenview, Ill.: Scott, Foresman, 1981.

Mones, Leon. "Teaching the Paragraph." *EJ*, 10 (1921), 456–60.

Moran, Michael G. "An Inductive Method of Teaching the Paragraph: The Paragraph Game." *NOTE*, 9 (1981), 12–14.

Murray, Lindley. *An English Grammar*. Vol. 1. York: Wilson, 1808, pp. 296–99.

Ney, James W. "On Not Practicing Errors." *CCC*, 14 (1963), 102–6.

Nicholas, J. Karl. "Handbooks and Horsesense." *FEN*, 2 (1973), 3–4.

Packard, Dennis J. "From Logic to Composition and Reading." *CCC*, 27 (1976), 366–72.

Perrin, Jay Kyle. "The Subject Isn't What It Seems." *EJ*, 61 (1972), 1334–37.

Pike, Kenneth. "Beyond the Sentence." *CCC*, 15 (1964a), 129–35.

———. "A Linguistic Contribution to Composition." *CCC*, 15 (1964b), 82–88.

Pincas, A. "Writing in Paragraphs." *Eng Lang Teach J*, 24 (1970), 182–85.

Pitkin, Willis L., Jr. "Discourse Blocs." *CCC*, 20 (1969), 138–48.

———. "Hierarchies and the Discourse Hierarchy." *CE*, 38 (1977a), 648–59.

———. "X/Y: Some Basic Strategies of Discourse." *CE* 38 (1977b), 660–72.

Read, Herbert. *English Prose Style*. New York: Pantheon, 1952, pp. 52–65.

Reising, R. W. "Turning the Corner: A Strategy for Teaching Paragaphing." *PJE*, 47 (1970), 308–9.

"The Rhetoric of the Paragraph: Principles and Practices." Report on *CCC* Workshop. *CCC*, 9 (1958), 191–92.

Rockas, Leo. "Further Comments on the Paragraph." *CCC*, 17 (1966), 148–51.

———. "The Persistent Ptolemy and the Paradox of the Paragraph." *CCC*, 19 (1968), 135–37.

———. "The Rhetoric of Doodle." *CE*, 40 (1978), 139–40.

Rodgers, Paul C., Jr. "Alexander Bain and the Rise of the Organic Paragraph." *QJS*, 51 (1965), 399–408.

———. "A Discourse-Centered Rhetoric of the Paragraph." *CCC*, 17 (1966), 2–11.

———. "The Stadium of Discourse." *CCC*, 18 (1967), 178–85.

Rogers, C. D. "The Sedulous but Successful Ape." *EJ*, 56 (1967), 1309–11.

Sauer, Edwin H. "The Cooperation Correction of Paragraphs." In *Essays on the Teaching of English*. Ed. E. J. Gordon and E. S. Noyes. New York: Appleton: Century-Crofts, 1960, pp. 138–49.

Schell, Leo M. "Paragraph Composition: A Suggested Sequential Outline." *Education*, 90 (1969), 158–60.

Schiff, Peter M. "Problem Solving and the Composition Model: Reorganization, Manipulation, Analysis." *RTE*, 12 (1978), pp. 203–10.

Scott, Fred N., and Joseph V. Denney. *Paragraph Writing: A Rhetoric for Colleges*. 3rd ed. Boston: Allyn, Bacon, 1893.

Selzer, Jack. "Another Look at Paragraphs in Technical Writing." *J Tech Writ Comm*, 10 (1980), 293–301.

Shearer, Ned. A. "Alexander Bain and the Genesis of Paragraph Theory."' *QJS*, 58 (1972), 408–17.

Sherman, L. A. *Analytics of Literature: A Manual for the Objective Study of English Prose and Poetry*. Boston: Ginn, 1983.

Sjogren, Douglas, and W. Timpson. "Frameworks for Comprehending Discourse: A Replication Study." *Am Educ Res J*, 16 (1979), 341–46.

Smith, Herbert Winslow. "Concerning Organization in Paragraphs." *EJ*, 9 (1920), 390–400.

Stanko, Thomas. "An Effective Opening." *CCC*, 20 (1969), 233–37.

Stern, Arthur A. "When Is a Paragraph?" *CE*, 27 (1976), 253–57.

Stratton, Beverly D., John Charlton-Seifert, and Maurice G. Williams. "Reading and Writing Shapes." *J Dev Rem Educ*, 3 (1980), 21–22.

Stronks, James. "Coherence in the Paragraph." In *Writing Exercises from Exercise Exchange*. Ed. Littleton Long. Urbana, Ill.: NCTE, 1976, pp. 48–51.

Tagliente, Jo. "The Edible Paragraph—Dagwood's Sandwich." *Elem Eng*, 50 (1973), 954–58.

Thaddeus, Janice. "Imitation and Independence." *Teachers and Writers Magazine*, 12 (1981), 2–6.

Thompson, C. J. "Thought-Building in the Paragraph." *EJ*, 5 (1916), 610–19.

Thorndyke, Perry. "Cognitive Structures in Comprehension and Memory of Narrative Discourse." *Cog Psychol*, 9 (1977), 77–110.

Trotsky, O.S., and C. C. Wood. "Nobody Writes a Paragraph." *Elem Eng*, 49 (1972), 372–75.

———. "Paragraph Writing: A Second Look." *Elem Eng*, 52 (1975), 197–200, 238.

Turner, E. G. *Greek Manuscripts of the Ancient World*. Princeton, N.J.: Princeton University Press, 1971, pp. 9–17.

Vande Kopple, William J. "Readability of Expository Paragraphs with Identical or Related Sentence Topics." *Psychol Rep*, 45 (1979), 947–52.

———. "Readability of a Rhetorically Linked Expository Paragraph." *Perc Motor Skills*, 51 (1980), 245–46.

———. "Functional Sentence Perspective, Composition, and Readings," *CCC*, 33 (1982), 50–63.

Vitanza, Victor J. "A Tagmemic Heuristic for the Whole Composition." *CCC*, 30 (1979), 270–74.

Waller, Marcie R., and F. L. Durley. "The Influence of Context on the Auditory Comprehension of Paragraphs by Aphasic Subjects." *J Speech Hear Res*, 21 (1978), 732–45.

Walpole, Jane R. "Rhetorical Form: A Crockful of Crots." *FEN*, 8 (1979), 1–2.

Warner, Richard. "Teaching the Paragraph as a Structural Unit." *CCC*, 30 (1979), 152–55.

Weathers, Winston. "Grammars of Style: New Options for Composition." *FEN*, 4 (1976), 4–12.

———. *An Alternative Style: Options for Composition*. Montclair, N.J.: Boynton/Cook, 1980.

———, and Otis Winchester. *Copy and Compose: A Guide to Prose Style*. Englewood Cliffs, N.J.: Prentice-Hall, 1969.

Wendell, Barrett. *English Composition*. New York: Ungar, 1963. First published as *Eight Lectures*, 1891.

Wensch, William. "What Reading Research Tells Us about Writing." 1979. ERIC ED 178 956.

Whitmore, Charles E. "A Doctrine of the Paragraph." *EJ*, 12 (1923), 605–10.

Whitten, M.E. *Creative Pattern Practice: A New Approach to Writing*. New York: Harcourt, Brace, World, 1966, pp. 187–200.

Wiener, Harvey S. "The Single Narrative Paragraph and College Remediation." *CE*, 33 (1972), 660–69.

Wilson, Thomas W. "Composition Where None Is Apparent: Contemporary Literature and the Course of Writing." *CCC*, 16 (1965), 70–75.

Williams, Joseph. "Nuclear Structures of Discourse." In *Selected Papers from the 1981*

Texas Writing Research Conference. Ed. Maxine C. Hairston and Cynthia L. Selfe. Austin: Texas Writing Research Group, 1981, pp. 165–89.

Winterowd, W. Ross. "The Grammar of Coherence." *CE*, 31 (1970), 828–35.

———. *The Contemporary Writer*. New York: Holt, Rinehart, Winston, 1976, pp. 110–35.

Witte, Stephen P., and Lester Faigley. "Coherence, Cohesion, and Writing Quality." *CCC*, 32 (1981), 189–206.

Wolfe, D. M. "Crucial First Assignment: Describing a Room." *Elem Eng*, 47 (1970), 784–86.

Young, Richard E., and Alton Becker. "The Role of Lexical and Grammatical Cues in Paragraph Recognitions." *Stud Lang & Lang Behav*, 2 (1966), 1–6.

———, Alton Becker, and Kenneth Pike. *Rhetoric: Discovery and Change*. New York: Harcourt, Brace, Jovanovich, 1970.

Appendices

Textbooks Revisited

DONALD C. STEWART

In the Fall of 1977 I examined a number of widely used textbooks for English composition classes to see whether they incorporated into their discussions of the composing process recent studies then being done on composition theory, particularly the work on invention by Richard Young and his colleagues at the University of Michigan. That research appeared in my article "Composition Textbooks and the Assault on Tradition" (1978).

At that time I discovered that only a small percentage of the books that were selling well were even slightly touched by contemporary theory, and I suggested that if composition teachers who were conversant with the new material ever began to have an impact on the textbook market, a number of widely selling books would quickly become obsolete.

This appendix is a follow-up to the previous essay, another look at textbooks, to see whether the conclusions that might be drawn today would be similar to or different from those I drew in 1977. My impression has been that things were changing, but that has been only an impression, unverified by any significant examination of current textbooks. Now, however, after repeating the research of 1977, with some additional variations, I have fresh observations to make about textbooks for writing courses.

I sent letters to 23 publishers, 16 of whom responded, asking them to name composition texts (the examples being books like James McCrimmon's *Writing with a Purpose* [1980], Sheridan Baker's *The Complete Stylist [1983]*, and Edward P. J. Corbett's *Classical Rhetoric for the Modern Student [1971]*) and handbooks that had sold well in the past ten years. As a very general figure, I suggested that sales of 100,000 copies or more would indicate fairly widespread regional or national use. One publisher informed me, however, that sales of 100,000 over ten years would not be considered successful by his company. I can accept that judgment from publishers who measured success in millions of copies sold, but I believe that 100,000 copies, even over ten years, suggests a book that has had some impact. I also asked them to list the titles of recent innovative texts whose sales were promising.

The publishers responded quickly and openly. They gave me more titles than I had time to examine, so I eventually settled on 14 widely selling rhetorics, 7 handbooks, and 9 innovative texts that seemed representative of the categories into which I had arbitrarily placed them. The complete list of these books appears in a list of textbooks cited at the end of this appendix.

In all, I examined 32 books, and I have grouped them as follows: (1) best-sellers that fall into three subcategories: generally traditional, slightly innovative, and considerably innovative; (2) handbooks; and (3) innovative texts that have shown promising sales but that do not yet compete with the books that dominate the market. In addition, I have looked at one new phenomenon: the university press composition textbook. Two recent examples make up the sample.

In my examination of these books I was concerned with three questions: (1) what is the author's definition of good writing; (2) what is the author's perception of the composing process and how is that related to the process of learning to write; and (3) what treatment is given to invention, arrangement, and style? The answers to these questions, as they developed in my examination of the 32 books I reviewed, provided me with considerable food for thought. (I was strongly tempted to deal with some of the questions Susan Miller raised in "Is There a Text in This Class?" [1982], but the philosophical issues in that paper are too removed from the immediate concerns of this one to permit me to discuss them.)

Best-sellers

Best-selling traditional rhetorics or composition texts, whichever one prefers to call them—and I include in this category the books by Sylvan Barnet and Marcia Stubbs (1980), Cleanth Brooks and Robert Warren (1979), David Skwire and Francis Chitwood (1981), one by Skwire alone (1982), Anthony Winkler and Jo Ray McCuen (1981), James McCrimmon (1980), and A. M. Tibbetts and Charlene Tibbetts (1979)—have a number of common features. (Although all books in this group do not contain all of these features, most of them contain a good number of them.) They treat the word, the sentence, the paragraph, or the whole theme, in that or reverse order and, in so doing, reveal their debt either to Barrett Wendell's *English Composition* (1891; rpt. 1963) or his pupil Henry Pearson's *Freshman Composition* (1897); take up the forms of discourse—narration, description, exposition (broken down usually into several patterns: comparison and contrast, cause and effect, definition, example, analysis of a process, and so on), and argument; and include special features such as the research paper, writing about literature, editing, writing examinations, and business communications. The distinctions between these books (organization of the sections, differences in the writing ability of the authors, and so on) are superficial.

The authors of these texts take a variety of stances, especially when they sense that something else is out there trying to undercut their market, but a certain tone prevails. Barnet and Stubbs (1980) exemplified this. It is the attitude that students have some very practical work to do for their teachers, and they can learn to do it by mastering a few essential principles of good writing. The authors, in effect, said to their readers, "We are not going to confuse you with a lot of pedagogical mumbo-jumbo; we are going about this in a no-nonsense way; writing in college is, in a general sense, writing practice for the tasks of life—those memos and reports which everybody, not just gifted writers, has to produce. What you need is training in the production of good, clean, economical prose." All of these remarks sound fine, but I believe that this kind of pedagogy has produced, more than anything else, generations of dull writers. Perhaps students need to learn something else.

These traditional texts usually define *good writing* by implication, rather than by direct definition, and the answer becomes this: good writing is characterized by having a point and by being responsive to an audience. Some books say something about the writers (they should take stances or roles), and they suggest that the kind of writing they are talking about—practical writing for college students—should be direct, clear, and utilitarian. Anyone can learn to write clearly, economically, purposefully, and effectively. The problem is that these books simpy do not deal with the writer in a very sophisticated way psychologically, they neglect invention terribly, they say nothing about organization that is not old hat, and their remarks on style are often simplistic.

Some qualifications are in order. We must ask how well acquainted with contemporary theory the writers of these texts are and whether or not the decision not to mention modern approaches to invention, arrangement, and style is made deliberately or out of ignorance. I do not know, personally, most of the writers of these books, but I do know Arnold and Charlene Tibbetts, and they have said, publicly, that their book (1979) is the one teachers will buy. Their conservatism is an informed one, dictated, in their judgment, by a market that is not overly receptive to new thinking about composition. That introduces another question. Who makes textbook decisions? Are the buyers of texts uninformed about what has been taking place in the field, particularly during the past 20 years, or do they choose to reject new knowledge in favor of the established paradigm that has come to them from late nineteenth-century texts? Are publishers themselves culpable because they perpetuate a status quo, preferring to continue with what is safe and avoiding the new and relatively unfamiliar?

The books I call "slightly innovative" best-sellers often contain the same kinds of topics, the same pattern of organization, and the same theoretical stance of the traditional books, but they offer occasional modifications that catch the attention of a textbook reader whose sensibility has been dulled by a repetition of the contents and methodologies of the traditional books. For example, Michael Adelstein and Jean Pival's *Writing Commitment* (1976) shows some awareness of early pre-writing work—the journal and the need for an authentic voice—and they have modern ideas about usage and grammar. They work in discussion of the Christensen cumulative sentence and its uses in descriptive writing, and they do have some specific if not particularly original answers to the question of what is good writing:

Good writing reflects the writer's ability to use the appropriate voice . . . . Good writing reflects the writer's ability to organize the material into a coherent whole so that it moves logically from a central dominant idea to the supporting points and finally to a consistent ending, conveying to the reader a sense of a well-thought-out plan. Good writing reflects the writer's ability to write clearly and unambiguously. . . . Good writing reflects the writer's pride in the manuscript. (p. xxi)

What they really mean is that good writers adjust their voices to the audience and situation, organize well, have command of the language, are persuasive, and are good at editing. That is about as profound as saying that good weather consists of temperatures in the low 70s, low humidity, and clear skies with little or no breeze. "There's ne'er a villain dwelling in all Denmark but he's an arrant knave," said Hamlet. To which Horatio aptly replies, "There needs no ghost, my lord, come from the grave to tell us this" (Act I, Scene v).

Jacqueline Berke's *Twenty Questions for the Writer* (1981) goes beyond traditional texts in its definition of good writing, its treatment of invention, and in some aspects its treatment of style. She called *rhetoric*, and by implication, good writing, "The art of using language to its best possible effect: to teach, to delight, to win assent, to 'energize' the truth, to move an audience to action—not ill-chosen or precipitous action, but considered and significant action" (pp. 3-4). Citing Kenneth Burke, she said that good writing promotes cooperation, it has integrity, and it appeals to reason. The introduction of the moral dimension into the definition of good writing is refreshing, particularly in an age that increasingly values amoral but effective managerial skills.

Her discussion of the way one learns to write does not leave me confident that she has progressed beyond the instrumental metaphor, the notion that writing is thought on paper, which was attacked by Robert Zoellner in his *College English* monograph "Talk-Write" in 1969, but her treatment of invention is good. She said that it can and must be dealt with systematically and creatively. She acknowledged the topics of classical rhetoric and then generated her own inventional procedure, the 20 questions, to which she gave high priority. This is focusing realistically on the question: where do writers get their subjects? The only problem is that she keyed several questions to the modes or forms of discourse, the efficacy of which in the teaching of writing has been questioned for the past 30 years. Her discussion of style does include mention of Francis Christensen's work, which is a hopeful sign, but despite the apparent modernity of this book, I find it more traditional, overall, than one would at first suspect.

Wilma and David Ebbitt's *Writer's Guide* (1978), a re-working of Porter Perrin's successful text (1942) by the same name, is commendable, despite the number of traditional features in the book, for its recognition that writing is highly idiosyncratic, its acknowledgment that a range of rhetorical, syntactic, and lexical choices are involved in any adjustment to a writing context, and its inclusion of some sentence-combining work in the section on style.

Hans Guth's *Words and Ideas* (1980) and Donald Hall's *Writing Well* (1982), the first in its fifth edition, the second in its fourth, are good examples of texts that are well written, essentially traditional, but slightly touched by recent research in composing. For example, Guth asserted that his book is process-based, in keeping with the trend in composition teaching over the past decade, and Hall showed awareness of recent studies in brain hemisphericity and its importance in composing, the recursive nature of the composing process, and the necessity of extending the time for pre-writing, but one feels that although he has been touched by recent work, he has not been touched very deeply or else one must accept the conclusion that the publisher told him to stick with the traditional stuff that sells well. Hall's textbook is one of the best written ones in the lot, a not surprising fact since he is an accomplished poet, but I have been continually puzzled by the simplistic ways in which he discussed the composing process. He knows better. But here is an author who can make even the old stuff interesting, and sales figures for his book testify to his ability to do that.

Guth is another interesting case. For example, his discussion of invention goes quickly into focusing on a topic; there is no real assimilation of the material Richard Young has been promoting. Arrangement is keyed to traditional categories: the modes of discourse and patterns of exposition that one is accustomed to finding in these books. There is no creative approach to arrangement or to real alternatives in it. Style is handled traditionally too. But anyone who has heard Guth speak at professional meetings knows that he is familiar with new work in a number of areas. I do not know, however, whether he chooses not to assimilate new material because he thinks it will make his book less saleable or whether he has reservations about its efficacy. Only one thing is certain: he does not omit it out of ignorance.

One other somewhat innovative text that has done well financially deserves mention here: Maxine Hairston's *Contemporary Rhetoric* (1982). It is my impression that successive editions of Hairston's book have been increasingly affected by new work in composition theory. For example, in this third edition we find mention of the processes of *preparation, incubation, illumination,* and *verification,* pre-writing terms that first appeared in textbooks in Young, Alton Becker, and Kenneth Pike's *Rhetoric* (1970) more than ten years ago. Hairston also included, in her discussion of invention, a modification of the Burke pentad, identified as "the journalists' questions," some of the topics of classical rhetoric, brainstorming, focused freewriting, capsuling, what she called "prism thinking," a reduction of Young, Becker, and Pike's tagmemic matrix, and even research and serendipity. The section on arrangement is not particularly new, but she did incorporate into her discussion of style material on sentence-combining.

Overall, one must say that this is essentially a traditional book, occasionally incorporating new theory. That is the author's choice. Her comments and bibliographies reveal that she, like Guth, is familiar with new material that she uses as she pleases. Her discussion of the metamorphosis of the topics of classical rhetoric into categories of exposition probably comes from Frank D'Angelo; Young's influence, as indicated, is here; Kenneth Burke's influence and that of the sentence-combiners have touched this book. It will be interesting to see what changes the author chooses to make in subsequent editions of the text.

There are two widely selling texts that I regard as more innovative than traditional: Dean Memering and Frank O'Hare's *Writer's Work* (1980), and W. Ross Winterowd's *Contemporary Writer* (1981). Although Memering and O'Hare's table of contents reveals a number of traditional headings, there are several aspects of the book that break away from the old paradigm. For example, when they say that writing is a process of mediating between choices, choices determined by one's perception of experience, purpose, code, audience, self, and the message, they are moving close to a context-oriented definition of good writing; I mean a complex understanding of context, not something simple that can be reduced to a formula such as writer, reader, message. Their discussion of the composing process is flawed, however, by the assumption so common to all textbooks on writing that movement from writing about personal exprience to writing on more abstract subjects is a movement from the simple to the complex, from the easier to the harder. I do not believe that assumption has been rigorously enough challenged in our writing classrooms. Writing about personal experience, which is often narrative and descriptive writing, requires as high a degree of skill in invention, arrangement, and style as impersonal academic writing. It is a different kind of writing, and it requires less research and assimilation of concepts by students, but getting it on the page so that the reader has a sense of an authentic voice reporting accurately, honestly, and aesthetically that which one sees, feels, and hears, is at least as difficult as getting on paper more impersonal prose.

Perhaps we confuse the difficulty one has in understanding certain kinds of concepts with the actual presentation of them, itself not so difficult a task given the nature of most academic prose. I do not, however, wish to give the impression that I am unfamiliar with recent work on both the linear and recursive nature of composing. One could say that understanding of difficult concepts occurs during the process of writing about them. But we have a tendency to minimize some composing difficulties when writing academic prose by reverting to a limited number of organizational "sets." Thus the writer of such work usually spends very little time worrying about the structure of the piece; he or she already knows that what is expected is a thesis statement, three to five supporting arguments, and a concluding remark. The writer of good narrative or descriptive prose has no such organizational security when composing. Much of our academic prose is in great need of re-charging. As it appears in books, articles, and government documents, it is frequently formulaic and dull.

Memering and O'Hare's discussion of invention includes brainstorming, concepts from Burke's pentad, and Young, Becker, and Pike's matrix. They are at their best, however, in their discussion of style in which they stress the need for an authentic voice and their discussion of sentence-combining, a particular strength of both authors. In their discussion of voice they fall into the trap of assuming that the several superficial voices of a person in a variety of roles are significantly different from the person's authentic voice. On the other hand, their discussion of sentence–combining specifically avoids a fault in many such texts: the impulse to identify, and to encourage students to identify, specific grammatical structures. They stress the combining of sentences into longer more complex units and do not worry about names for the subsections of sentences. The traditional composition teacher, steeped in a methodology that has stressed grammar, cannot resist the impulse to take time sorting out the adjective and adverbial clauses, participial phrases, gerunds, absolutes, and other structures at the expense of the more important exercise: combining chunks of material into more and more complex sentences. Those who have depth in this area can do no service of greater importance than stressing the need for backing off from the game of identifying grammatical structures as a part of sentence-combining. The actual exercise itself is sufficient.

Winterowd's book (1981) implies that good writing is that which most effectively solves the problems posed by any compositional situation. The problems are numerous— from concerns with language to larger conceptual matters—and varied. A good writer, he implied, knows how to identify and solve these problems. This is an excellent comprehensive notion about good writing.

Winterowd said that the writing process consists of pre-writing, writing, re-writing, and editing, and he amplified these concepts. His discussion of pre-writing includes brainstorming, clustering, both the journalist's questions and Burke's pentad, even the ratios of the pentad, something most other books avoid, and the tagmemic matrix of Young, Becker, and Pike. He has a good chapter on journal writing, sensible advice about outlining, writing about literature, the research paper, and logic, readability, and emphasis (the latter a response to Hirsch's *Philosophy of Composition* [1977]). His discussions of the paragraph and of style are less interesting than his material on invention, but he offered one generalization about language structures that should be memorized by every teacher of composition at every level: "No language form is good or bad *out of context*" (p. 441; italics mine). The implications of that remark are so far reaching that they are likely to be overlooked. It finally refutes an absolutist position in matters of language use. Taking the statement to its logical conclusion, one could even say that "He done real good" was an effective and acceptable expression in a particular context: as a judgment of someone's performance by one relatively uneducated person speaking to another. The message gets through; the level of usage may be one with which both the speaker and the listener are comfortable. In that context, the sentence is fine. Used by superintendents of schools to describe the performance of a teacher would be a disaster;

it would offend their listeners and cause them to have serious reservations about their competency for the job.

The best aspect of Winterowd's book, whether or not one is reading his presentation of innovative or traditional material, is the reader's sense that the writer knows, in detail, far more than is here and that he has assimilated much contemporary research and made it palatable as well as practical.

University Press Composition Texts

The phenomenon of university presses publishing textbooks for English composition is somewhat novel. Traditionally, they have supported non-profitable scholarship by subsidizing it. I wonder if the appearance of textbooks is now a signal that university presses need to make money on some of their books or that they have recognized that the teaching of writing is becoming a respectable subject. Whatever the reasons, I looked at Irvin Hashimoto, Barry Kroll, and John Schafer's *Strategies for Academic Writing* (1982) and Susan Horton's *Thinking Through Writing* (1982). They present some striking contrasts. Hashimoto and his colleagues, who developed their book while teaching at Michigan, offered a predictable rationale for their text: it is concerned with academic writing because that is the kind of work students in college will do most of the time, it helps students learn to think in the ways specialists in their particular disciplines think, and it is a significant part of a student's life. They said that such writing is more concerned with exposition and argument than with narration and description and implied that the latter is less difficult to do than the former, a position I have already discussed in this appendix. After studying the book's rationale, organization, and discussion of the composing process, I have concluded that despite the excuses that might be offered because the book limits itself to academic writing, it has severe limitations: (1) the authors never defined good writing; their assumption seems to have been that it is clear, informative, and interesting academic prose; (2) on the composing process they offered material that has been in textbooks for several generations, some of which has been challenged in the past 20 years; and (3) their treatment of invention is non-existent, a particular irony because their book comes from Michigan, the place where, in the mid-1960s, Richard Young and his colleagues began their assault on the deficiencies of contemporary thinking about invention. Was it possible to teach writing at Michigan and be untouched by Richard Young's ideas when he was there? Apparently, the answer is yes.

Horton's *Thinking Through Writing* (1982) is a different matter. This is less a text and more a statement about writing, and it is a very good statement. The author was influenced in her thinking by Ann Berthoff, who is an active and creative member of the Conference on College Composition and Communication. One may not always agree with Berthoff— she is controversial—but she is knowledgeable. There are many things I found to like about Horton's book. "Good writing has to do with putting together what is there in a plausible, interesting, and persuasive way" (p. 4). She was opposed to simplistic definitions, particularly error-oriented descriptions of the writing process. She took cognizance of the way physical behavior generates writing; she noted the importance of seeing what one writes so that one can proceed to more complex ideas; she accepted the uniqueness and eccentricity of the process for each person; she defined writing as a process of recognizing and solving problems; she implied that learning to write involves a sustained and elaborate effort of thinking, essentially concept forming. An essay may serve, she said, to inform; to instruct; to persuade; to solve a problem; to speculate about an issue;

to theorize about what has happened, what is happening, what will happen; to retrieve relevant information; to analyze problematic or troubling data; to discover new concepts; and so on. This is one of the few books I have seen that goes into concept formation as conceived by Jerome Bruner and elaborated by Gordon Rohman and Albert Wlecke (1964). She stressed the point that people are given certain concepts by their environment, that they may find them challenged, that their responsibility is to think through their ways of seeing and defining the world and the ways they think.

In her chapter on the whole essay the author described the writing process as a mess and a mystery. She also recognized the recursive nature of the process. She did not really do a lot with traditional concepts of organization and style; most of her effort was in the new work on process and invention. The people cited in her bibliography give some evidence of her reading and the reasons for the modernity of the book: James Britton, Janet Emig, Walter Ong, E. D. Hirsch, Janice Lauer, Lev Vygotsky, Thomas Kuhn. Other names in the bibliography suggest that this author consciously attempted to avoid the kind of writing instruction found in texts that are the carriers of the nineteenth-century tradition in the teaching of writing.

In the first scrimmage between university presses, then, between Michigan and Johns Hopkins, the latter wins by four touchdowns.

Innovative Texts

A number of less than best-selling but promising texts have been or are coming into the composition market at this time. Some of them are very good, and one wants them to succeed. I am less enthusiastic about others. Nonetheless, they represent some significant changes taking place in the market. In this list I include Edward P. J. Corbett's *Classical Rhetoric for the Modern Student* (1971); Frank D'Angelo's *Process and Thought in Composition* (1980); Jim Corder's *Contemporary Writing* (1979); Elizabeth Cowan and Greg Cowan's *Writing;* (1980); Linda Flower's *Problem-Solving Strategies for Writing* (1981); A. D. Van Nostrand, C. H. Knoblauch, and Joan Pettigrew's *Process of Writing* (1982); Peter Elbow's *Writing with Power* (1981); and Robert Scholes and Nancy Comley's *Practice of Writing* (1981).

Of Corbett's book (1971) one can say only the obvious: it has been with us for some time and most people in the profession know it well. It remains one of the very best, if not the best, expositions of classical rhetorical theory in a modern textbook for undergraduates. Corbett's treatment of invention, arrangement, and style is deep and thorough; his brief history of rhetoric is informative and useful. The book has been the source for more recent adaptations of classical rhetoric into modern textbooks.

D'Angelo's book (1980) is also classically oriented—he took up invention, arrangement, and style—and it is thorough. What separates it from other recent texts are a few features that either originated with him or have been emphasized by him to the extent that others have begun to listen. For example, the book is D'Angelo's platform for arguing that the modes of discourse are also patterns of thinking that develop naturally from the nature of the inquiry each initiates. "Thus, paradigms are on the one hand patterns of thought that give to your writing a determinate direction, and on the other hand formal patterns that help you to order your ideas" (p. 98). This is a position he first argued in *A Conceptual Theory of Rhetoric* (1975). D'Angelo has also been most persistent in calling attention to the recursive nature of the writing process, noting that invention, arrangement, style, and revision are often going on at once.

His discussion of arrangement contains the beginning, middle, and end pattern that appears so briefly in Plato's *Phaedrus*, but I do not sense that D'Angelo perceives this as an organic instead of a mechanical concept. Overall, however, the book is challenging and informed by much of the thinking going on in contemporary writing circles.

Corder's *Contemporary Writing* (1979) is a pleasing book to read: it includes a great deal of recent material on invention—journal keeping, existential sentences (which he called "Charlie Brown sentences"), word associations, question asking, journalist's questions, some topics from classical rhetoric, and some problem-solving techniques.

Although his discussion of arrangement is keyed to the five-part classical rhetorical pattern (introduction, background, argument, refutation, and conclusion), he offered a number of alternatives to suit a variety of occasions, a flexibility that is commendable. The section on style is adequate but not as strong as the others.

Despite the text's habit of interrupting the flow of its discussion of important concepts with inserts, blocks, and other diversions, the book profits from the author's congenial style, his flexibility, and his recognition that writing varies with individuals and that no single method will ever be adequate to cover all possible rhetorical situations that any person faces.

The Cowans's book (1980), the main disadvantage of which is its sheer bulk, is praiseworthy for its thorough discussion of the writing process. Invention is given much space (brainstorming, looping, cubing, the pentad, tagmemic applications, all are represented); its discussion of arrangement is keyed to the needs of a particular context; paragraphing is discussed in a non-dogmatic manner—they are the first, to my recollection, to say bluntly that the traditional paragraph form is suited to perhaps 50 percent of writing occasions and that paragraphing occurs for many more reasons than are usually given in composition textbooks; style is adjusted to context. In sum, this is a refreshing book, full of clever diagrams and good advice and lacking the formulaic dogmatic tone of so many single-method texts.

Flower's book (1981) is very different from any of the others. Her perception of the composing process, for example, is a considerable advancement over that of the more traditional books in the field. She was concerned with analyzing a piece of organized rhetoric not to see how it is put together but to discover how it was created. Collaboration with John Hayes, a cognitive psychologist, has informed her approach to the writing process. Thus instead of telling students to find a thesis, she showed them how to recognize and define a problem and then solve it. Six steps are given: (1) define the conflict or key issue; (2) place the problem in a larger context; (3) make your problem definition more operational; (4) explore the parts of the problem; (5) generate alternative solutions; (6) come to a well-supported conclusion.

In dealing with writer's block, she drew on the process articulated in Young, Becker, and Pike's *Rhetoric: Discovery and Change* (1970): preparation, incubation, illumination, and verification. The basic point is that she did not oversimplify or underconceptualize the actual process of composing.

Flower was continuously attentive to the needs of both writer and reader—the terms *reader-based* and *writer-based prose* inform her book—and her treatment of invention is deep and skillful.

Her discussion of organization is less impressive. She assumed that good writing is organized logically, and that writing which lacks this organization will be troubling to a reader. She might concede that some writer-based prose will contain illogicalities, acceptable because they will not trouble the writer-reader, but in the practical world, reader-based prose must be logical. But she failed to be daring enough on this point.

Her concept of style is essentially Spencerian: use language that requires a minimum of mental energy to comprehend and thus allows the reader maximum energy for coping with the ideas presented. On the whole, this is a good book; it does not rely, in its conception or organization, on traditional models.

Van Nostrand and colleagues offer a book (1982) that is not as innovative as they would have liked it to be. Some good concepts are in it, however. For example, they, too, recognized the recursive nature of the writing process. Their definition of *composing* as the forming of relationships among pieces of information and their observation that in composing the writer will often discover relationships hitherto unnoticed or unsuspected is good, but the rest of the book is not so fresh or so interesting.

Peter Elbow (1981) did not answer the question, what is good writing, directly; his answer seems to be scattered throughout his book. Good writing has voice, the voice you speak with that gets transferred to the paper, and it makes a point, but he was aware of the varied contexts in which writing does this. At times one has the opportunity to be subtle; at other times, just to get it straight and not confuse the reader. He obviously thought people should write about things that interest them and are important to them, but although we tend to think this is a modern concept, it can be found in Richard Whately's *Elements of Rhetoric* (1846) in the first half of the nineteenth century.

The point he made about voice is worth noting, because he is one of the few to recognize that one essential voice underlies the many voices we use in the various roles we play in our daily lives.

Another point of interest in this text is the author's recognition that the creative and critical faculties, both of which are needed by the writer, operate against each other while composing is occurring. He recommended suspending the critical faculty while composing, advice that runs counter to that of those who point to the recursive nature of composing and who would assert that one cannot, even if he or she wishes to, completely suspend those critical faculties when writing. As Father Ong has pointed out in *The Barbarian Within* (1962), a writer is both a writer and a reader; that is, while composing writers are playing the words going onto the page back to themselves and reviewing them while moving forward with the composing effort itself. All of this merely suggests the rich complexity of the composing process, a complexity skated over by more traditional texts. My view is that in composing, even if one has a tendency to do some mental editing as the process goes along, it is better to ride the crest of a momentum that one can build up in a composing effort.

Elbow had some good observations, also, on the ways one learns to write. He made the analogy between learning to write and learning to speak to a new person in a new situation. Writing is not like learning a new language. He then offered a large number of strategies—looping, quick revising, freewriting, editing, and developing voice—that are rarely found in traditional textbooks but that are psychologically truer to what happens than what is reported in those books.

He never really got into a discussion of invention, arrangement, or style, as such, and I doubt that these subjects interest him a great deal. I think he believes that they will take care of themselves if the writer takes control of his or her work.

In many ways Elbow's work, like Horton's book (1982), is not really a textbook. It is a statement of Elbow's observations, perceptions, and convictions about the writing process.

Robert Scholes and Nancy Comley (1981) gave us a new term, *extraordinary writing*, to describe the kinds of work college students do. I take it to mean writing that is out of the normal pattern of a student's experience. Their perception of writing appears to be influenced by speech-act theory. They divide the writing process into four categories: writer, reader, topic, and text, each of which is self-evident. Implicit, however, and this seems to be a real strength in this text, is their recognition that the writing process is constantly mediating between these factors. They seemed very strongly context oriented, and they identified forms of discourse that they called "writer-oriented," "reader-oriented," and "topic-oriented." *Writer-oriented forms* of discourse are expression and reflection. *Reader-oriented forms* are direction and persuasion. *Topic-oriented forms* are those one is most accustomed to seeing in textbooks: argumentation, description, narration, classification, analysis, and synthesis. This book contains a curious mix of classical topics metamorphosed and the nineteenth-century forms of discourse.

The refreshing part of their presentation is that they have asked the questions James Britton believed were essential: what needs of both the writer and the reader are fulfilled by a particular piece of discourse? Scholes and Comley became more traditional when they said that the function of writing is to organize, to order, and to clarify. They did not say a lot new about purpose, thesis, unity of voice, tone, perspective, coherence and development, or words and sentences. But their unwillingness to present traditional views on the paragraph is commendable. They accepted the fact that the modern paragraph is much more difficult to define than many texts would have us believe.

Invention, arrangement, and style are not dealt with directly in the book. The authors said almost nothing about the ways in which one develops material for a subject, assuming, I suppose, that the assignments given and the students' understanding of the kind of discourse they are producing will generate the material. None of the recent material on invention is here. The section on argumentation contains elements of the classical paradigm, but they seemed to be encouraging the notion that proving a point, or keeping the writing in focus, will direct the organization. Style is also dealt with briefly.

Although the book lacks some features I would like to see, it does represent some innovation in addressing the needs of both writer and reader in realistic ways, and it has been influenced, to some extent, by portions of modern theory. It mutes elements of nineteenth-century theory and could not be said to be much in the line of traditional textbooks of the twentieth century.

Handbooks

If we use the *Harbrace Handbook* by Hodgin and Whitten as a model of the kinds of things one usually finds in handbooks, we must come to some melancholy conclusions. Here is the kind of book that is a publisher's bread and butter. Their sales are astronomical. *They make money.* But what do they celebrate? They emphasize the preoccupation—the American *obsession*—with superficial mechanical correctness. In *Writing with Power* (1981) Elbow called the material handbooks contain *grammar*, but he used the term as a blanket for not only grammar but punctuation, spelling, and mechanics (he knew the definitions of *grammar*, but he was just explaining his particular use of the term in a special context). "Like it or not," he said, "there is a deep psychic importance to that whole set of rules and conventions for writing which we tend to sum up loosely as grammar. Grammar is glamour. . . . Writing without errors doesn't make you anything, but writing with errors—if you give it to other people—makes you a hick, a boob, a bumpkin. . . . The only way to make grammar disappear—to keep the surface of your writing from distracting readers away from your message—is to make it right'' (p. 168).

He is absolutely right. But why? Who caused this to happen? What set of circumstances? A complete answer would involve the history of the evolution of literacy in England and America, class consciousness, the desire for upward mobility, and a lot of other things. But it also takes us back to the early composition courses and their emphases that are still with us. The pity is that English teachers and the American public ignored advice given by Fred Newton Scott of Michigan in a paper he wrote for the *School Review* in 1909:

It is of course necessary that our young people should spell and punctuate properly, should make the verb agree with its subject, should use words in their dictionary senses and write sentences that can be read aloud without causing unnecessary pain to the mandibles. They should also know the meanings of the words in the poetry and prose that they read, and understand the allusions to things ancient and modern. But these matters, after all, are subsidiary and must be treated as such. They are means to an end. To treat them as an end in and for themselves is to turn education in this subject upside down. The main purpose of training in composition is free speech, direct and sincere communion with our fellows, that swift and untrammeled exchange of opinion, feeling, and experience which is the working instrument of the social instinct and the motive power of civilization. The teacher of composition who does not somehow make his pupils realize this and feel that all of the verbal machinery is but for the purpose of fulfilling this great end, is false to his trust. (p. 19)

Despite the progress we have made, the sales of handbooks tell us that we have scarcely dented, in the minds of many English teachers and the general public, the sense that mechanical correctness is the primary virtue of writing. What of the handbooks' treatment of the writing process? It is generally superficial: invention gets reduced to "choose and limit a subject" (one that you like); arrangement to "make an outline," and style to clichés about word choice and sentence and paragraph structure. In spite of this we are told, in the eighth edition of the *Harbrace Handbook* (1977), "Although shorter than the Seventh Edition, the Eighth still covers all the basic principles of effective writing to which instructors usually refer, as shown by a comprehensive examination of student papers" (p. v). *All* of the basic principles? Hardly any are dealt with. "To which instructors refer." Which instructors? In what schools?

Handbooks suggest the correlation between knowledge of grammar and good writing, a notion that had been discredited for several decades until challenged by Martha Kolln in the May 1981 issue of *College Composition and Communication*. She found the research designs of many studies on the subject flawed, but she did not include in her sample the most comprehensive piece of work on this subject in recent years: Warwick Elley's three-year study in New Zealand between 1972 and 1975. Untroubled by that omission, Kolln called those who question the value of grammatical knowledge to writers "alchemists," a position I find analogous to that of one who tells the owner of a car to "get a horse."

Handbooks also contain Wendell's unity, coherence, and emphasis and the Bain paragraph but rarely any sentence-combining.

I cannot conclude my discussion of handbooks without a note on William Strunk and E. B. White's *Elements of Style* (1979), "one of the most widely used style manuals in the country today. . . . It has helped millions to improve and refine their writing style" its advertisements say. Who can read this book without remembering what Monroe Beardsley said in "Style and Good Style" (1965)? He noted that in Rule 14, "Use the active voice," they recommended changing "There were a great number of dead leaves lying on the ground" to "Dead leaves covered the ground" (p. 19). In Rule 15 Strunk and White said, "Put statements in positive form" (p. 19). That means changing "He was not very often on time" to "He usually came late." Putting into practice Rule 16, "Use definite, specific, concrete language," they changed "A period of unfavorable weather set in" to "It rained every day for a week" (p. 21). In all three examples, as Beardsley pointed out, we are not offered a better way of saying something; we are offered a significantly changed *meaning*. For example, when one says "Dead leaves covered the ground," one is saying more than "A great number of dead leaves were lying on the ground." In the latter there are some open spaces. The revisions suggested for Rules 15 and 16 are equally flawed. They significantly alter *meaning*. E. B. White may have liked Professor Strunk's dogmatism, but advice on style is a strange thing, as Beardsley pointed out, if it asks you to mean something other than what you intended to mean. For such reasons, I am not particularly fond of the Strunk and White manual.

White's contribution, an essay on style, isn't bad, and I accept his notion that style is something intangible, but he failed to make his point with paraphrases of Thomas Paine: "Times like these try men's souls"; "How trying it is to live in these times!"; "These are trying times for men's souls"; and "Soulwise, these are trying times!" These sentences are poor substitutes for "These are the times that try men's souls," said White. Why? He observed that we could "talk about 'rhythm' and 'cadence,' but the talk would be vague and unconvincing." We certainly could, but I see no reason in the world why it should be either vague or unconvincing. Look at the four paraphrases again, with their accents marked:

> Tímes liƙe thése trý mén's sóuls.
>
> Hŏw trýinğ iť iš tŏ líve ĭn thése tiḿes!
>
> Thése aŕe trýinğ tiḿes fŏr mén's soúls.
>
> Soúlwiše, thése aŕe trýinğ tiḿes.

Everyone of them is herky-jerky in its rhythm. There is no regularity to the pattern of accents, unless you want to consider the four straight stresses in the first version. In Paine's sentence, however, a clear and very predictable pattern of stressed and unstressed syllables is established, and this pattern gives the lines their stately dignity: 'Thése aŕe thĕ tiḿes thăt trý mĕn's sóuls.'' Sentence rhythm and cadence are exactly what make the difference. White should have chosen a different example to illustrate the intangible qualities of good style.

The authors of handbooks will argue that the purpose of such books is not to provide comprehensive treatments of rhetoric. My rejoinder: Do the purpose and popularity of handbooks suggest something about the priorities of those who teach composition? I think they do, and I do not care for the priorities they suggest.

That brings us to some summary judgments about textbooks and handbooks for English composition. What is the current state of affairs? The forms of discourse, the methods of exposition, the word, the sentence, and the paragraph, and a concern for superficial mechanical correctness are still the staples of the most commercially successful texts. Promising inroads are being made by the kinds of texts I have cited in the section on innovative books, but they are still inroads. One should never underestimate the inertia of a profession that has defined its pedagogy in a particular way for nearly five generations. It will not be changed overnight. But we do seem to be moving closer to a significant breakthrough, despite a return to "the basics," which usually are not basics at all but only the most trivial aspects of writing. There are a number of new people entering the profession who have had professional preparation in the teaching of writing that is nearly the equivalent of their professional training in literature, and they will not long be satisfied with the old paradigm. So change is on the wing, and it will come but quite literally over the dead bodies of some who are fiercely resistant to new ways of doing things.

We must ask, again, what is the role of publishers in this matter? To protect their markets, do they perpetuate old ideas? Are they keeping teachers who might be responsive to new ideas philosophically and theoretically in jail because it is profitable to do so, or are they merely recognizing that new ideas have not won sufficient assent from a large enough base of the profession to gain acceptance? I do not know the answer, but I am aware of the problems.

Textbooks Cited

Adelstein, Michael E., and Jean G. Pival. *The Writing Commitment*. New York: Harcourt, 1976.

Baker, Sheridan. *The Complete Stylist*. 3rd Ed. New York: Harper, Row, 1983.

———. *The Practical Stylist*. 5th Ed. New York: Harper, Row, 1981.

Barnet, Sylvan, and Marcia Stubbs. *Practical Guide to Writing*. 3rd ed. Boston: Little, Brown, 1980.

Berke, Jacqueline. *Twenty Questions for the Writer*. 3rd ed. New York: Harcourt, 1981.

Brooks, Cleanth, and Robert Penn Warren. *Modern Rhetoric*. 4th ed. New York: Harcourt, 1979.

Corbett, Edward P. J. *Classical Rhetoric for the Modern Student*. 2nd ed. New York: Oxford University Press, 1971.

Corder, Jim W. *Contemporary Writing*. Glenview, Ill.: Scott, Foresman, 1979.

Cowan, Elizabeth, and Greg Cowan. *Writing*. New York: Wiley, 1980.

D'Angelo, Frank J. *Process and Thought in Composition*. 2nd ed. Cambridge, Mass.: Winthrop, 1980.

Ebbitt, Wilma R., and David R. Ebbitt. *Writer's Guide*. 6th ed. Glenview, Ill.: Scott, Foresman, 1978.

Elbow, Peter. *Writing With Power: Techniques for Mastering the Writing Process*. New York: Oxford University Press, 1981.

Elsbree, Langdon, Neil G. Altizer, and Paul V. Kelley. *The Heath Handbook of Composition*. 10th ed. Lexington, Mass.: Heath, 1981.

Flower, Linda. *Problem-Solving Strategies for Writing*. New York: Harcourt, 1981.

Guth, Hans. *Words and Ideas*. 5th ed. Belmont, Calif.: Wadsworth, 1980.

Hairston, Maxine. *Contemporary Rhetoric*. 3rd ed. Boston: Houghton Mifflin, 1982.

Hall, Donald. *Writing Well*. 4th ed. Boston: Little, Brown, 1982.

Hashimoto, Irvin Y., Barry Kroll, and John C. Schafer. *Strategies for Academic Writing*. Ann Arbor: University of Michigan Press, 1982.

Hodges, John C., and Mary E. Whitten. *The Harbrace College Handbook*. 8th ed. New York: Harcourt, 1977.

Horton, Susan R. *Thinking Through Writing*. Baltimore: Johns Hopkins University Press, 1982.

Leggett, Glenn, C. David Mead, and William Charvat. *Prentice-Hall Handbook for Writers*. 8th ed. Englewood Cliffs, N.J.: Prentice-Hall, 1982.

McCrimmon, James. *Writing with a Purpose*. 7th ed. Boston: Houghton Mifflin, 1980.

Memering, Dean, and Frank O'Hare. *The Writer's Work: Guide to Effective Composition*. Englewood Cliffs, N.J.: Prentice-Hall, 1980.

Pearson, Henry Greenleaf. *Freshmen Composition*. Boston: Heath, 1897.

Perrin, Porter Gale. *Writer's Guide and Index to English*. Chicago: Scott, Foresman, 1942.

Scholes, Robert, and Nancy R. Comley. *The Practice of Writing*. New York: St. Martin's, 1981.

Skwire, David. *Writing with a Thesis: A Rhetoric and Reader*. 3rd ed. New York: Holt, Rinehart, Winston, 1982.

———, and Frances Chitwood. *Student's Book of College English*. 3rd ed. New York: Macmillan, 1981.

Strunk, William, and E. B. White. *The Elements of Style*. 3rd ed. New York: Macmillan, 1979.

Tibbetts, A. M., and Charlene Tibbetts. *Strategies of Rhetoric*. 3rd ed. Glenview, Ill.: Scott, Foresman, 1979.

Van Nostrand, A. D., C. H. Knoblauch, and Joan Pettigrew. *The Process of Writing: Discovery and Control*. 2nd ed. Boston: Houghton Mifflin, 1982.

Watkins, Floyd C., William B. Dillingham, and Edwin T. Martin. *Practical English Handbook*. 5th ed. Boston: Houghton Mifflin, 1978.

Wendell, Barrett. *English Composition*. New York, 1891; rpt. New York: Ungar, 1963.

Willis, Hulon, and Enno Klammer. *A Brief Handbook of English*. 2nd ed. New York: Harcourt, 1981.

Willson, Robert F., John M. Kierzek, and Walker Gibson. *The Macmillan Handbook of English*. 7th ed. New York: Macmillan, 1982.

Winkler, Anthony C., and Jo Ray McCuen. *Rhetoric Made Plain*. 3rd ed. New York: Harcourt, 1981.

Winterowd, W. Ross. *The Contemporary Writer*. 2nd ed. New York: Harcourt, 1981.

References

Beardsley, Monroe. "Style and Good Style." In *Reflections on High School English: NDEA Institute Lectures*. Ed. Gary Tate. Tulsa: University of Tulsa, 1966, pp. 91–105. Rpt. in *Contemporary Essays on Style*. Ed. Glen A. Love and Michael Payne. Glenview, Ill.: Scott, Foresman, 1969, pp. 3–15.

D'Angelo, Frank. *A Conceptual Theory of Rhetoric*. Cambridge, Mass.: Winthrop, 1975.

Elley, W. B., I. H. Barham, H. Lamb, and M. Wylie. "The Role of Grammar in a Secondary School English Curriculum." *RTE*, 10 (1976), 5–21.

Hirsch, E. D., Jr. *The Philosophy of Composition*. Chicago: University of Chicago Press, 1977.

Kolln, Martha. "Closing the Books on Alchemy." *CCC*, 32 (1981), 139–51.

Miller, Susan. "Is There a Text in This Class?" *FEN*, 11 (1982), 20–24.

Ong, Walter. *The Barbarian Within*. New York: Macmillan, 1962.

Rohman, D. Gordon, and Albert Wlecke. "Pre-Writing: The Construction and Application of Models for Concept Formation in Writing." HEW Cooperative Research Project No. 2174. East Lansing: Michigan State University, 1964.

Scott, Fred Newton. "What the West Wants in Preparatory English." *Sch Rev*, 17 (1909), 10–20.

Spencer, Herbert. "The Philosophy of Style." *Westminster Rev*, 114 (1852), 234–47.

Stewart, Donald C. "Composition Textbooks and the Assault on Tradition." *CCC*, 29 (1978), 171–76.

Whately, Richard. *Elements of Rhetoric*. 7th ed. London: Parker, 1846.

Young, Richard, Alton Becker, and Kenneth Pike. *Rhetoric: Discovery and Change*. New York: Harcourt, 1970.

Zoellner, Robert. "Talk-Write: A Behavioral Pedagogy for Composition." *CE*, 30 (1969), 267–320.

Evaluating Usage Manuals

MARVIN K. L. CHING

To select the best usage manual for their needs, users, whether they are professional linguists or college students, should consider five general factors. First, users should evaluate their own particular needs and interests. A professional linguist will want a different approach than a student in freshman English. Second, they should determine their particular philosophical orientation regarding usage. They will choose a different type of manual if they prefer a descriptive approach that records and explains actual usage than they will if they prefer a prescriptive, pedagogical approach that emphasizes correctness. Third, they should consider the scope of the subjects covered. Some books cover only a few essentials, while others attempt to examine the subject exhaustively. A student in freshman English trying to determine the difference between *lie* and *lay* will not appreciate a detailed discussion of regional differences in usage of these verbs. Fourth, users should consider the depth of treatment. Do they prefer the manual to cover each area exhaustively with ample details or more selectively with fewer specifics? Fifth, they should consider the style and tone of the manuals. Some are witty, idiosyncratic, and prescriptive; others are less distinguished stylistically but more objective and factual.

Users should therefore select the most suitable manual with these general guidelines in mind.

Books for the Scholar, Researcher, or Teacher

The most descriptive—factually objective—books for scholarly pursuits are Margaret M. Bryant's *Current English Usage* (1962), Roy H. Copperud's *American Usage and Style* (1980), and the sixth edition of Wilma R. Ebbitt and David R. Ebbitt's *Writer's Guide and Index to English* (1978).

Undoubtedly, Bryant's work is a distinguished piece of scholarship that carefully differentiates between writing and speech and the formal and the informal levels. When examples are cited for generalizations, the rhetorical context of the kind of writing is always given. Bryant's work contains data from various linguistic atlases, including the files of those not yet published, as well as information from learned journals. The results of studies are published quantitatively in percentage figures. Good historical reasons are given for various usages: for example, why *dare* acts like modals in lacking an inflectional *-s* marker for the third person singular and why certain adverbs, especially in speech, do not use the *-ly* ending. Good observations are made about when exceptions to rules occur and about where they tend to occur. Although now out of date, it is still worth consulting because of the precision of its generalizations and the good data upon which pronouncements are based. Although learned and scholarly in tone, the style is clear and unpretentious.

Roy Copperud's *American Usage and Style* (1980), an update of the author's previous books on usage, compares the various opinions of handbooks and dictionaries currently available at the time when he wrote it. Copperud is refreshingly modern, taking a more progressive stance on many items when opinions conflict. His prose is lucid, direct, and forceful.

The sixth edition of Wilma Ebbitt and David Ebbitt's *Writer's Guide and Index to English* (1978), an updated edition of the Porter Perrin series, is better than the current seventh edition because the most recent text does not cite the sources upon which the judgments on usage are made. The sixth edition, therefore, although meant for college freshmen, is an excellent source not only for examples of various items of usage in published prose but also for the sources that led the authors to arrive at their conclusions about various items of usage. Distinctions in usage appropriate to the formality of different situations are stressed. However, the language of this textbook is at times more suitable for the professional or the exceptional student than the average college freshman, the intended audience.

Although Copperud's and Ebbitt and Ebbitt's advice may not always follow actual use, at least they acknowledge their deviations from a descriptive orientation when they are prescriptive and identify writers' options when there is divided usage. They are thus more objective—descriptive—than authors of the other books in this section.

The usage manuals that are more subjective, which make pronouncements contrary to actual use, vary widely in degree of prescriptivism—in the specific items toward which they show an amazing tolerance and in the specific items against which they are rigidly opposed. Michael Montgomery and John Stratton's *Writer's Hotline Handbook* (1981) and Bergen Evans and Cornelia Evans's *Dictionary of Contemporary American Usage* (1957) are by far less prescriptive than most of these manuals. Theodore Bernstein's *Careful Writer* (1965) and his *Miss Thistlebottom's Hobgoblins* (1971) are midway in the prescriptive range. Wilson Follett's *Modern American Usage* (1966) and H. W. Fowler's *Dictionary of Modern English Usage* (1965) are definitely prescriptive.

An outgrowth of a telephone hotline service sponsored by the University of Arkansas of Little Rock for secretaries, businessmen, and the community, Michael Montgomery and John Stratton's *Writer's Hotline Handbook* (1981) cites the principal questions asked by non-language specialists about usage. This book is more lucid, readable, and succinct than other manuals currently available. Moreover, it cites ways to circumvent grammatically correct but awkward phrasing. In many instances it fulfills its promise "to be authoritative without being authoritarian" by enumerating the options, the levels of formality, and the contexts in which various words or constructions are used. In some instances, however, it is prescriptive, even more so than the *American Heritage Dictionary*. It is superior in its discussion of the subjunctive; *shall/should* and *will/would*; the type of audience that accepts a naturalized plural noun and the type of audience that retains the foreign plural form; the indefinite use of pronouns; and sexist language.

Bergen Evans and Cornelia Evans's *Dictionary of Contemporary American Usage* (1957), another slightly prescriptive book, is strong in the following areas: the discussion of various usage items pertaining to structure (for example, absolutes, sentence adverbs, and adjectives as adverbs), the confusion between words because of similarity of pronunciation, words close in meaning but differentiated in use, and clichés. The book also differentiates between British and American usage. Although the writers recognize that the best usage guide is based on actual use, they also give their own preference at times. Generally, however, the explanations of historical change in English make the language of the book objective, clear, and convincing.

Of books in the midrange of prescriptivism, both Bernstein's *Careful Writer* and *Miss Thistlebottom's Hobgoblins* possess trenchant wit, stylistic grace, and lucidity. However, both possess a bewildering schizophrenia in their decisions of leniency for certain items and in their pronouncements of undue severity against other items.

In the introduction to *The Careful Writer*, Bernstein recognized the midrange—a wide range between casual and formal registers—as the reputable range for most writing. The formal level today is restricted to baccalaureate addresses, court decisions, specialized papers in learned journals, and only a few other uses. He was liberal in this respect but troubled about linguists' descriptive advice based on statistical evidence. He was amazingly liberal on many items: tolerance of broad reference for *which* and the use of *whose* for an inanimate possessive pronoun, for example. But he maintained distinctions even though good writers may not do so: the differentiation between *flaunt* versus *flout*, for example. Another instance of both openness and restrictiveness is his acknowledgement that *contact* will gradually be accepted as a verb in the language but his rejection of *cope* in its intransitive form as in "She simply couldn't cope."

Although *Miss Thistlebottom's Hobgoblins* possesses an iconoclastic intent to eradicate "the superstitions of usages," "mere personal prejudices," and "misguided pedantry passed on from one generation to another," Bernstein bemoaned the collapsing of distinctions and begrudgingly said that the new must be accepted while holding out for some of his own personal preferences (p. xi). The book has virtues, however: its pronouncements when they are descriptive, its clarity, its presentation of the complexities of various problems, and the qualifications of certain generalizations.

The most prescriptive books are Wilson Follett's *Modern American Usage* (1966) and H. W. Fowler's *Dictionary of Modern Usage* (1965), which evoke interest because of their highly polemical language, categorical statements, and Shavian flavor. Although sounding learned in their judgments, both reveal deep, ill-founded prejudices, and their prose is ponderous. Exceptions to these generalizations, however, appear from time to time.

Follett's *Modern American Usage* advocates keeping distinctions whenever they fill a need despite current usage. The introduction to the text is highly militant, attacking linguists for denying any notion of correctness by treating even slips of the tongue as acceptable. Extremely traditional, the introduction also advocates the study of Latin to understand the definitions and distinctions made in English.

Fowler's *Dictionary of Modern English Usage*, like Follett's work, espouses distinctions no longer made by speakers and writers. Advice given often seems to follow the vagaries of the author and the reviser of the book. Although this reference guide's distinctions of shades of meanings and of various words are highly questionable, it is one of the popular sources that editors and lay people consult—probably because of their attraction to dogmatism and definitive answers even when usage is divided. Sometimes, however, the book seems shockingly radical, as in the acceptance of *burgle* as legitimate.

Books for the College Student

Like dictionaries, college freshman usage books are not accessible, as one reviewer of a certain text has perceptively observed, to those in most need of such books: remedial, below-average, and average students do not understand the explanations of such texts without considerable teacher help. Another problem most students encounter is that they do not already possess an adequate command of rhetoric and usage terminology to ask the right questions, including the headings under which their problems may be solved. Usage books, then, for a significant number of students do not serve their intended function as handbooks. Moreover, books trying to be simple often end up being simplistic, thus actually causing confusion, compounding some problems, and perpetuating out of date prescriptive admonitions that do not really matter but that are incorporated in a text only because of the demand of naive and uninformed pedagogues who little understand language change, language variation, and appropriate usage determined by rhetorical context. Another problem, moreover, is the unevenness in the scope and the quality of the subjects treated in usage texts.

Undoubtedly, the most thorough and accurate usage texts are Marcella Frank's *Modern English* (1972) and the sixth (rather than the current seventh) edition of Wilma R. Ebbitt and David R. Ebbitt's *Writer's Guide and Index to English* (1978). Both show an understanding of the new linguistics but discuss matters in traditional terminology. Glenn Leggett and colleagues' *Prentice-Hall Handbook for Writers* (1982) is superior in descriptive orientation and scope of subjects discussed but not as thorough as the other two in the treatment of each subject.

Frank's *Modern English* (1972), designed for students of English as a second language, treats comprehensively these matters with all their complexities: legitimate and appropriate uses of the passive; syntactic and semantic uses of the modals; idiomatic uses of prepositions with verbs and prepositions. Throughout, the lexical items and grammatical constructions cited are discussed in terms of the rhetorical effect they produce in style and variety of English. Although no separate glossary of usage is incorporated, discussion throughout concerns words and phrases that are most significant and not the inconsequential matters all too often included in student texts. This book is truly a linguist's dream. Although thorough in describing generalizations and presenting many illustrative examples, the book is clear.

Although the seventh edition of Ebbitt and Ebbitt's *Writer's Guide and Index* (1978) is the edition available, the sixth edition (1978) is better because of the identification of the sources upon which judgments are made for various items in the glossary of usage and because of the unabridged chapters in the text. Generalizations concerning this text in the previous section on books for the professional also hold true for this section. Moreover, this book is the text par excellence for varieties of English—especially how diction works together with punctuation, sentence patterns, and transitional devices to create different styles or varieties of English. Appropriateness according to rhetorical context is emphasized at all times. The discussion on modals is adequate, and the treatment of reference of pronouns teaches how clarity may be achieved without pomposity. The glossary of usage identifies sources that object to more liberal uses, and when there is divided usage, the authors always note the discrepancy. The only drawback to this book is that the language is at times not comprehensible to poor and average students.

Glenn Leggett and colleagues' *Prentice-Hall Handbook for Writers* (1982) possesses the virtues of clarity, simplicity, succinctness, and truthfulness to the facts of usage. The discussion of varieties of English and levels of usage is excellent, showing the complexities in categorizing the different varieties, illustrating degrees of overlap, citing the types of discourse in which each variety appears, and using the accepted terminology of modern usage studies. The sections citing prepositions following certain verbs and adjectives provides sentences in which the idioms occur to help the reader deduce when a certain preposition and not another one should be used to convey the intended meaning. Although the glossary of usage identifies the objections of the traditional stylists and popular pundits of language, it truthfully states that these admonitions are contrary to actual use or the admonitions of dictionaries. The discussion of modal auxiliaries and legitimate and appropriate uses of the passive is not as complete, however, as it could be.

Other usage texts, in general, tend to be much less objective than any of the ones named above. These more prescriptive books are discussed below in alphabetical order of publisher. I have selected for discussion several representative books.

John C. Hodges and Mary E. Whitten's *Harbrace College Handbook* (1983) has the virtue of succinctness with its attendant problem of not being complex enough. Although clear in style, the glossary of usage is inconsistent in prescriptive or descriptive orientation. Often, however, the discussion notes that some authorities make distinctions when its admonitions contradict actual practice. The text's discussion on levels of usage and appropriateness to rhetorical context is noticeably inadequate in giving the true and complex picture of what actually occurs in different kinds of writing.

Langdon Elsbree and colleagues' *Heath Handbook of Composition* (1981) is excellent in discussing legitimate and appropriate uses of the passive and good in explaining varieties of English and levels of usage—the overlapping of different varieties and the wide range within a variety. The prose is clear with sufficient examples. The glossary of usage is prescriptive, however.

William Herman's *Portable English Handbook* (1982) is a succinct indexed paperback covering various usage matters. In many areas the brevity is achieved without sacrificing complexity. The explanations on varieties of English and levels of usage and legitimate and appropriate uses of the passive are amazingly clear without being simplistic. The section on idiomatic prepositions following certain verbs and adjectives is well illustrated with sentences containing different prepositions for a given verb or adjective. But the appendixed glossary of usage at the end of the book negates the beautiful descriptive treatment of varieties of English and levels of usage in the body of the book. The admonitions and illustrative examples in the appendix, much too simplistic and prescriptive, should have been correlated with differences in rhetorical context and varieties of English.

Sylvan Barnet and Marcia Stubbs's *Practical Guide to Writing* (1983) is expressed in trenchant, clear prose. Although the glossary of usage is surprisingly liberal for some items, it is definitely reactionary for other entries, a mere reflection of the authors' vagaries when compared to actual use. The generalizations, admonitions, and illustrative materials about finding the appropriate level of language are excellent, but the terminology calling the most casual level *vulgar* is definitely passé and unfortunate in connotation.

H. Ramsey Fowler's *Little, Brown Handbook* (1983) is adequate in generalizations and examples about legitimate and appropriate uses of the passive, but the information is unfortunately scattered in four parts of the book, never neatly placed together in one place. Its glossary of usage is definitely prescriptive, preserving distinctions no longer preserved in actual use. Much to be desired is a section that would integrate the matters presently discussed under diction and tone and that would show a true picture of the complexities in overlapping varieties and levels of English in actual usage. The prose is reasonably clear.

James A. W. Hefferman and John E. Lincoln's *Writing* (1982) is remarkably clear and eloquent in demonstrating all of the complexities in legitimate and appropriate uses of the passive. The section on diction is also a tour de force in explaining varieties of English and levels of usage, with exceptions and overlapping of levels clarified and illustrated. Much in need of improvement, however, is its prescriptive, reactionary glossary of usage. The prose of this text is lucid and graceful.

Frederick Crews's 1980 Random House Handbook's best usage section is on problems of agreement, especially with collective nouns, nouns of quantity, mathematical relations, and troublesome words like *none*, which can be either singular or plural, depending upon how the subject is viewed. The prose is generally clear, although the content is not always as illuminating as it should be.

Hans P. Guth's *New English Handbook* (1982) is good on the legitimate and appropriate uses of the passive, although the subject could be treated even more completely. The glossary of usage is inconsistent in its admonitions—ranging from descriptive to extreme prescriptive judgments. Although the text lists in phrasal contexts the prepositions that follow verbs and adjectives, only one preposition follows each verb or adjective entry, even when there are more prepositions that can be legitimately used with each entry.

Manuals Cited

Barnet, Sylvan, and Marcia Stubbs. *Practical Guide to Writing*. 4th ed. Boston: Little, Brown, 1983.

Bernstein, Theodore. *The Careful Writer: A Modern Guide to English Usage*. New York: Atheneum, 1965.

————. *Miss Thistlebottom's Hobgoblins: The Careful Writer's Guide to the Taboos, Bugbears and Outmoded Rules of English Usage*. New York: Farrar, Straus, Giroux, 1971.

Bryant, Margaret M. *Current English Usage*. New York: Funk, Wagnalls, 1962.

Copperud, Roy H. *American Usage and Style: The Consensus*. New York: Van Nostrand Reinhold, 1980.

Crews, Frederick. *The Random House Handbook*. 3rd ed. New York: Random House, 1980.

Ebbitt, Wilma R., and David R. Ebbitt. *Writer's Guide and Index to English*. 6th ed. Glenview, Ill.: Scott, Foresman, 1978.

Elsbree, Langdon, et al. *The Heath Handbook of Composition*. 10th ed. Lexington, Mass.: Heath, 1981.

Evans, Bergen, and Cornelia Evans. *A Dictionary of Contemporary American Usage*. New York: Random House, 1957.

Follett, Wilson. *Modern American Usage: A Guide*. Ed. and completed by Jacques Barzun. New York: Hill, Wang, 1966.

Fowler, H. Ramsey. *The Little, Brown Handbook*. 2nd ed. Boston: Little, Brown, 1983.

Fowler, H. W. *A Dictionary of Modern English Usage*. 2nd ed. Rev. and ed. Sir Ernest Gowers. New York: Oxford University Press, 1965.

Frank, Marcella. *Modern English: A Practical Reference Guide*. Englewood Cliffs, N.J.: Prentice-Hall, 1972.

Guth, Hans P. *New English Handbook*. Belmont, Calif.: Wadsworth, 1982.

Hefferman, James A. W., and John E. Lincoln. *Writing: A College Handbook*. New York: Norton, 1982.

Herman, William. *The Portable English Handbook: An Index to Grammar, Usage, and the Research Paper*. 2nd ed. New York: Holt, Rinehart, Winston, 1982.

Hodges, John C., and Mary E. Whitten. *Harbrace College Handbook*. 9th ed. New York: Harcourt, 1983.

Leggett, Glenn, et al. *Prentice-Hall Handbook for Writers*. 8th ed. Englewood Cliffs, N.J.: Prentice-Hall, 1982.

Montgomery, Michael, and John Stratton. *The Writer's Hotline Handbook*. New York: New American Library, 1981.

Author Index

Subject Index

About the Contributors

DAVID J. BARTHOLOMAE is Associate Professor of English and Director of Composition at the University of Pittsburgh. He is a member of the Executive Committee of the Conference on College Composition and Communication and of the Board of Directors of the National Council of Writing Program Administrators. He has published essays on error, basic writing, writing assignments, and the relationship between reading and writing.

LYNN DIANNE BEENE is an Assistant Professor of Language and Literature and the Director of the Communication Skills Testing Program at the University of New Mexico. Her principal research interests range from linguistic pragmatics and discourse analysis to rhetorical and linguistic aspects of technical writing. She is the author of several articles on language structure and composition theory.

JAMES S. BEGGS is a Lecturer of English at the University of North Carolina at Charlotte. His special interests include teaching English as a second language, dialect interference, and learning disabilities.

LYNN Z. BLOOM is Professor of English at Virginia Commonwealth University, where she chairs the English Department. She has directed the writing programs at the University of New Mexico and the College of William and Mary. She has published widely in literature and composition and is the author of *Strategic Writing*.

JOHN C. BRIGGS is Assistant Professor of English at the University of California, Riverside, where one of his responsibilities is to direct the Basic Writing Program. He is currently involved in a study of Renaissance conceptions of rhetoric.

CHRISTOPHER C. BURNHAM is Assistant Professor of English and Director of the Freshman Writing Program at New Mexico State University and was formerly Director of Writing at Stockton State College (New Jersey). His scholarship has focused on the relations between cognitive devel
opment and writing, the function of expressive writing in all the disciplines, and on Walt Whitman's composing process.

MARVIN K. L. CHING, Associate Professor of English at Memphis State University, teaches linguistics and serves as the school's Director of Freshman and Sophomore English. Interested in applying linguistic theory to the study of literature, dialectology, and composition, he has authored articles appearing in *American Speech, Centrum,* and *College Composition and Communication.*

FRANK J. D'ANGELO is Professor of English at Arizona State University where he directs the Ph.D. program in rhetoric and composition. He is a former Chair of the Conference on College Composition and Communication and an Executive Committee member of the MLA Writing Division. He has published widely in rhetoric, composition, and stylistics, and he is the author of *A Conceptual Theory of Rhetoric* and *Process and Thought in Composition.*

GLYNDA A. HULL is a Post-doctoral Fellow at the Learning Research and Development Center and a teacher of writing in the Department of English, both at the University of Pittsburgh. She has published essays on writing pedagogy and writing research. Her current research centers on computer-assisted editing instruction and error in writing.

GRETA D. LITTLE is Associate Professor of English and Linguistics at the University of South Carolina. She is currently engaged in research investigating the use, perception, and acquisition of punctuation.

RONALD F. LUNSFORD is Associate Professor of English at Clemson University where he directs the Composition and Rhetoric Program and the Clemson Writing Project. He has published articles in linguistics, stylistics, and composition and is the co-author of *Writing: Discovering Form and Meaning.*

MARY HURLEY MORAN is Assistant Professor of English at Clemson University where she has coordinated the Writing Laboratory. Her research interests include basic writing and twentieth-century British literature, and she is the author of *Margaret Drabble: Existing within Structures.*

MICHAEL G. MORAN is Assistant Professor of English at Clemson University where he has directed the Composition and Rhetoric Program. Since completing a Post-doctoral Fellowship in Composition at the University of Kansas, his main research interests have been in rhetorical invention and the rhetoric of scientific writing, and he has published essays in composition theory and pedagogy, technical communication, and business writing.

JASPER NEEL is Professor and Chairman of English at Francis Marion College. He has taught at Baylor, New York University, and served as Director of ADE. He edited *Options for the Teaching of English: Freshman Composition* and has published several articles both on composition and on the relationship between composition theory and reading theory. He is currently completing a book on the relationship between critical theory and composition theory.

LOUISE WETHERBEE PHELPS is Assistant Professor of English at the University of Southern California and was formerly Director of the Writing Lab at Cleveland State University. She is the author of articles in various journals on the philosophy and psychology of composition and editor of a recently published special issue of *Pre/Text* on Paul Ricoeur and rhetoric. She is currently completing a book-length study of composition as a discipline and developing a hermeneutical theory to explain how teachers read student writing.

ROBERT W. REISING is Professor of Communicative Arts at Pembroke State University, where he teaches courses in writing, English education, American Indian literature, and education. He co-directs the North Carolina Writing Project at PSU and is the author of numerous professional articles and of several books, including two on Jim Thorpe, the American Indian athlete. He has recently co-authored *Writing for Learning in the Content Areas*.

BENJAMIN J. STEWART is a Teacher of English at Pine Forest Senior High School in Fayetteville, NC, where he has served for eighteen years. He also has been a part-time Instructor in the English Department of Methodist College. His principal research interest involves the effects of peer revision strategies on the writing of high school seniors, and he has published professional articles on composition.

DONALD C. STEWART is a Professor of English at Kansas State University. He is the author of *The Authentic Voice* and numerous articles on composition history and theory, some of which have appeared in *College Composition and Communication, College English, English Education, Research in the Teaching of English,* and *The English Journal.* In 1983 he was Chair of the Conference on College Composition and Communication.

WILLIAM L. STULL is Assistant Professor of English and Director of the Writing Program at the University of Hartford. He is the author of a textbook, *Combining and Creating: Sentence Combining and Generative Rhetoric*, as well as articles on literature, composition, and academic administration.

JOHN WARNOCK is Associate Professor of English and Law at the University of Wyoming where he has directed Freshman English, the Writing Center, the Wyoming Conference on Freshman and Sophomore English, and the Legal Writing Program and where in 1978 he started the Wyoming Writing Project. He has published fiction and articles on rhetoric, writing, learning, and teaching. In Summer 1984, he directed an NEH Summer Seminar for College Teachers entitled ''The Writing Process: A Humanistic View.''